Chiara Lagani   Mara Cerri

MY BRILLIANT FRIEND

FROM THE NOVEL BY ELENA FERRANTE

*TRANSLATED FROM THE ITALIAN
BY ANN GOLDSTEIN*

Europa
editions

Europa Editions
27 Union Square West, suite 302
New York N.Y. 10003
www.europaeditions.com
info@europaeditions.com

This book is a work of fiction. Any references to historical events, real people, or real locales are used fictitiously.

First Publication 2023 by Europa Editions

Translation by Ann Goldstein
Original title: *L'amica geniale*

Library of Congress Cataloging in Publication Data is available
ISBN 978-1-60945-946-8

Cerri, Mara & Lagani, Chiara
Adapted from the novel by Elena Ferrante, *L'amica geniale*
© Edizioni E/O, 2011
First US edition *My Brilliant Friend* © 2012 by Europa Editions

Book design, font, and adaptation: Leonardo Guardigli
Art direction: Davide Reviati

Cover illustration by Mara Cerri

Additional design by Ginevra Rapisardi

Prepress by Grafica Punto Print - Rome

Printed in Italy

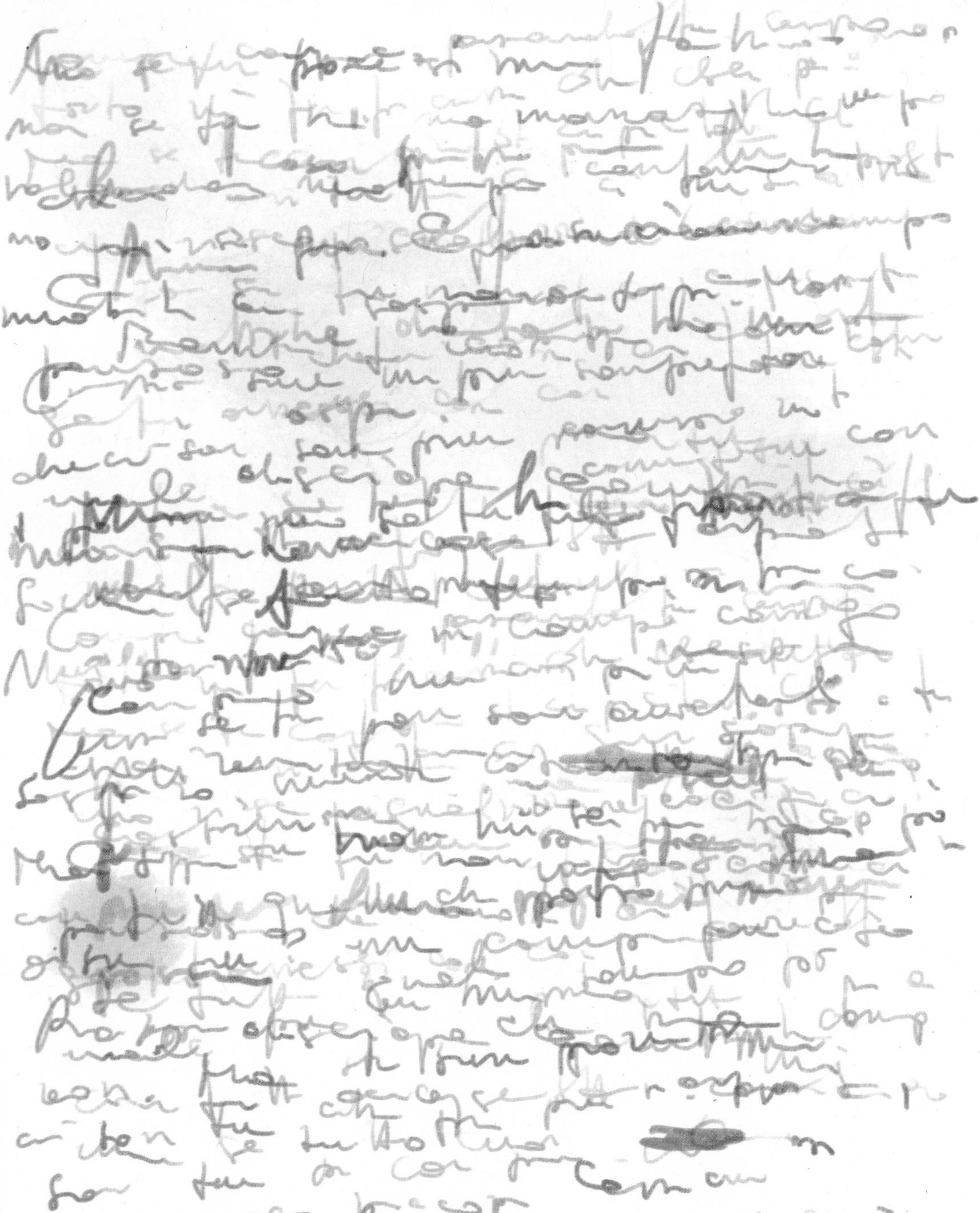

MY BRILLIANT FRIEND

FOR CINCILLA.
FOR FIORENZA.

Prologue

- ELIMINATING ALL THE TRACES -

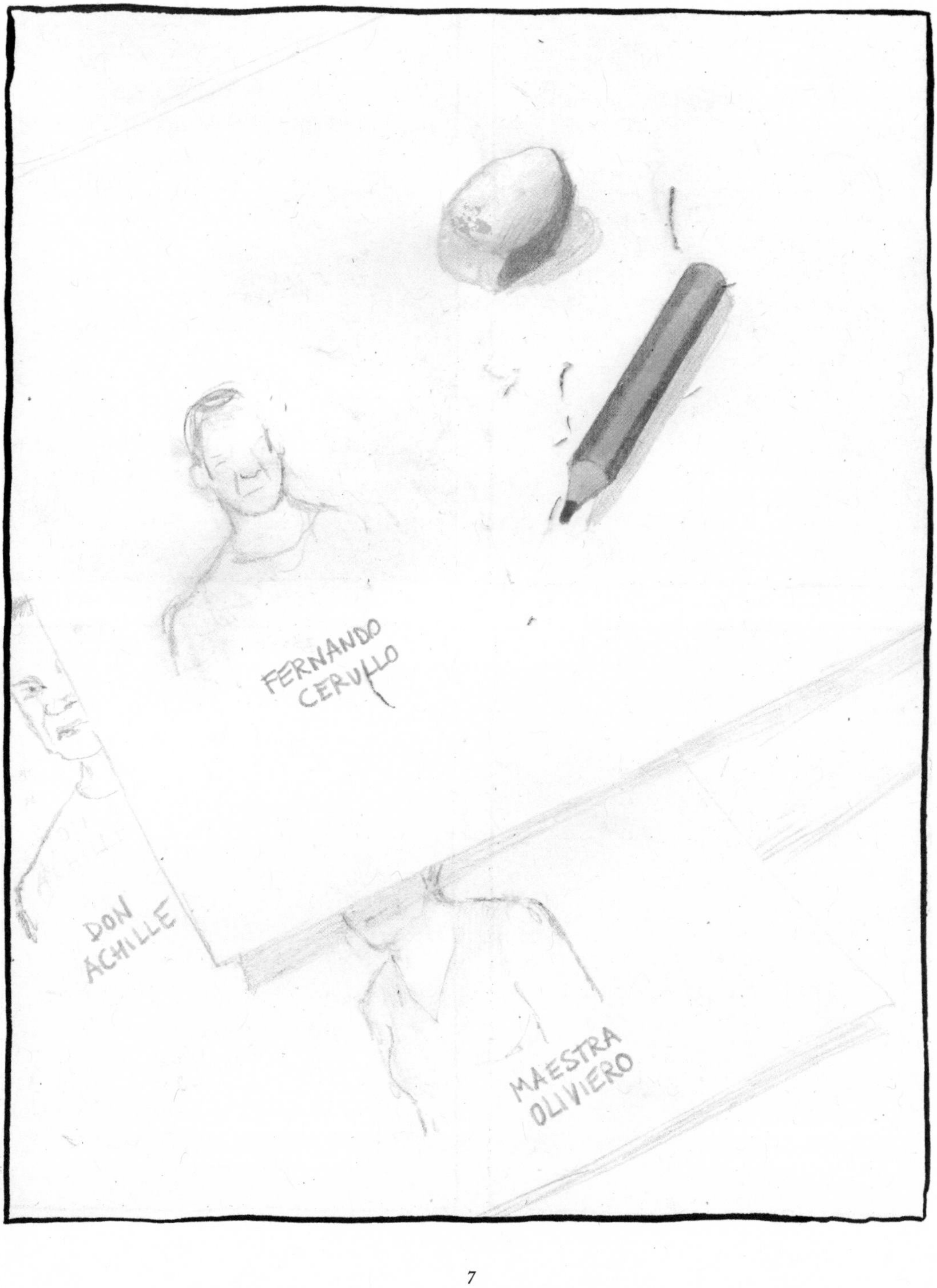
FERNANDO CERULLO
DON ACHILLE
MAESTRA OLIVIERO

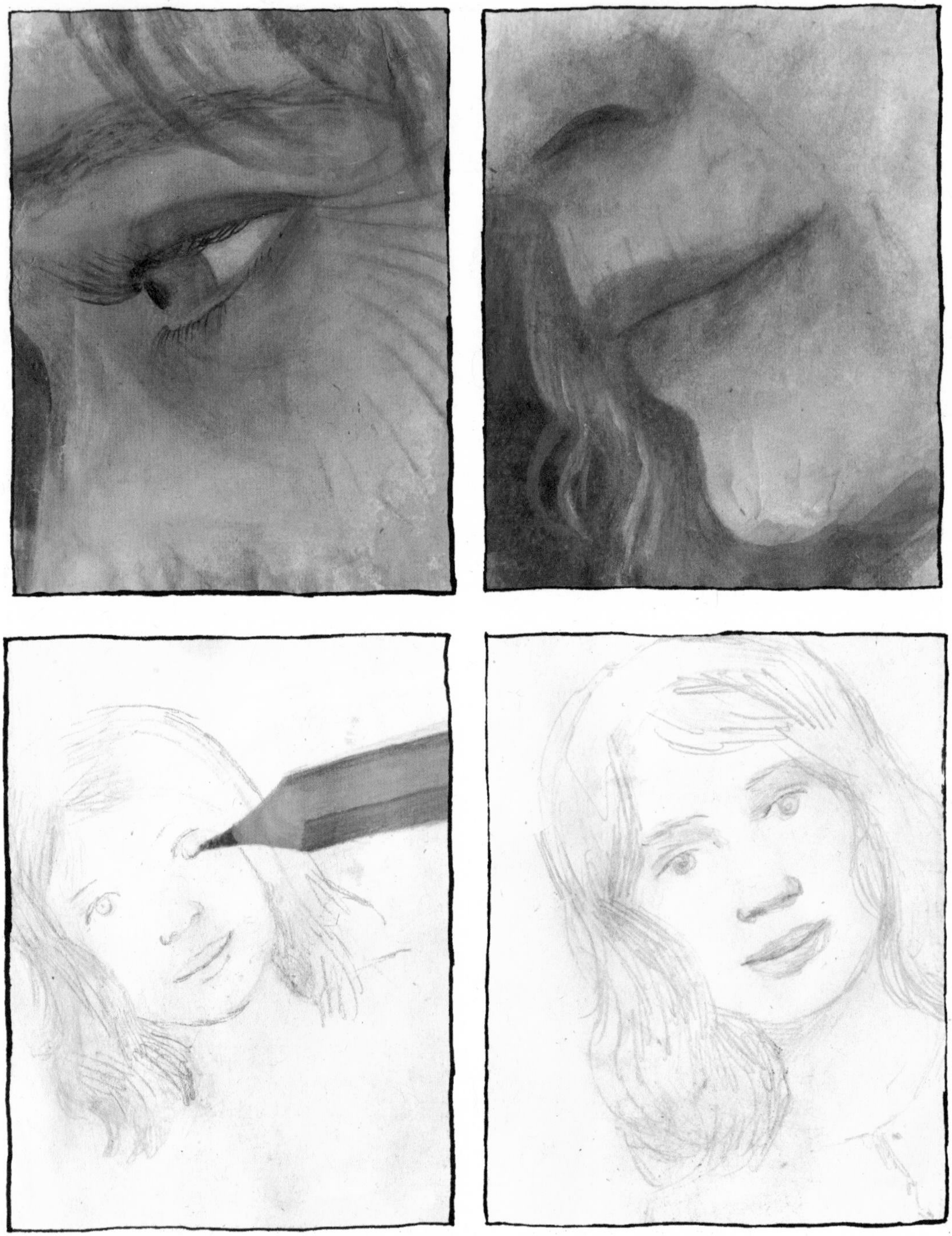

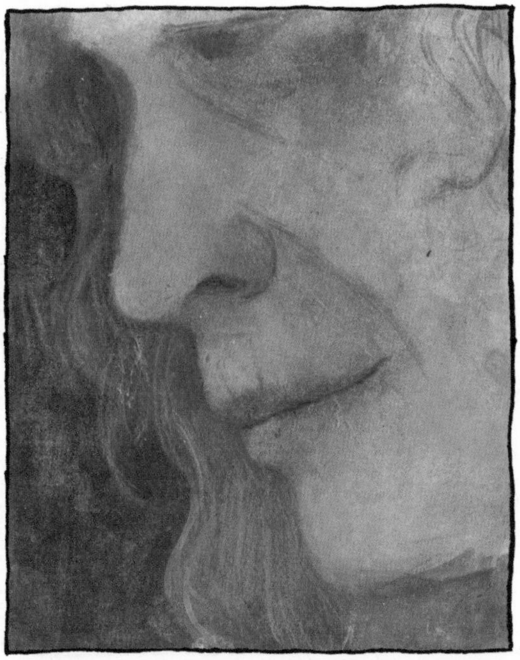

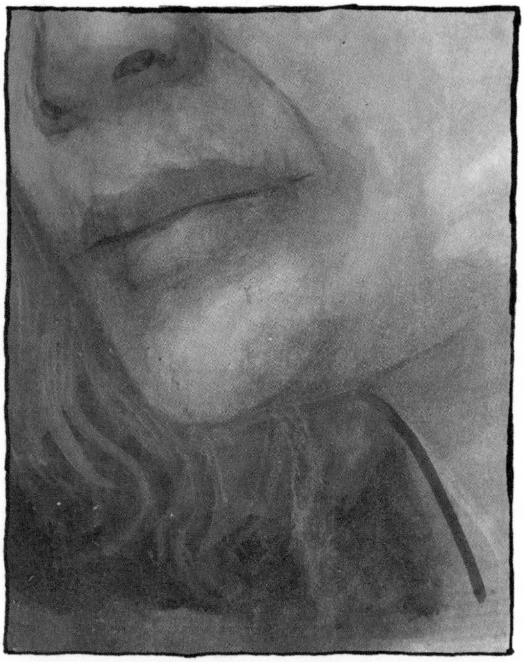

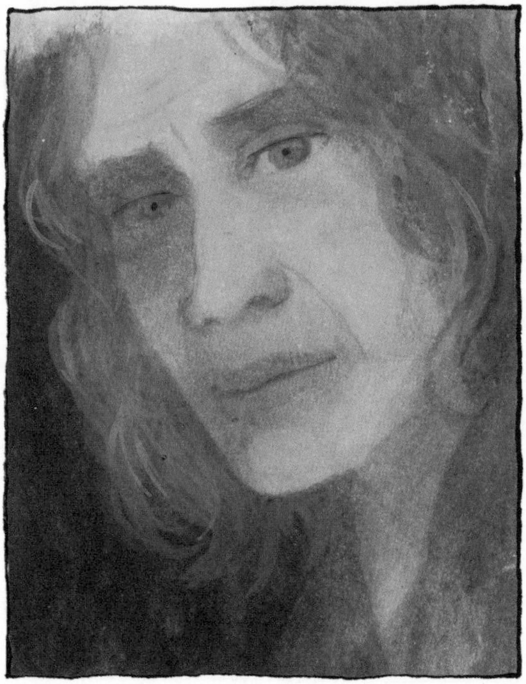

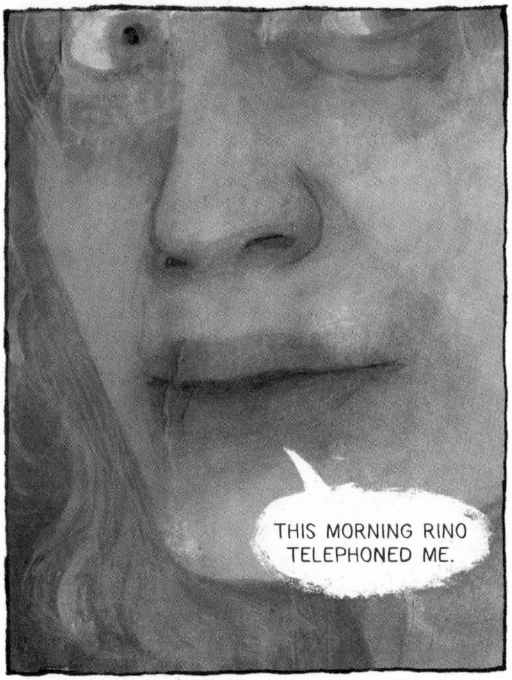
THIS MORNING RINO TELEPHONED ME.

I THOUGHT HE WANTED MORE MONEY AND I WAS READY TO SAY NO.

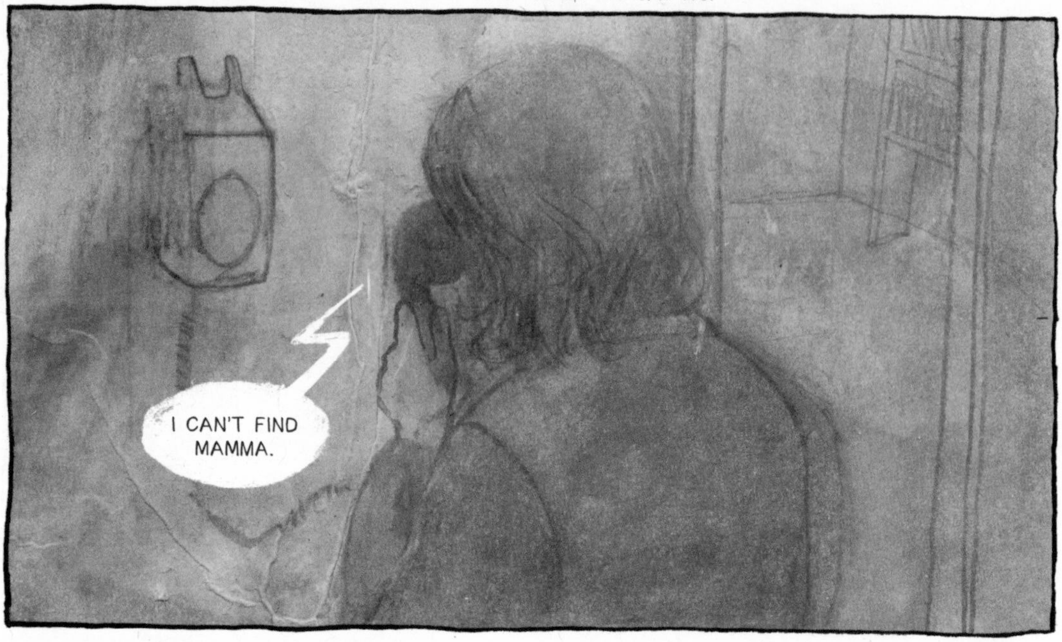
I CAN'T FIND MAMMA.

BUT THAT WASN'T WHY HE'D CALLED.

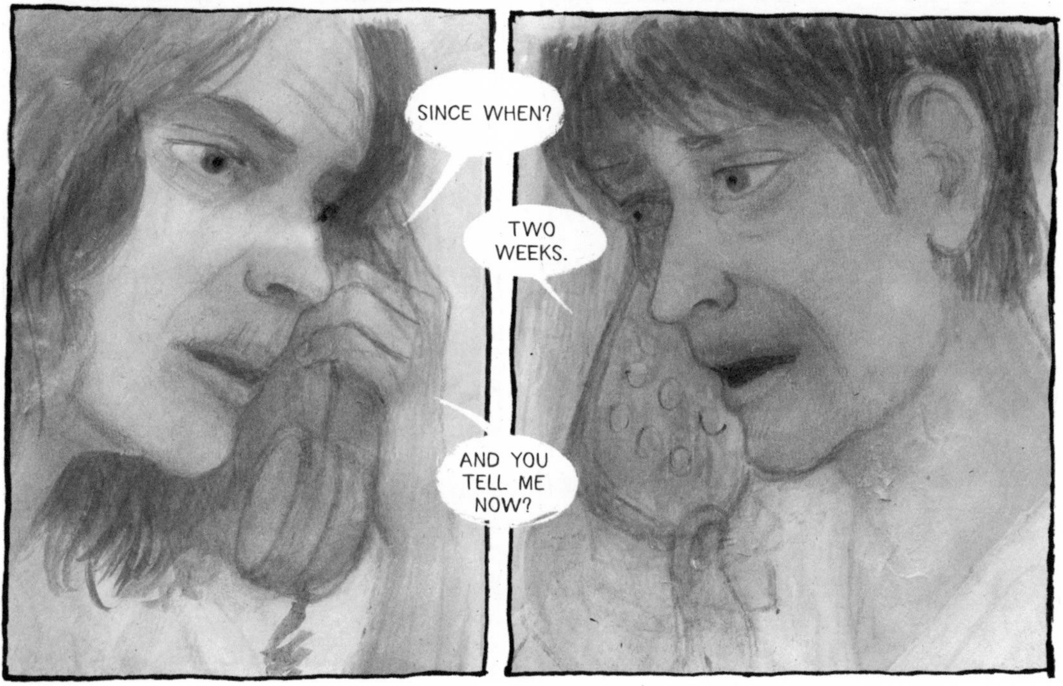
SINCE WHEN?
TWO WEEKS.
AND YOU TELL ME NOW?

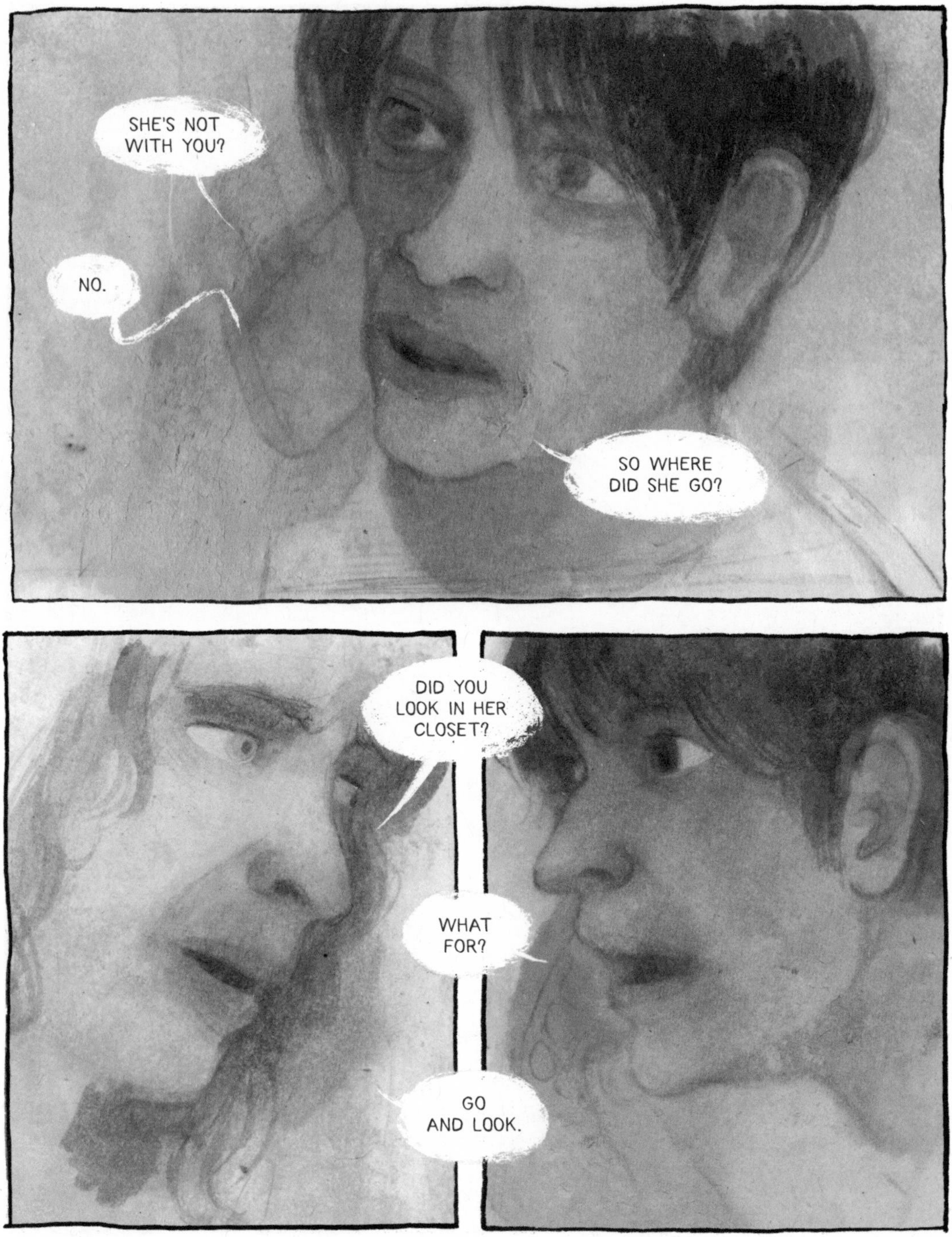
SHE'S NOT WITH YOU?
NO.
SO WHERE DID SHE GO?
DID YOU LOOK IN HER CLOSET?
WHAT FOR?
GO AND LOOK.

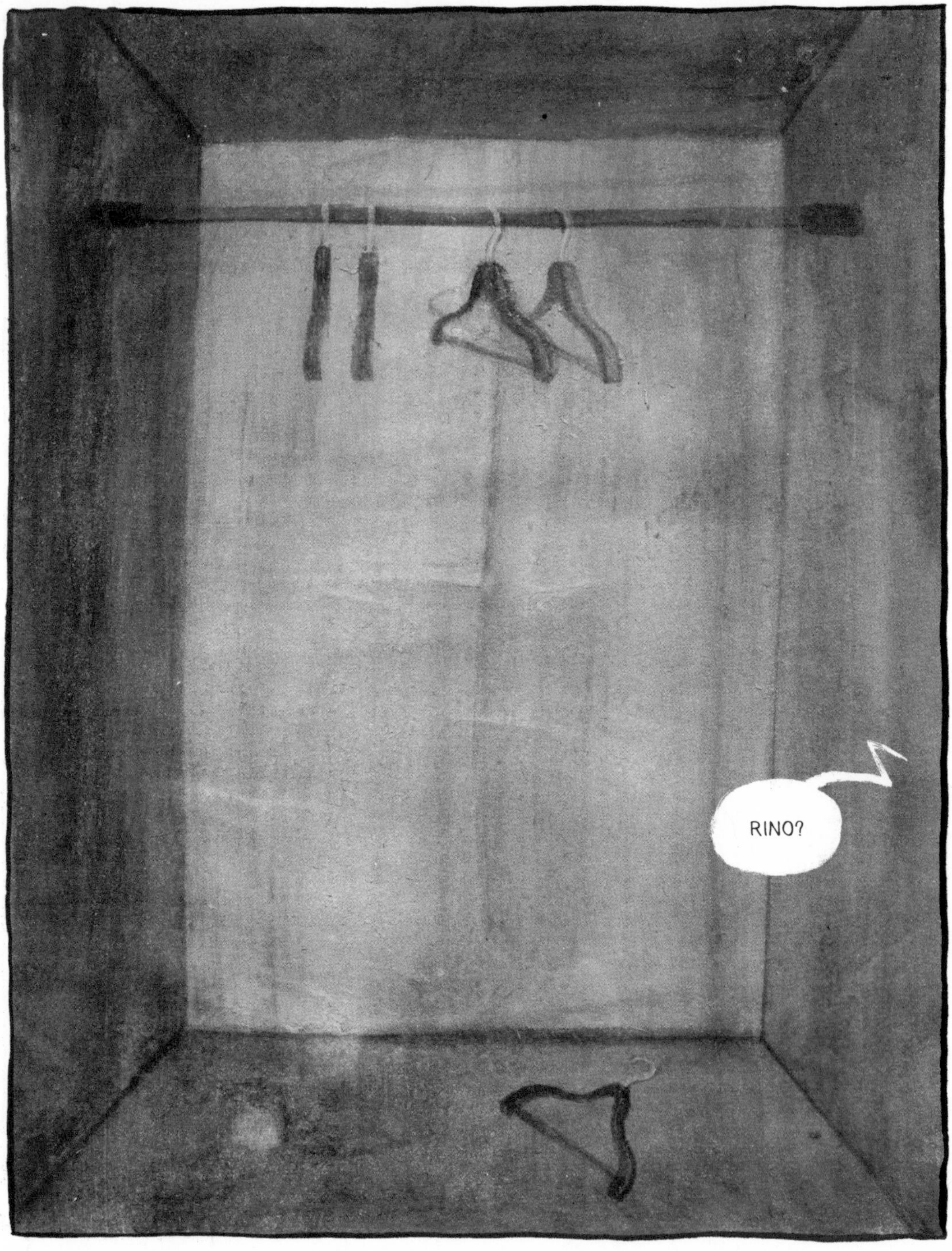
RINO?

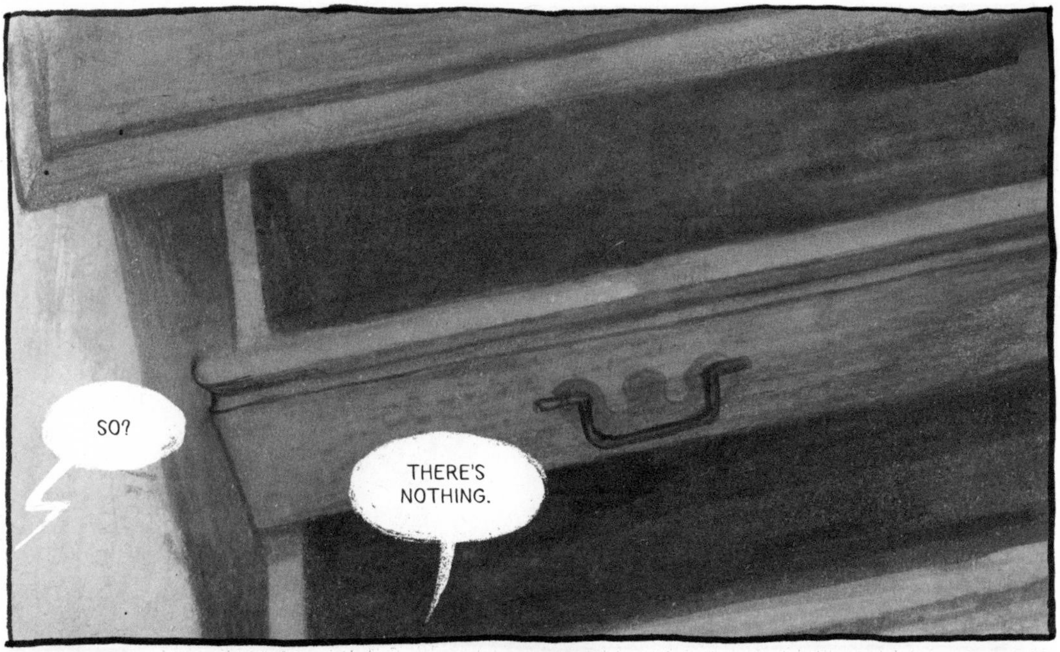
SO?
THERE'S NOTHING.

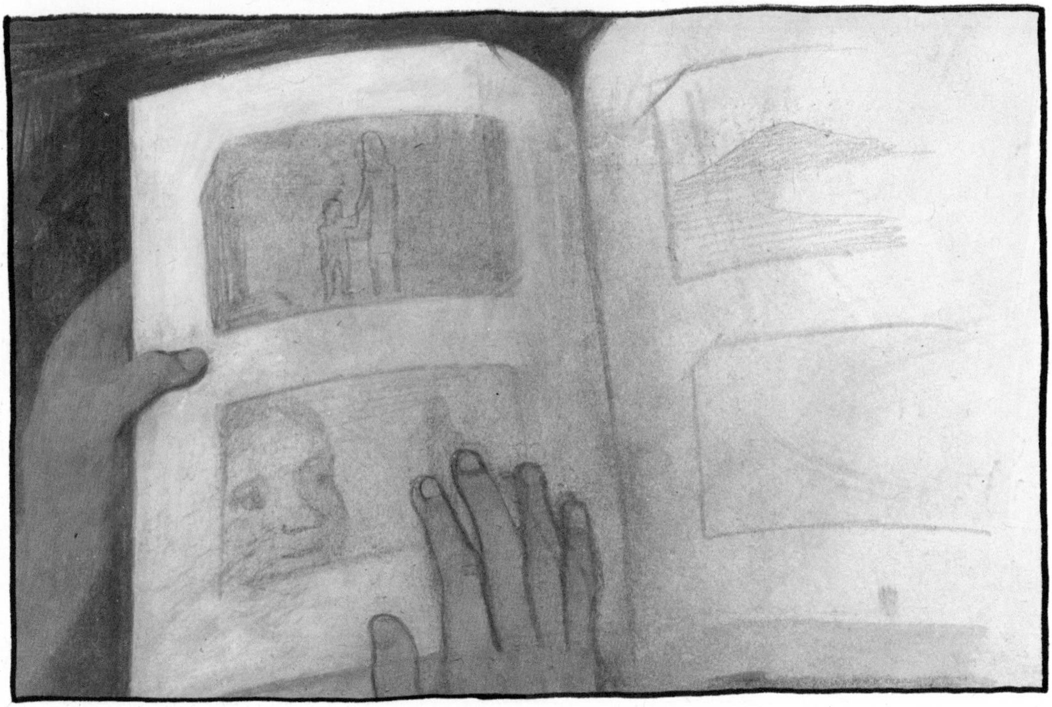

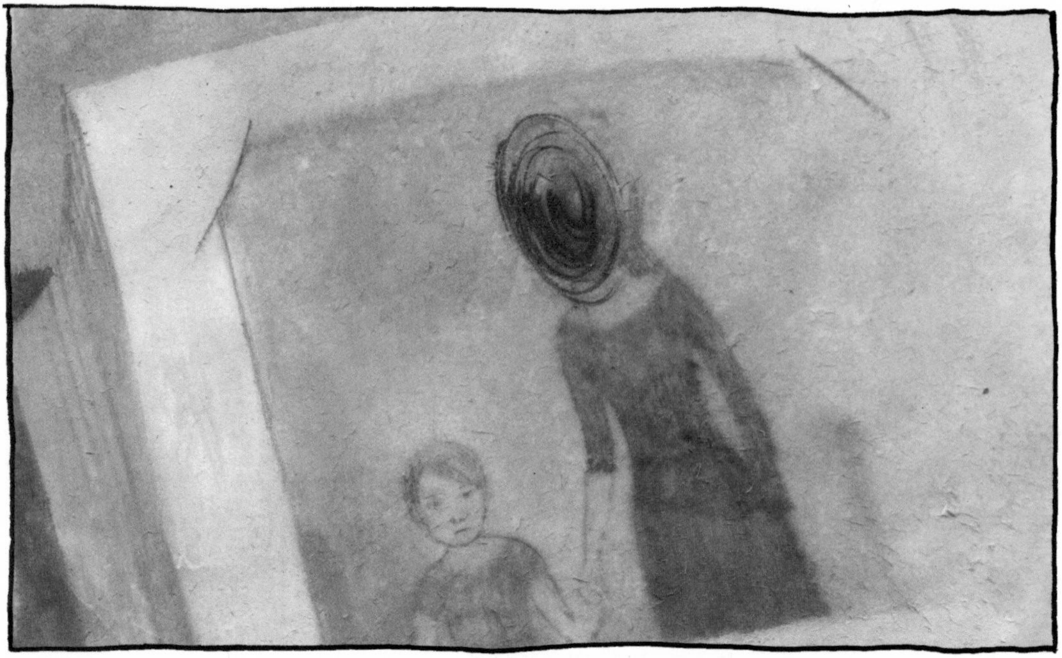

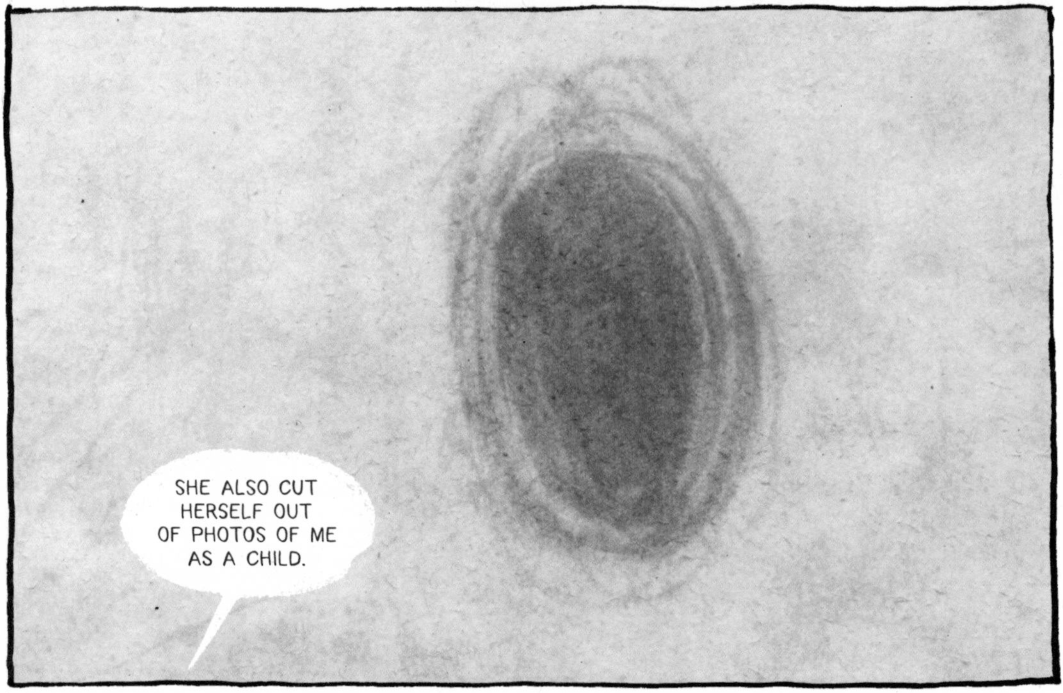
SHE ALSO CUT HERSELF OUT OF PHOTOS OF ME AS A CHILD.

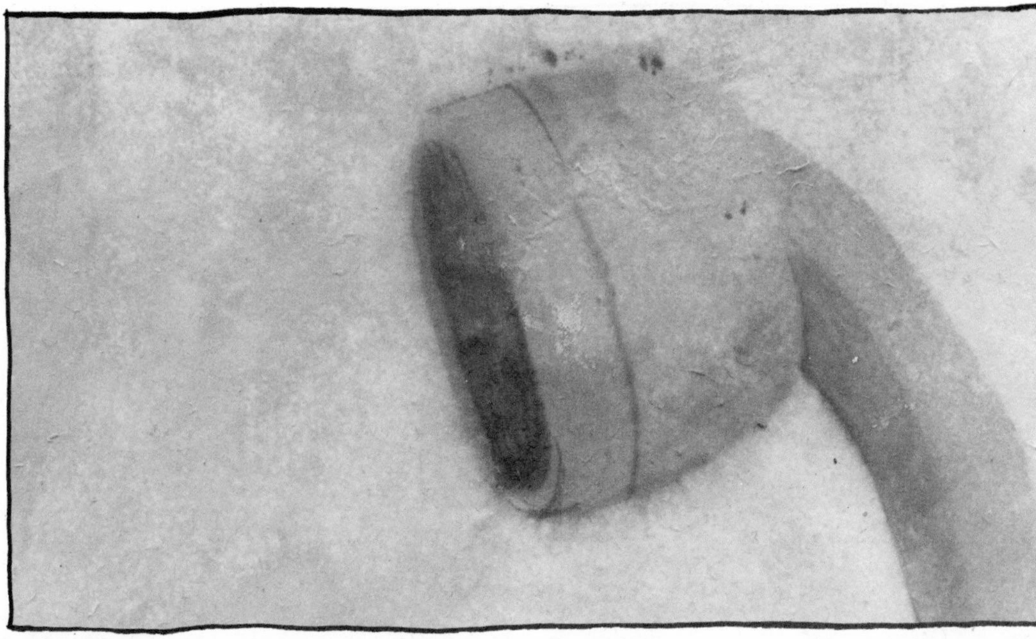

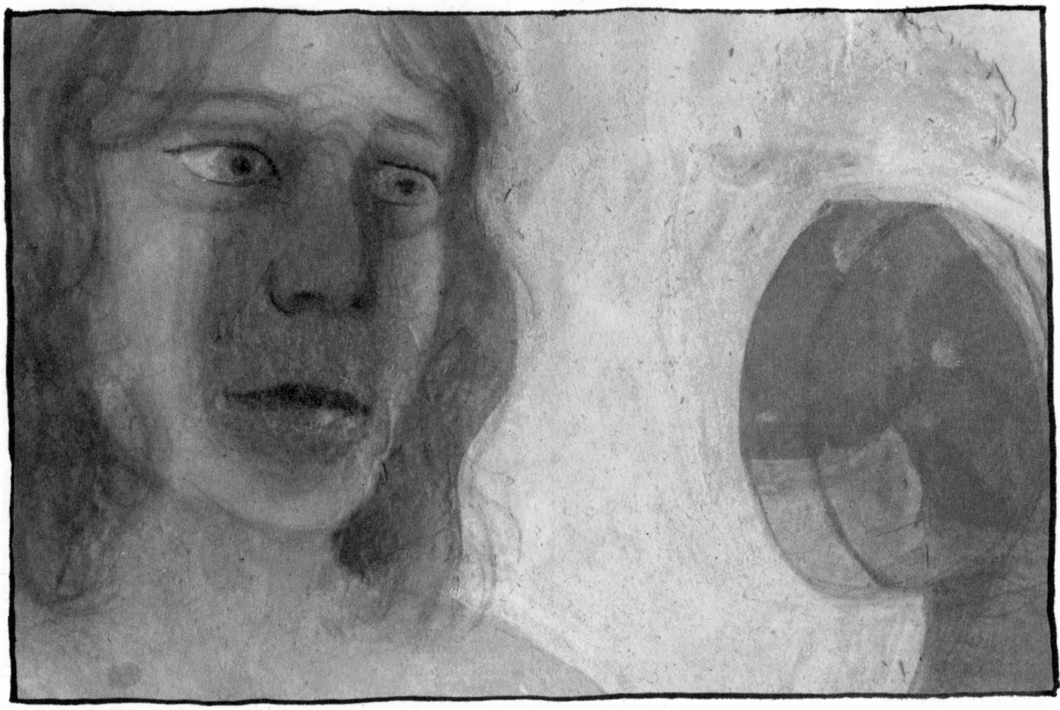

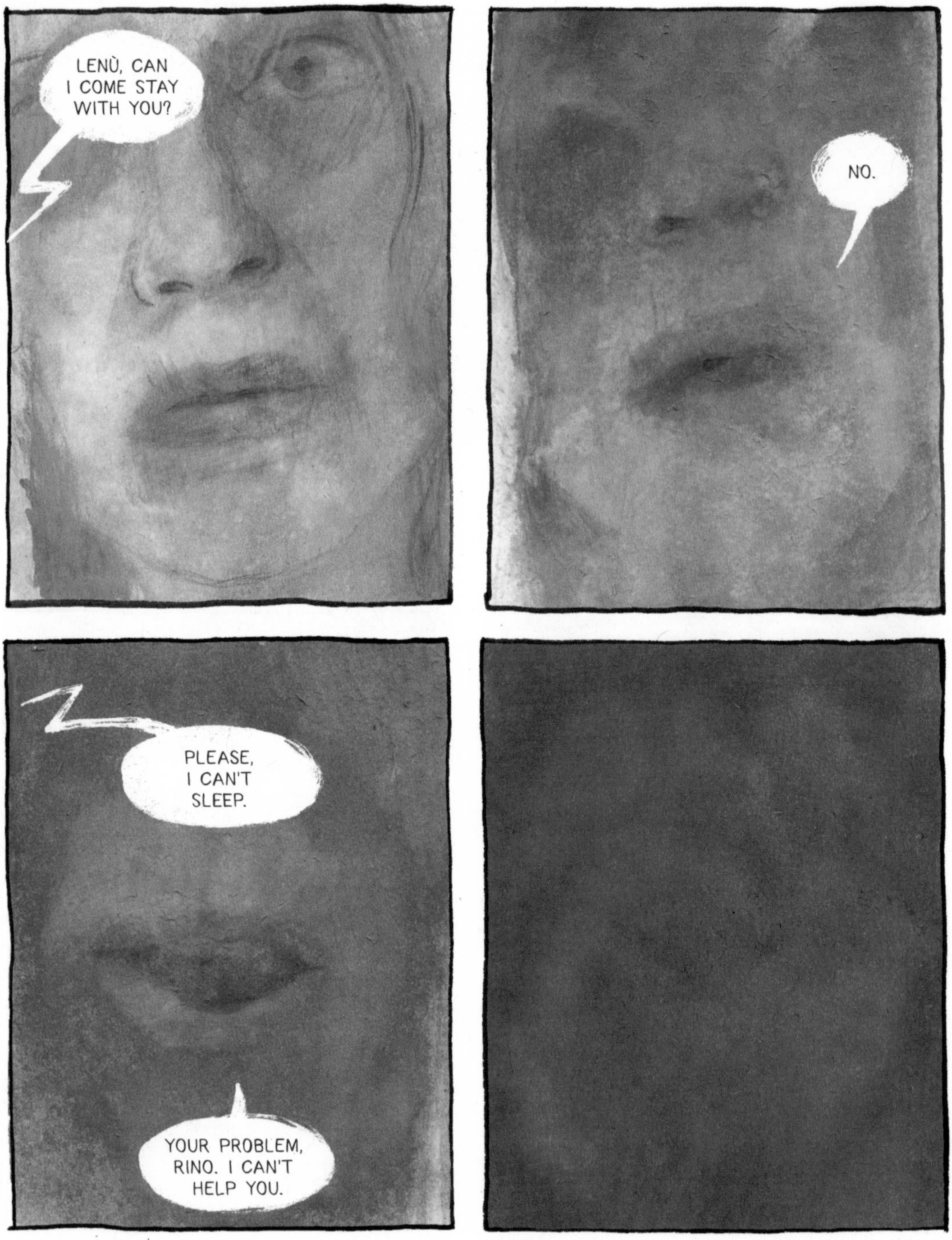
LENÙ, CAN I COME STAY WITH YOU?
NO.
PLEASE, I CAN'T SLEEP.
YOUR PROBLEM, RINO. I CAN'T HELP YOU.

RINO'S MOTHER IS NAMED RAFFAELLA CERULLO, BUT EVERYONE HAS ALWAYS CALLED HER LINA. NOT ME. TO ME, FOR MORE THAN SIXTY YEARS, SHE'S BEEN LILA.

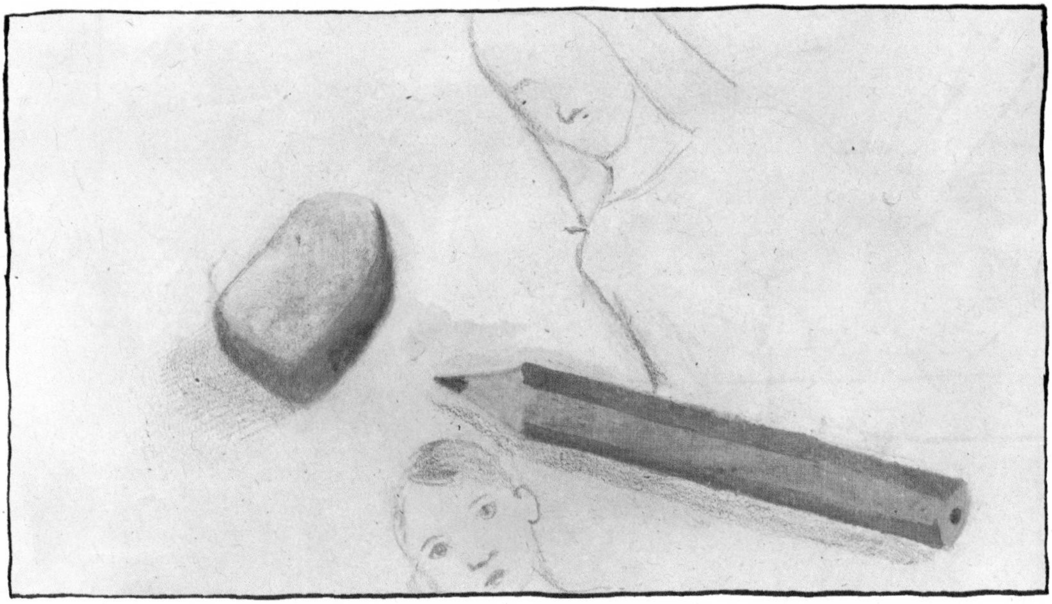

FOR AT LEAST THREE DECADES SHE'S SAID SHE WANTED TO DISAPPEAR WITHOUT A TRACE...

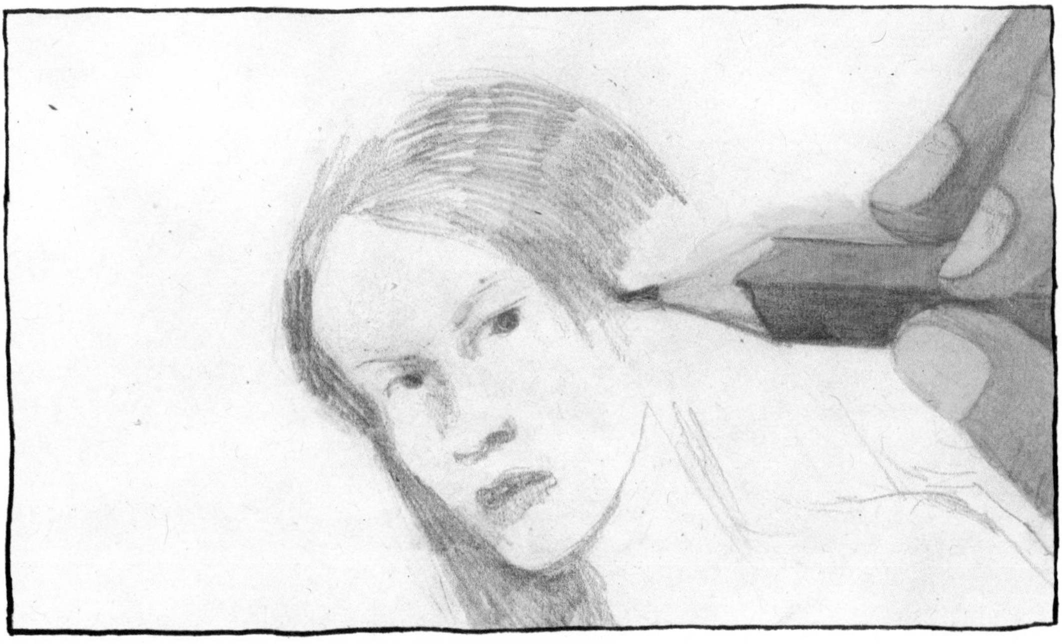

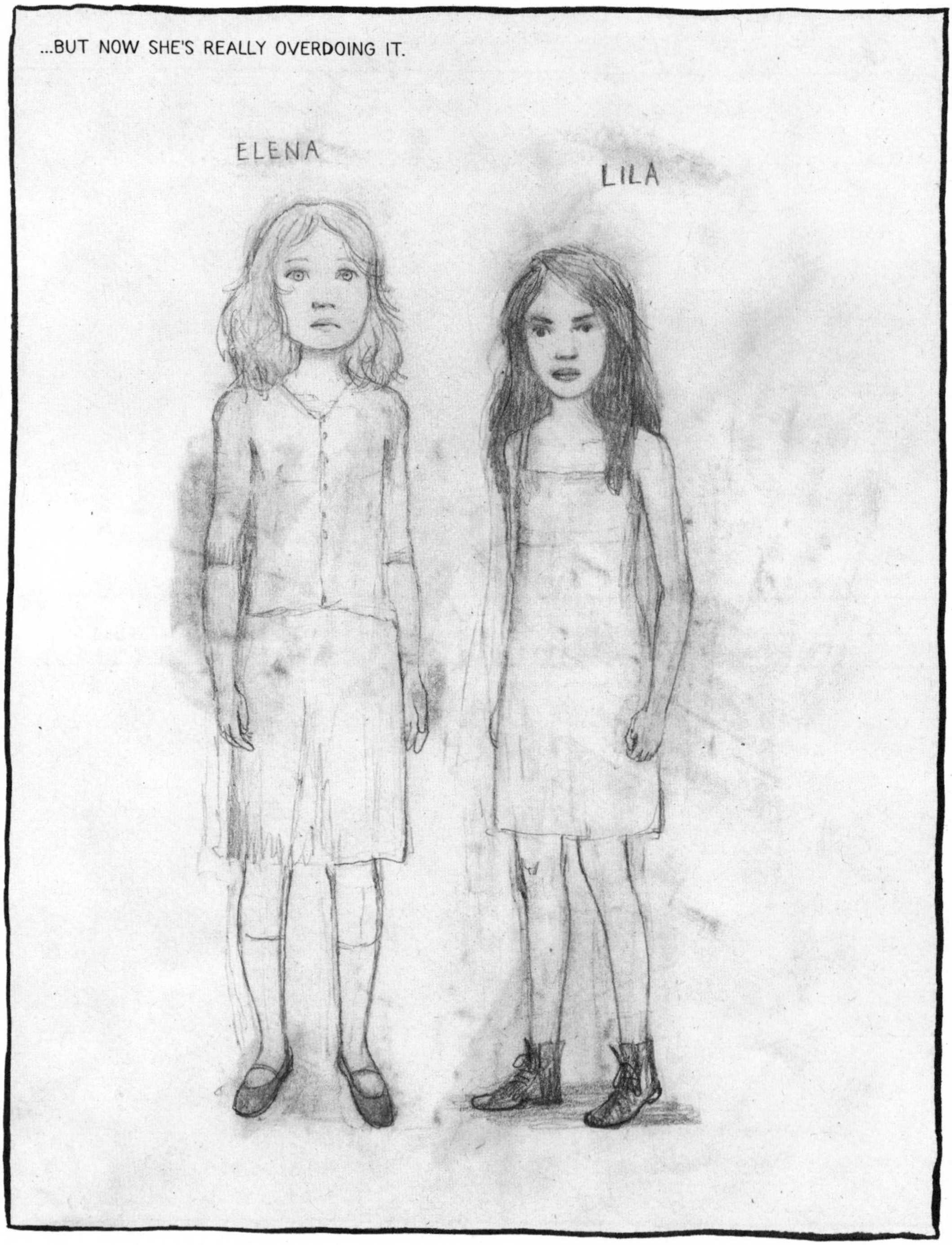
...BUT NOW SHE'S REALLY OVERDOING IT.
ELENA
LILA

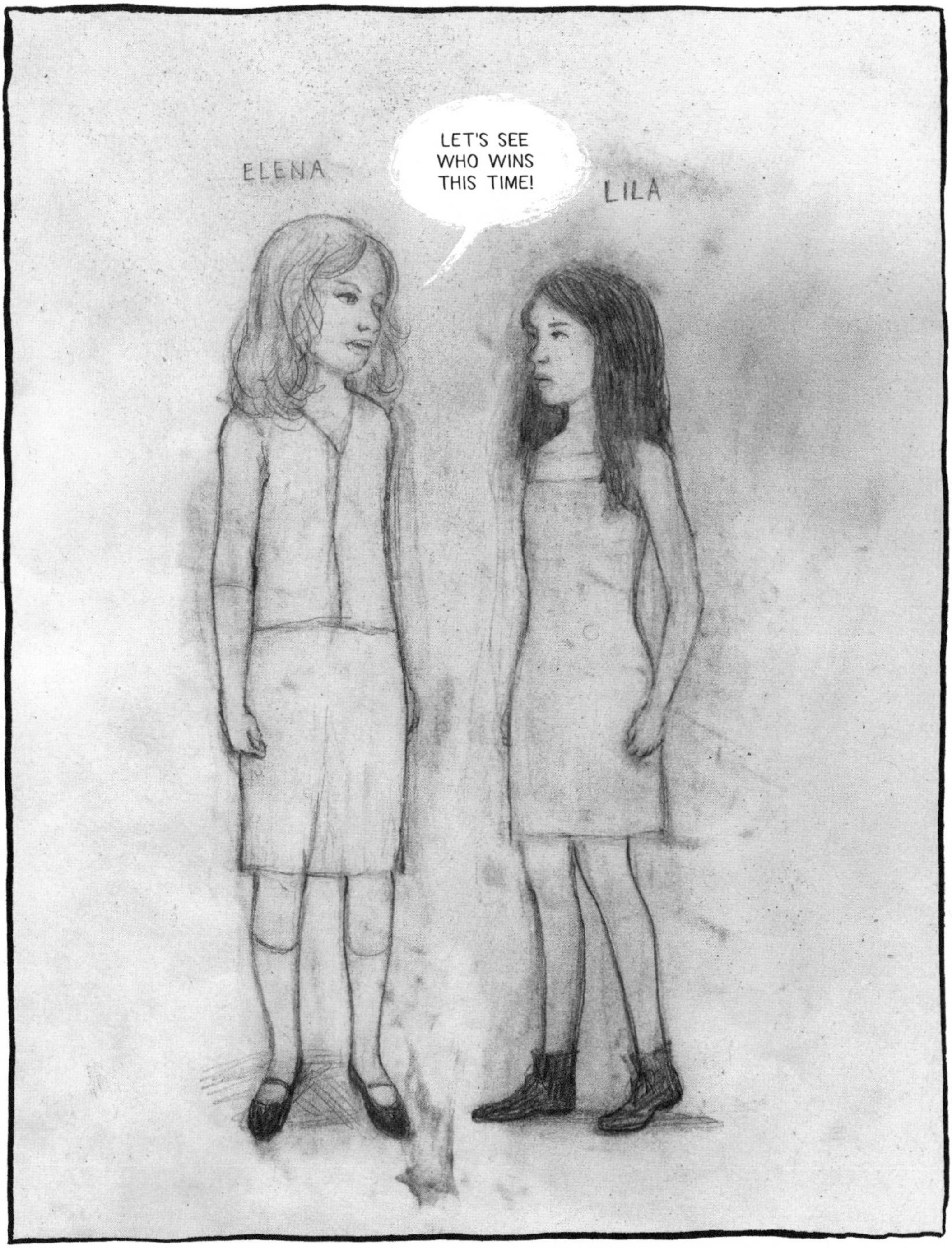
ELENA
LET'S SEE WHO WINS THIS TIME!
LILA

Childhood

- THE STORY OF DON ACHILLE -

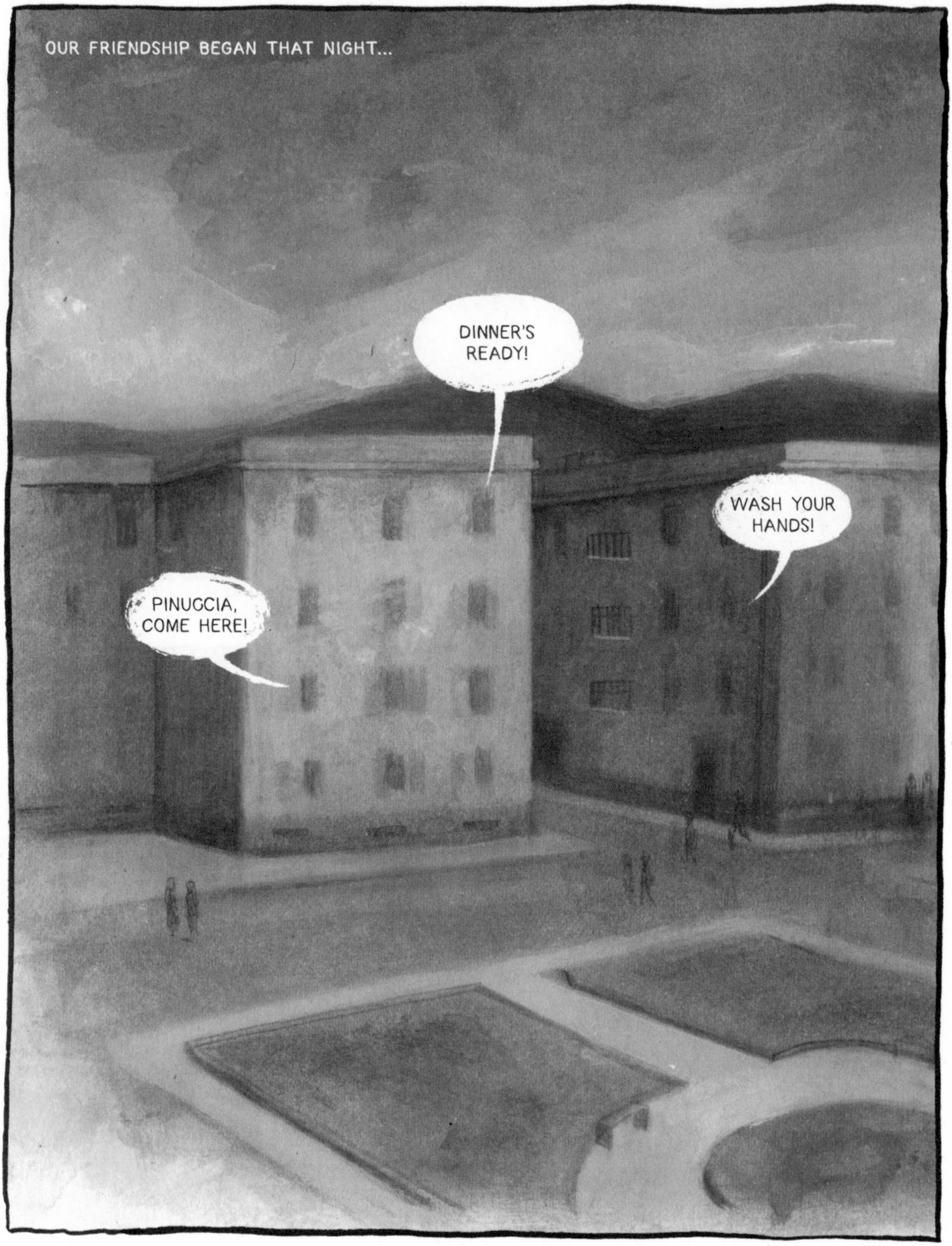
OUR FRIENDSHIP BEGAN THAT NIGHT...
DINNER'S READY!
PINUCCIA, COME HERE!
WASH YOUR HANDS!

IT WAS TIME TO GO HOME...

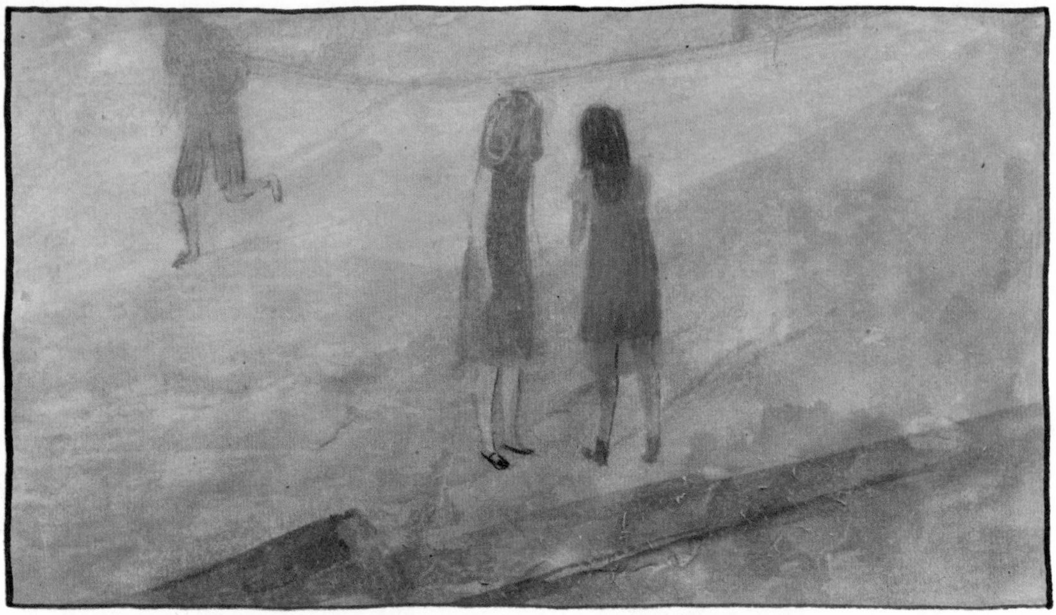

...BUT WE DELAYED, CHALLENGING EACH OTHER, TESTING OUR COURAGE.

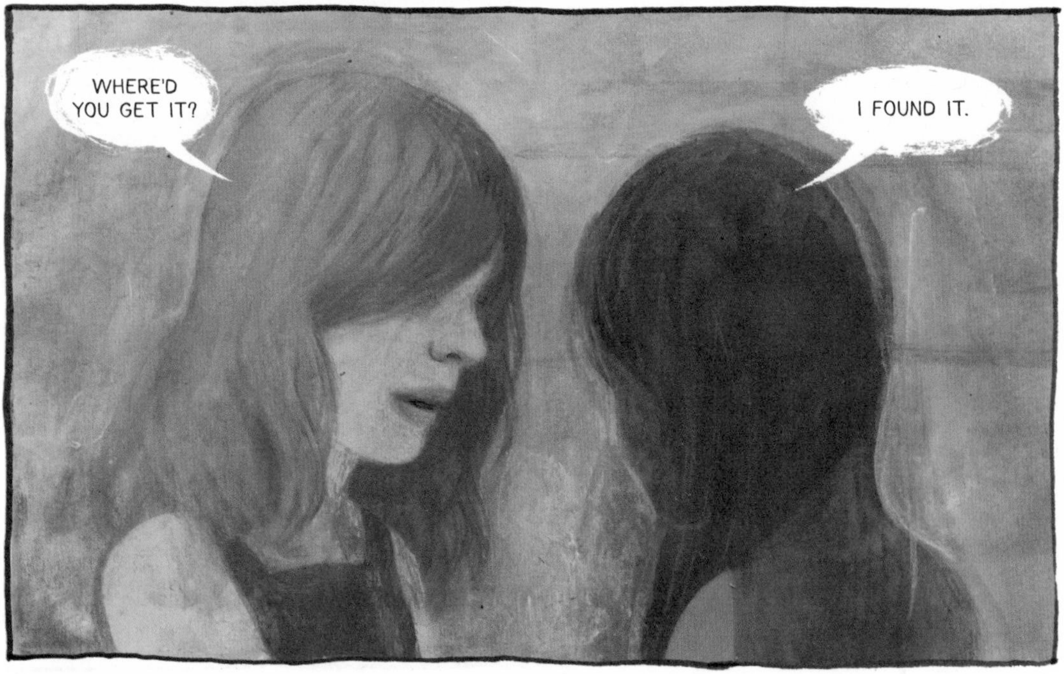
WHERE'D YOU GET IT?
I FOUND IT.

LILA KEPT THAT RUSTED SAFETY PIN LIKE THE GIFT OF A FAIRY GODMOTHER...

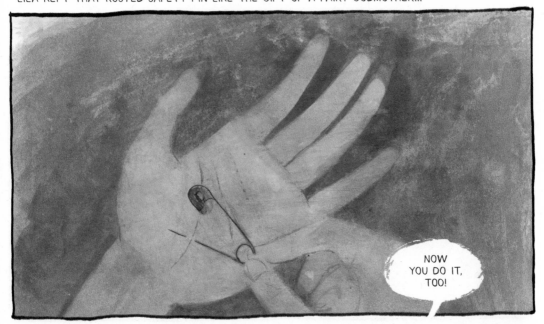

NOW
YOU DO IT,
TOO!

25

AT SOME POINT SHE GAVE ME ONE OF HER LOOKS.

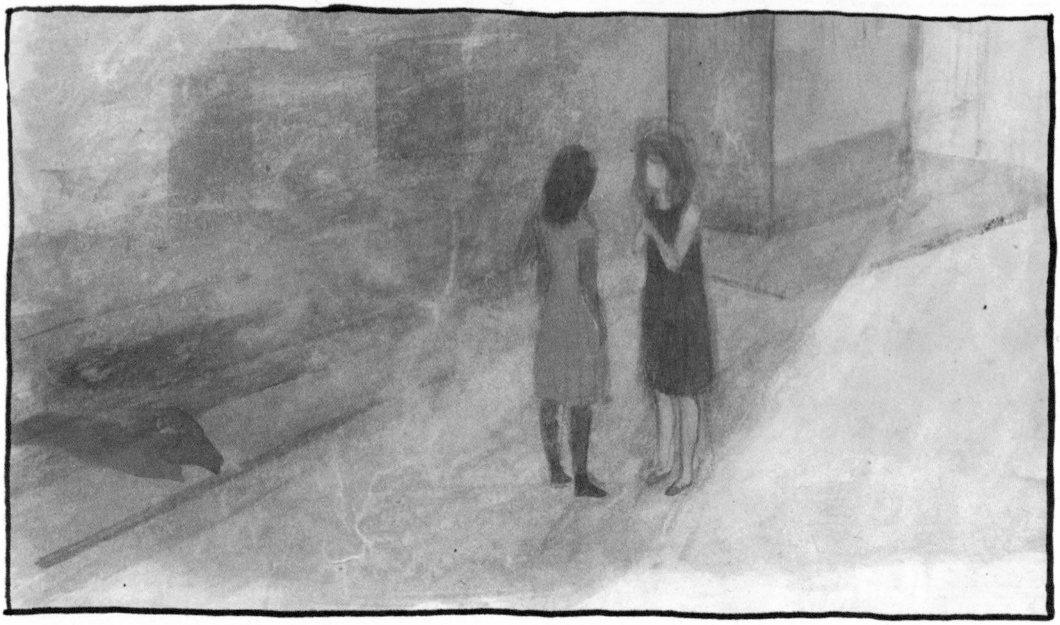

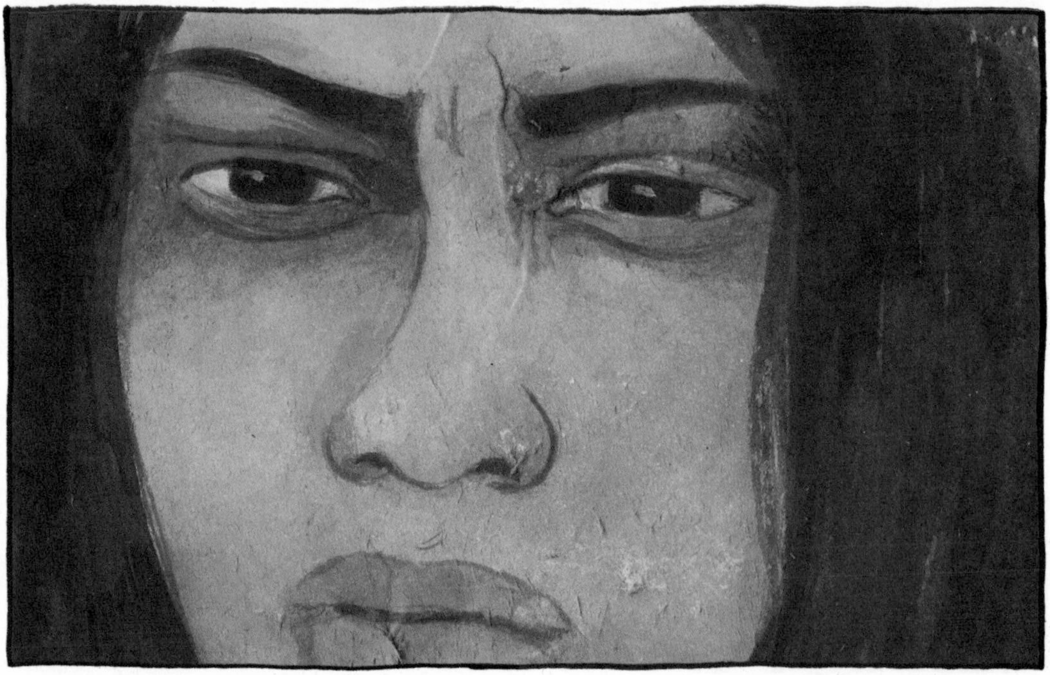

THEN SHE HEADED TOWARD THE BUILDING WHERE DON ACHILLE LIVED.

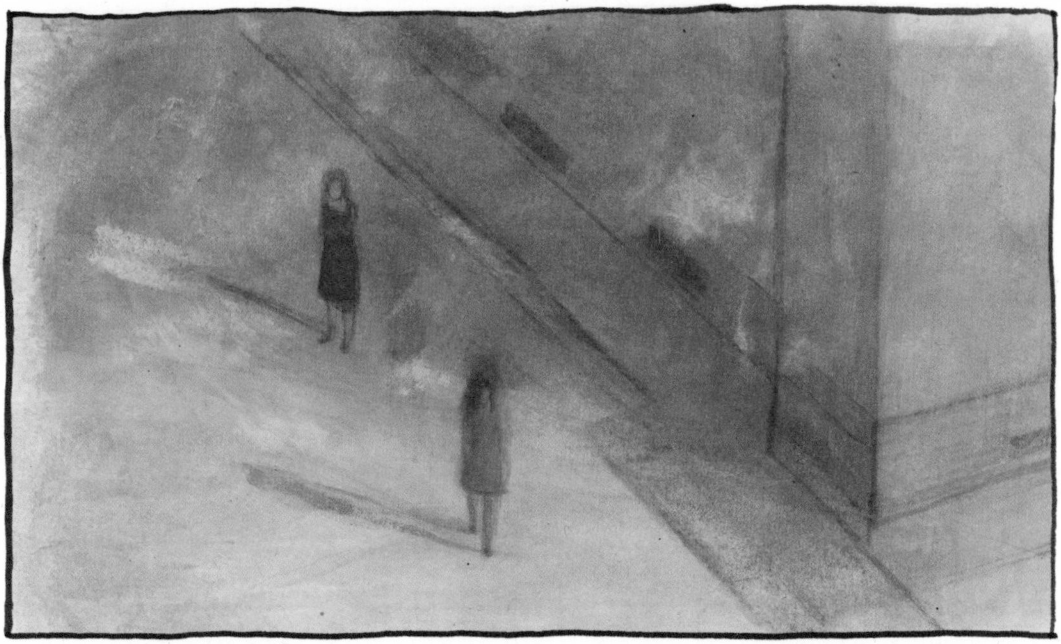

I WAS FROZEN WITH FEAR.

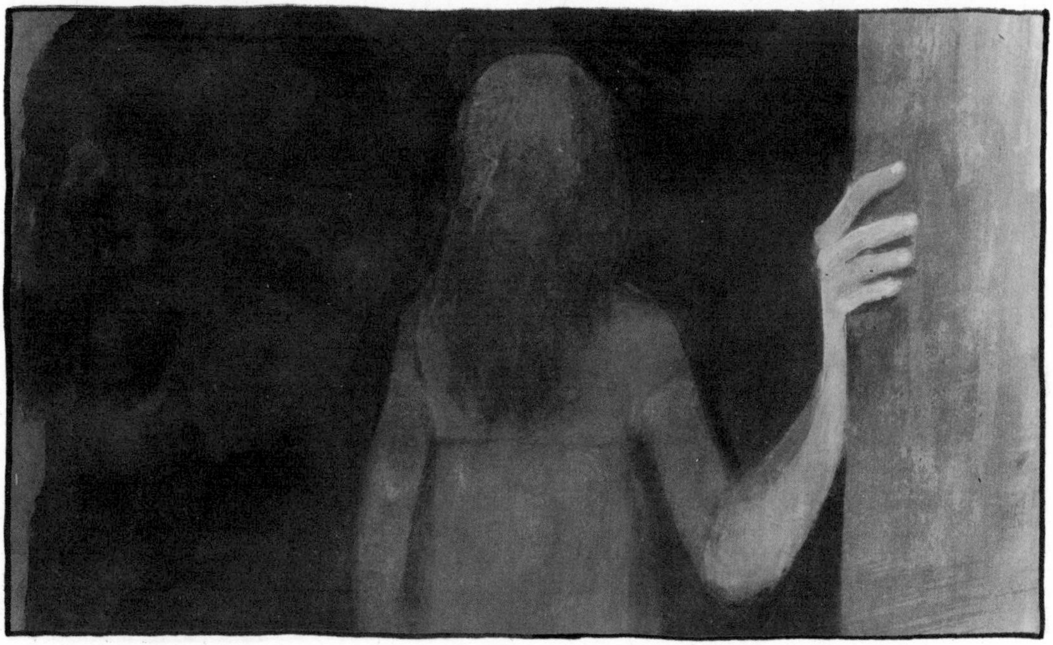

DON ACHILLE WAS THE OGRE OF FAIRY TALES.

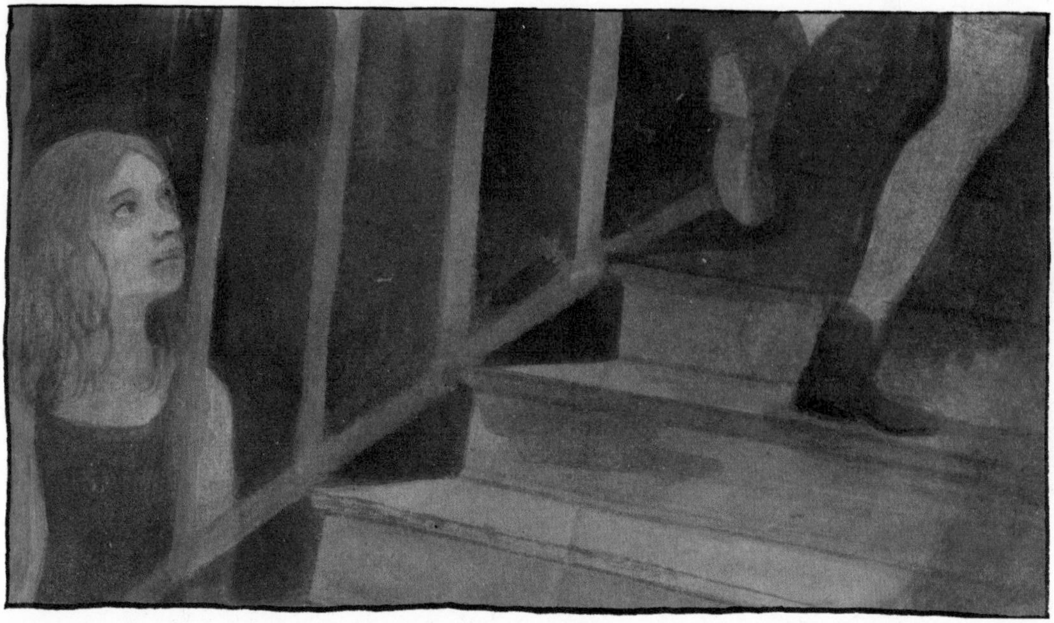

IF I WAS MAD ENOUGH TO APPROACH HIS DOOR, HE WOULD KILL ME.

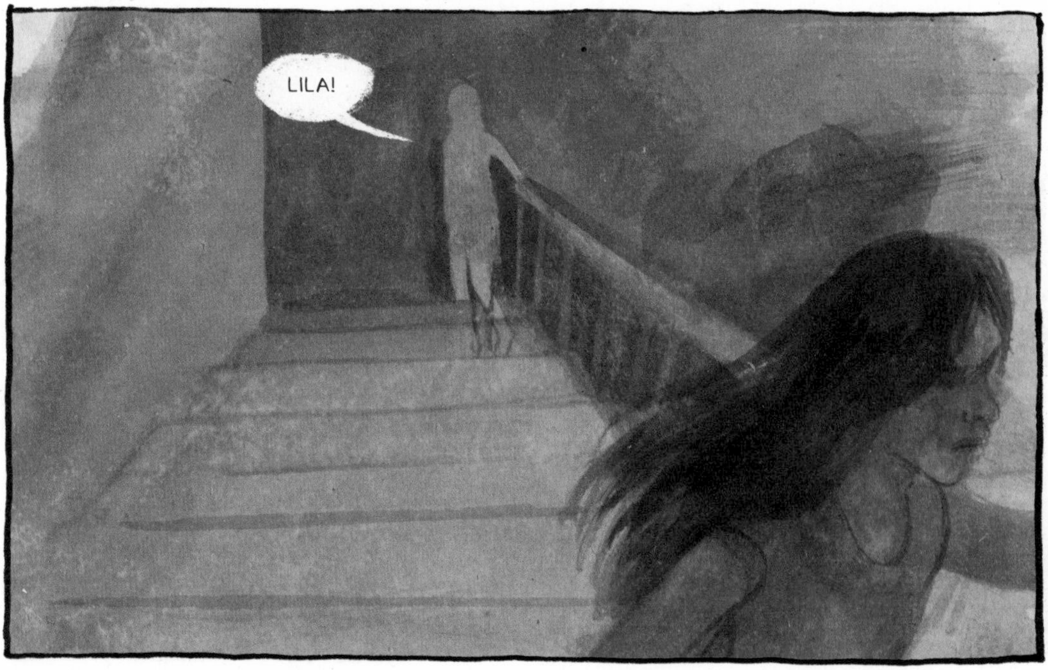
LILA!

REGARDING HIM THERE WAS, IN MY HOUSE BUT NOT ONLY MINE...

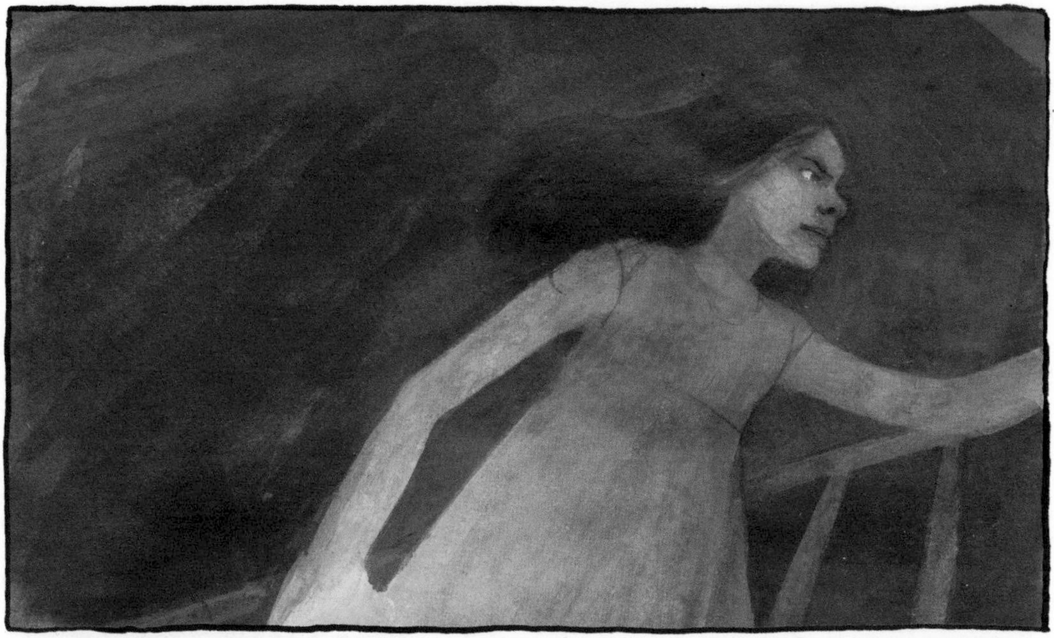

...A FEAR AND A HATRED WHOSE ORIGIN I DIDN'T KNOW.

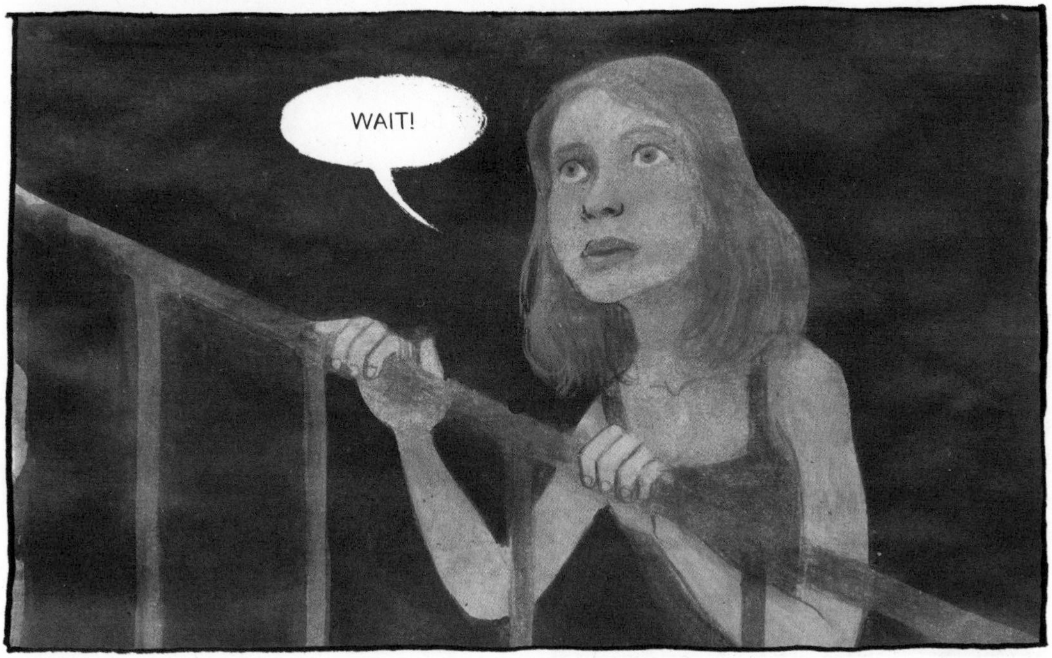
WAIT!

I WAS ABSOLUTELY FORBIDDEN TO GO NEAR HIM.

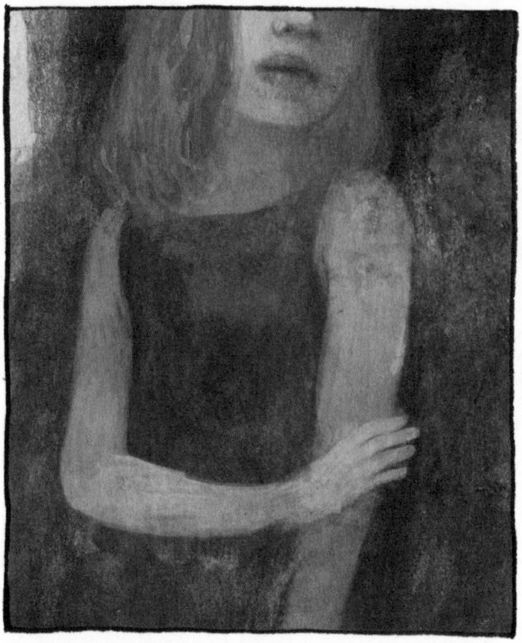

SPEAK TO HIM, SPY ON HIM...

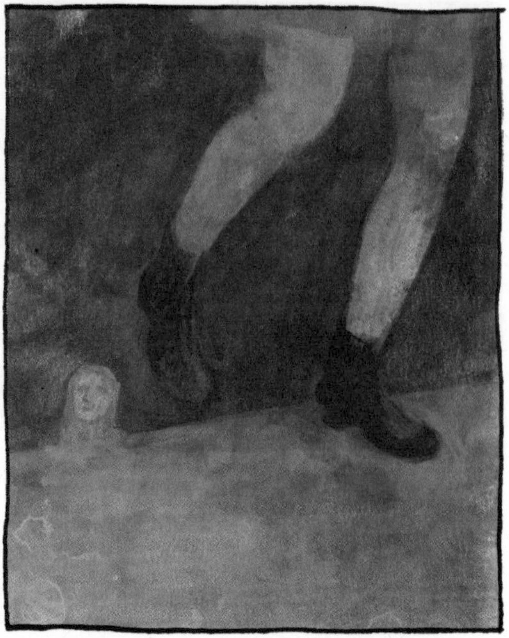

I WAS TO ACT AS IF HE DIDN'T EXIST.

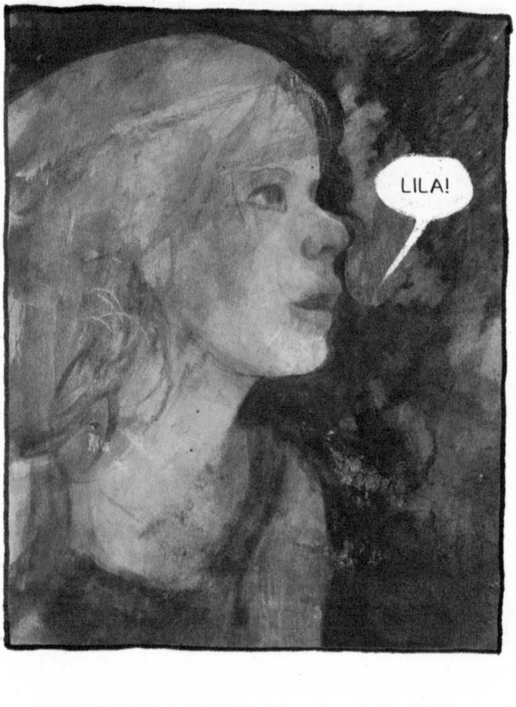
LILA!

IF I MERELY SAW HIM FROM A DISTANCE...

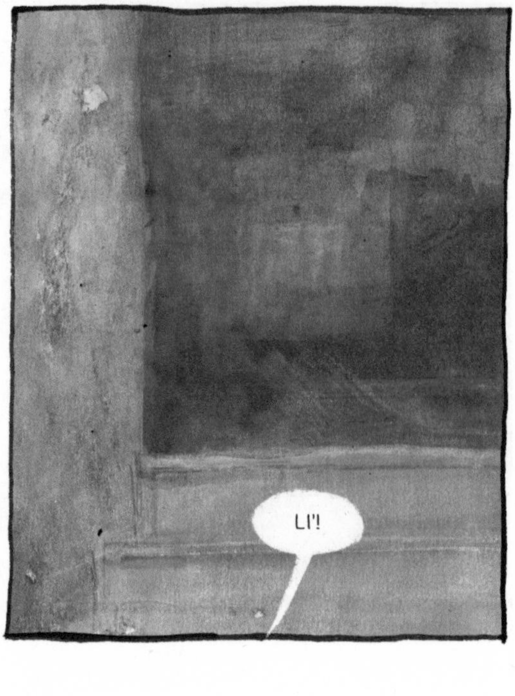
LI'!

...HE WOULD DRIVE SOMETHING SHARP AND BURNING INTO MY EYES.

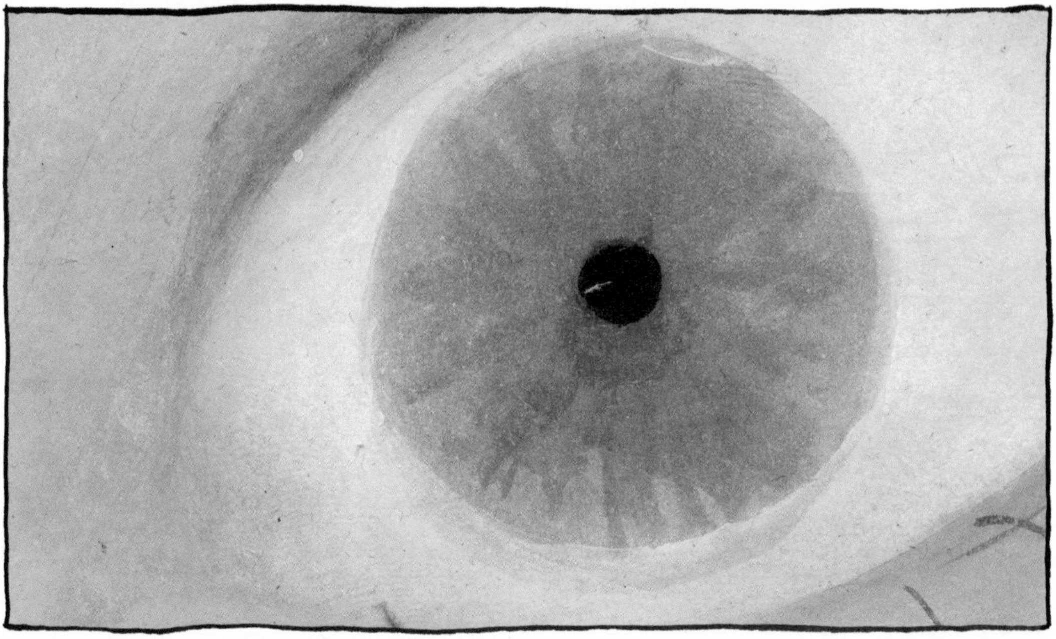

SUDDENLY THE LIGHT ON THE STAIRS CAME ON.

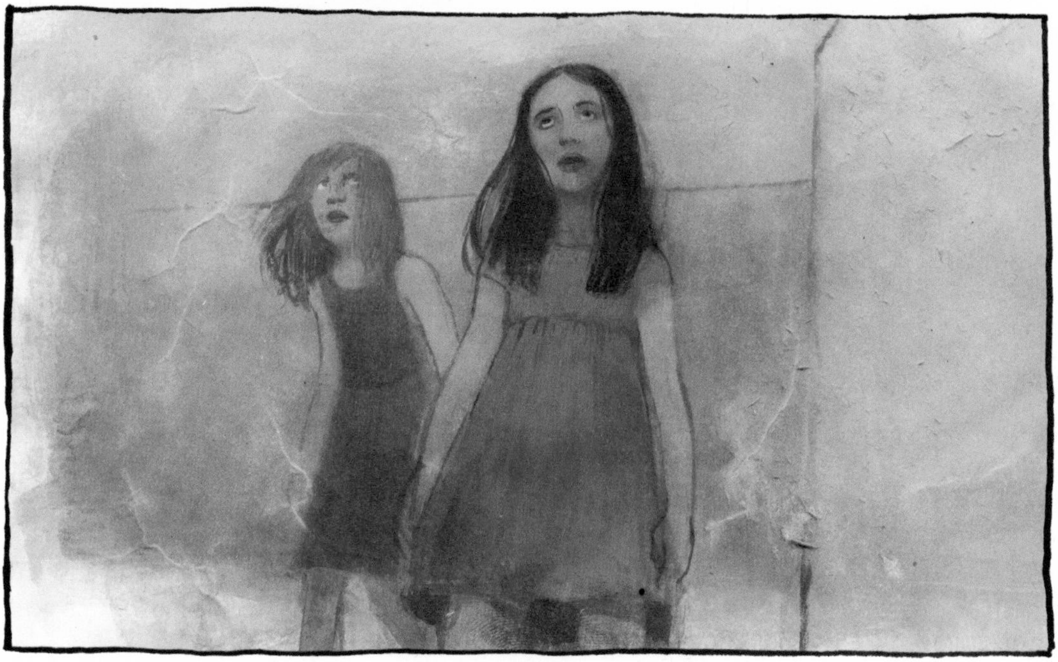

WAS IT DON ACHILLE WHO HAD TURNED THE SWITCH?

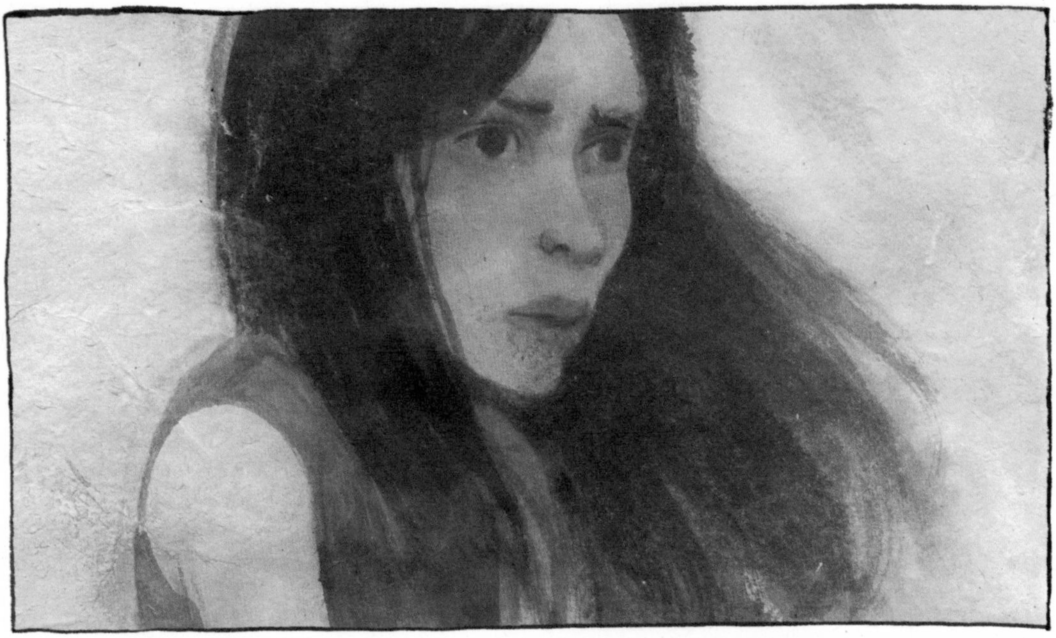

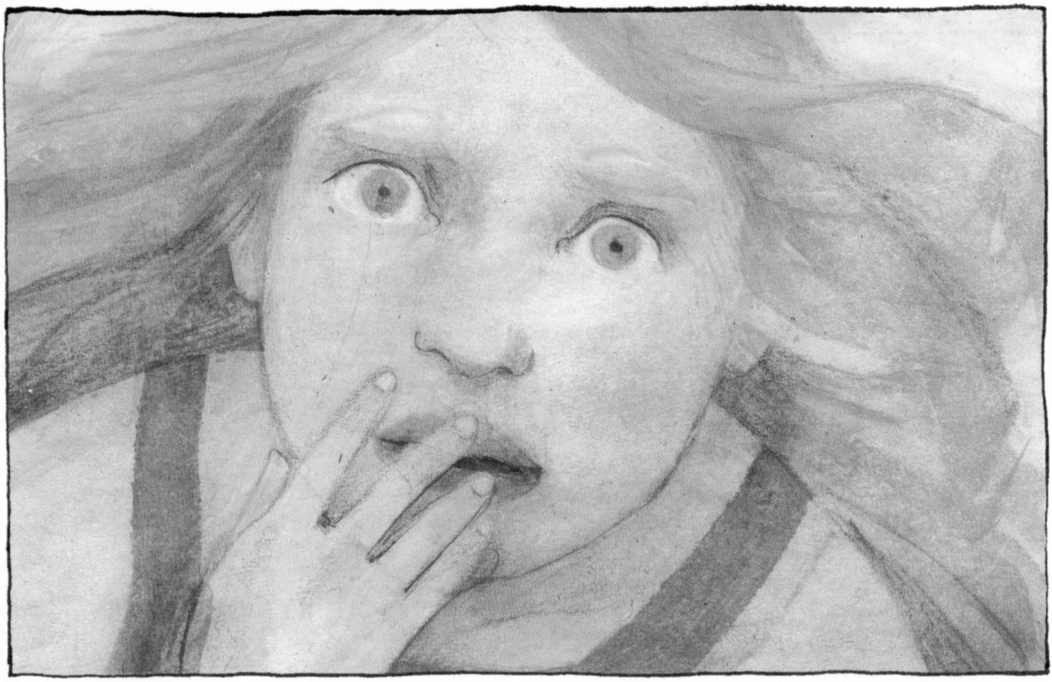

WE WAITED, BUT WE HEARD NOTHING.

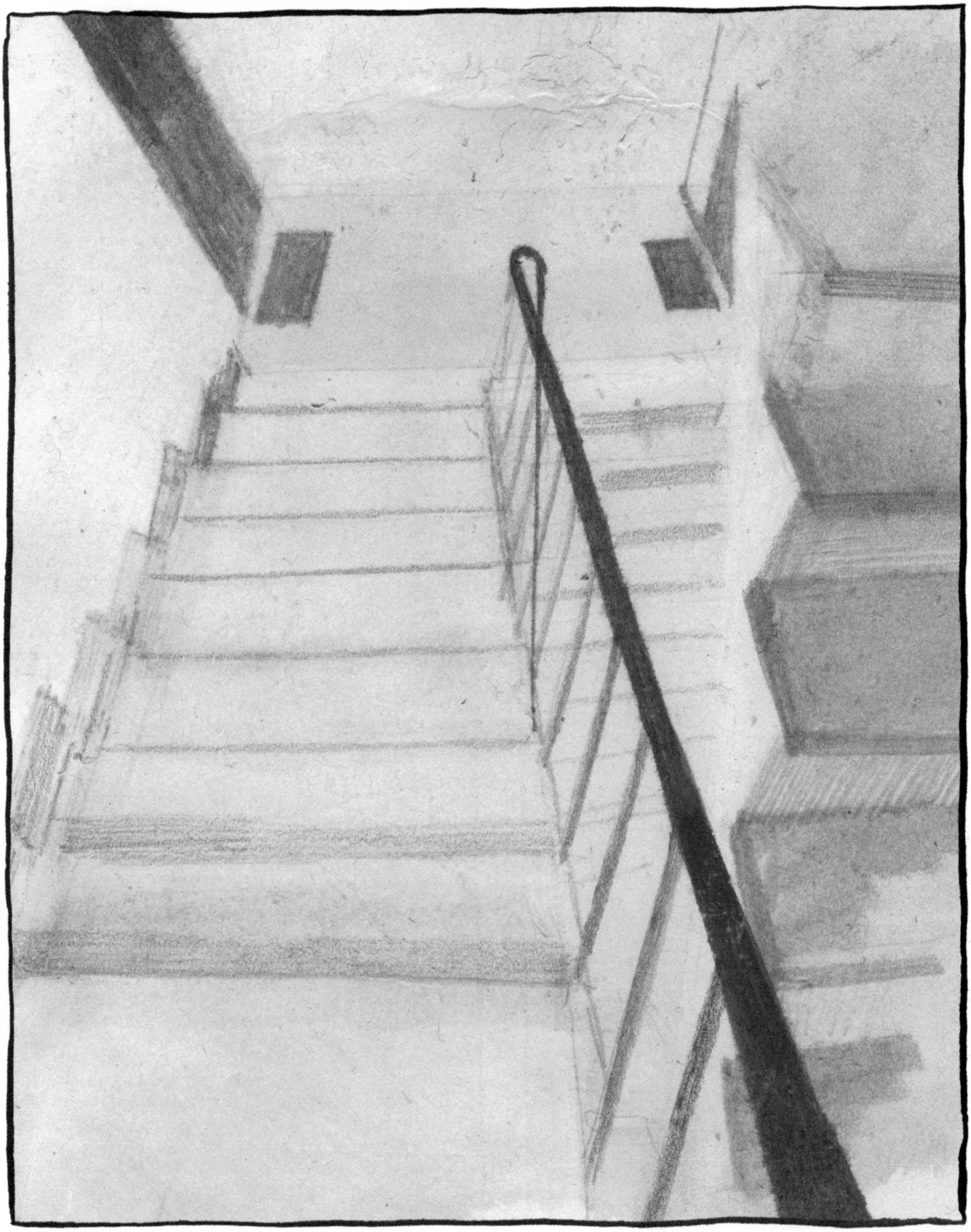

THEN SHE CONTINUED ON, AND I FOLLOWED.

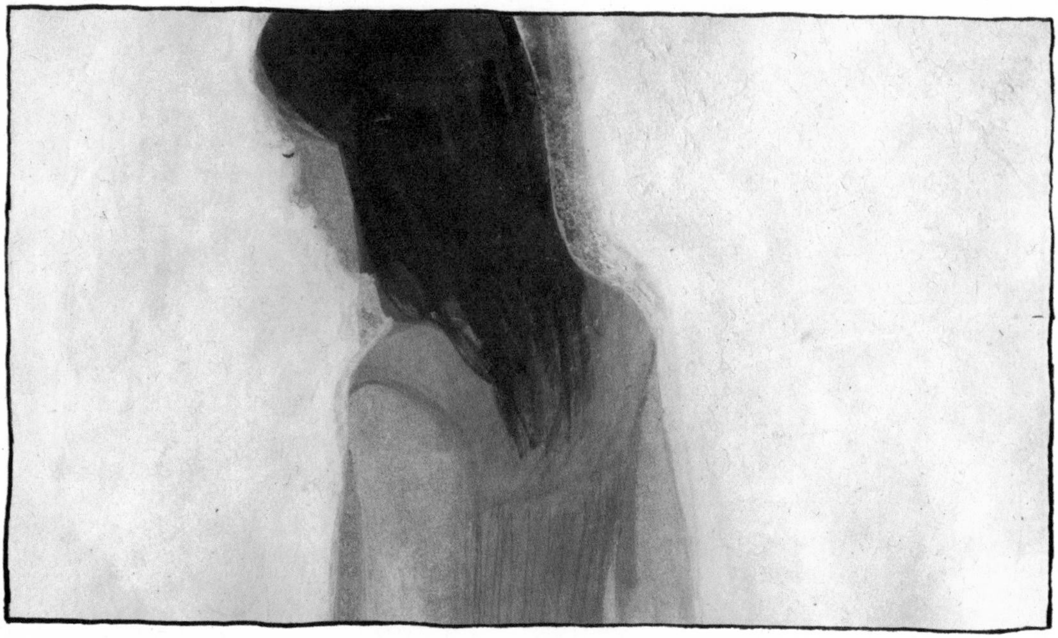

AT THE FOURTH FLIGHT...

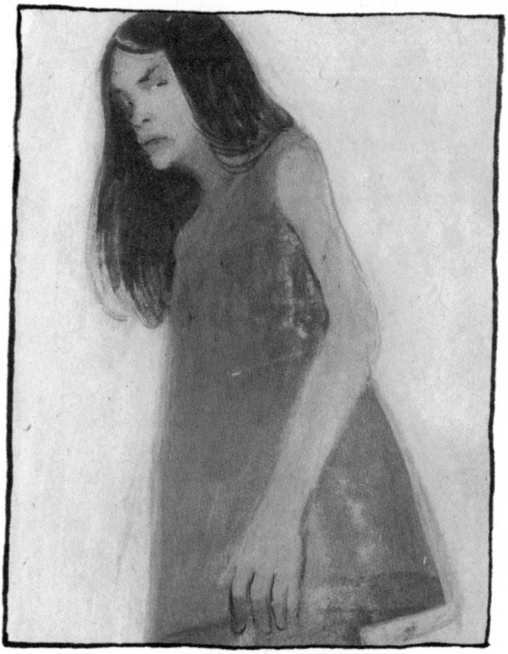

...SHE DID SOMETHING UNEXPECTED.

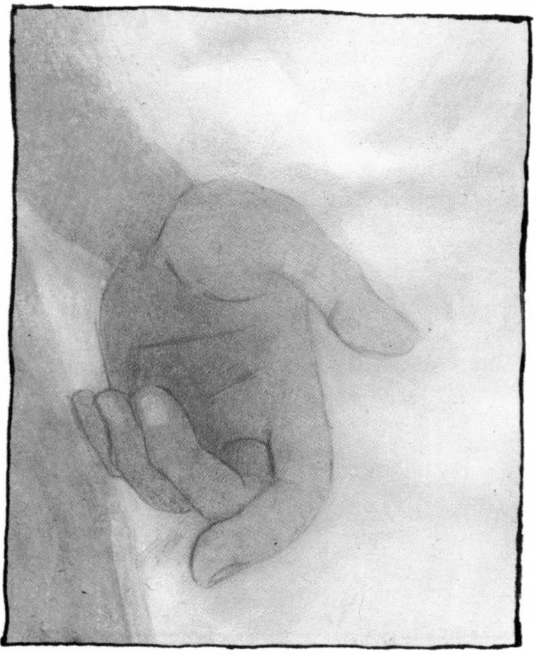

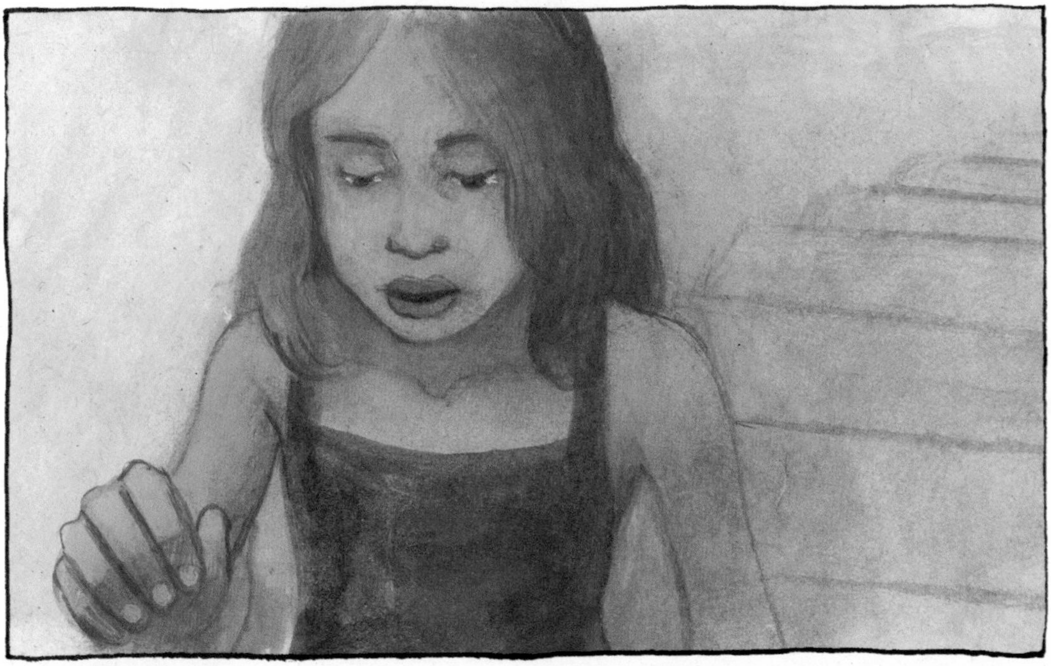

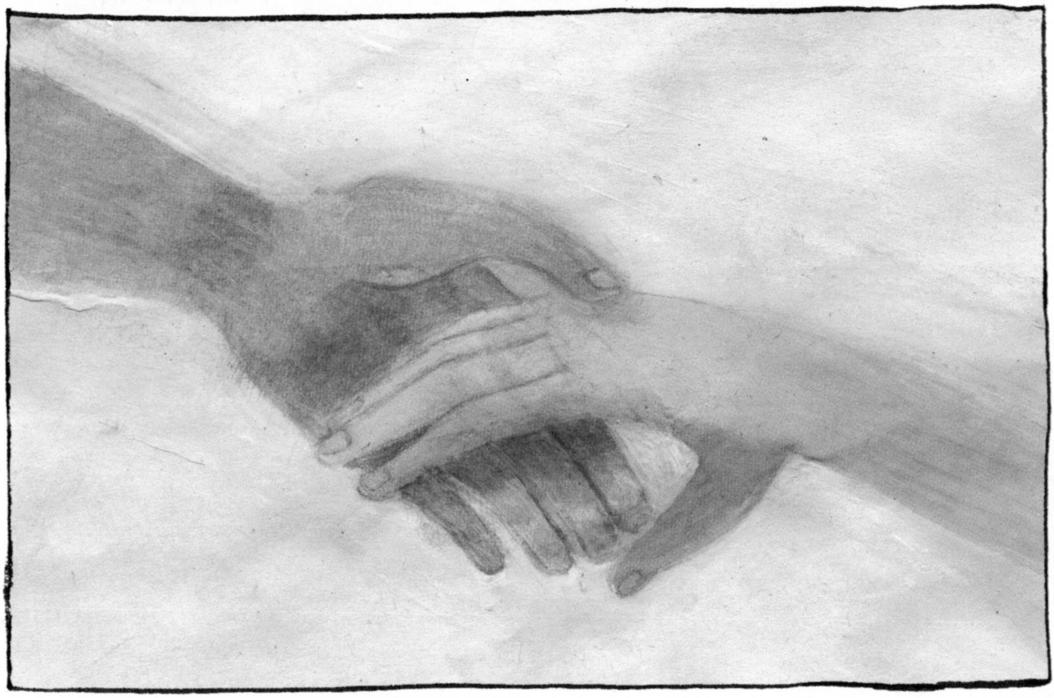

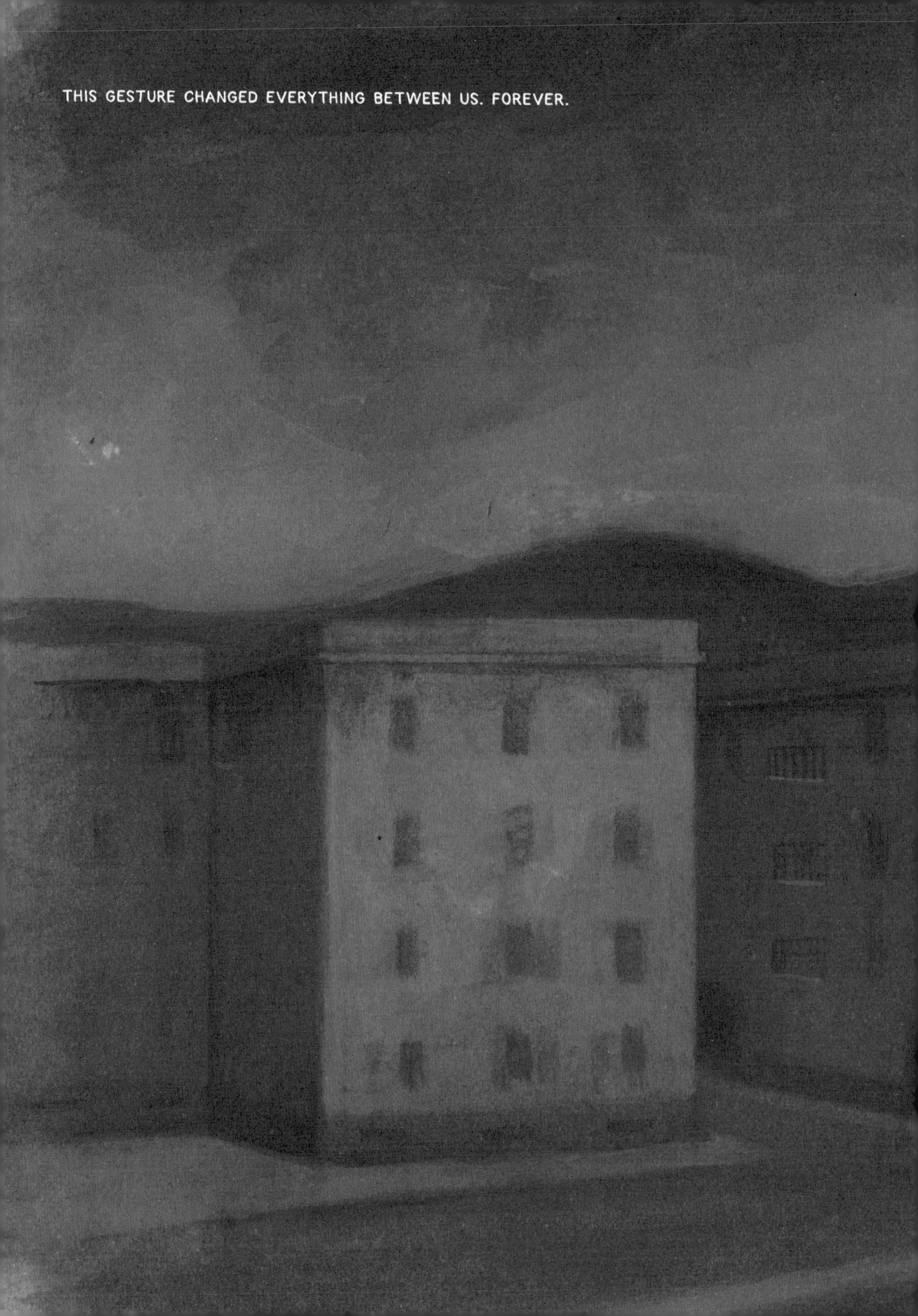
THIS GESTURE CHANGED EVERYTHING BETWEEN US. FOREVER.

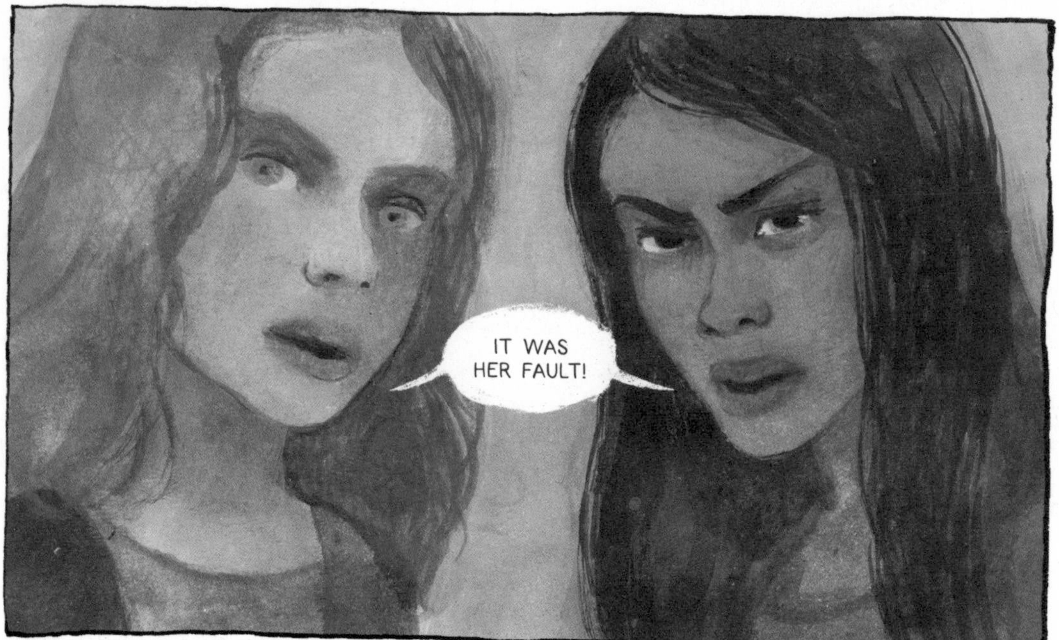
IT WAS HER FAULT!

NOT TOO LONG BEFORE—TEN DAYS, A MONTH, WHO CAN SAY...

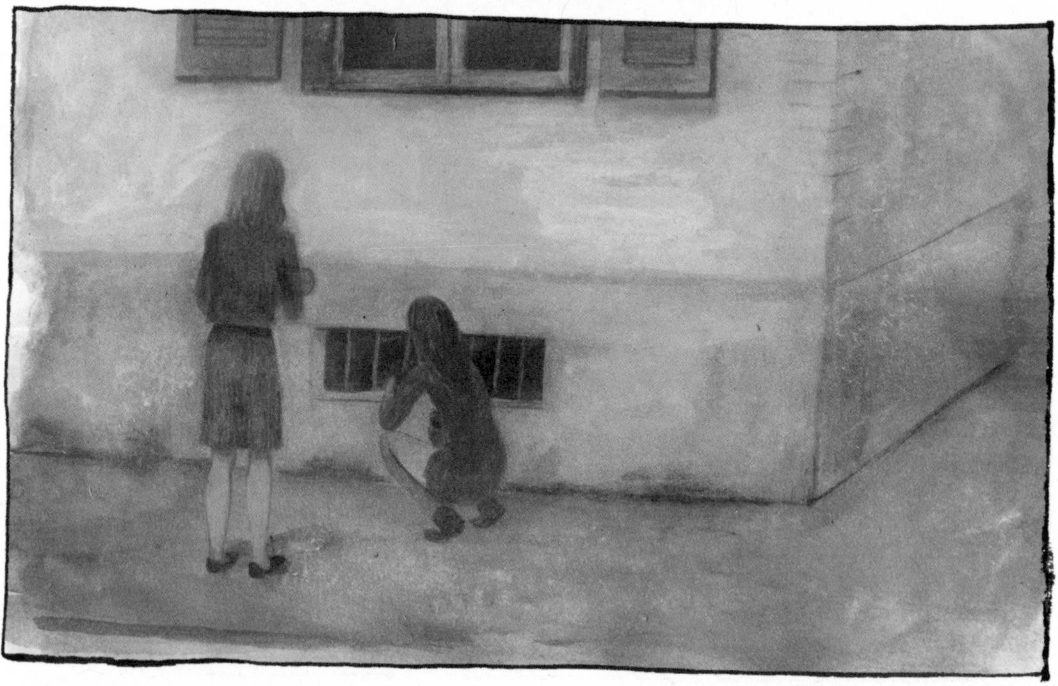

...WE WERE PLAYING IN THE COURTYARD,

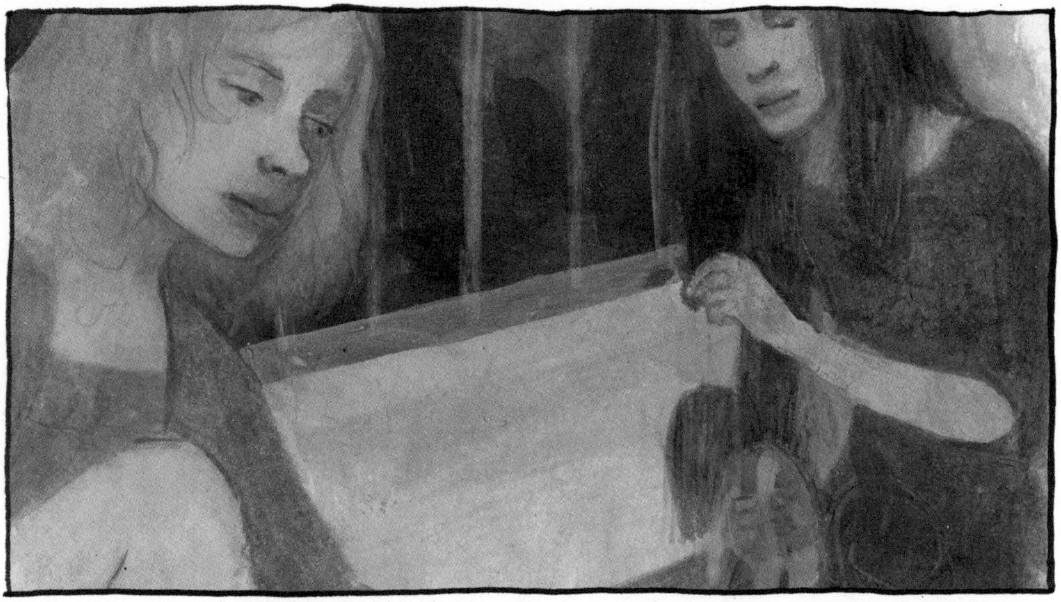

BUT AS IF WE WEREN'T PLAYING TOGETHER.

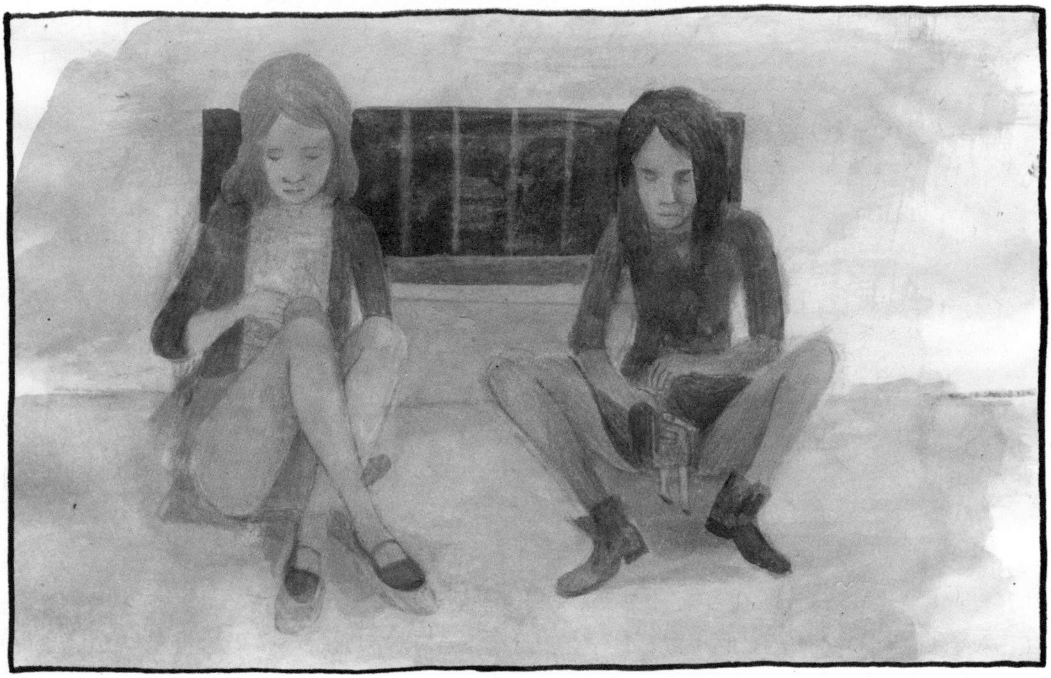

MY DOLL HAD A PLASTIC FACE AND PLASTIC EYES. HER NAME WAS TINA.

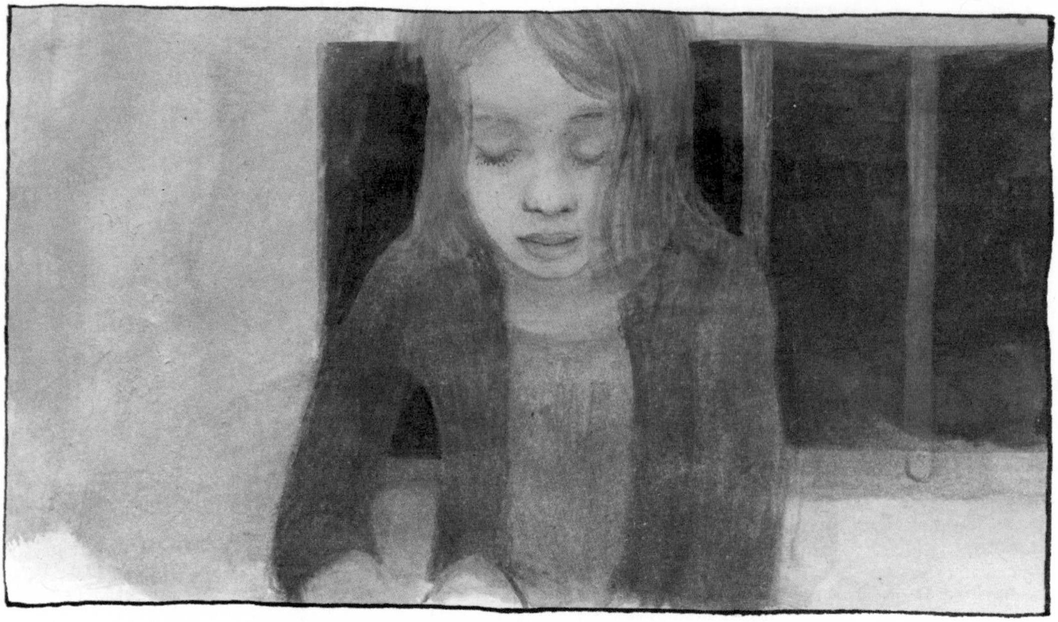

HER DOLL HAD A YELLOWISH CLOTH BODY, FILLED WITH SAWDUST. HER NAME WAS NU.

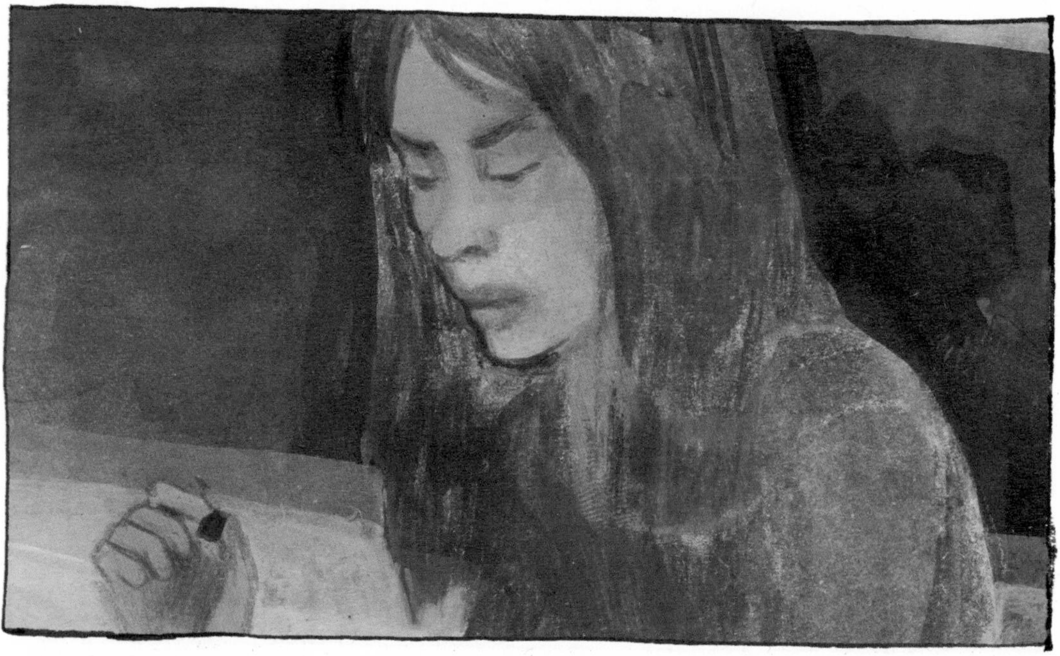

TINA AND NU WEREN'T HAPPY.

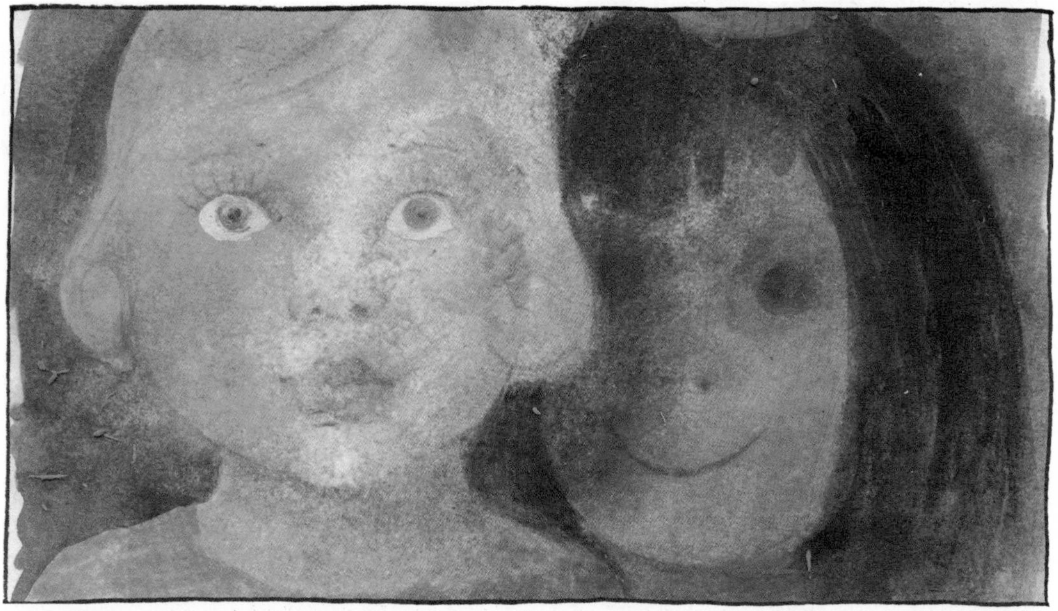

OUR TERRORS WERE THEIRS.

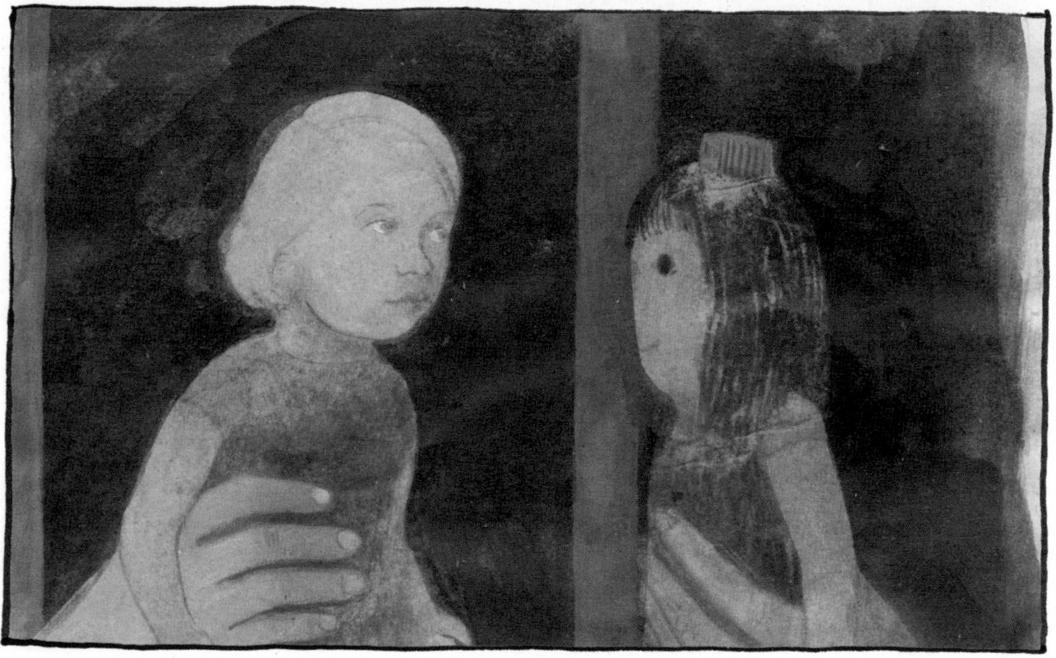

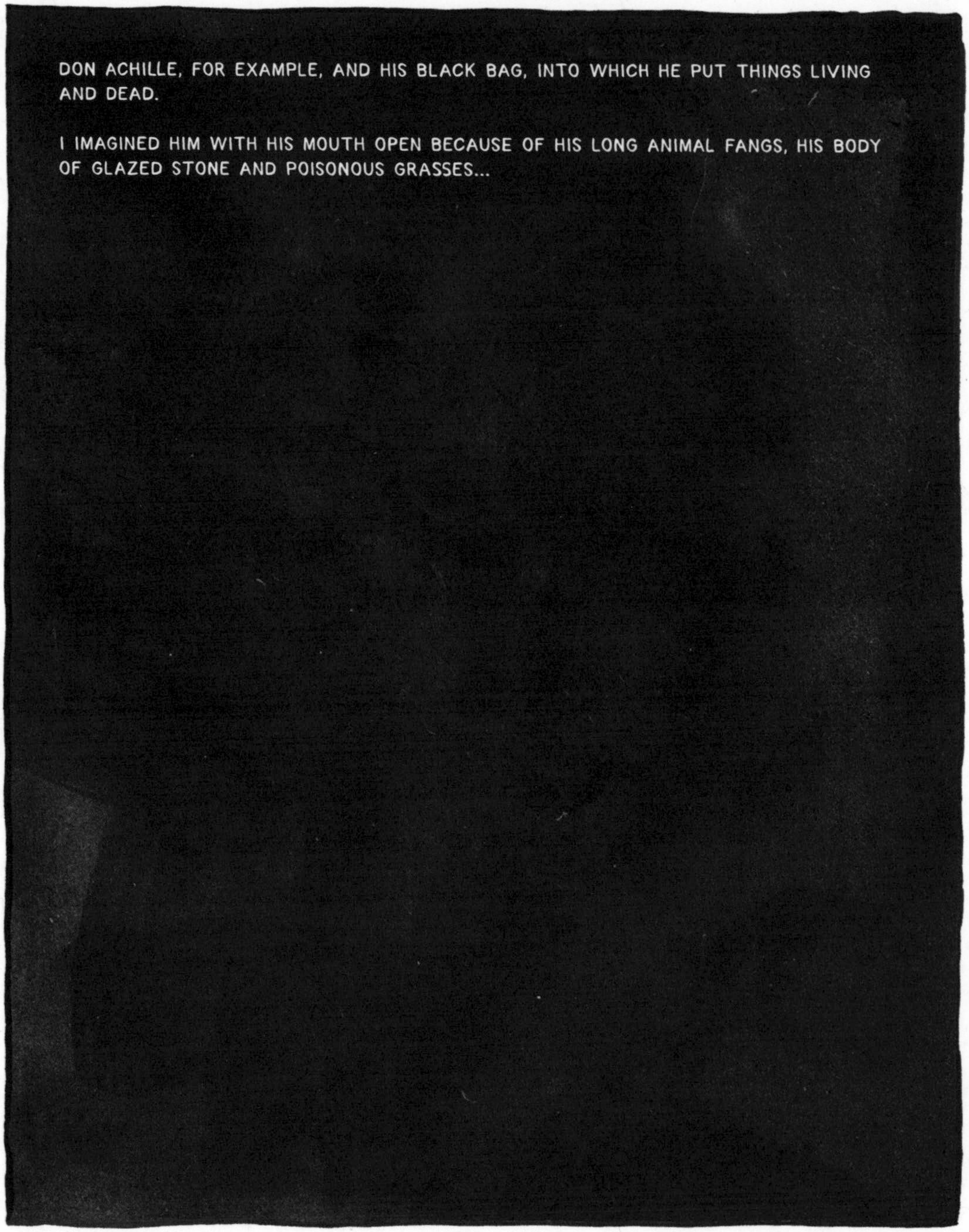
DON ACHILLE, FOR EXAMPLE, AND HIS BLACK BAG, INTO WHICH HE PUT THINGS LIVING AND DEAD.
I IMAGINED HIM WITH HIS MOUTH OPEN BECAUSE OF HIS LONG ANIMAL FANGS, HIS BODY OF GLAZED STONE AND POISONOUS GRASSES...

LILA KNEW I HAD THAT FEAR.

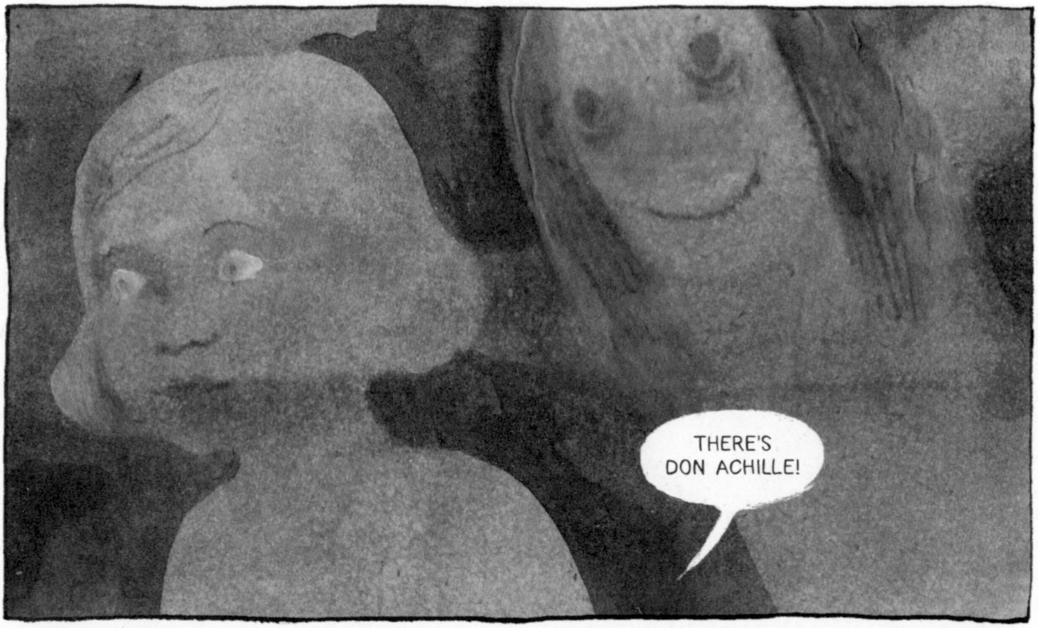
THERE'S DON ACHILLE!

TINA AND NU TALKED ABOUT IT OUT LOUD.

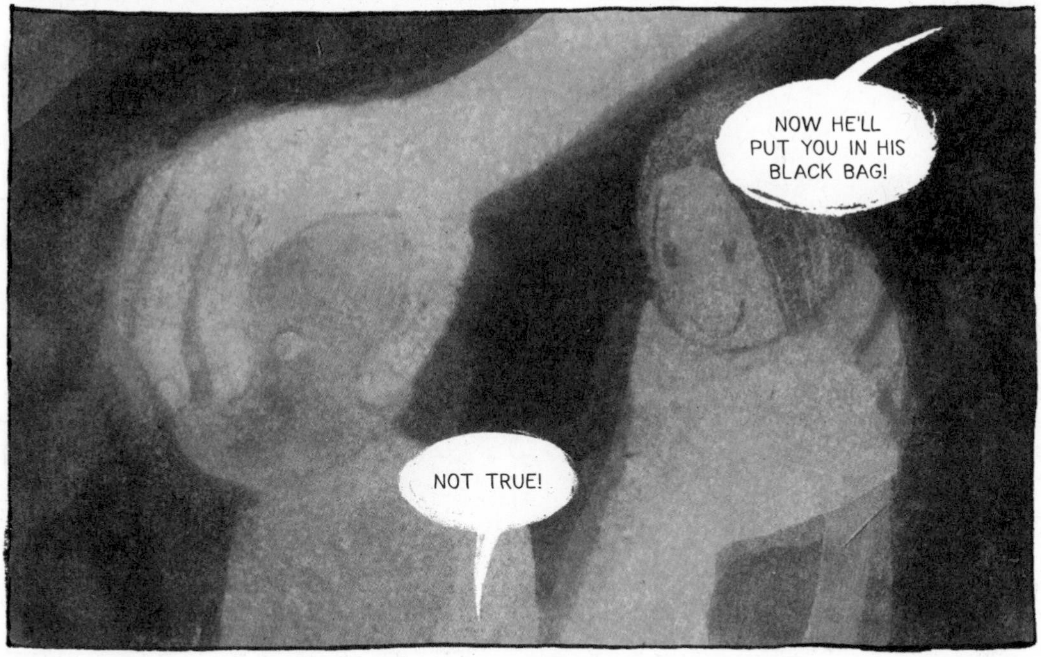
NOW HE'LL PUT YOU IN HIS BLACK BAG!
NOT TRUE!

THAT'S WHY, WHEN SHE PROPOSED THAT WE EXCHANGE DOLLS...

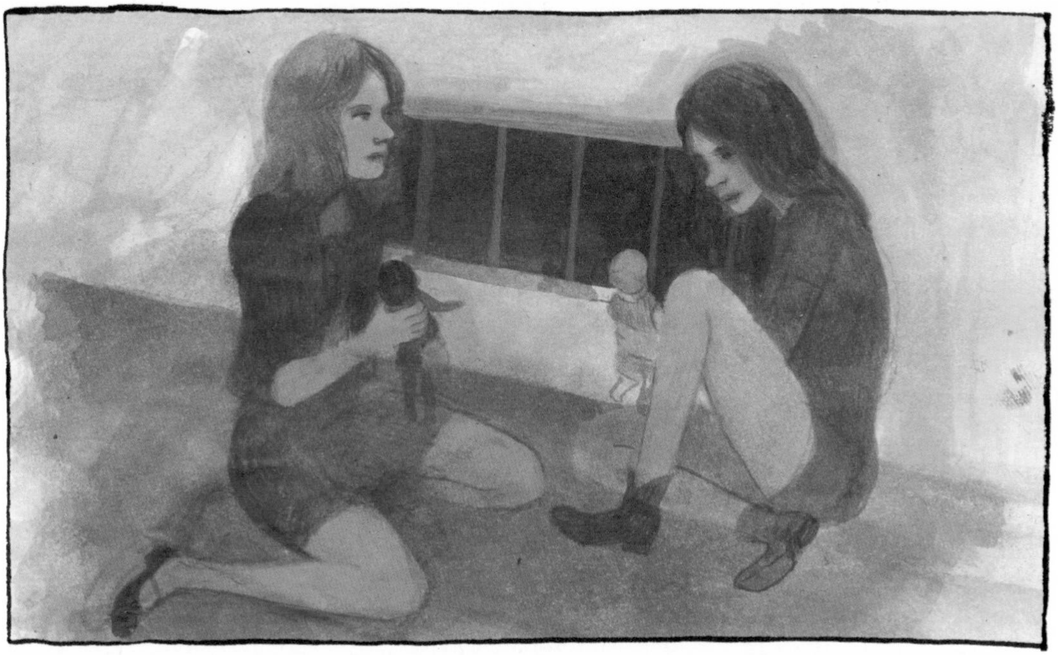

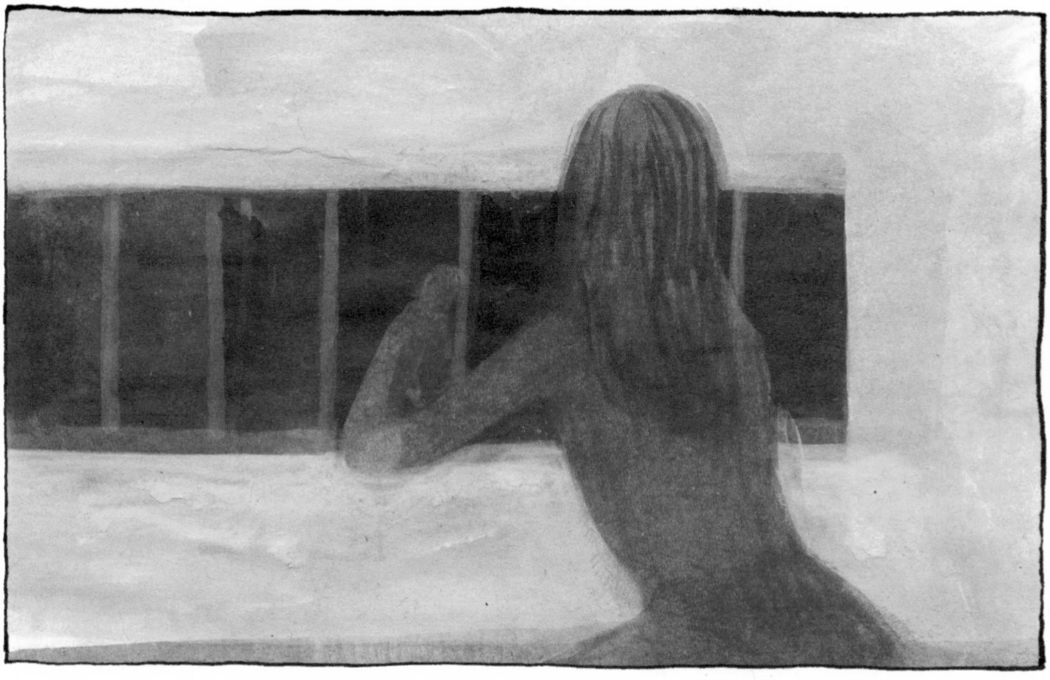

...AS SOON AS SHE HAD TINA SHE PUSHED HER THROUGH THE GRATE.

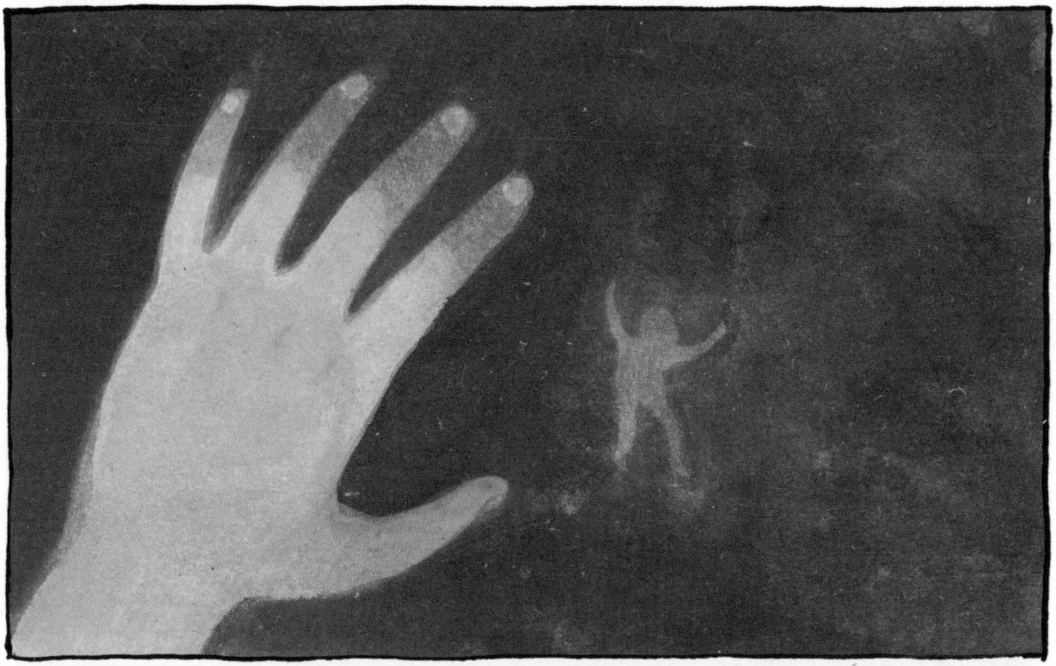

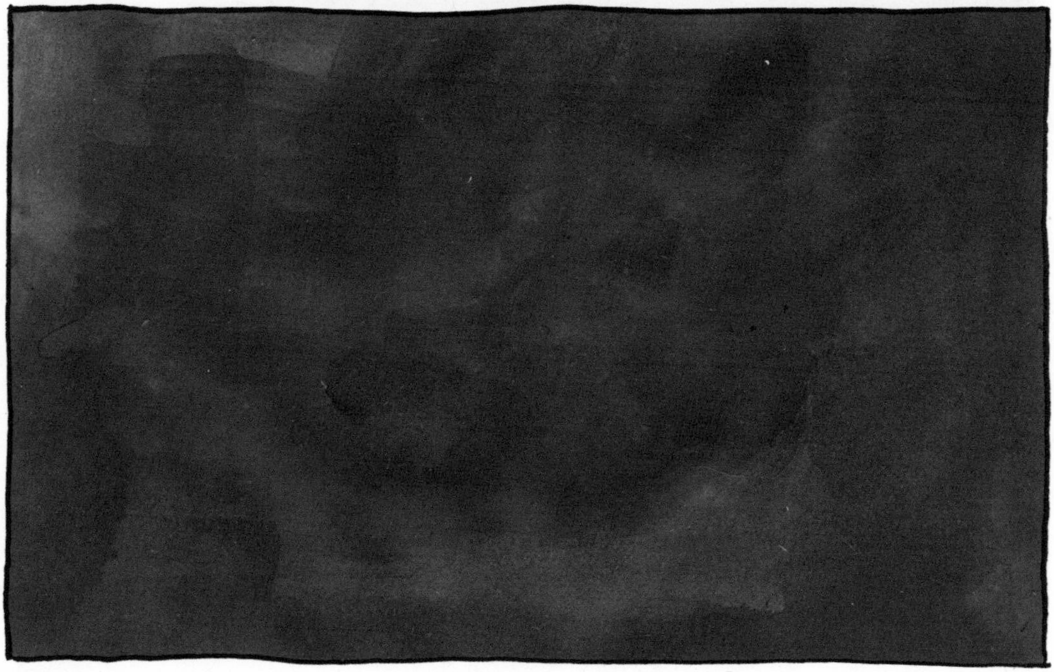

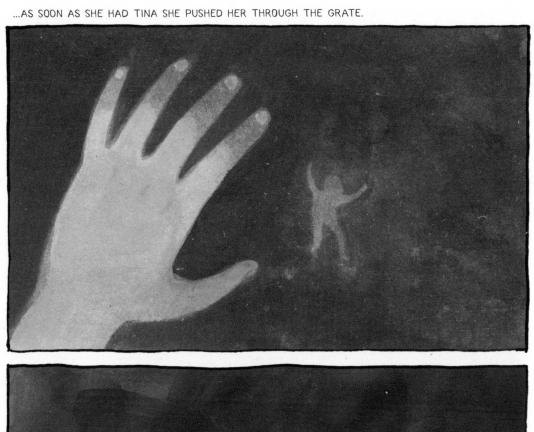

I KNEW LILA WAS BAD...

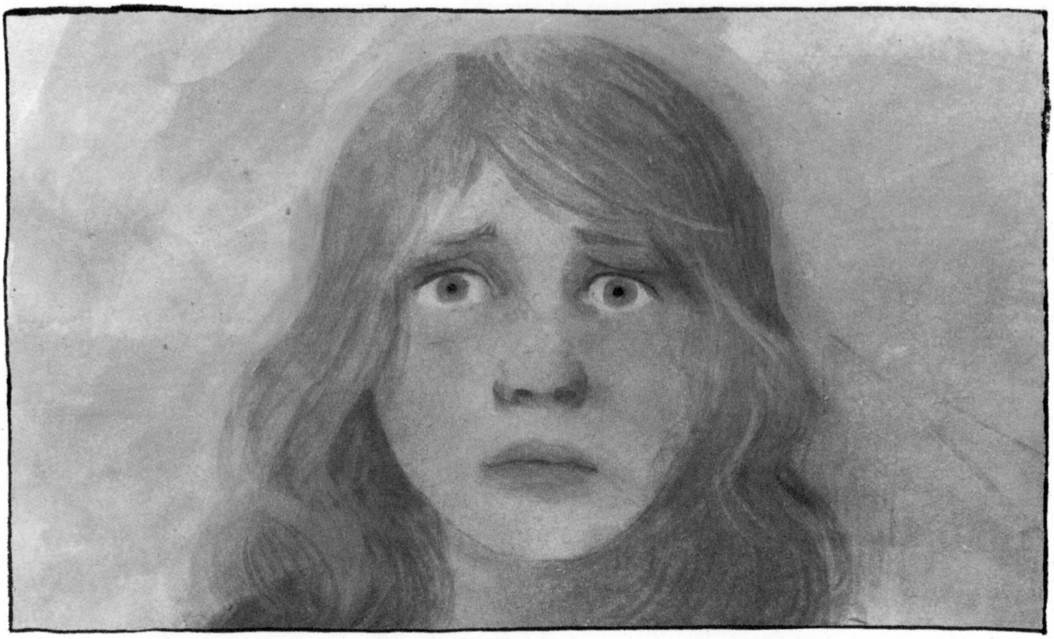

...BUT I NEVER THOUGHT SHE'D DO SOMETHING SO MEAN.

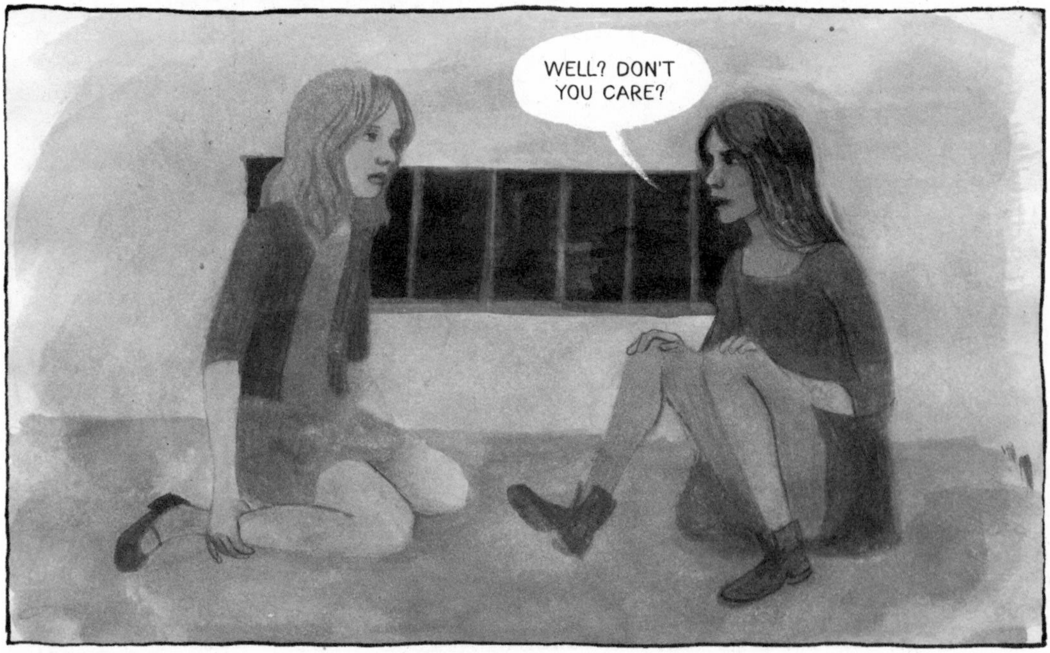
WELL? DON'T YOU CARE?

I SAID NOTHING. I ONLY ACTED, WITHOUT SPITE, AS IF IT WERE NATURAL,

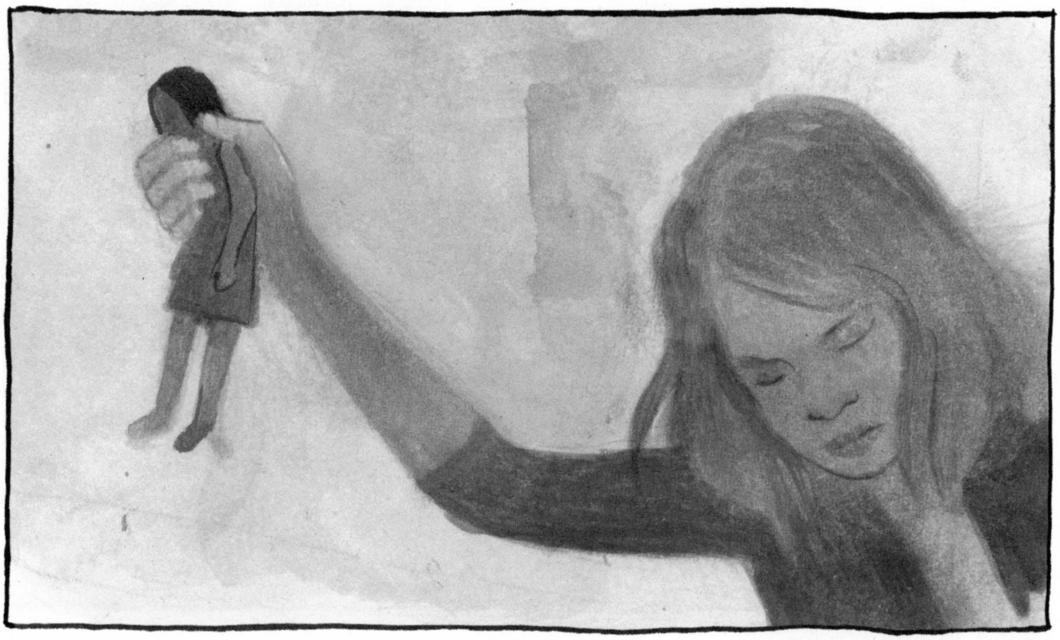

EVEN IF IT WASN'T NATURAL.

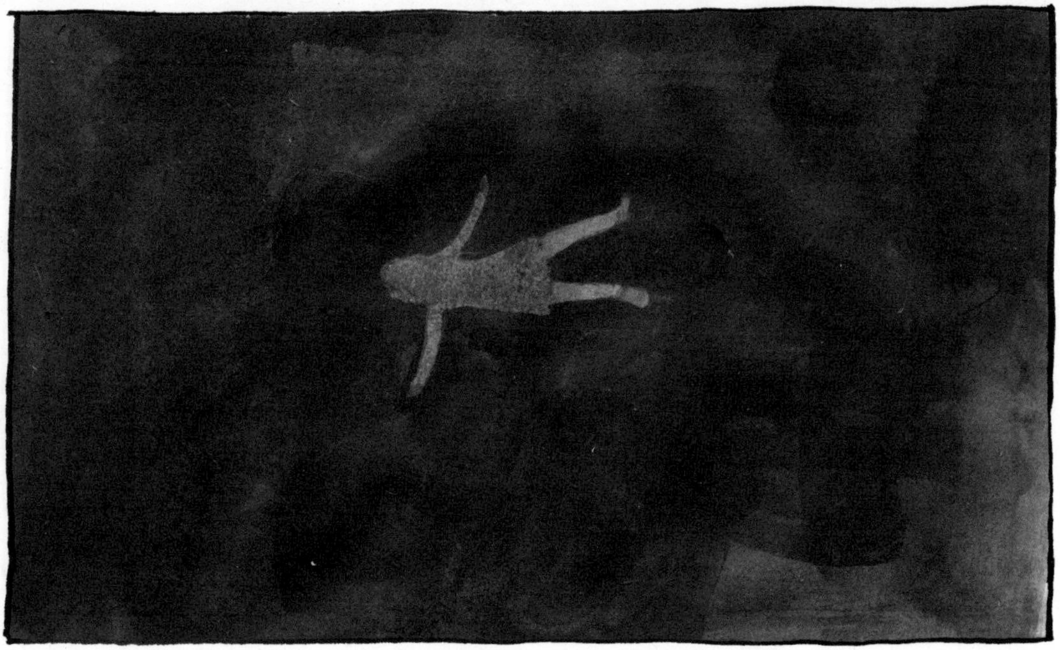

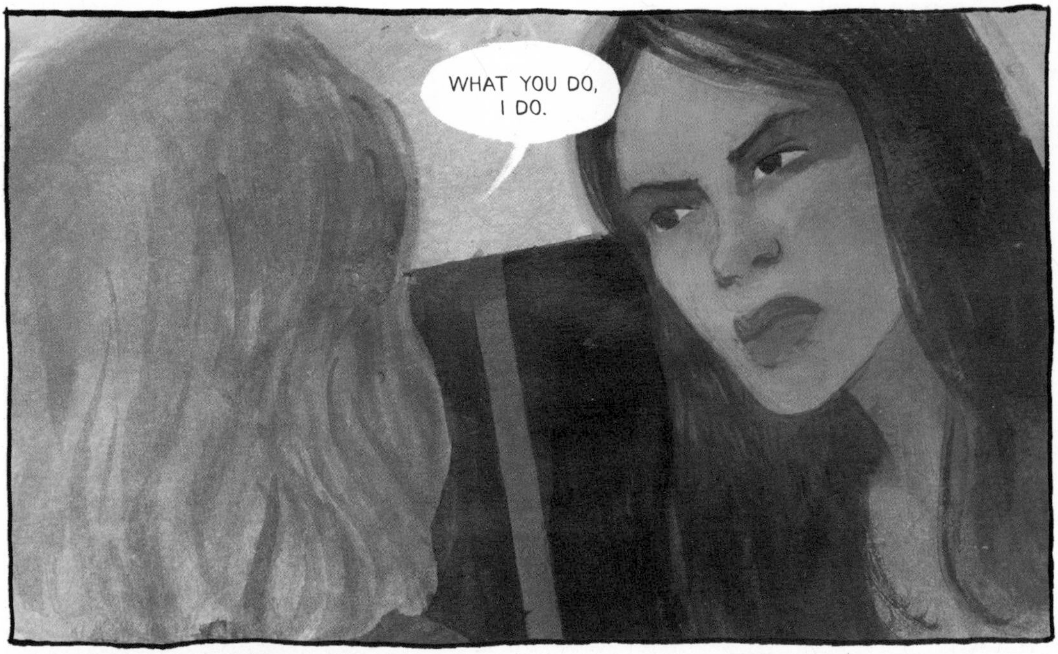
WHAT YOU DO,
I DO.

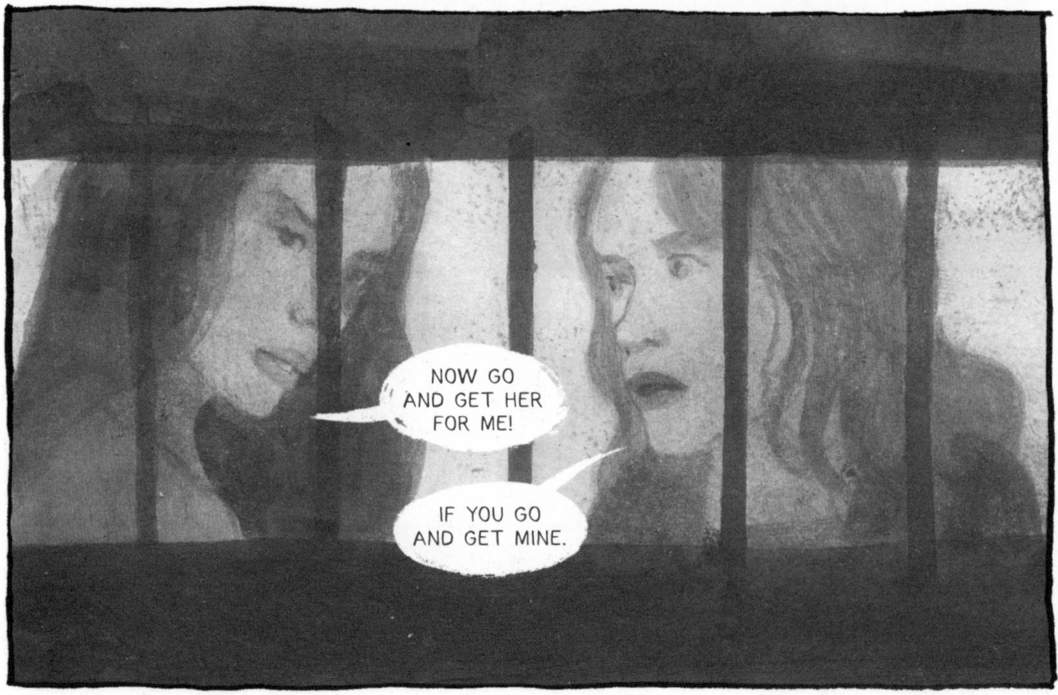
NOW GO
AND GET HER
FOR ME!
IF YOU GO
AND GET MINE.

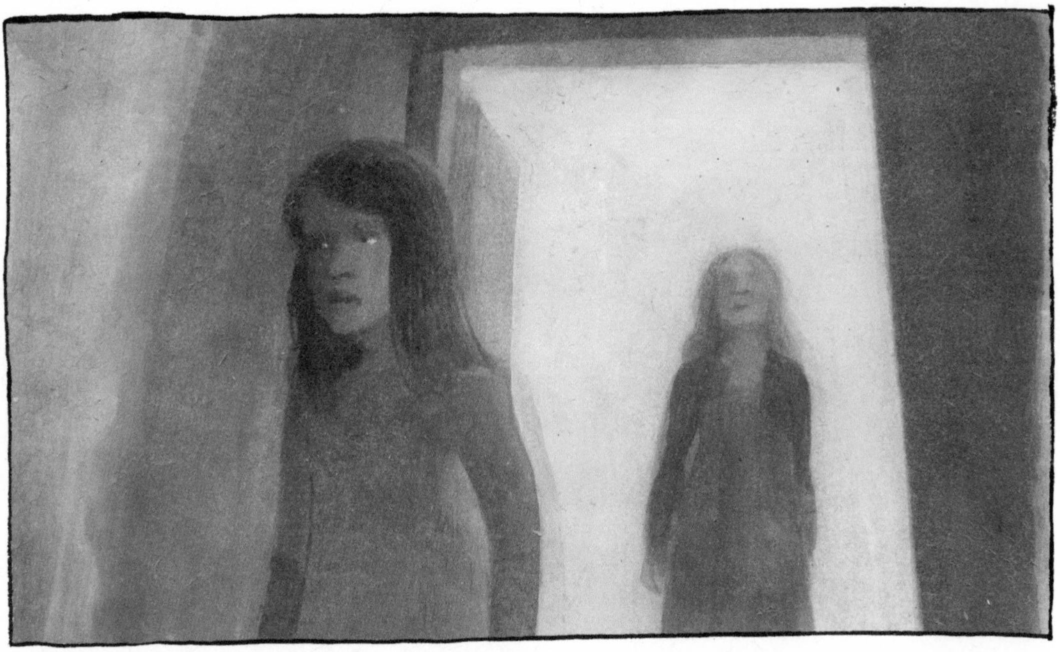

WE WENT TOGETHER.

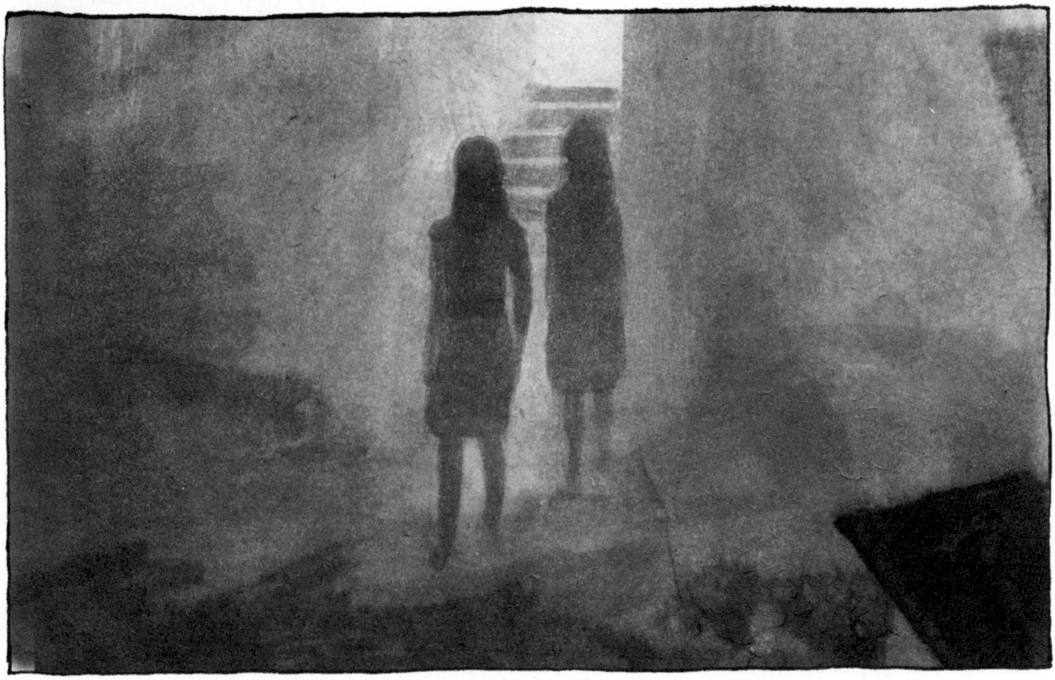

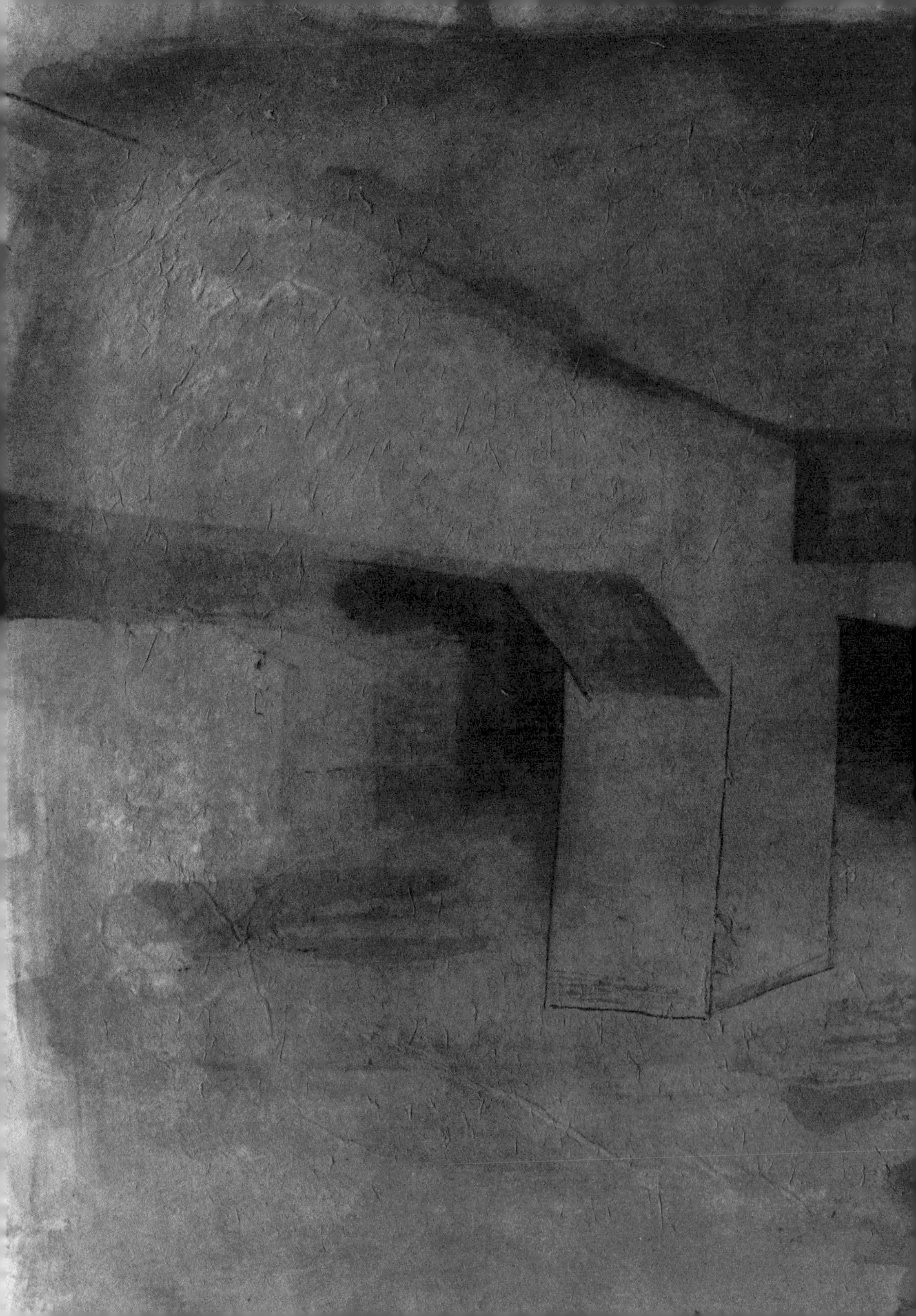

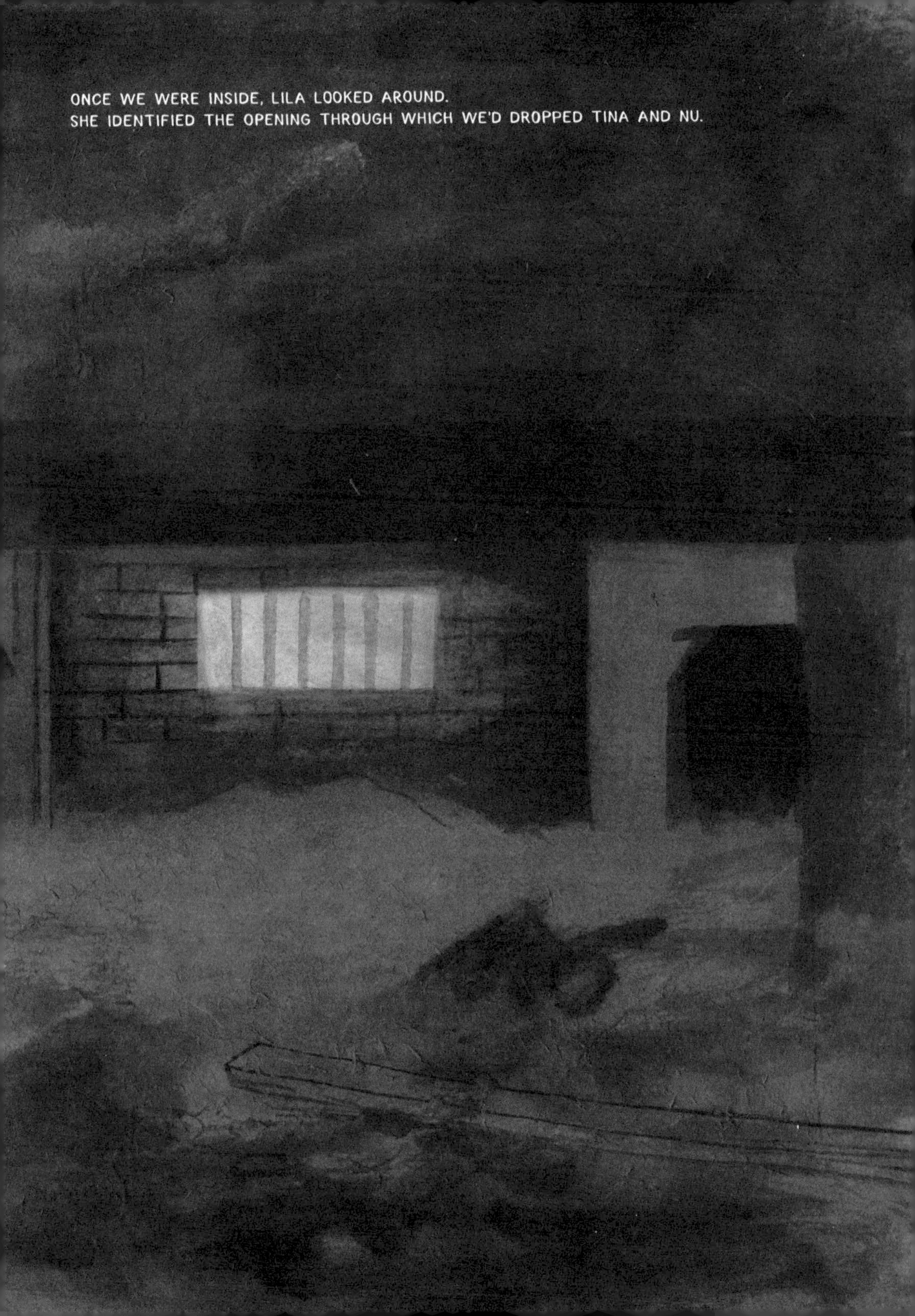
ONCE WE WERE INSIDE, LILA LOOKED AROUND.
SHE IDENTIFIED THE OPENING THROUGH WHICH WE'D DROPPED TINA AND NU.

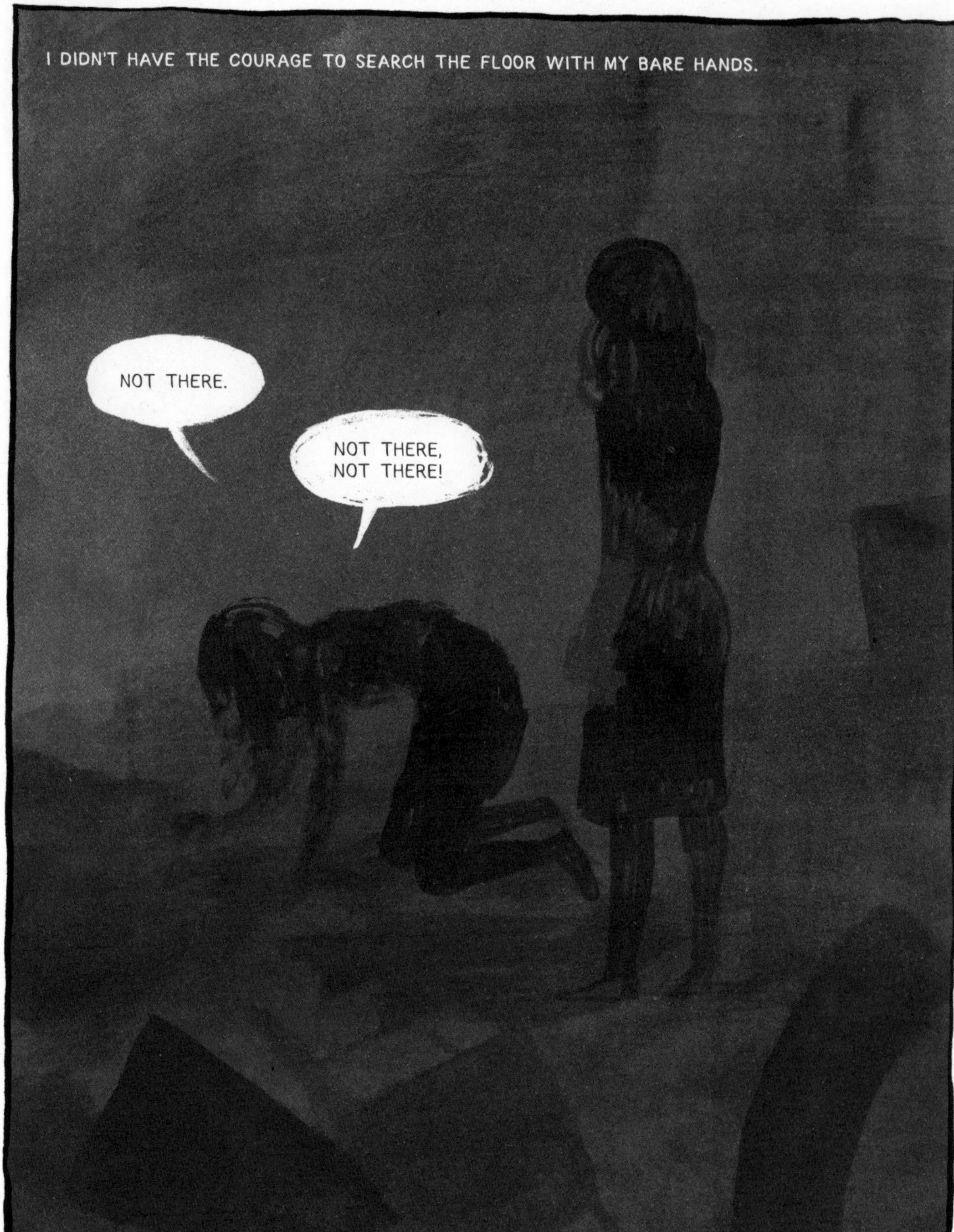
I DIDN'T HAVE THE COURAGE TO SEARCH THE FLOOR WITH MY BARE HANDS.
NOT THERE.
NOT THERE, NOT THERE!

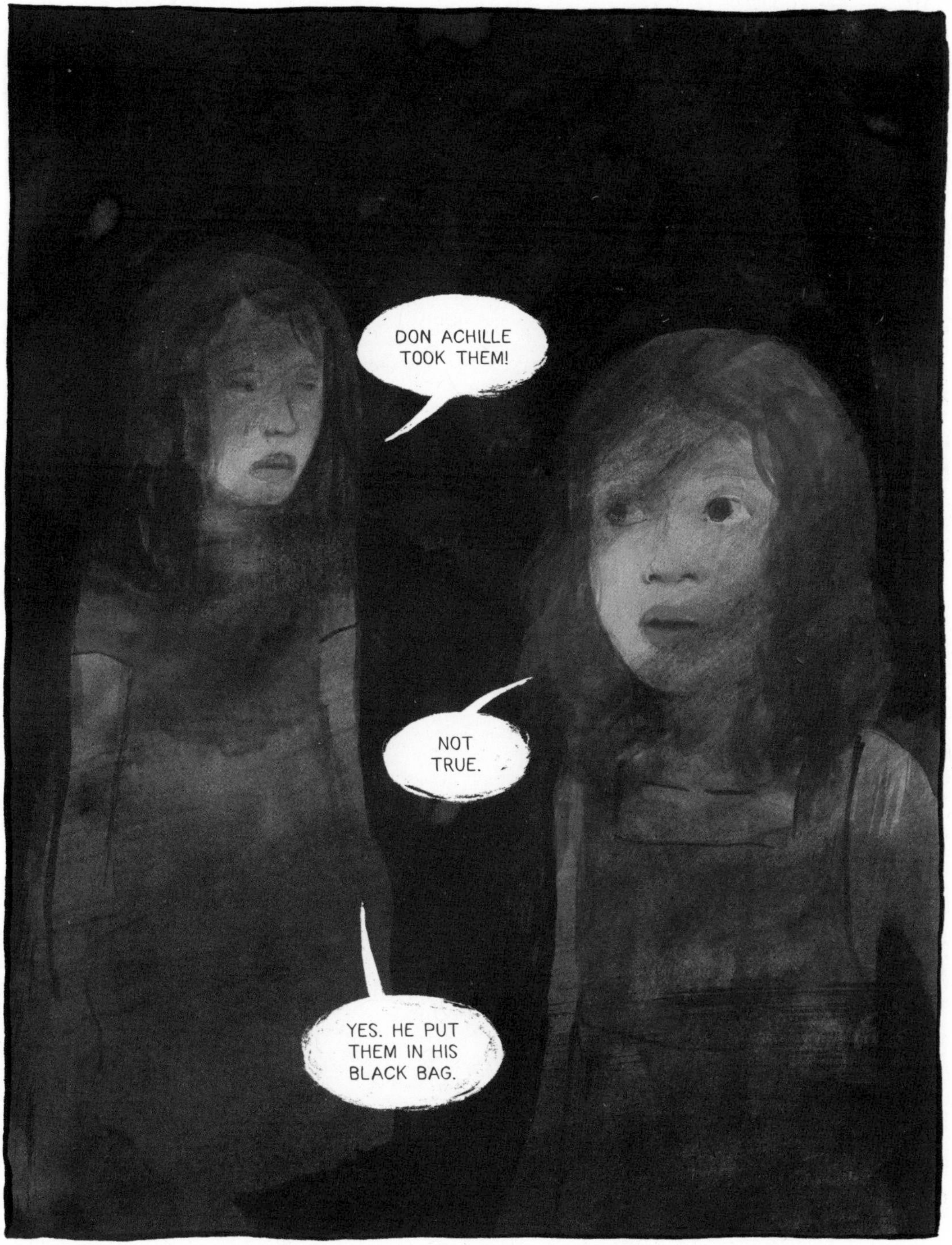
DON ACHILLE TOOK THEM!
NOT TRUE.
YES. HE PUT THEM IN HIS BLACK BAG.

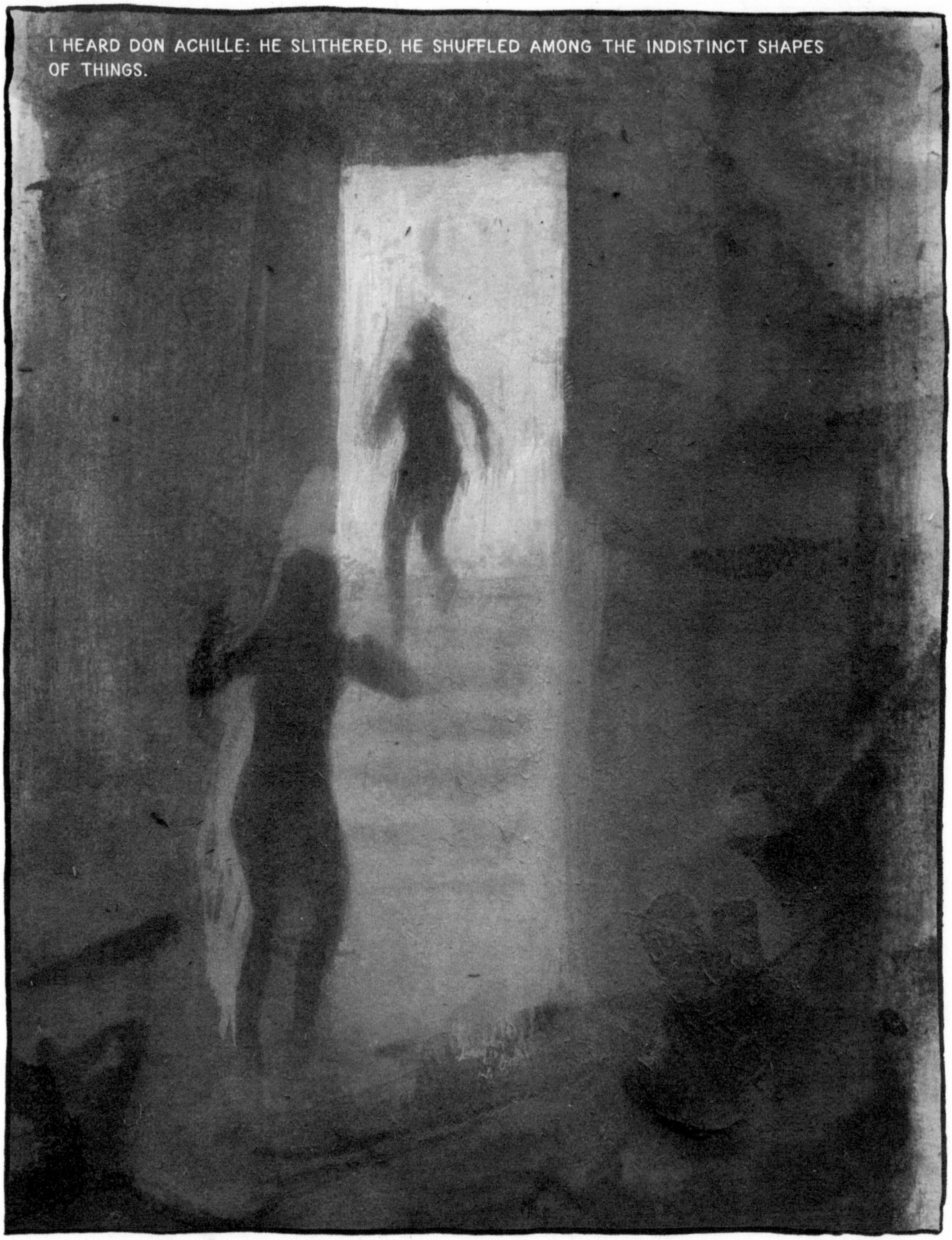
I HEARD DON ACHILLE: HE SLITHERED, HE SHUFFLED AMONG THE INDISTINCT SHAPES OF THINGS.

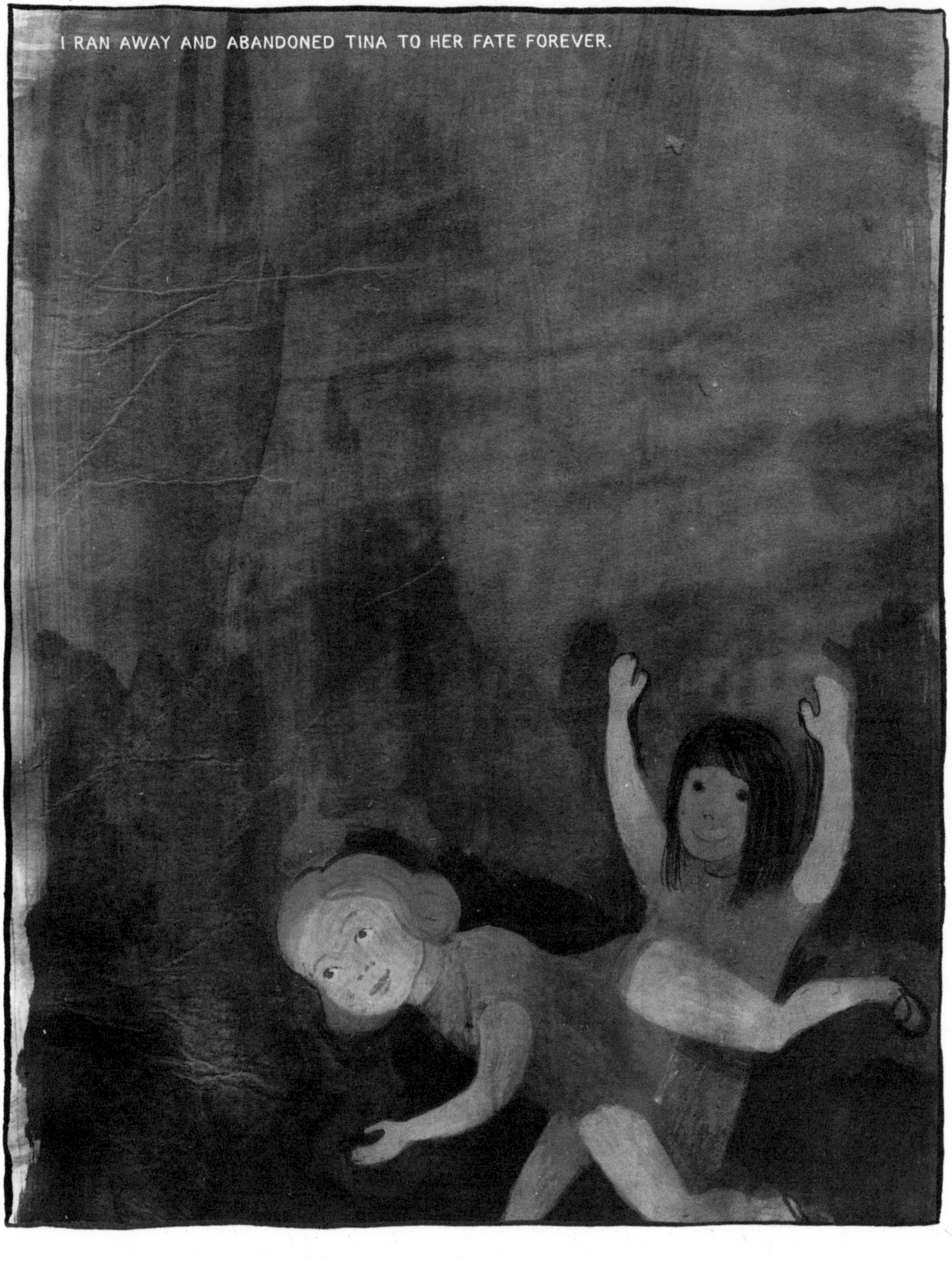
I RAN AWAY AND ABANDONED TINA TO HER FATE FOREVER.

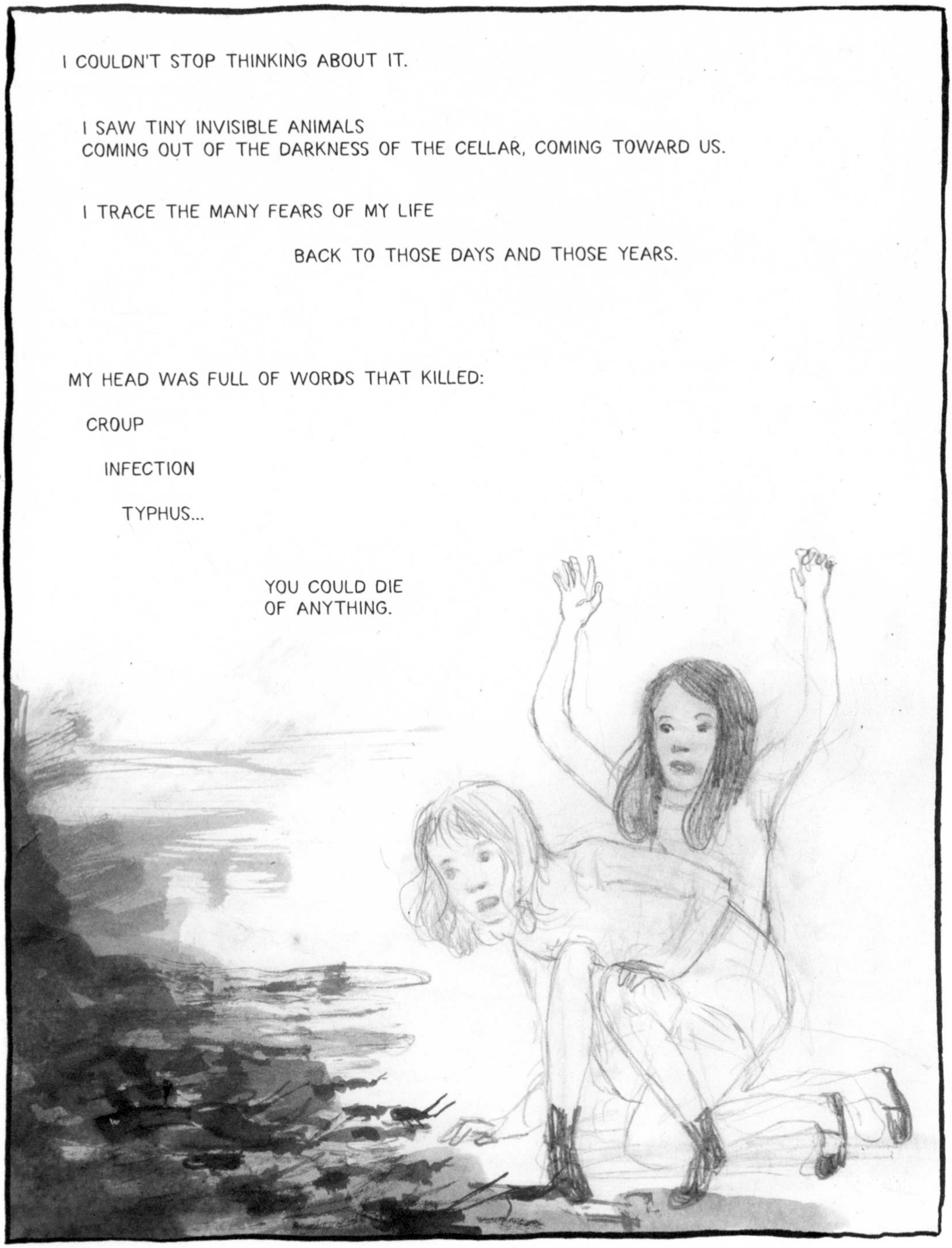
I COULDN'T STOP THINKING ABOUT IT.
I SAW TINY INVISIBLE ANIMALS
COMING OUT OF THE DARKNESS OF THE CELLAR, COMING TOWARD US.
I TRACE THE MANY FEARS OF MY LIFE
BACK TO THOSE DAYS AND THOSE YEARS.
MY HEAD WAS FULL OF WORDS THAT KILLED:
CROUP
INFECTION
TYPHUS...
YOU COULD DIE
OF ANYTHING.

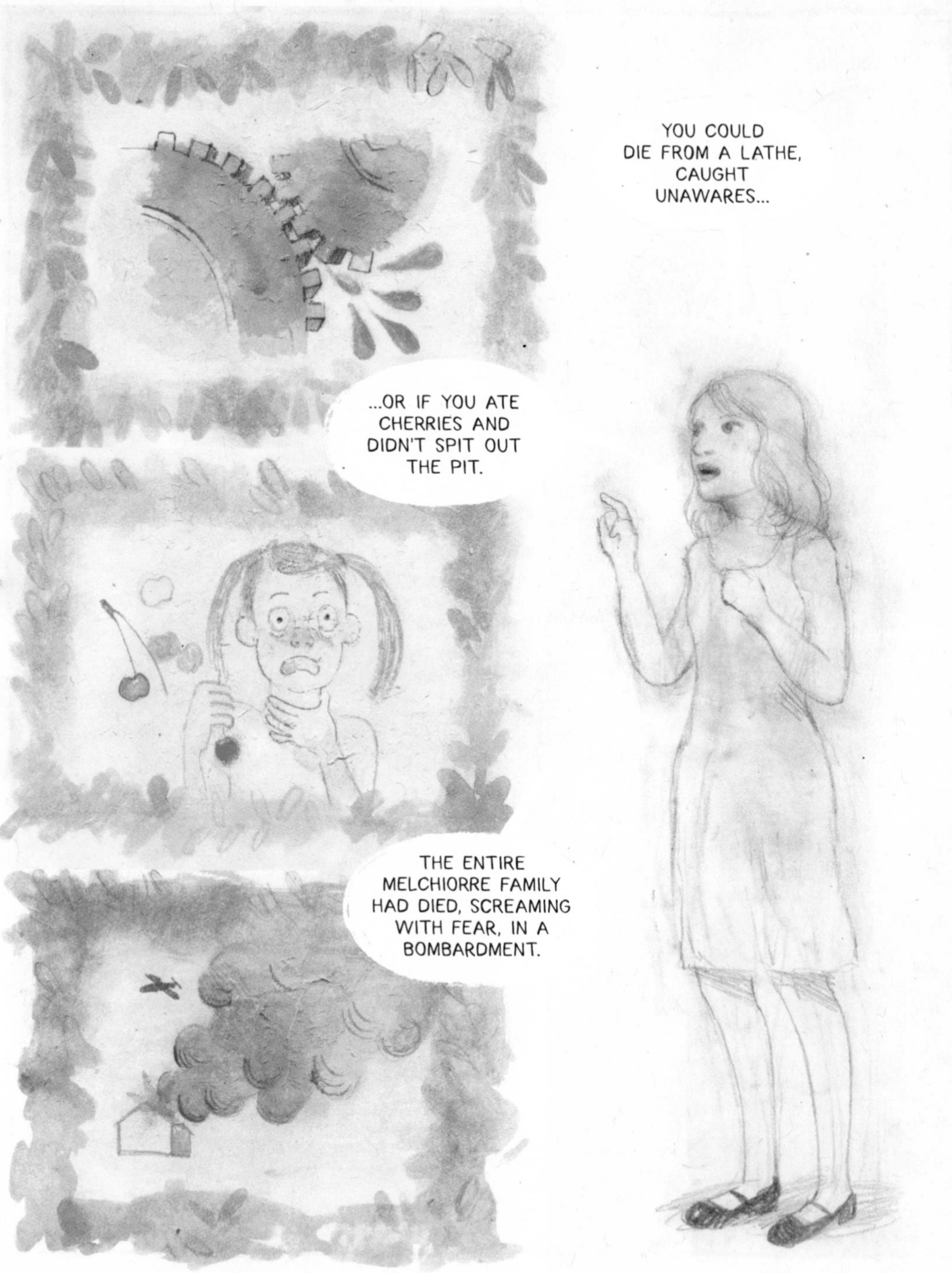
YOU COULD DIE FROM A LATHE, CAUGHT UNAWARES...
...OR IF YOU ATE CHERRIES AND DIDN'T SPIT OUT THE PIT.
THE ENTIRE MELCHIORRE FAMILY HAD DIED, SCREAMING WITH FEAR, IN A BOMBARDMENT.

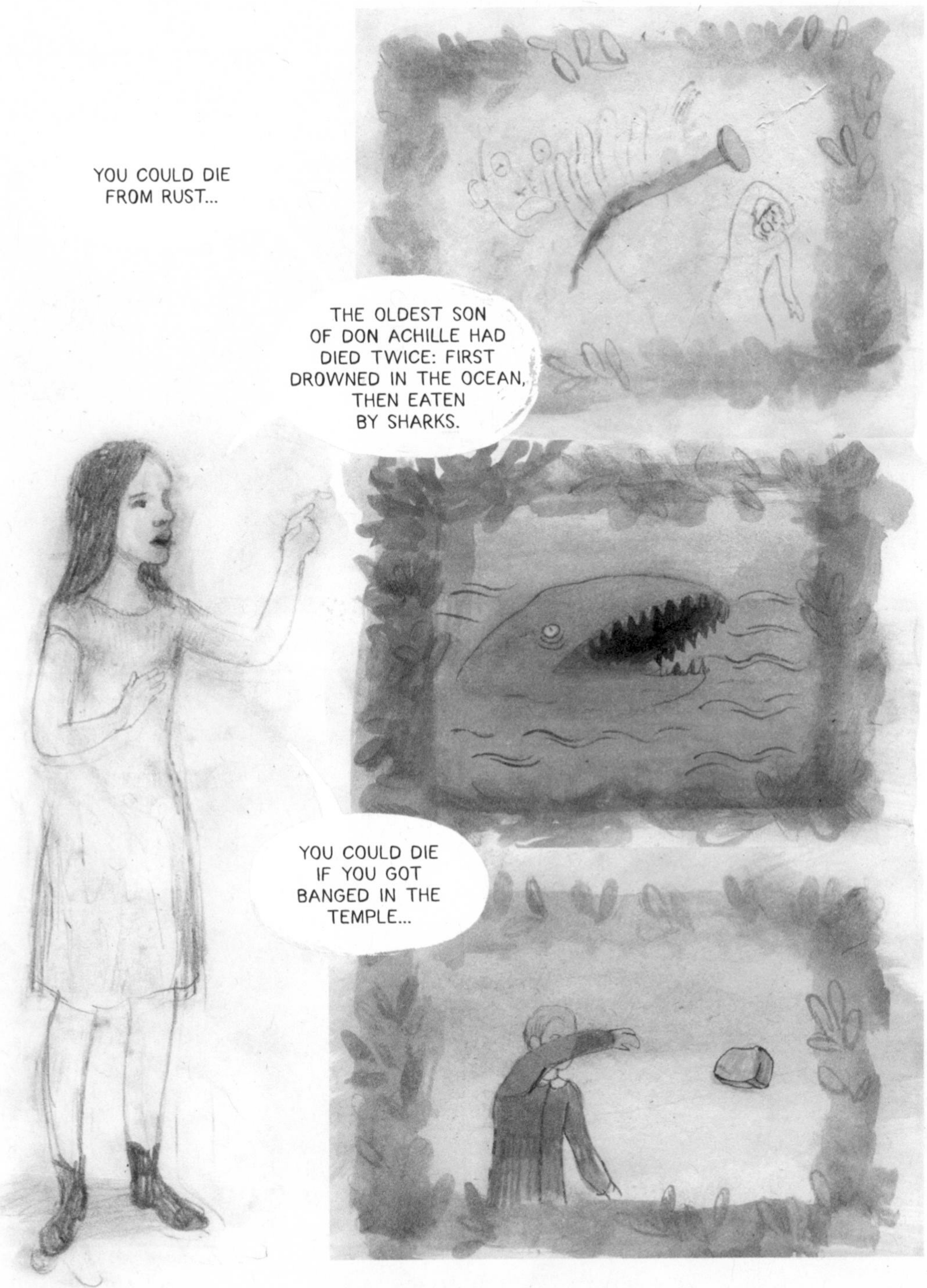
YOU COULD DIE FROM RUST...
THE OLDEST SON OF DON ACHILLE HAD DIED TWICE: FIRST DROWNED IN THE OCEAN, THEN EATEN BY SHARKS.
YOU COULD DIE IF YOU GOT BANGED IN THE TEMPLE...

YOU COULD BE HIT BY A STONE.

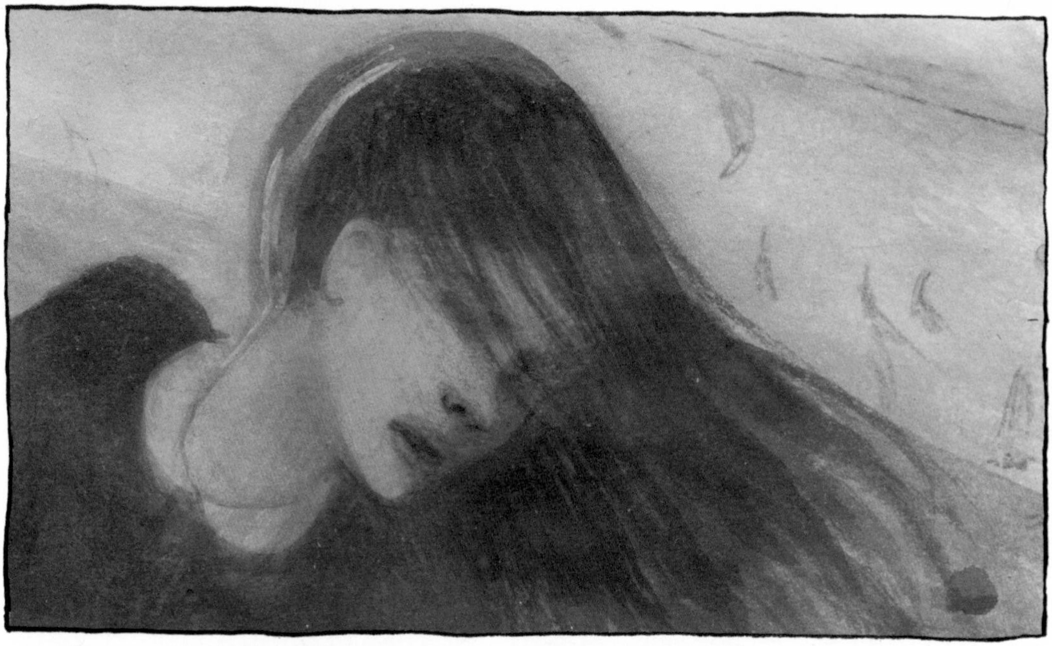

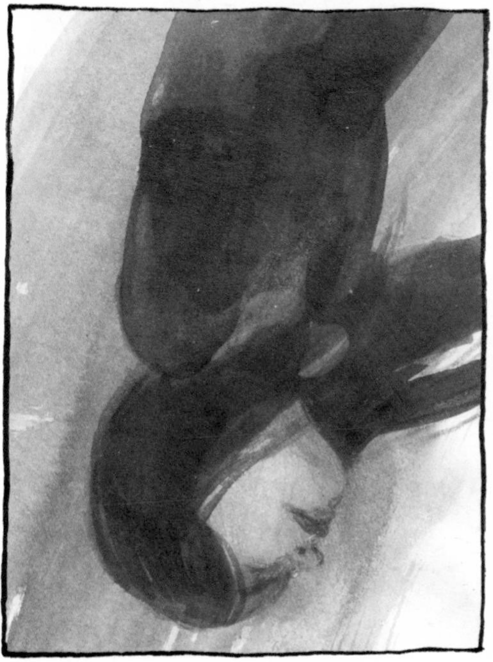

AND THROWING STONES WAS THE NORM.

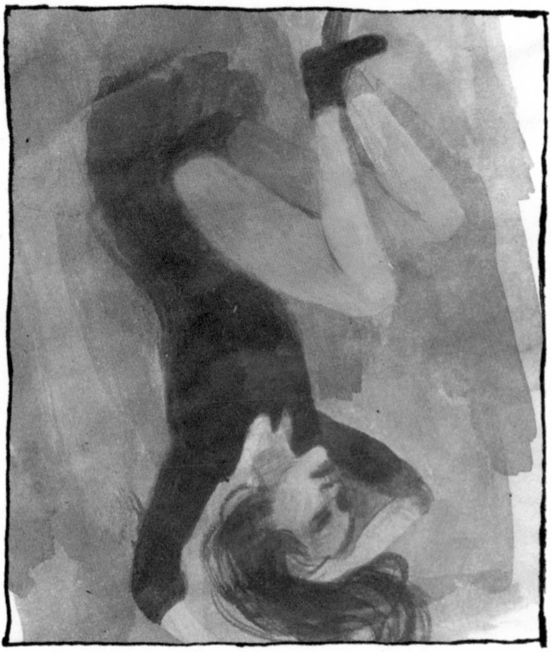

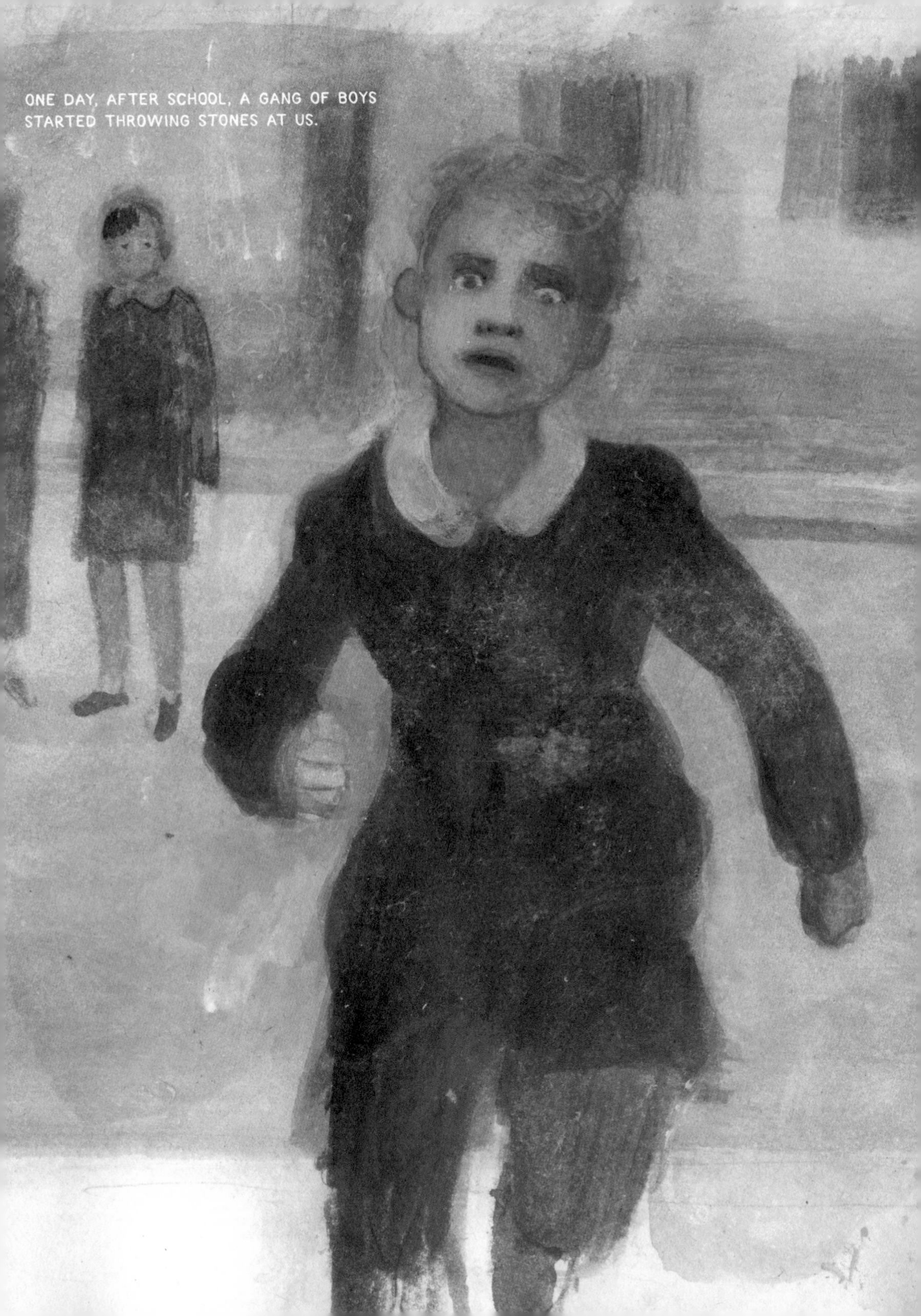
ONE DAY, AFTER SCHOOL, A GANG OF BOYS STARTED THROWING STONES AT US.

THEY WERE ANGRY BECAUSE WE WERE SMARTER IN SCHOOL.

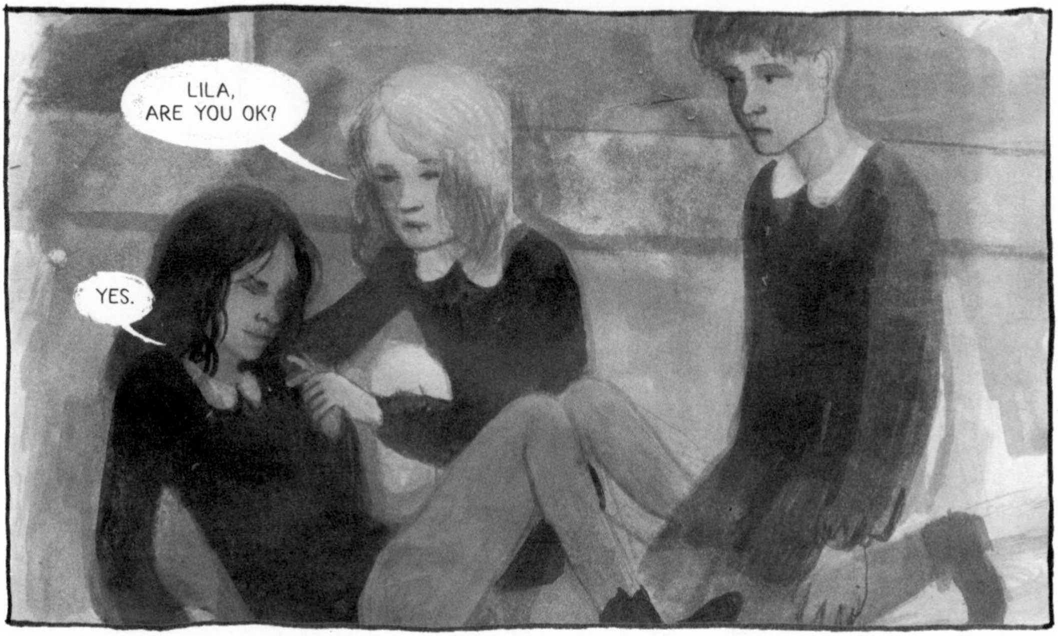
LILA,
ARE YOU OK?
YES.

ENZO, THE LEADER, WAS A DANGEROUS TYPE.

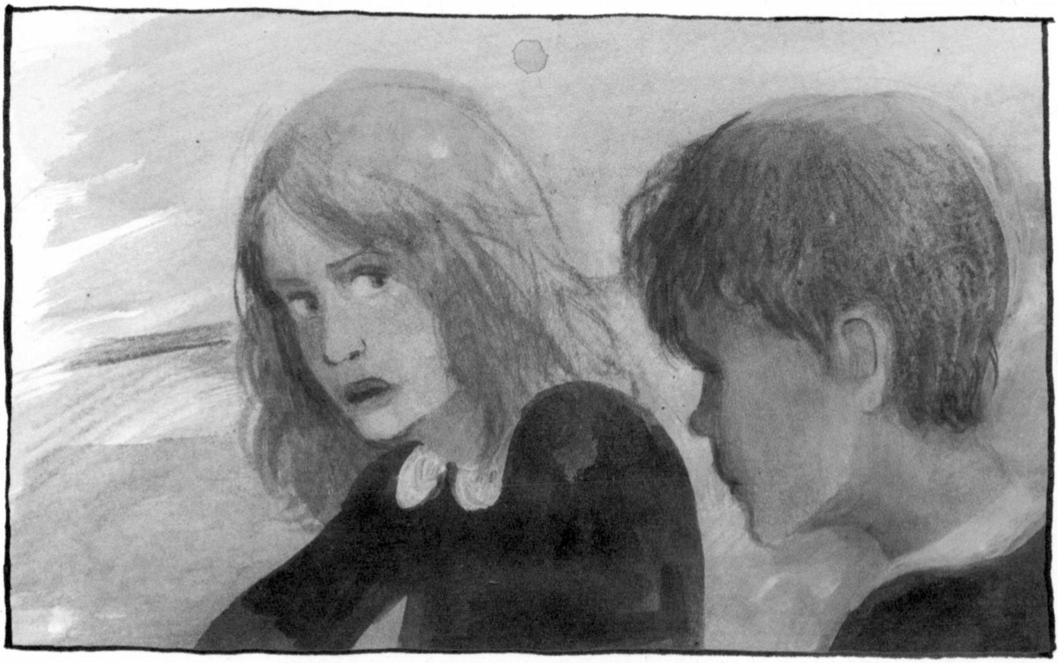

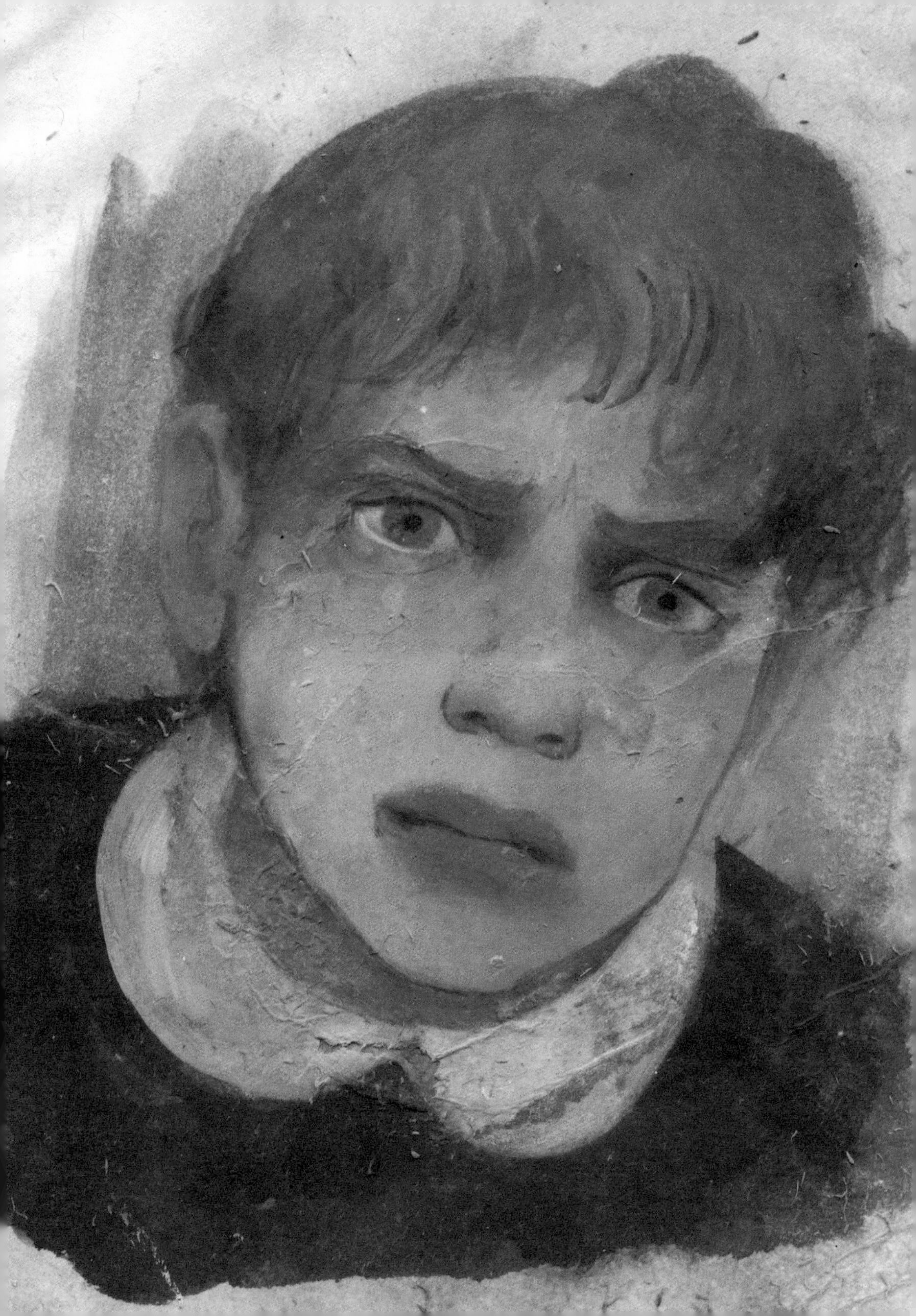

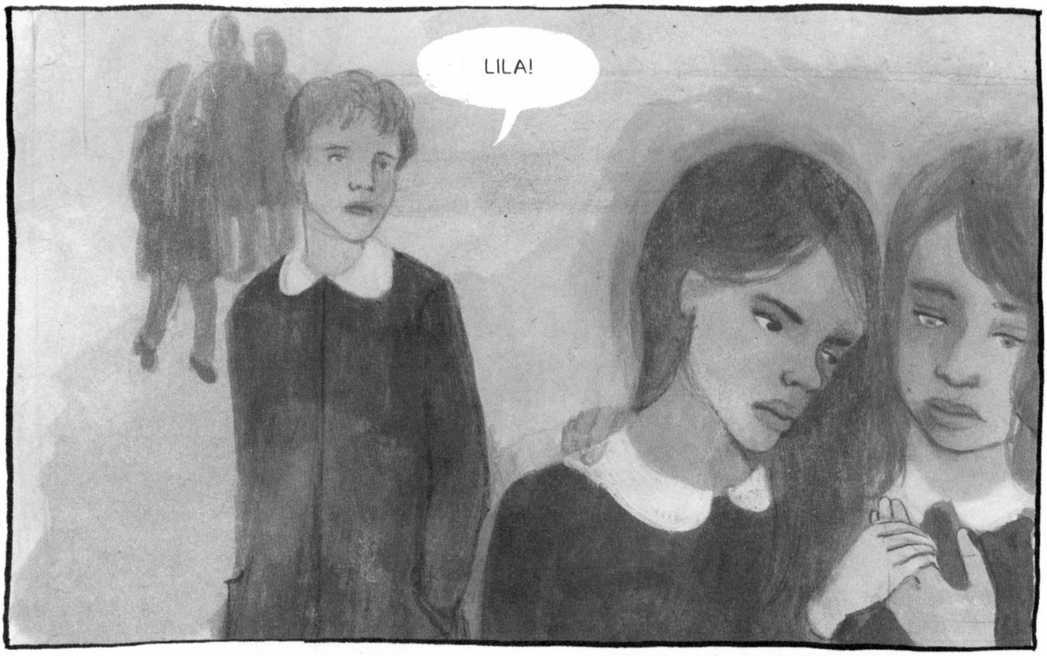
LILA!

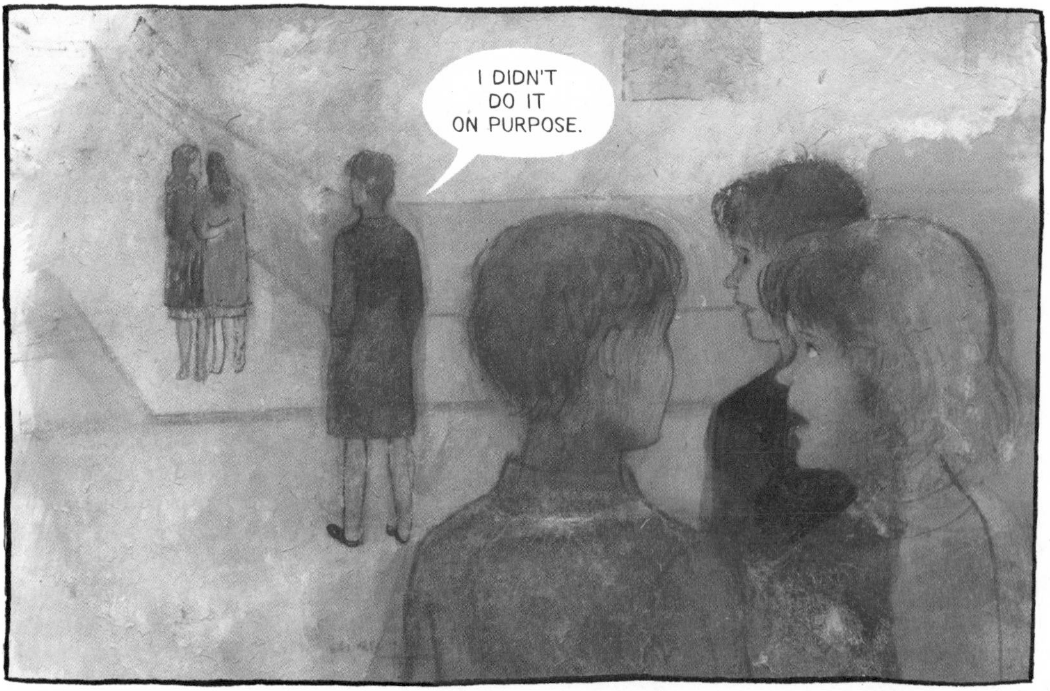
I DIDN'T DO IT ON PURPOSE.

SOME TIME LATER ENZO DID A THING THAT SEEMED WONDERFUL TO ME.

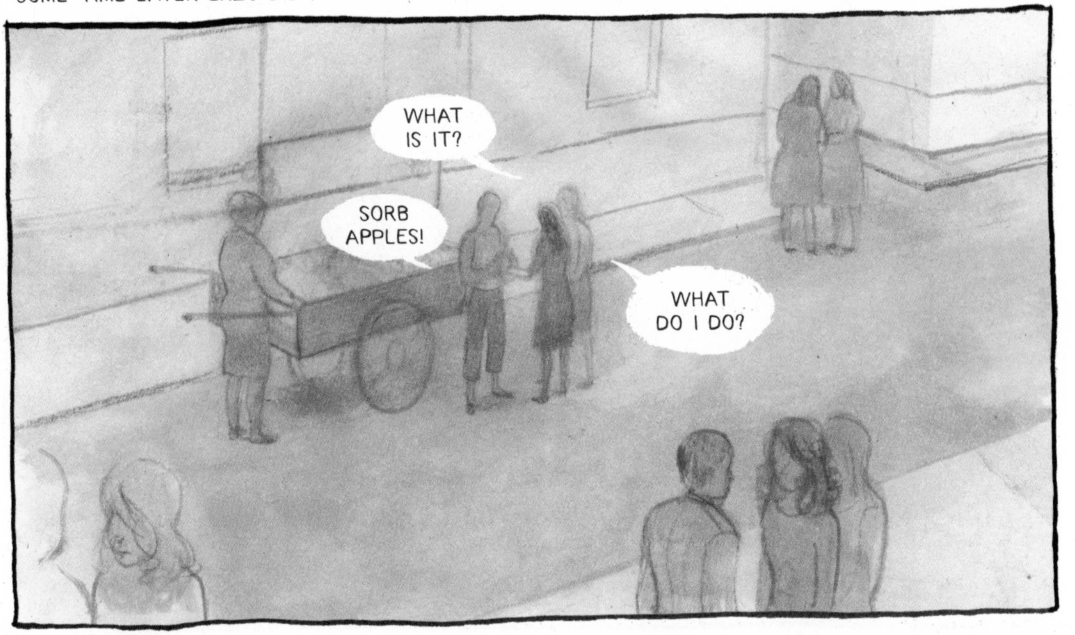
WHAT IS IT?
SORB APPLES!
WHAT DO I DO?

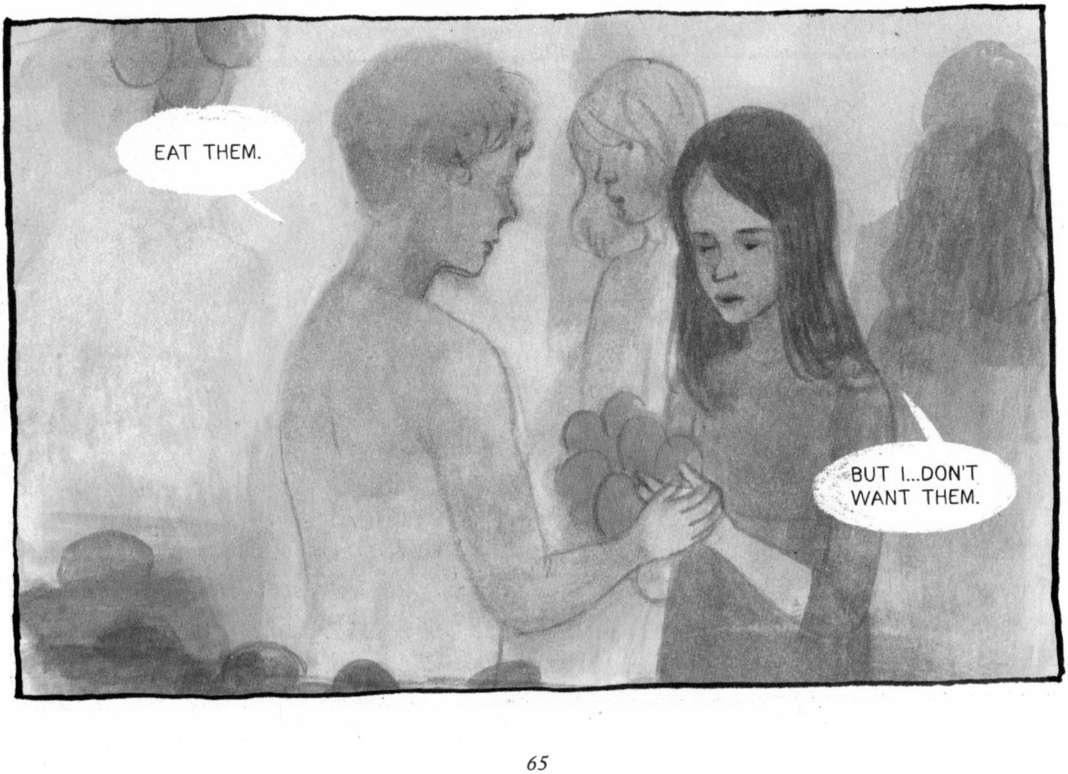
EAT THEM.
BUT I...DON'T WANT THEM.

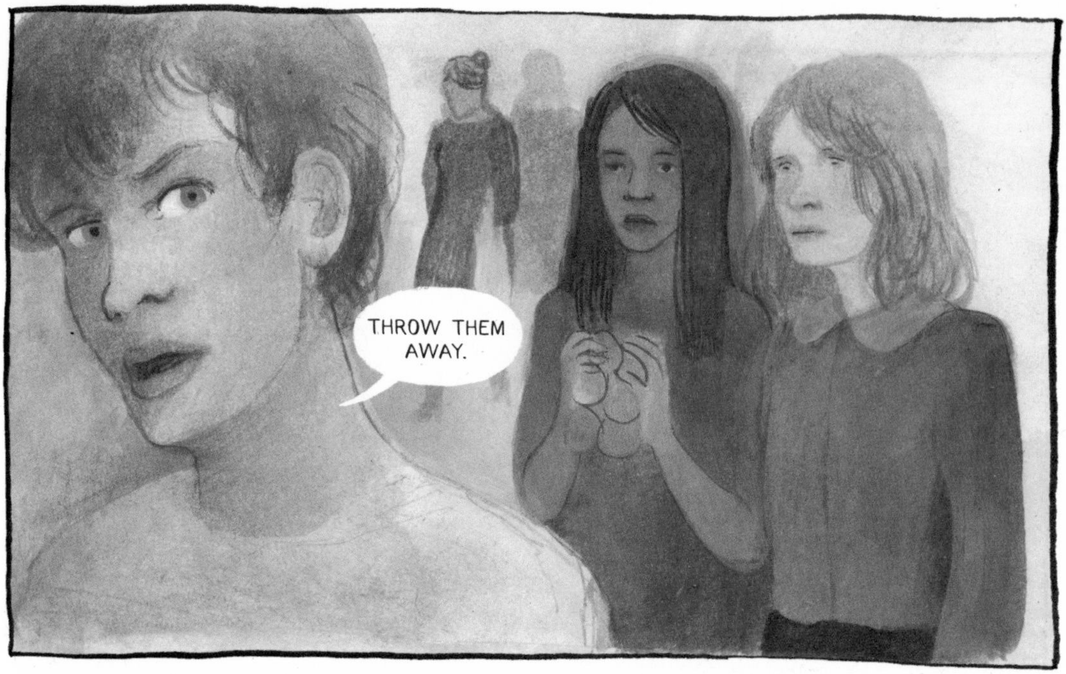
THROW THEM AWAY.

I HOPED THAT LILA WOULD SAY: HERE, YOU TAKE THEM.

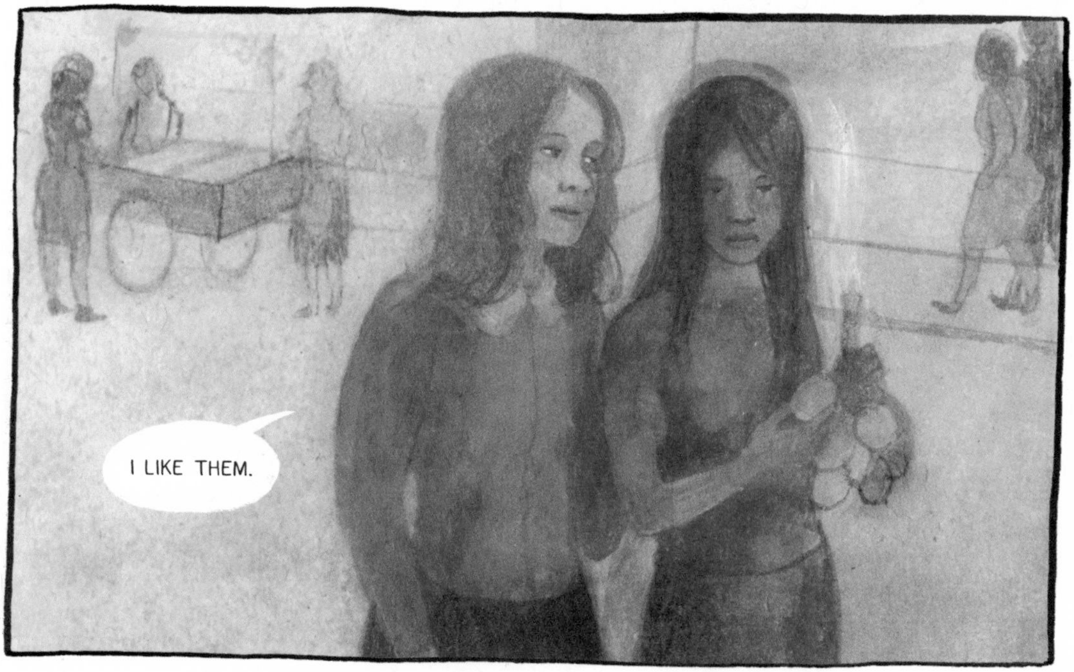
I LIKE THEM.

BUT SHE DIDN'T.

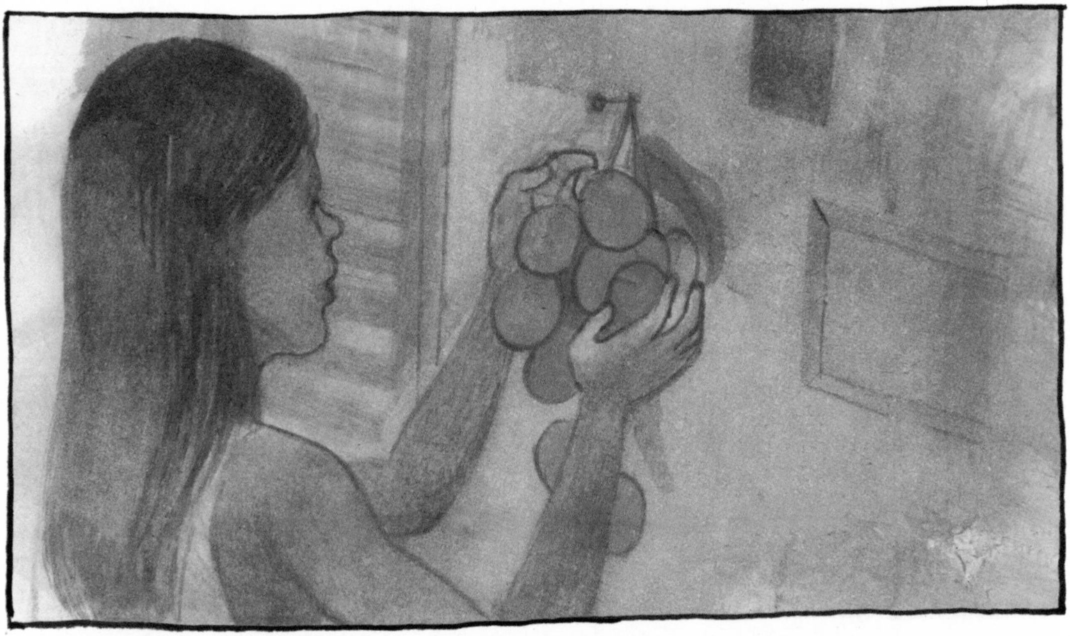

AFTER THAT ENZO DIDN'T GIVE HER ANY MORE GIFTS.

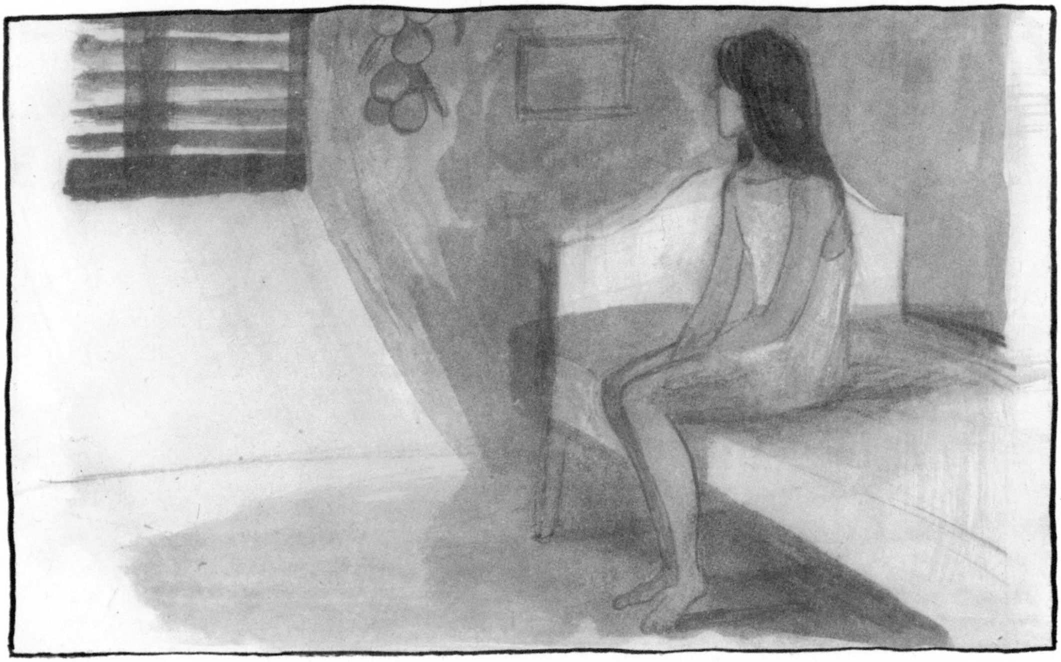

WE SAW HIM LESS AND LESS: HE'D LEFT SCHOOL FOR THE FRUIT CART.

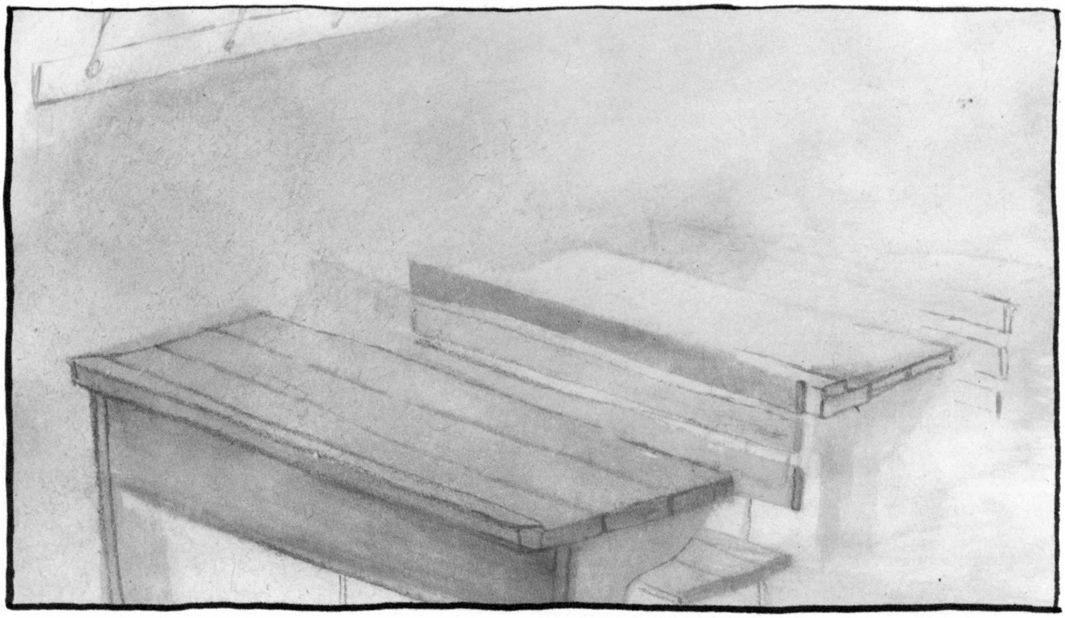

AS FOR US, WHEN WE HAD ALMOST FINISHED FIFTH GRADE, THE TEACHER ASKED OUR PARENTS TO LET US CONTINUE IN SCHOOL.

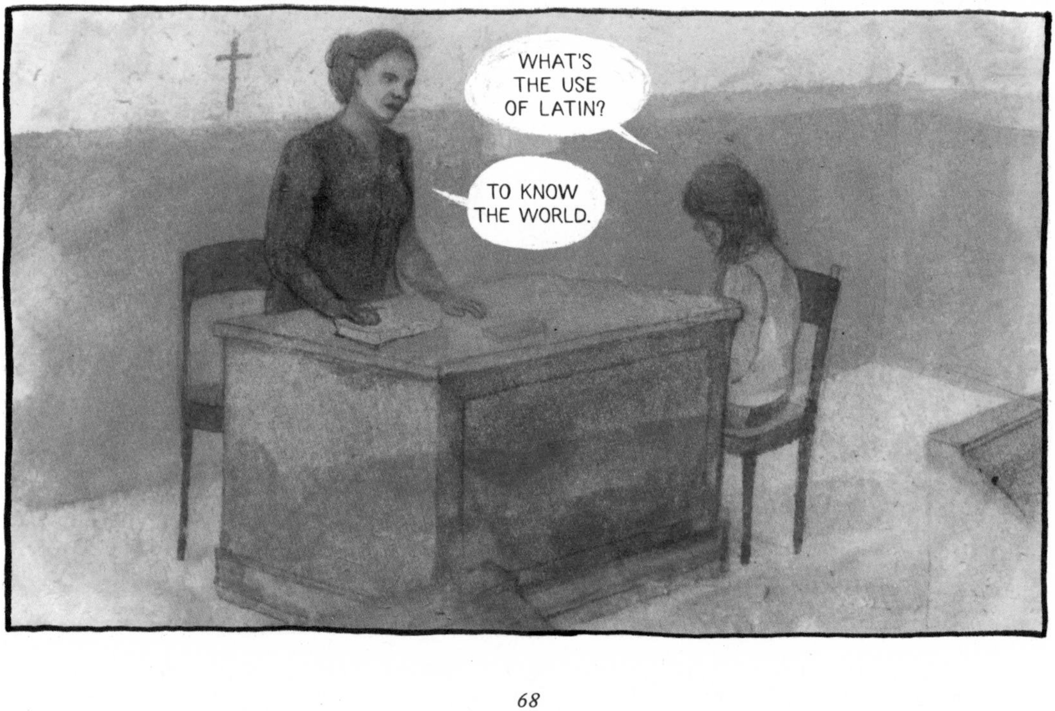
WHAT'S THE USE OF LATIN?
TO KNOW THE WORLD.

AT FIRST MY FATHER WAS UNCERTAIN.

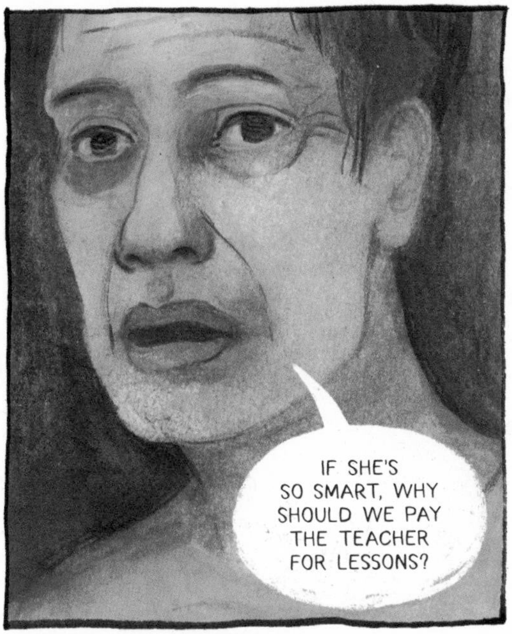
IF SHE'S SO SMART, WHY SHOULD WE PAY THE TEACHER FOR LESSONS?

MY MOTHER, HOWEVER, WAS AGAINST IT.

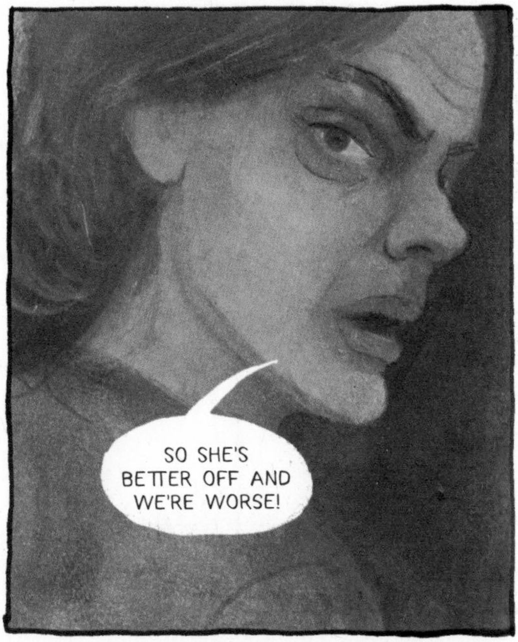
SO SHE'S BETTER OFF AND WE'RE WORSE!

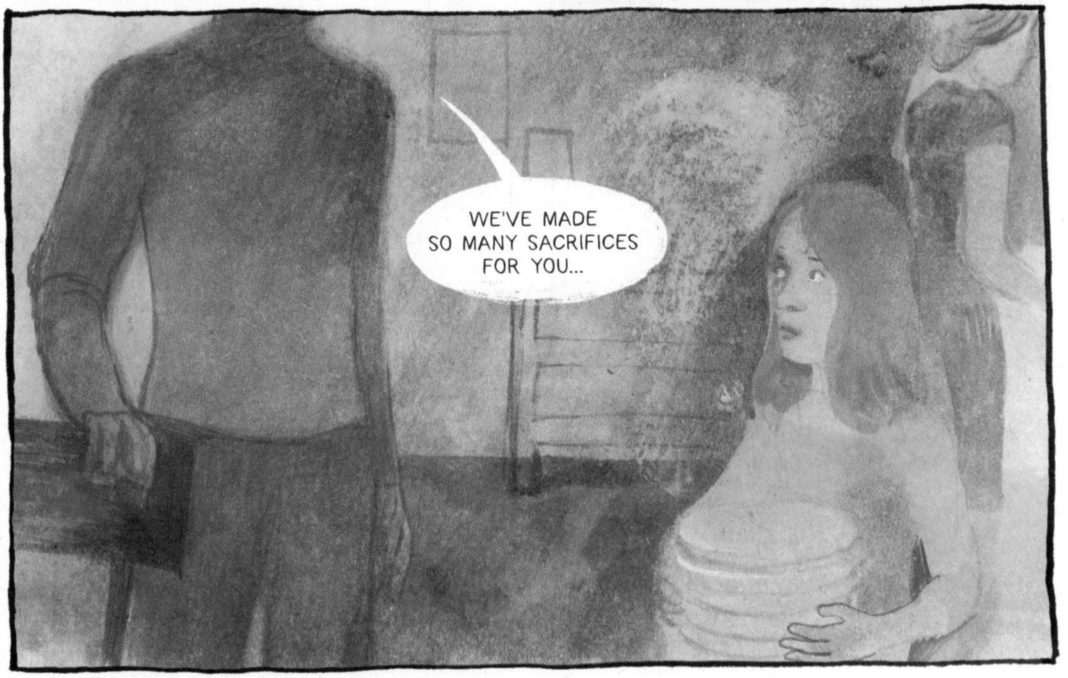
WE'VE MADE SO MANY SACRIFICES FOR YOU...

FINALLY THEY DECIDED TO LET ME TAKE THE MIDDLE-SCHOOL ADMISSION EXAM.

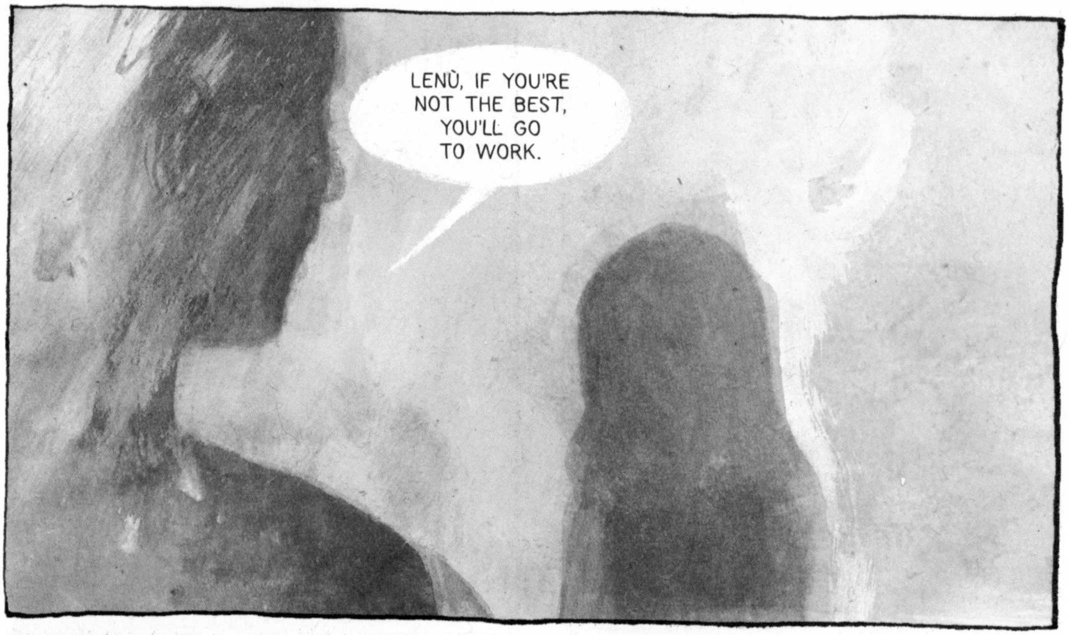
LENÙ, IF YOU'RE NOT THE BEST, YOU'LL GO TO WORK.

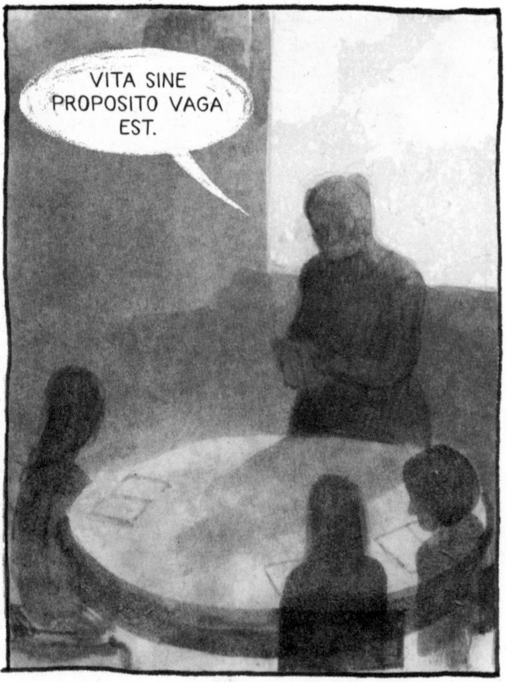
VITA SINE PROPOSITO VAGA EST.

I STARTED GOING TO MAESTRA OLIVIERO'S HOUSE EVERY AFTERNOON.

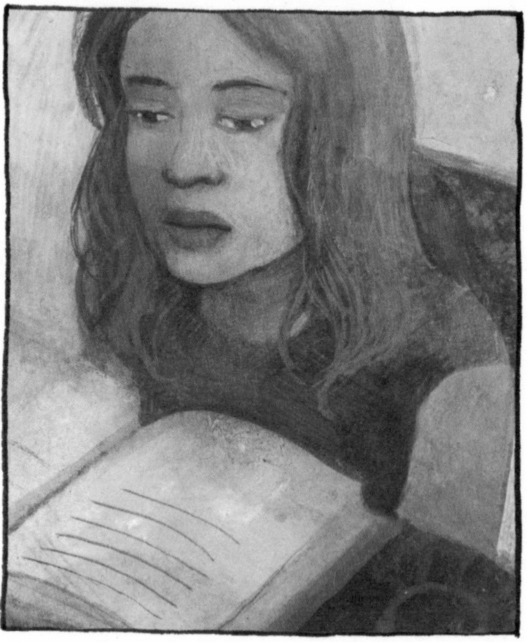

BUT LILA DIDN'T COME. HER FATHER WOULDN'T EVEN DISCUSS IT. ONLY HER BROTHER RINO DEFENDED HER.

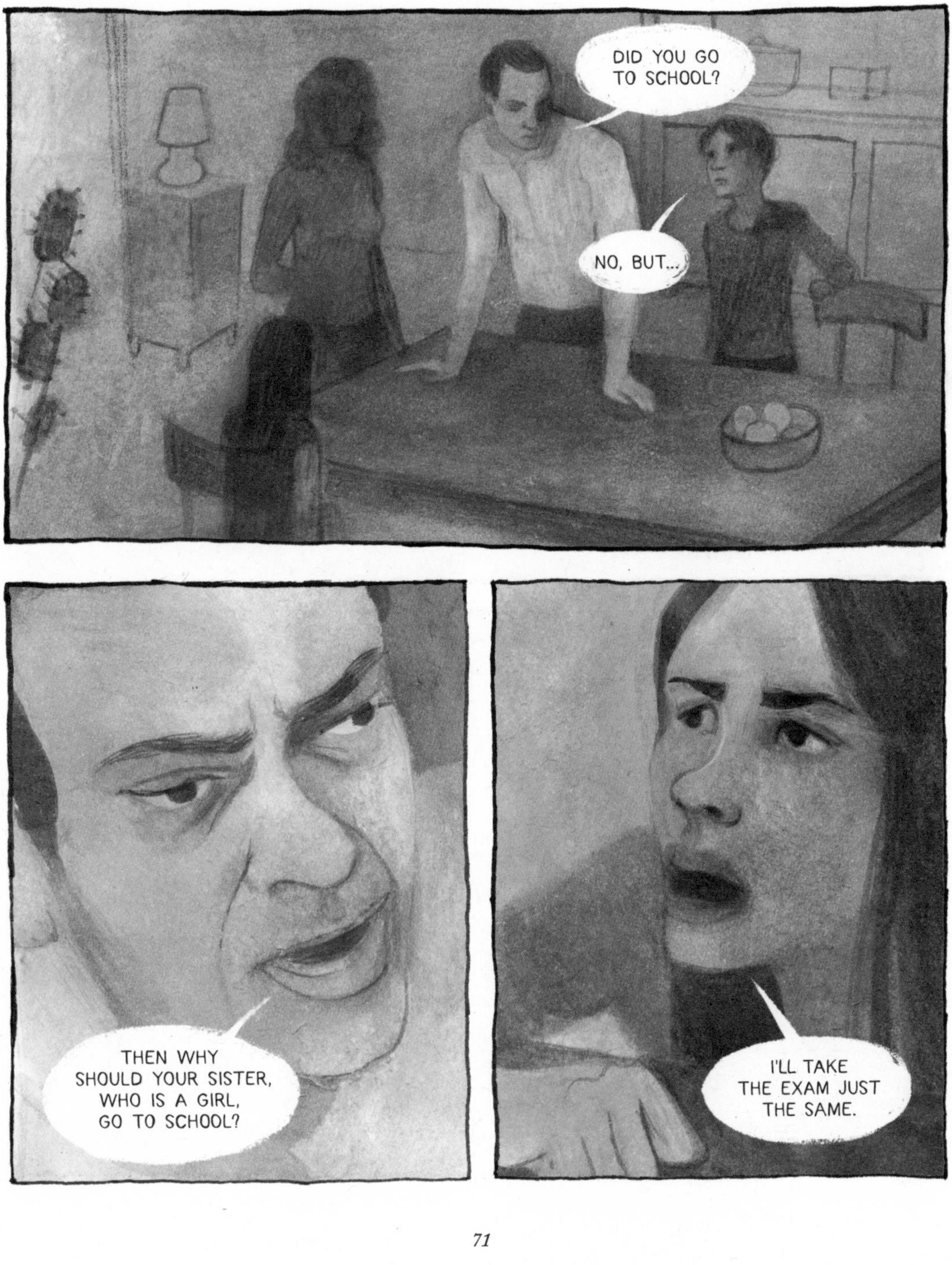
DID YOU GO TO SCHOOL?
NO, BUT...
THEN WHY SHOULD YOUR SISTER, WHO IS A GIRL, GO TO SCHOOL?
I'LL TAKE THE EXAM JUST THE SAME.

THE TEACHER COULDN'T ACCEPT THAT DECISION, EITHER. SHE HAD UNDERSTOOD THAT LILA WAS THE BEST SINCE THE FIRST DAY OF SCHOOL.

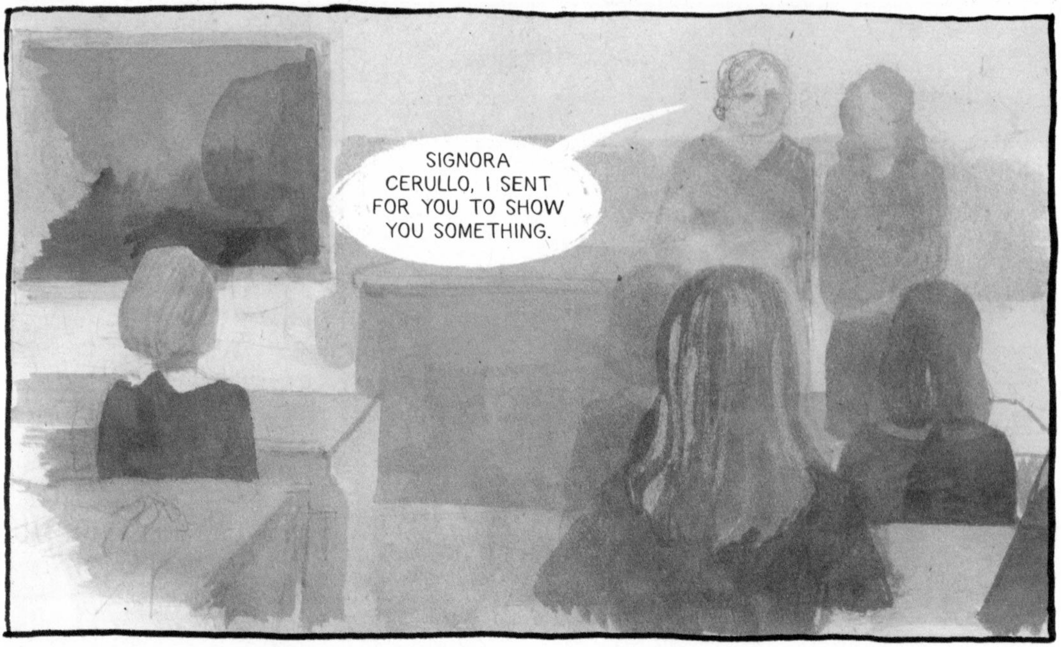
SIGNORA CERULLO, I SENT FOR YOU TO SHOW YOU SOMETHING.

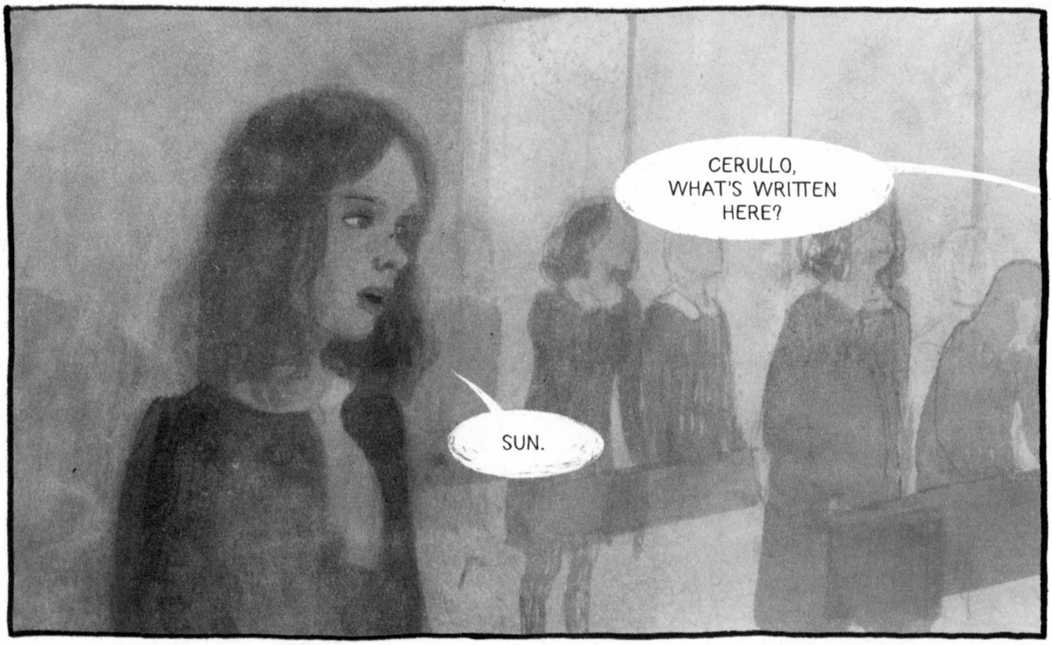
CERULLO, WHAT'S WRITTEN HERE?
SUN.

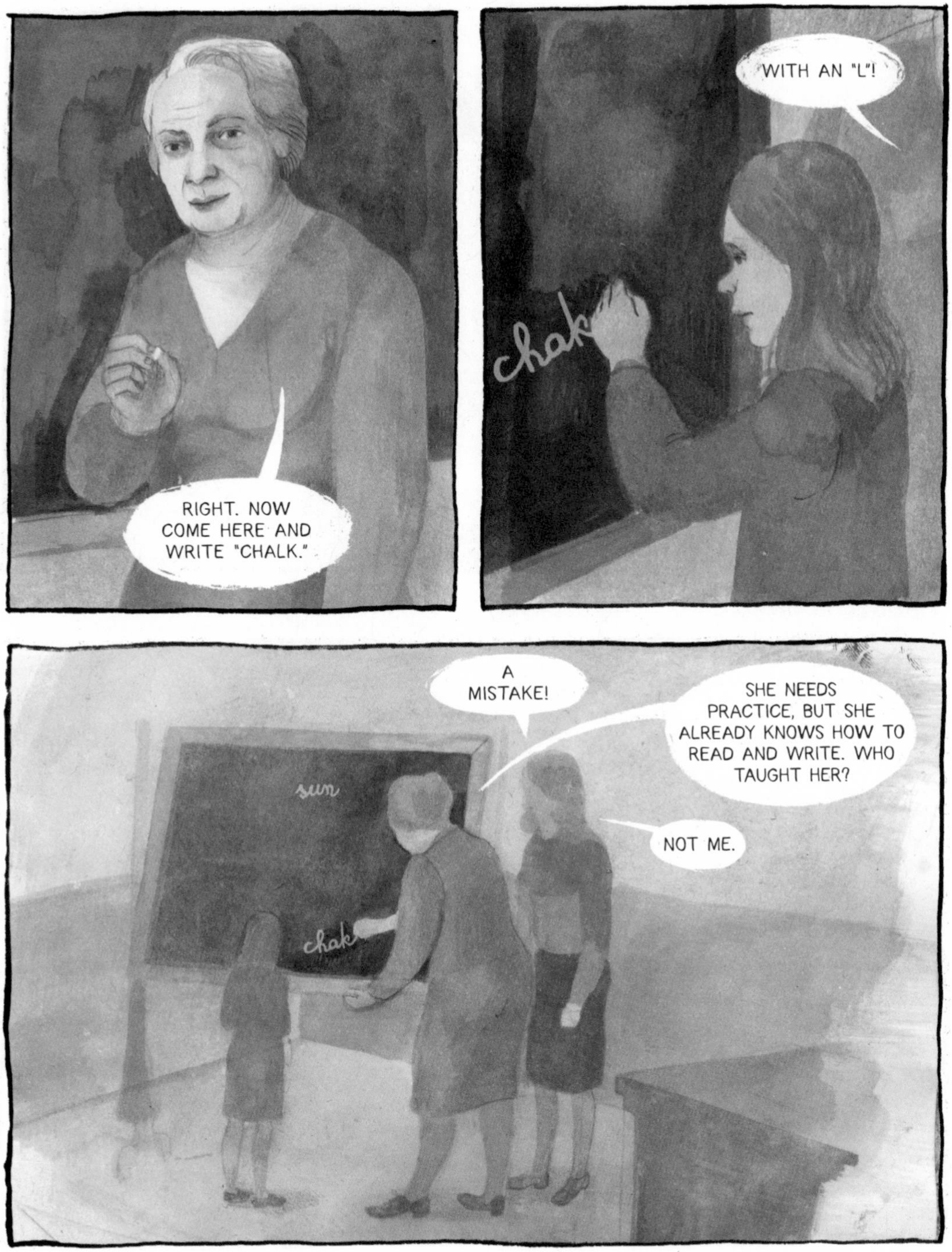
RIGHT. NOW COME HERE AND WRITE "CHALK."
chak
WITH AN "L"!
sun
chak
A MISTAKE!
SHE NEEDS PRACTICE, BUT SHE ALREADY KNOWS HOW TO READ AND WRITE. WHO TAUGHT HER?
NOT ME.

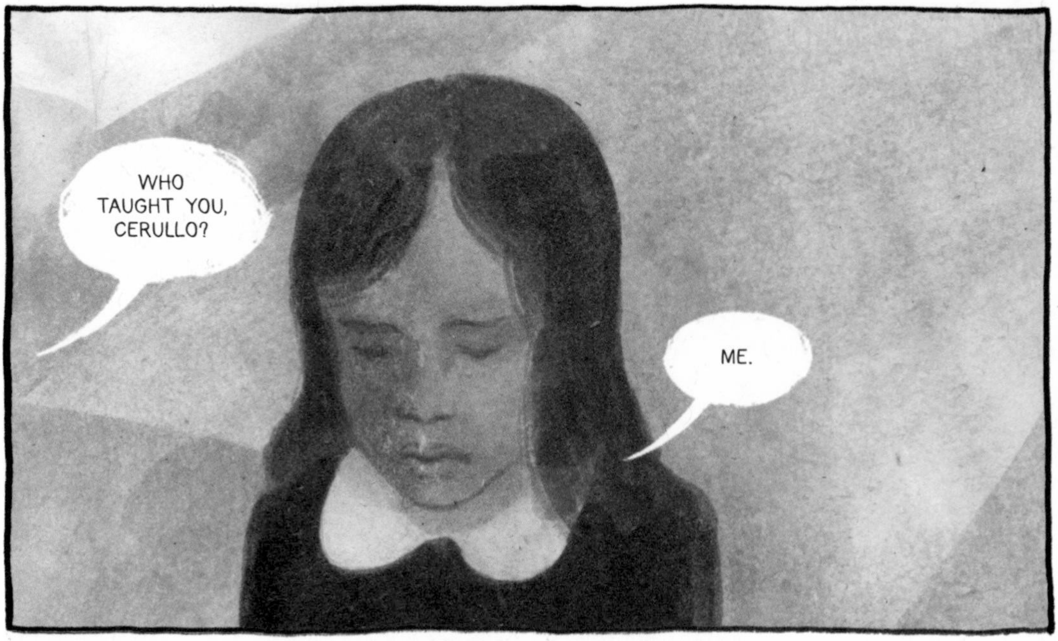
WHO TAUGHT YOU, CERULLO?
ME.

ACCORDING TO RINO, LILA HAD LEARNED BY LOOKING AT THE LETTERS IN HIS PRIMER.

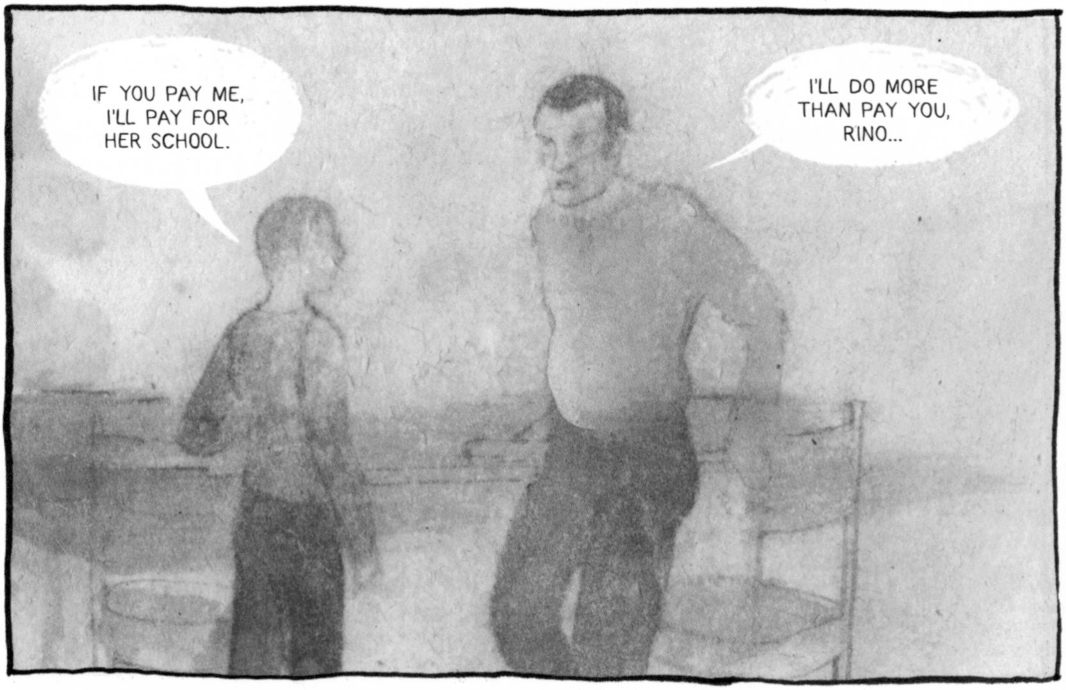
IF YOU PAY ME, I'LL PAY FOR HER SCHOOL.
I'LL DO MORE THAN PAY YOU, RINO...

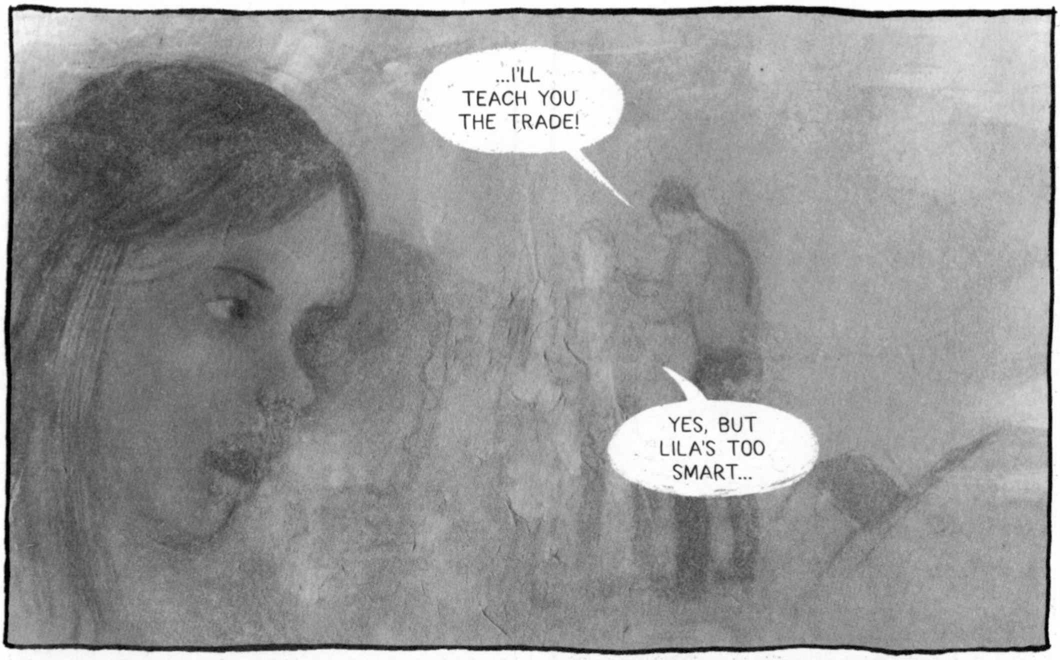
...I'LL TEACH YOU THE TRADE!
YES, BUT LILA'S TOO SMART...

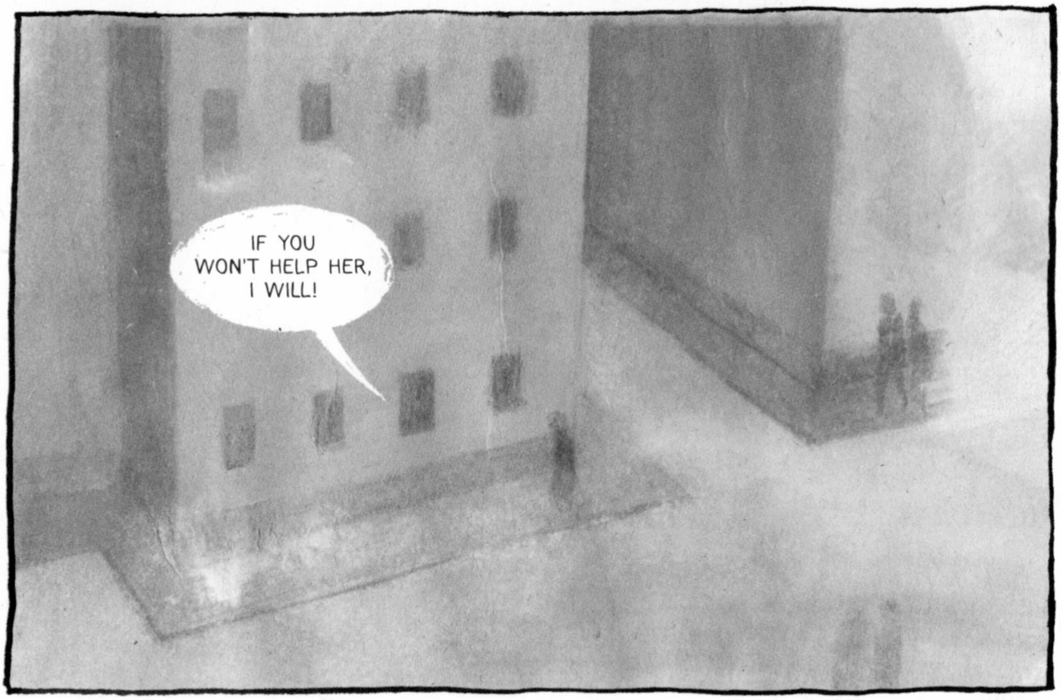
IF YOU WON'T HELP HER, I WILL!

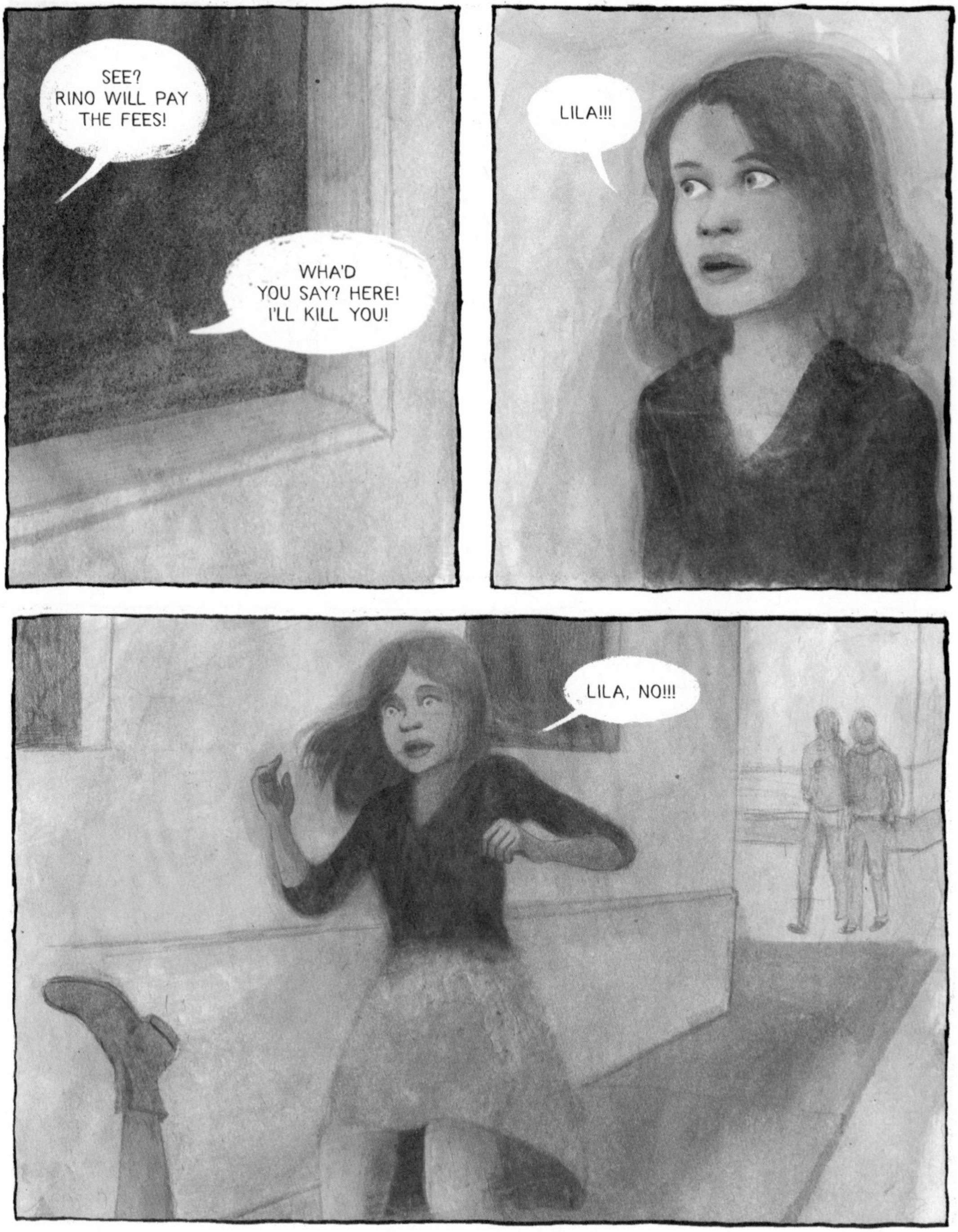
SEE? RINO WILL PAY THE FEES!
WHA'D YOU SAY? HERE! I'LL KILL YOU!
LILA!!!
LILA, NO!!!

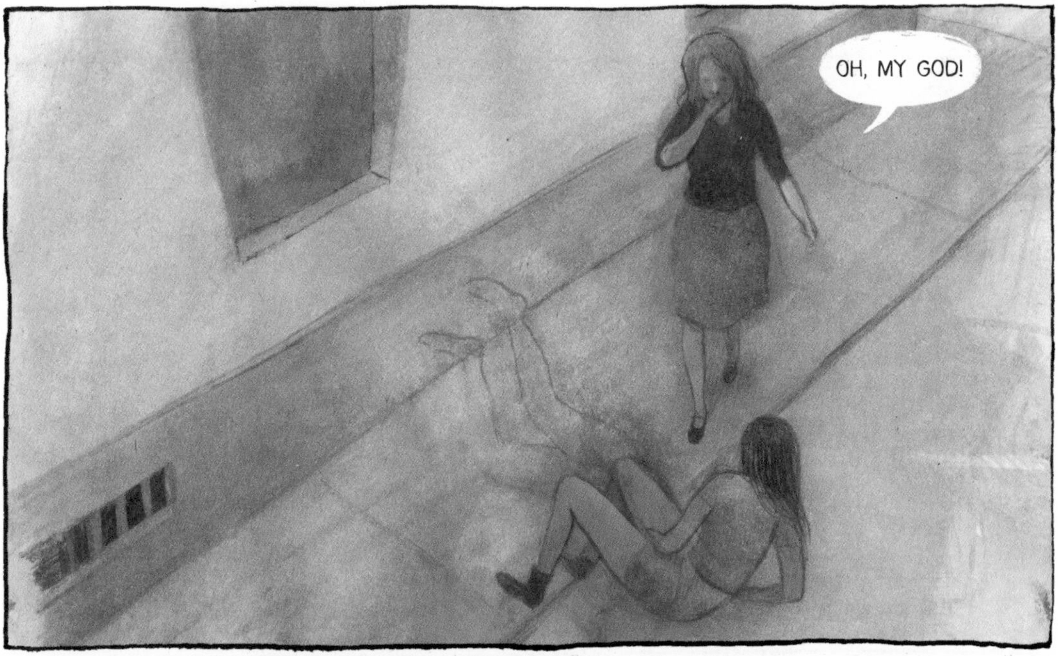
OH, MY GOD!

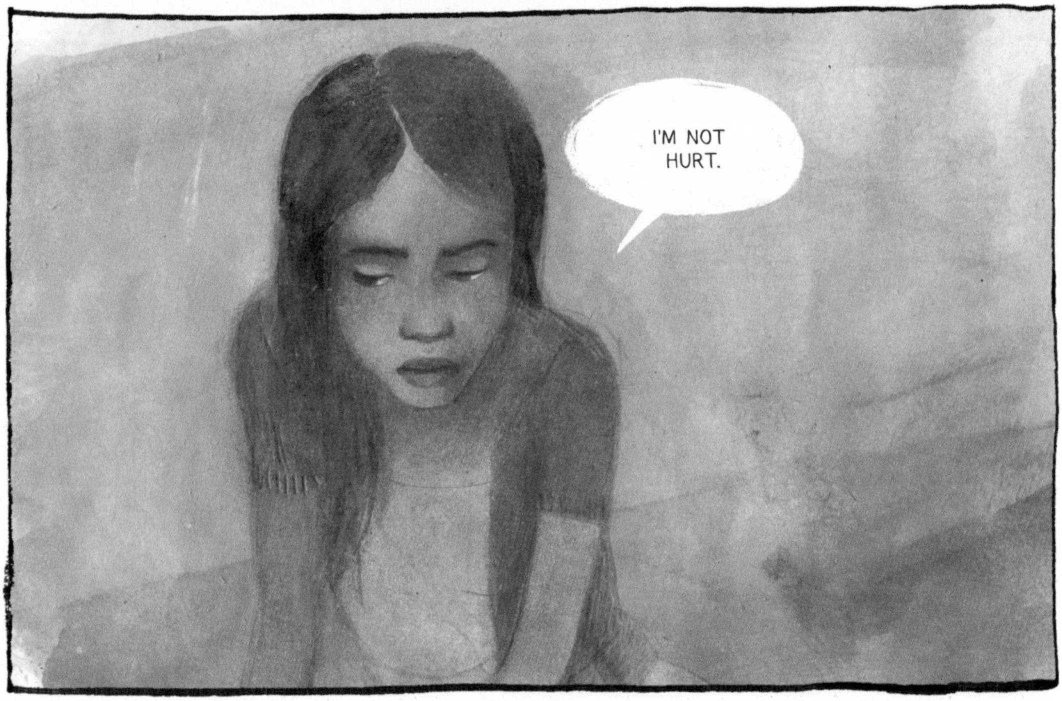
I'M NOT HURT.

FATHERS COULD DO WHATEVER THEY LIKED TO DISOBEDIENT GIRLS WHO DID THINGS THAT WERE FORBIDDEN.

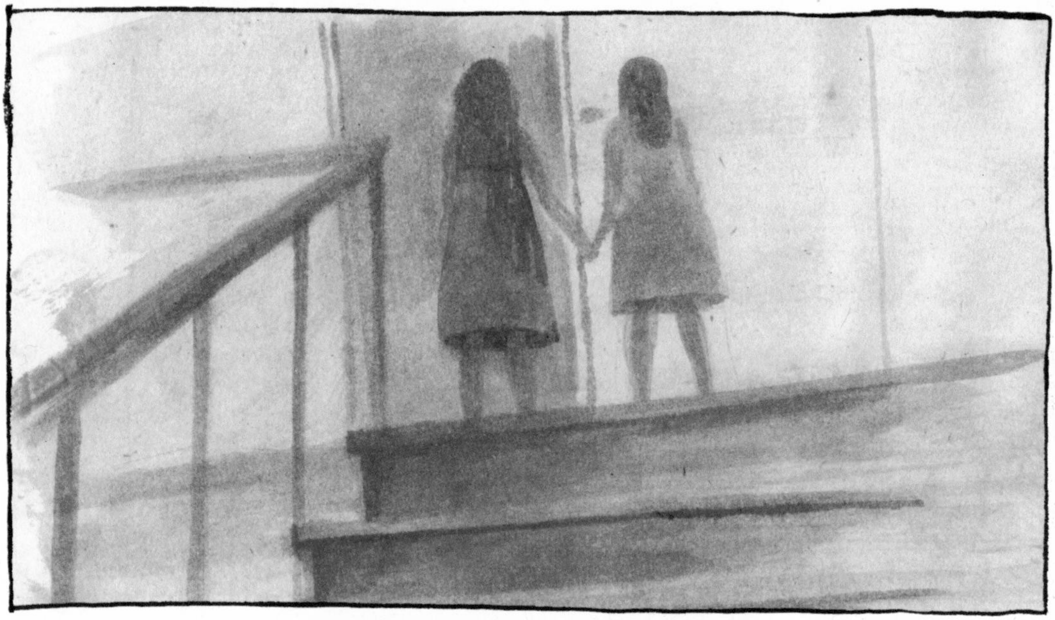

AND GOING TO DON ACHILLE WAS FORBIDDEN.

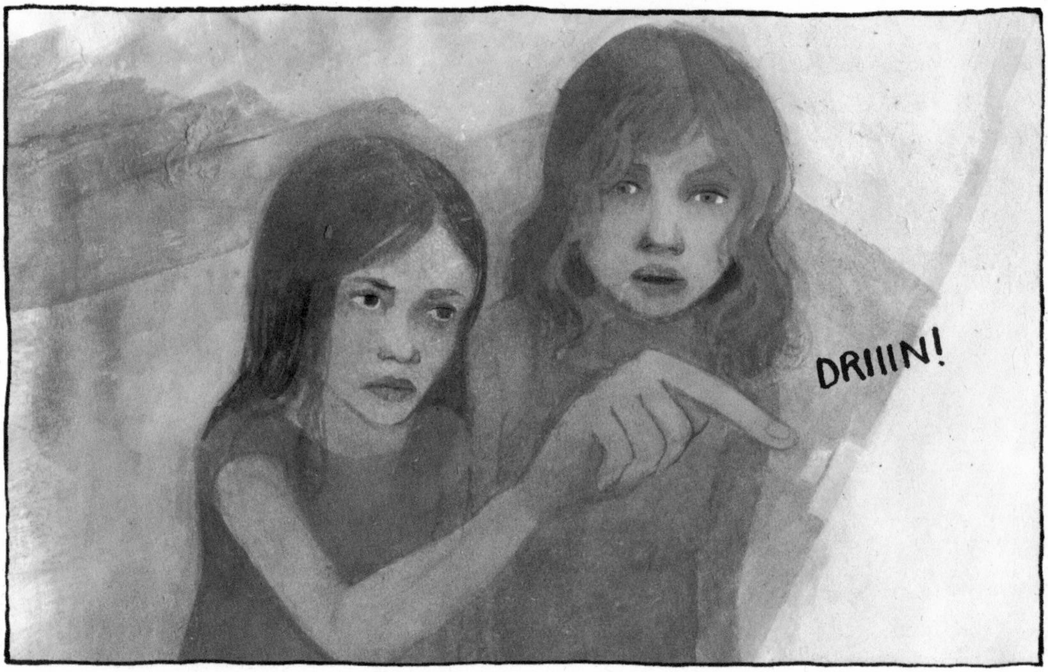
DRIIIN!

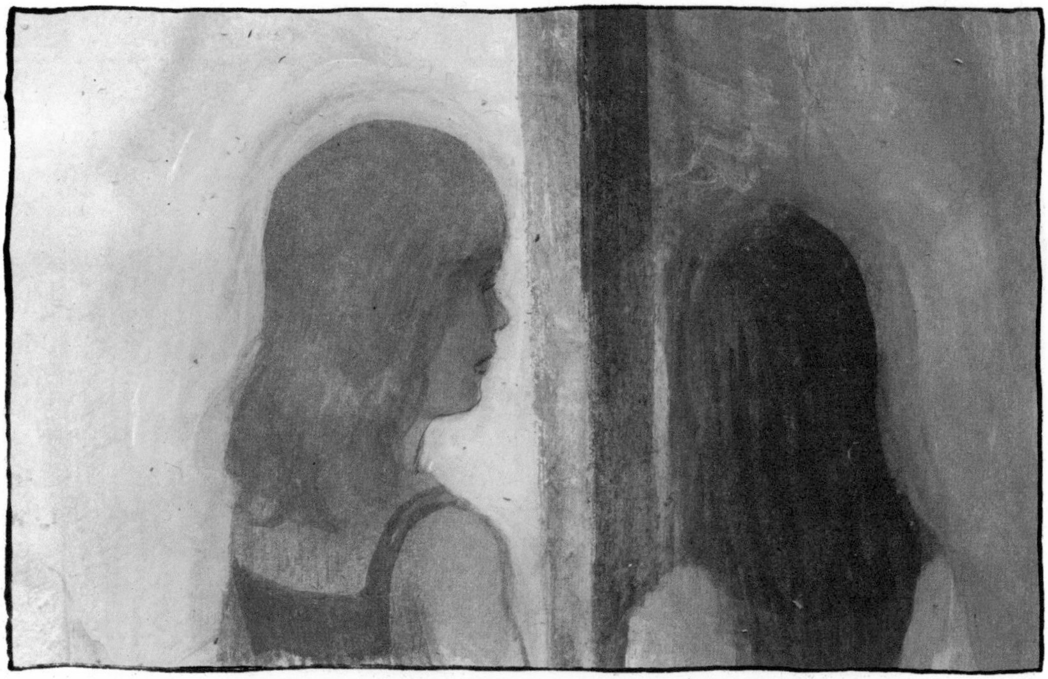

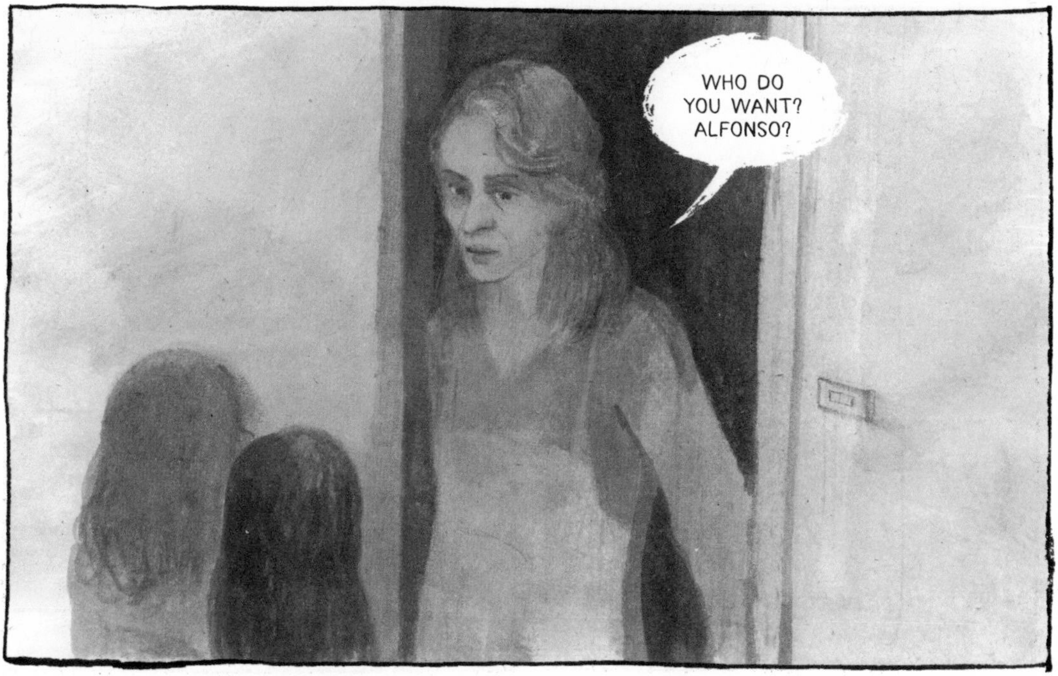
WHO DO YOU WANT? ALFONSO?

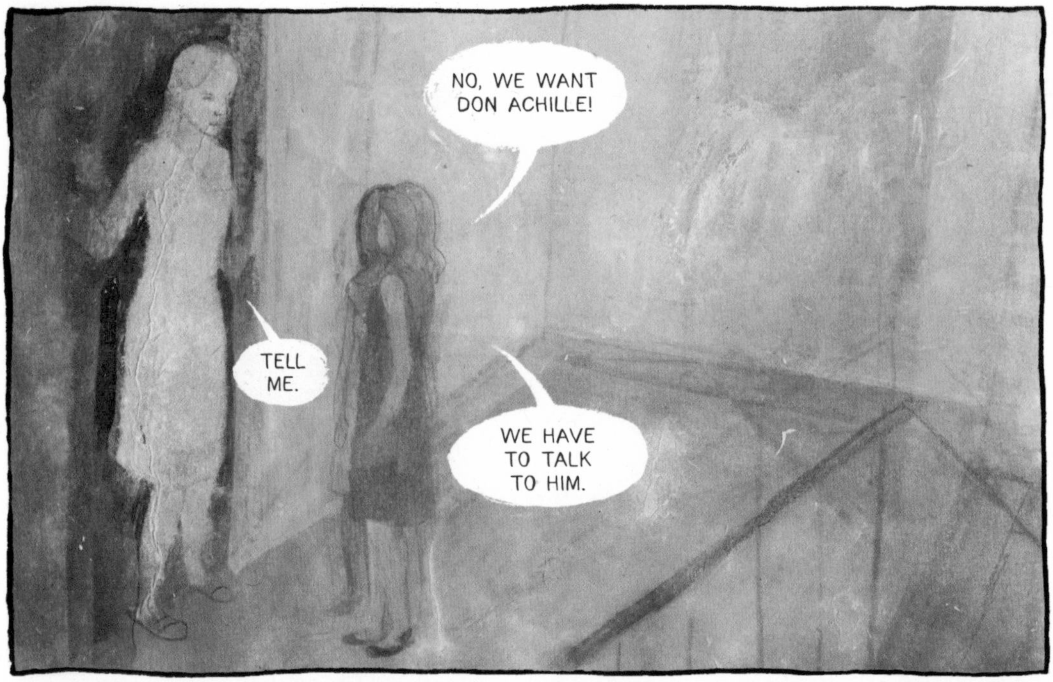
NO, WE WANT DON ACHILLE!
TELL ME.
WE HAVE TO TALK TO HIM.

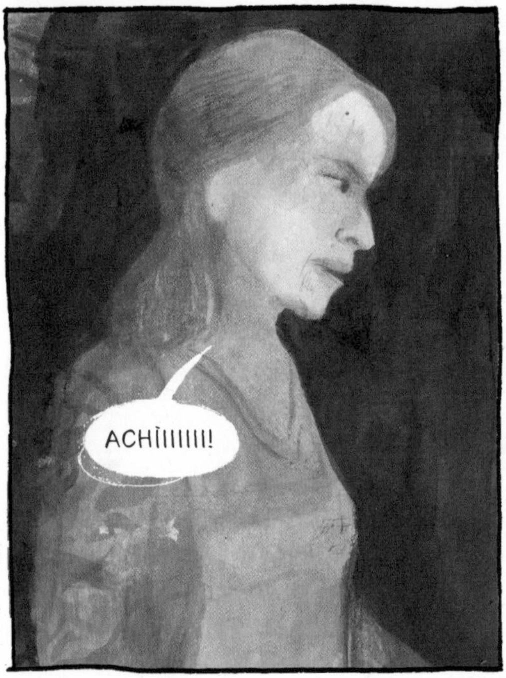
ACHÌIIIIIII!

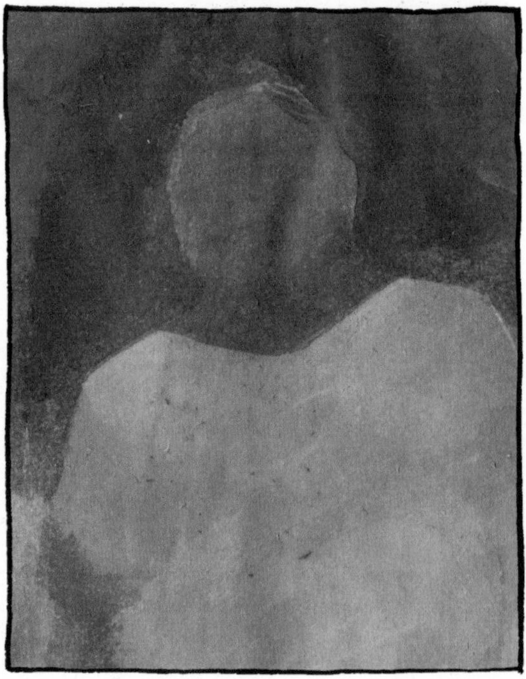

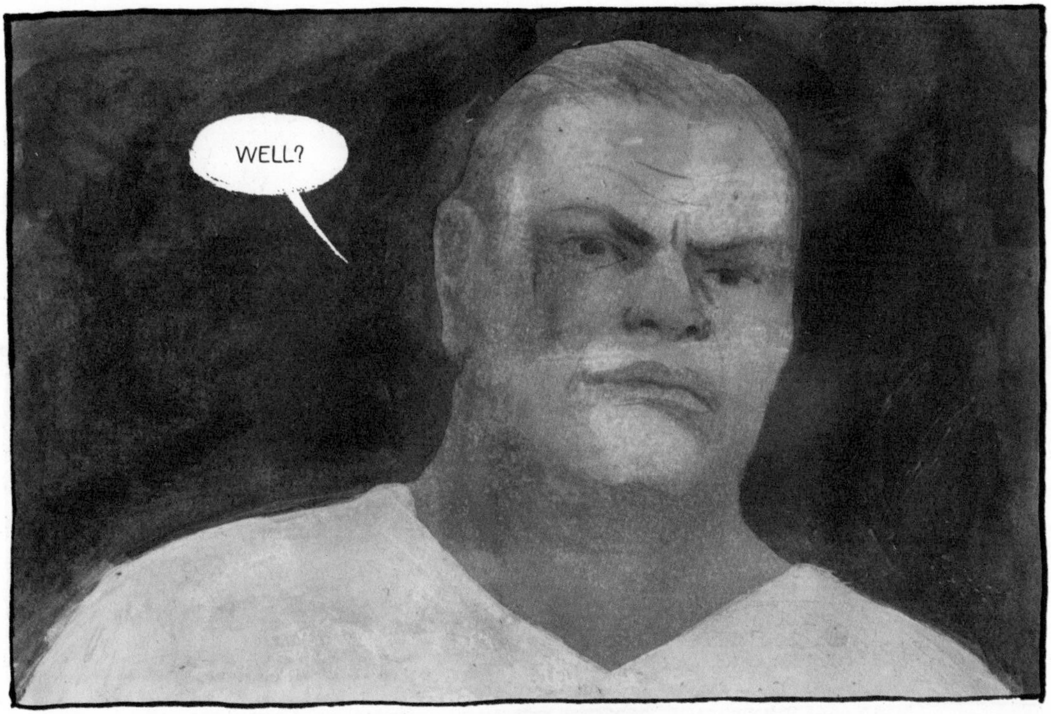
WELL?

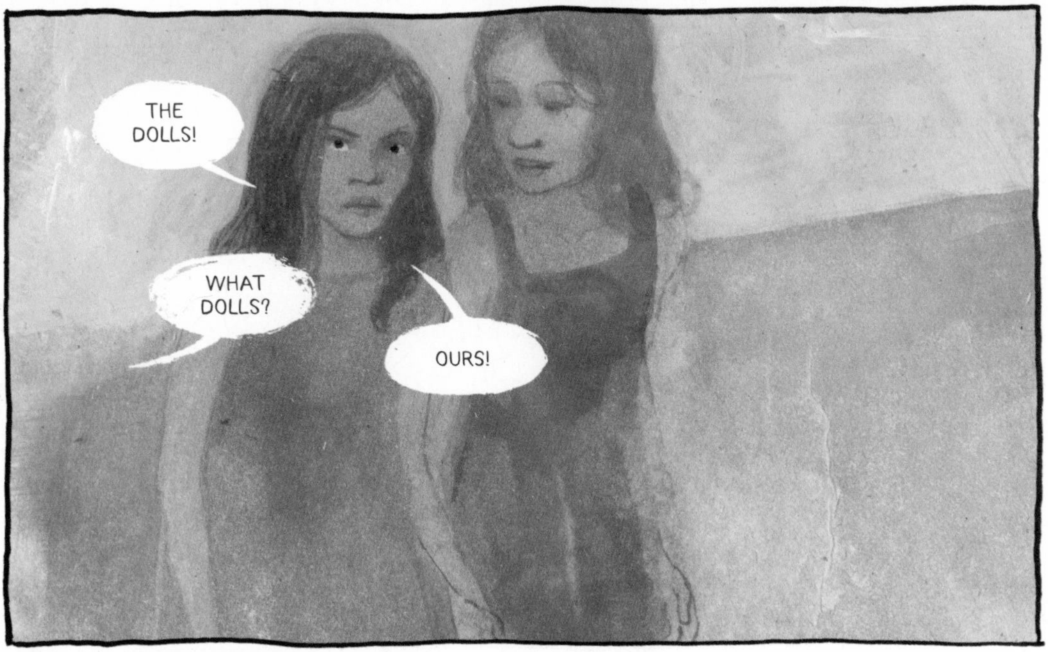
THE DOLLS!
WHAT DOLLS?
OURS!

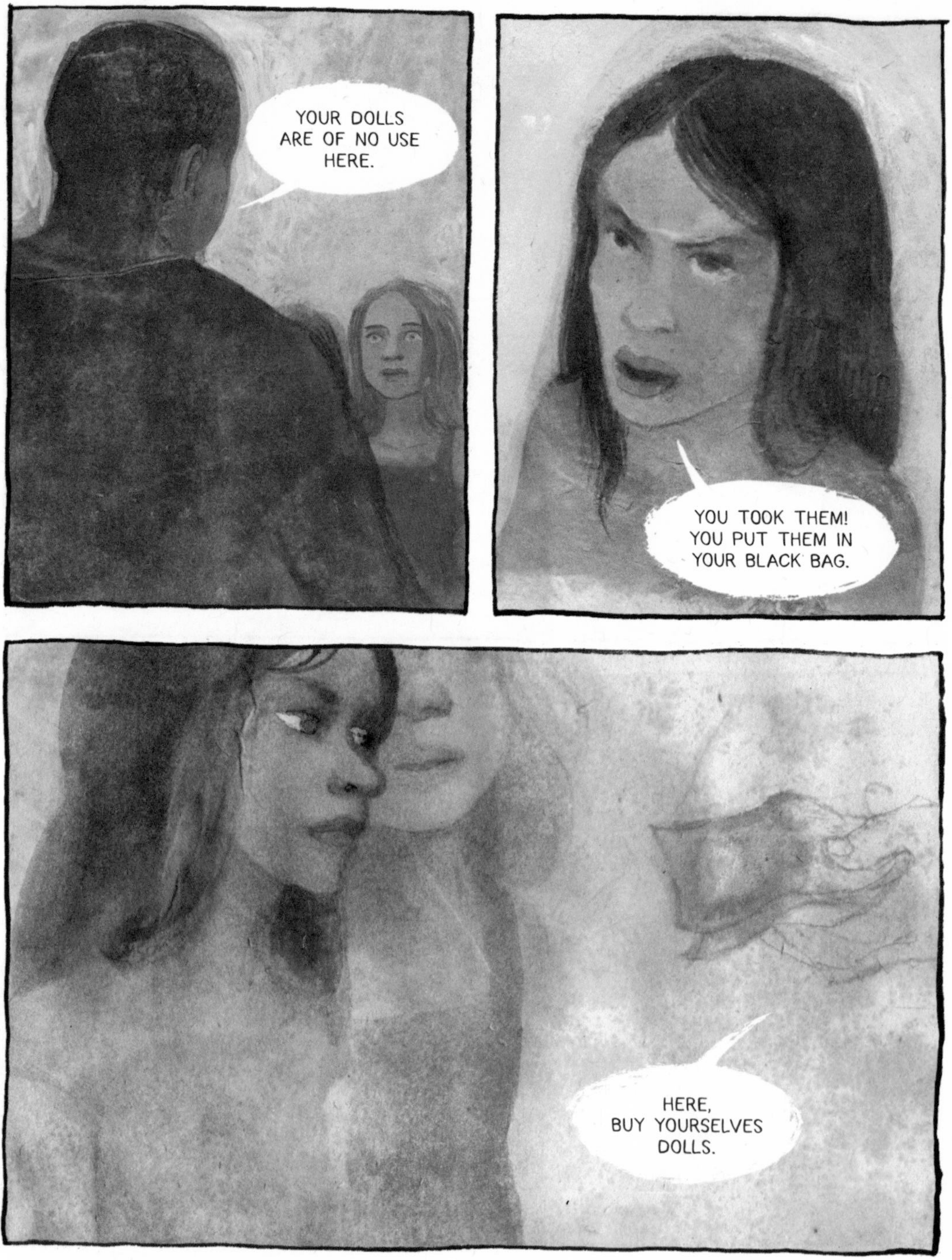
YOUR DOLLS ARE OF NO USE HERE.
YOU TOOK THEM! YOU PUT THEM IN YOUR BLACK BAG.
HERE, BUY YOURSELVES DOLLS.

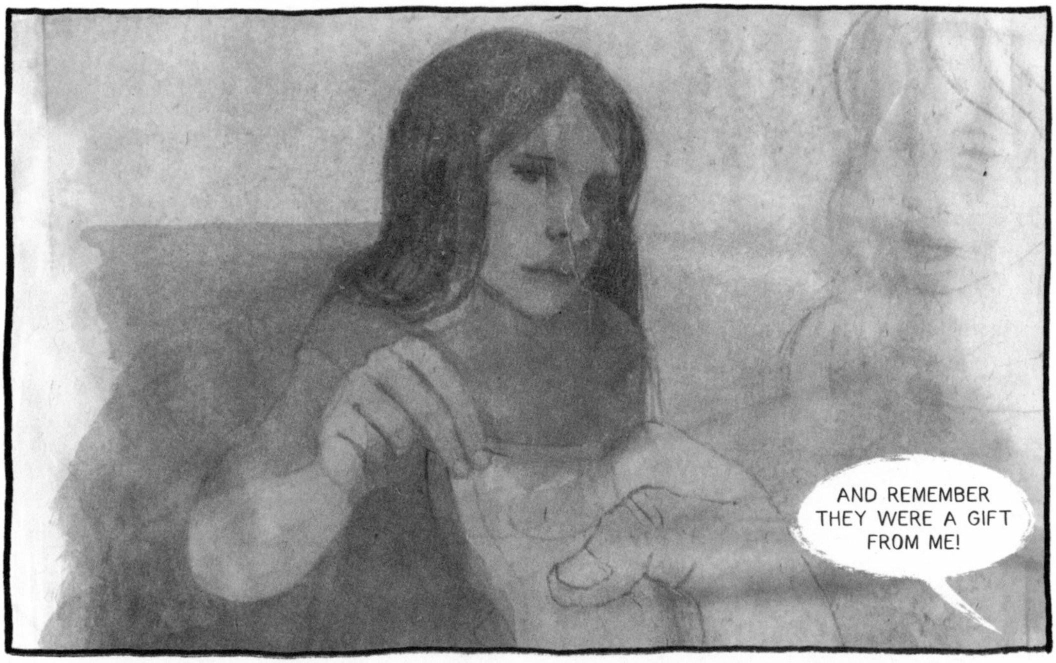
AND REMEMBER THEY WERE A GIFT FROM ME!

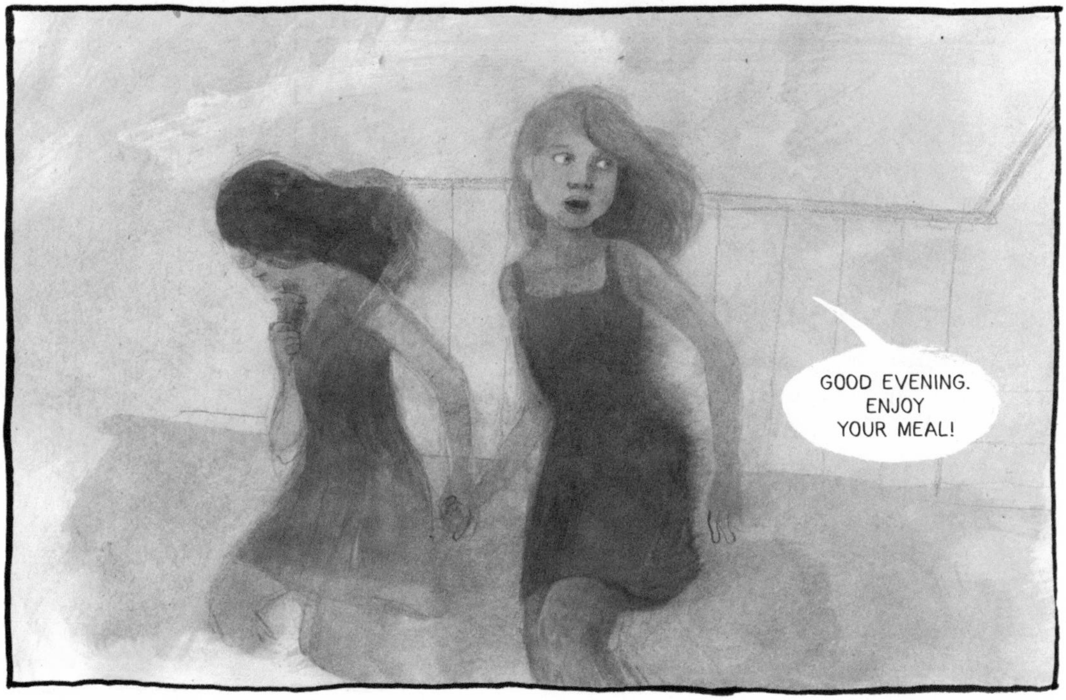
GOOD EVENING. ENJOY YOUR MEAL!

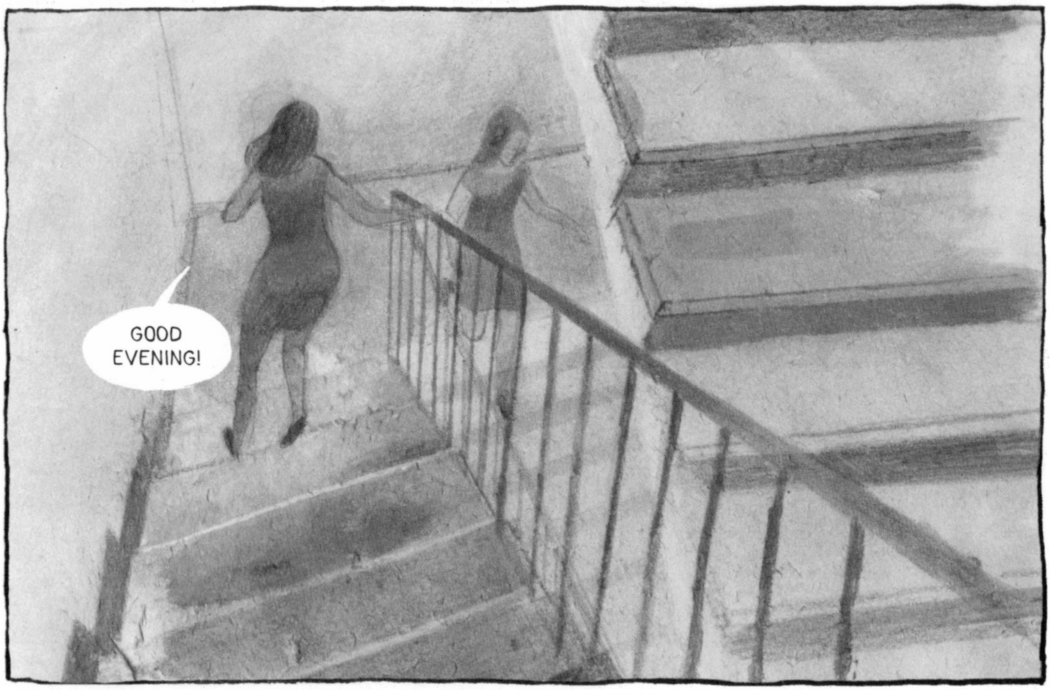
GOOD EVENING!

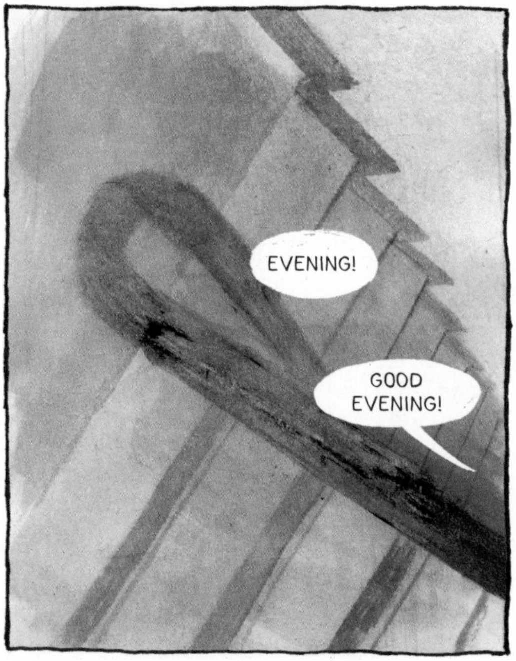
EVENING!
GOOD EVENING!

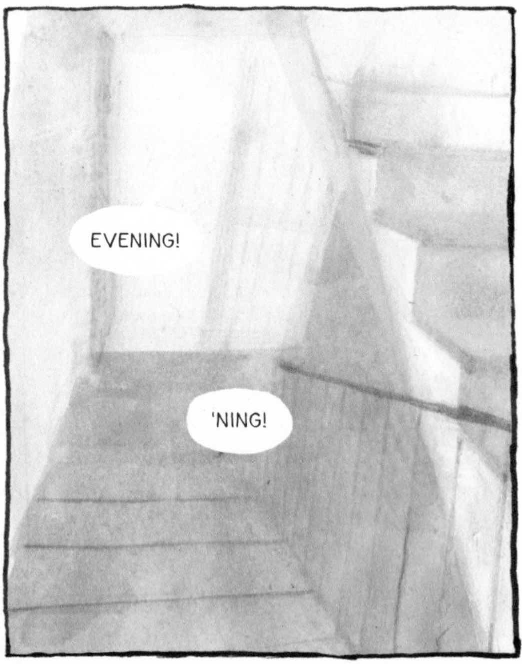
EVENING!
'NING!

BUT WE DIDN'T BUY DOLLS WITH THAT MONEY...

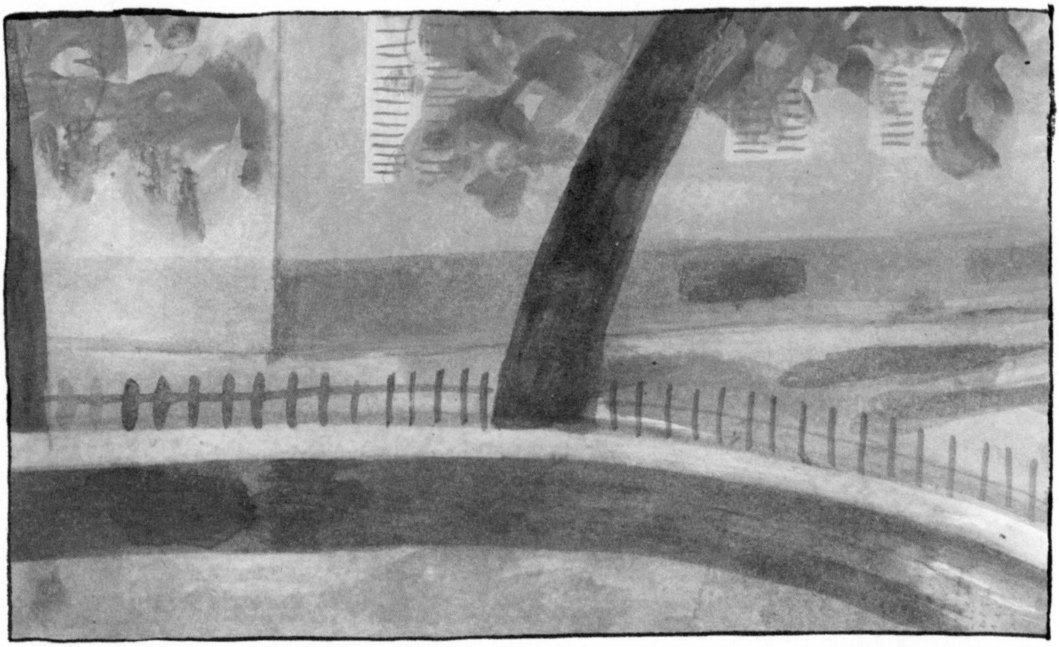

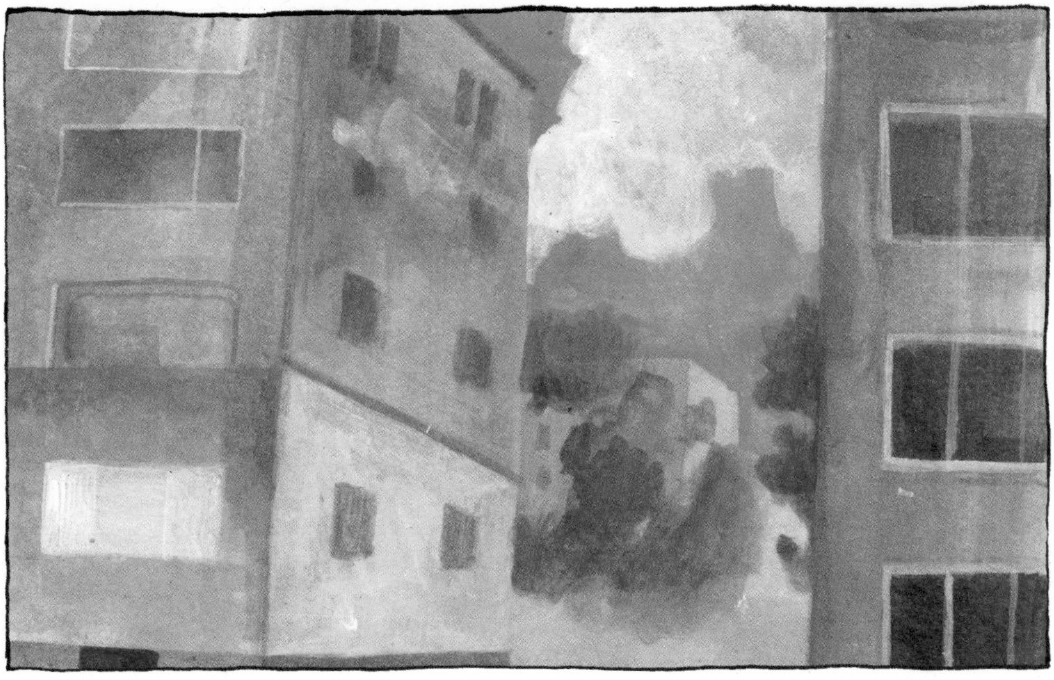

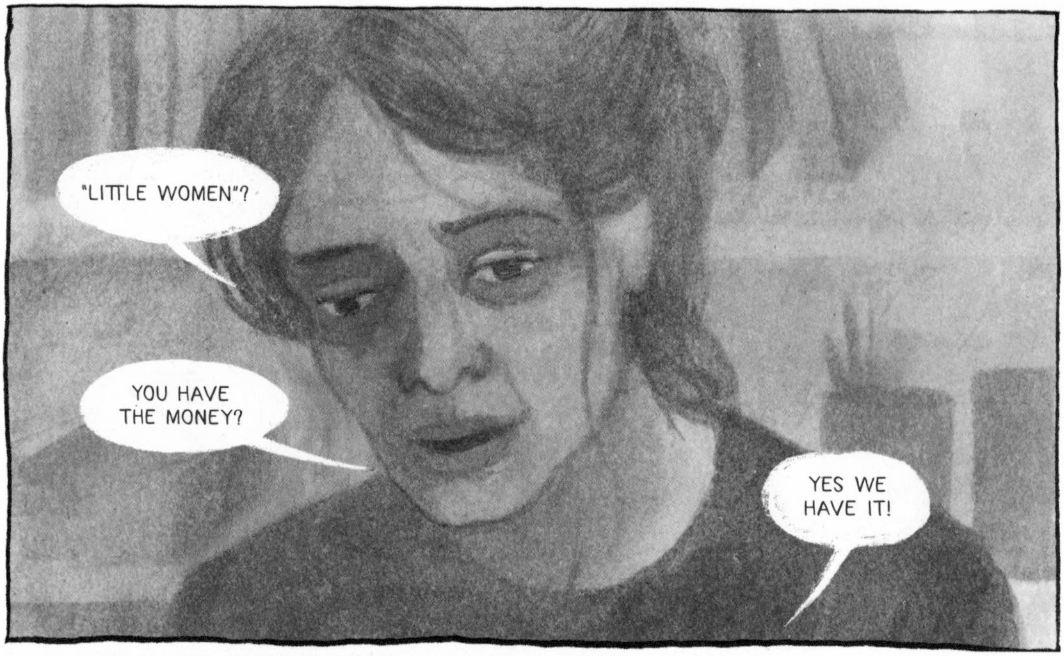
"LITTLE WOMEN"?
YOU HAVE THE MONEY?
YES WE HAVE IT!

HOW COULD WE HAVE REPLACED TINA AND NU?

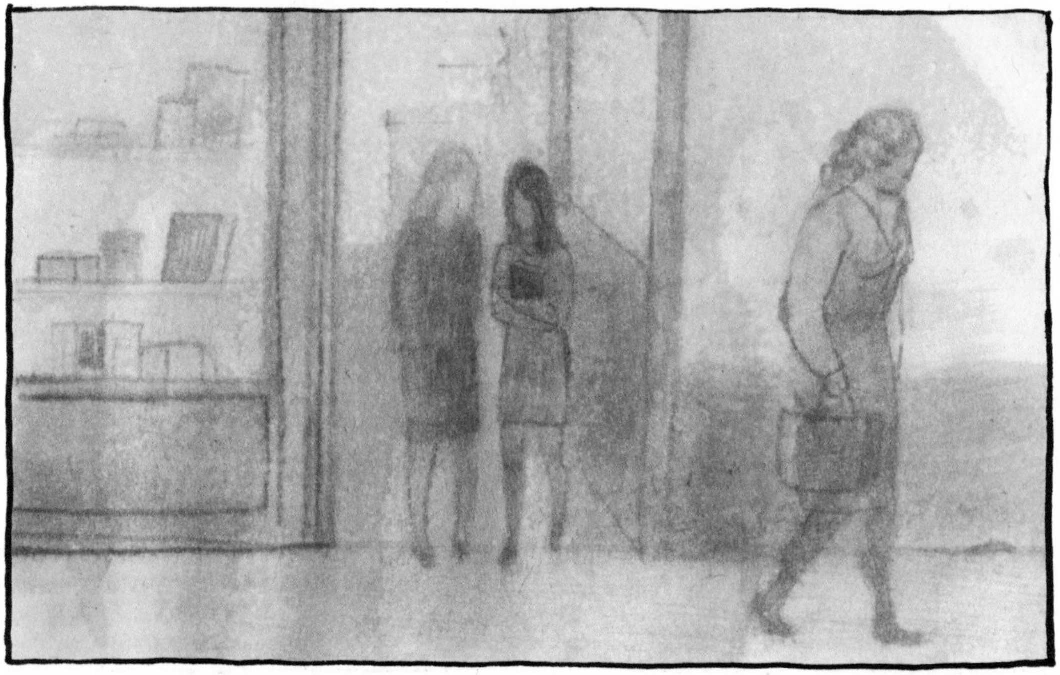

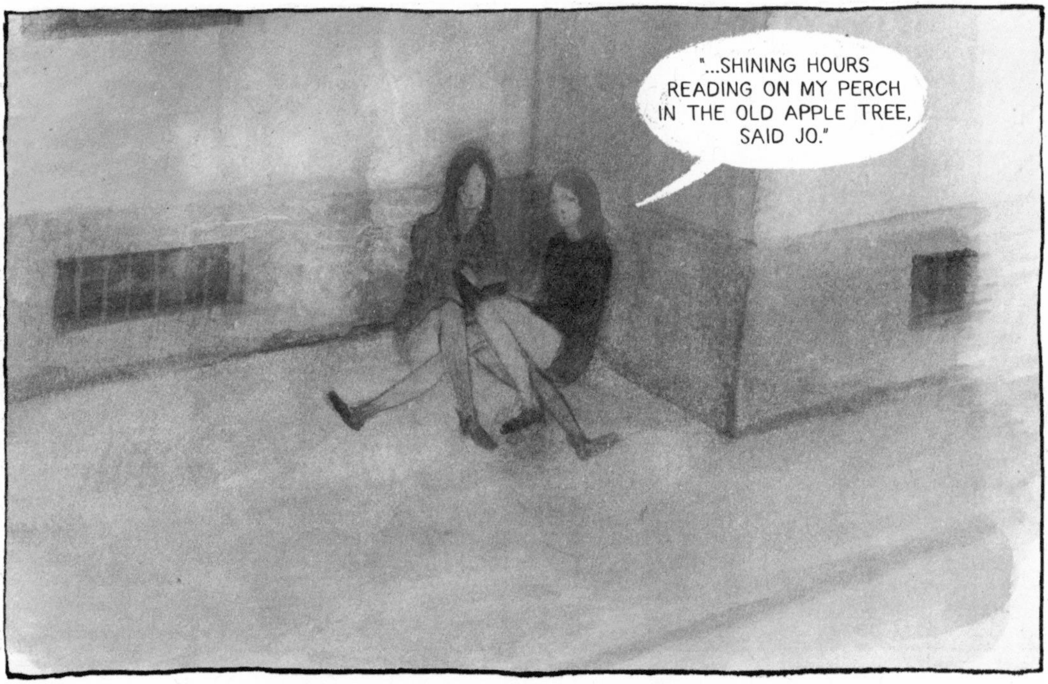
"...SHINING HOURS READING ON MY PERCH IN THE OLD APPLE TREE, SAID JO."

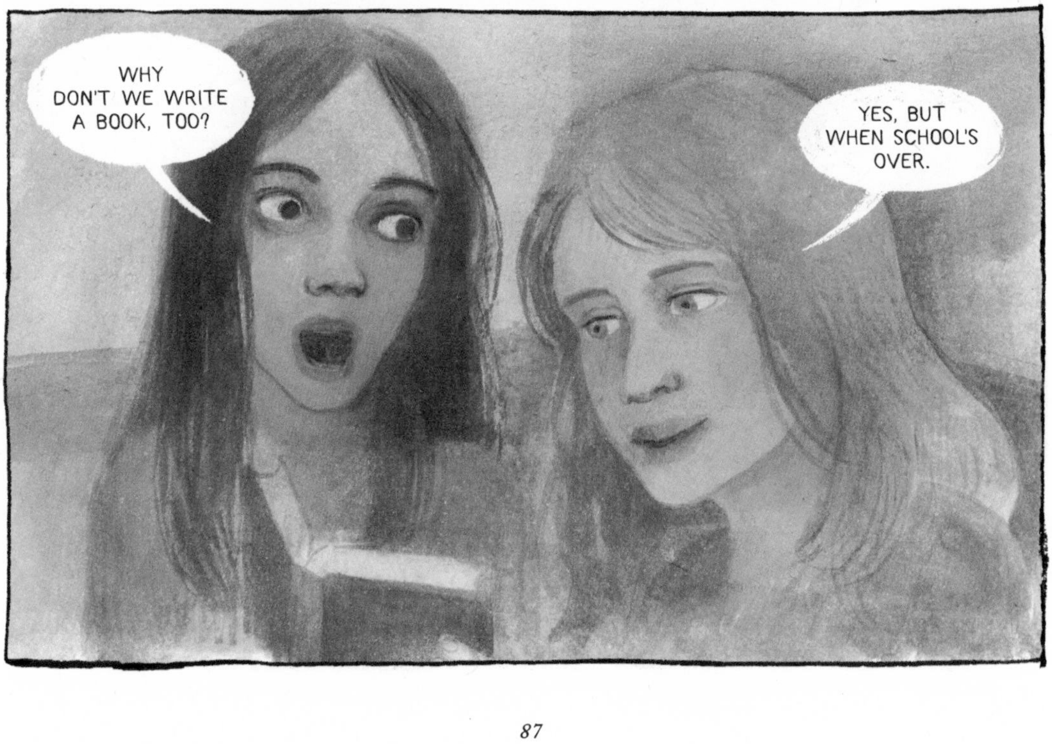
WHY DON'T WE WRITE A BOOK, TOO?
YES, BUT WHEN SCHOOL'S OVER.

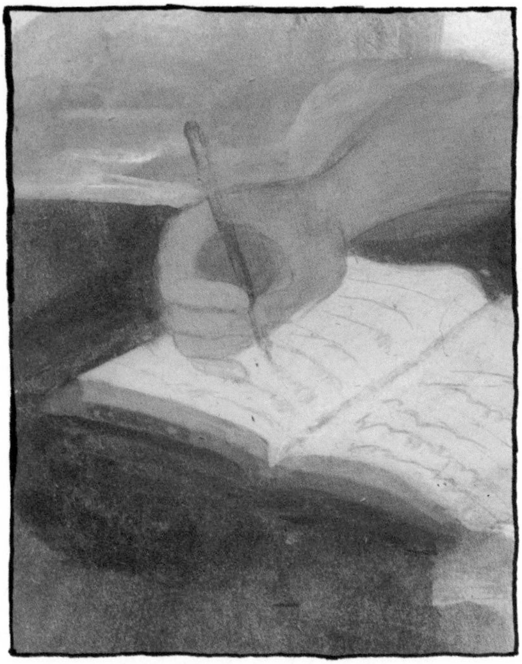

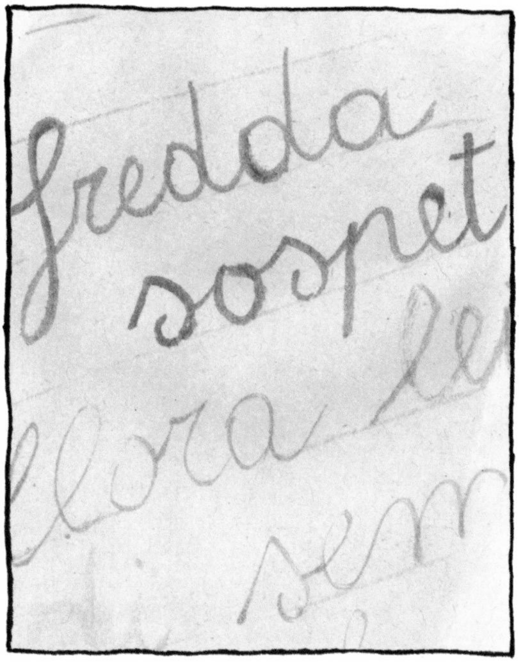
fredda
sospet

SHE HAD PROMISED, BUT SHE COULDN'T WAIT.

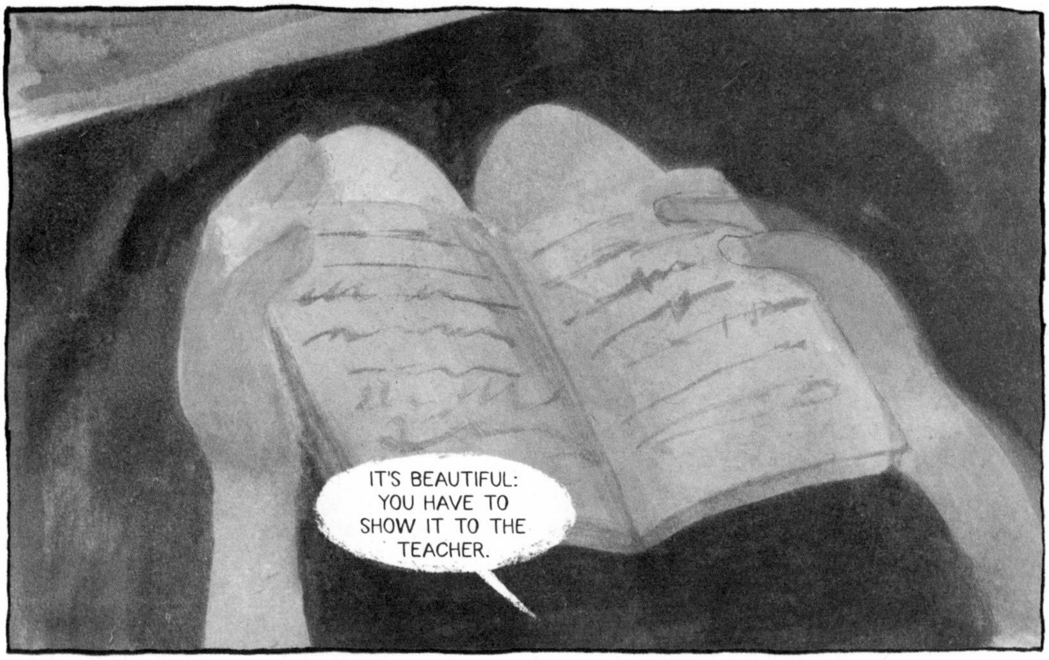
IT'S BEAUTIFUL: YOU HAVE TO SHOW IT TO THE TEACHER.

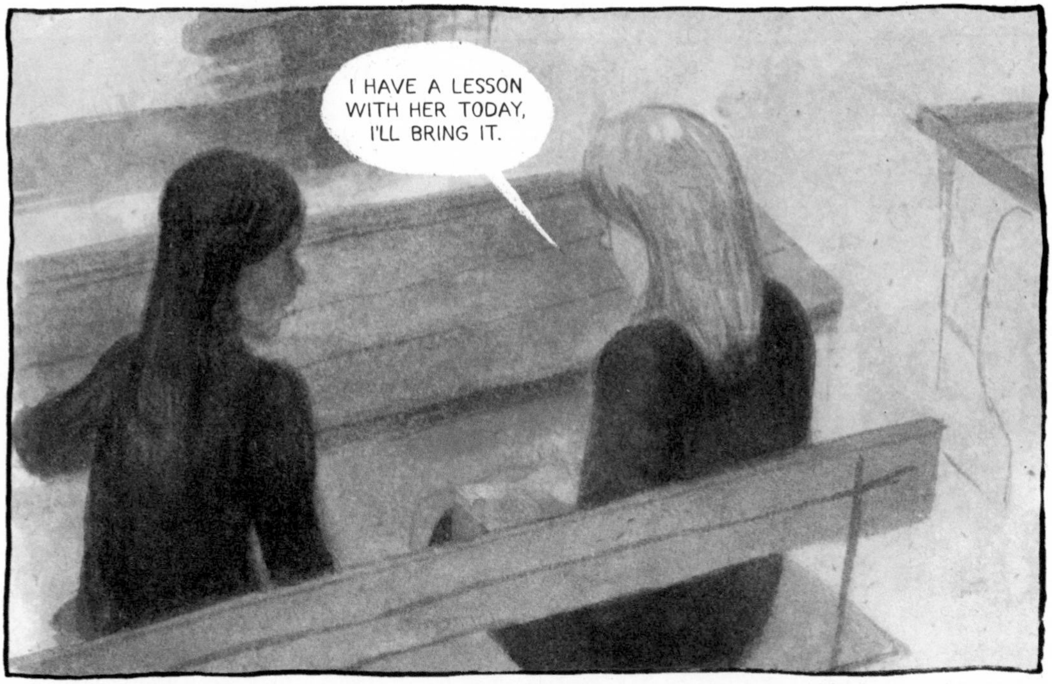
I HAVE A LESSON WITH HER TODAY, I'LL BRING IT.

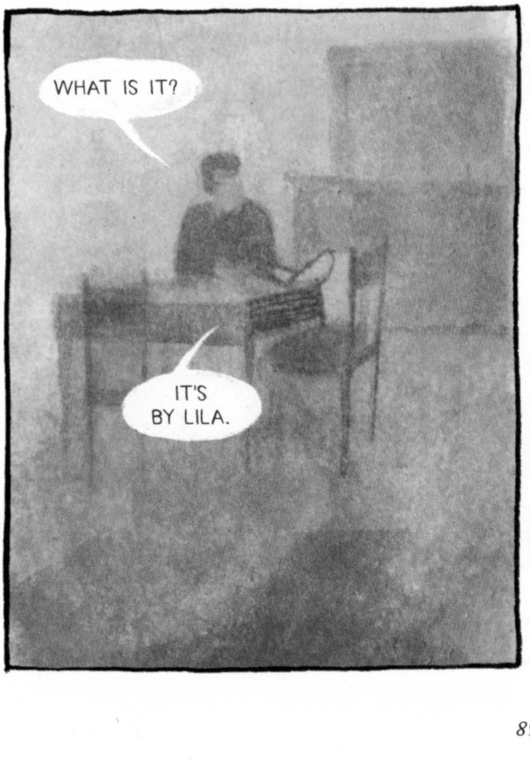
WHAT IS IT?
IT'S BY LILA.

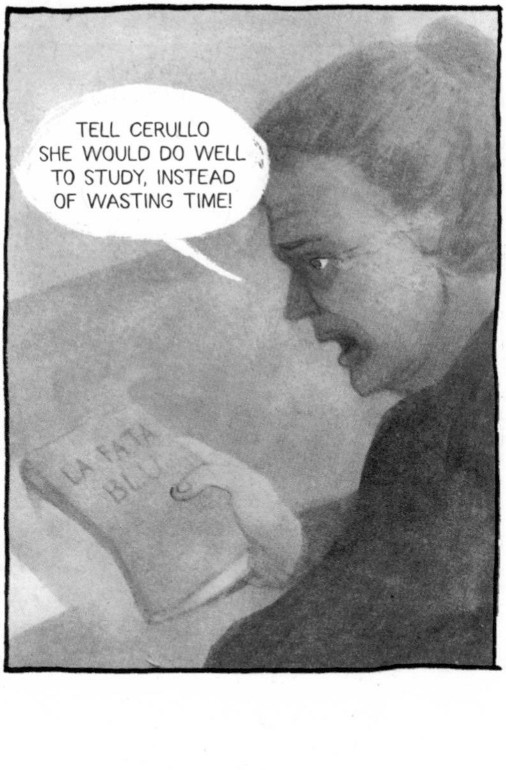
TELL CERULLO SHE WOULD DO WELL TO STUDY, INSTEAD OF WASTING TIME!
LA FATA BLU

THE TEACHER SAID NOTHING MORE ABOUT "THE BLUE FAIRY."

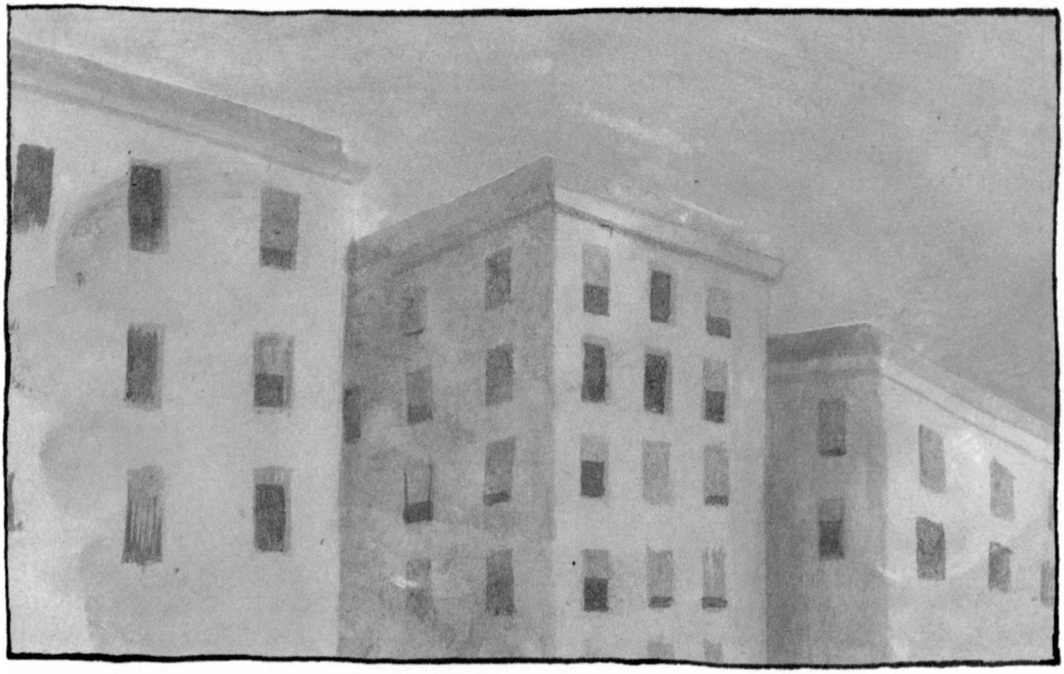

LILA ASKED ME ABOUT IT A COUPLE OF TIMES, THEN SHE LET IT GO.

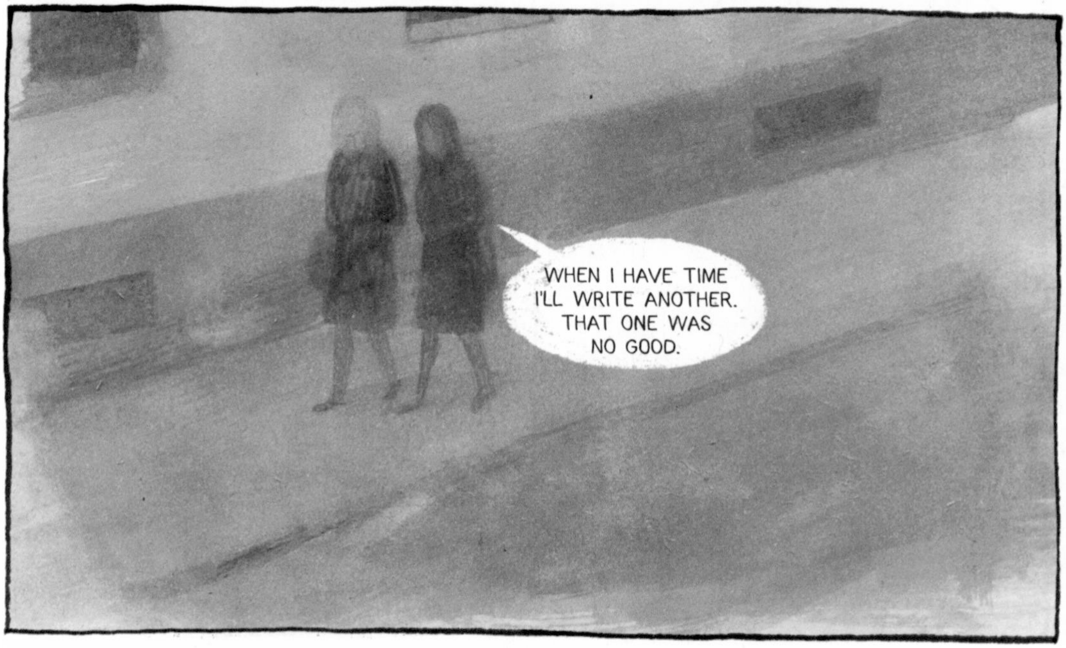
WHEN I HAVE TIME I'LL WRITE ANOTHER. THAT ONE WAS NO GOOD.

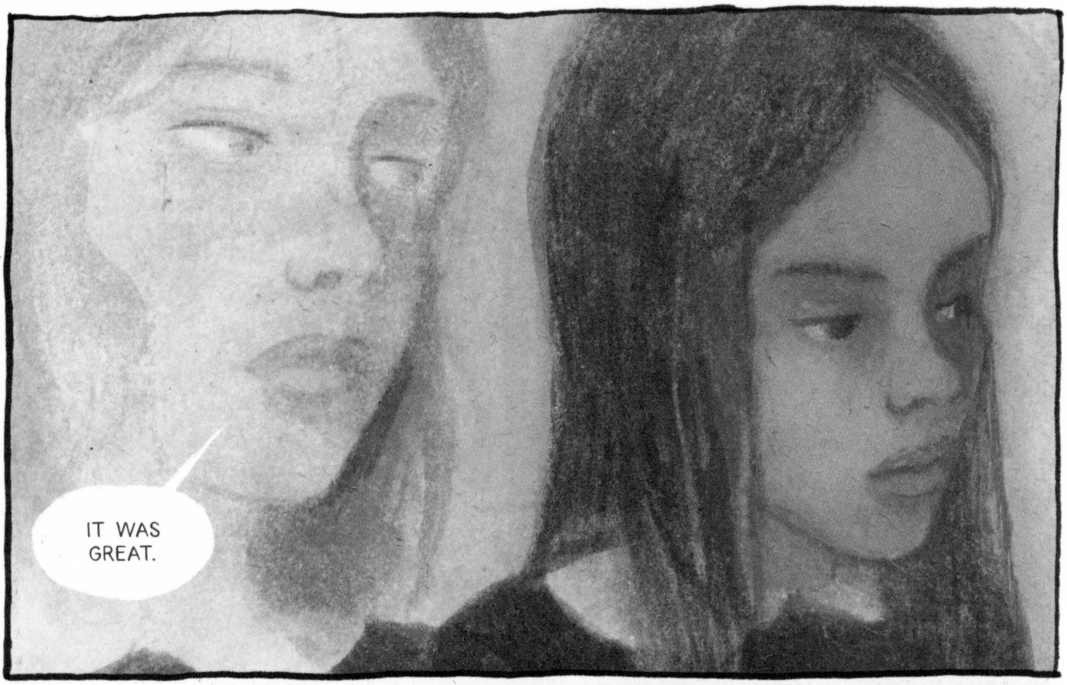
IT WAS GREAT.

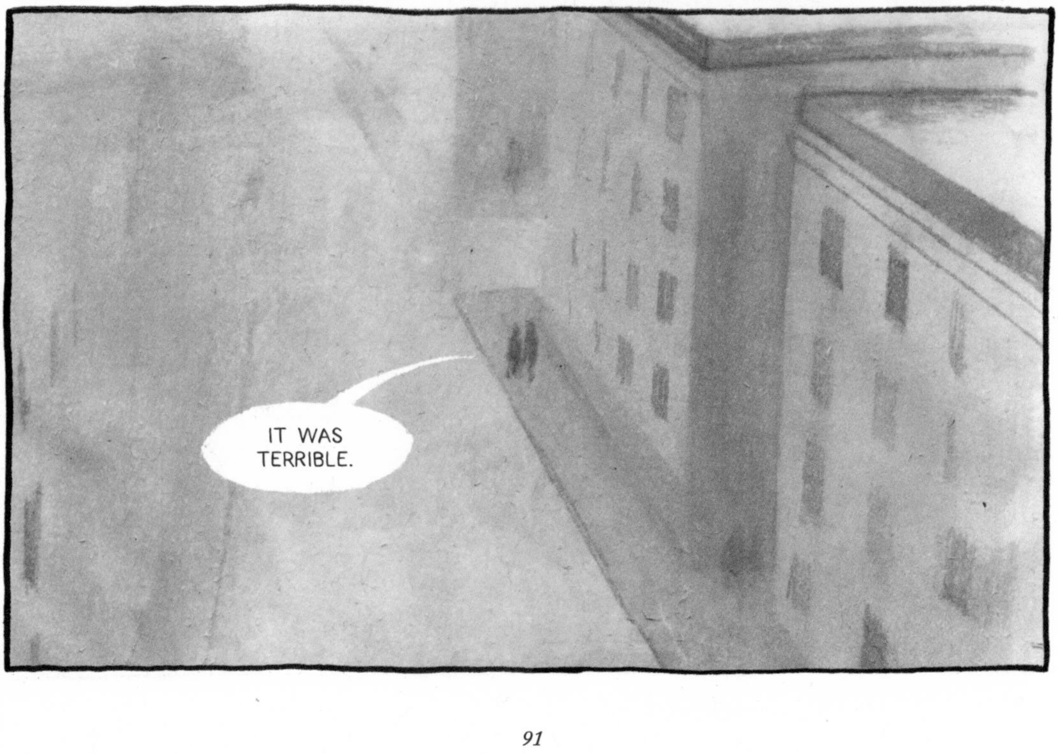
IT WAS TERRIBLE.

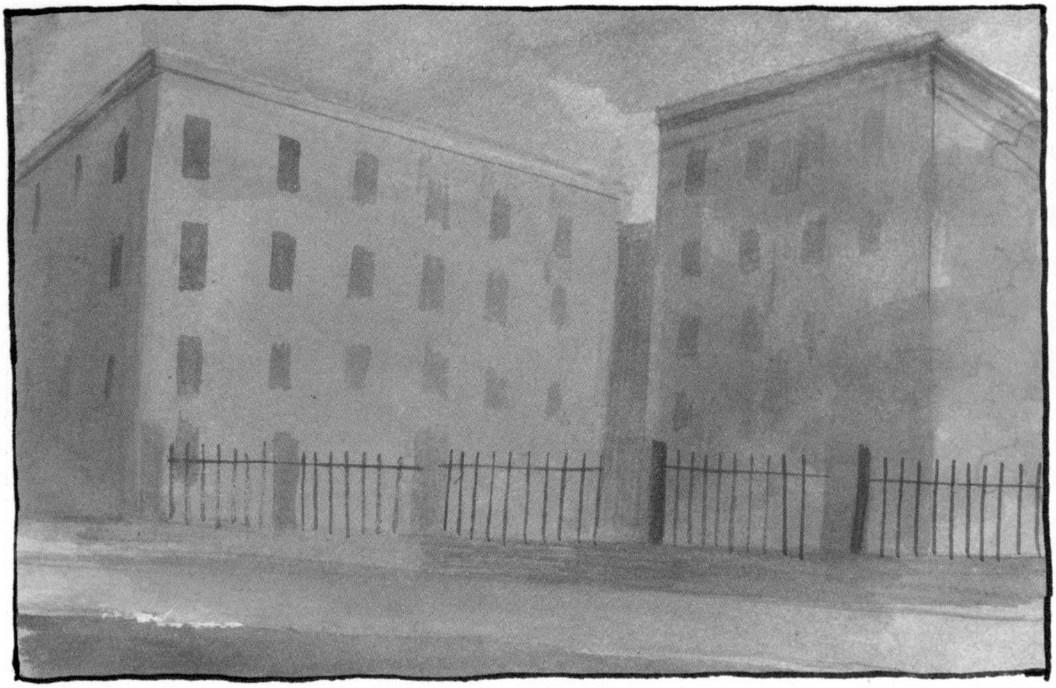

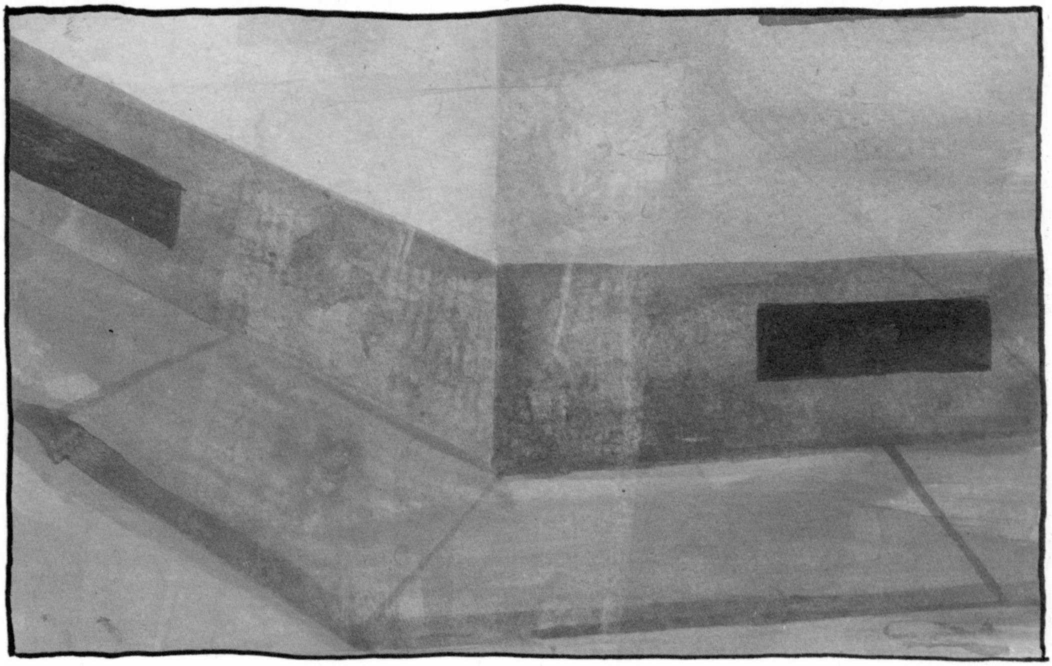

SHORTLY BEFORE THE FINAL TEST IN ELEMENTARY SCHOOL...

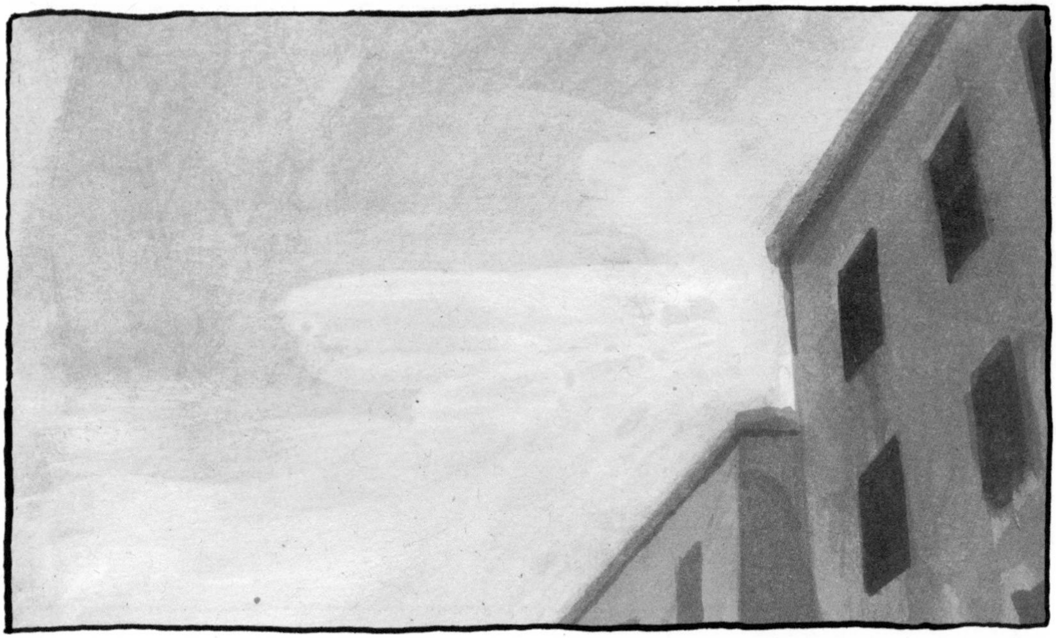

...LILA PUSHED ME TO DO SOMETHING ELSE...

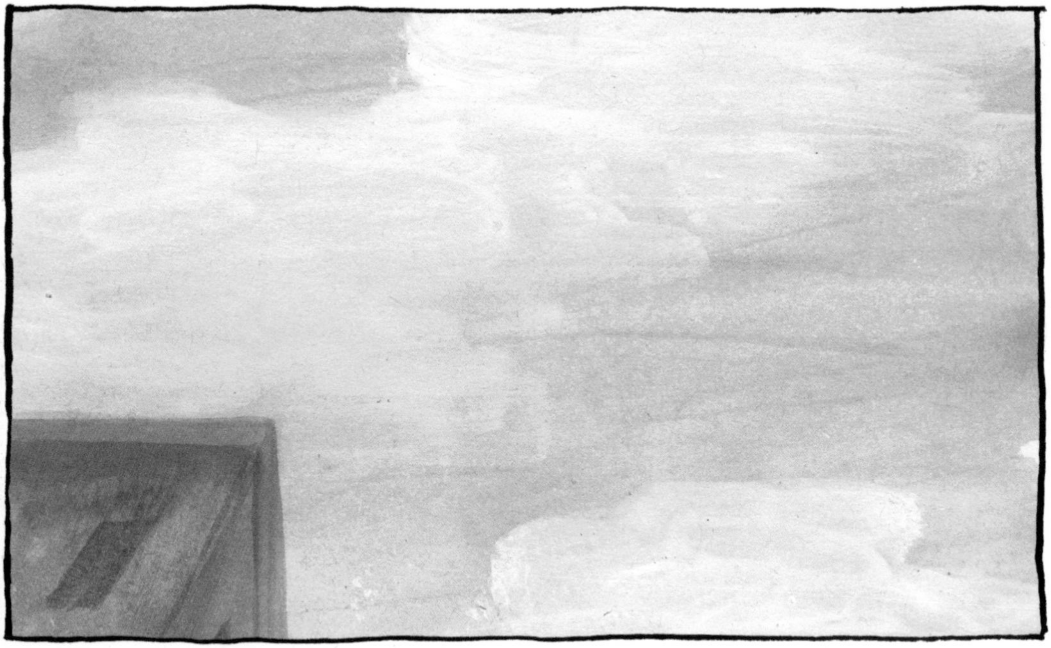

...THAT I WOULD NEVER HAVE HAD THE COURAGE TO DO BY MYSELF:

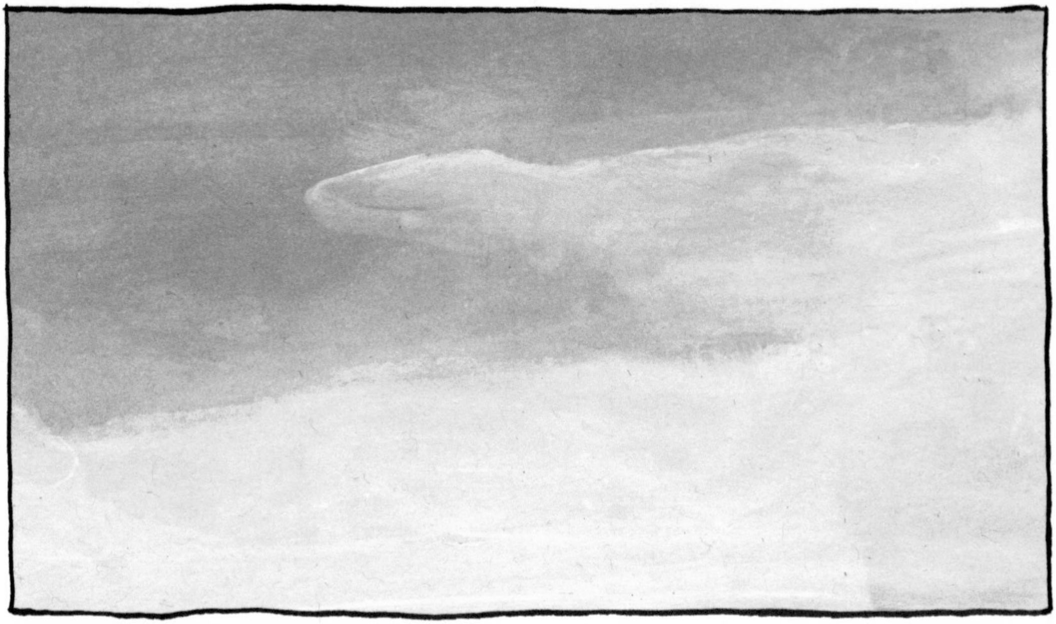

CROSS THE BOUNDARIES OF THE NEIGHBORHOOD.

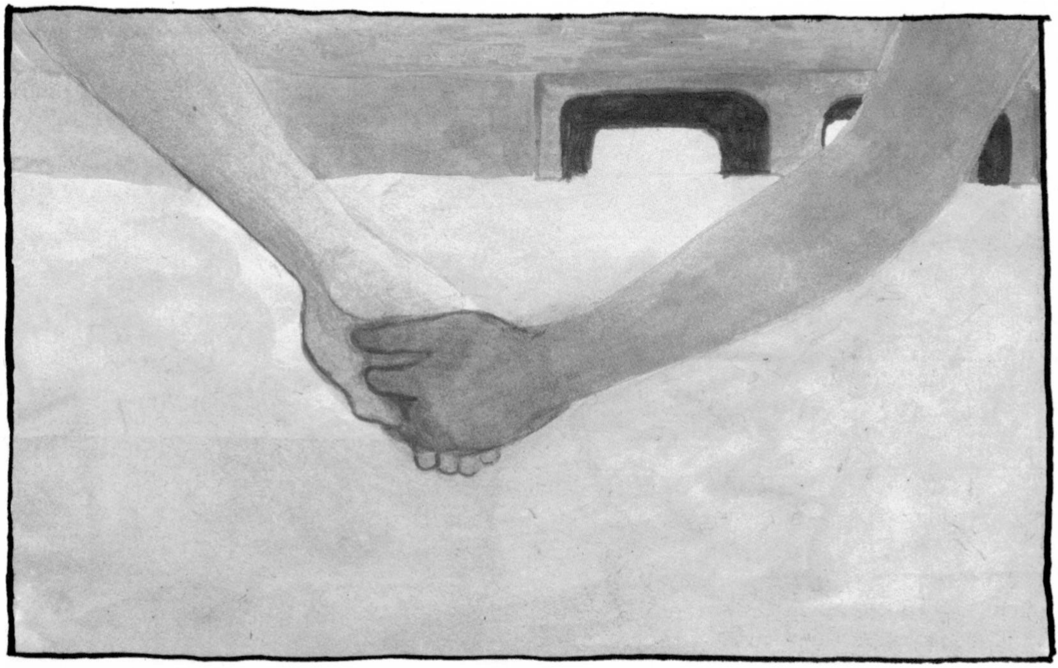

I HAD NEVER LEFT THE FOUR-STORY WHITE APARTMENT BUILDINGS,

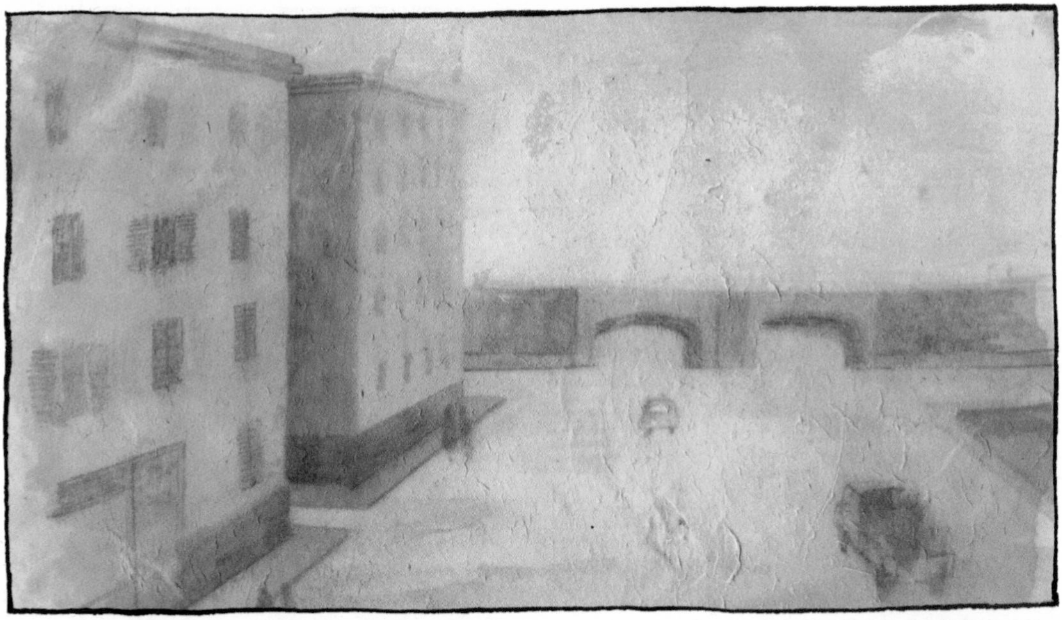

THE COURTYARD, THE PARISH CHURCH, THE GARDENS.

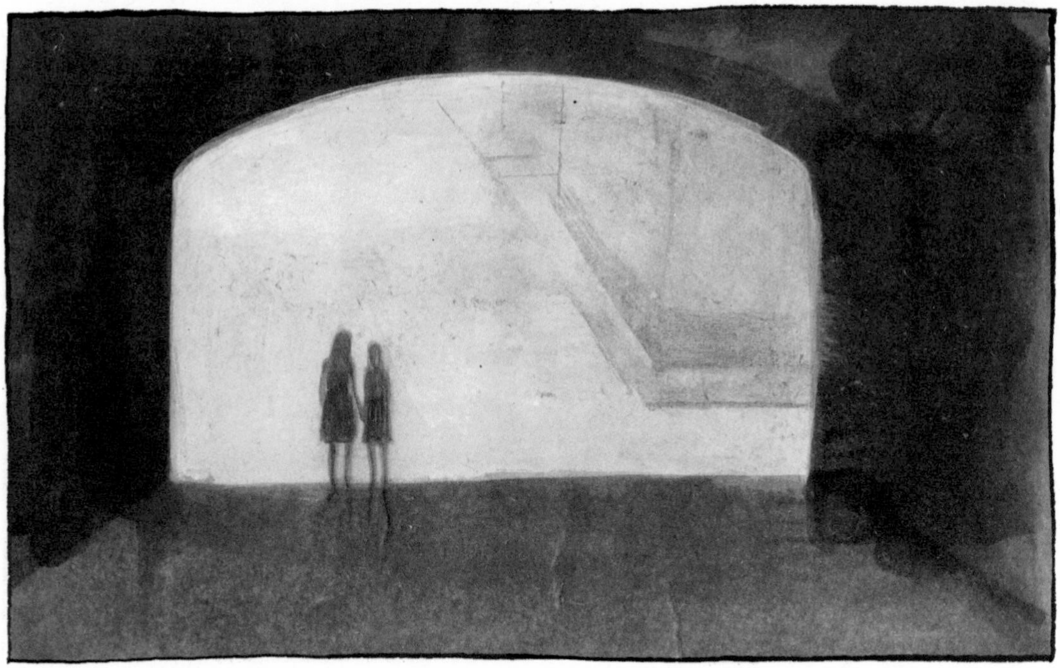

CARS AND TRUCKS PASSED BY CONTINUOUSLY ON THE OTHER SIDE OF THE TUNNEL.

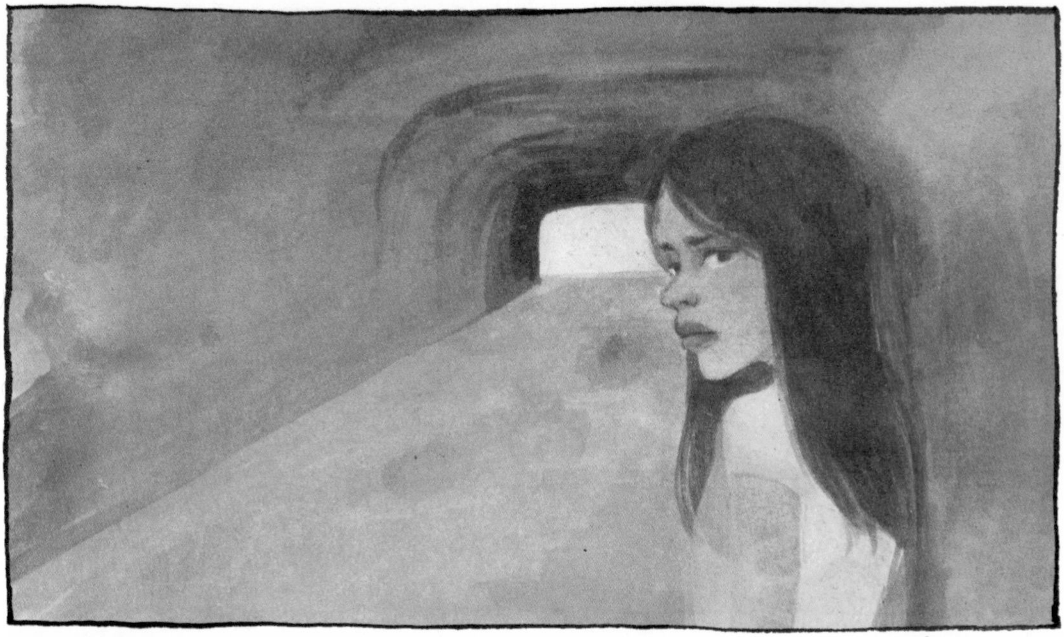

AND YET I DON'T REMEMBER EVER ASKING MYSELF...

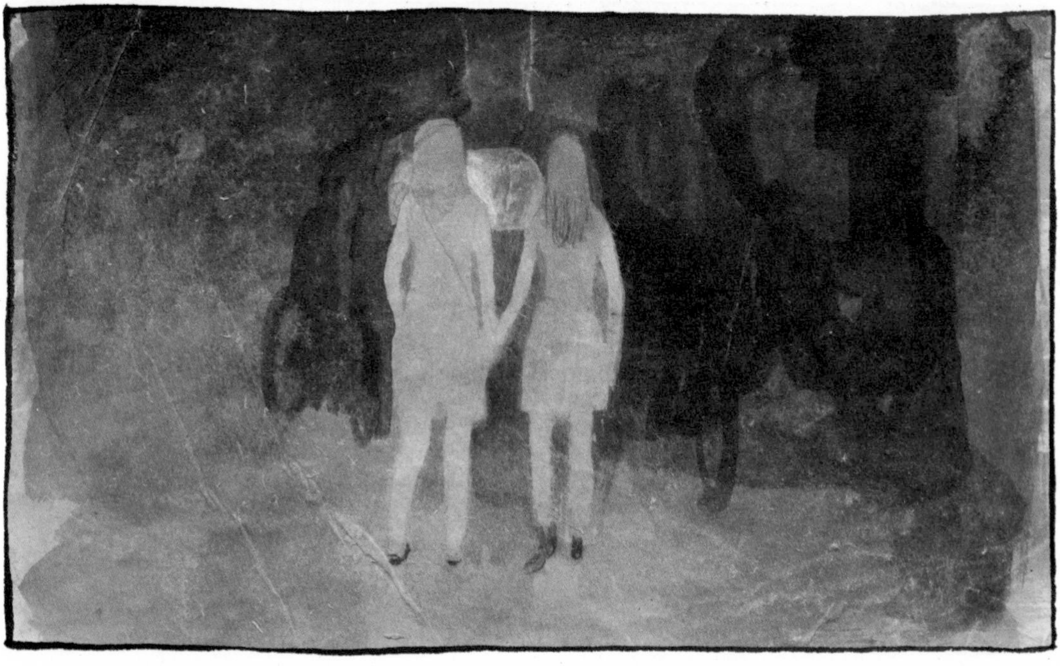

...WHERE ARE THEY GOING?

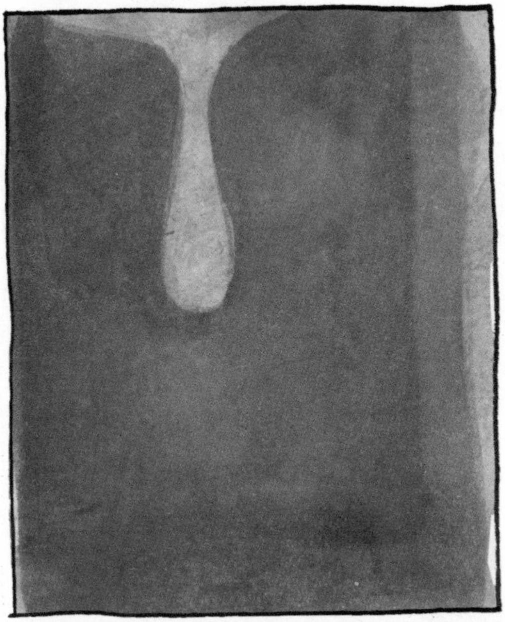

TO WHAT CITY?

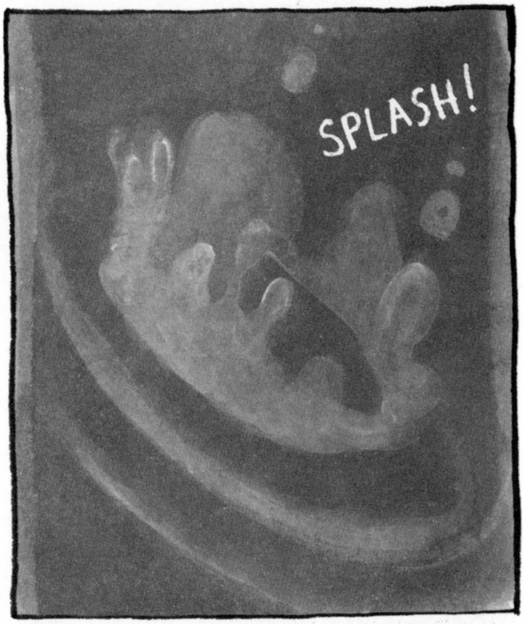
SPLASH!

TO WHAT WORLD?

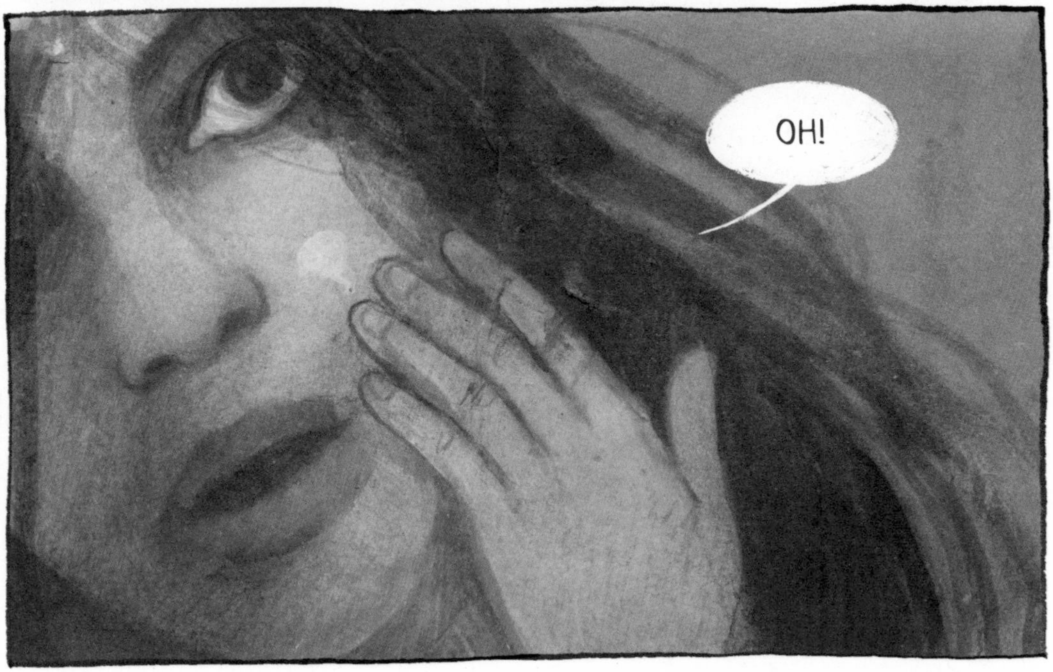
OH!

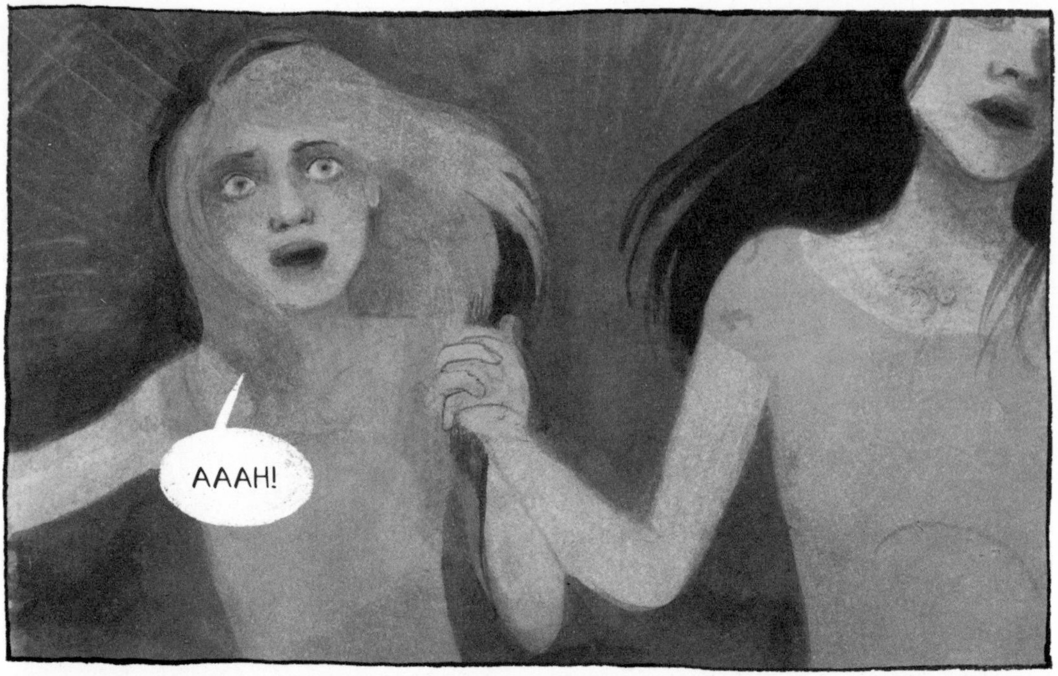
AAAH!

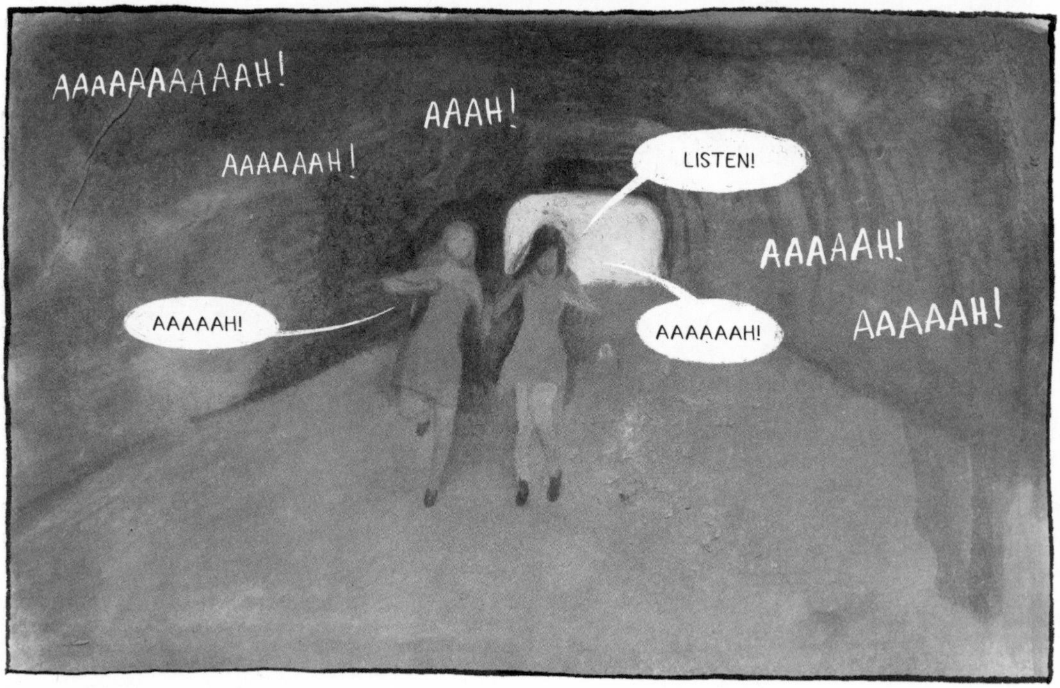
AAAAAAAAAAH!
AAAH!
AAAAAAH!
LISTEN!
AAAAAH!
AAAAAH!
AAAAAAH!
AAAAAH!

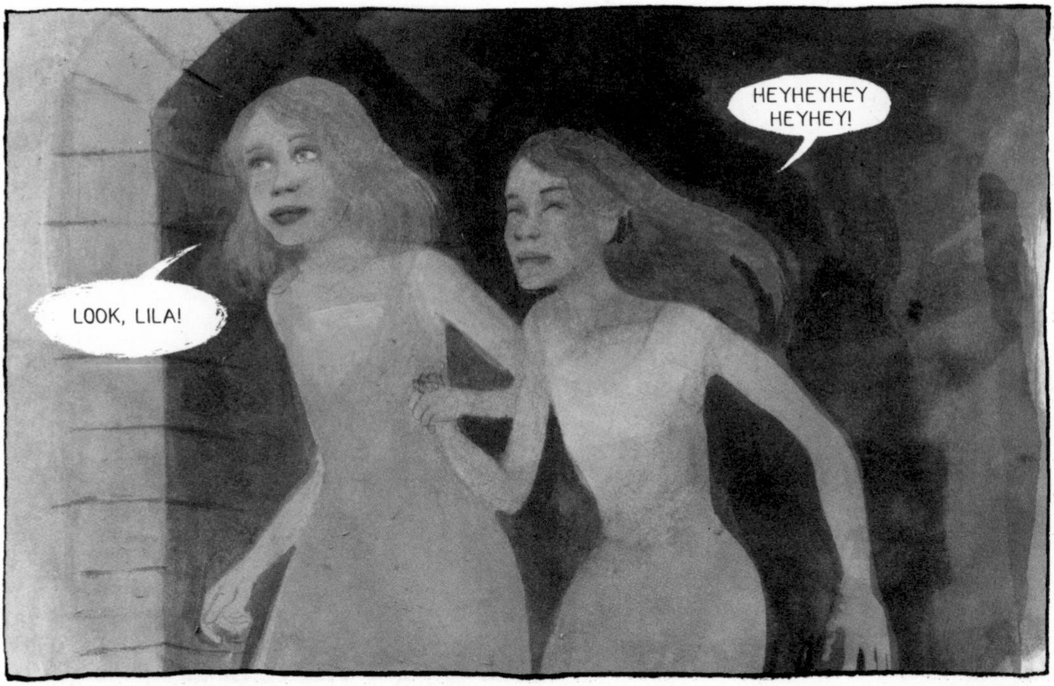
LOOK, LILA!
HEYHEYHEY
HEYHEY!

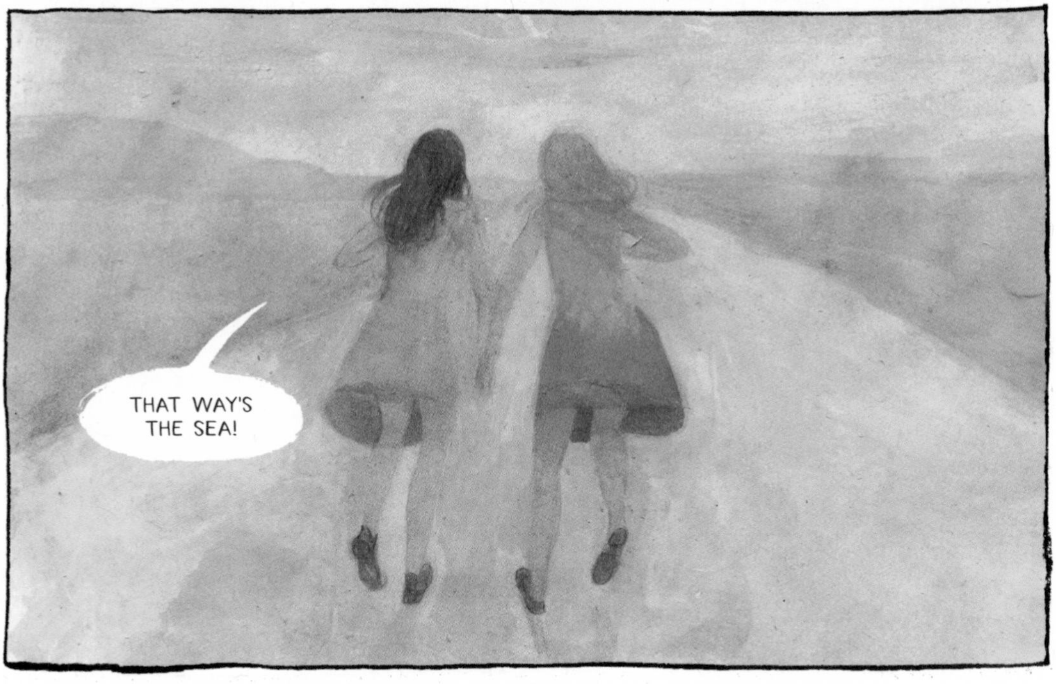
THAT WAY'S
THE SEA!

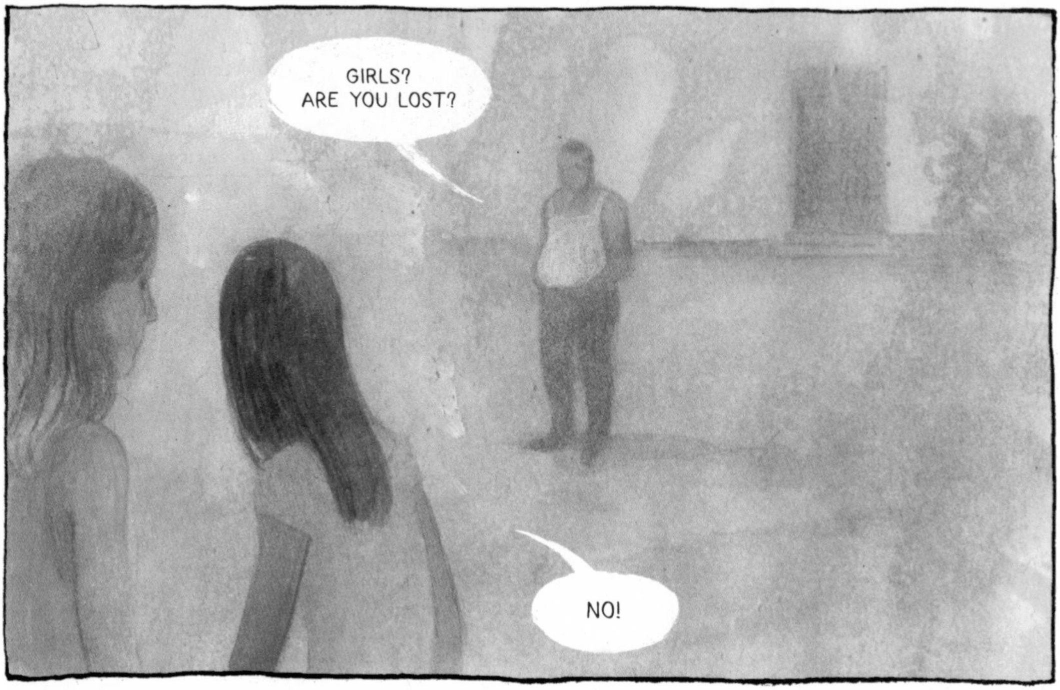
GIRLS?
ARE YOU LOST?
NO!

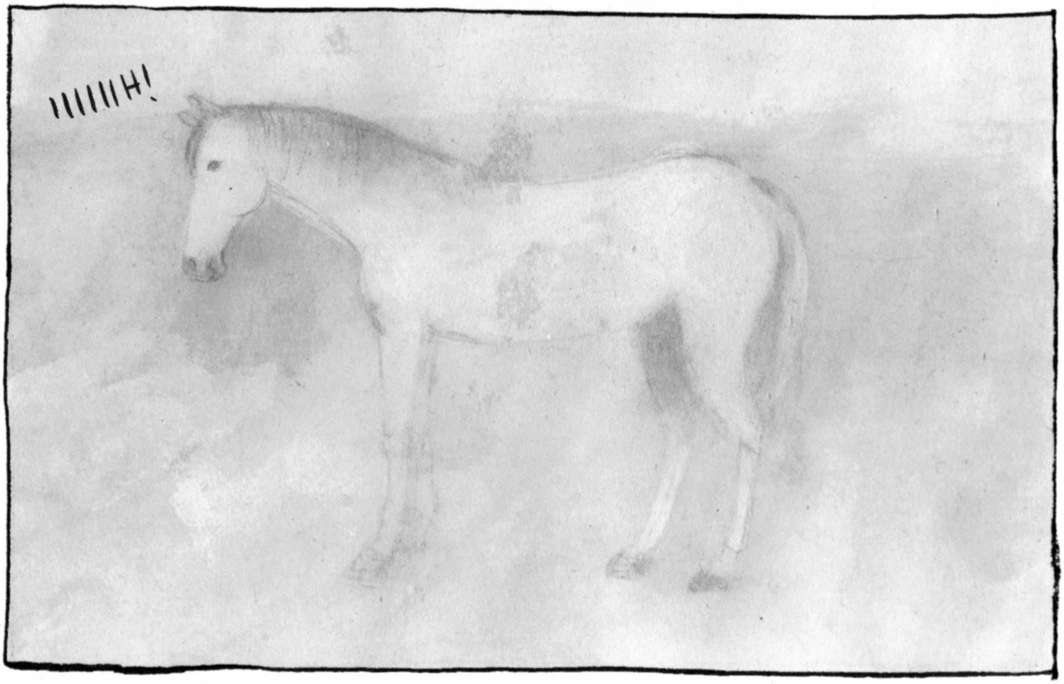
IIIIIIH!

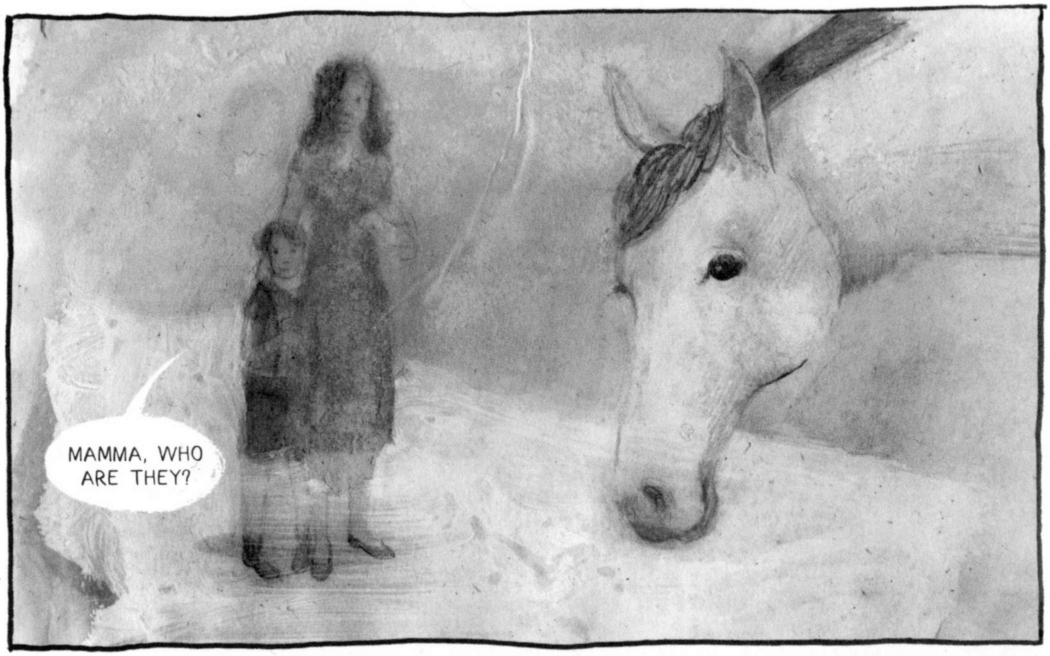
MAMMA, WHO ARE THEY?

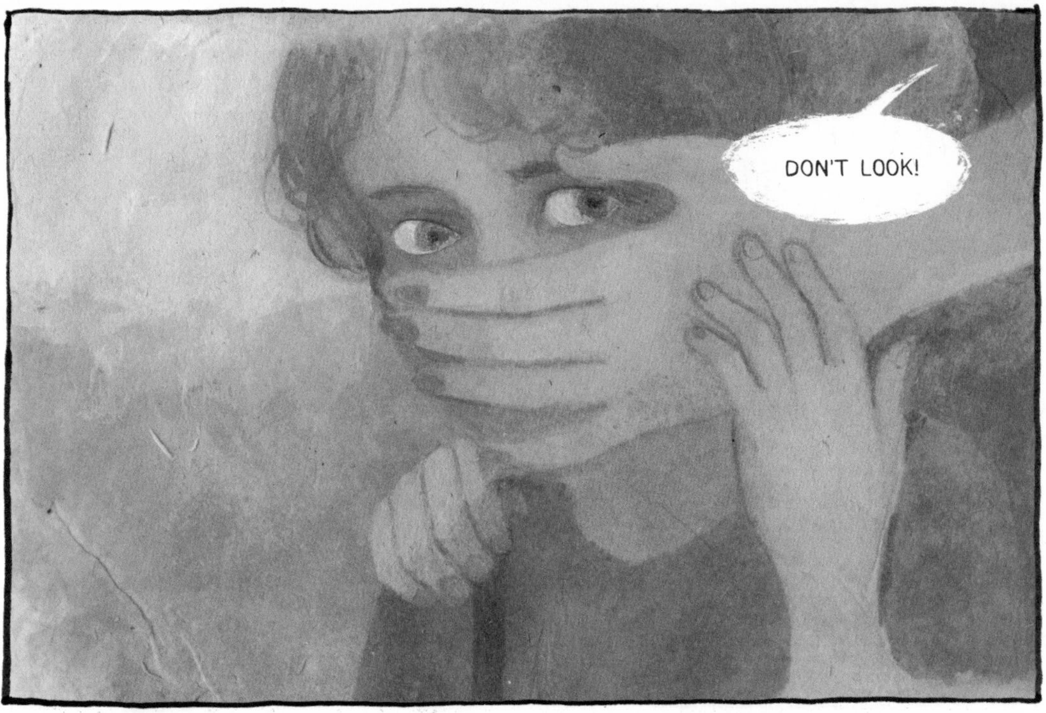
DON'T LOOK!

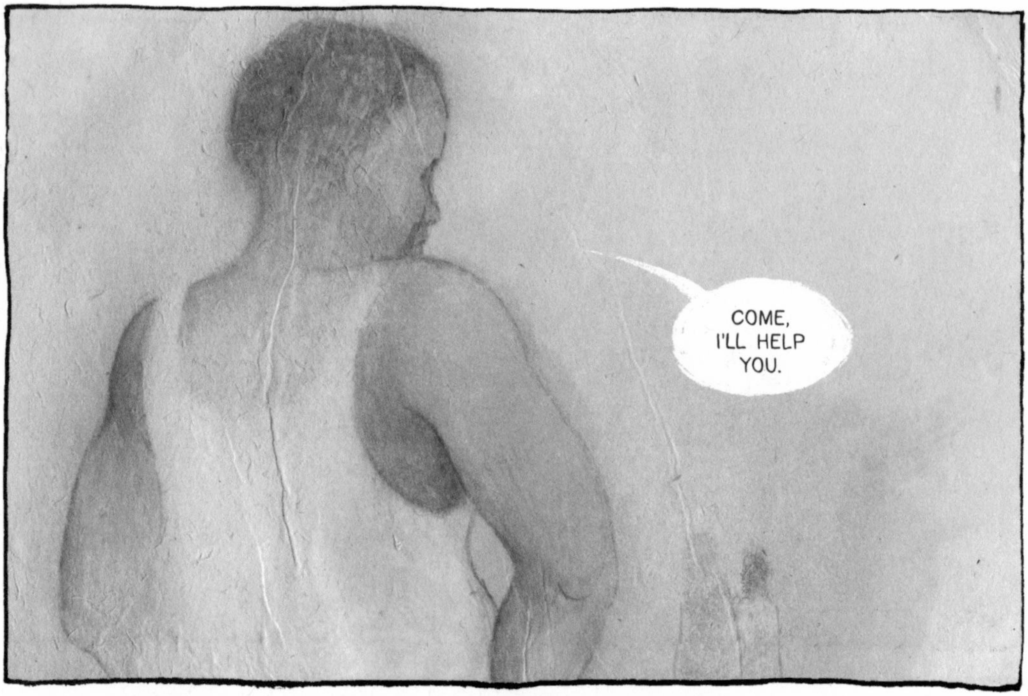
COME, I'LL HELP YOU.

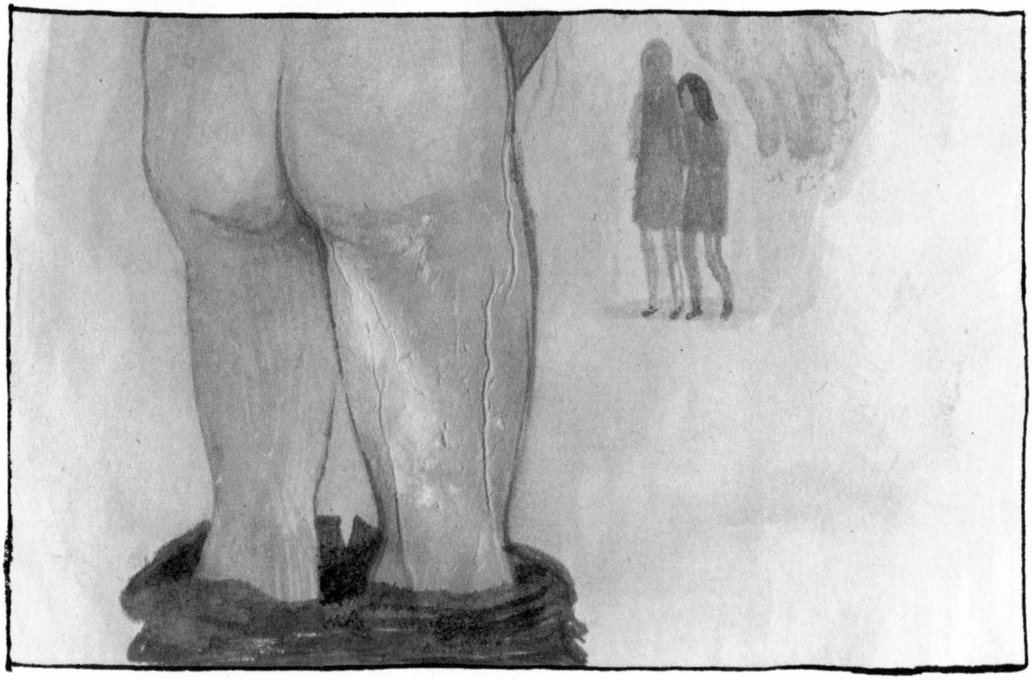

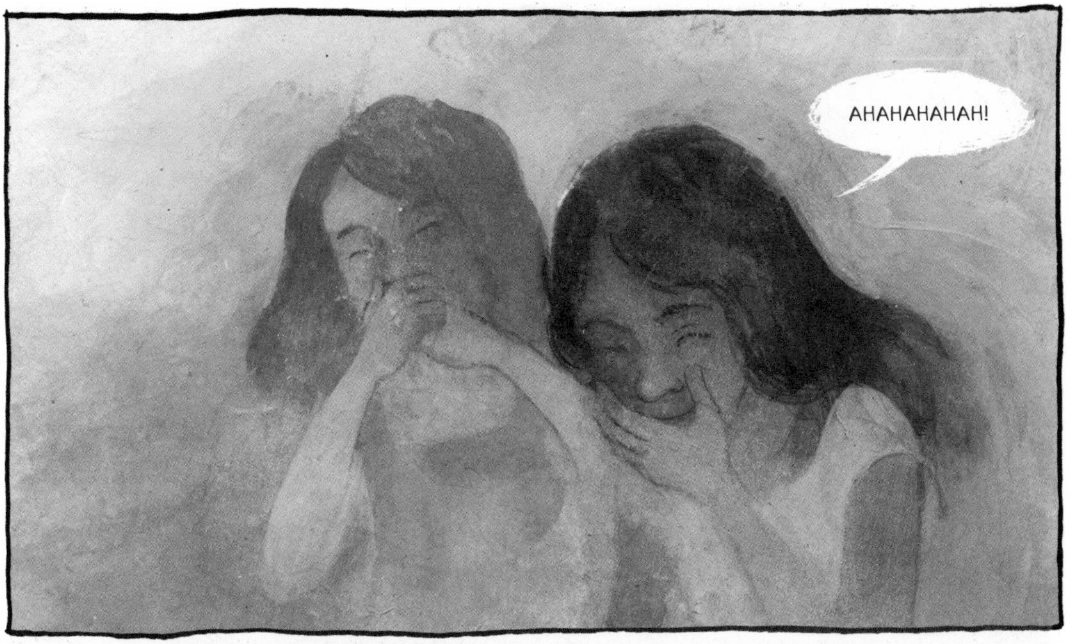

AHAHAHAHAH!

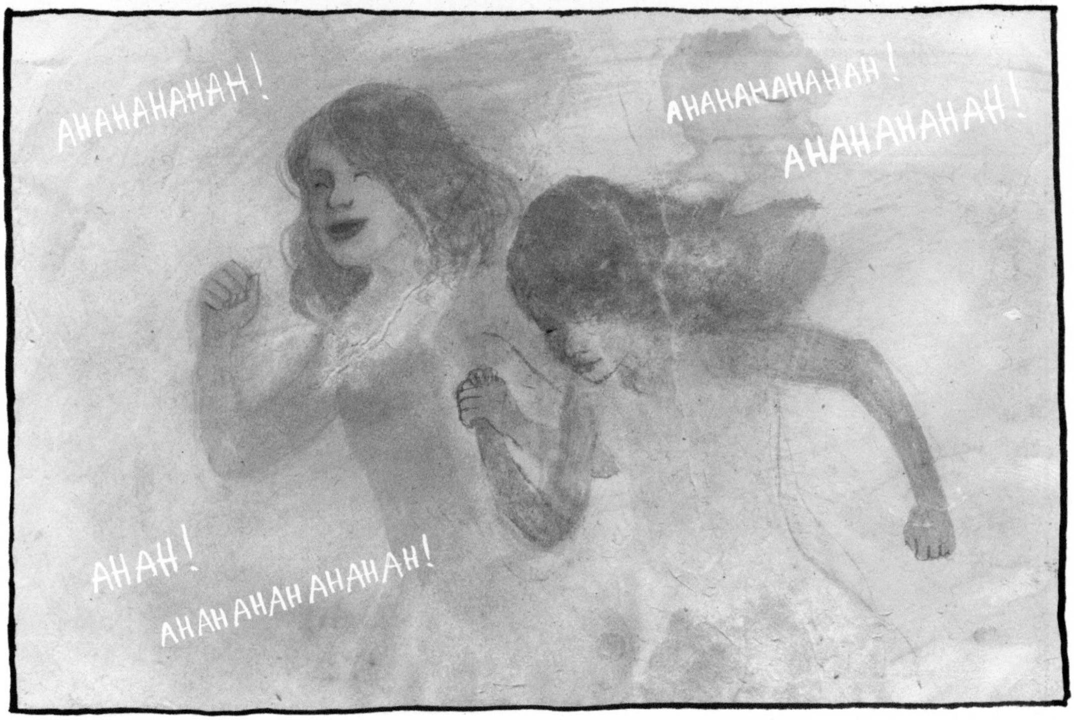

AHAHAHAHAH!
AHAHAHAHAHAH!
AHAHAHAHAH!
AHAH!
AHAHAHAH AHAHAH!

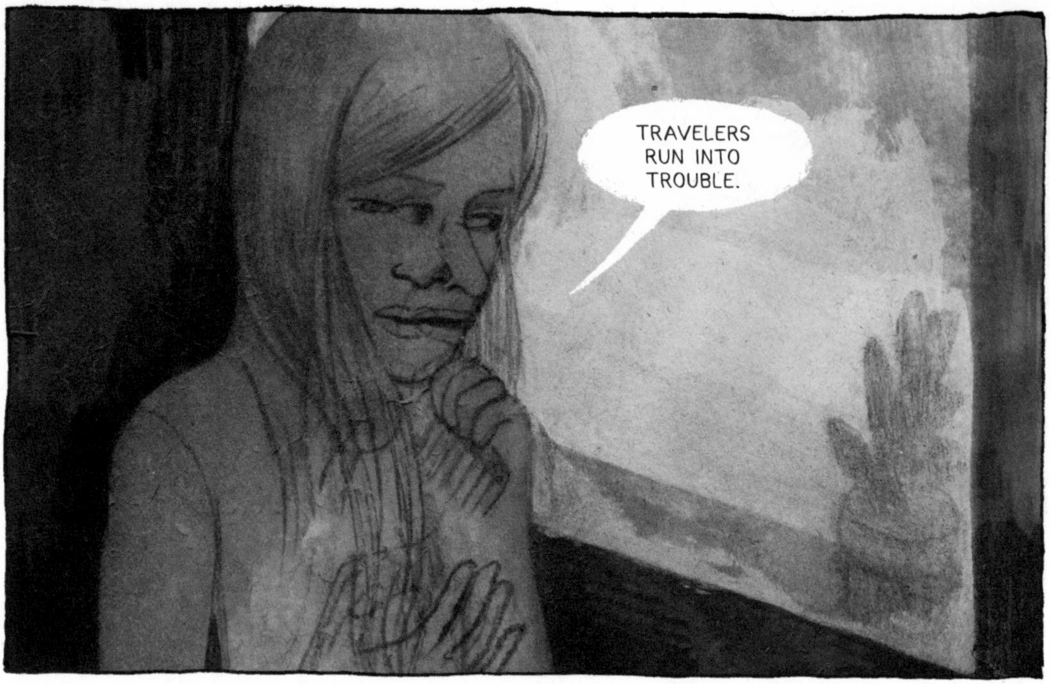
TRAVELERS RUN INTO TROUBLE.

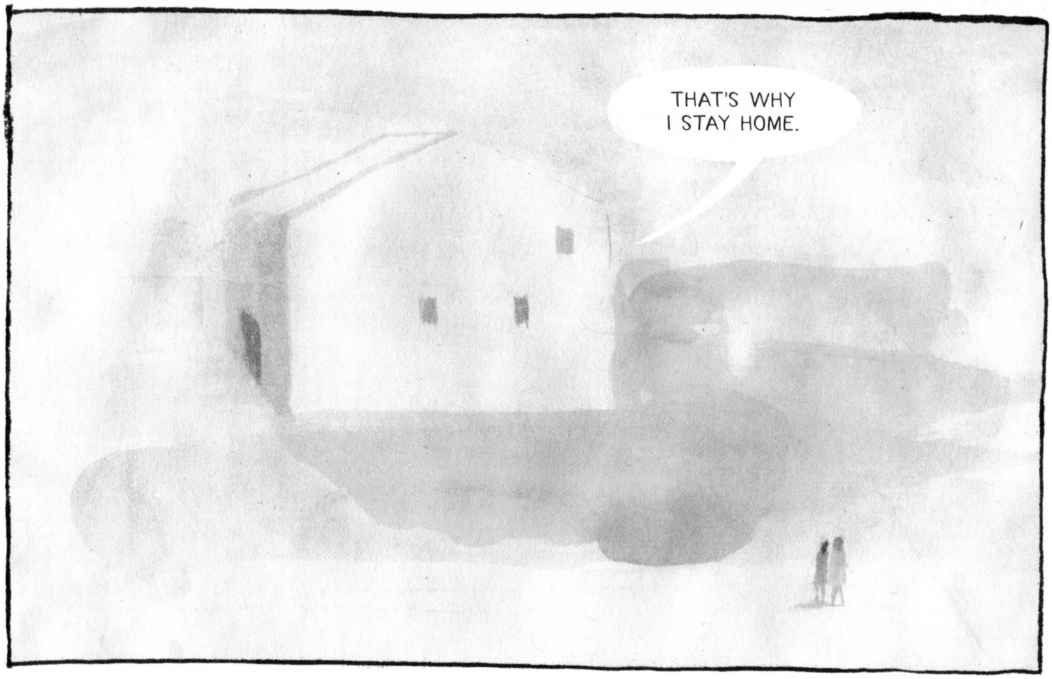
THAT'S WHY I STAY HOME.

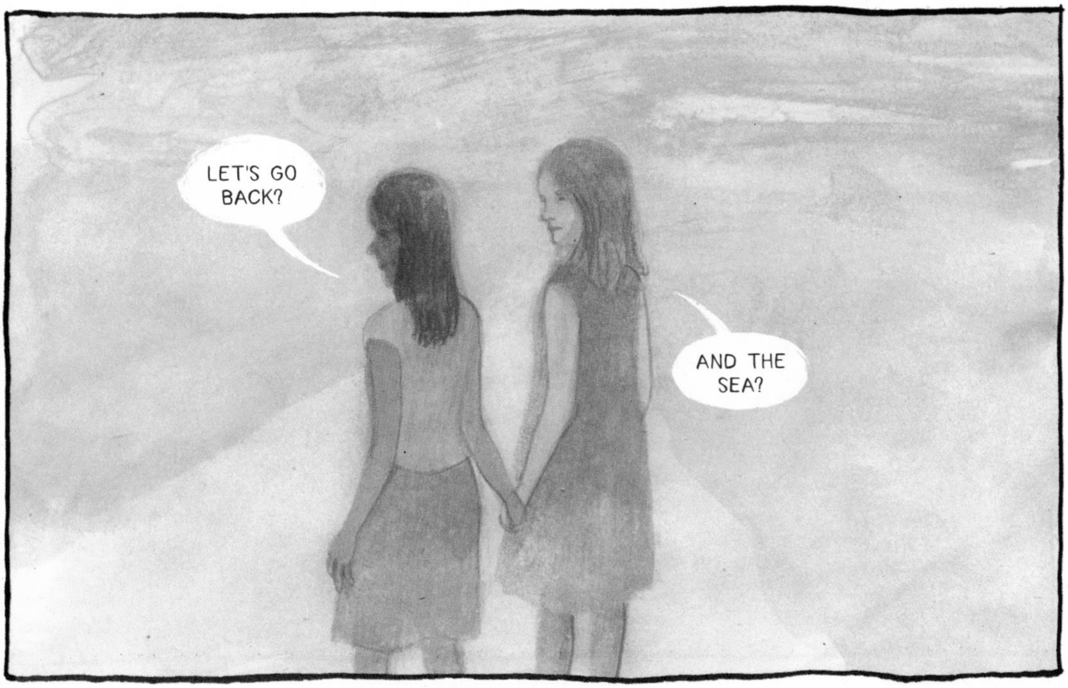
LET'S GO BACK?
AND THE SEA?

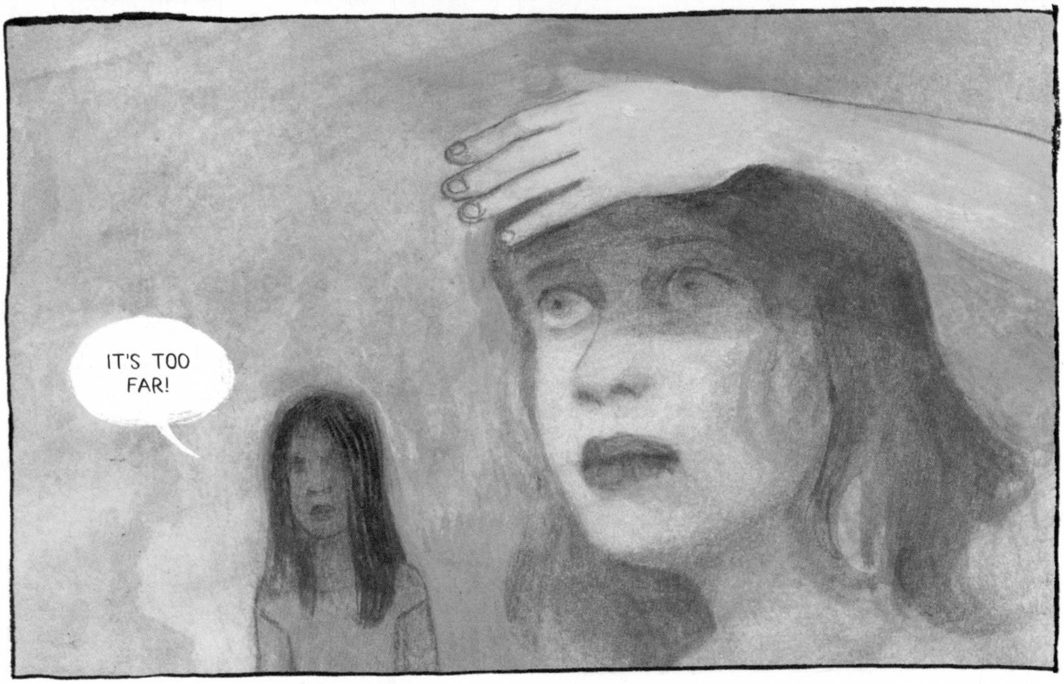
IT'S TOO FAR!

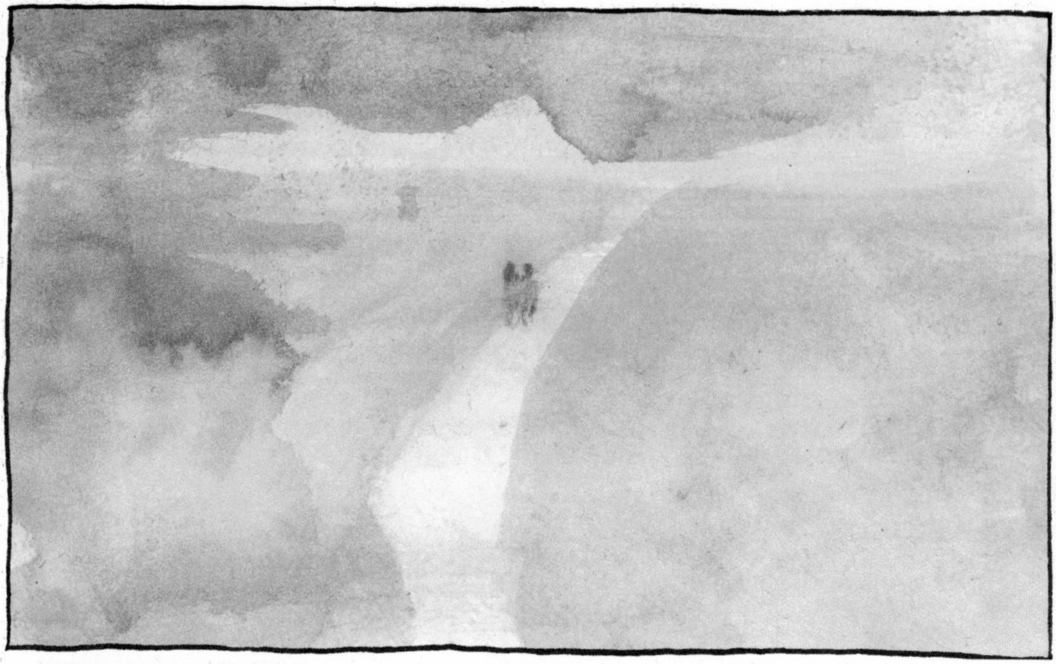

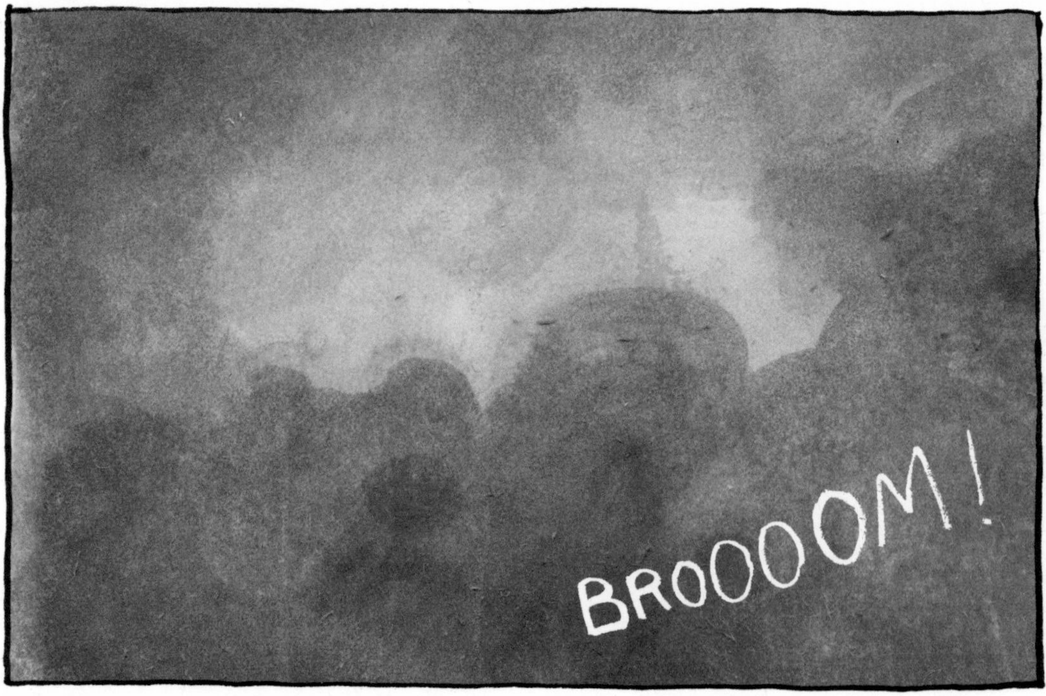
BROOOOM!

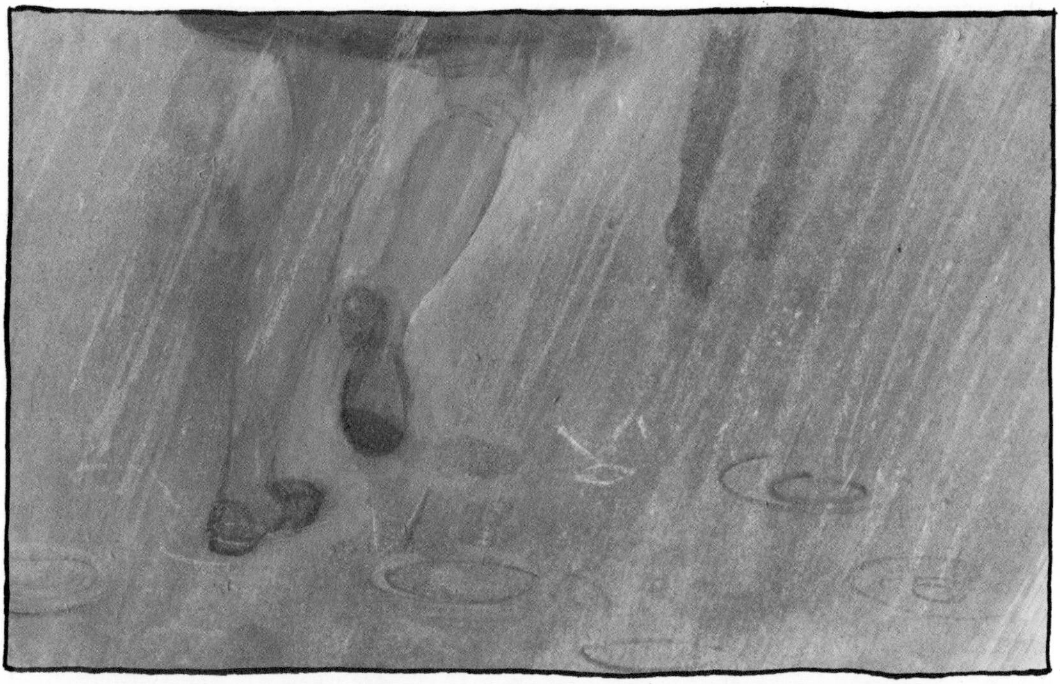

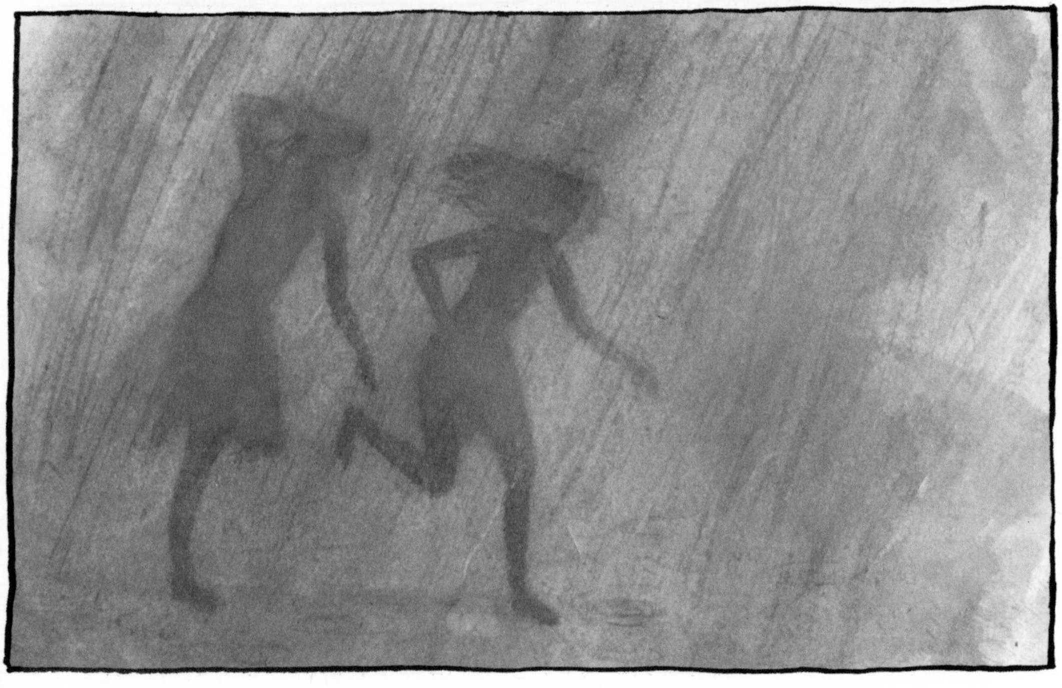

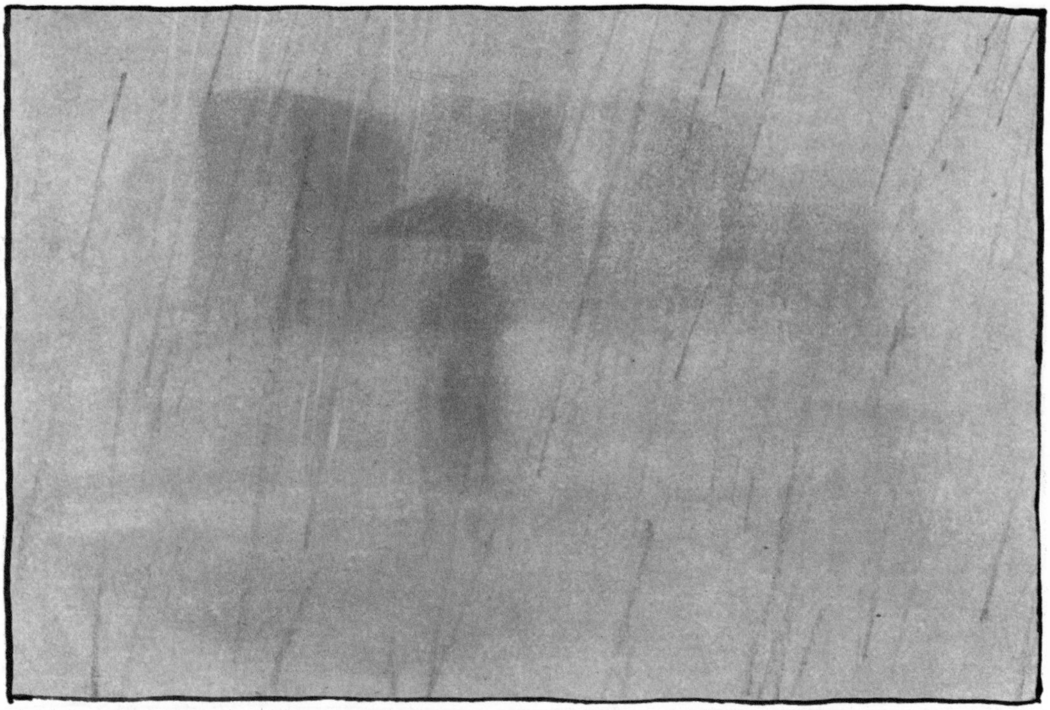

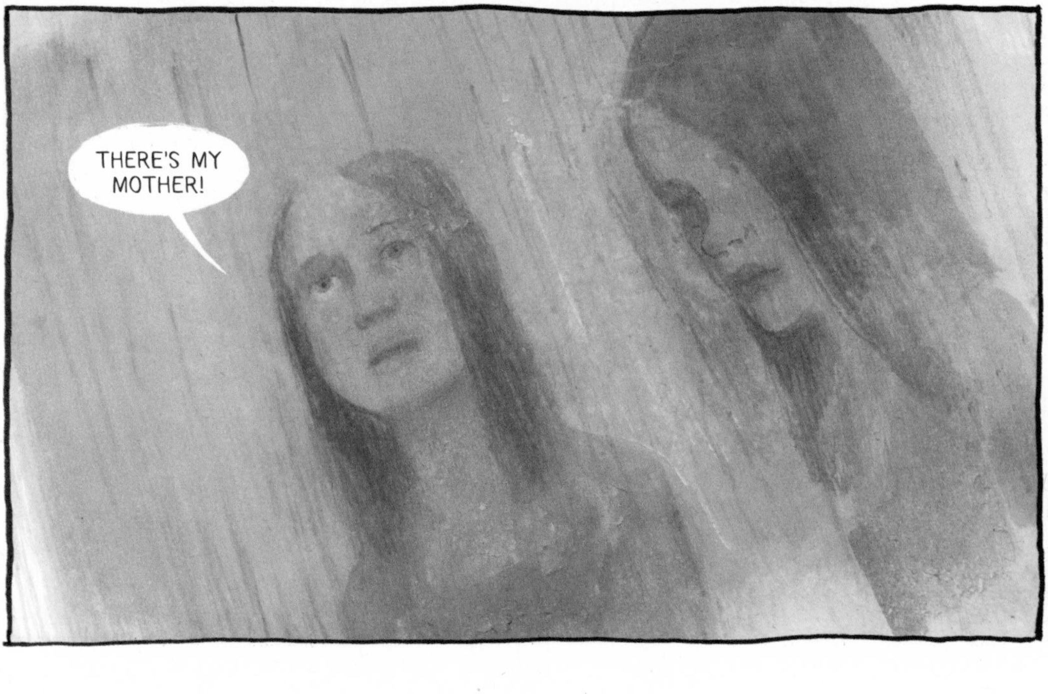
THERE'S MY MOTHER!

I'D TOLD HER WE WERE STUDYING AT THE TEACHER'S.

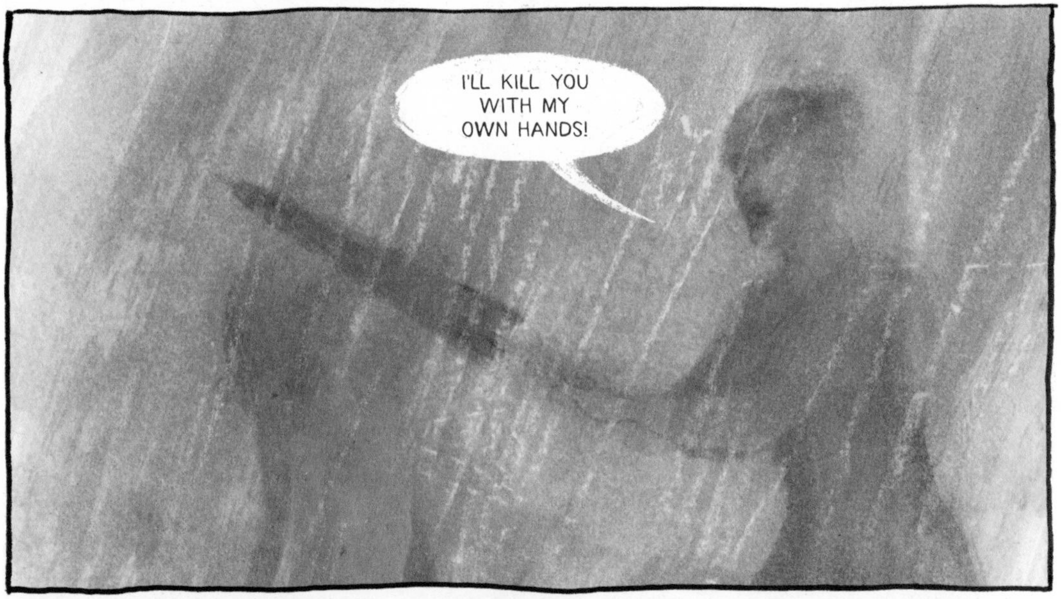
I'LL KILL YOU WITH MY OWN HANDS!

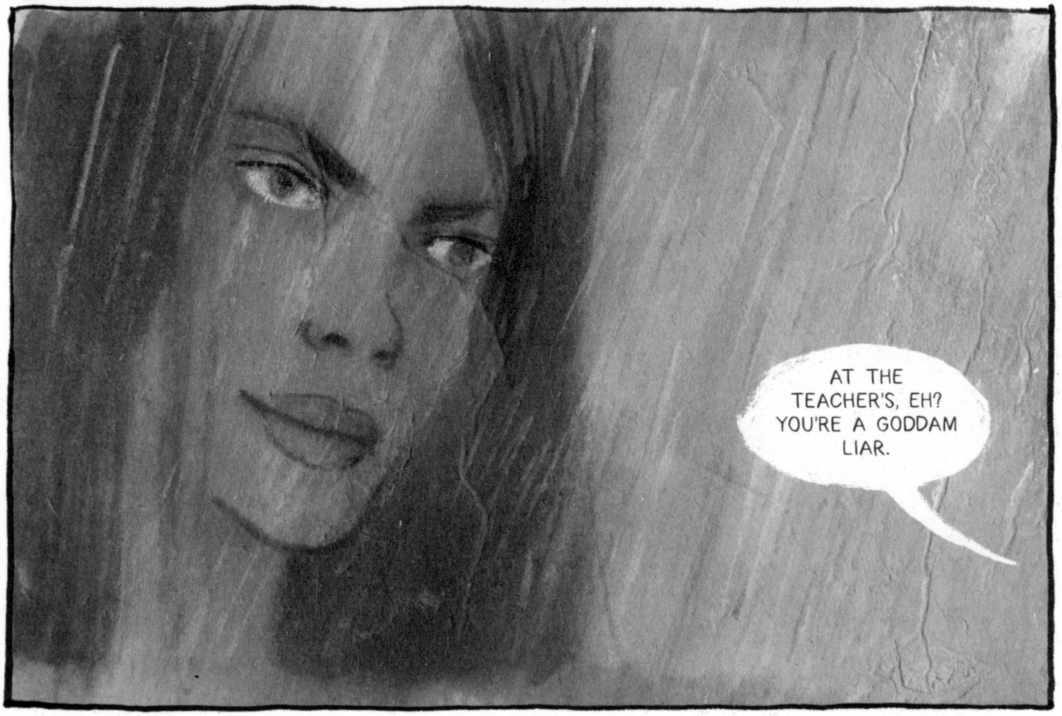
AT THE TEACHER'S, EH? YOU'RE A GODDAM LIAR.

THE NEXT DAY LILA WANTED TO SEE THE BRUISES I HAD ON MY ARMS.

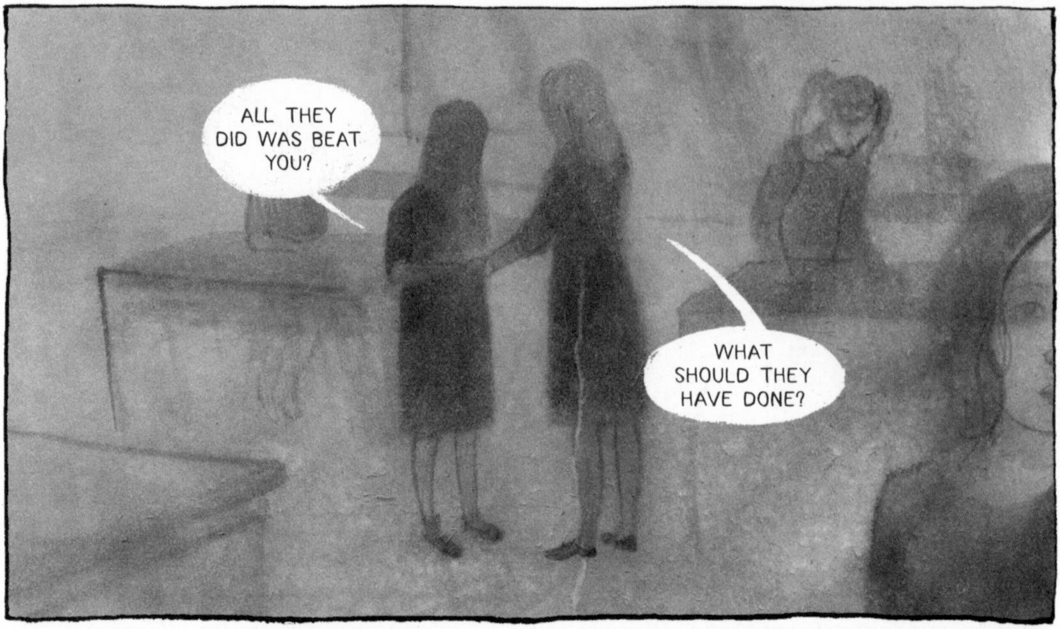
ALL THEY DID WAS BEAT YOU?
WHAT SHOULD THEY HAVE DONE?

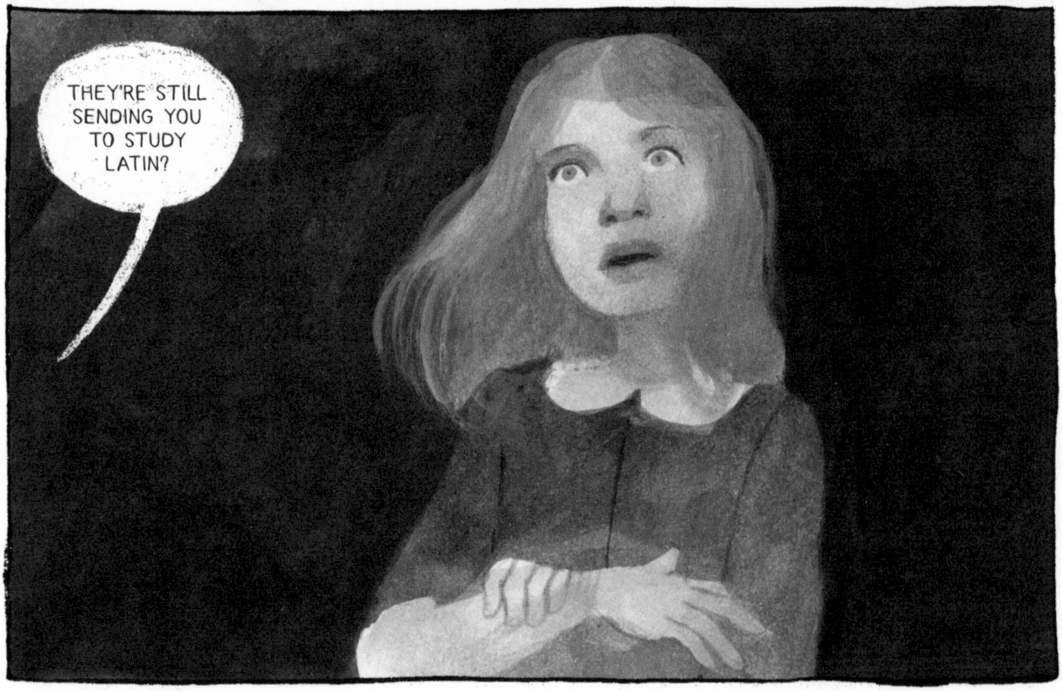
THEY'RE STILL SENDING YOU TO STUDY LATIN?

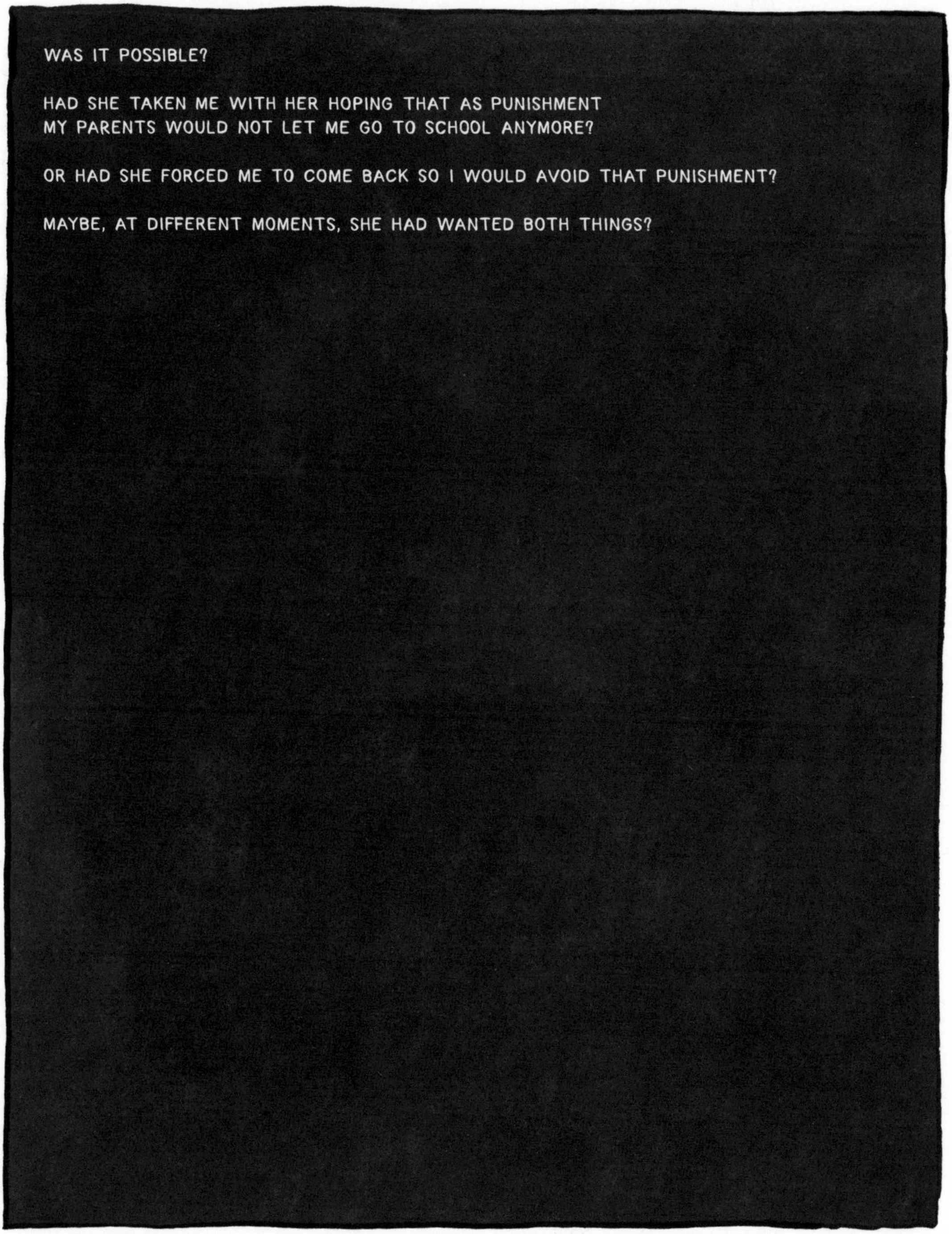
WAS IT POSSIBLE?
HAD SHE TAKEN ME WITH HER HOPING THAT AS PUNISHMENT MY PARENTS WOULD NOT LET ME GO TO SCHOOL ANYMORE?
OR HAD SHE FORCED ME TO COME BACK SO I WOULD AVOID THAT PUNISHMENT?
MAYBE, AT DIFFERENT MOMENTS, SHE HAD WANTED BOTH THINGS?

Adolescence

- THE STORY OF THE SHOES -

RIGHT IN THE MIDDLE OF THAT LONG SEASON MANY THINGS CHANGED.
THE TERRIBLE DON ACHILLE WAS MURDERED IN HIS HOUSE IN THE EARLY AFTERNOON ON A WARM RAINY DAY. THE CARABINIERI CARRIED OFF THE CARPENTER, SIGNOR PELUSO, WHO LET OUT HOARSE, FRIGHTENING CRIES, AAAH, AND SWORE THAT HE WAS INNOCENT.

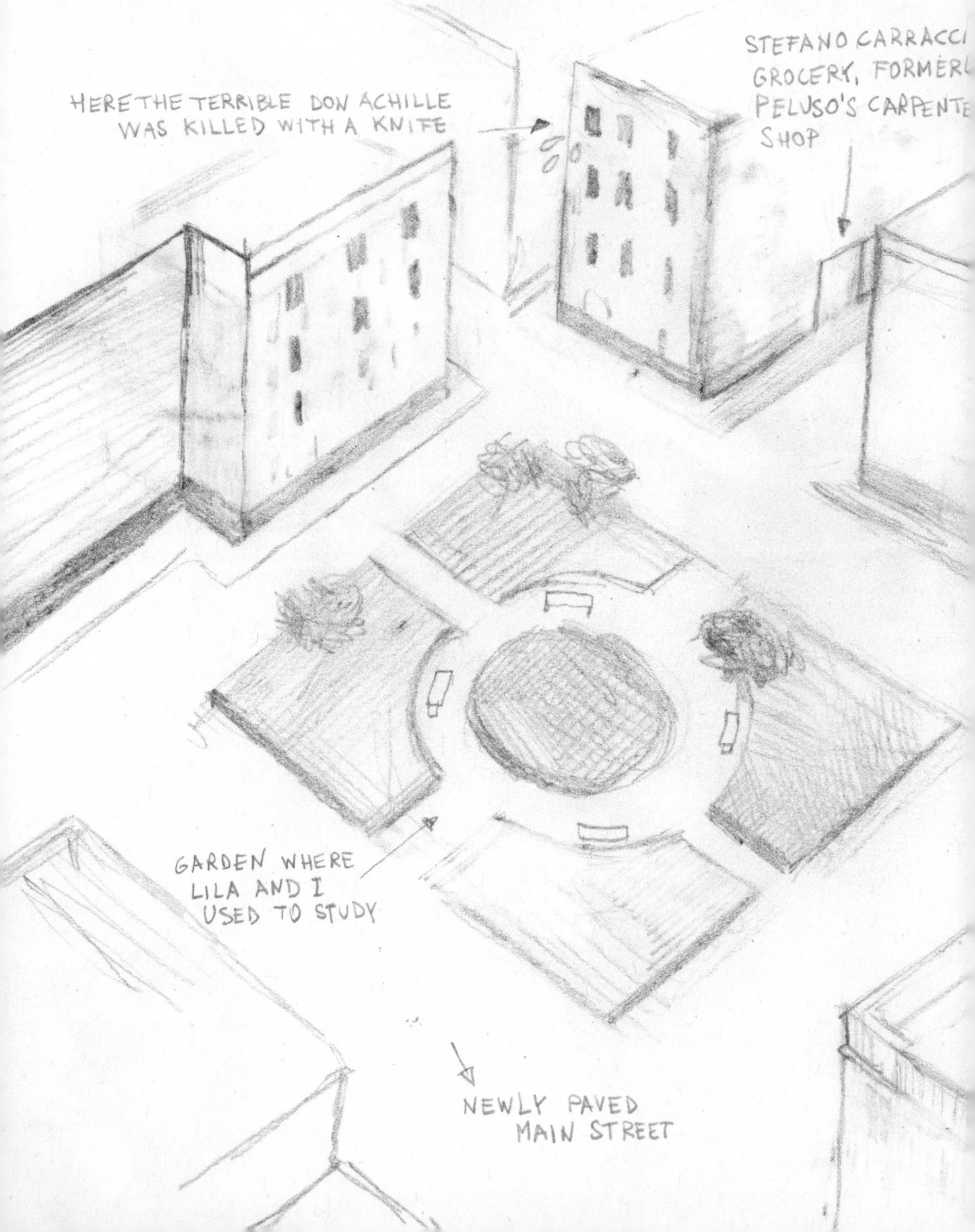
STEFANO CARRACCI GROCERY, FORMERLY PELUSO'S CARPENTE SHOP
HERE THE TERRIBLE DON ACHILLE WAS KILLED WITH A KNIFE
GARDEN WHERE LILA AND I USED TO STUDY
NEWLY PAVED MAIN STREET

THE SOLARA FAMILY'S BAR BECAME A WELL-STOCKED PASTRY SHOP. THE TWO SONS, MARCELLO
AND MICHELE, BOUGHT A FIAT 1100 IN WHICH THEY PARADED AROUND THE NEIGHBORHOOD.
SIGNOR PELUSO'S CARPENTER SHOP WAS TRANSFORMED INTO A GROCERY, WHICH WAS MANAGED
BY DON ACHILLE'S SON STEFANO CARRACCI.

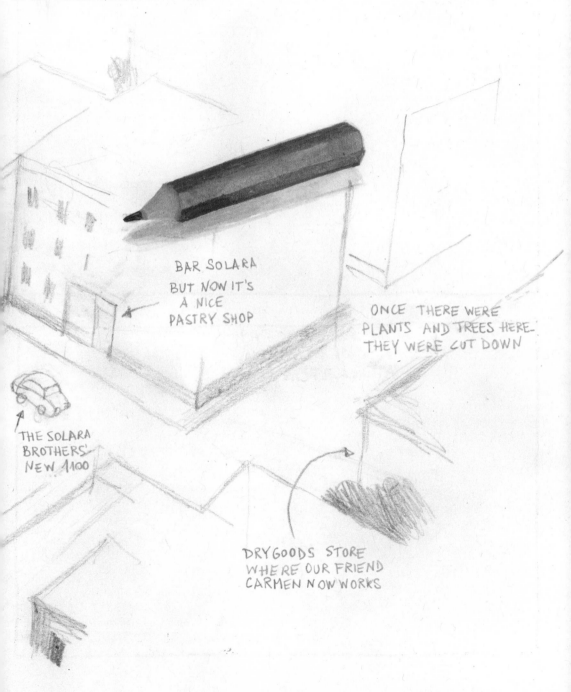

BAR SOLARA
BUT NOW IT'S
A NICE
PASTRY SHOP

ONCE THERE WERE
PLANTS AND TREES HERE.
THEY WERE CUT DOWN

THE SOLARA
BROTHERS'
NEW 1100

DRY GOODS STORE
WHERE OUR FRIEND
CARMEN NOW WORKS

THUS MANY THINGS CHANGED RIGHT BEFORE OUR EYES, BUT DAY BY DAY,

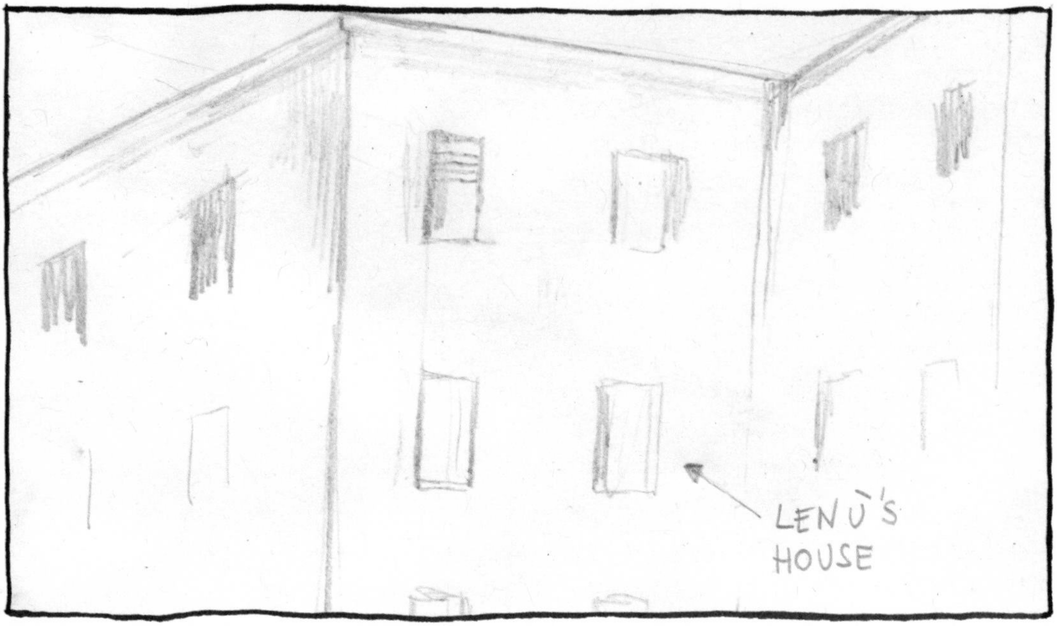
LENÙ'S
HOUSE

SO THAT THEY DIDN'T SEEM TO US LIKE REAL CHANGES.

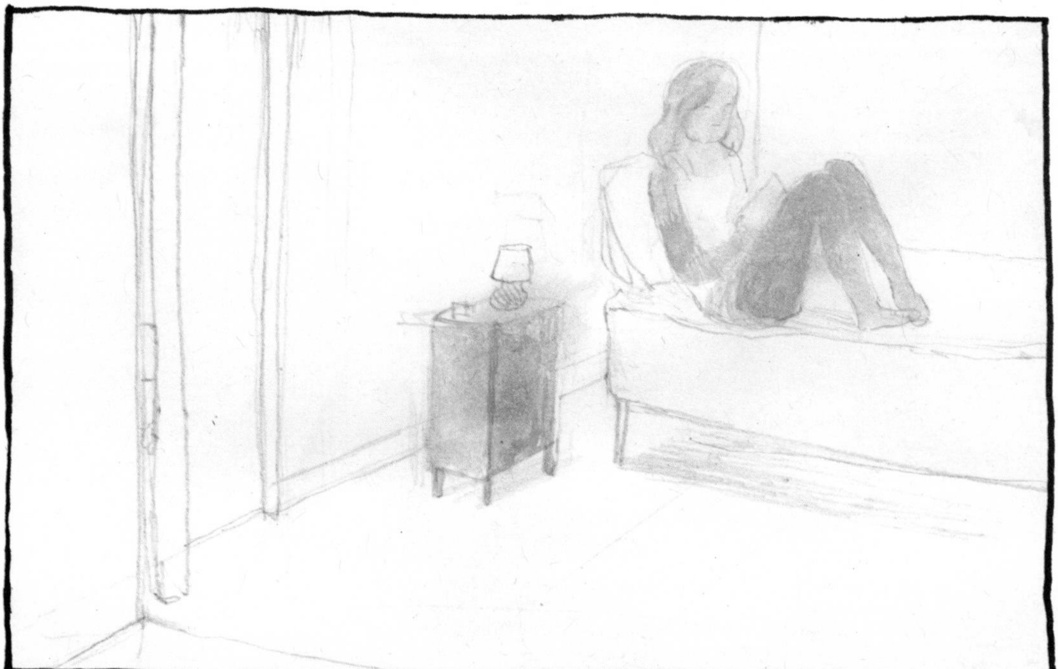

AND YET EVERYTHING AND EVERYONE WAS DIFFERENT...

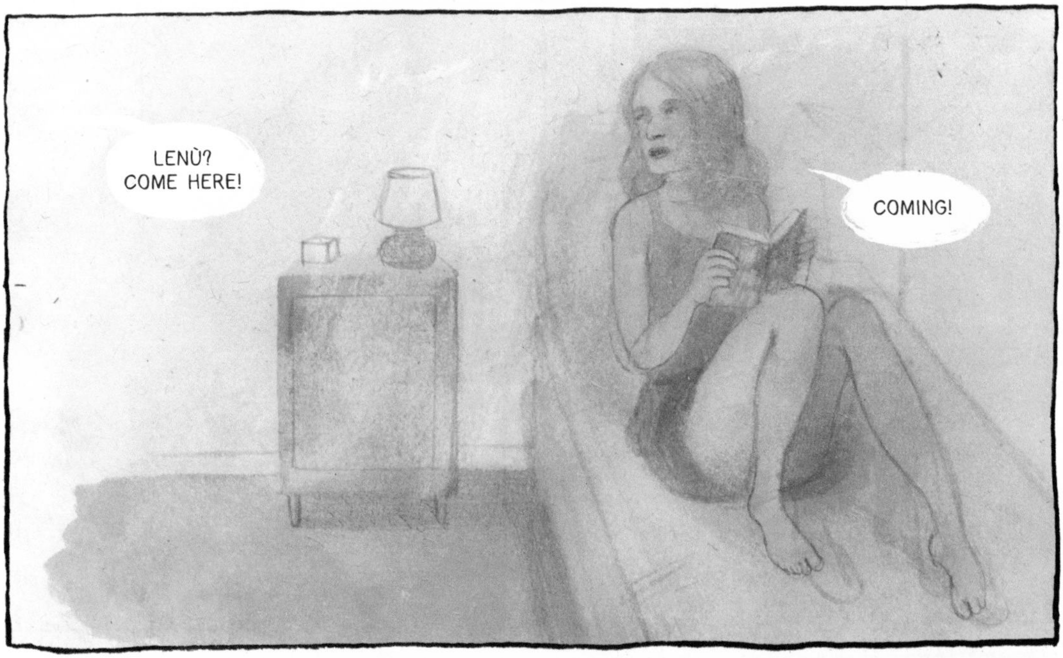
LENÙ?
COME HERE!
COMING!

INCLUDING US.

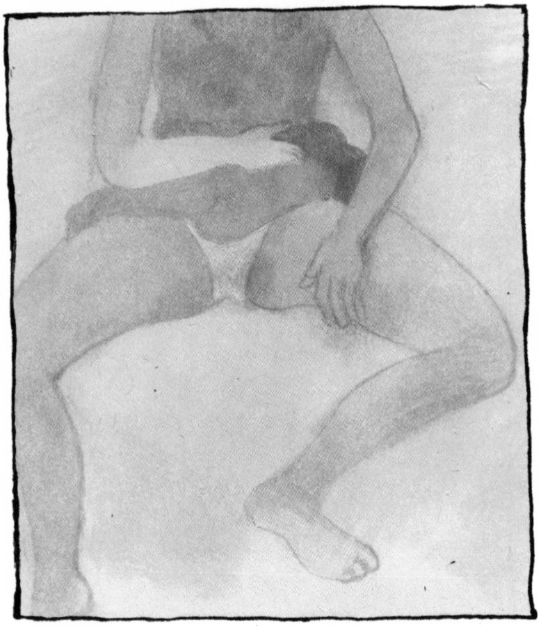

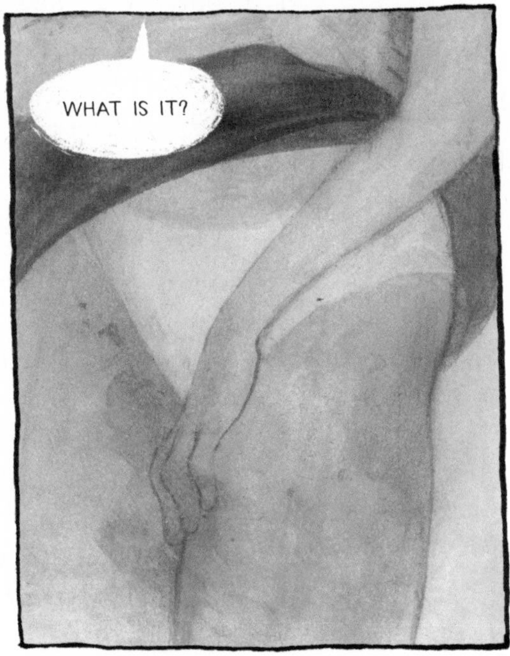
WHAT IS IT?

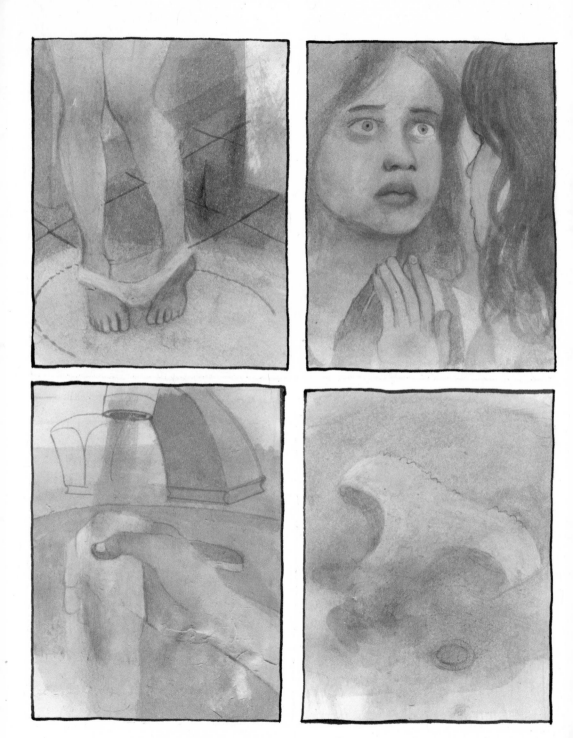

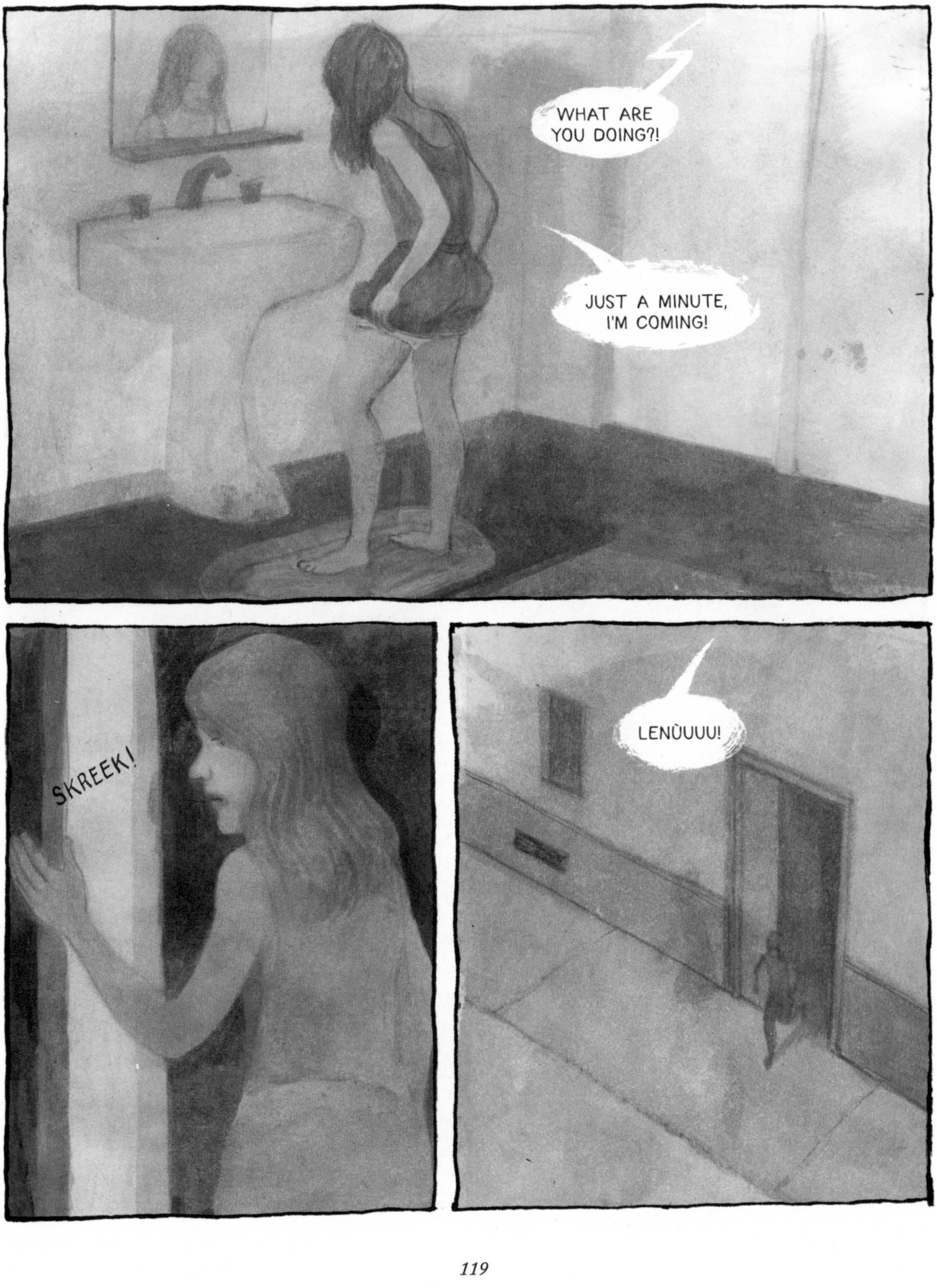
WHAT ARE YOU DOING?!
JUST A MINUTE, I'M COMING!
SKREEK!
LENÙUUU!

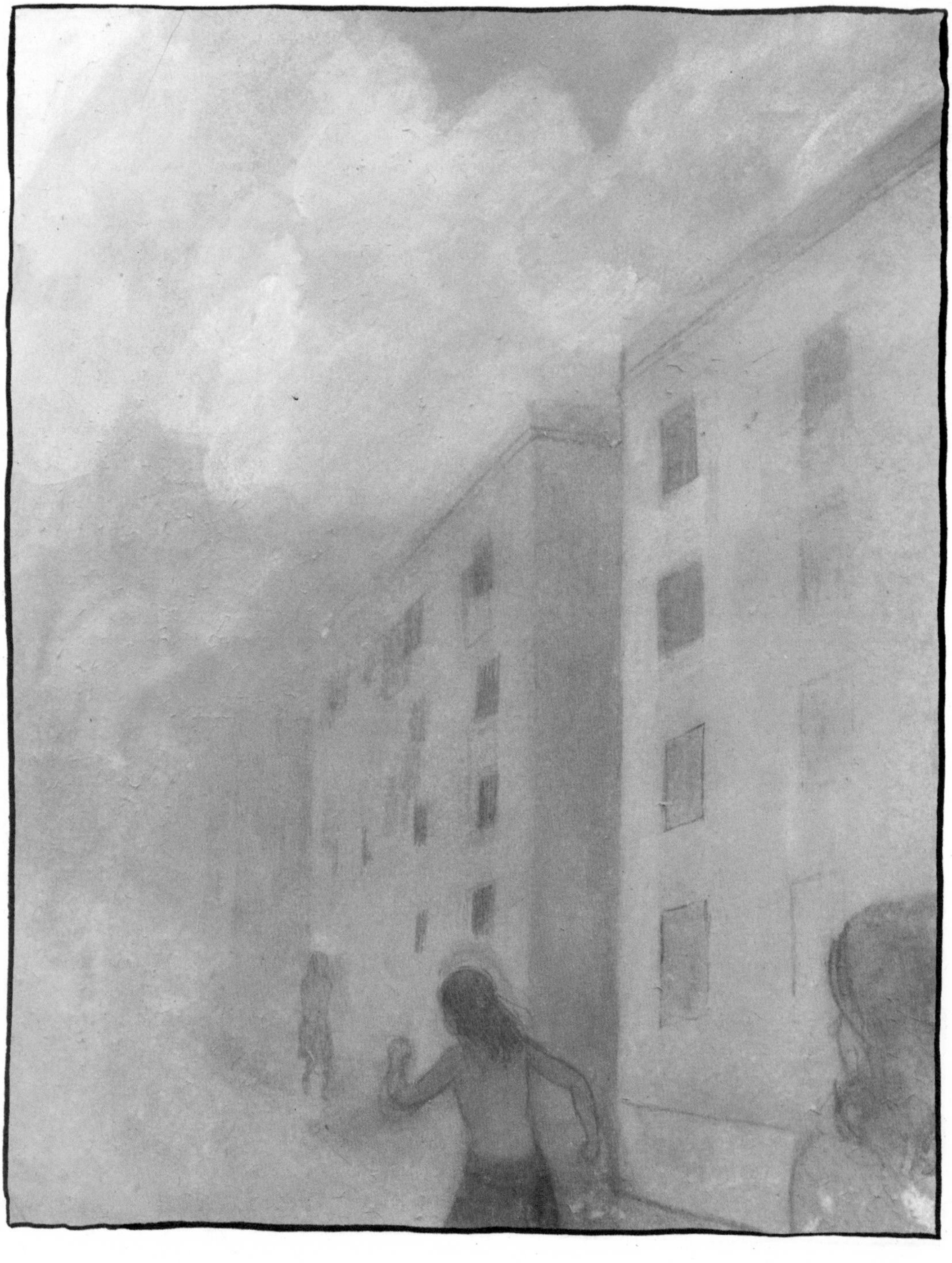

IN FRONT OF THE CHURCH I MET LILA, WHO WAS WALKING WITH CARMELA, SIGNOR PELUSO'S DAUGHTER.

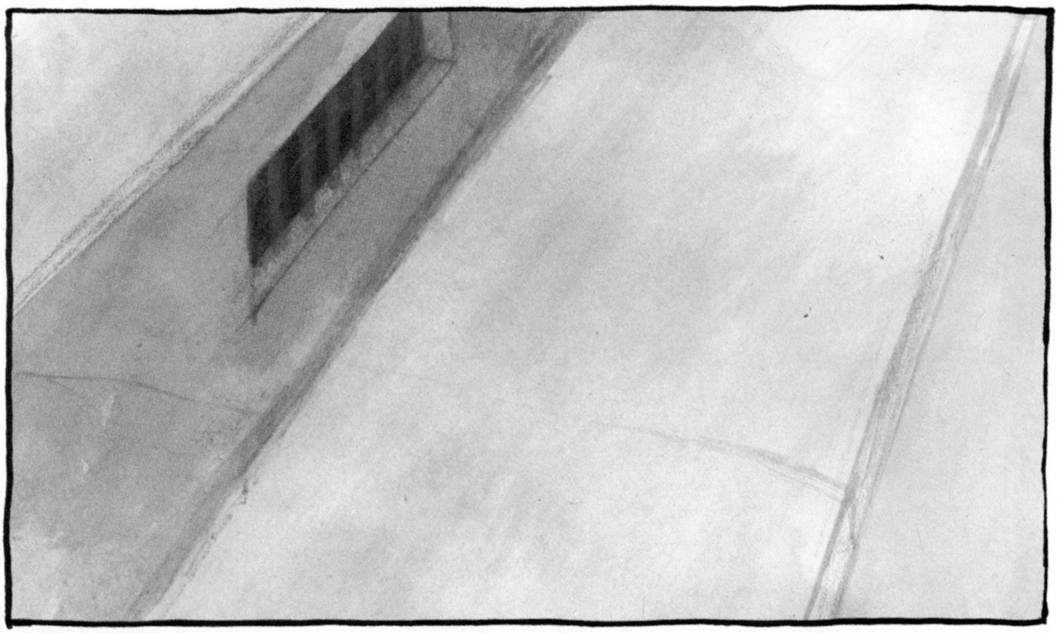

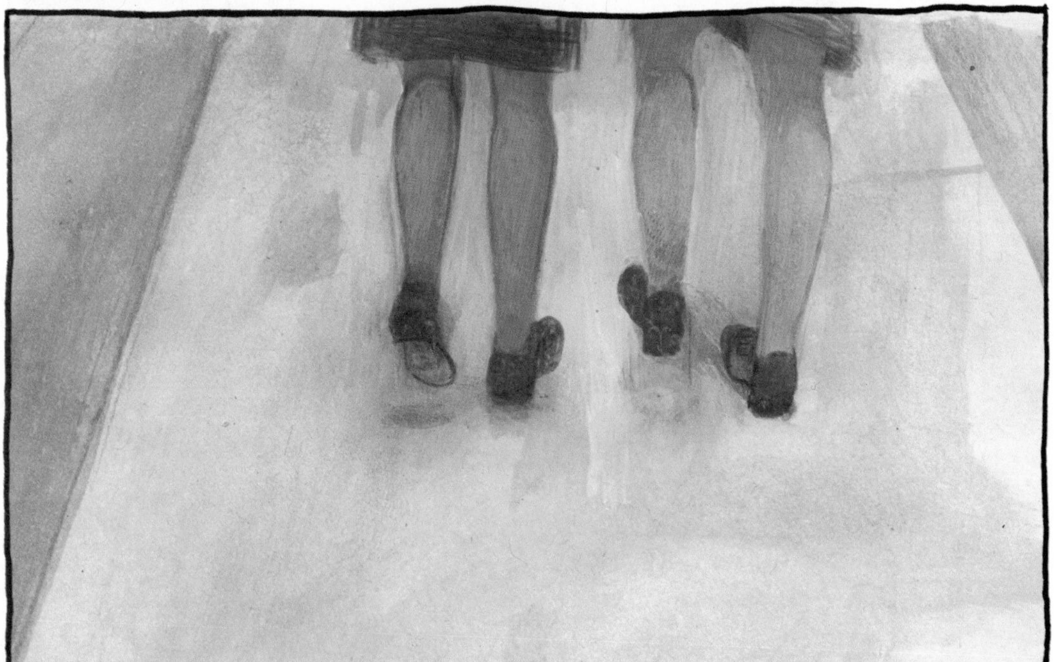

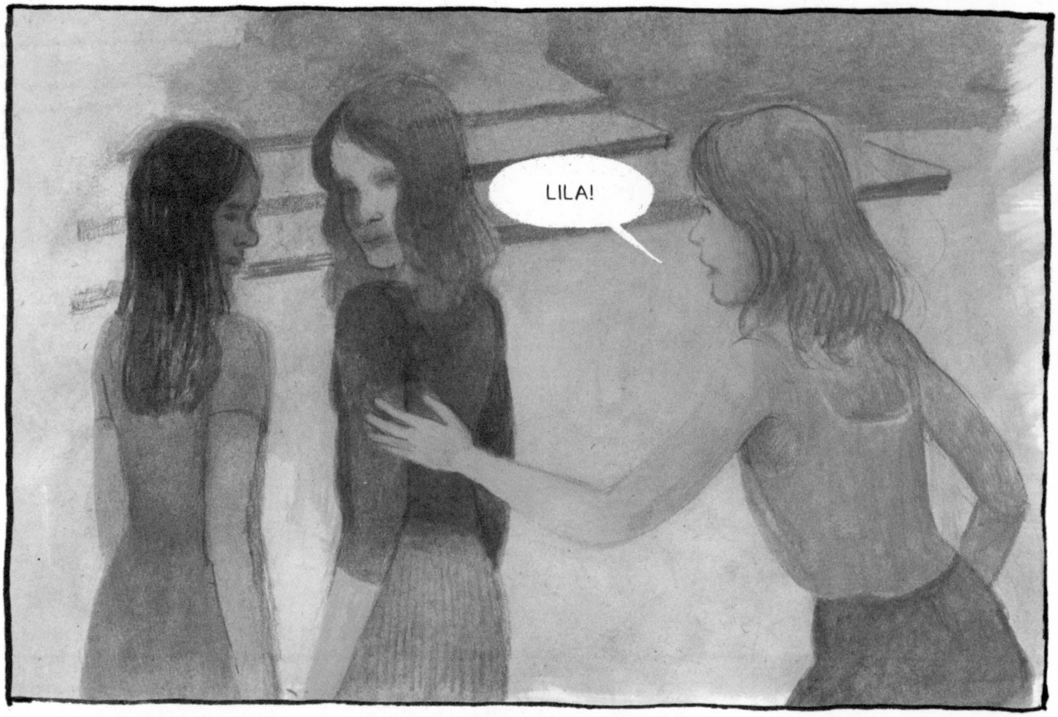
LILA!

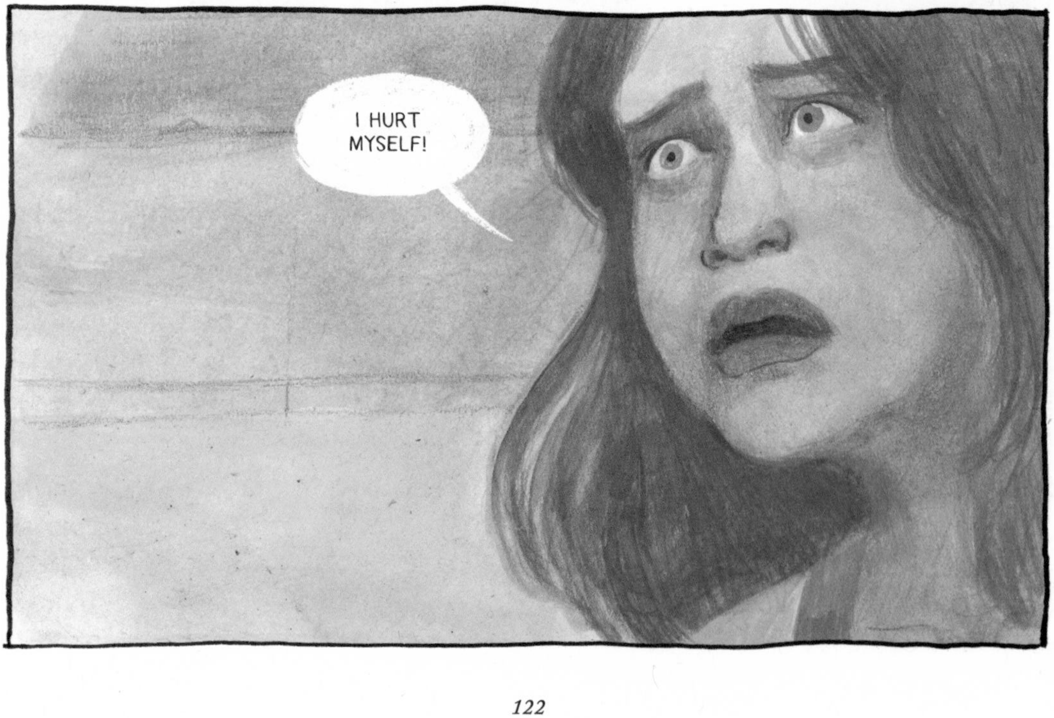
I HURT MYSELF!

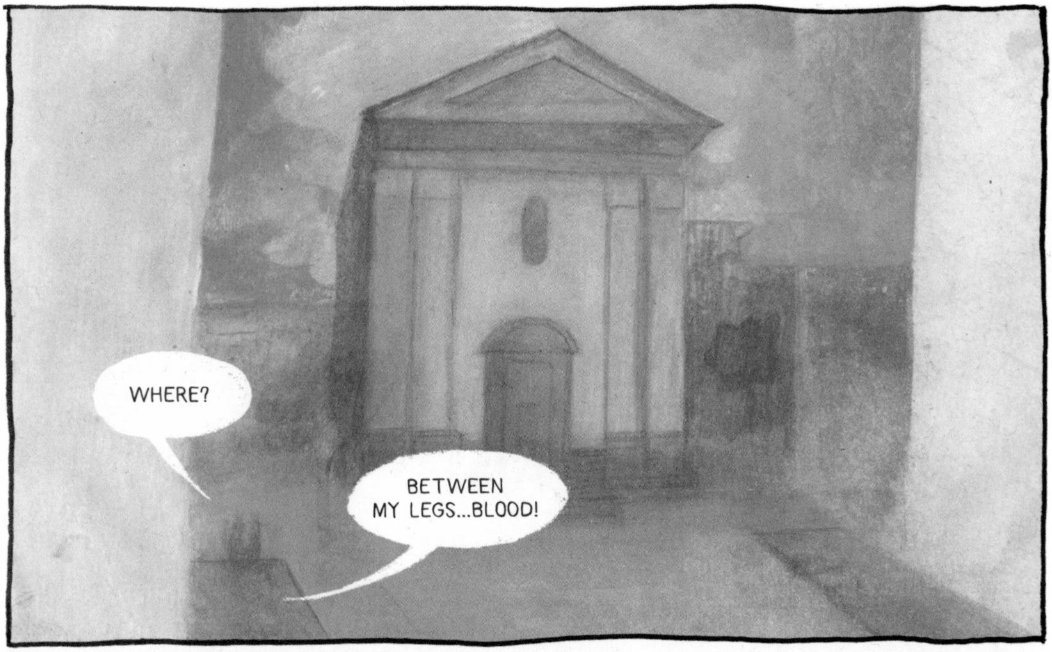
WHERE?
BETWEEN MY LEGS...BLOOD!

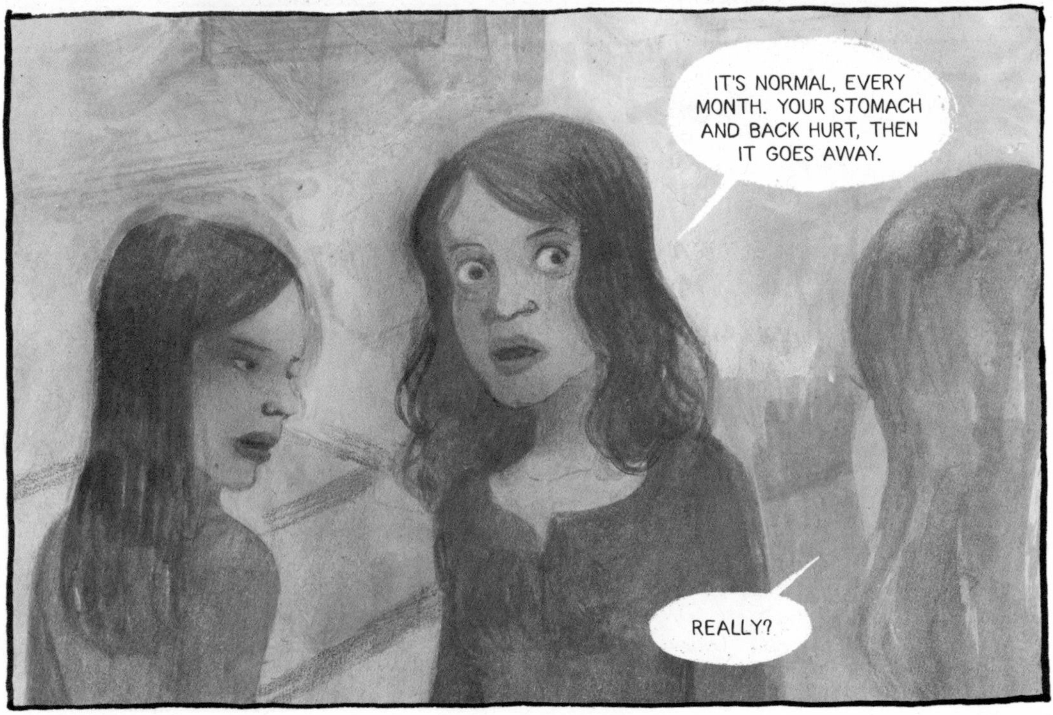
IT'S NORMAL, EVERY MONTH. YOUR STOMACH AND BACK HURT, THEN IT GOES AWAY.
REALLY?

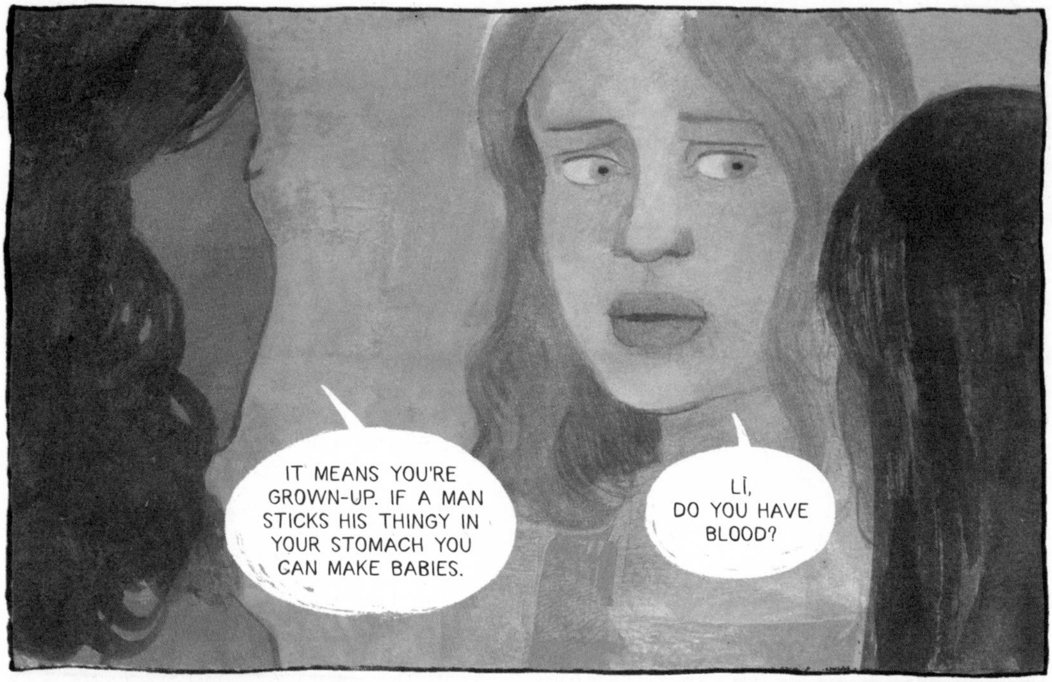
IT MEANS YOU'RE GROWN-UP. IF A MAN STICKS HIS THINGY IN YOUR STOMACH YOU CAN MAKE BABIES.
LÌ, DO YOU HAVE BLOOD?

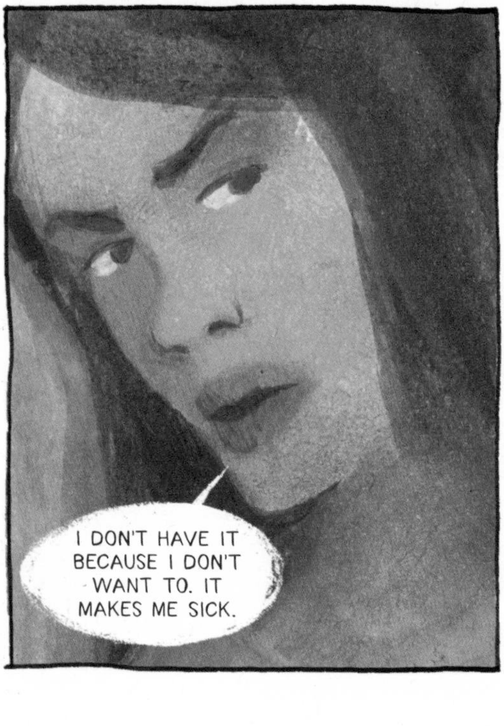
I DON'T HAVE IT BECAUSE I DON'T WANT TO. IT MAKES ME SICK.

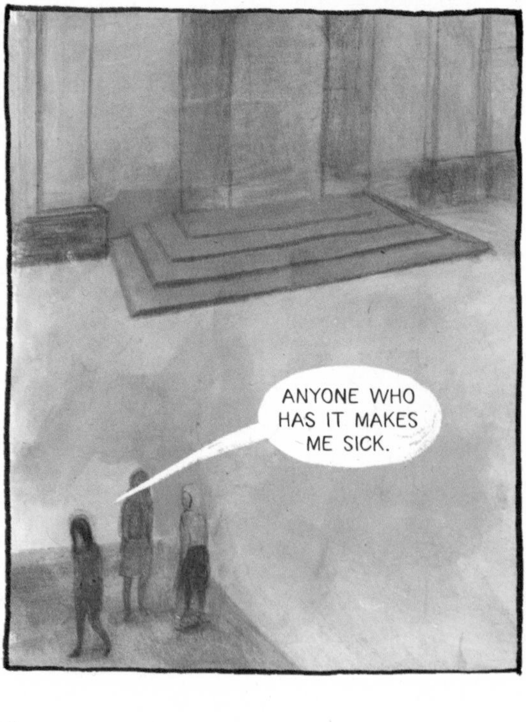
ANYONE WHO HAS IT MAKES ME SICK.

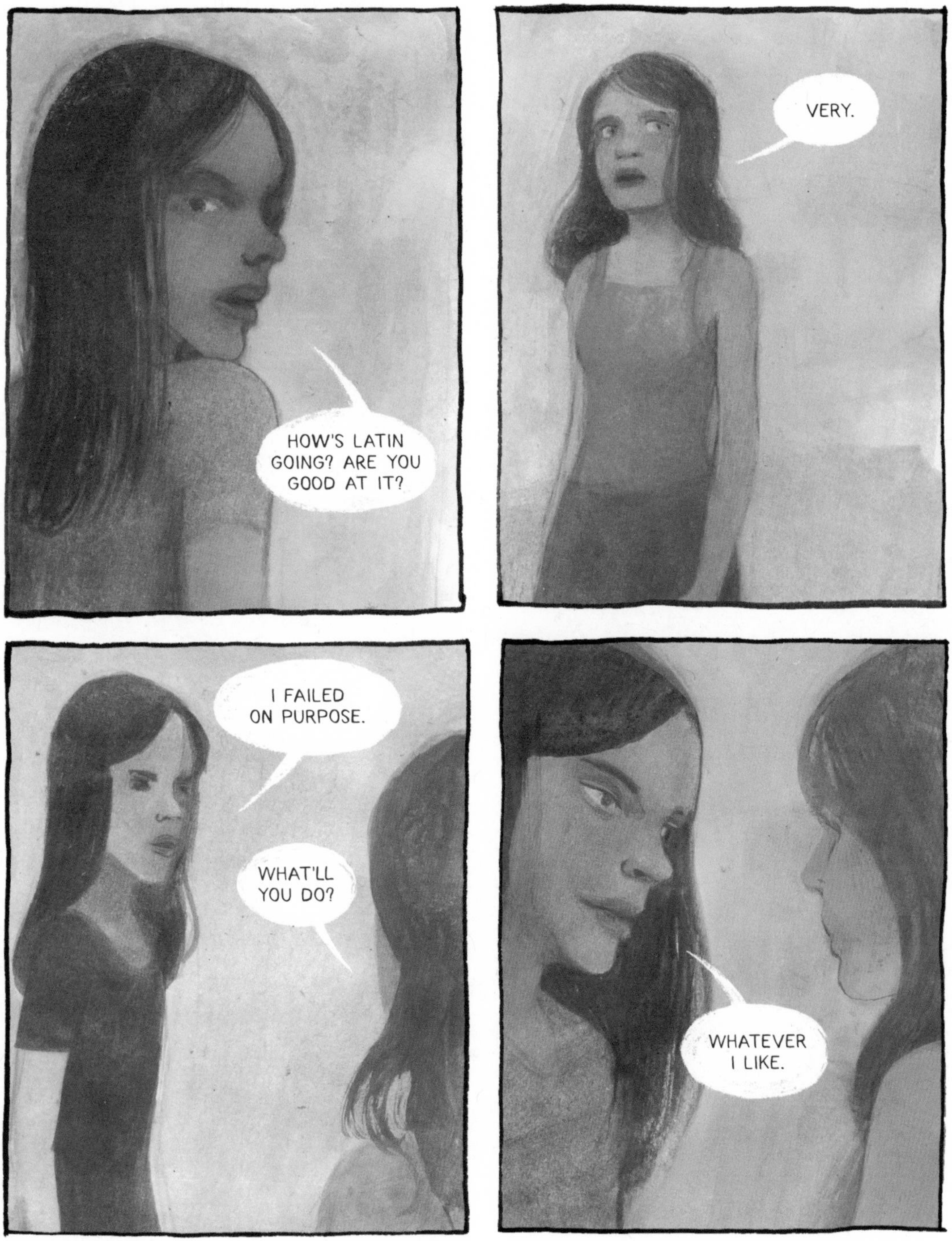
HOW'S LATIN GOING? ARE YOU GOOD AT IT?
VERY.
I FAILED ON PURPOSE.
WHAT'LL YOU DO?
WHATEVER I LIKE.

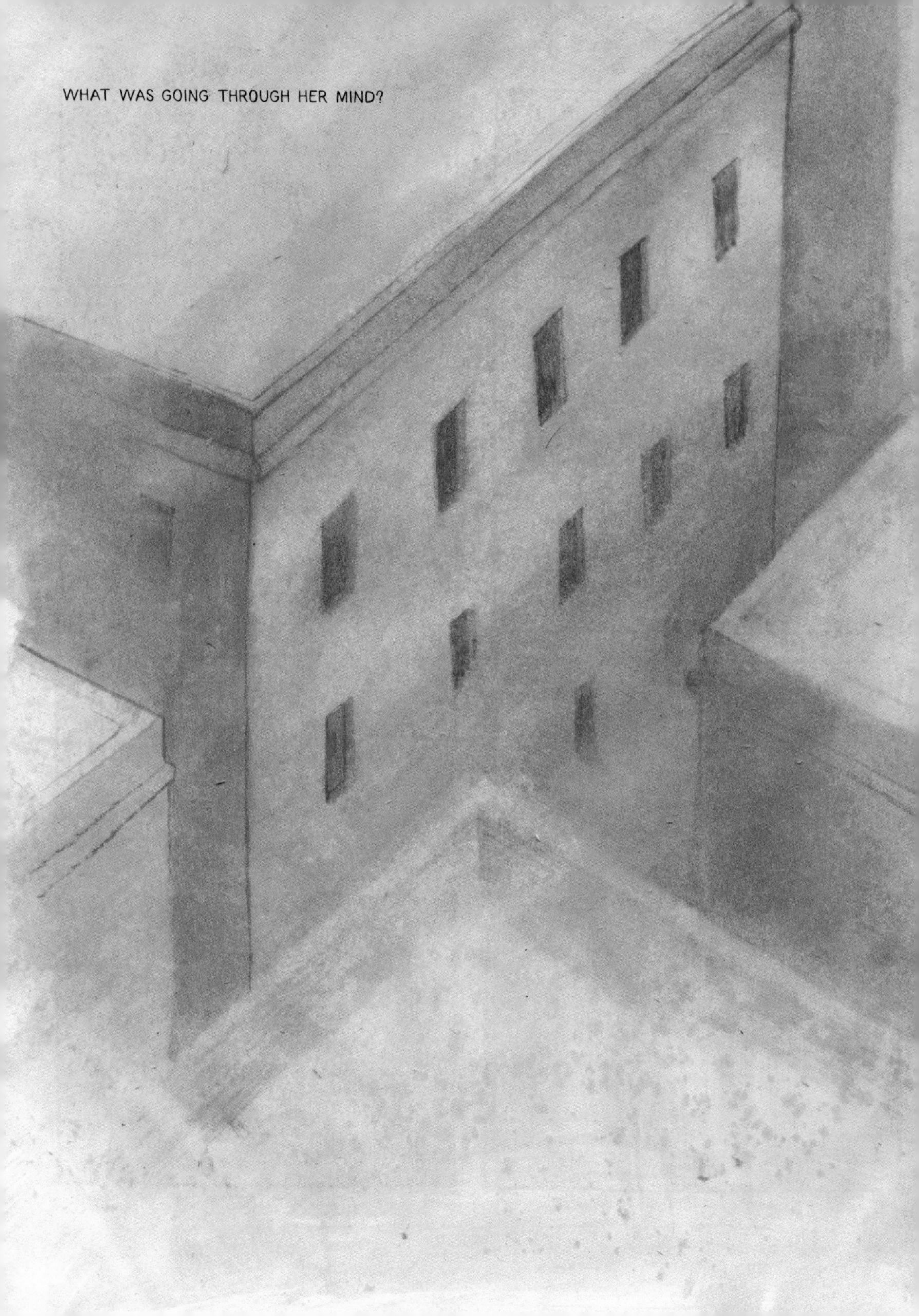
WHAT WAS GOING THROUGH HER MIND?

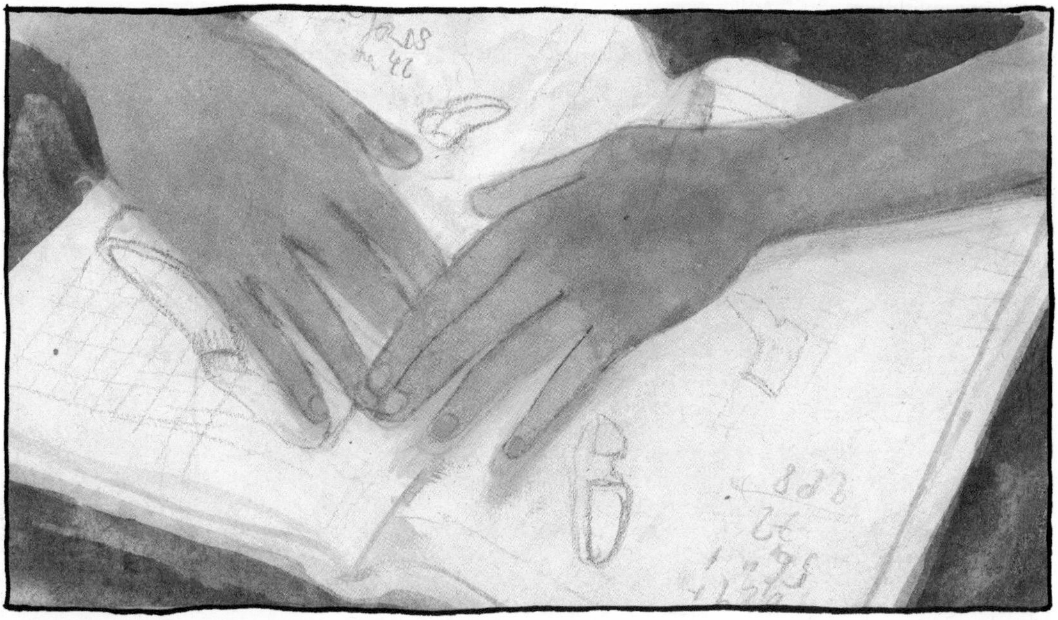

IT DIDN'T TAKE LONG TO FIND OUT...

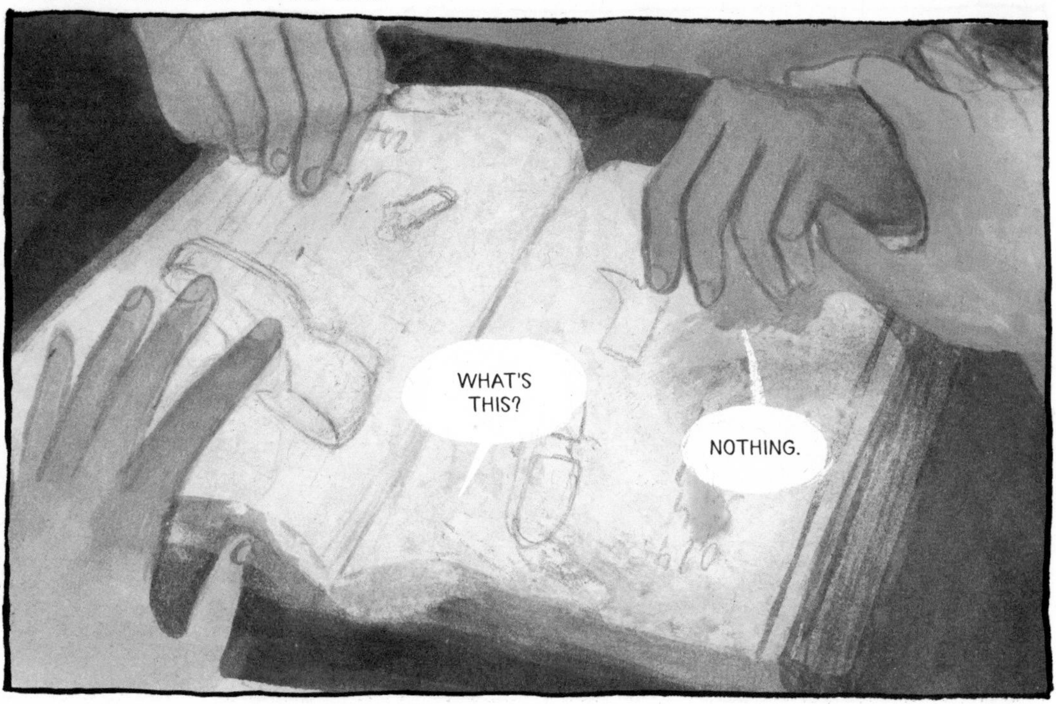
WHAT'S THIS?
NOTHING.

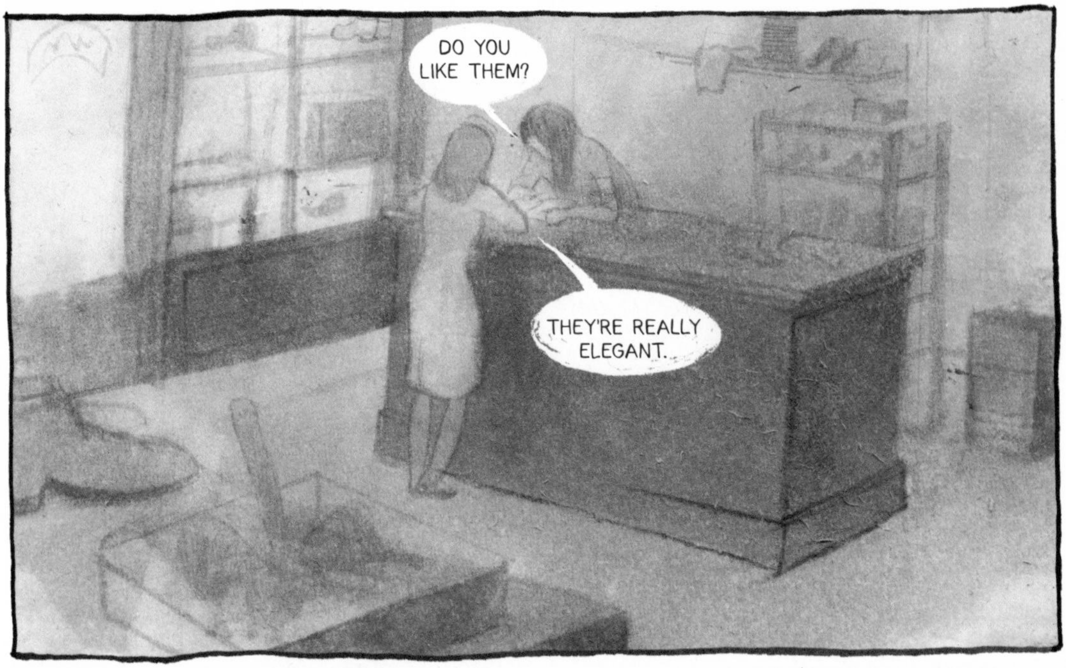
DO YOU LIKE THEM?
THEY'RE REALLY ELEGANT.

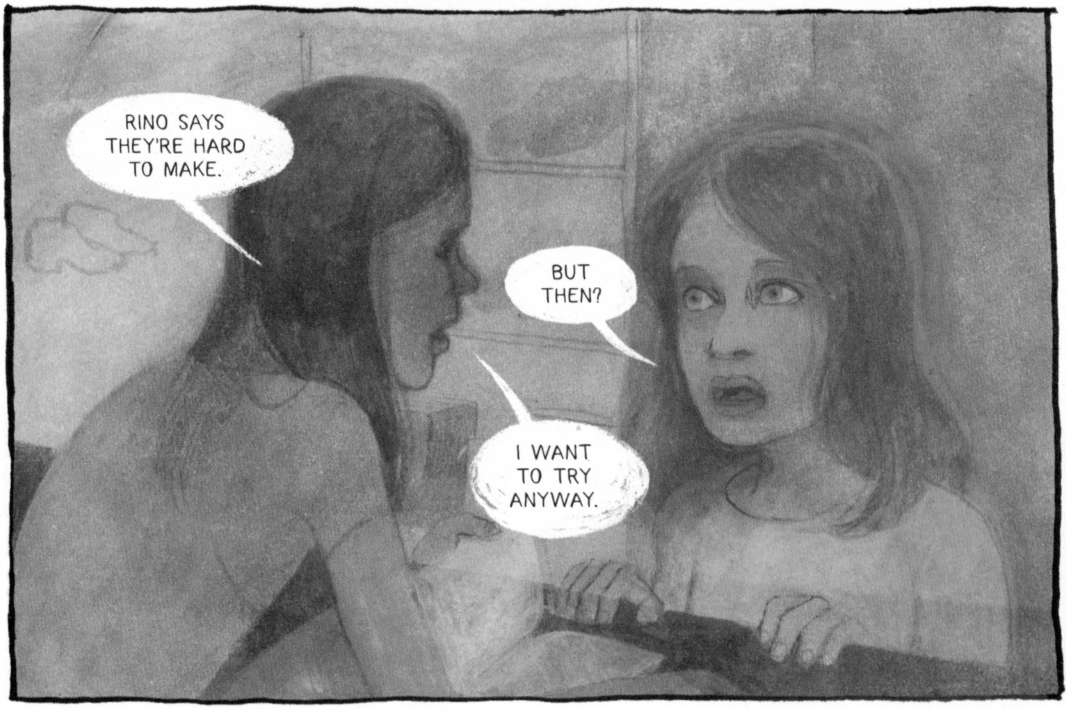
RINO SAYS THEY'RE HARD TO MAKE.
BUT THEN?
I WANT TO TRY ANYWAY.

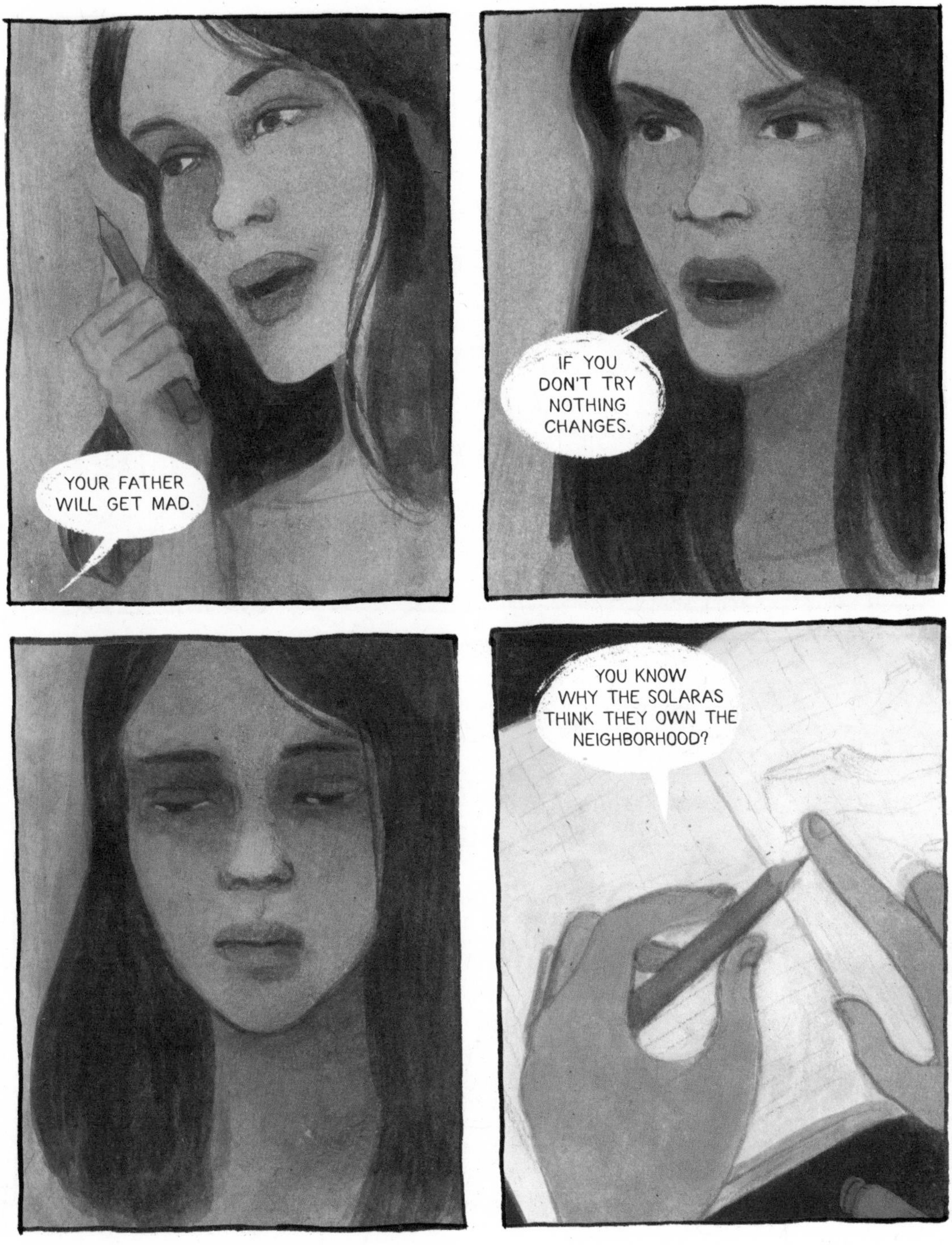
YOUR FATHER WILL GET MAD.
IF YOU DON'T TRY NOTHING CHANGES.
YOU KNOW WHY THE SOLARAS THINK THEY OWN THE NEIGHBORHOOD?

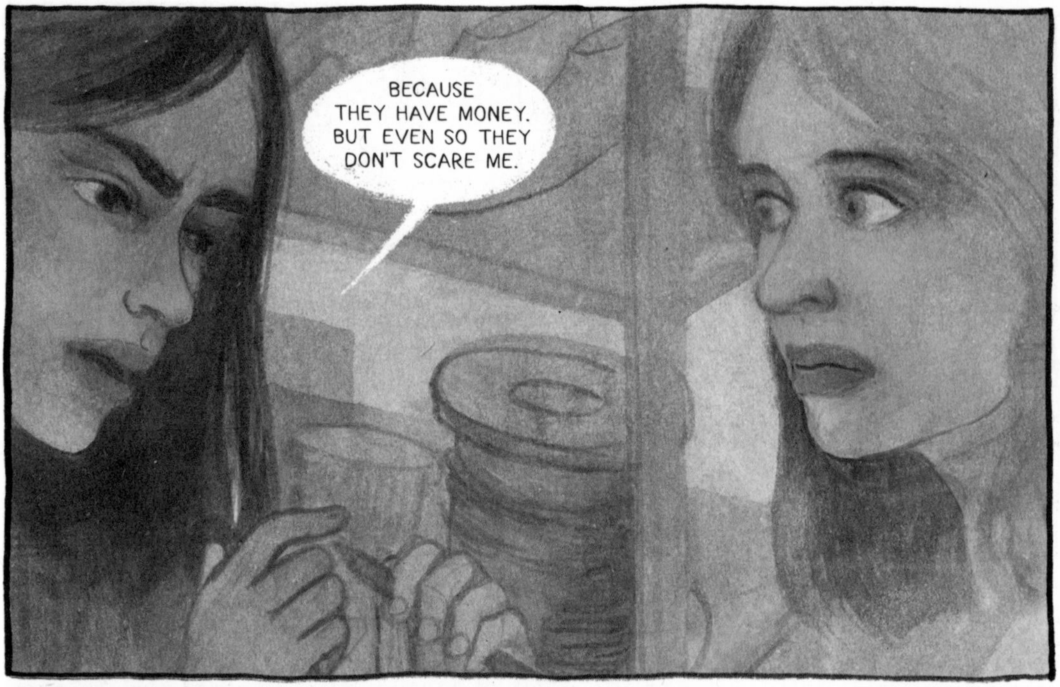
BECAUSE THEY HAVE MONEY. BUT EVEN SO THEY DON'T SCARE ME.

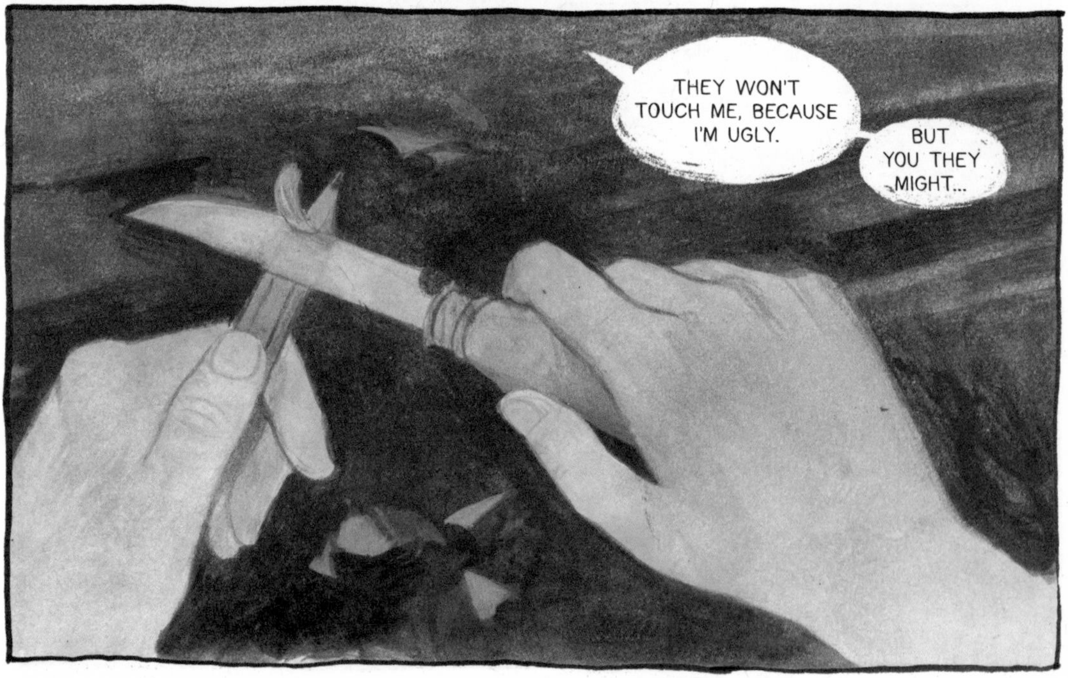
THEY WON'T TOUCH ME, BECAUSE I'M UGLY.
BUT YOU THEY MIGHT...

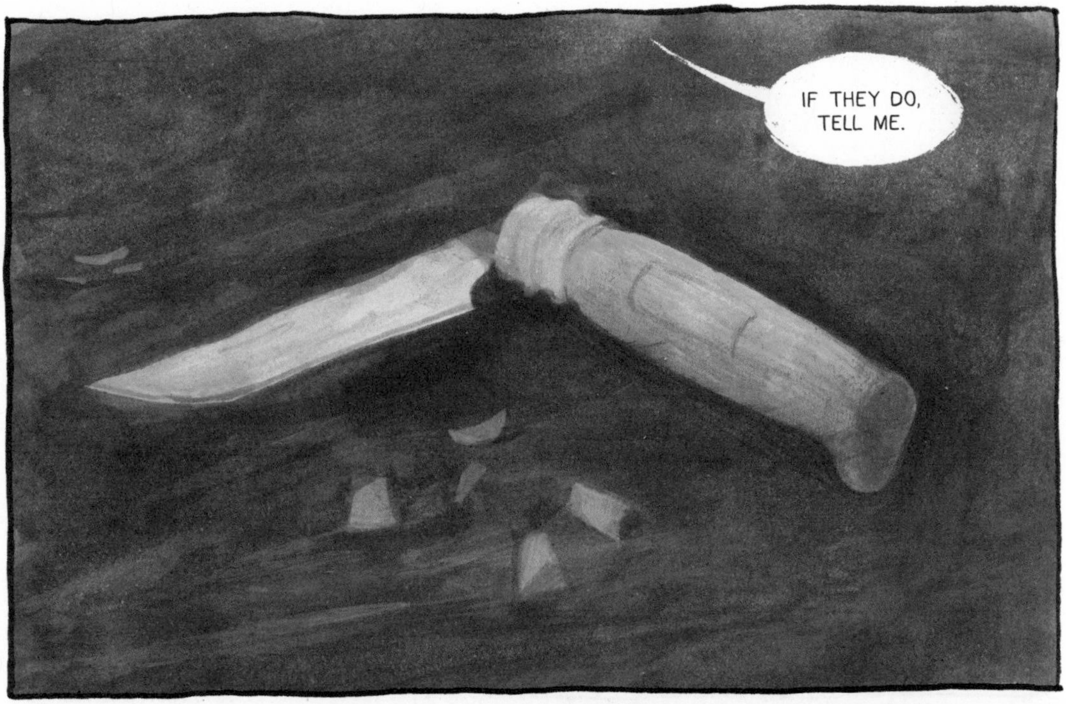
IF THEY DO, TELL ME.

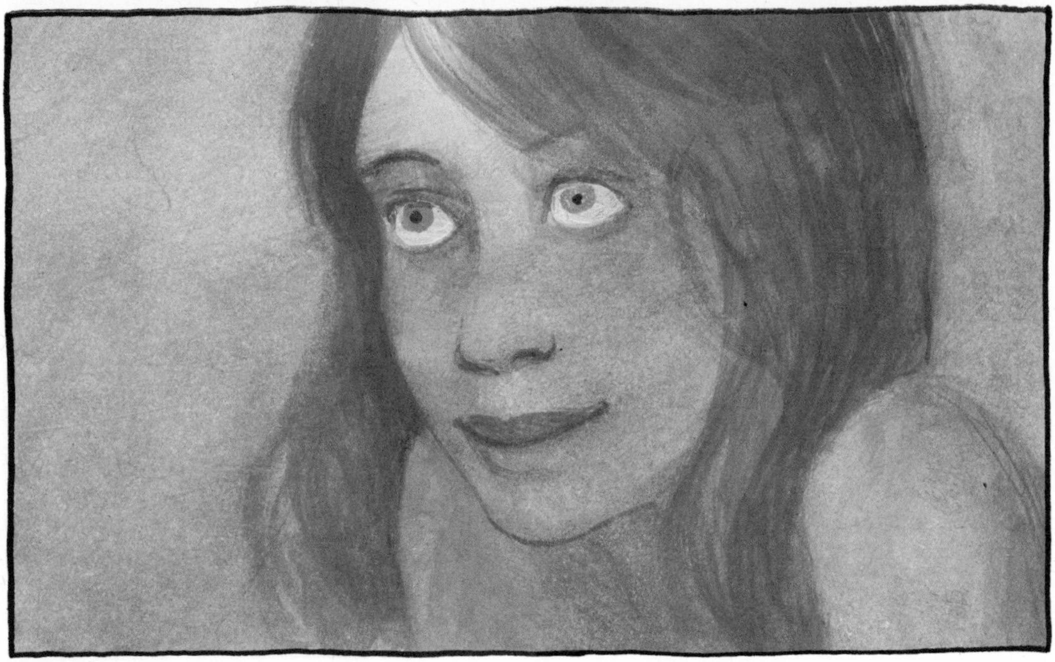

I DIDN'T DO WELL MY FIRST YEAR OF MIDDLE SCHOOL. WITHOUT LILA, I THOUGHT I'D BE THE BEST.

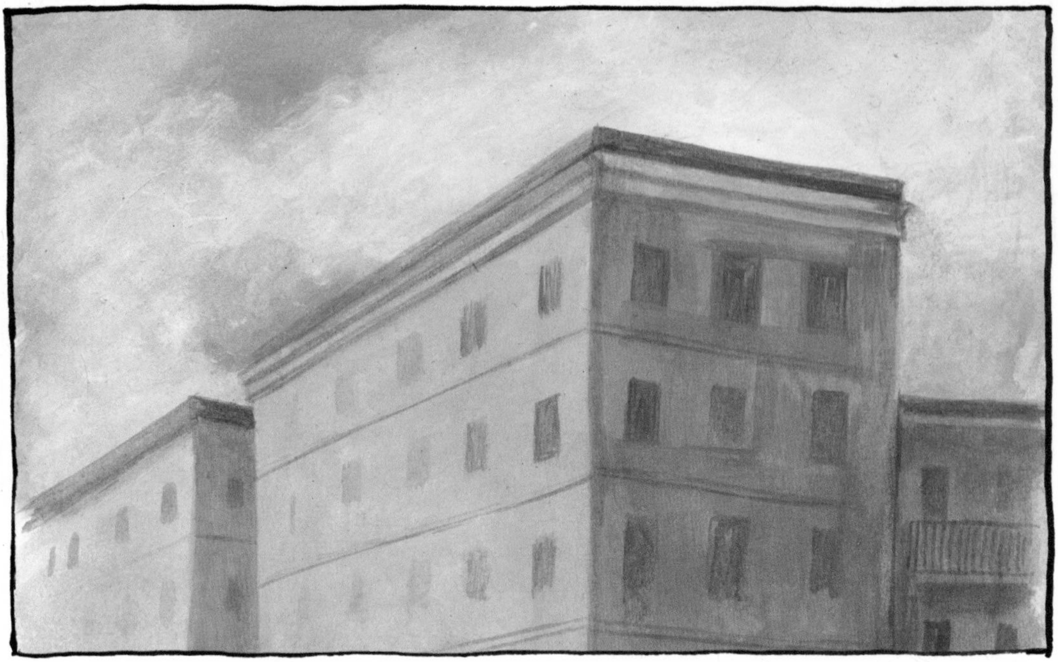

INSTEAD EVERYTHING SEEMED BLURRED. FROM THE TEXTBOOKS EVERY PROMISE HAD FLED, ALL ENERGY.

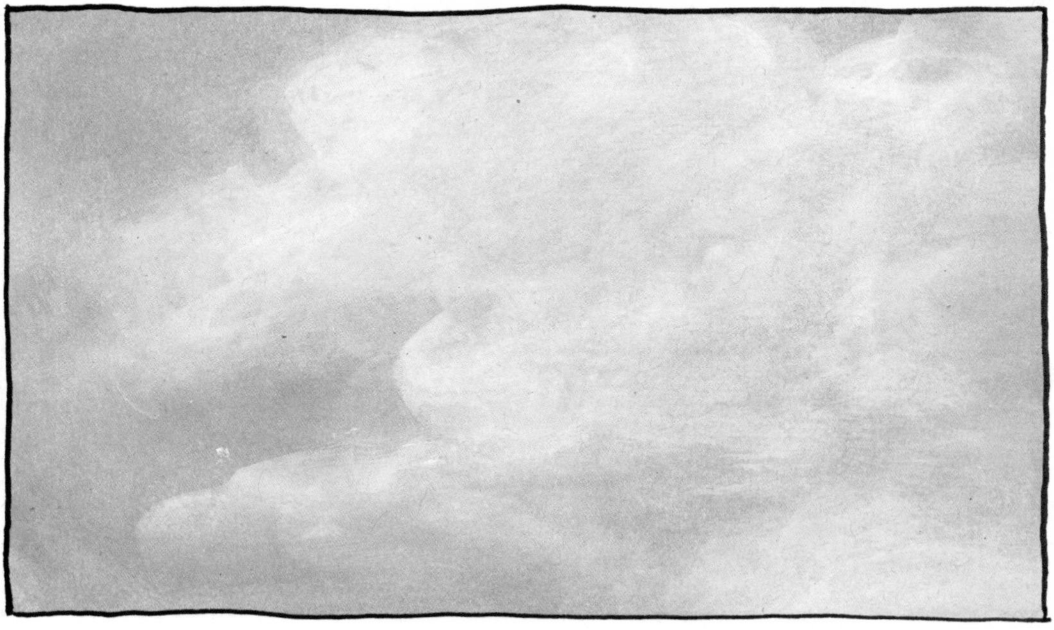

AT THE END OF THE YEAR I FAILED LATIN.

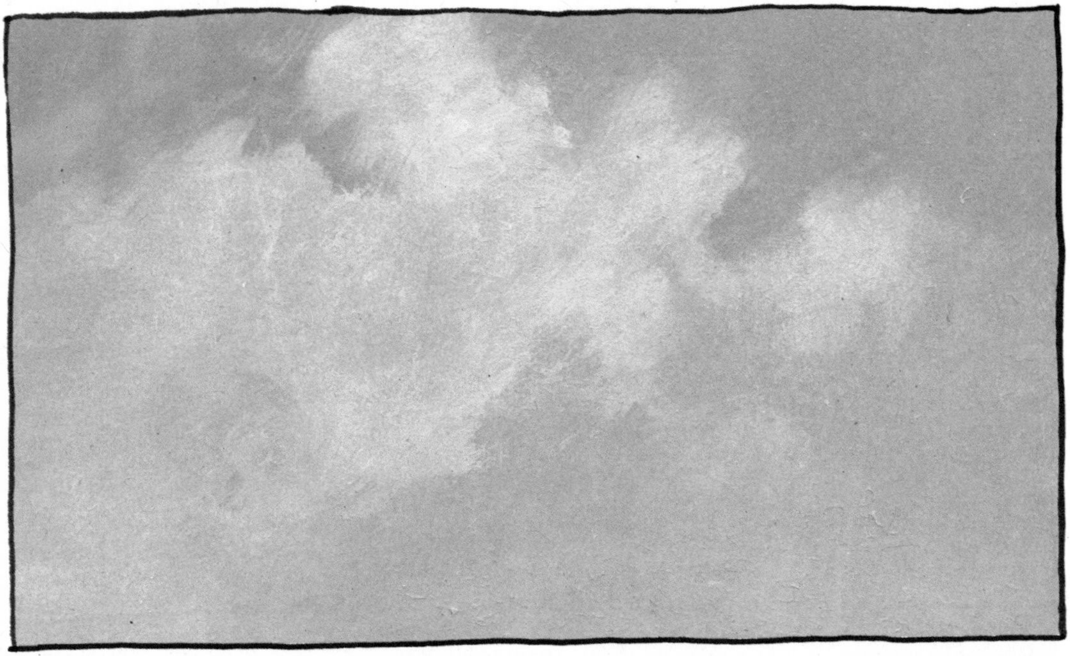

LILA CAME LOOKING FOR ME: AT THAT TIME WE DIDN'T SEE EACH OTHER EVERY DAY AS BEFORE.

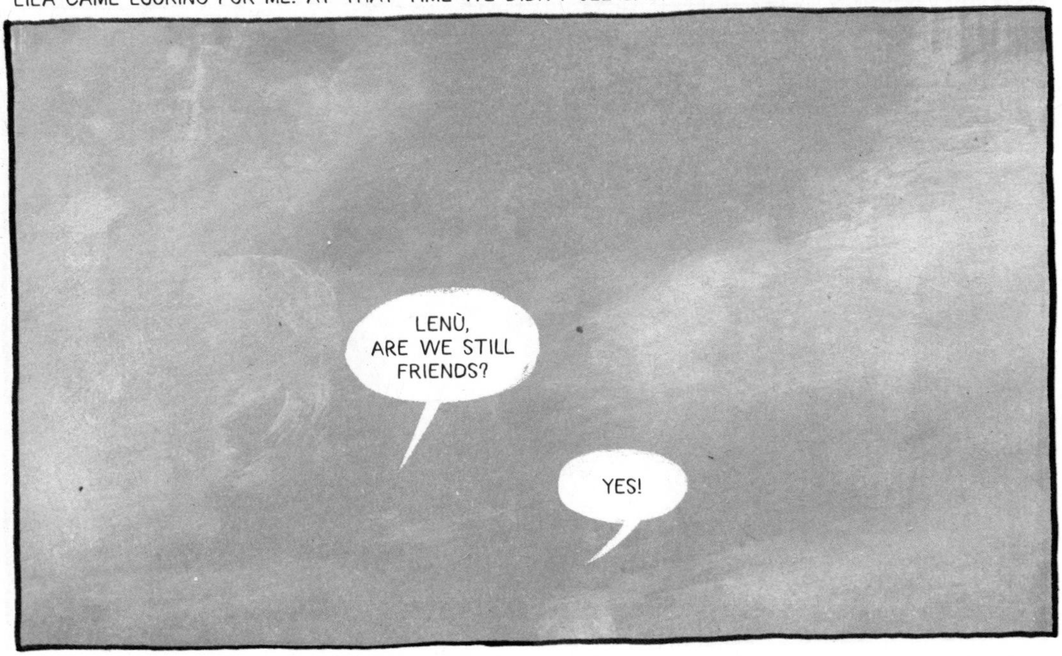
LENÙ, ARE WE STILL FRIENDS?
YES!

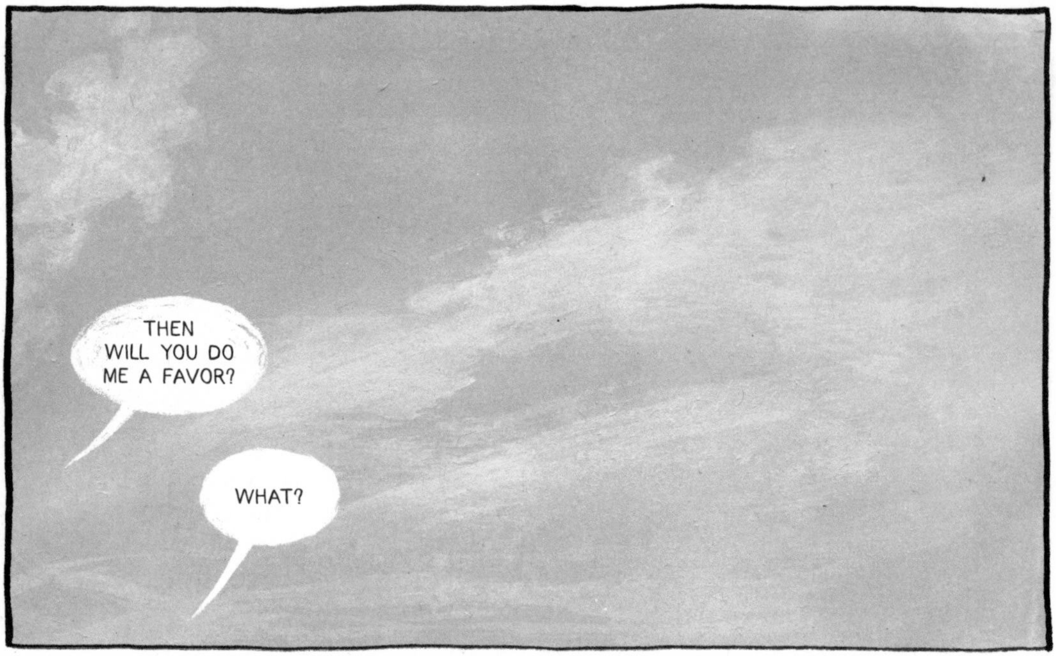
THEN WILL YOU DO ME A FAVOR?
WHAT?

I WOULD HAVE DONE ANYTHING FOR HER: RUN AWAY FROM HOME, LEAVE THE NEIGHBORHOOD, SLEEP IN FARMHOUSES, DESCEND INTO THE SEWERS...

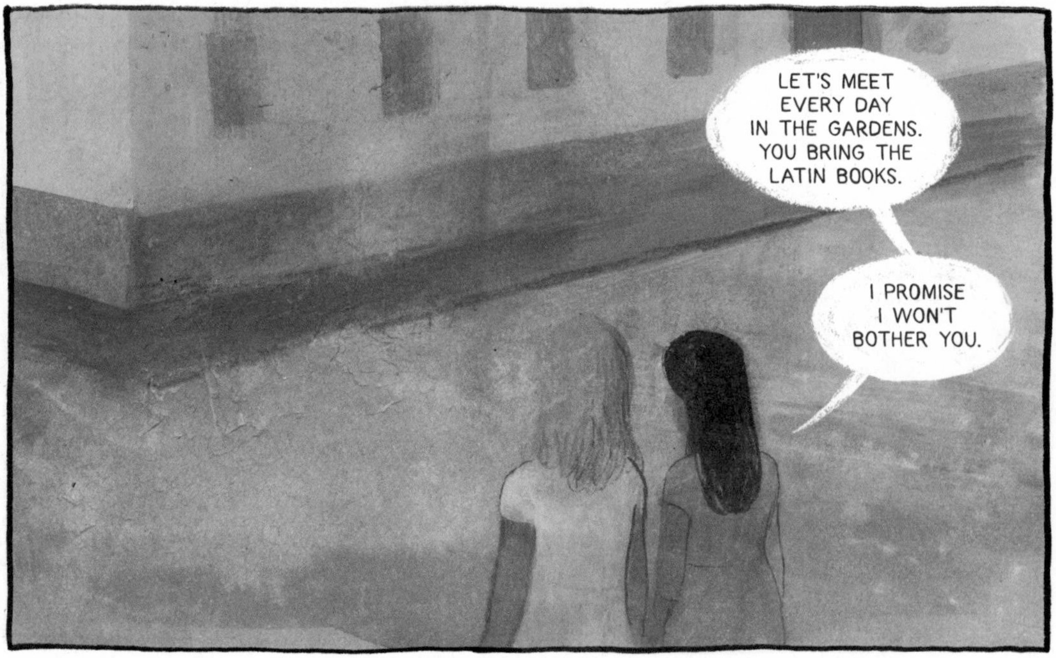
LET'S MEET EVERY DAY IN THE GARDENS. YOU BRING THE LATIN BOOKS.
I PROMISE I WON'T BOTHER YOU.

WE MET EVERY AFTERNOON, I SAW IMMEDIATELY THAT SHE KNEW MORE THAN I DID. WHERE HAD SHE LEARNED IT?

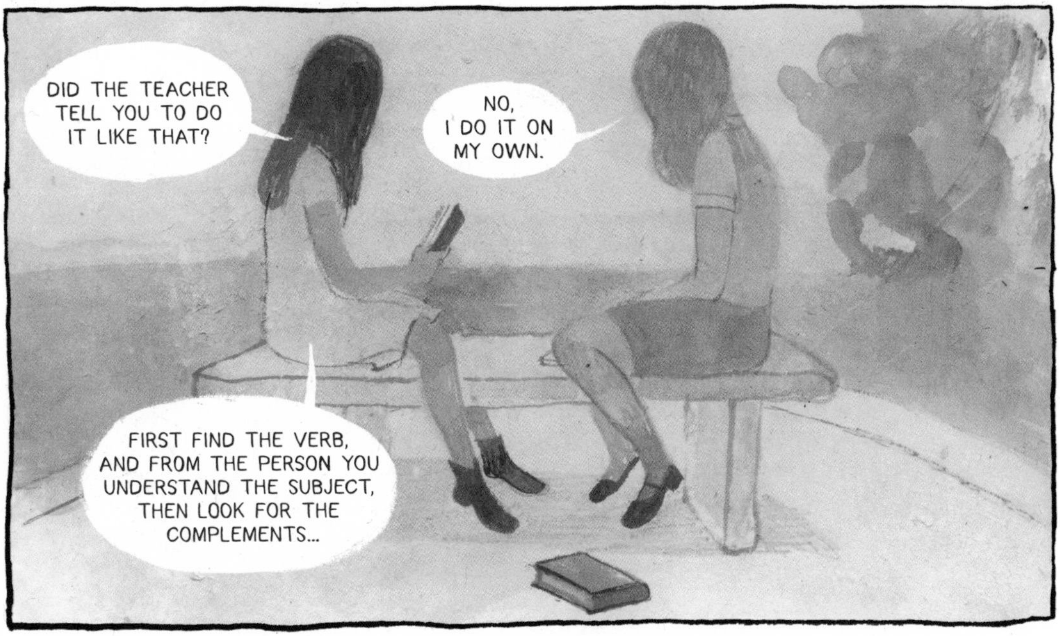
DID THE TEACHER TELL YOU TO DO IT LIKE THAT?
NO, I DO IT ON MY OWN.
FIRST FIND THE VERB, AND FROM THE PERSON YOU UNDERSTAND THE SUBJECT, THEN LOOK FOR THE COMPLEMENTS...

I TRIED.

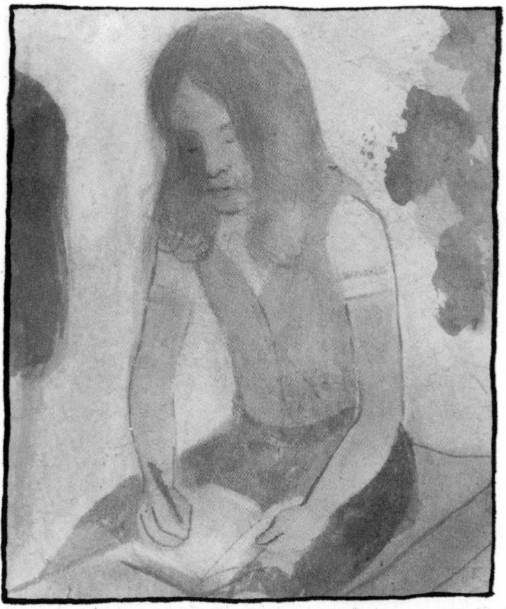

SUDDENLY TRANSLATING SEEMED EASY!

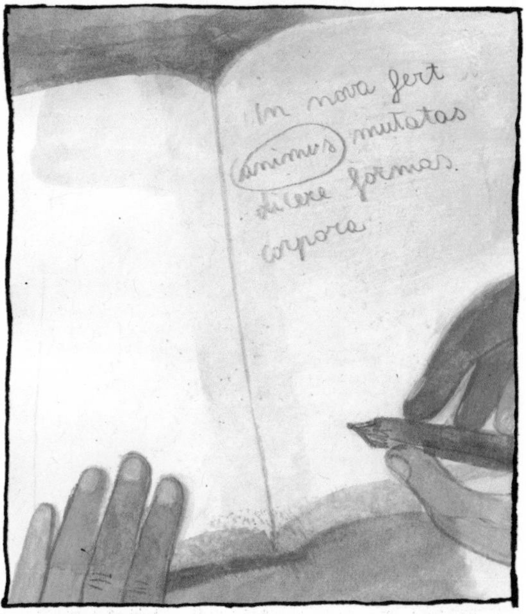
In nova fert
animus mutatas
dicere formas.
corpora

IN SEPTEMBER I PASSED THE EXAM: I DID THE WRITTEN PART WITH NO MISTAKES AND ANSWERED ALL THE QUESTIONS IN THE ORAL PART. LILA WAITED FOR ME OUTSIDE.

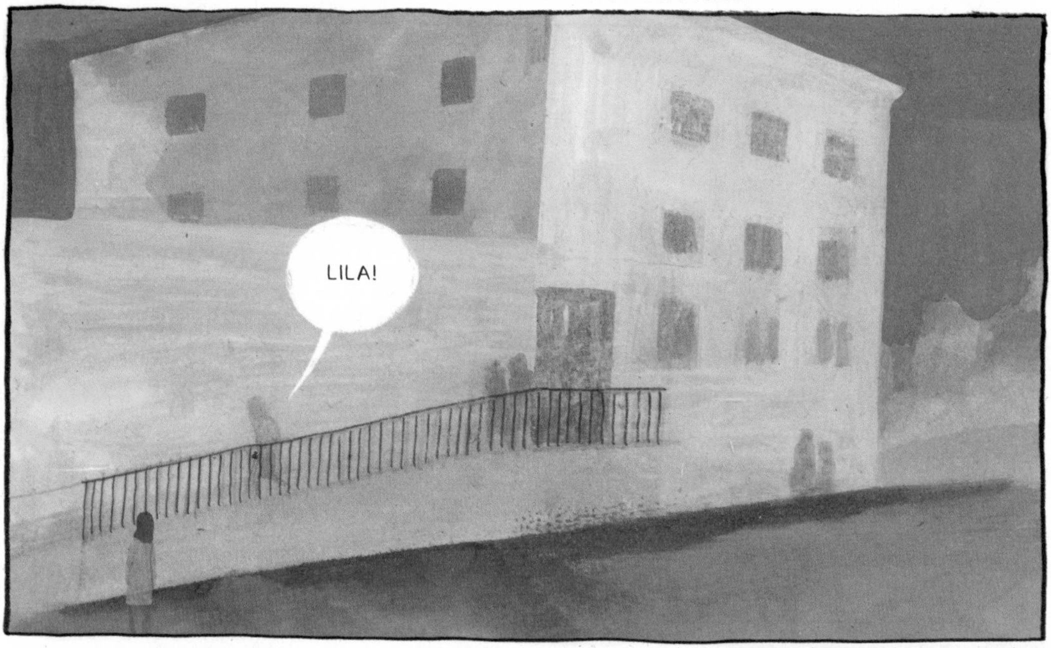
LILA!

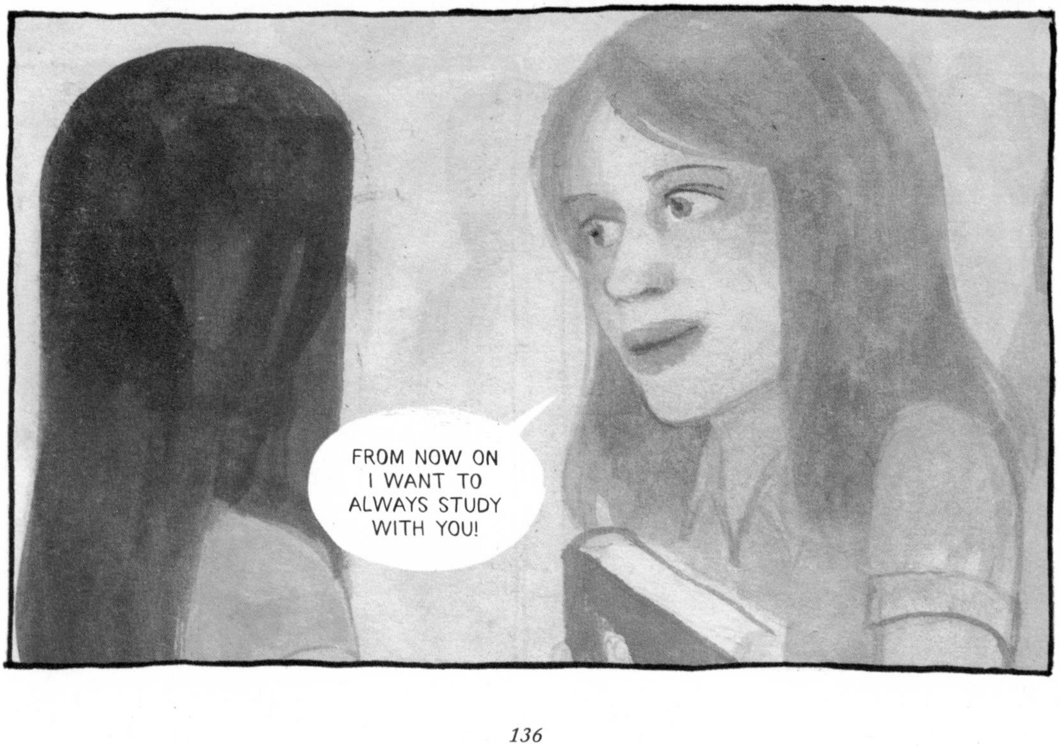
FROM NOW ON I WANT TO ALWAYS STUDY WITH YOU!

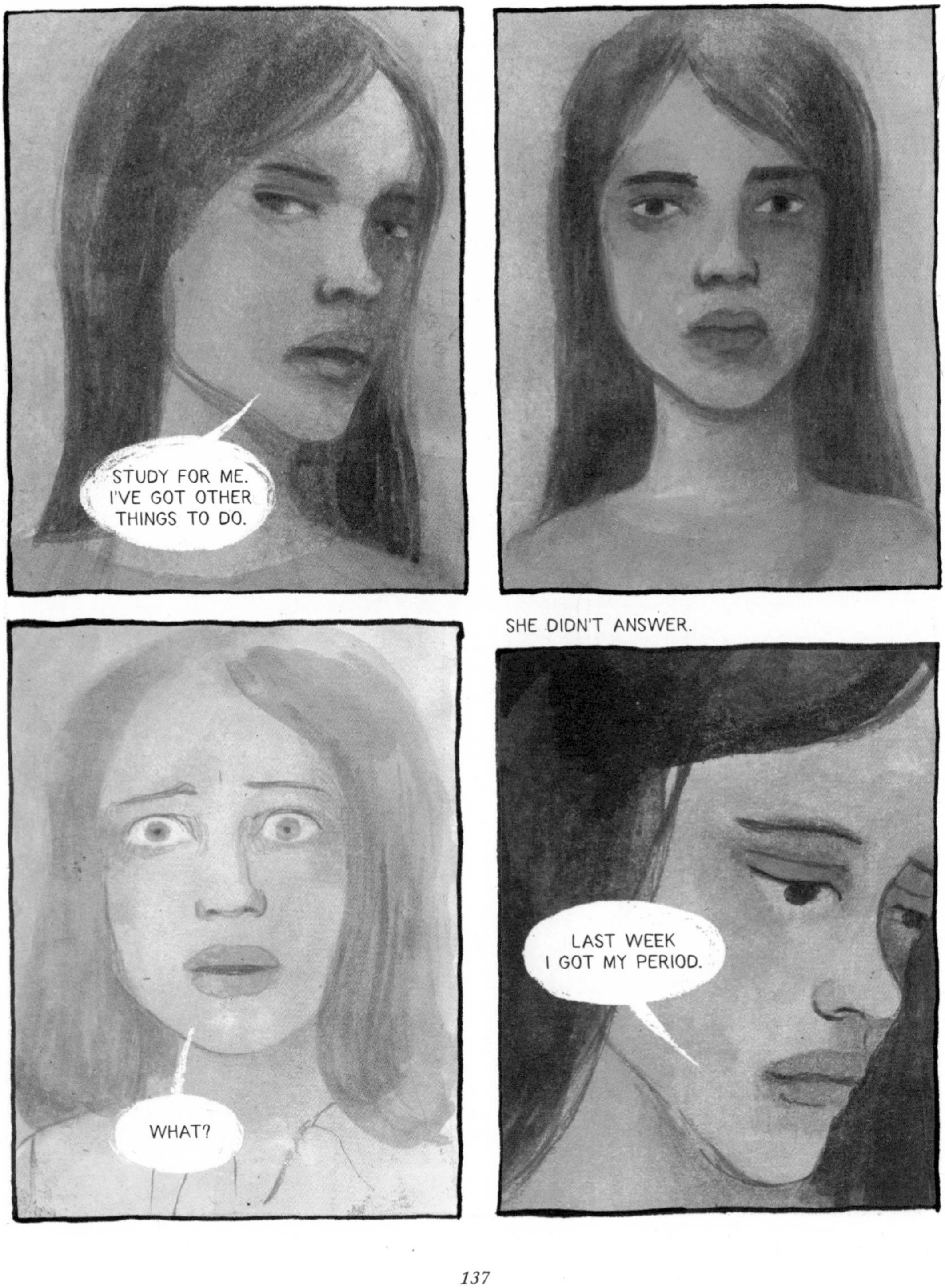
STUDY FOR ME. I'VE GOT OTHER THINGS TO DO.
WHAT?
SHE DIDN'T ANSWER.
LAST WEEK I GOT MY PERIOD.

SO NOW SHE WAS BLEEDING, TOO.

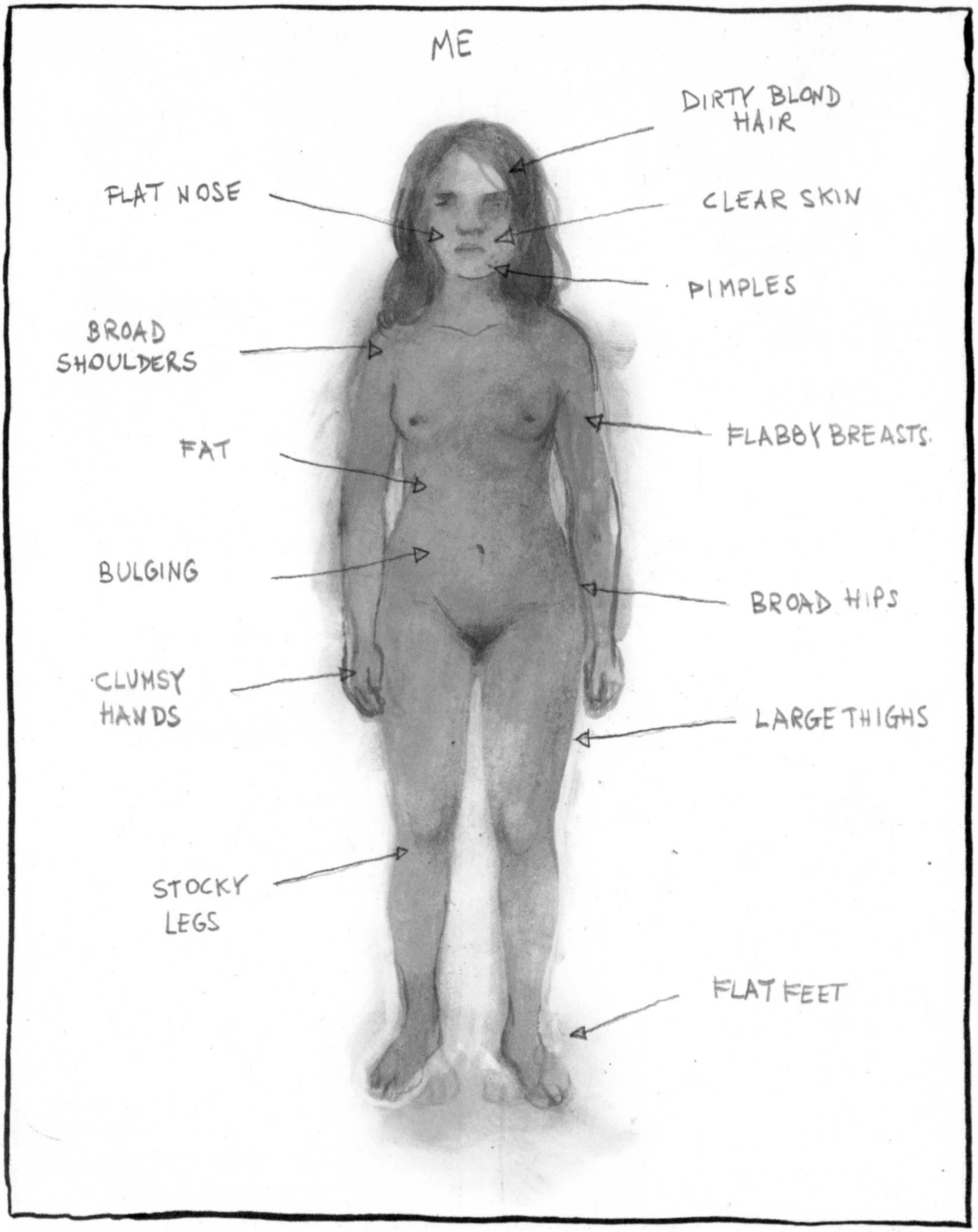
ME
DIRTY BLOND HAIR
FLAT NOSE
CLEAR SKIN
PIMPLES
BROAD SHOULDERS
FLABBY BREASTS.
FAT
BULGING
BROAD HIPS
CLUMSY HANDS
LARGE THIGHS
STOCKY LEGS
FLAT FEET

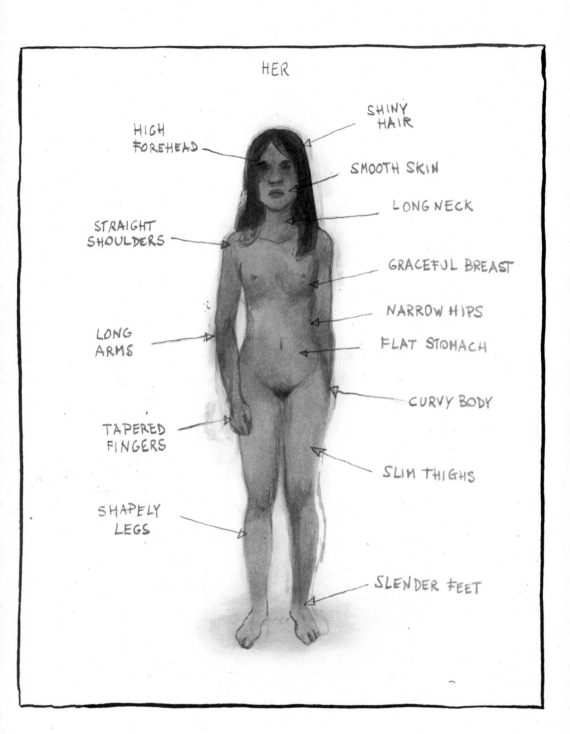

HER

SHINY HAIR

HIGH FOREHEAD

SMOOTH SKIN

LONG NECK

STRAIGHT SHOULDERS

GRACEFUL BREAST

LONG ARMS

NARROW HIPS

FLAT STOMACH

TAPERED FINGERS

CURVY BODY

SLIM THIGHS

SHAPELY LEGS

SLENDER FEET

IT HAD ARRIVED LIKE THE TREMOR OF AN EARTHQUAKE...

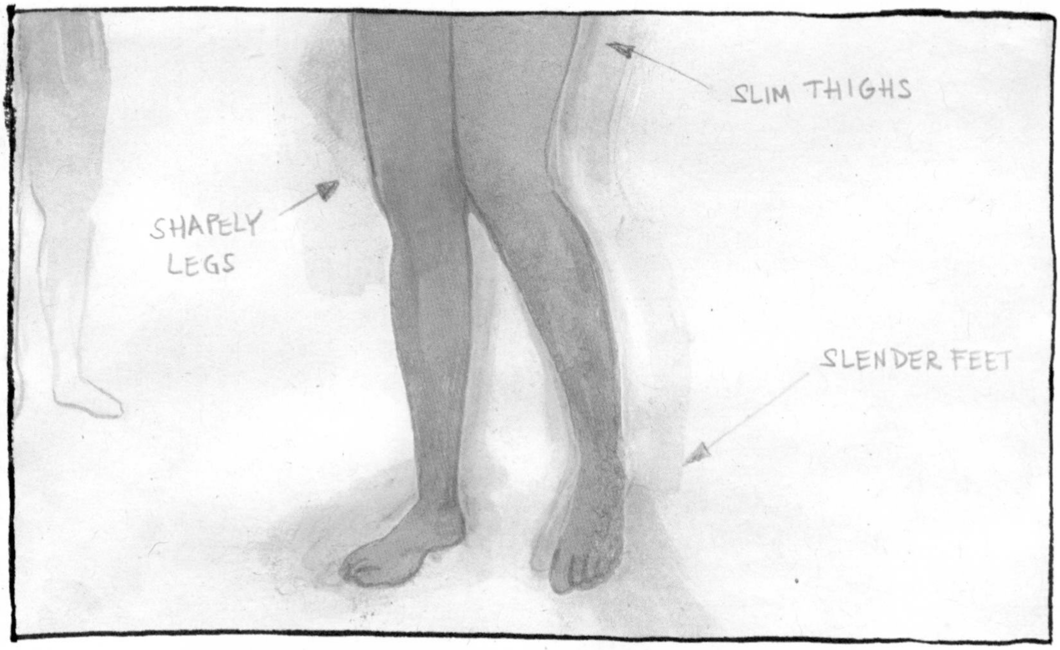
SLIM THIGHS
SHAPELY LEGS
SLENDER FEET

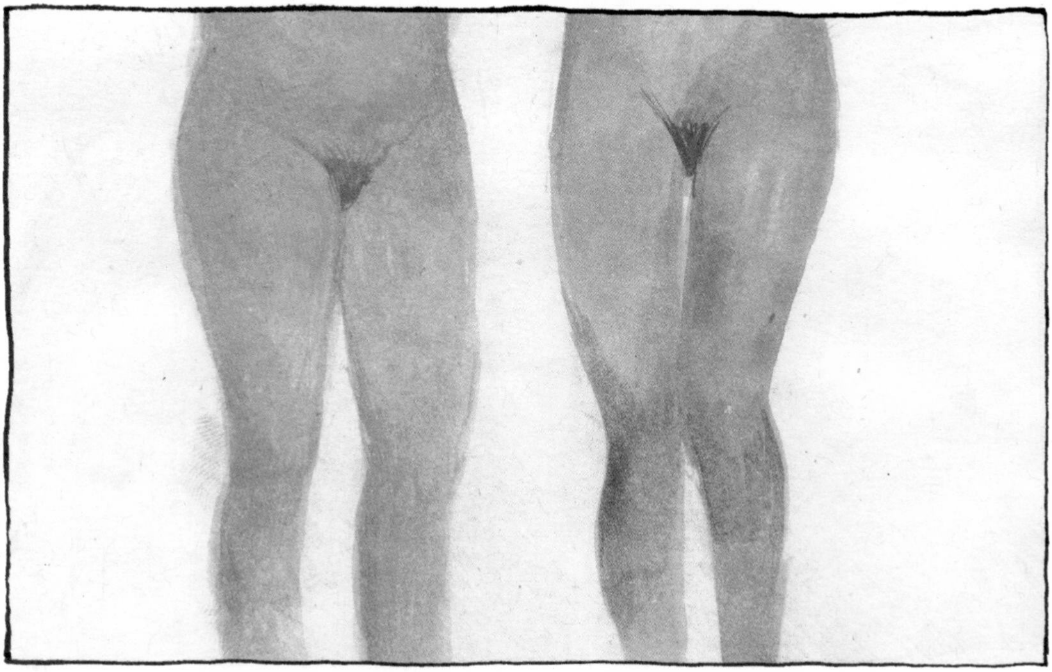

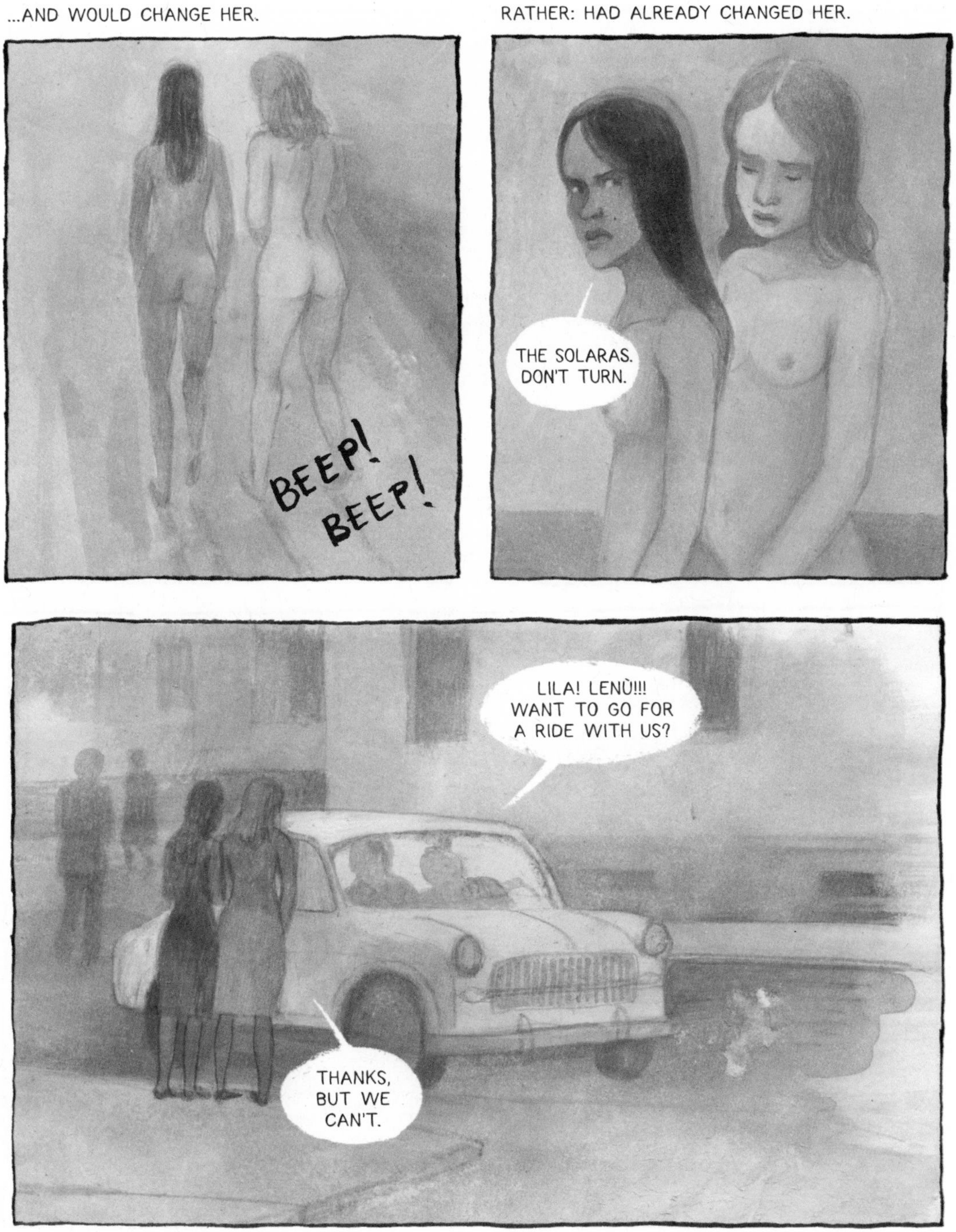
...AND WOULD CHANGE HER.
BEEP! BEEP!
RATHER: HAD ALREADY CHANGED HER.
THE SOLARAS. DON'T TURN.
LILA! LENÙ!!! WANT TO GO FOR A RIDE WITH US?
THANKS, BUT WE CAN'T.

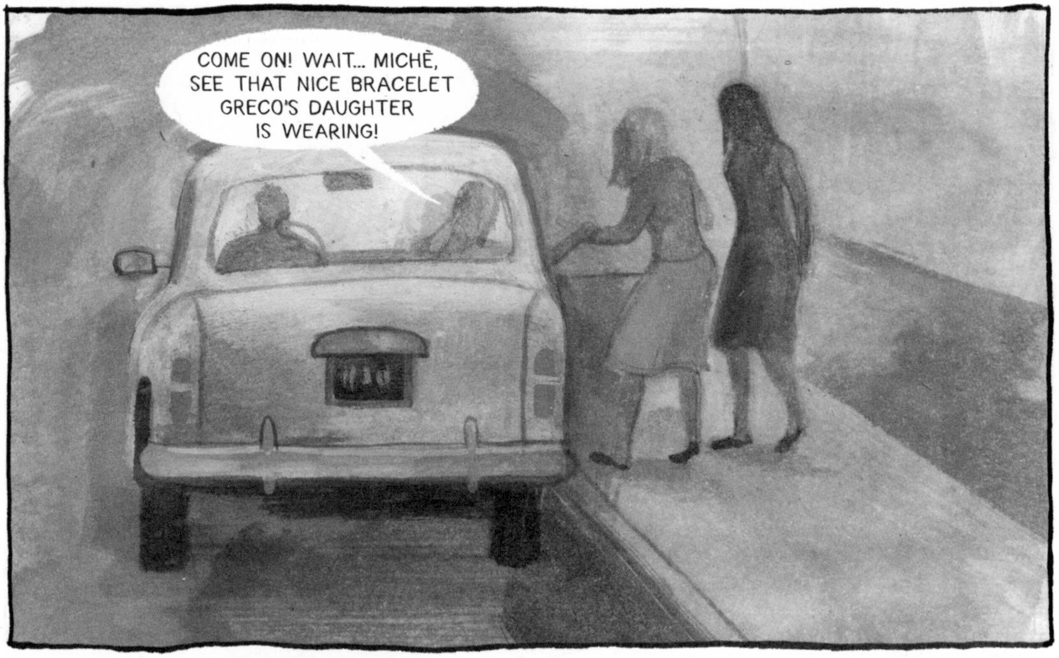
COME ON! WAIT... MICHÈ, SEE THAT NICE BRACELET GRECO'S DAUGHTER IS WEARING!

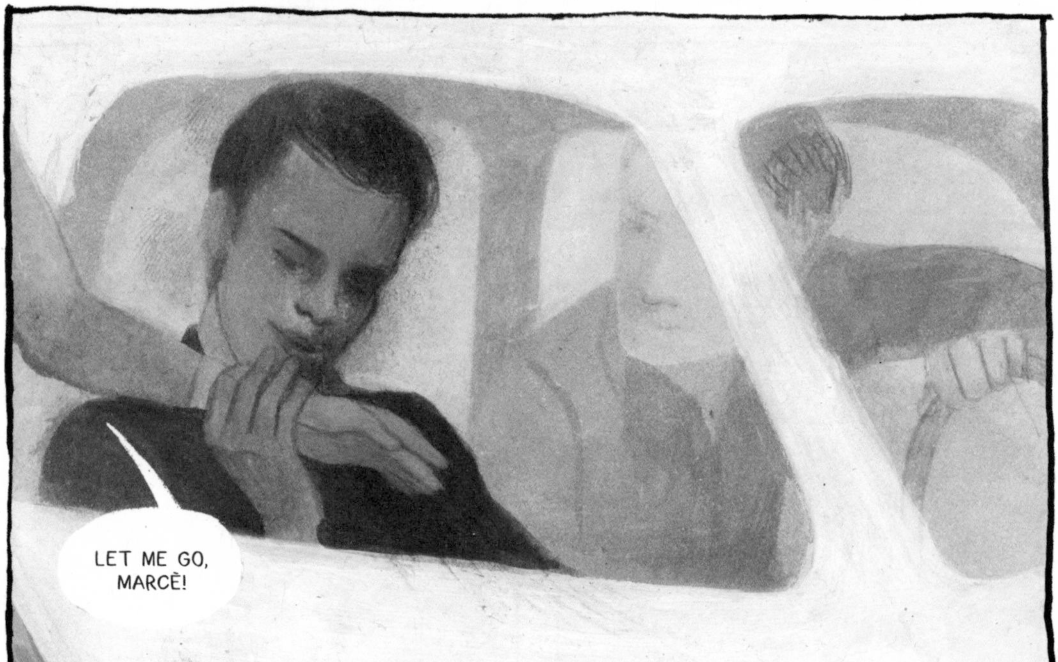
LET ME GO, MARCÈ!

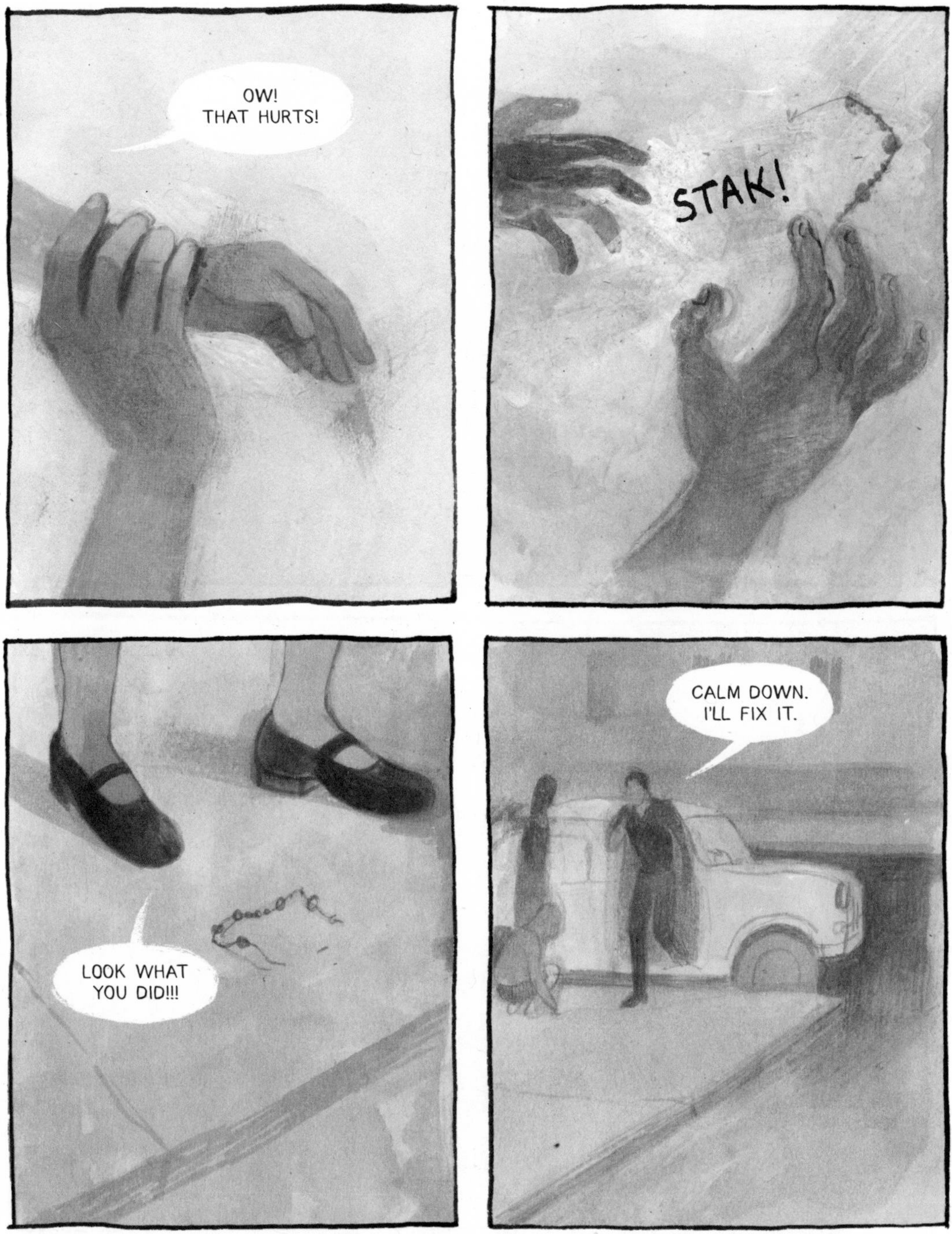
OW!
THAT HURTS!
STAK!
LOOK WHAT
YOU DID!!!
CALM DOWN.
I'LL FIX IT.

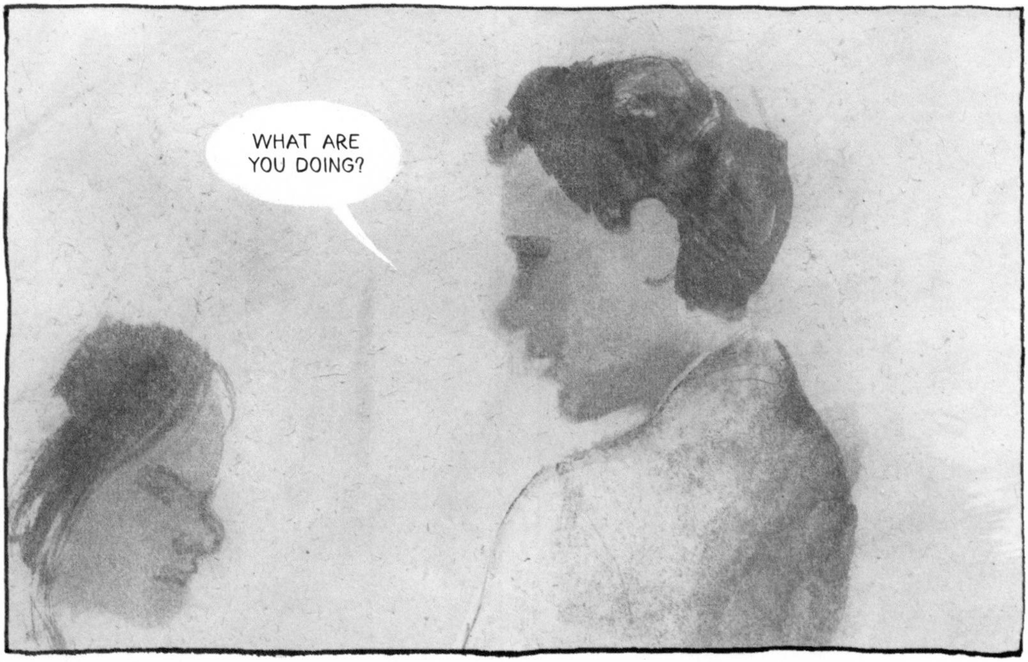
WHAT ARE YOU DOING?

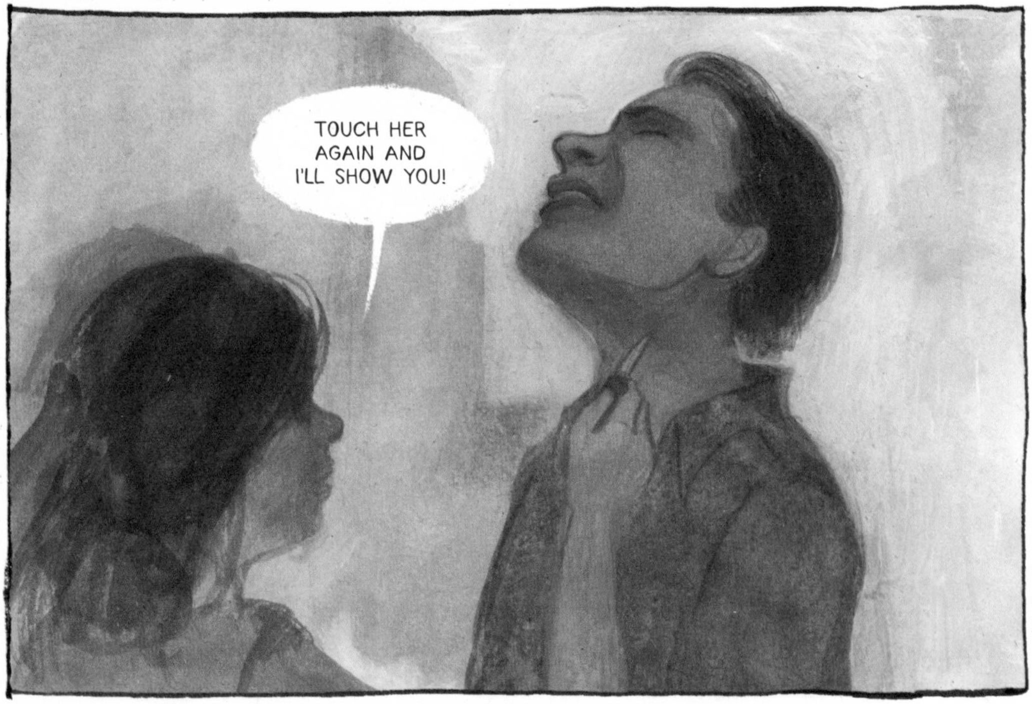
TOUCH HER AGAIN AND I'LL SHOW YOU!

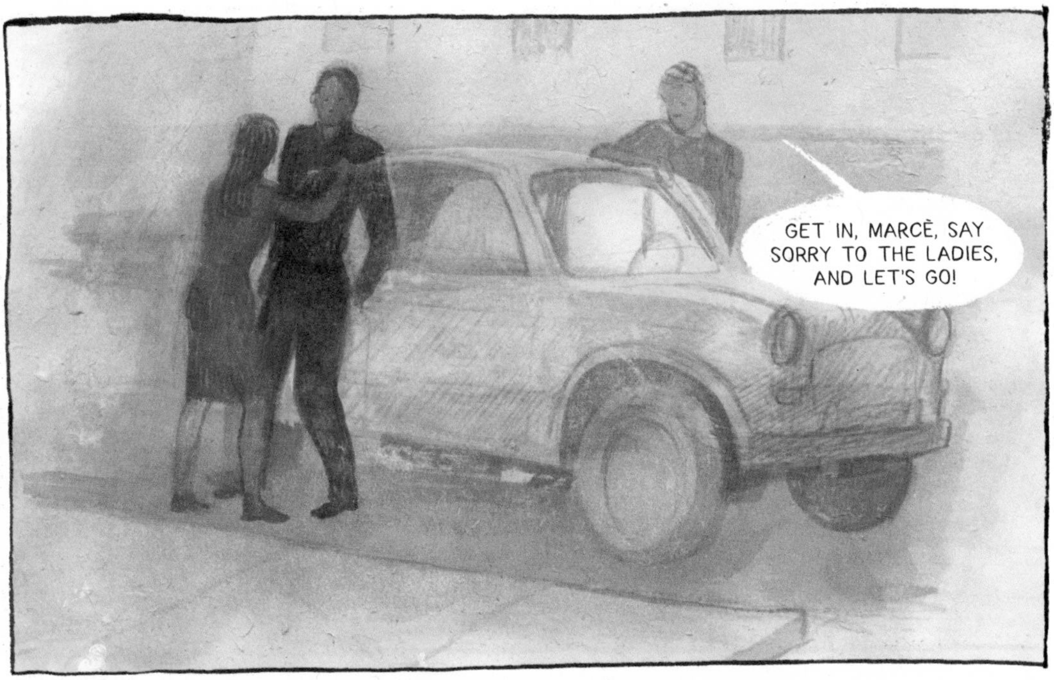
GET IN, MARCÈ, SAY SORRY TO THE LADIES, AND LET'S GO!

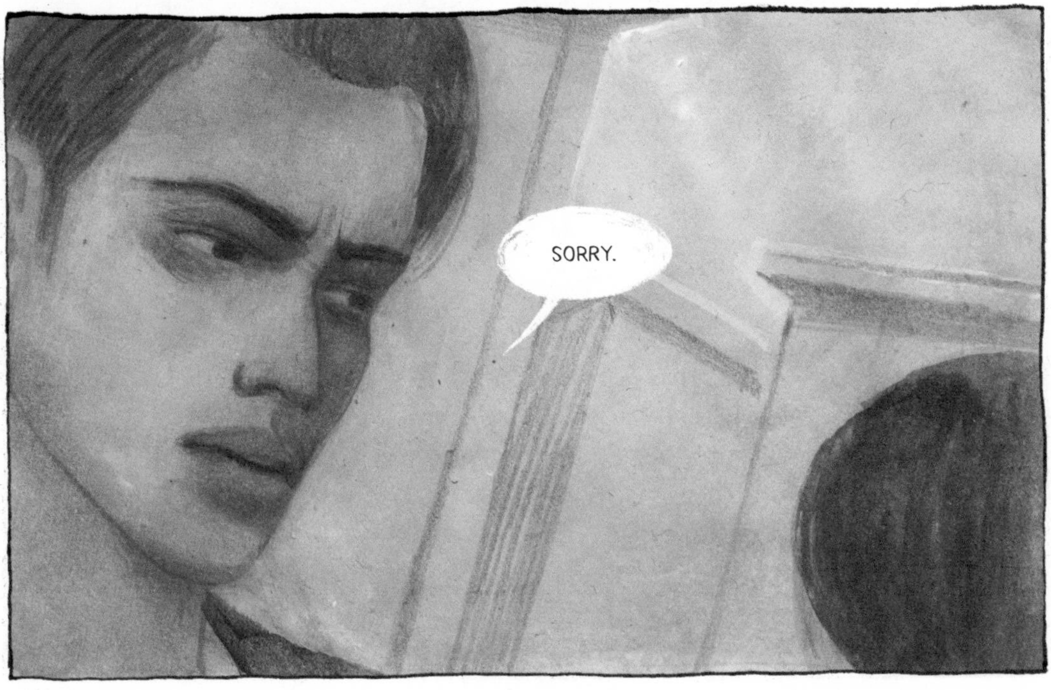
SORRY.

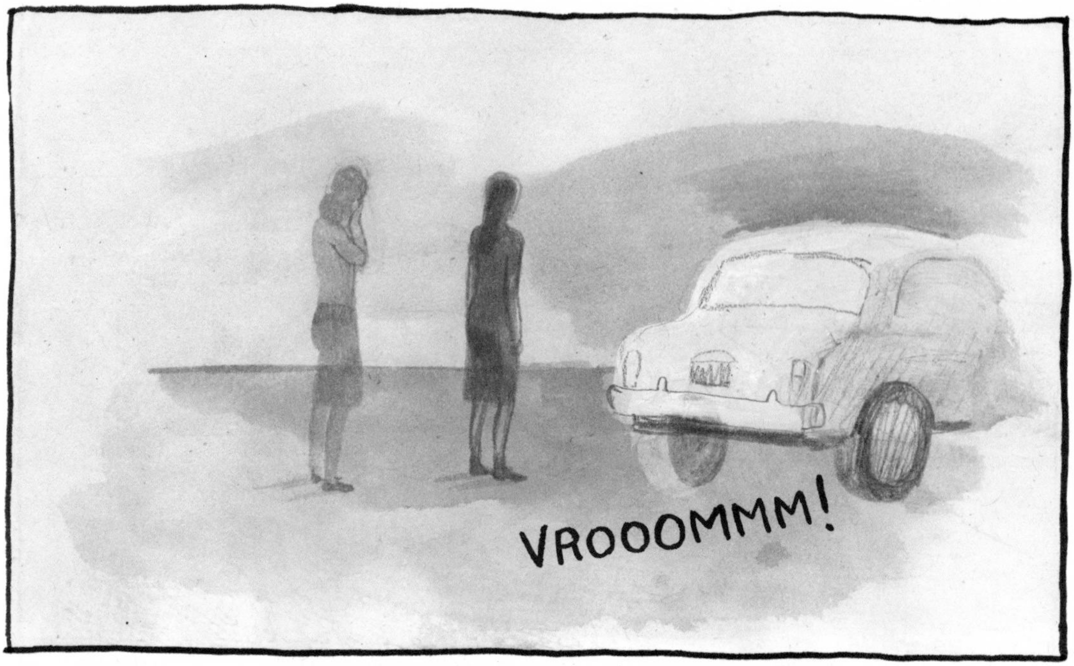
VROOOMMM!

EVEN MARCELLO SOLARA HAD REALIZED IT: LILA WAS TRULY BAD.

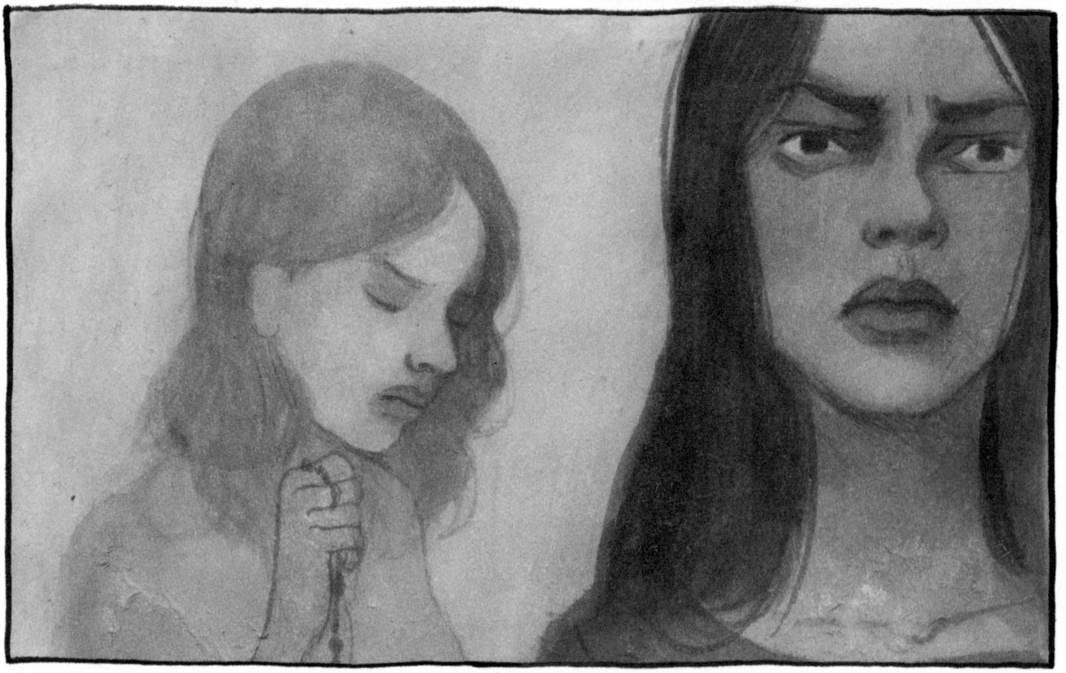

SHE KNEW HOW TO WOUND WITH WORDS.

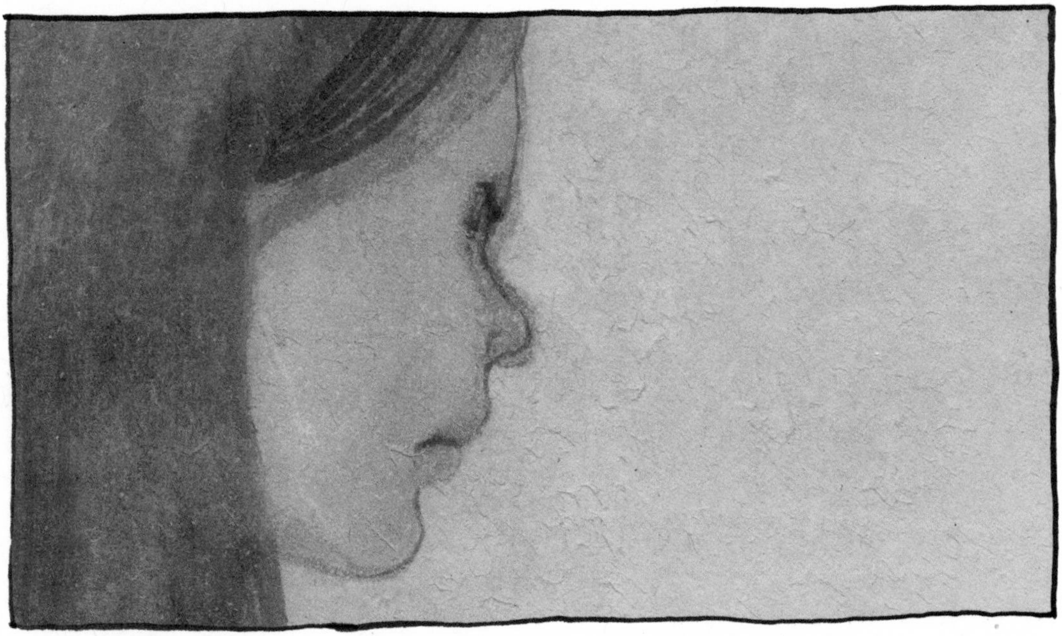

BUT SHE COULD ALSO GO SO FAR AS TO KILL.

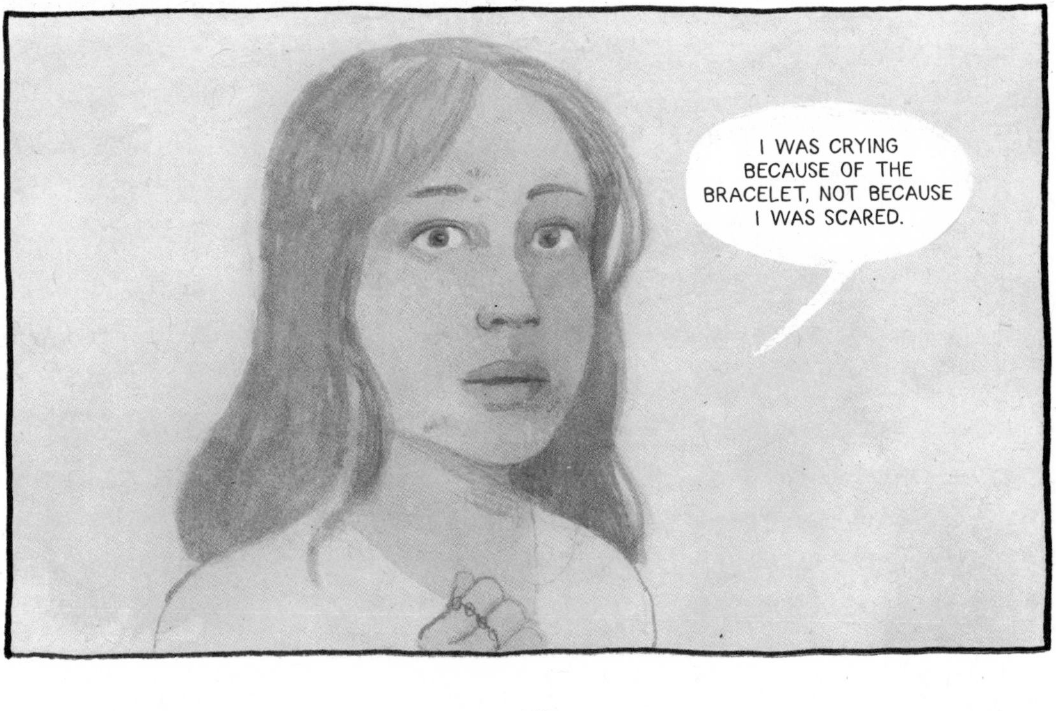
I WAS CRYING BECAUSE OF THE BRACELET, NOT BECAUSE I WAS SCARED.

AT THAT TIME SHE BEGAN DRAGGING ME TO PARTIES IN THE NEIGHBORHOOD BUILDINGS.

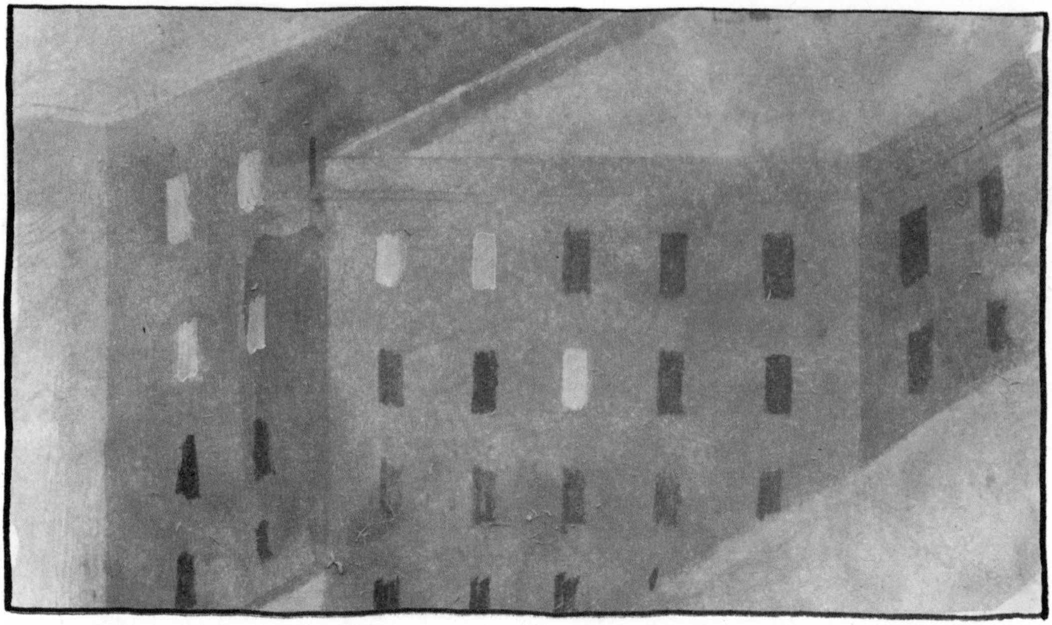

I WENT WITH A PERMANENT SENSE OF SHAME.

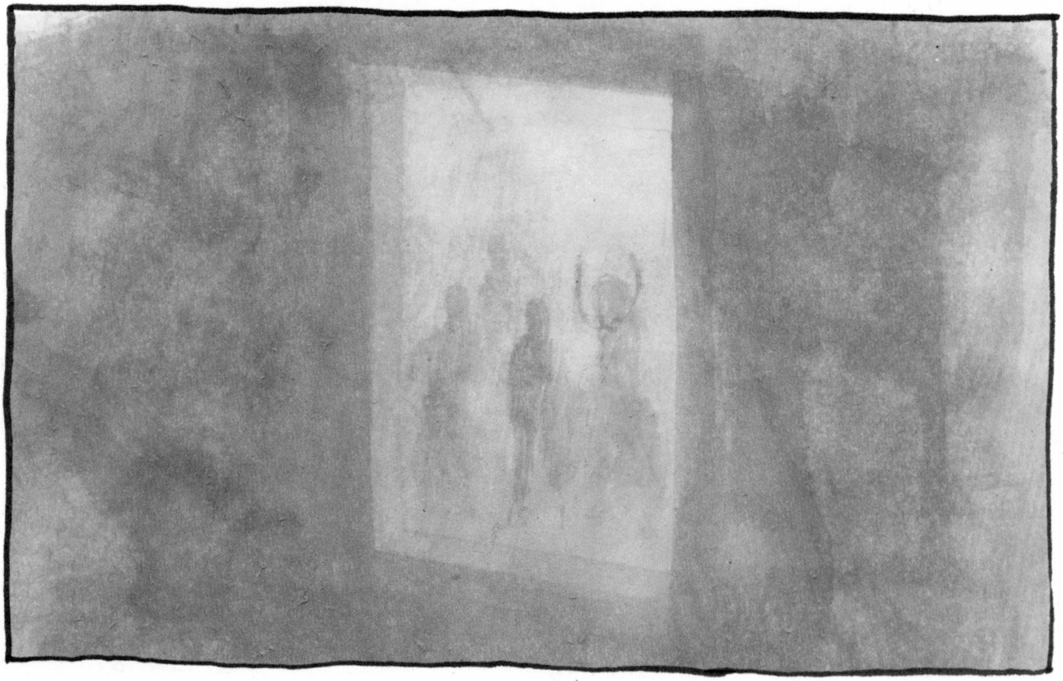

THOSE WHO KNEW HOW TO DANCE DANCED AND THOSE WHO DIDN'T LEARNED.

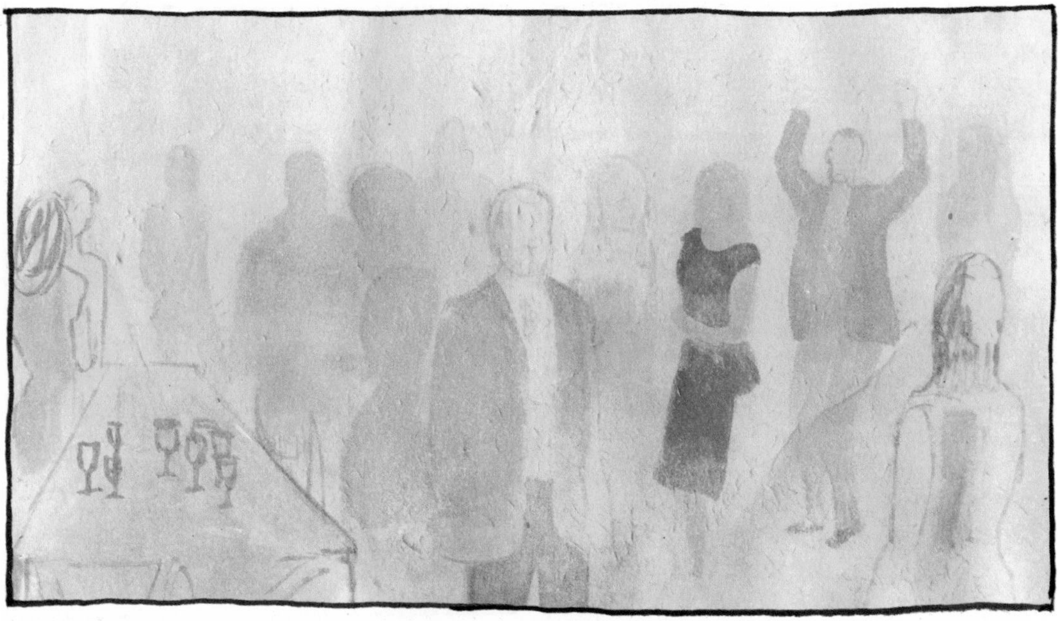

I FELT FRAGILE, EXPOSED TO EVERYTHING.

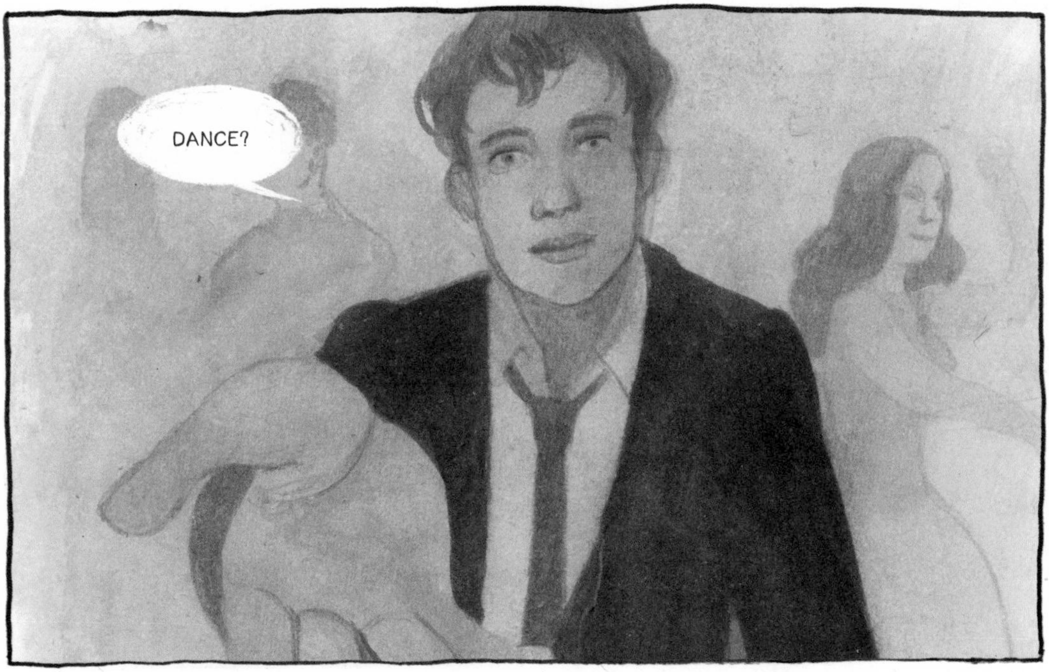
DANCE?

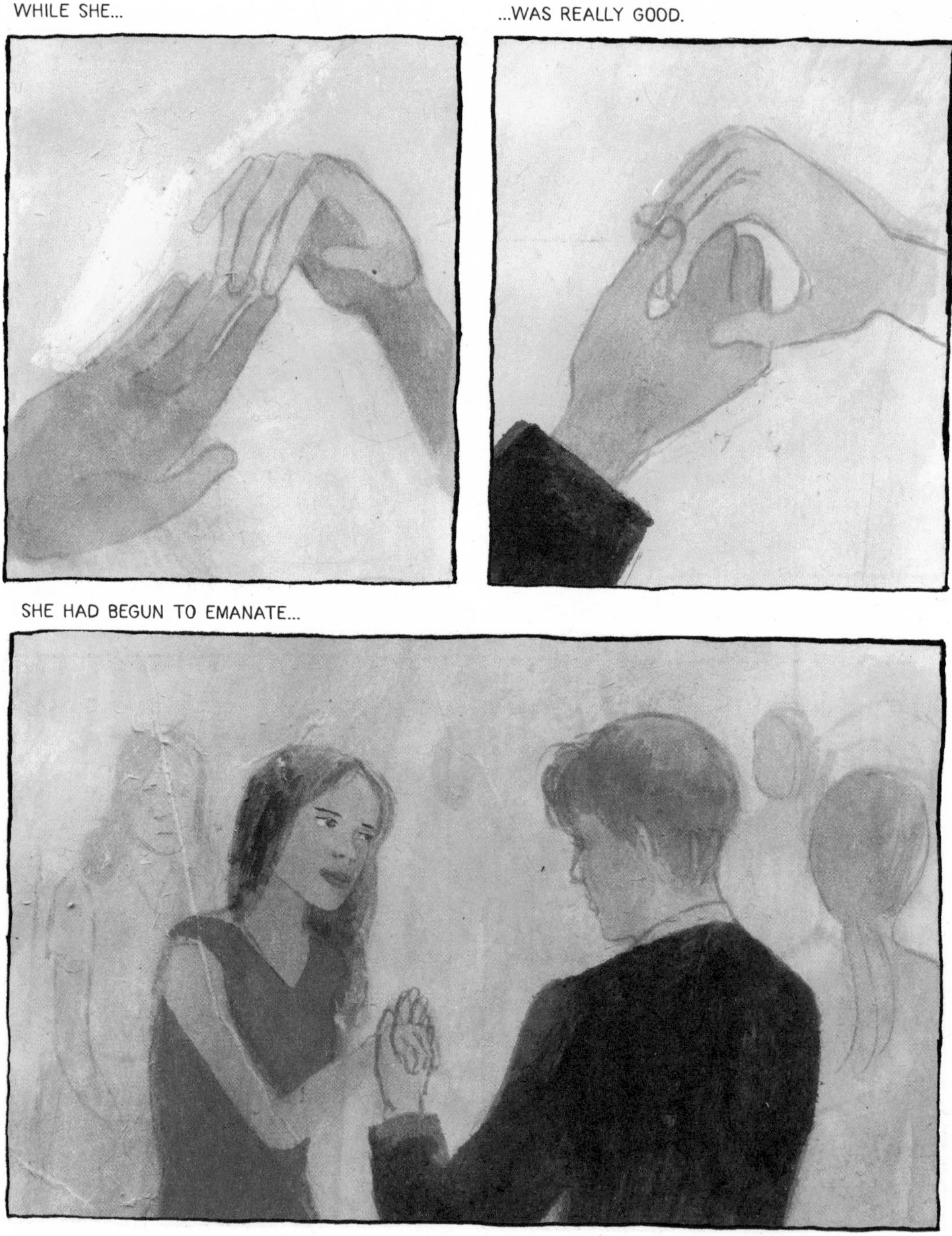
WHILE SHE...
...WAS REALLY GOOD.
SHE HAD BEGUN TO EMANATE...

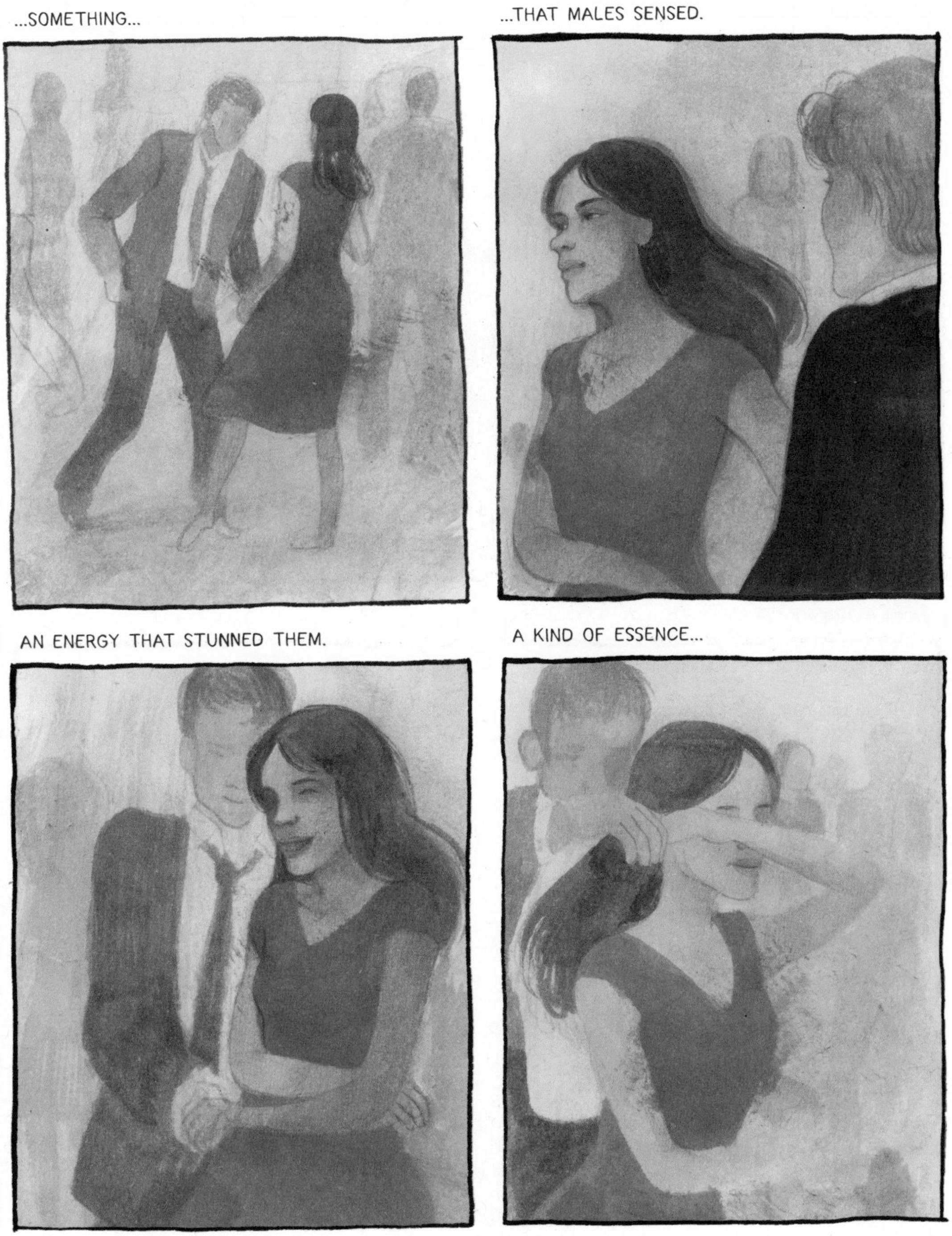
...SOMETHING...
...THAT MALES SENSED.
AN ENERGY THAT STUNNED THEM.
A KIND OF ESSENCE...

...SEDUCTIVE...

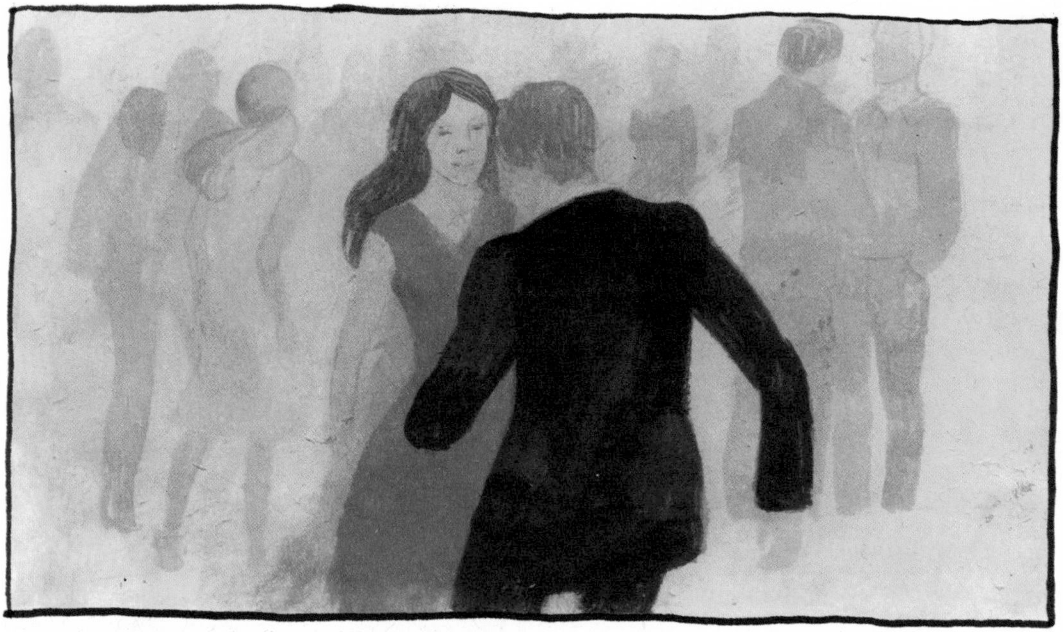

...AND DANGEROUS.

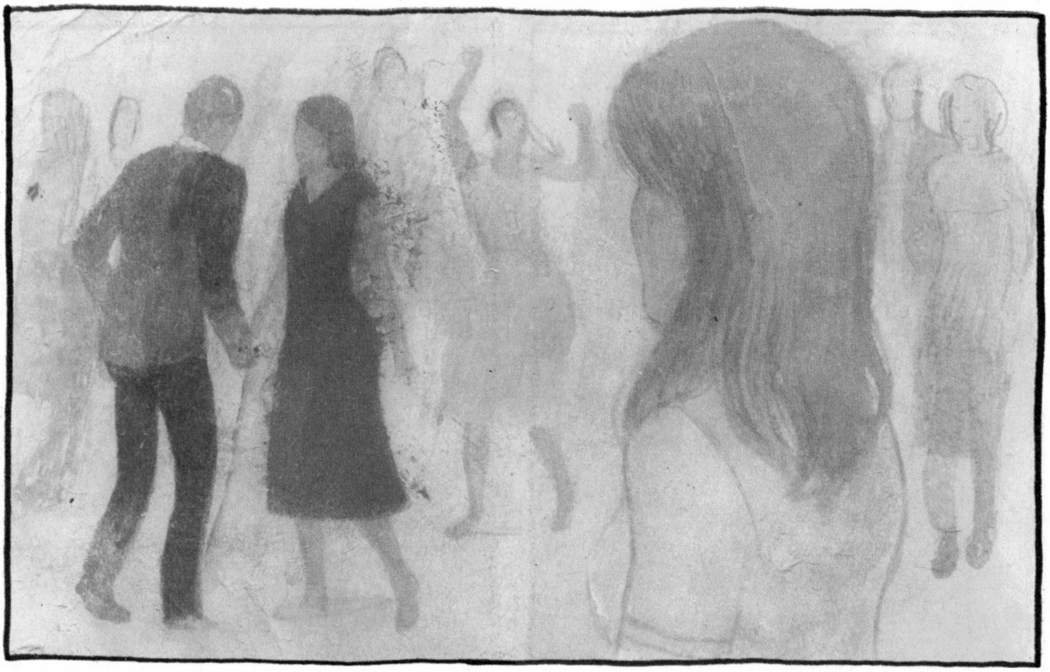

I REALIZED THAT THE BOYS, LOOKING AT HER, SAW MUCH MORE THAN I DID.

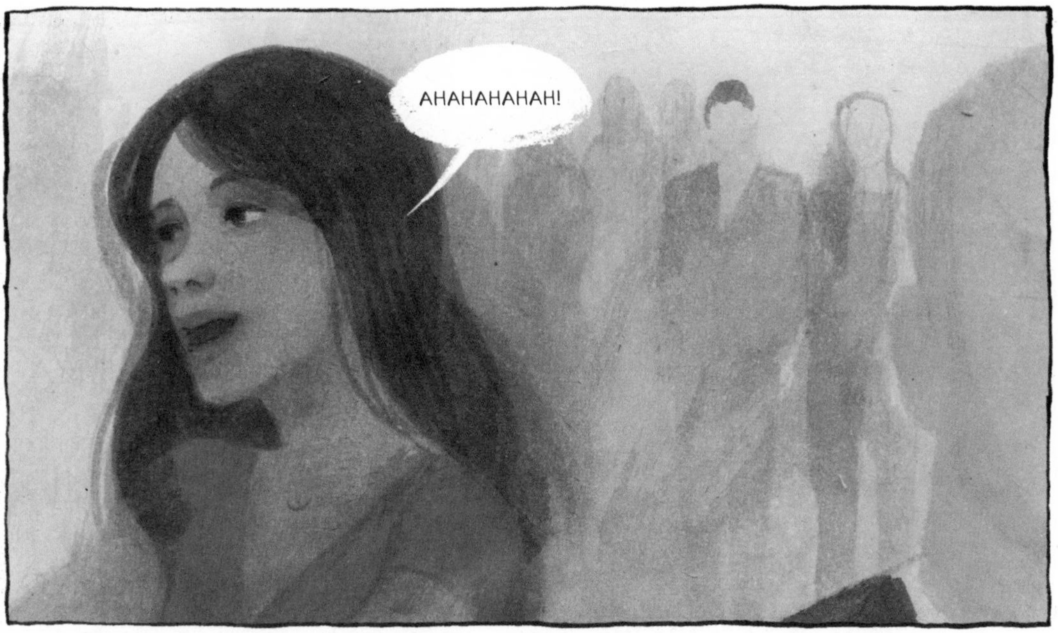
AHAHAHAHAH!

ENZO, ESPECIALLY.

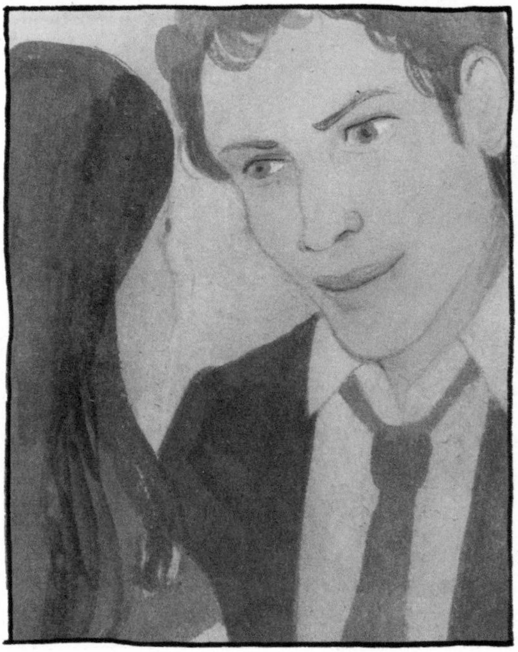

BUT ALSO STEFANO, THE SON OF DON ACHILLE.

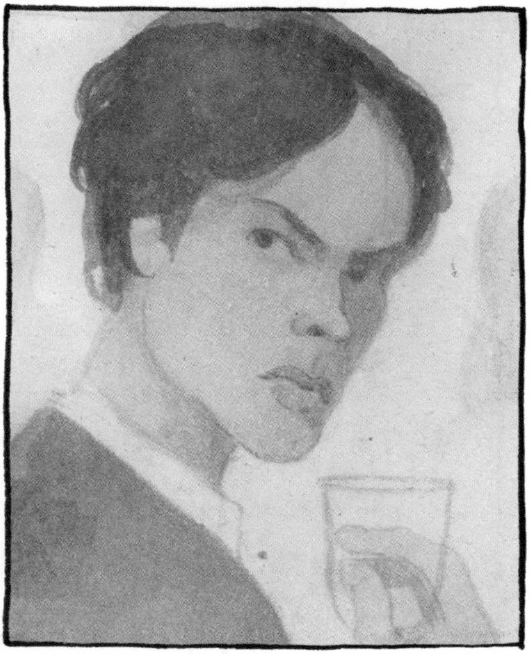

EVEN THE SOLARA BROTHERS HAD EYES ONLY FOR HER.

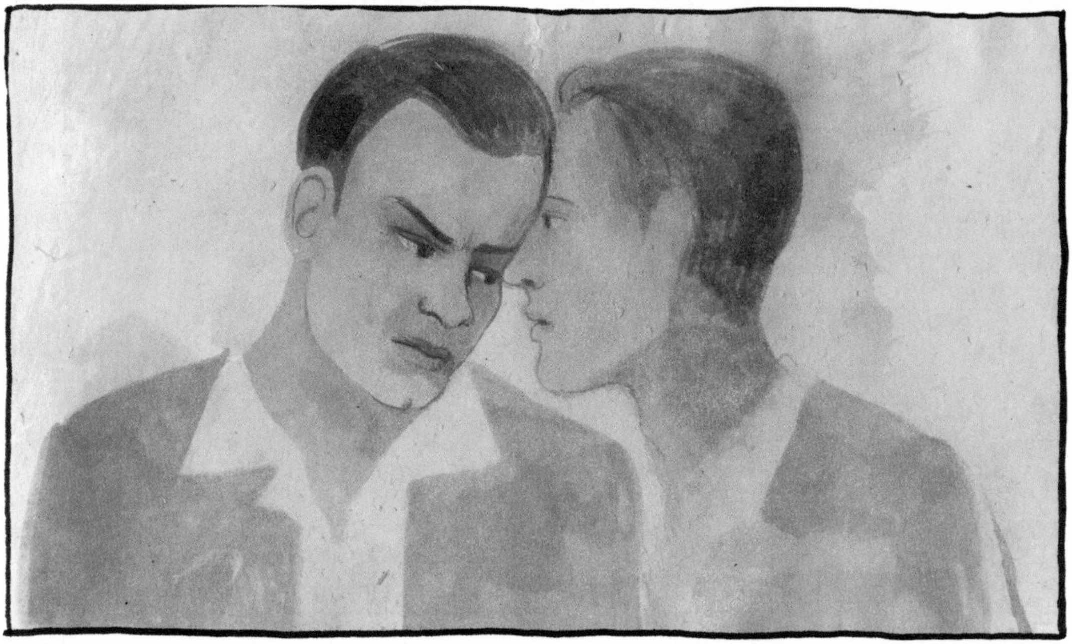

PASQUALE, CARMEN'S BROTHER, COULDN'T STOP STARING AT HER.

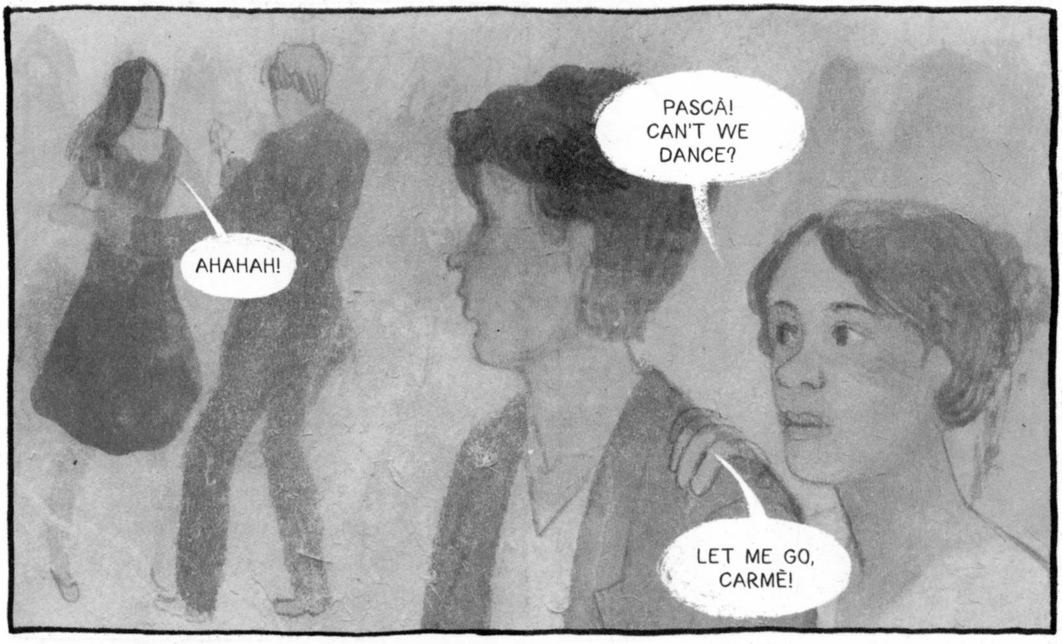
AHAHAH!
PASCÀ! CAN'T WE DANCE?
LET ME GO, CARMÈ!

LILA TOOK IN THEIR LOOKS,

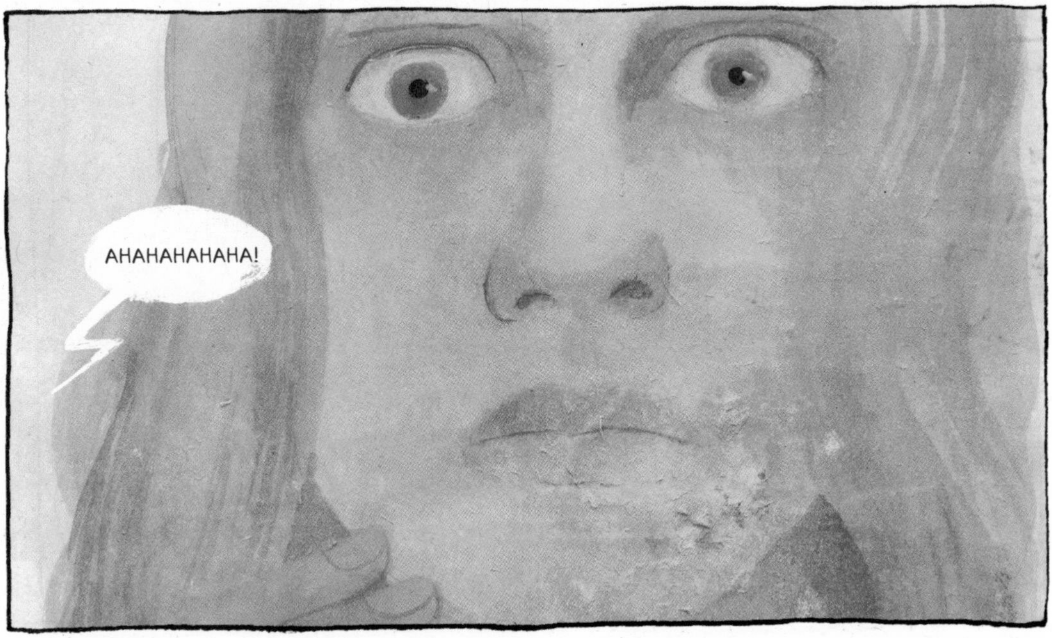
AHAHAHAHAHA!

SHE GRABBED THEIR HANDS AS IF THEY WERE MERELY HANDS.

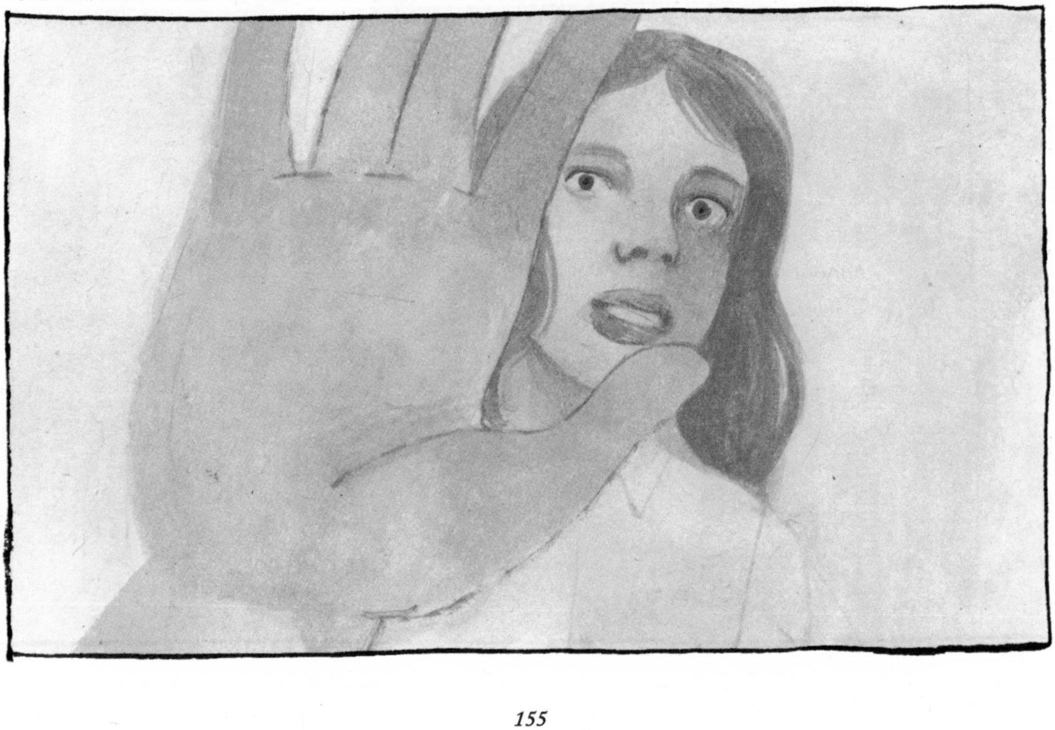

AS IF BEYOND THERE WERE NOT ARMS,

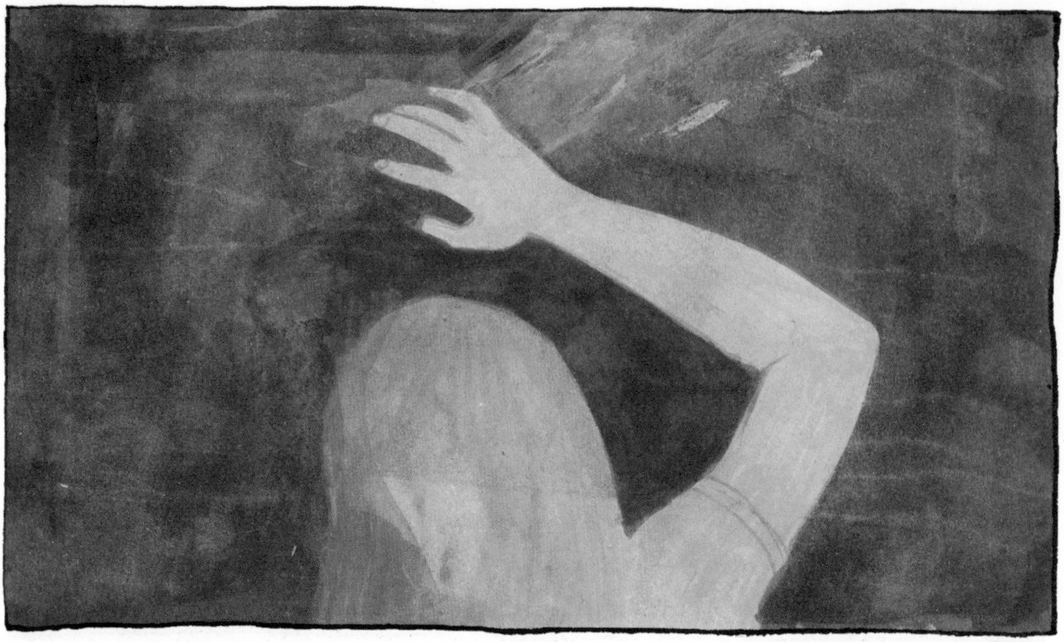

BODIES.

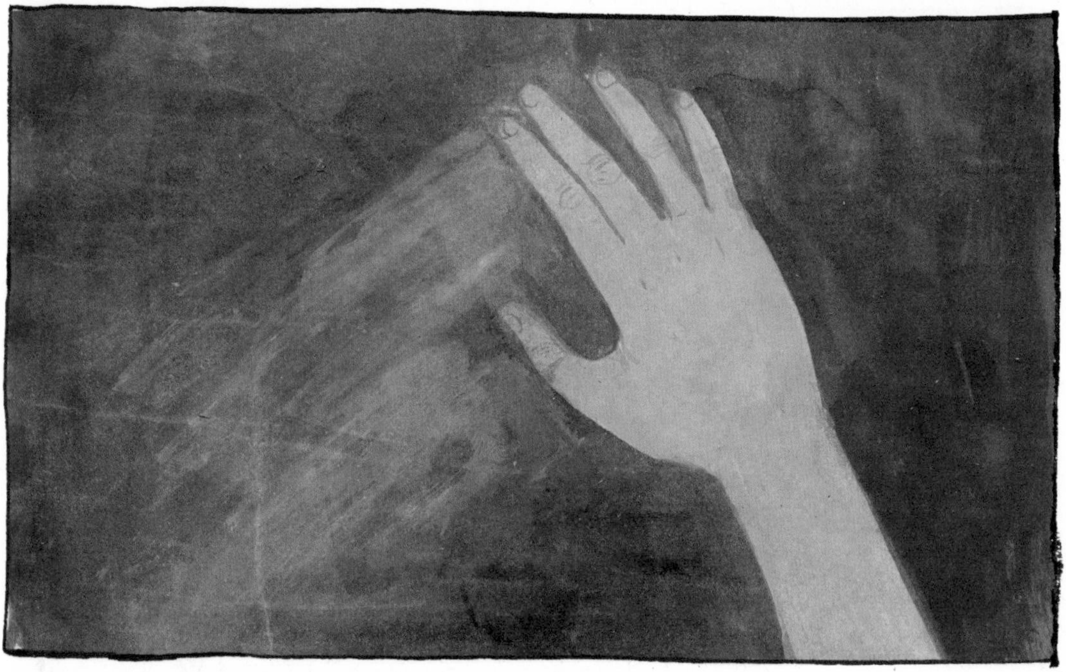

THE ONLY THING THAT COUNTED FOR HER WAS DANCING.

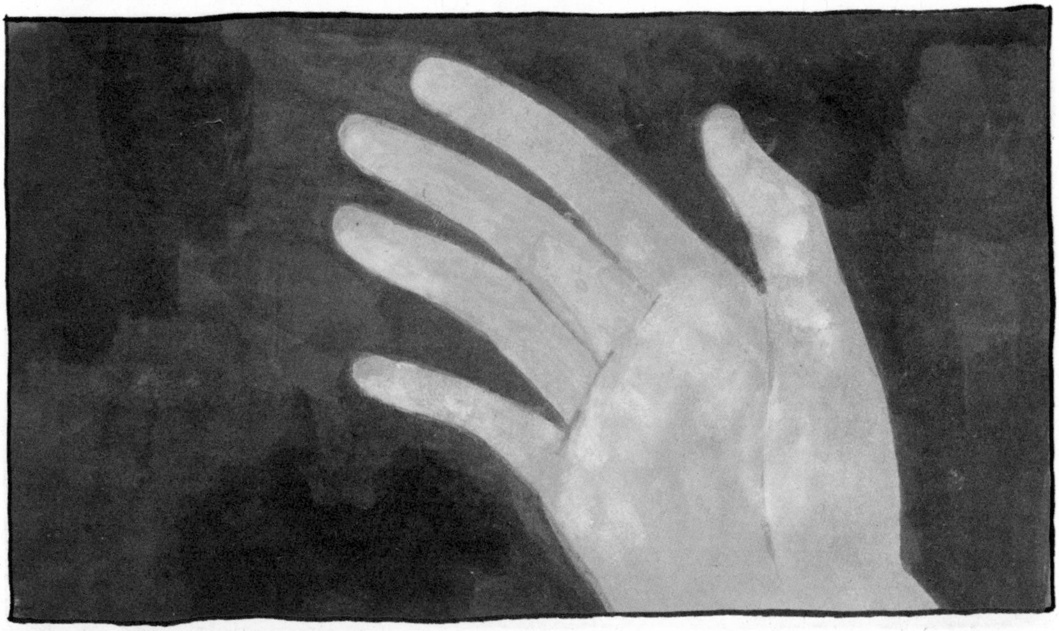

I COULDN'T BEAR HER, I WANTED HER TO DISAPPEAR!

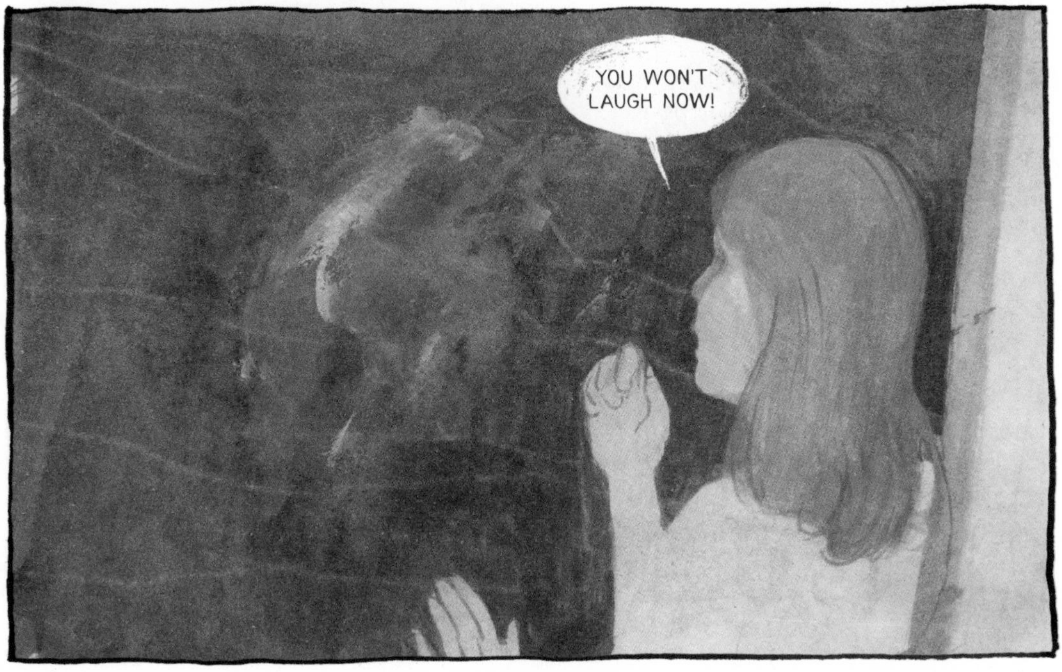
YOU WON'T LAUGH NOW!

BUT LILA WOULDN'T BE ELIMINATED.

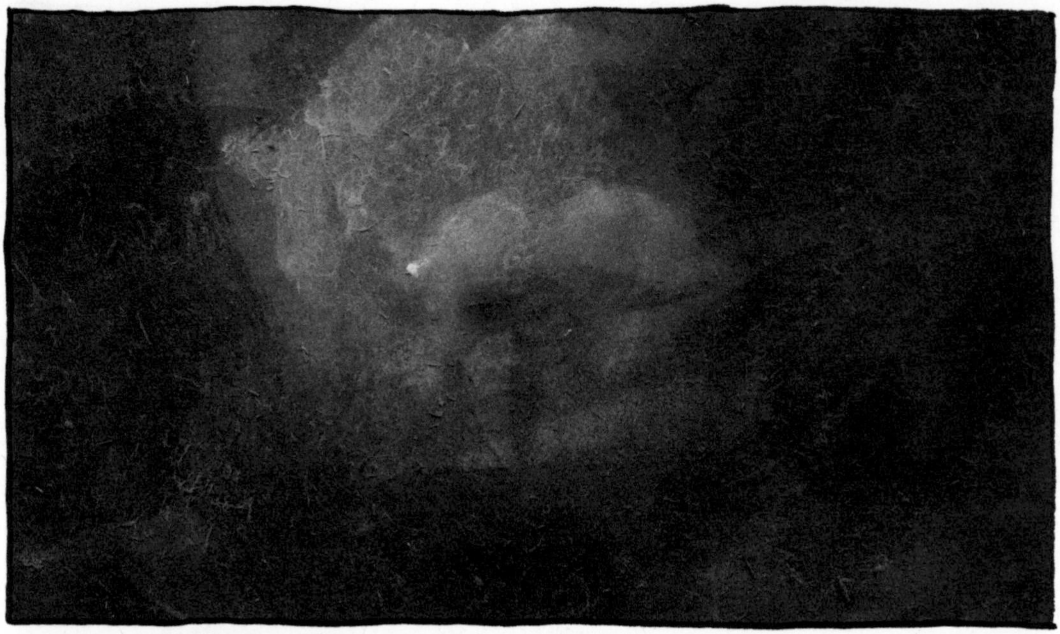

SHE ALWAYS CAME BACK.

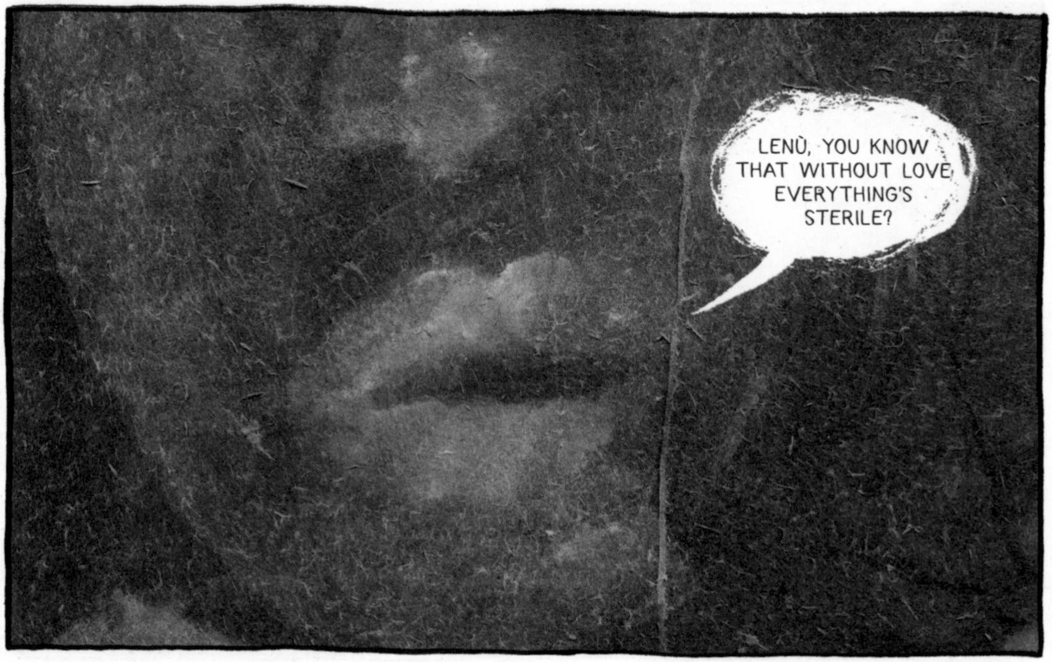
LENÙ, YOU KNOW THAT WITHOUT LOVE EVERYTHING'S STERILE?

I LISTENED TO HER WORDS, I REPEATED THEM, I MADE THEM MINE. EVEN AT SCHOOL.

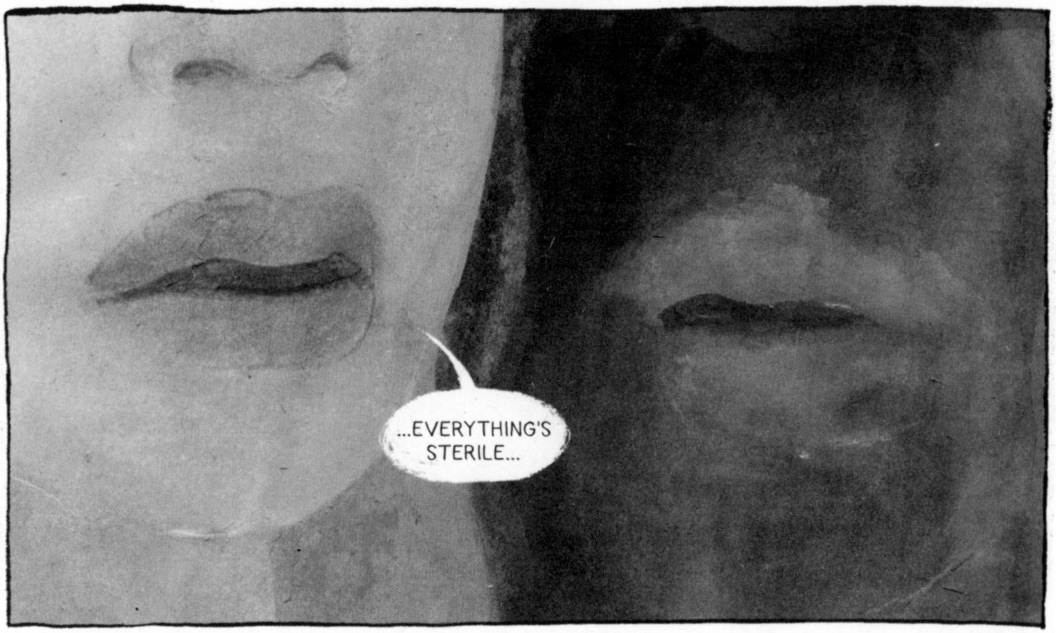
...EVERYTHING'S STERILE...

I WAS IN HIGH SCHOOL NOW.

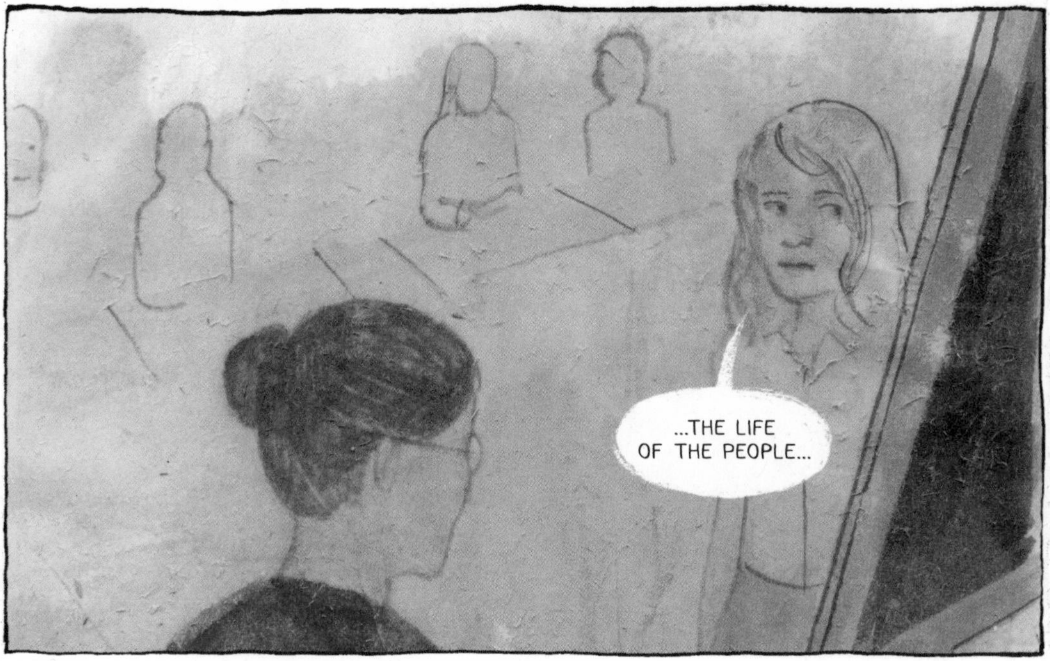
...THE LIFE OF THE PEOPLE...

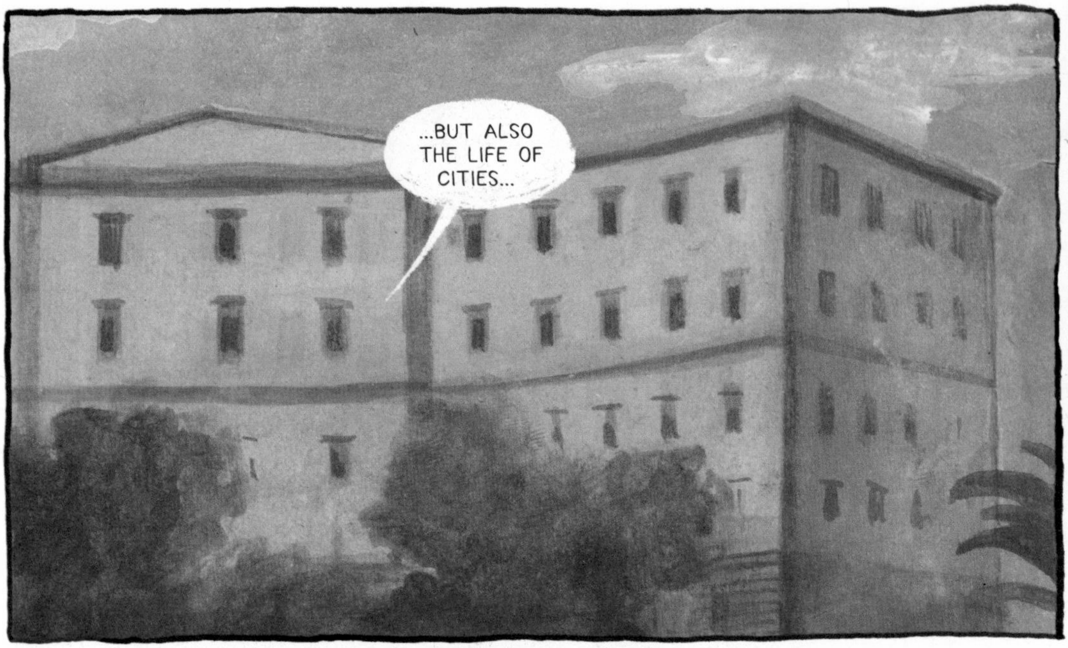
...BUT ALSO THE LIFE OF CITIES...

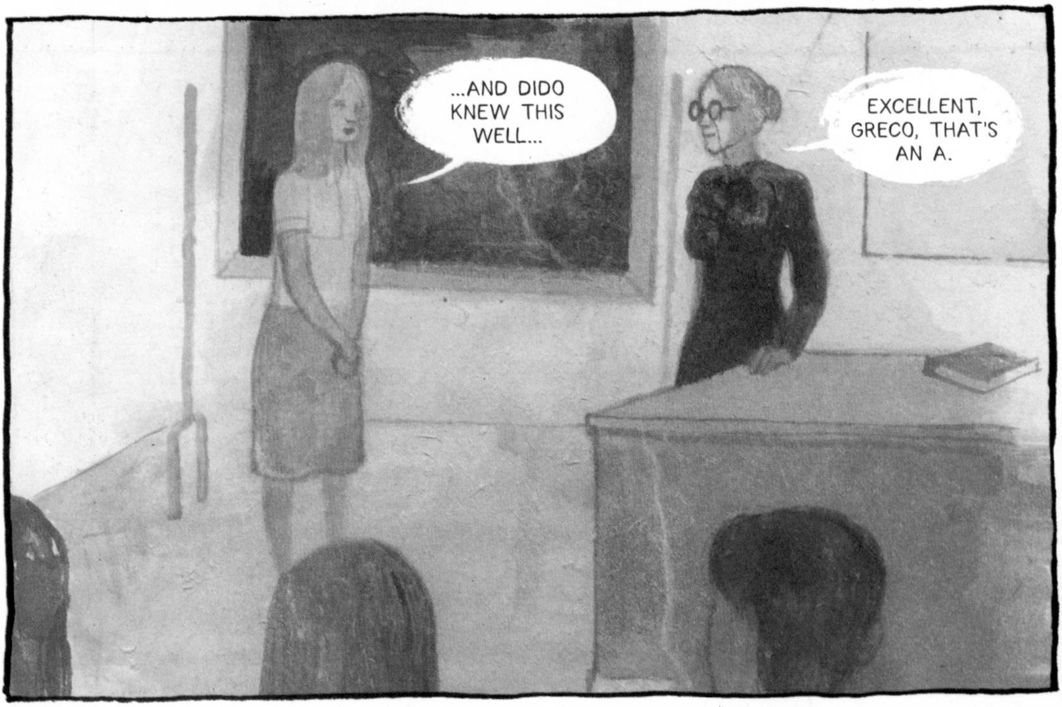
...AND DIDO KNEW THIS WELL...
EXCELLENT, GRECO, THAT'S AN A.

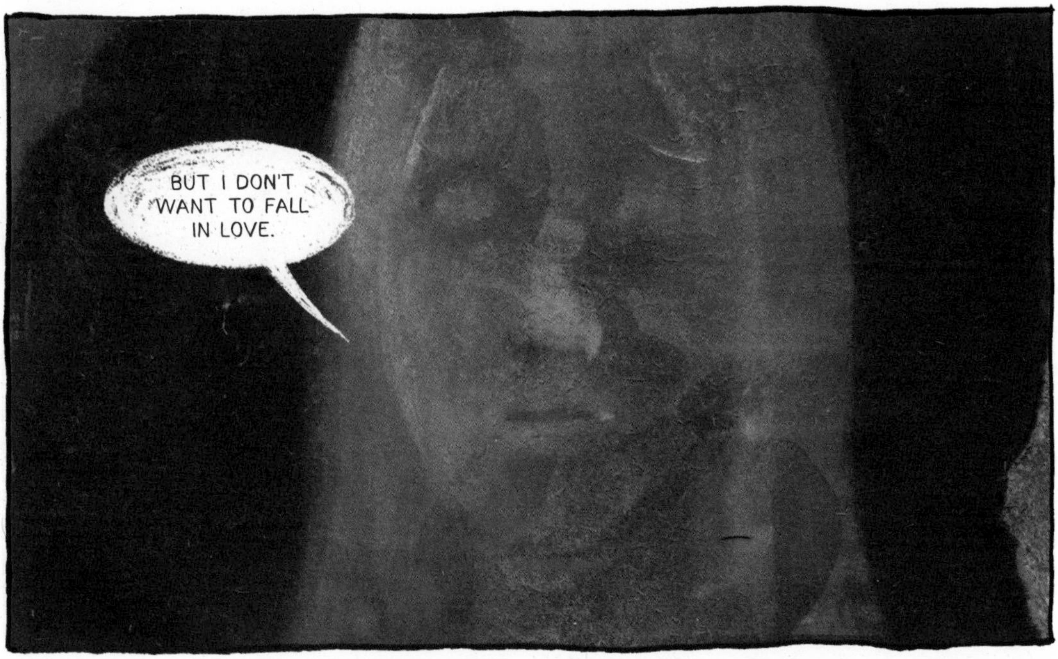
BUT I DON'T WANT TO FALL IN LOVE.

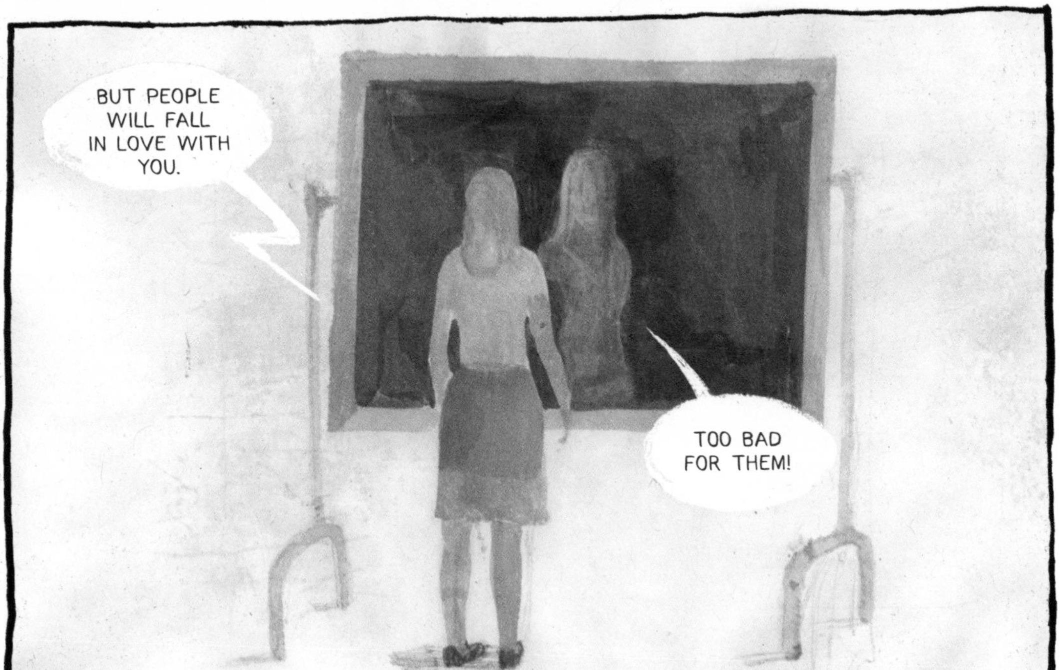
BUT PEOPLE WILL FALL IN LOVE WITH YOU.
TOO BAD FOR THEM!

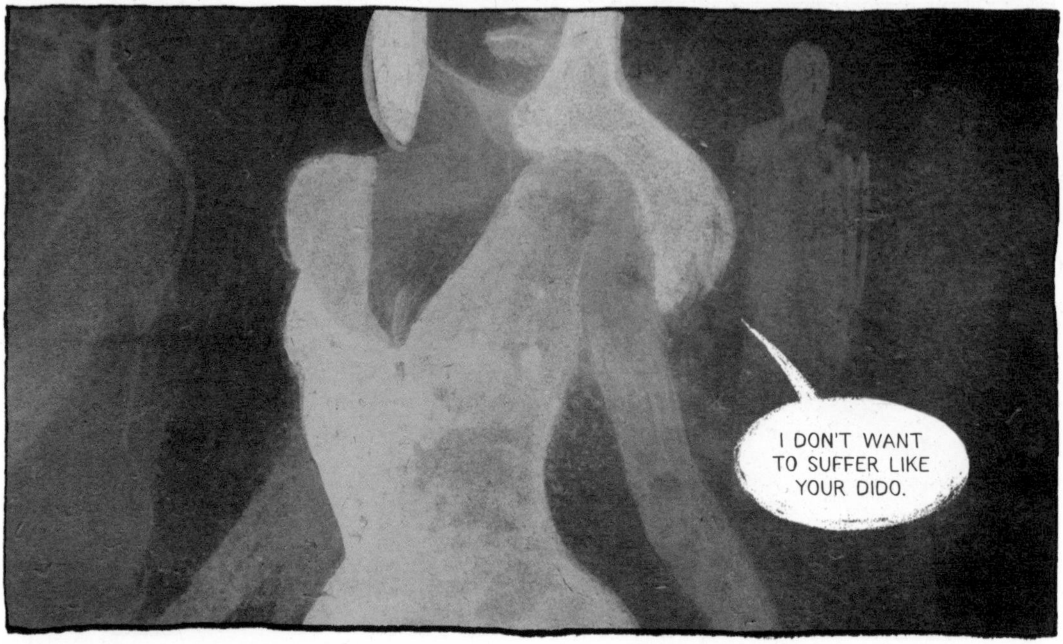
I DON'T WANT TO SUFFER LIKE YOUR DIDO.

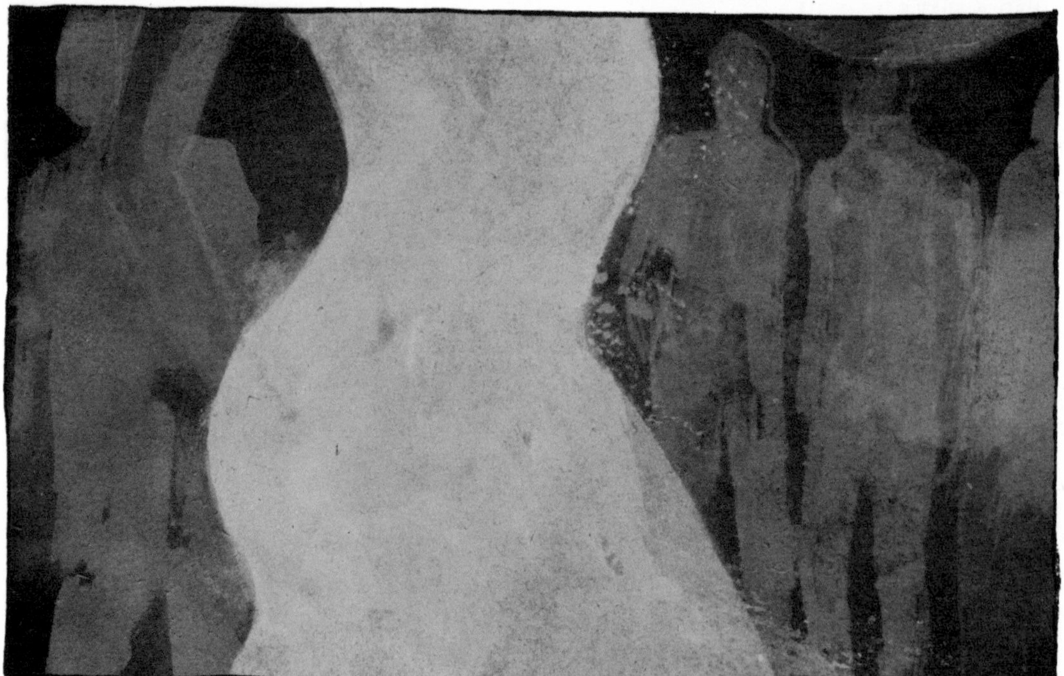

BUT I DIDN'T BELIEVE HER.

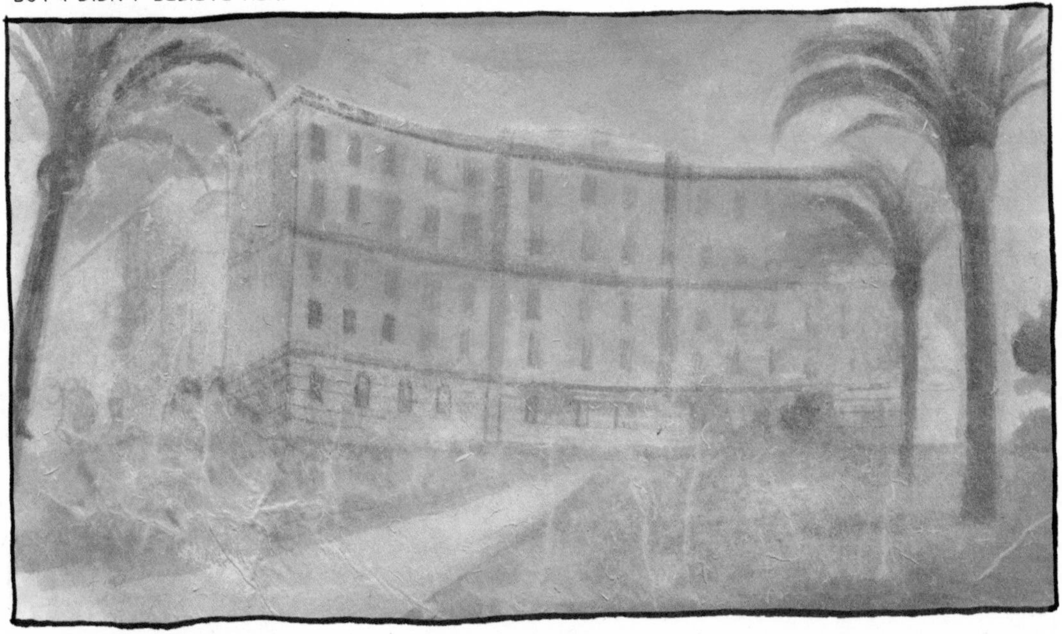

I HAD A SINGLE THOUGHT.

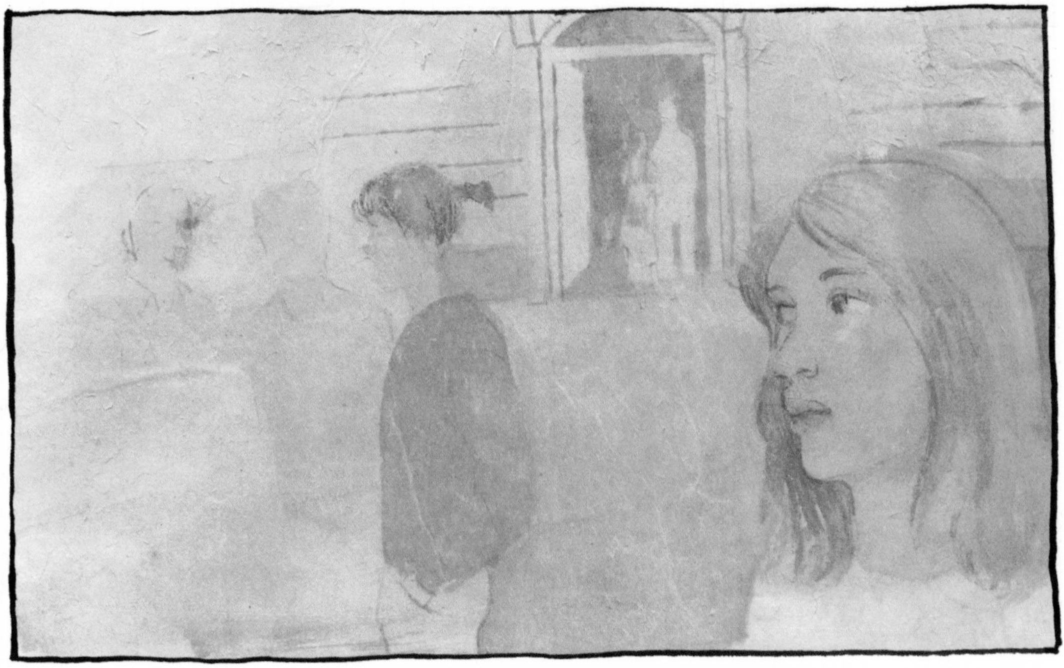

TO FIND A BOYFRIEND BEFORE SHE DID.

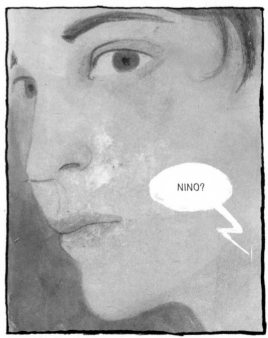

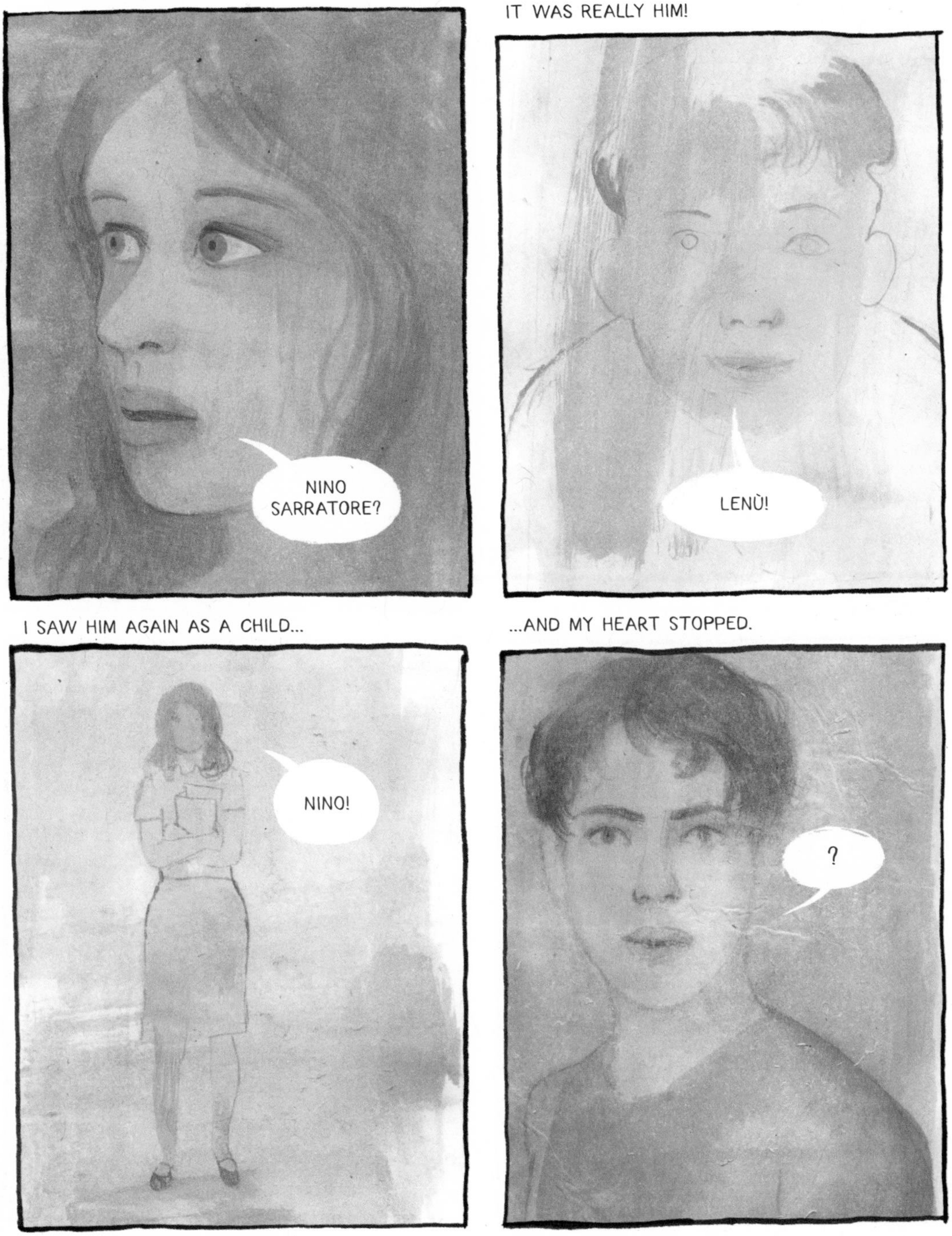
NINO SARRATORE?
IT WAS REALLY HIM!
LENÙ!
I SAW HIM AGAIN AS A CHILD...
NINO!
...AND MY HEART STOPPED.
?

HIS FAMILY HAD LEFT THE NEIGHBORHOOD YEARS EARLIER...

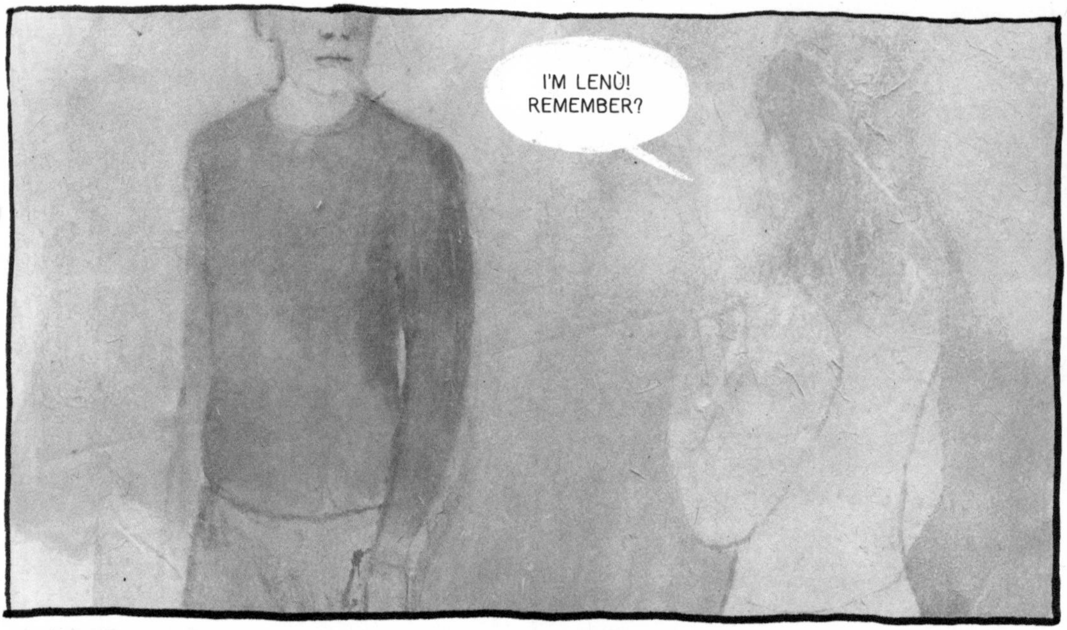
I'M LENÙ!
REMEMBER?

IN ELEMENTARY SCHOOL HE'D ASKED ME TO MARRY HIM: HOW COULD HE NOT RECOGNIZE ME NOW?

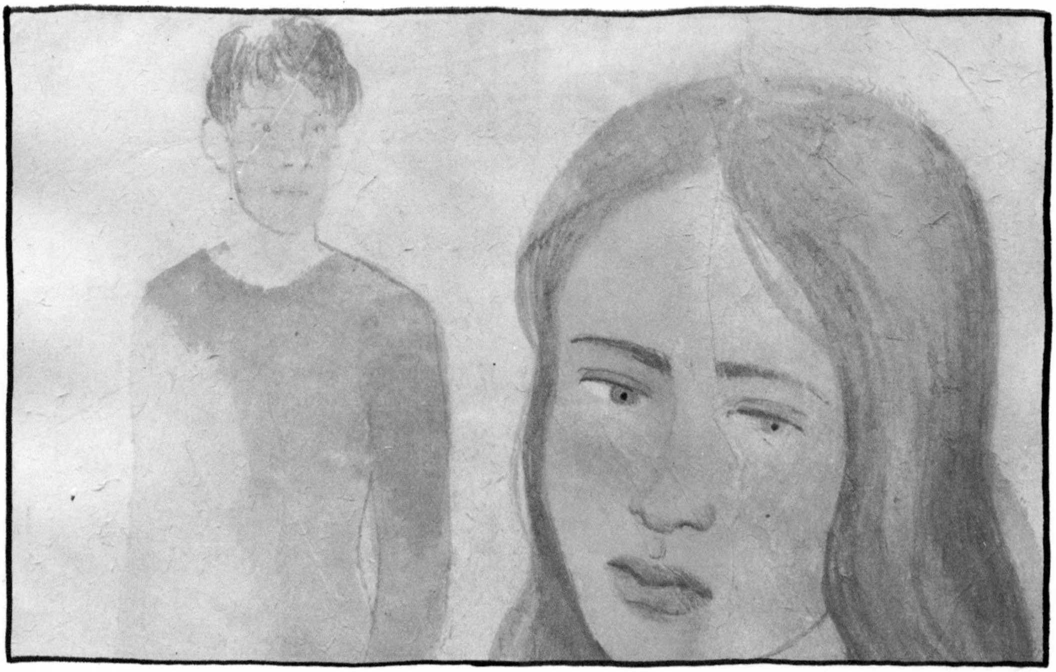

I HAD A VIOLENT IMPULSE TO SEE LILA RIGHT AWAY.

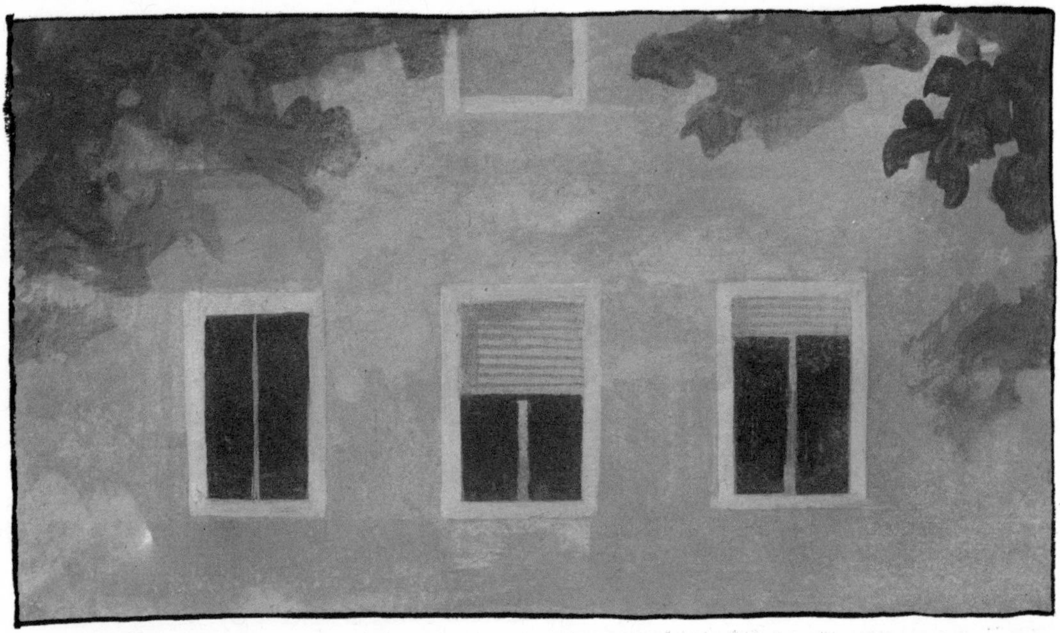

I WANTED TO TELL HER ABOUT NINO.

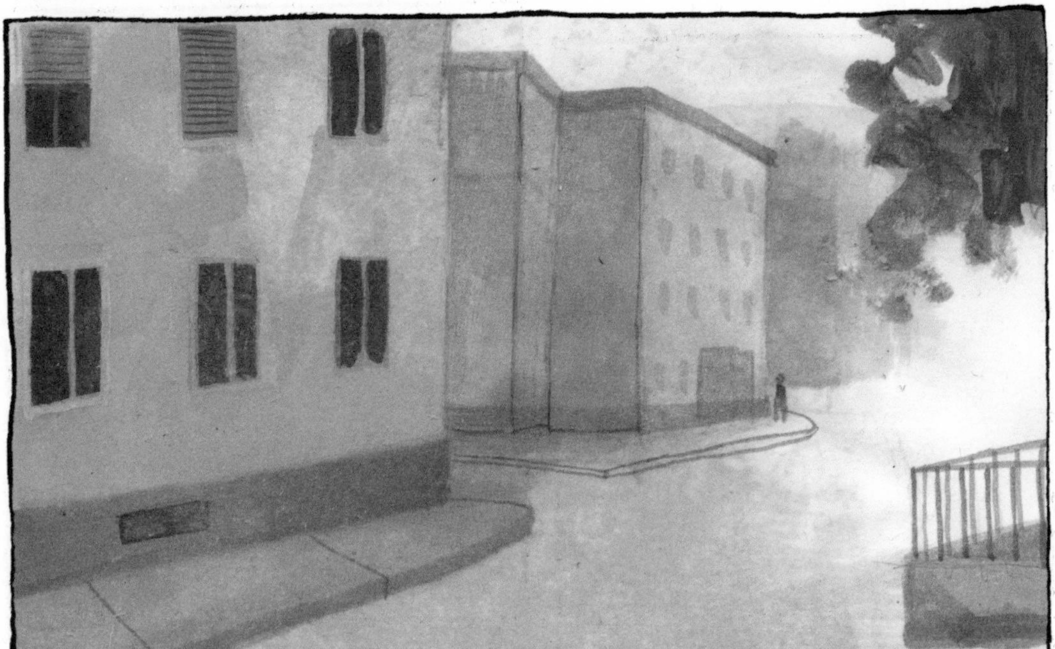

BUT I ALREADY KNEW WHAT WOULD HAPPEN: SHE WOULD ASK TO SEE HIM AND HE...

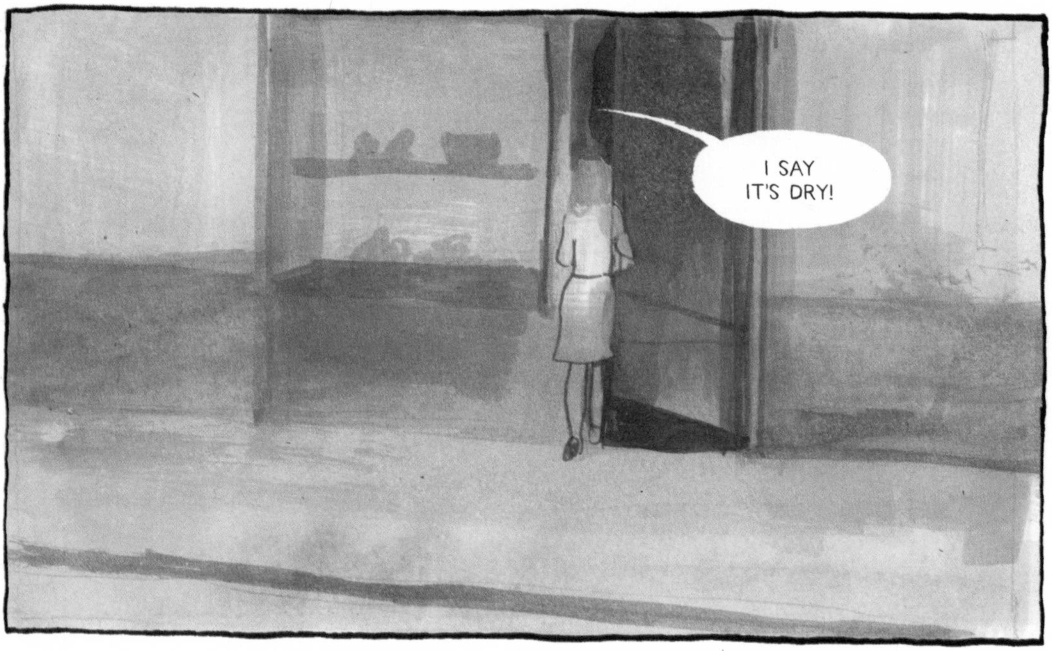
I SAY IT'S DRY!

...WOULD FALL IN LOVE WITH HER, LIKE THE REST.

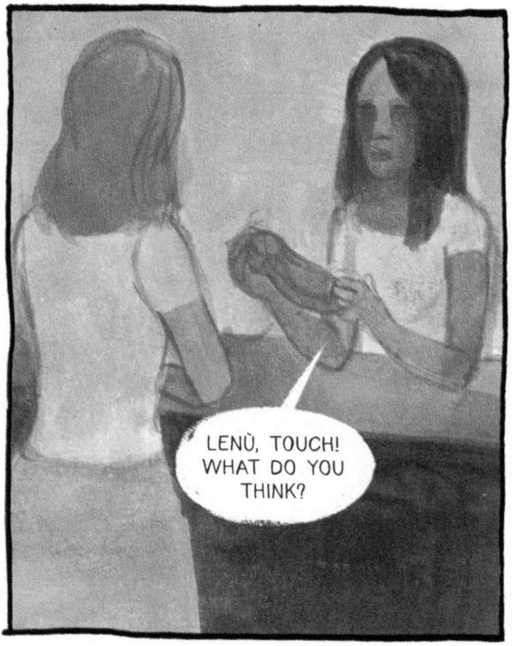
LENÙ, TOUCH! WHAT DO YOU THINK?

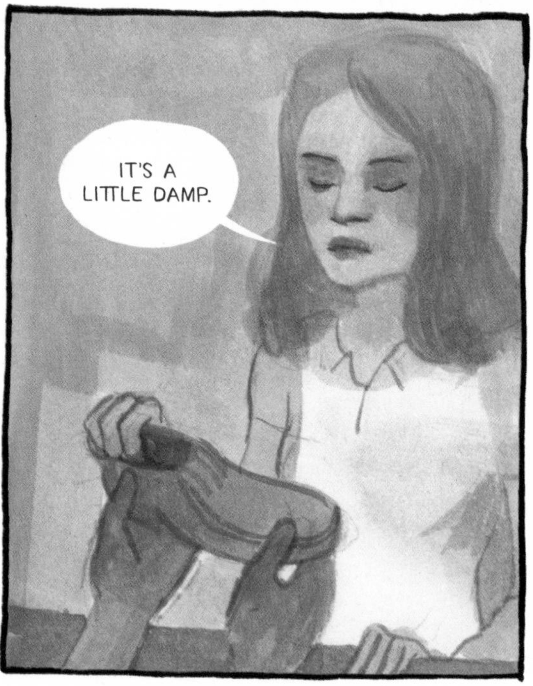
IT'S A LITTLE DAMP.

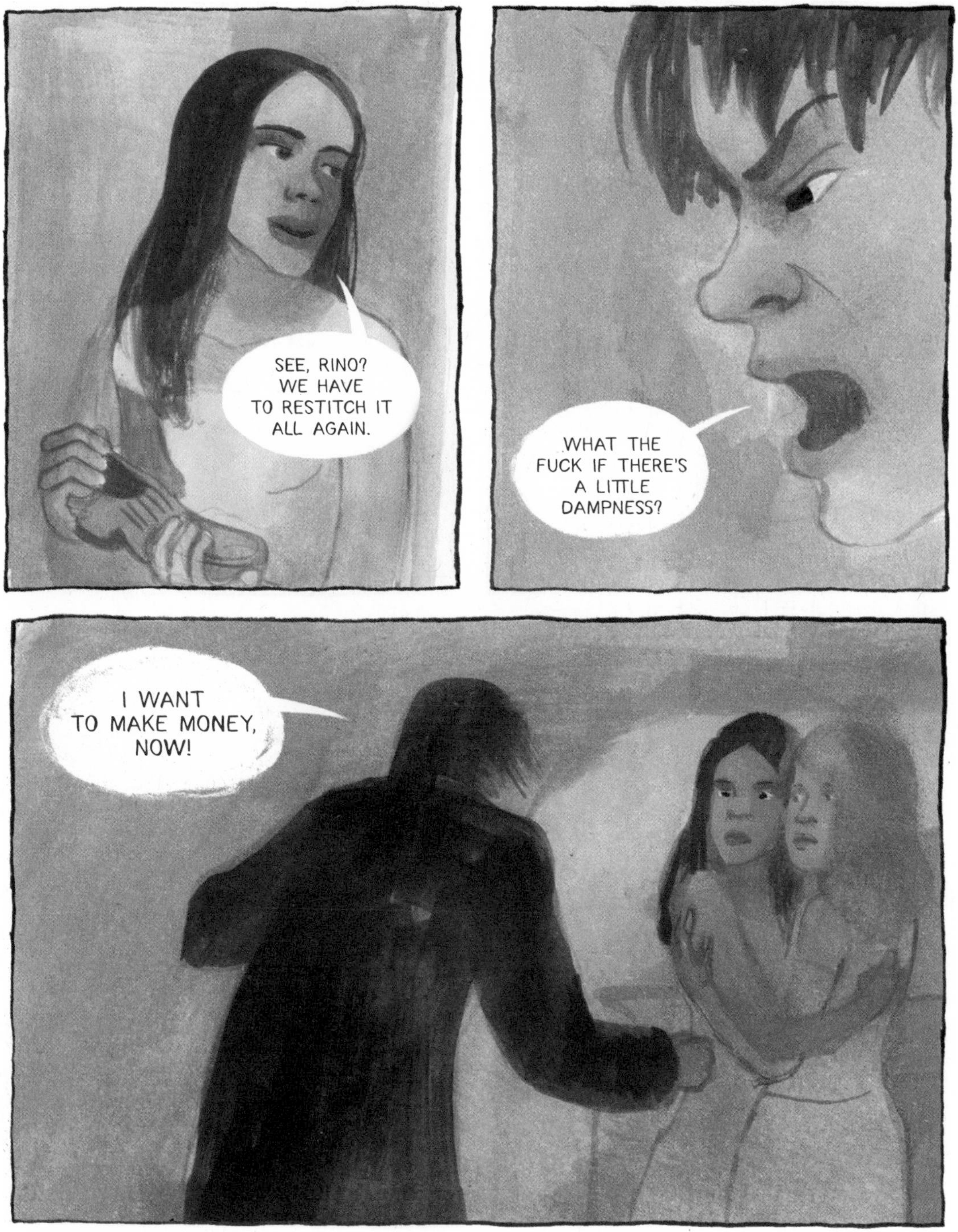
SEE, RINO? WE HAVE TO RESTITCH IT ALL AGAIN.
WHAT THE FUCK IF THERE'S A LITTLE DAMPNESS?
I WANT TO MAKE MONEY, NOW!

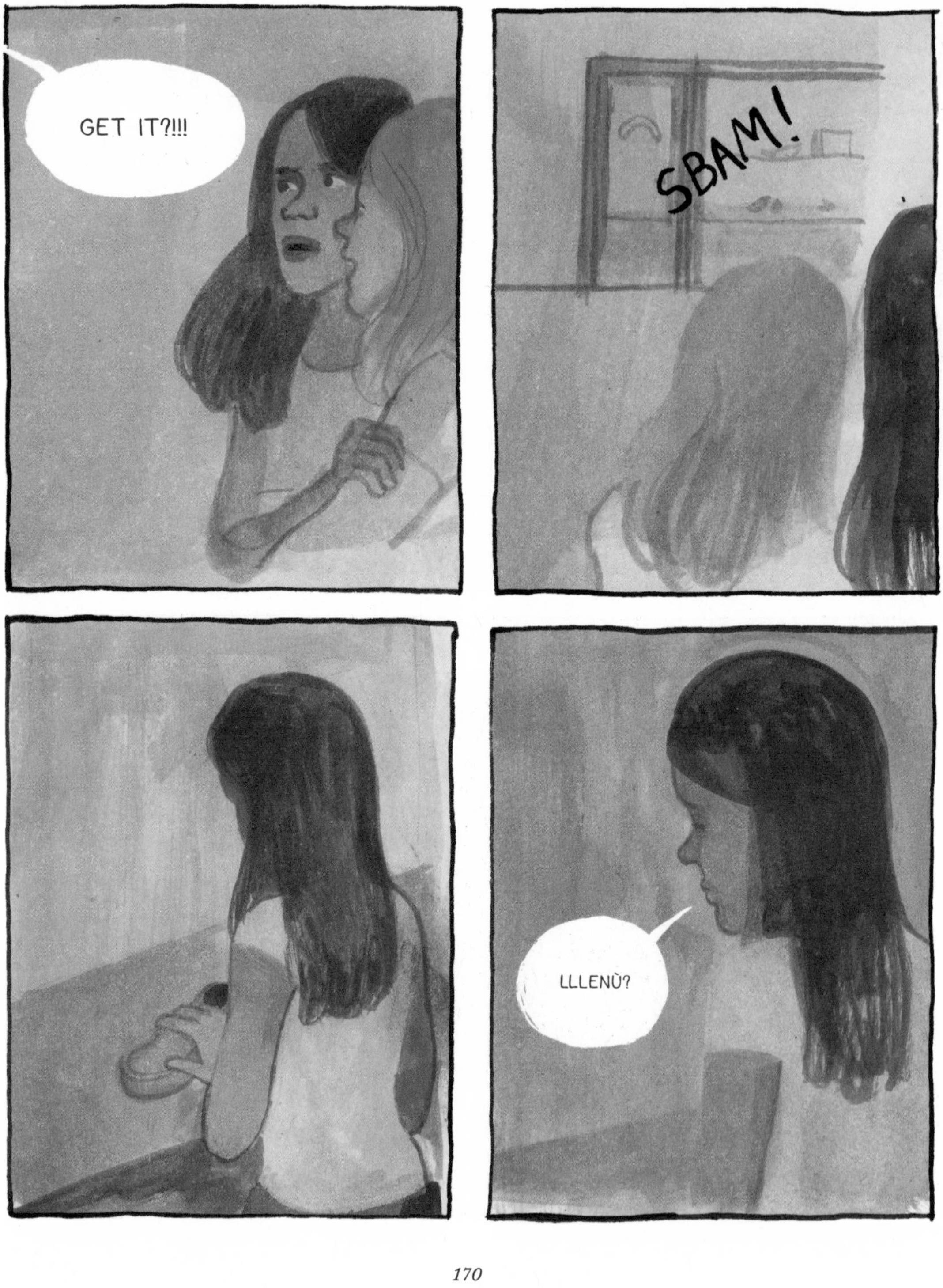
GET IT?!!!
SBAM!
LLLENÙ?

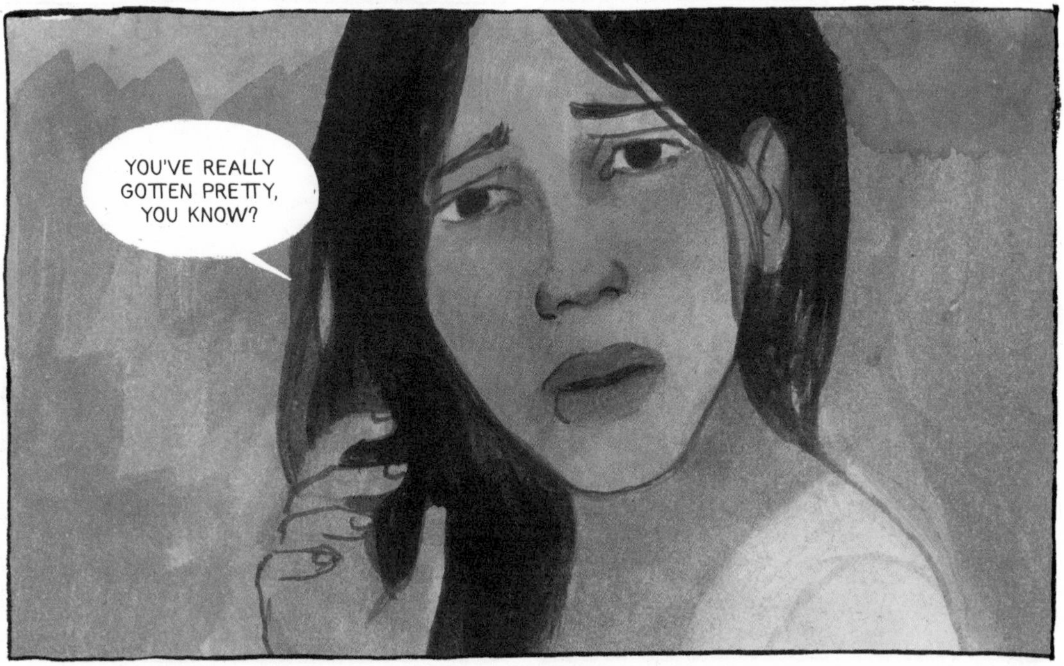
YOU'VE REALLY GOTTEN PRETTY, YOU KNOW?

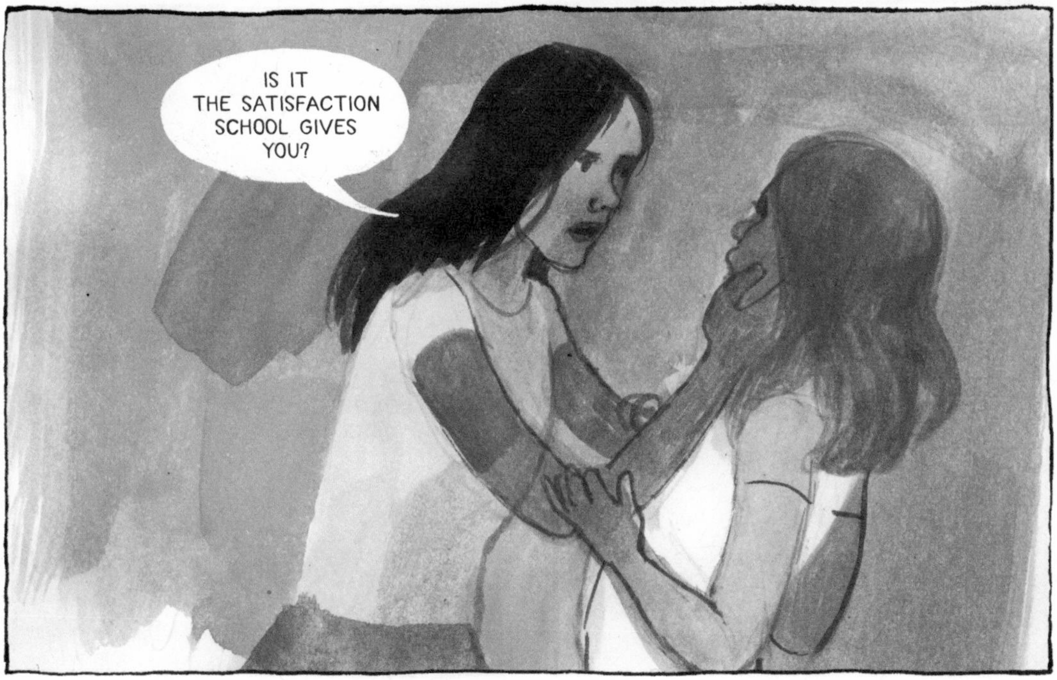
IS IT THE SATISFACTION SCHOOL GIVES YOU?

OR LOVE?

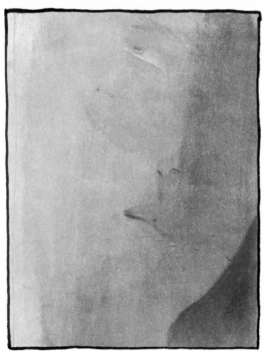

LENÙ, SWEAR WE'LL NEVER LEAVE EACH OTHER!

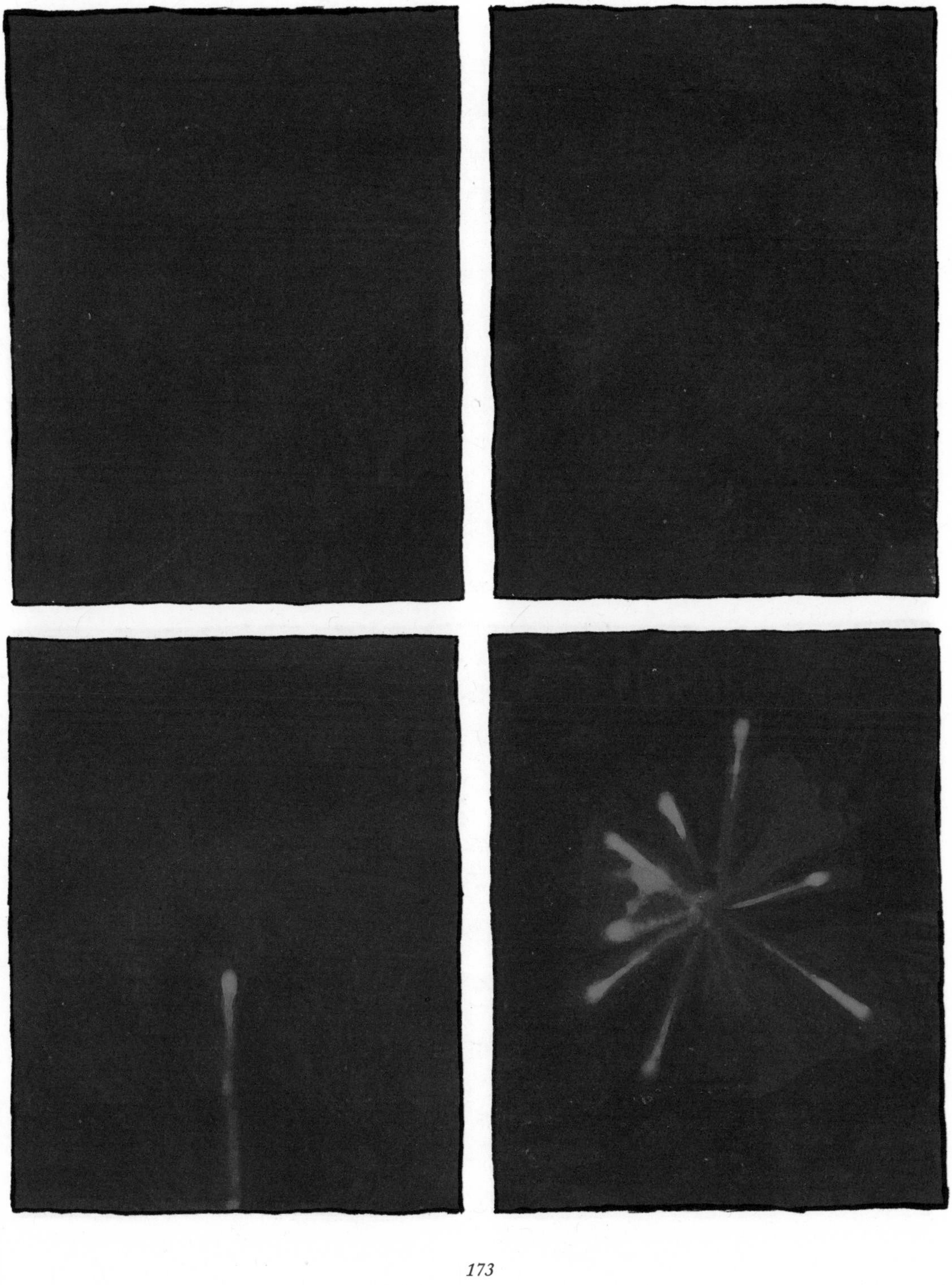

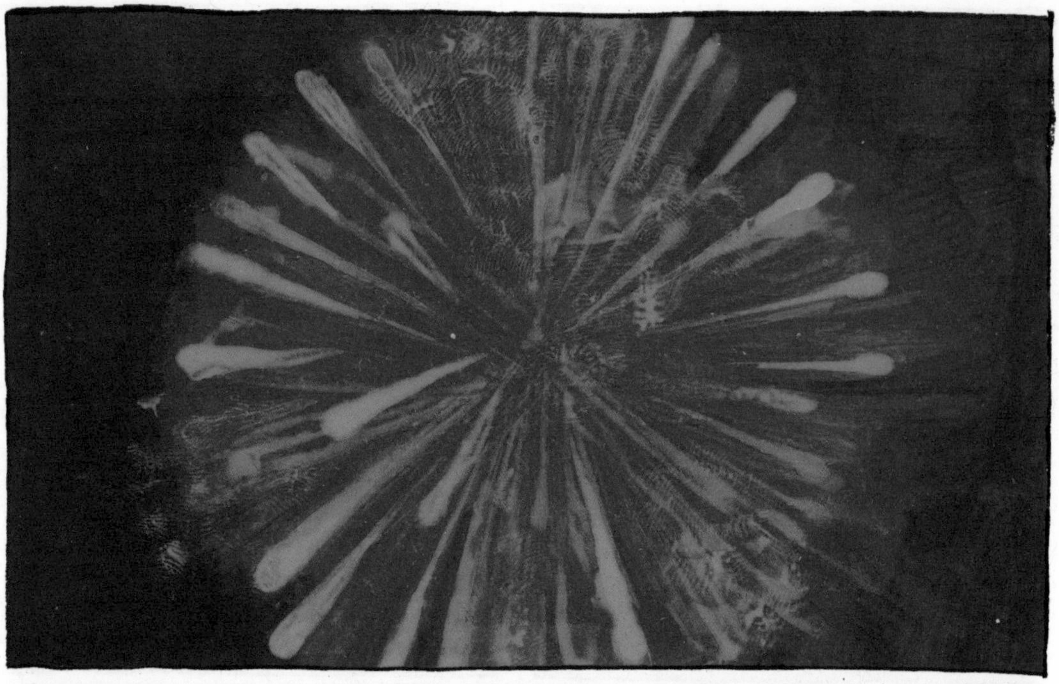

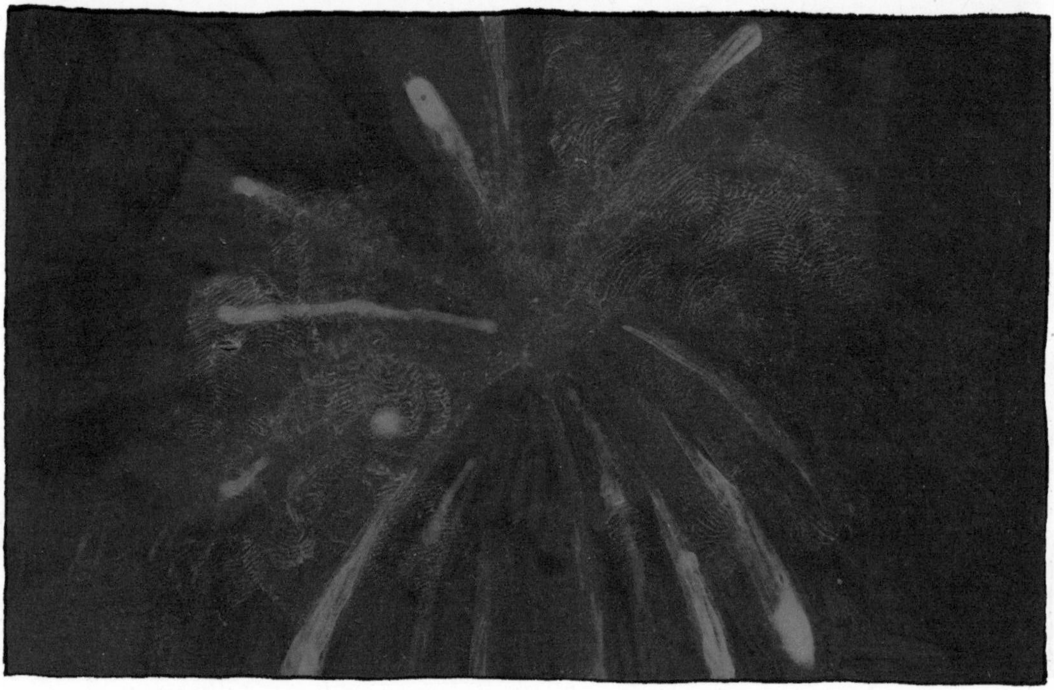

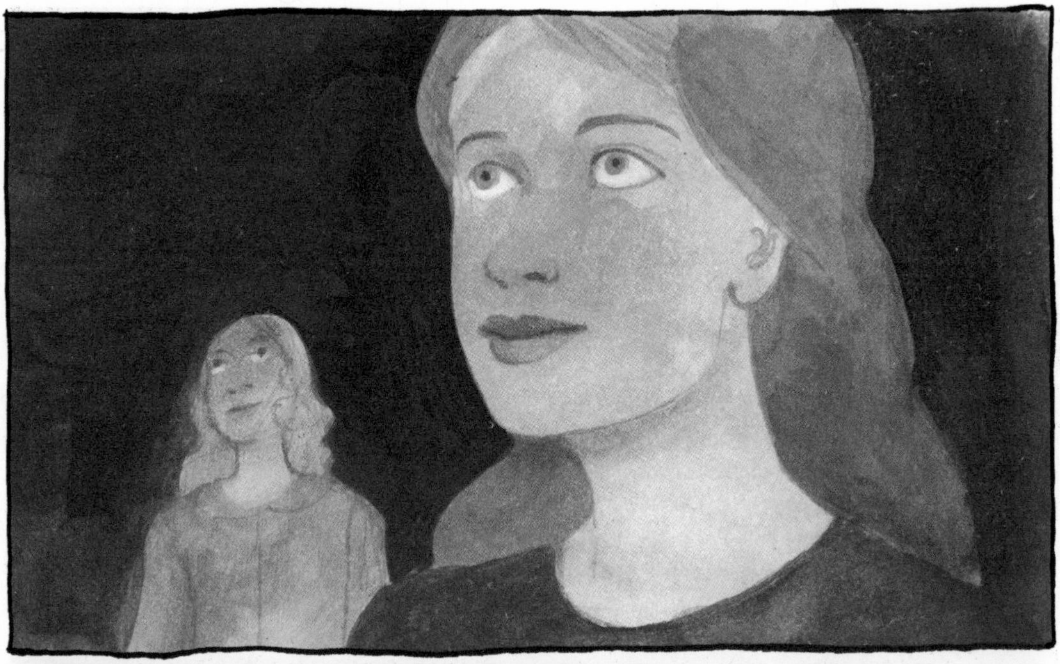

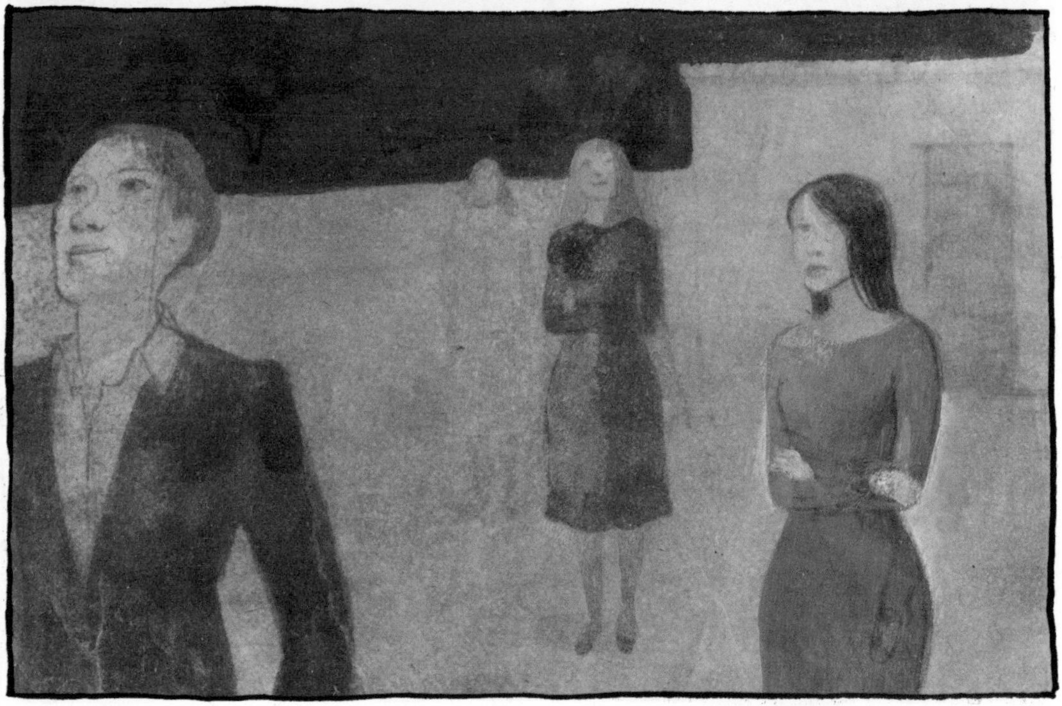

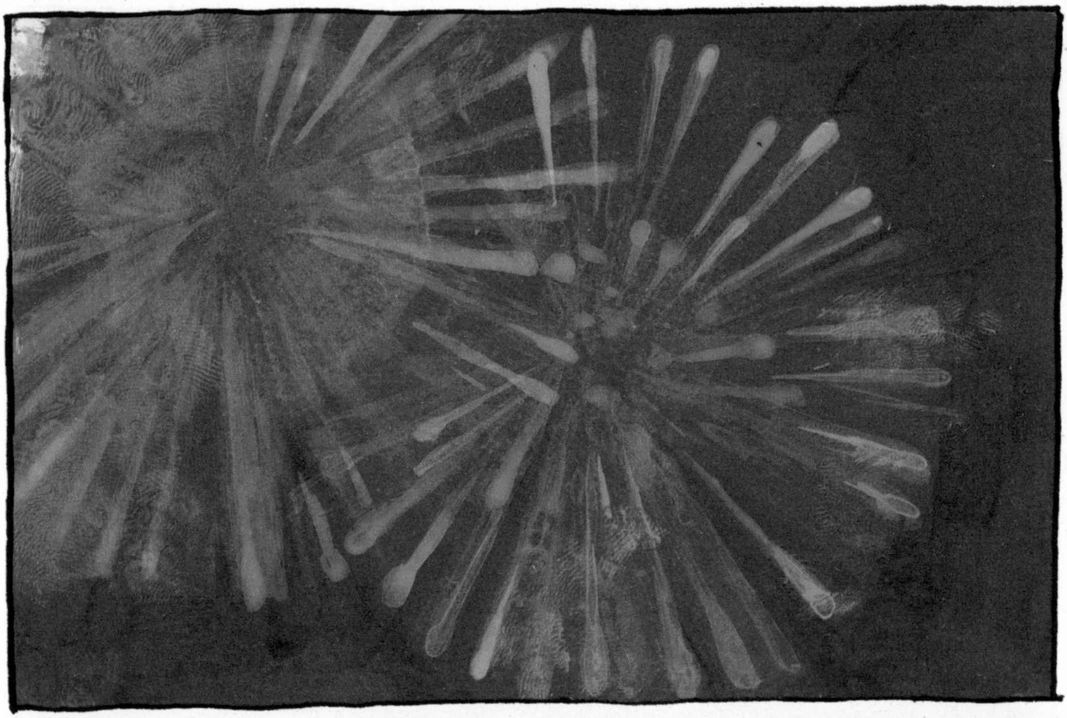

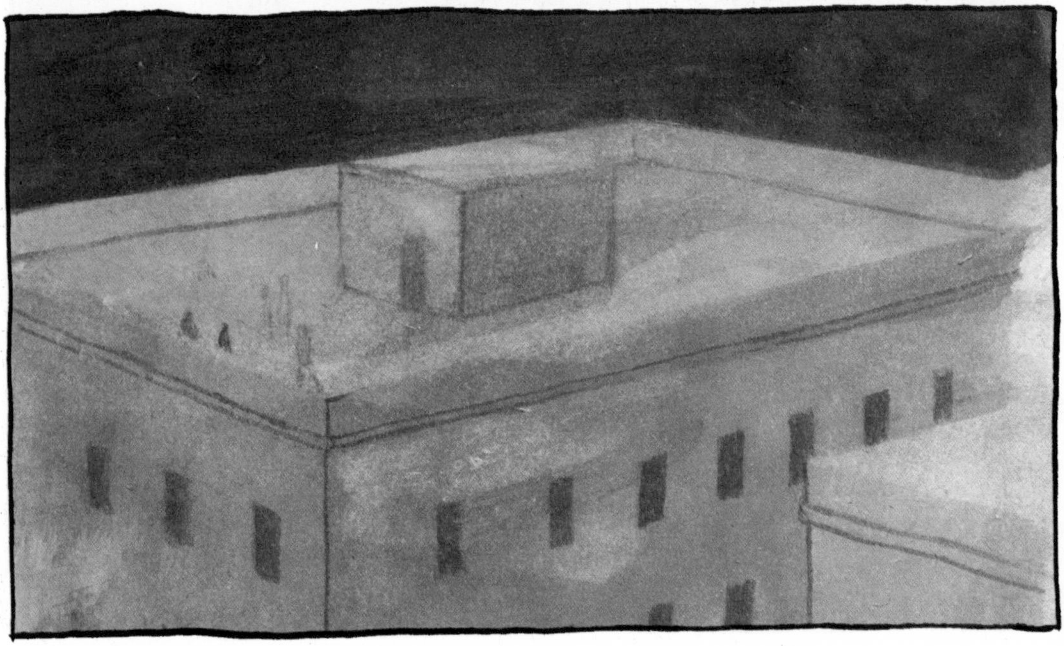

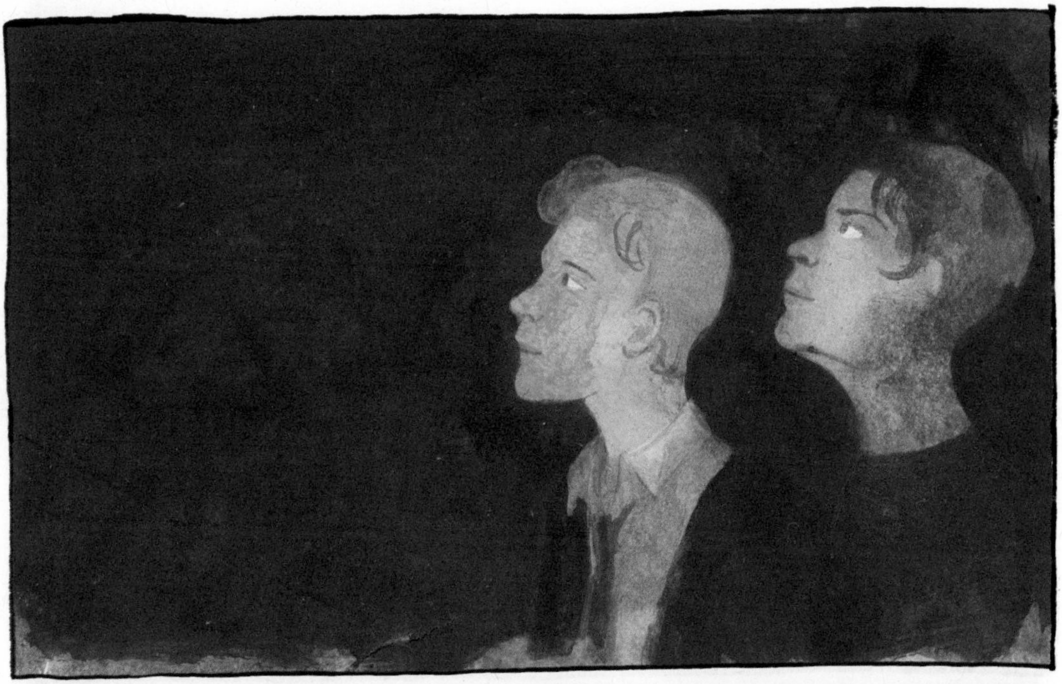

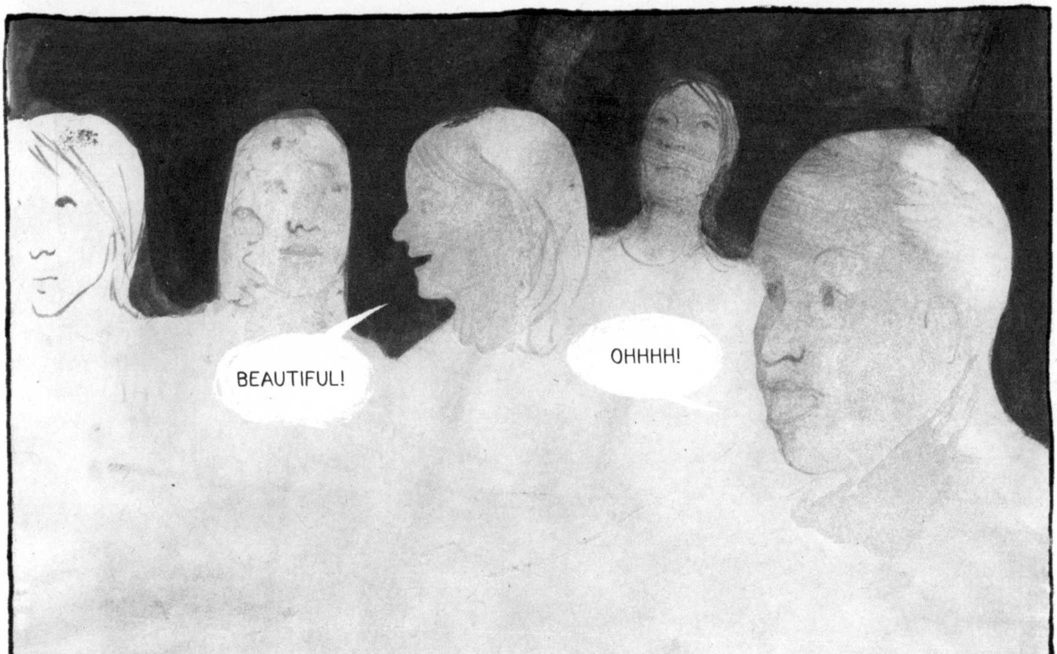
BEAUTIFUL!
OHHHH!

ON DECEMBER 31, 1958, LILA HAD HER FIRST EPISODE OF DISSOLVING BOUNDARIES.

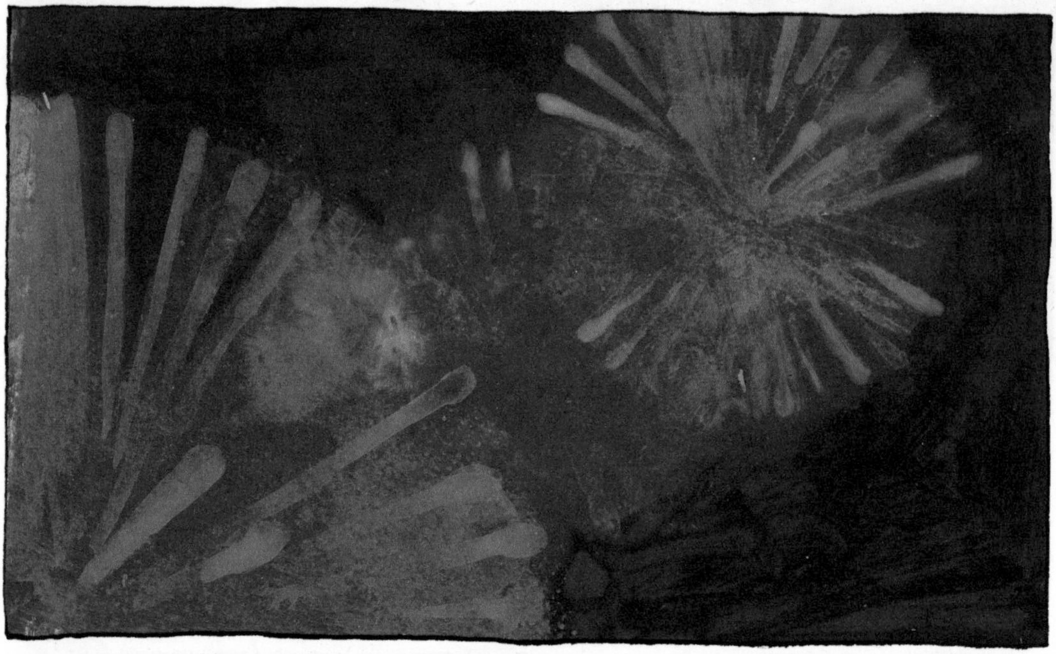

WE WERE AT STEFANO CARRACCI'S HOUSE.

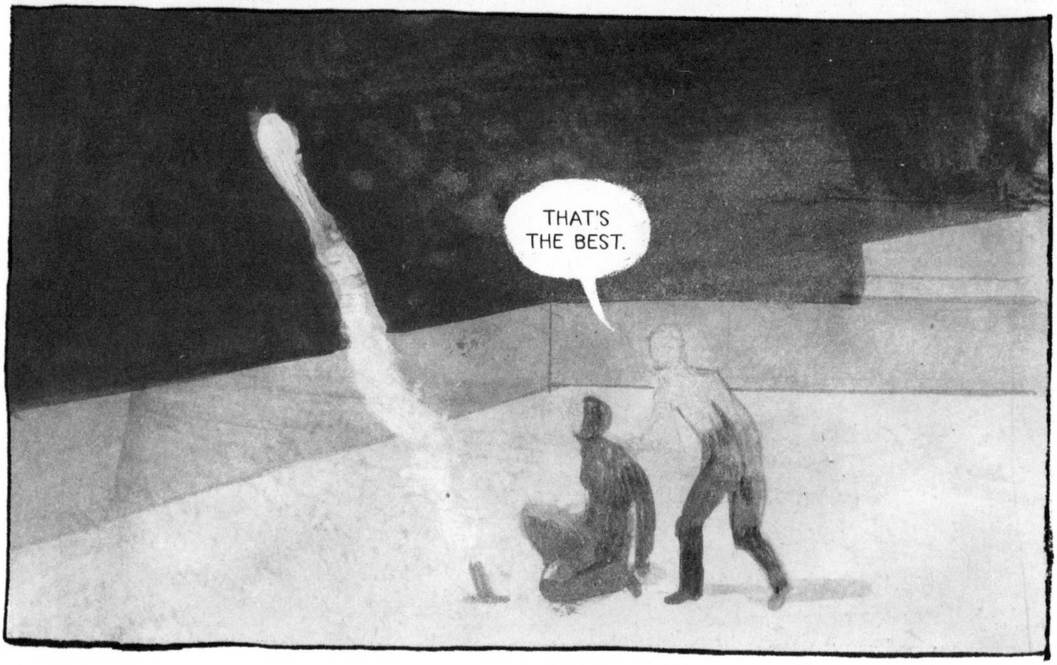

THAT'S THE BEST.

SUDDENLY SHE WAS COVERED WITH SWEAT.

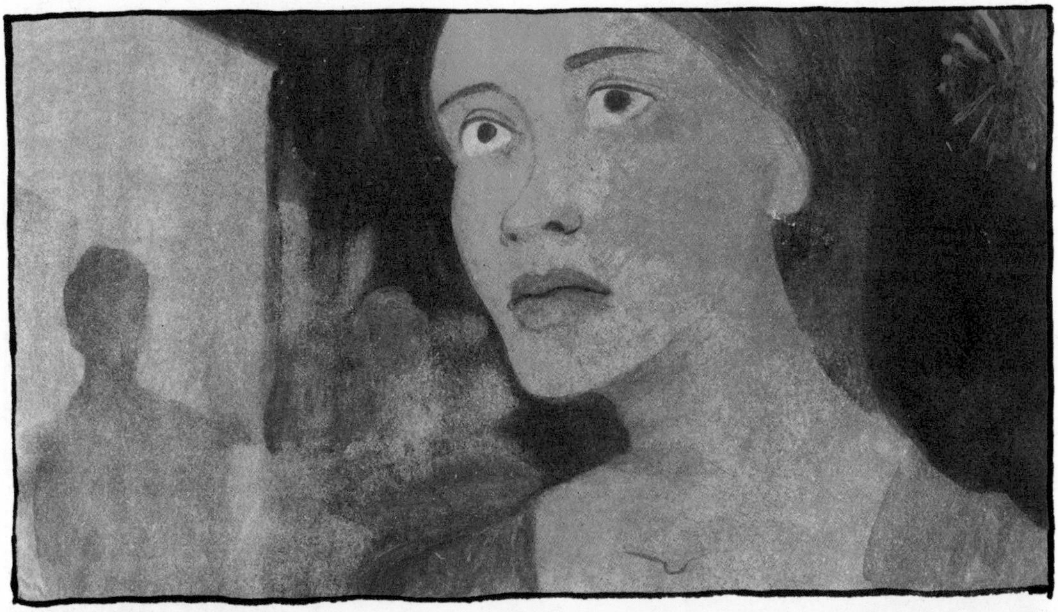

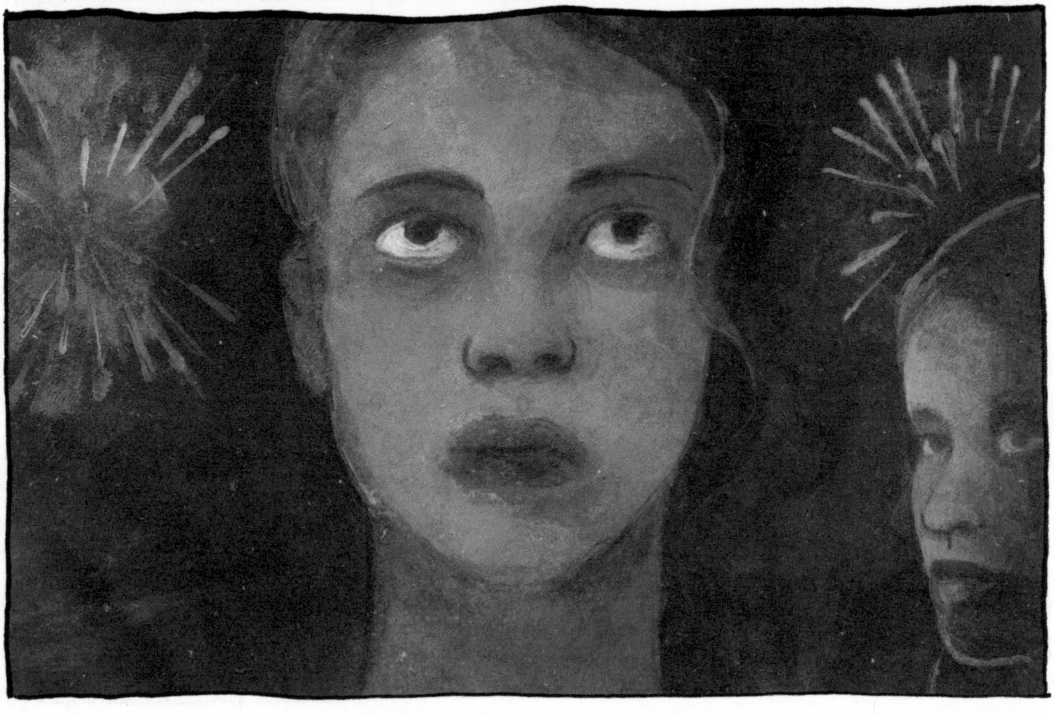

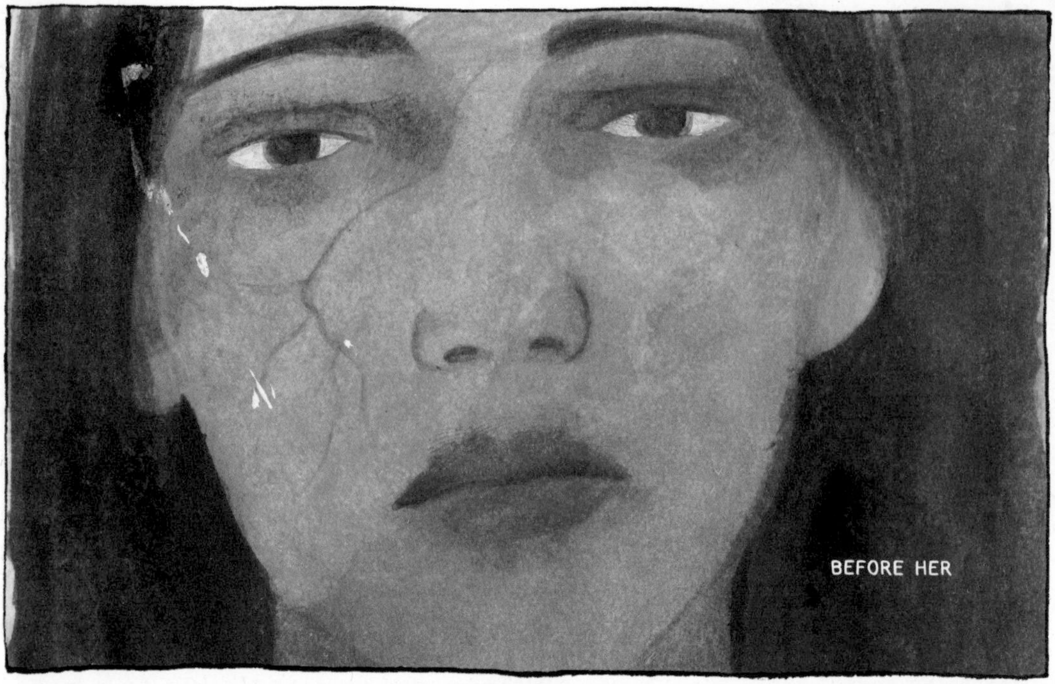
BEFORE HER

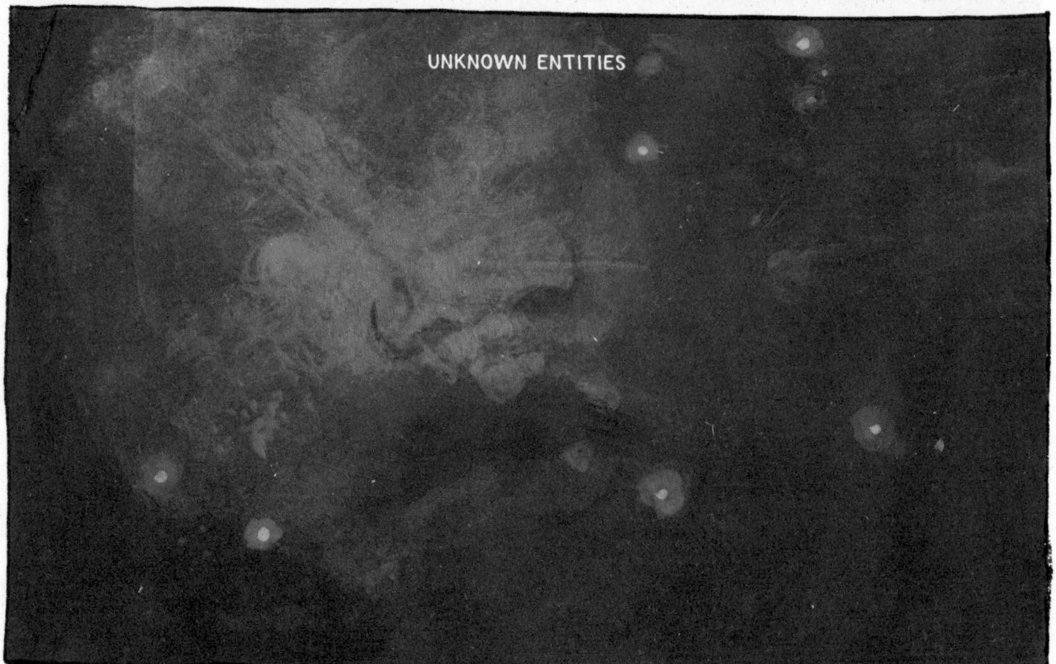
UNKNOWN ENTITIES

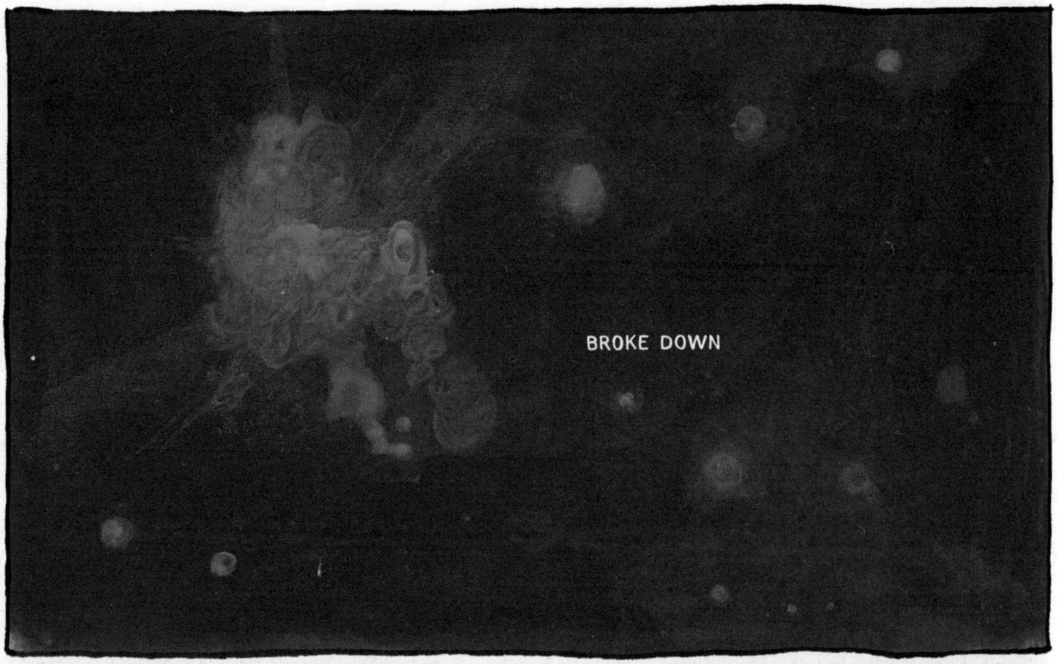
BROKE DOWN

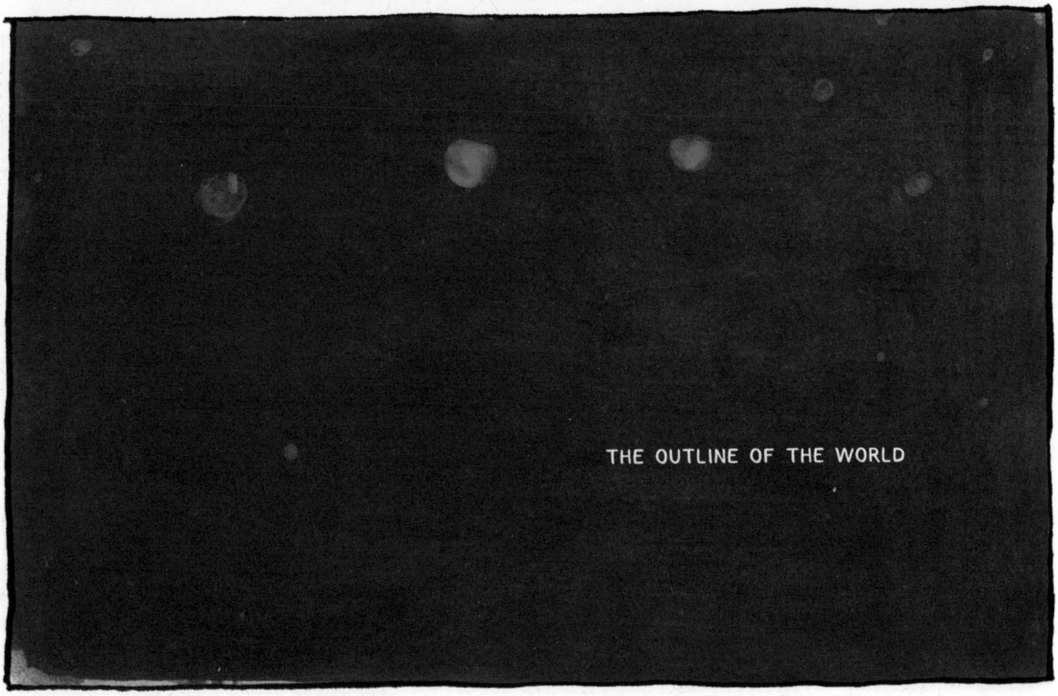
THE OUTLINE OF THE WORLD

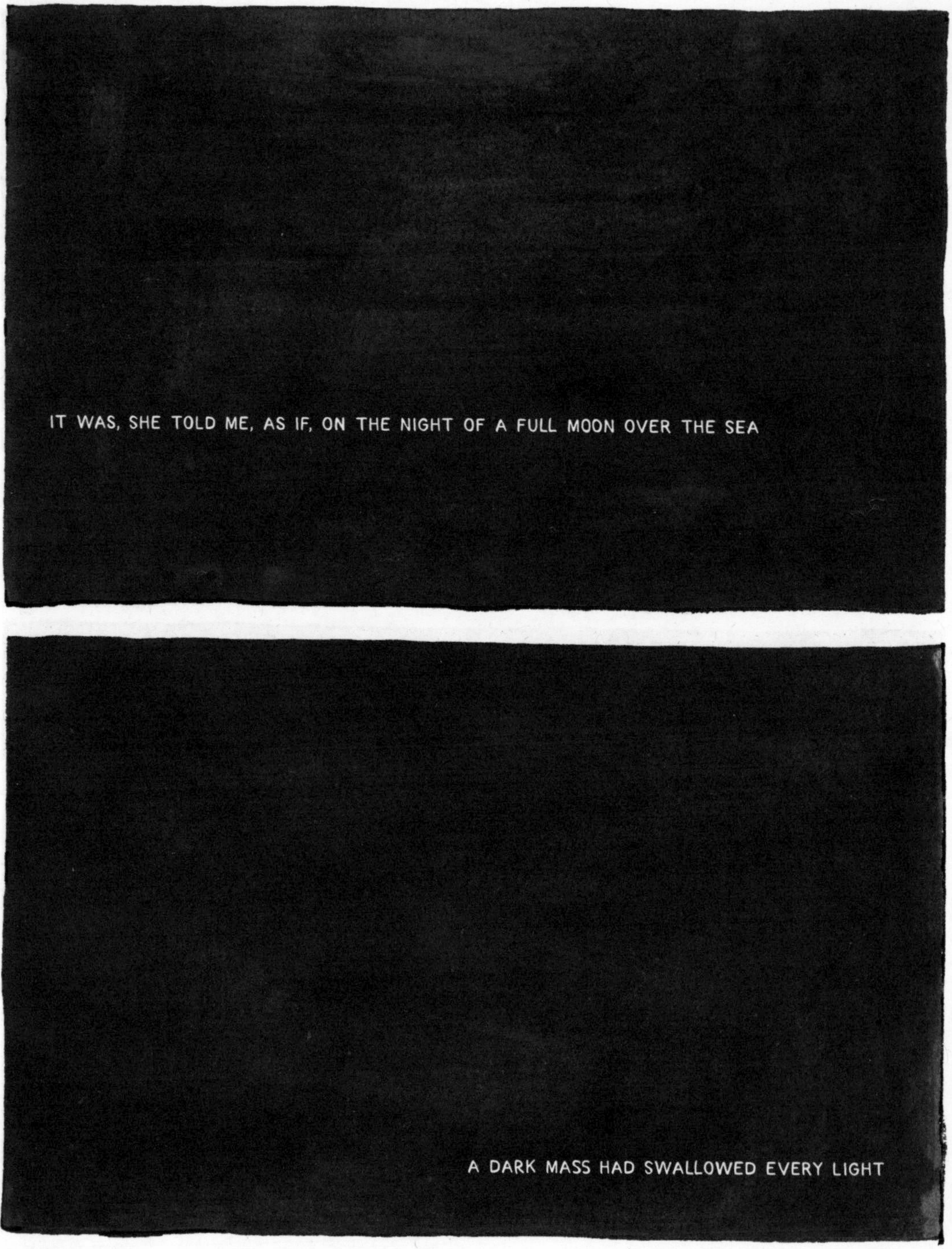
IT WAS, SHE TOLD ME, AS IF, ON THE NIGHT OF A FULL MOON OVER THE SEA
A DARK MASS HAD SWALLOWED EVERY LIGHT

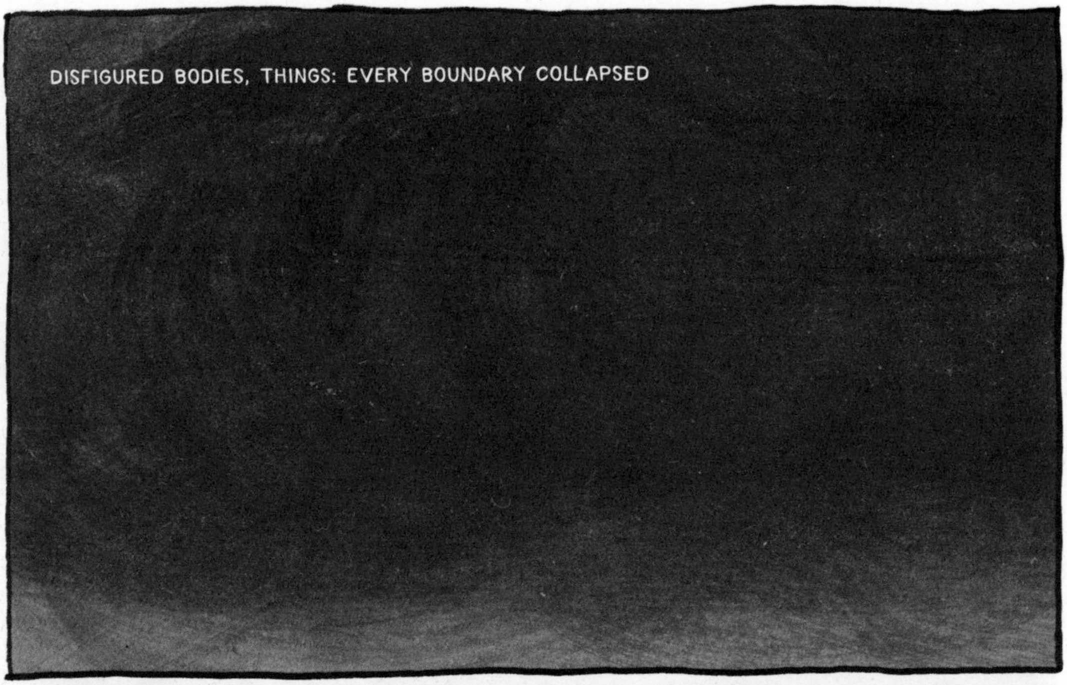
DISFIGURED BODIES, THINGS: EVERY BOUNDARY COLLAPSED

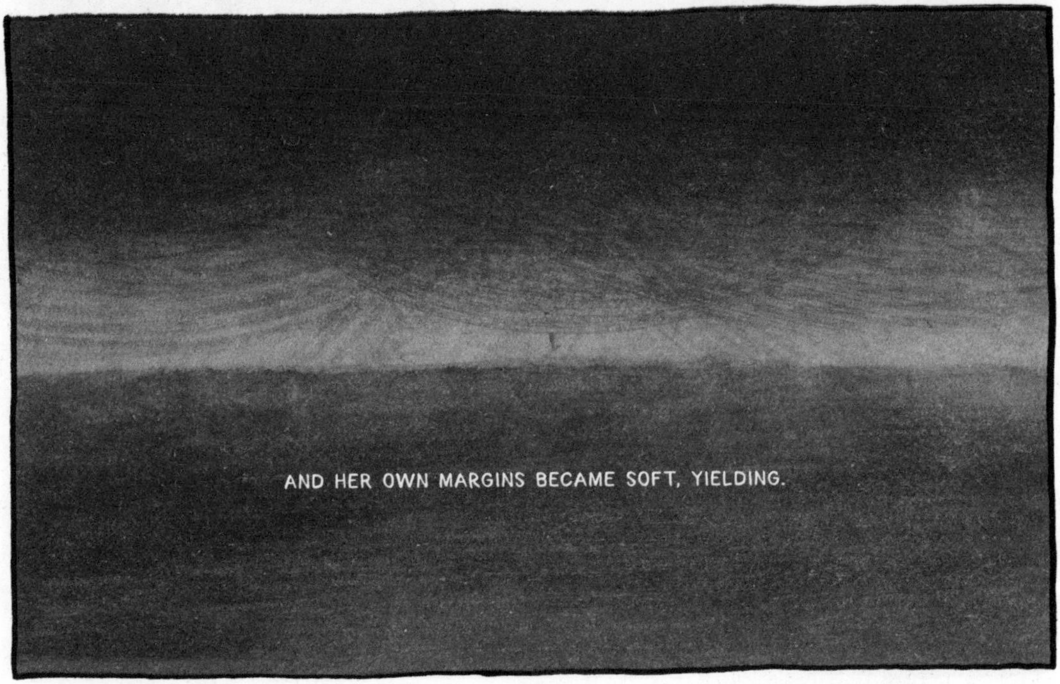
AND HER OWN MARGINS BECAME SOFT, YIELDING.

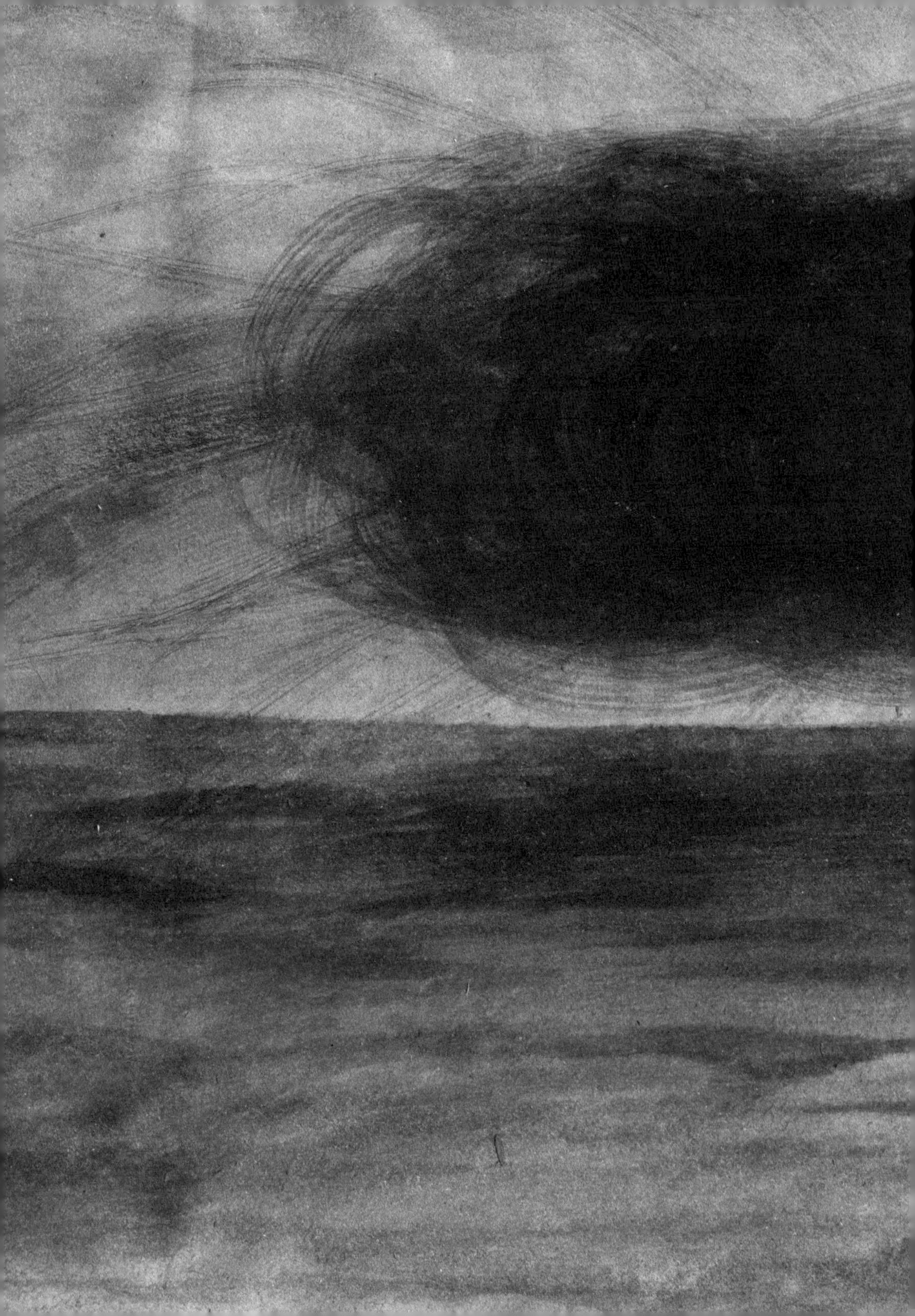

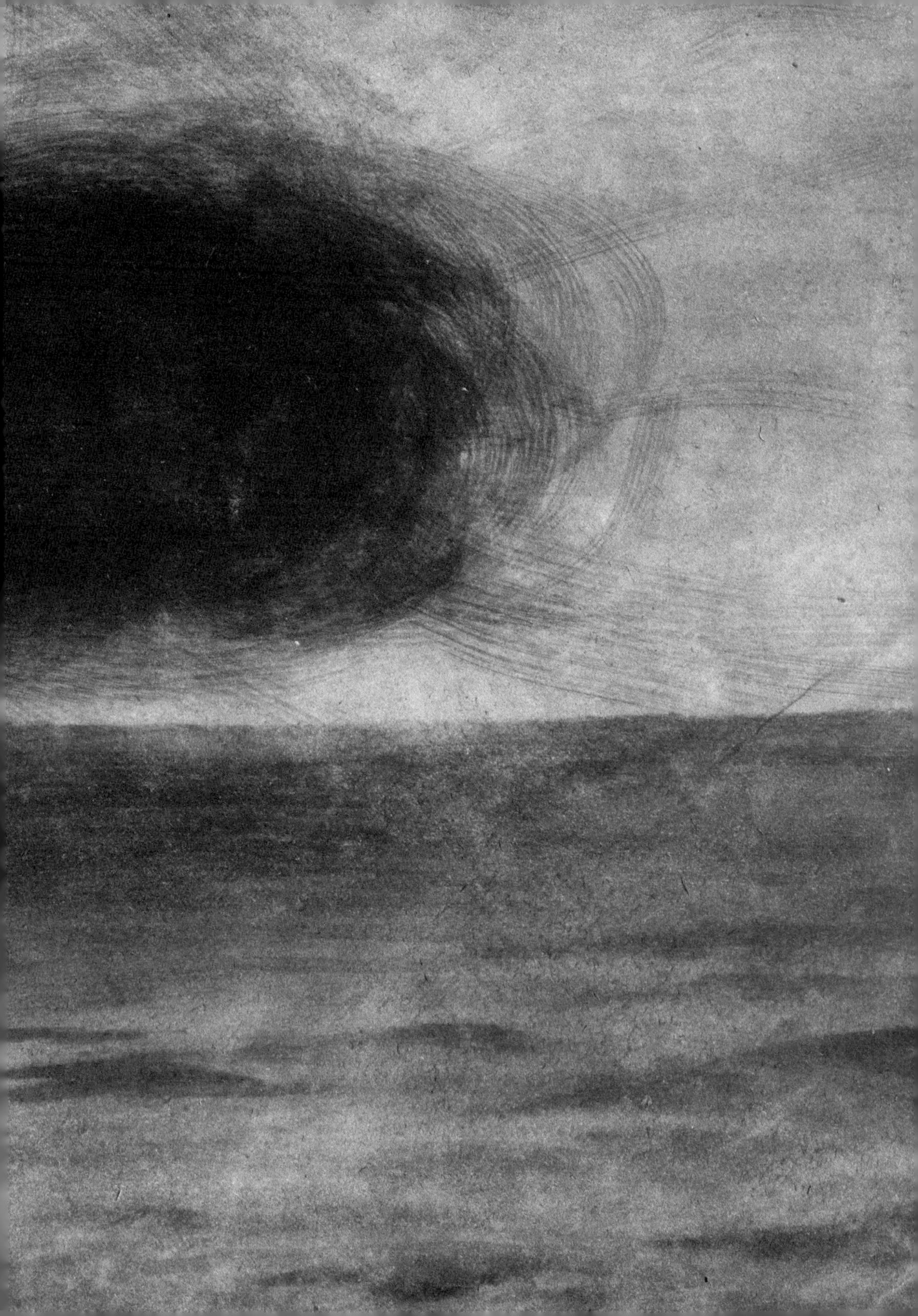

THAT NIGHT WE HAD A CONTEST OF EXPLOSIONS: WHOEVER HAD MORE MONEY SET OFF MORE.

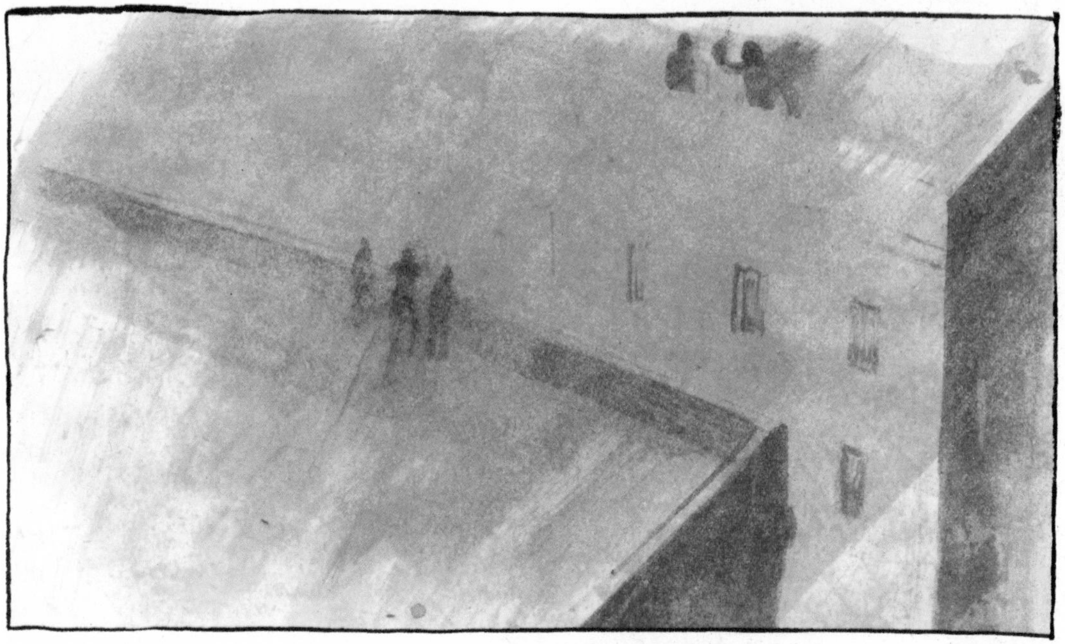

IT WAS US AGAINST THE SOLARAS.

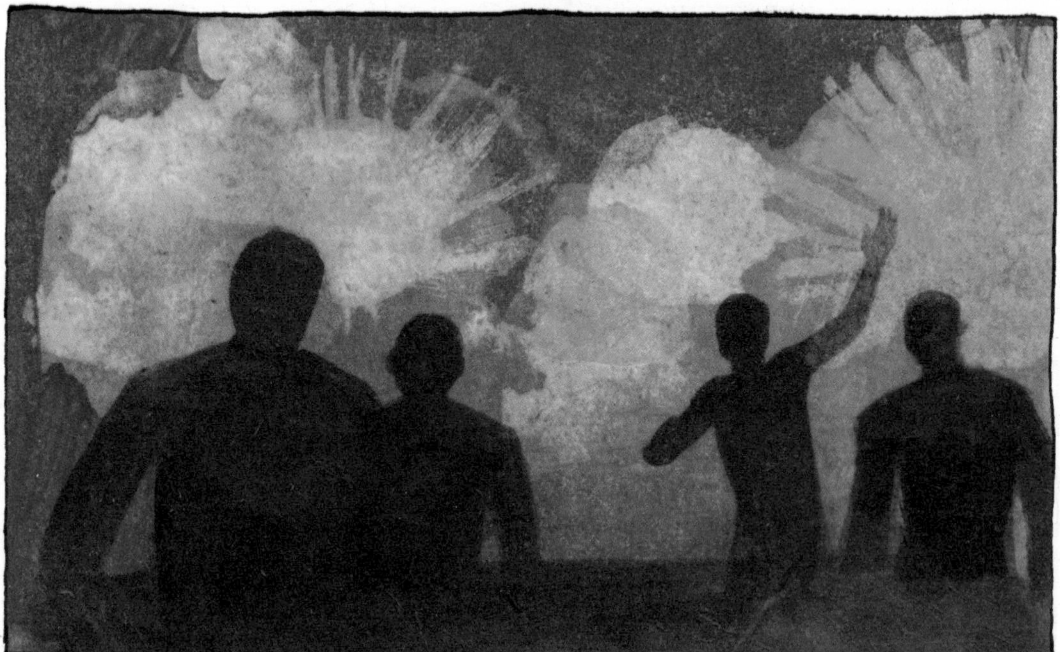

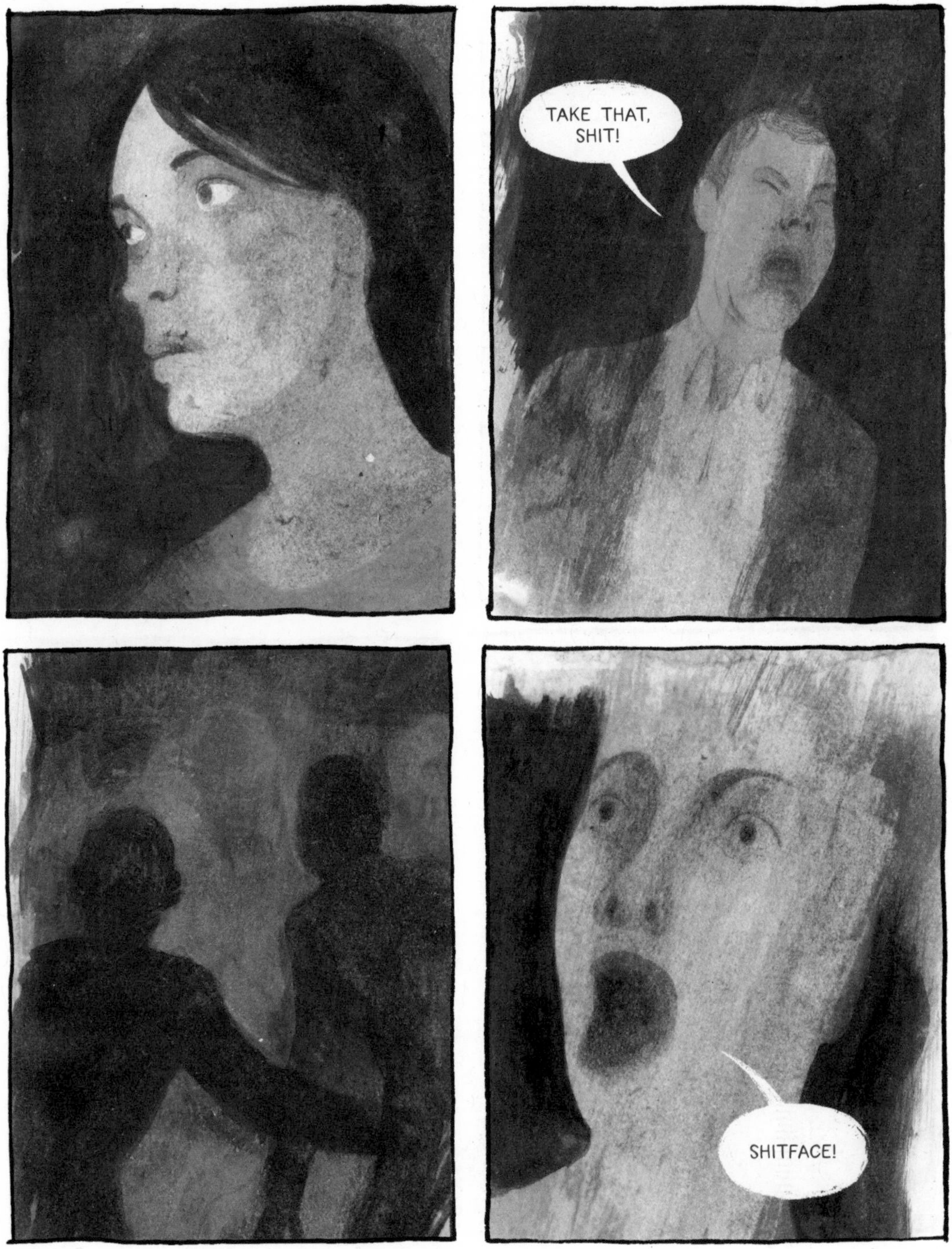
TAKE THAT, SHIT!
SHITFACE!

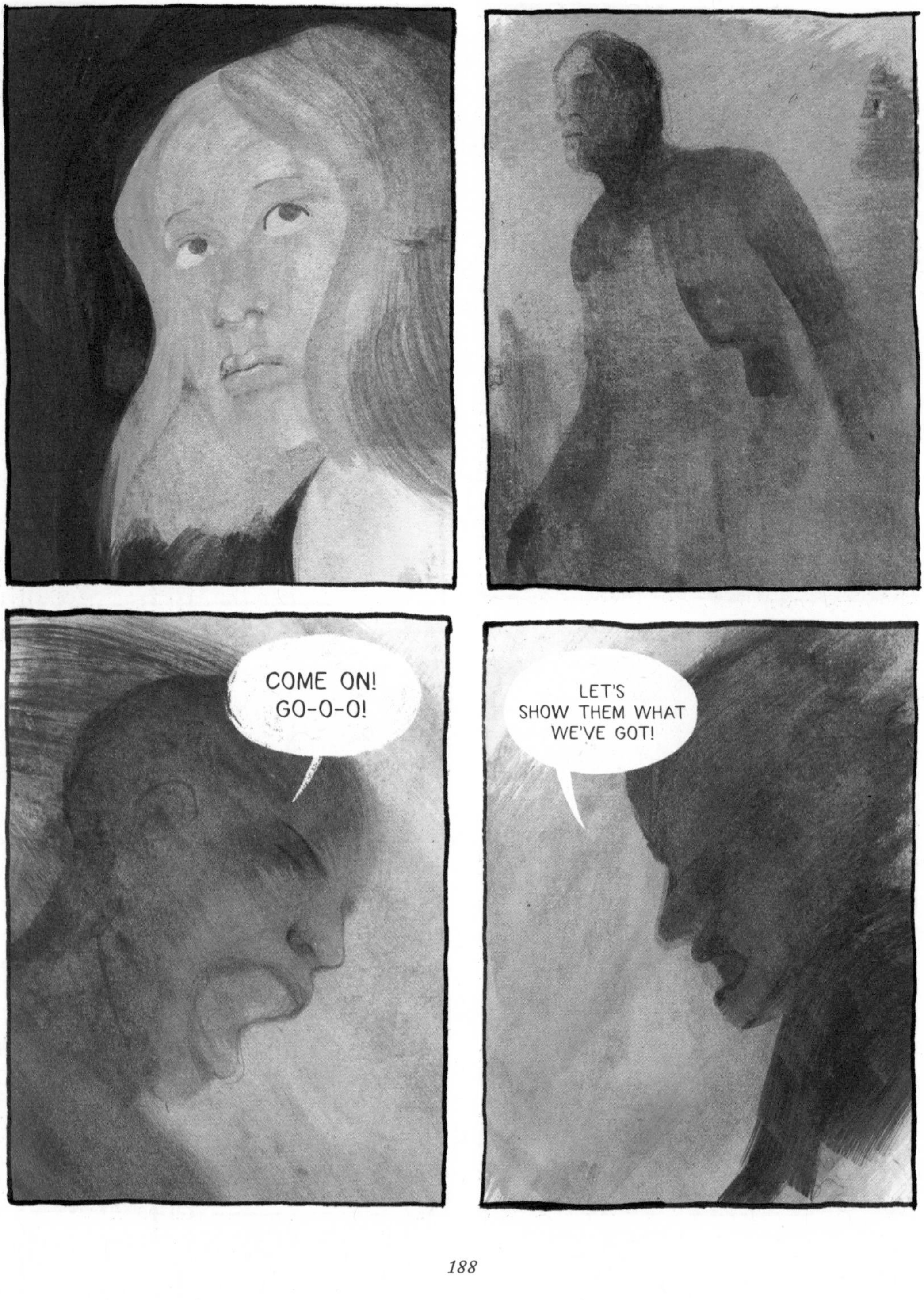
COME ON! GO-O-O!
LET'S SHOW THEM WHAT WE'VE GOT!

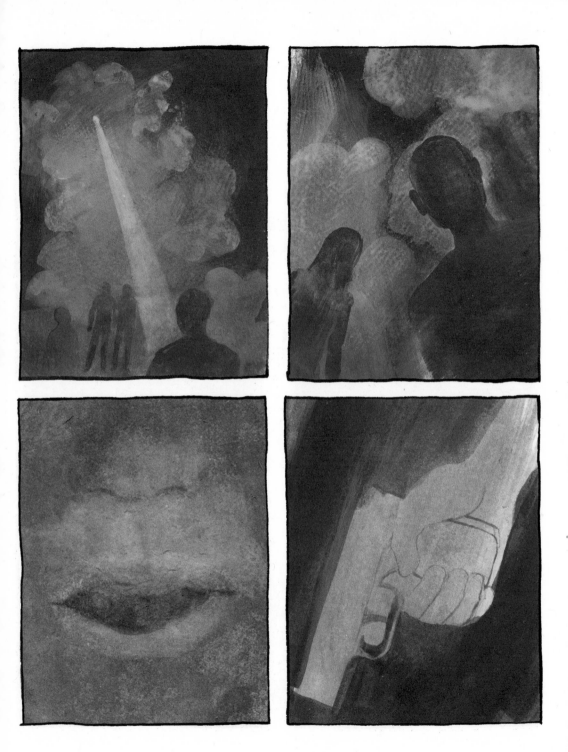

SUDDENLY THERE WAS SILENCE.

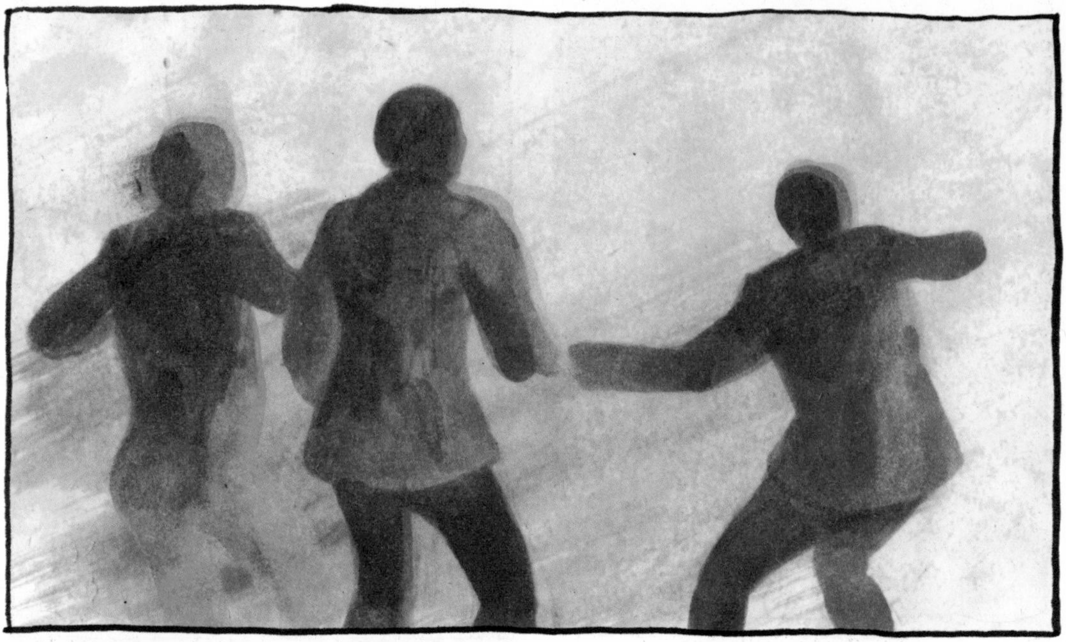

BUT IT DIDN'T LAST.

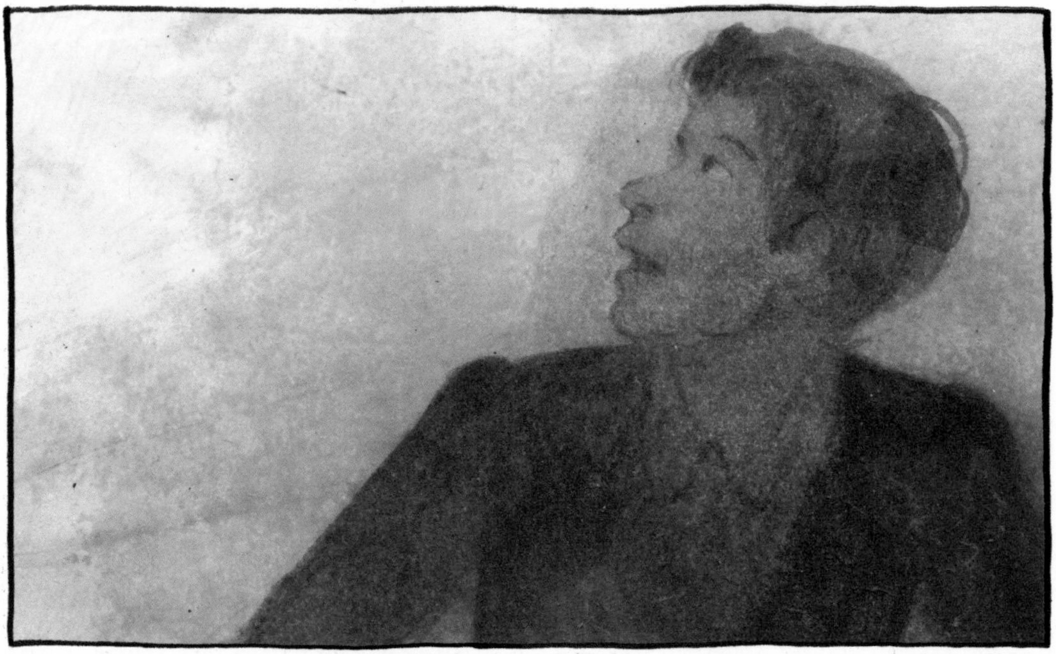

ON THE SOLARAS' BALCONY THE FLASHES QUICKLY APPEARED AGAIN.

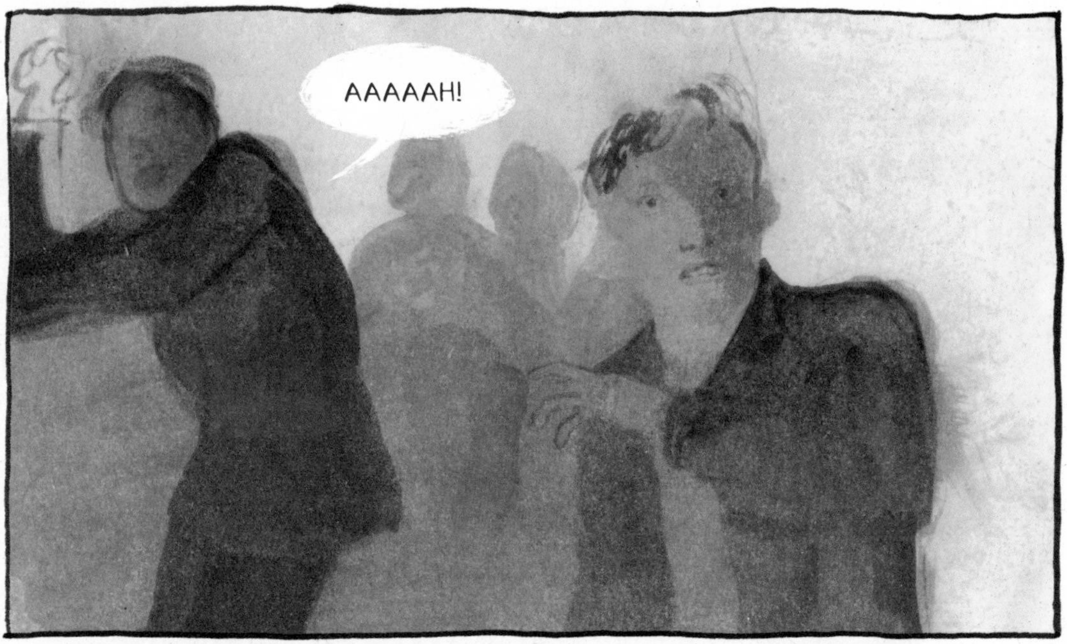
AAAAAH!

FOLLOWED BY SHARP SOUNDS, PAH, PAH.

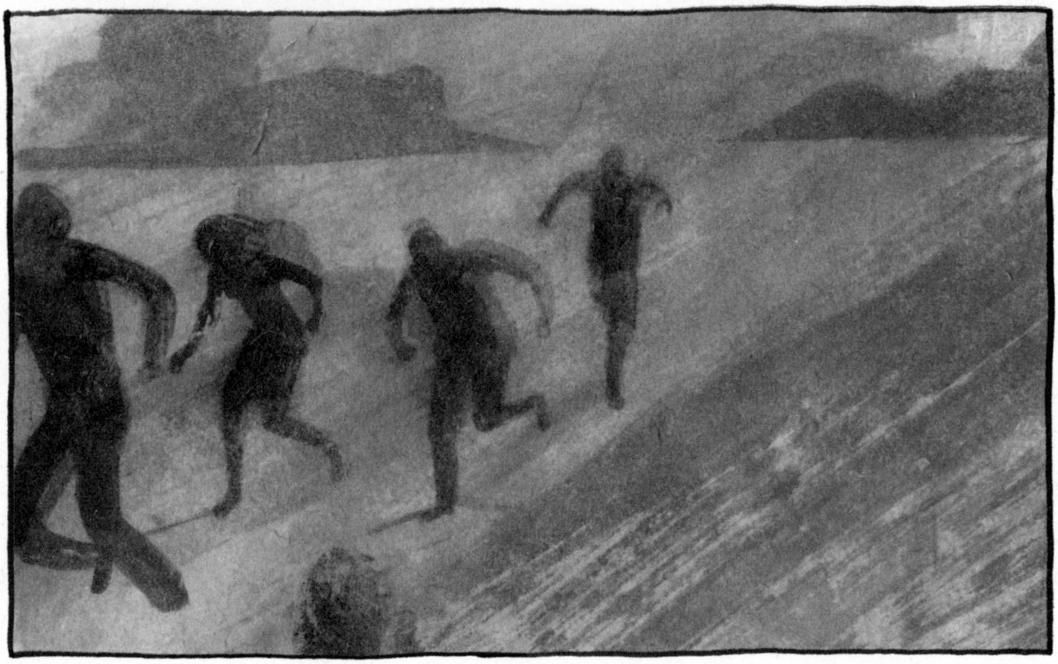

THE SOLARAS HAD USED UP THEIR SUPPLIES AND WERE SHOOTING AT US.

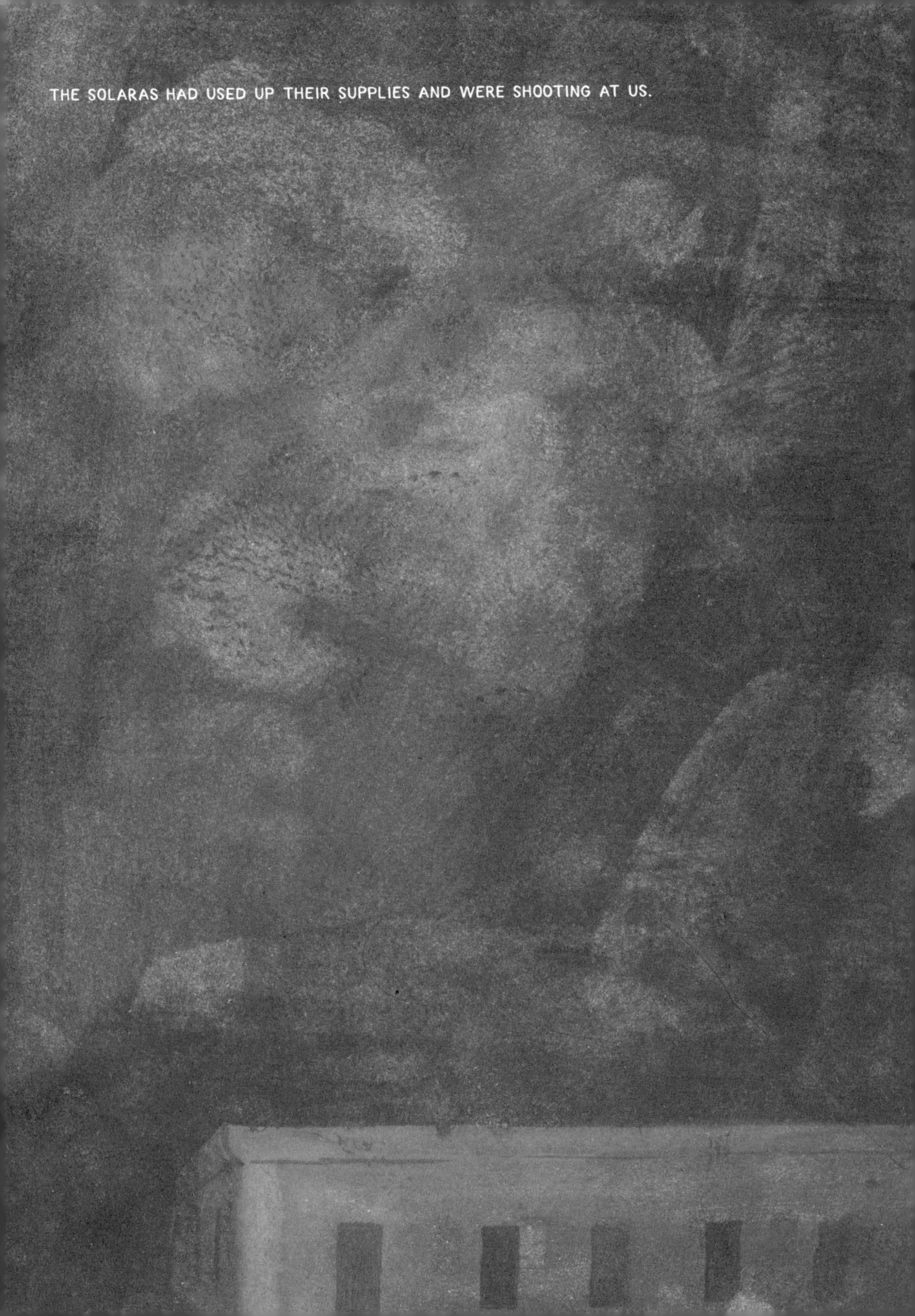

AFTER THAT NIGHT LILA BECAME LAZY, LETHARGIC.

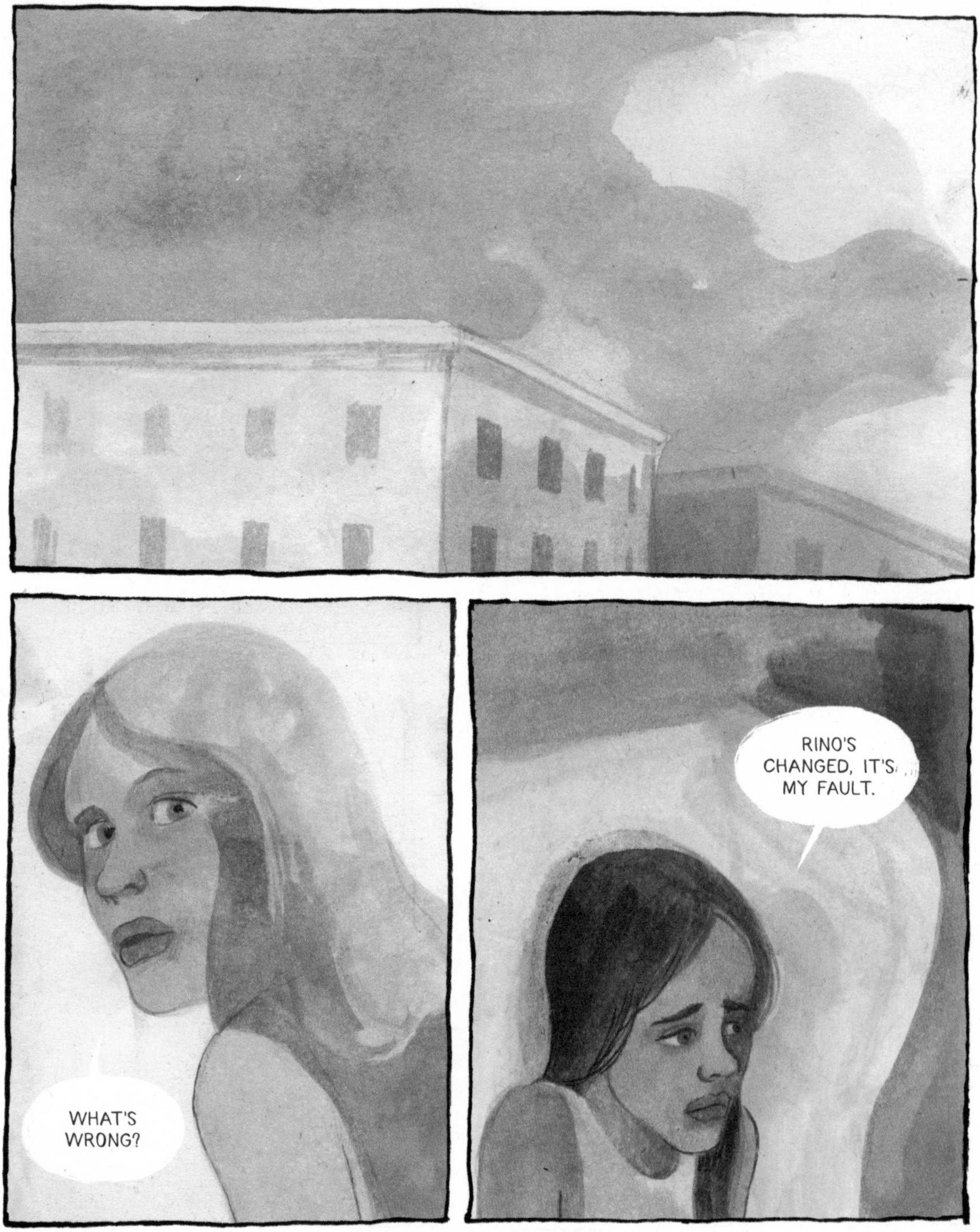
WHAT'S WRONG?
RINO'S CHANGED, IT'S MY FAULT.

SHE SAW HIM DIFFERENTLY. A SQUAT, CLUMSY HOWLING ANIMAL FORM. HE SEEMED TO HER THE FIERCEST, THE MEANEST OF ALL AND SHE NO LONGER RECOGNIZED HIM.

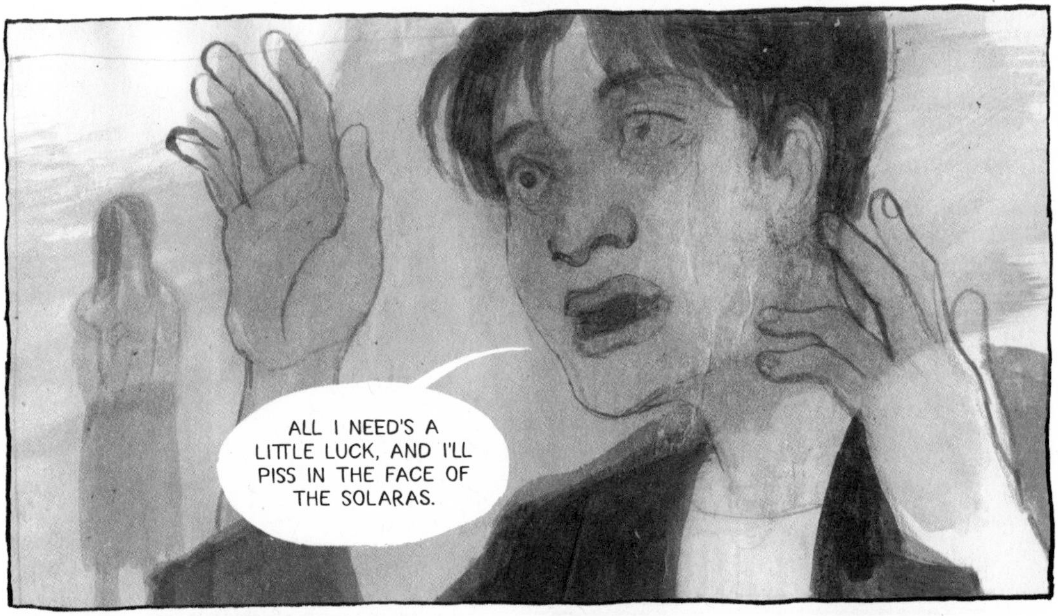
ALL I NEED'S A LITTLE LUCK, AND I'LL PISS IN THE FACE OF THE SOLARAS.

SHE THOUGHT SHE'D DONE HIM MORE HARM THAN GOOD.

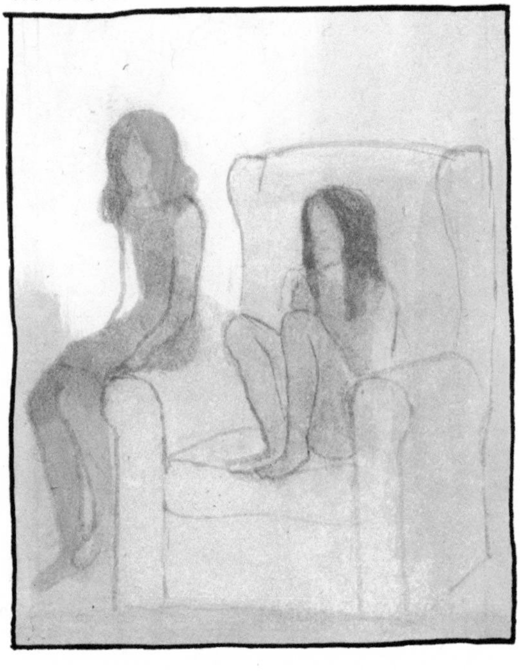

THE BUSINESS OF THE SHOES HAD RUINED HIM.

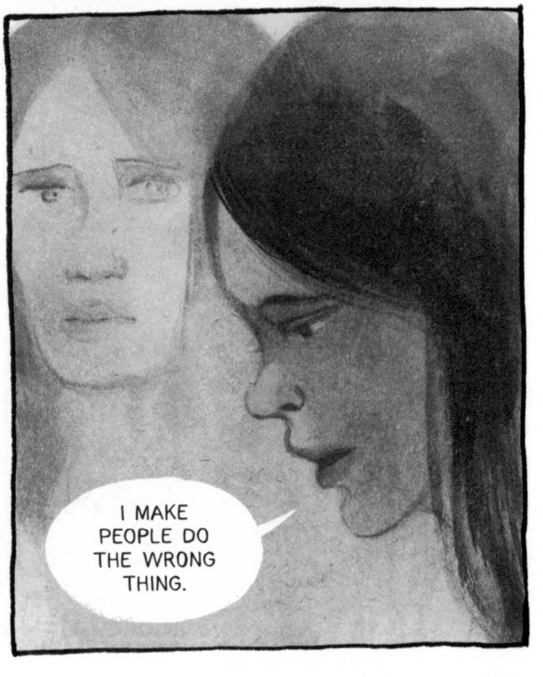
I MAKE PEOPLE DO THE WRONG THING.

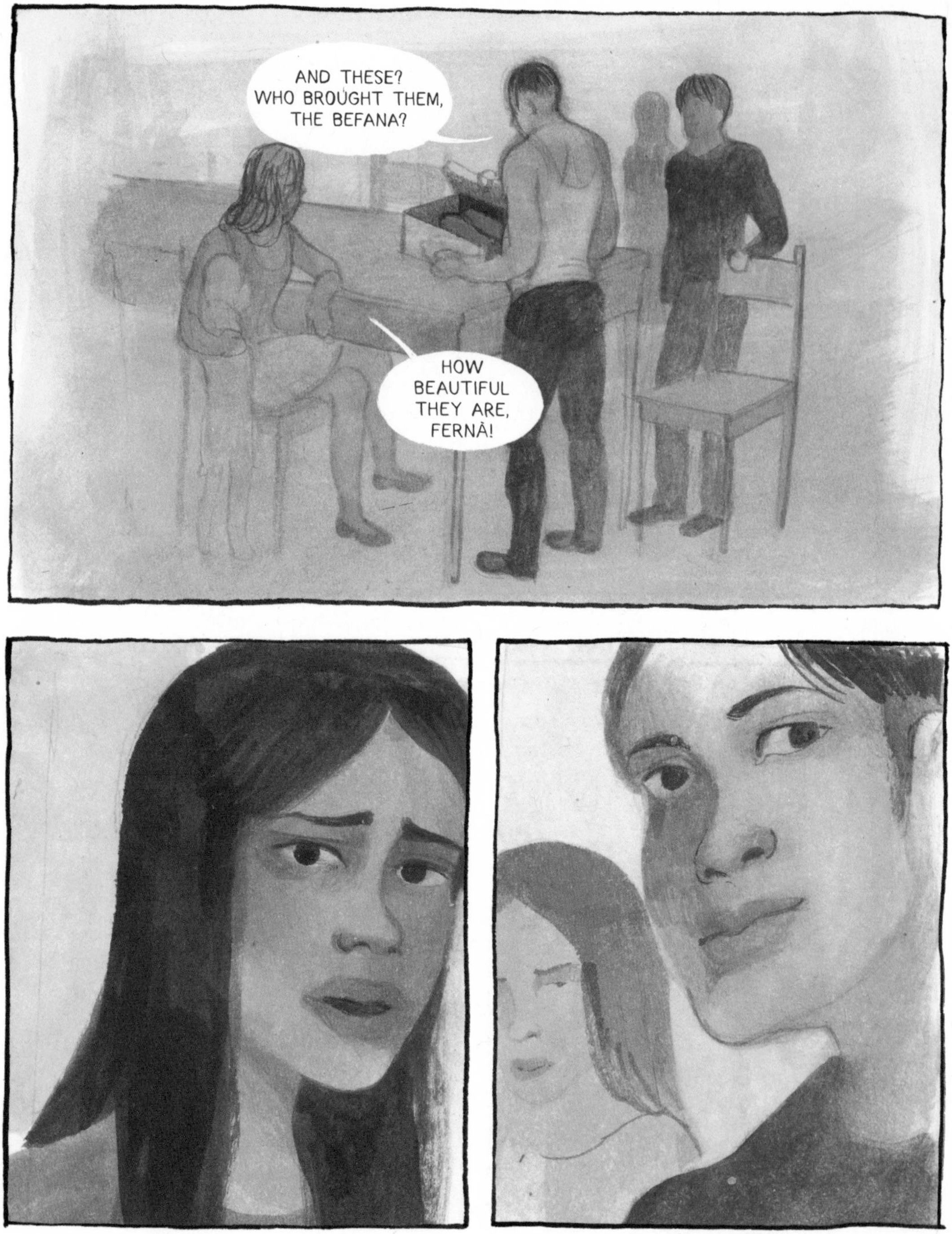
AND THESE? WHO BROUGHT THEM, THE BEFANA?
HOW BEAUTIFUL THEY ARE, FERNÀ!

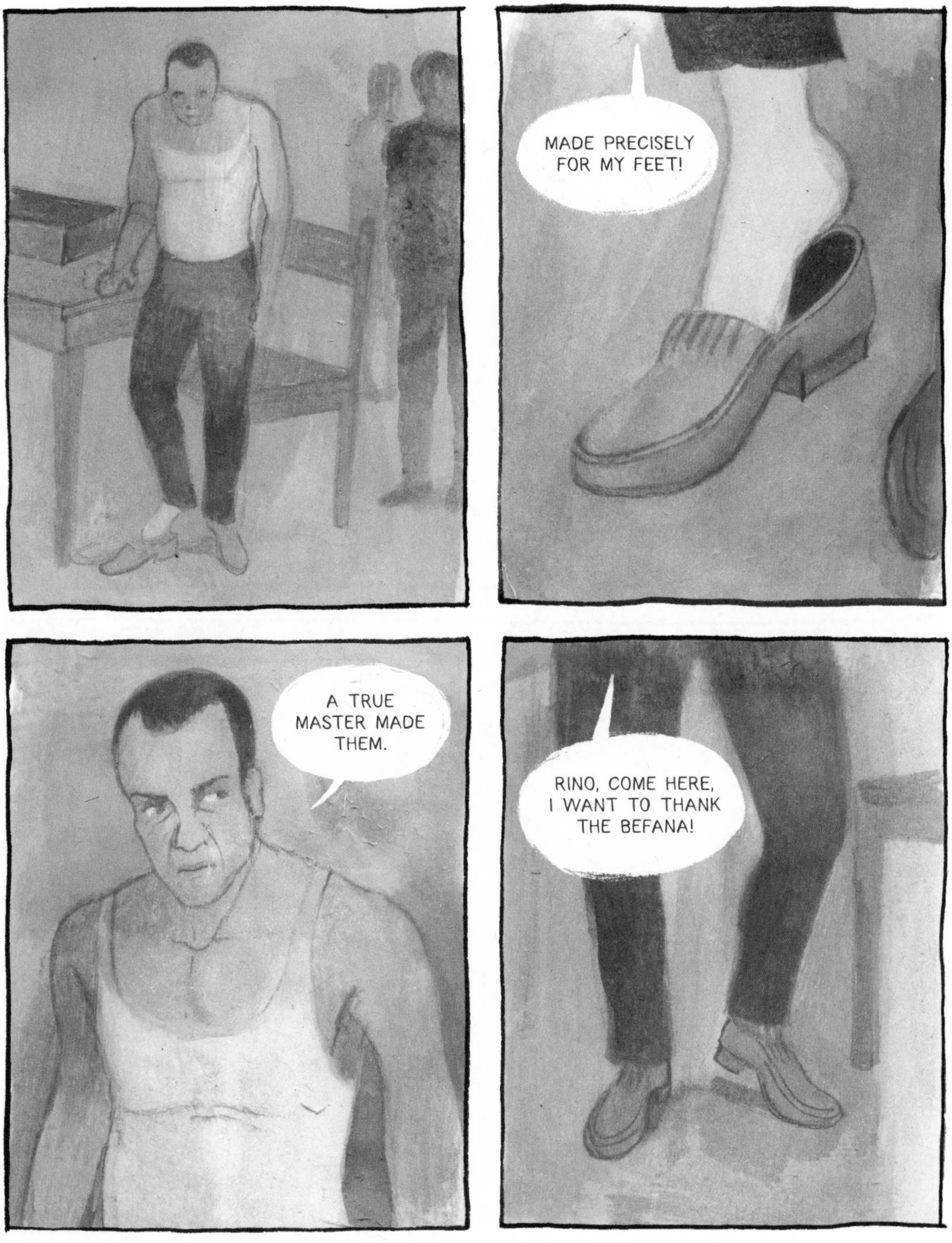
MADE PRECISELY FOR MY FEET!
A TRUE MASTER MADE THEM.
RINO, COME HERE, I WANT TO THANK THE BEFANA!

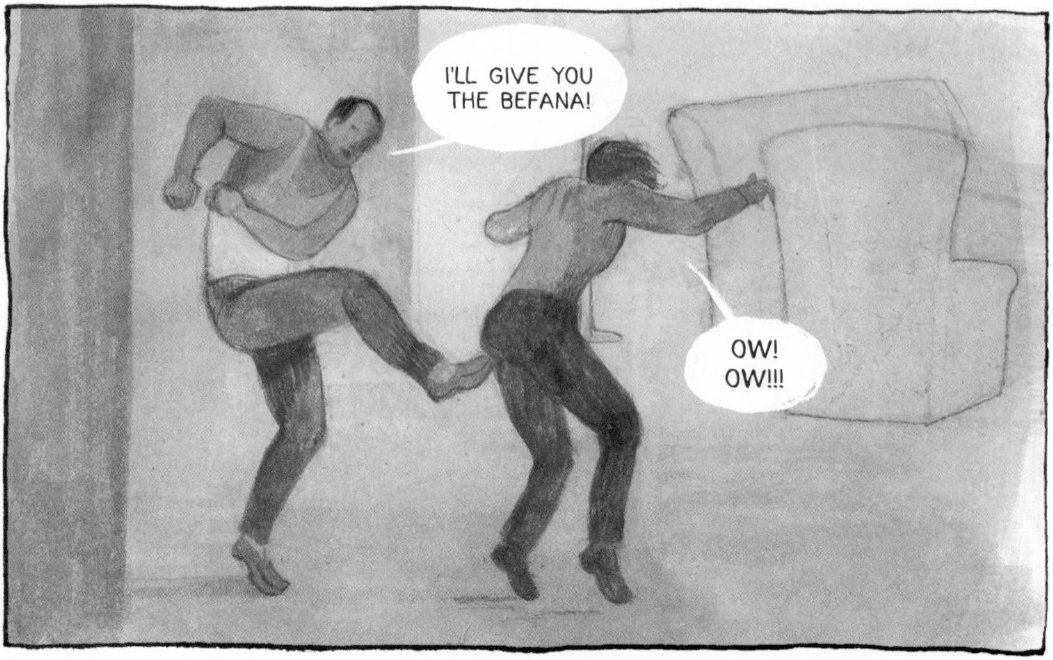
I'LL GIVE YOU THE BEFANA!
OW! OW!!!

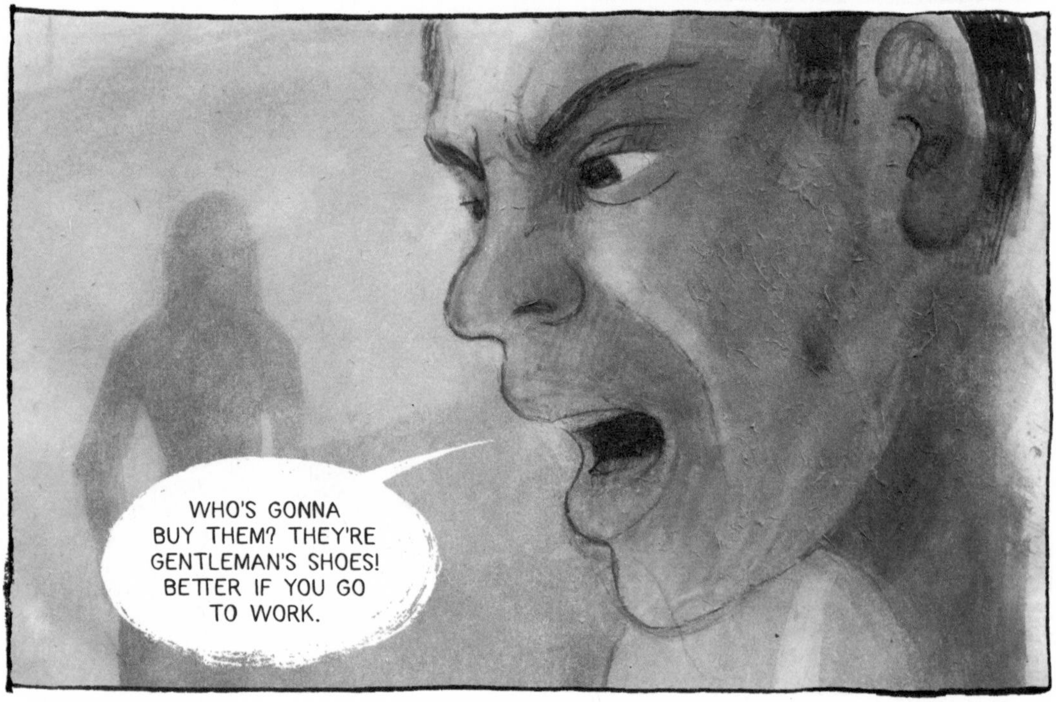
WHO'S GONNA BUY THEM? THEY'RE GENTLEMAN'S SHOES! BETTER IF YOU GO TO WORK.

THEN THEY WENT BACK TO THE SHOP, MUTE, SHUT INSIDE THEIR DESPERATIONS.

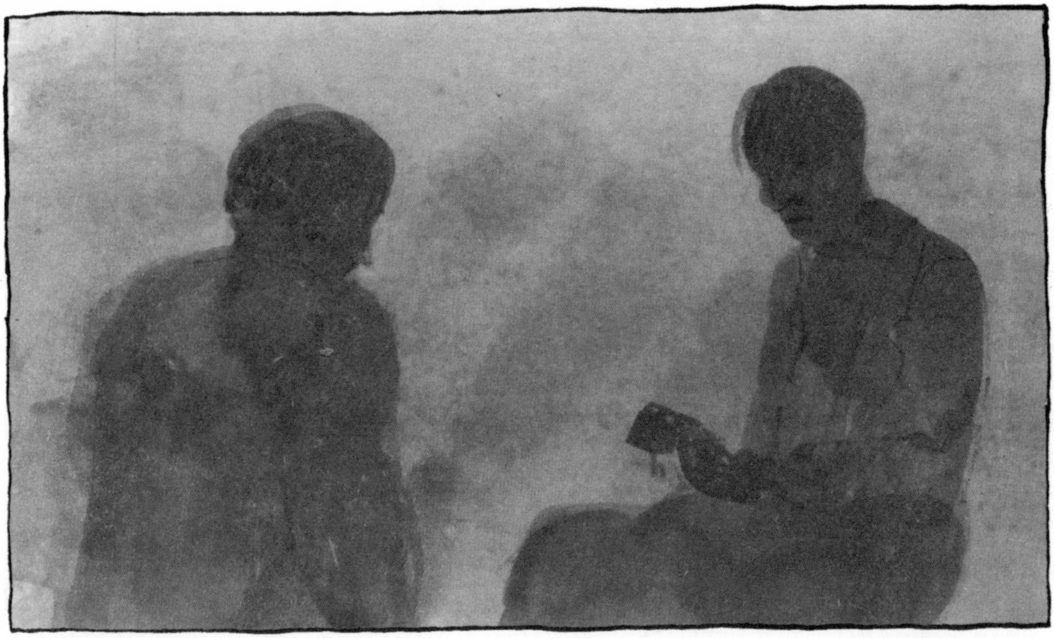

SOMETIMES WHEN LILA WAS ALONE IN THE HOUSE SHE'D TAKE OUT THE SHOES...

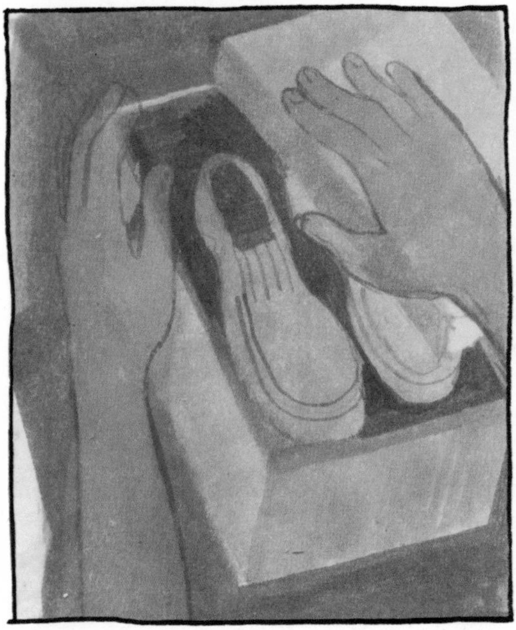

...WHICH SHE'D PUT AWAY IN A SECRET HIDING PLACE, AND LOOK AT THEM IN WONDER.

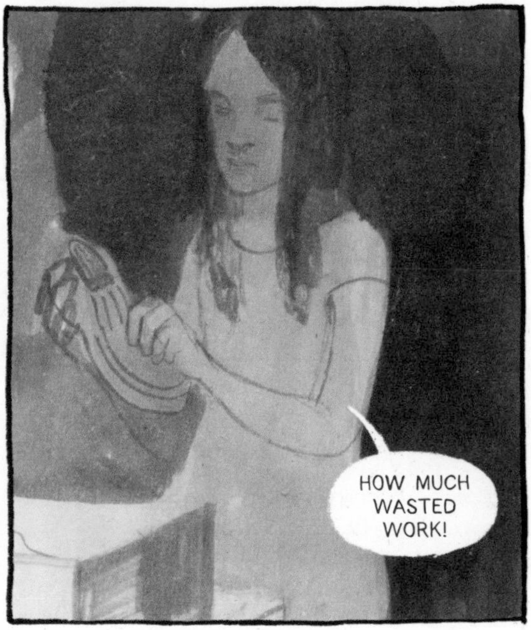
HOW MUCH WASTED WORK!

FOR HIS PART RINO WASN'T RESIGNED. HE'D STARTED SPENDING TIME WITH MARCELLO, WHO SUPPORTED HIM, BECAUSE FOR A WHILE HE'D HAD AN EYE ON HIS SISTER.

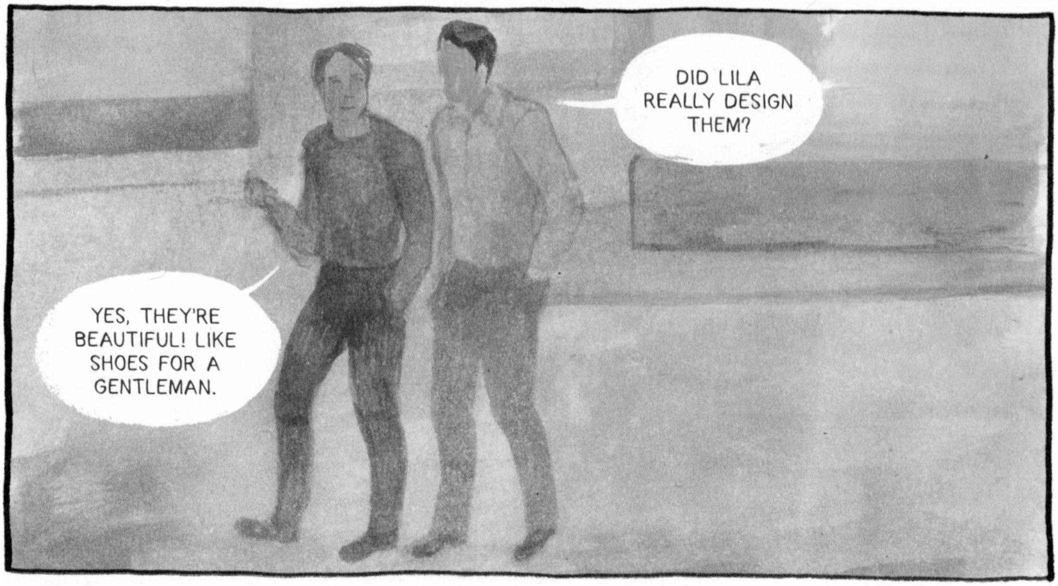
DID LILA REALLY DESIGN THEM?
YES, THEY'RE BEAUTIFUL! LIKE SHOES FOR A GENTLEMAN.

SOMETIMES HE EVEN BROUGHT HIM HOME, AND THEN FERNANDO INVITED HIM TO DINNER: MARCELLO WAS RICH AND POWERFUL, FRIENDSHIP WITH HIM SHOULD BE ENCOURAGED.

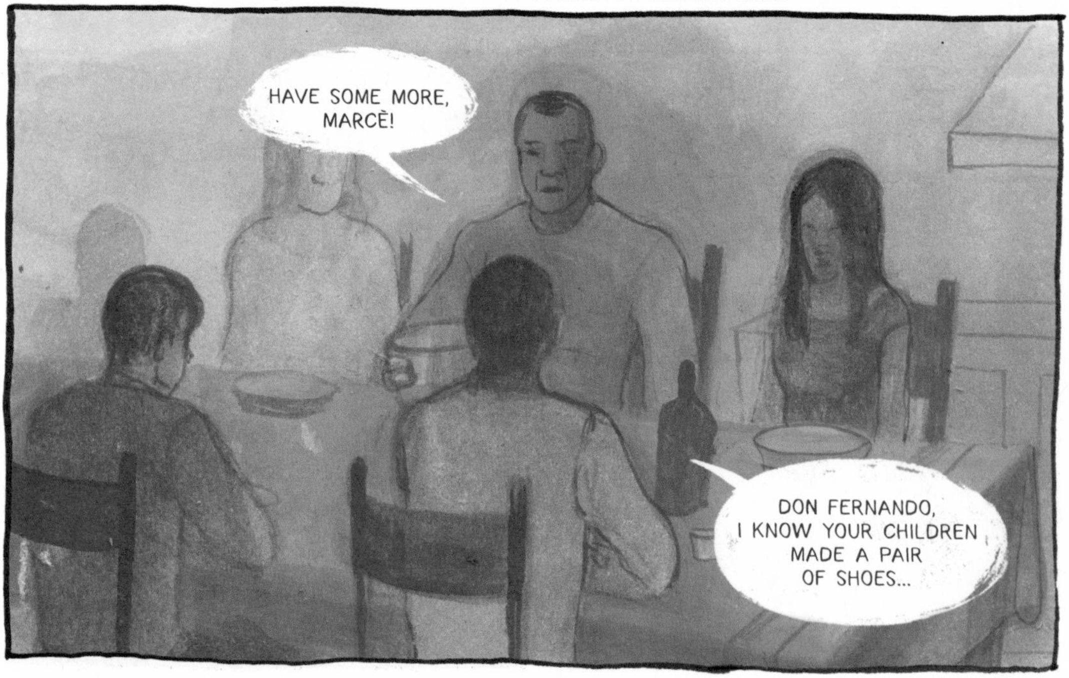
HAVE SOME MORE, MARCÈ!
DON FERNANDO, I KNOW YOUR CHILDREN MADE A PAIR OF SHOES...

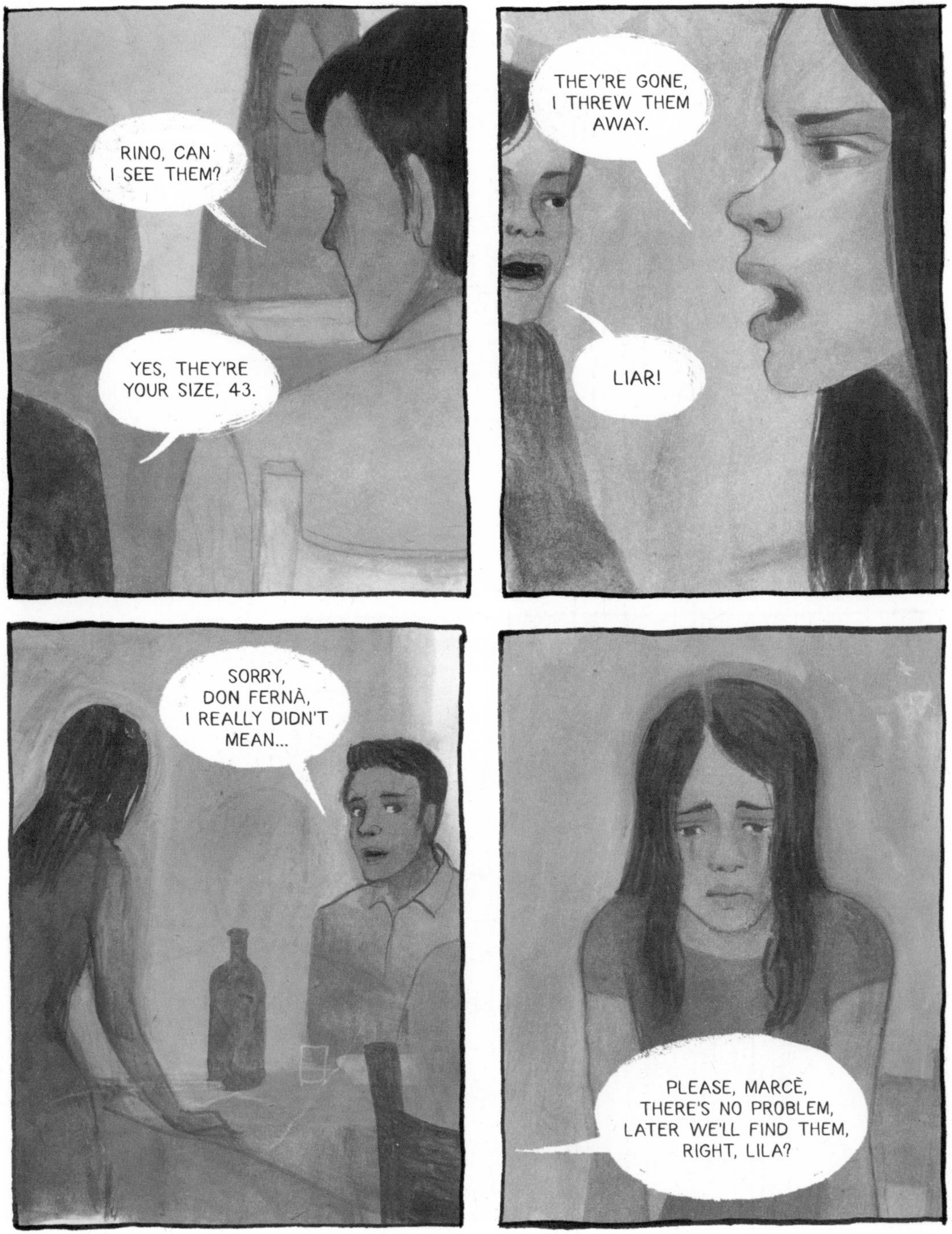
RINO, CAN I SEE THEM?
YES, THEY'RE YOUR SIZE, 43.
THEY'RE GONE, I THREW THEM AWAY.
LIAR!
SORRY, DON FERNÀ, I REALLY DIDN'T MEAN...
PLEASE, MARCÈ, THERE'S NO PROBLEM, LATER WE'LL FIND THEM, RIGHT, LILA?

THE NEXT DAY THE SHOES WERE IN THE SHOP WINDOW.

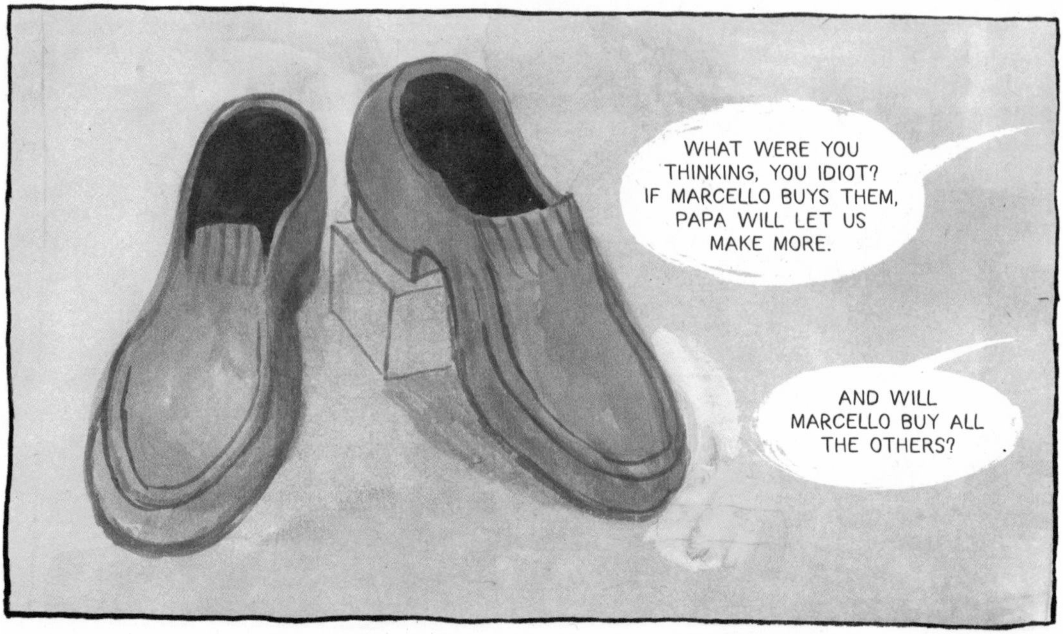
WHAT WERE YOU THINKING, YOU IDIOT? IF MARCELLO BUYS THEM, PAPA WILL LET US MAKE MORE.
AND WILL MARCELLO BUY ALL THE OTHERS?

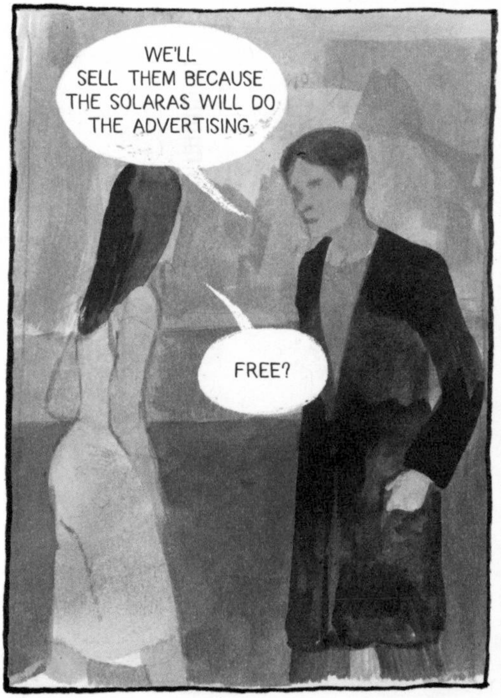
WE'LL SELL THEM BECAUSE THE SOLARAS WILL DO THE ADVERTISING.
FREE?

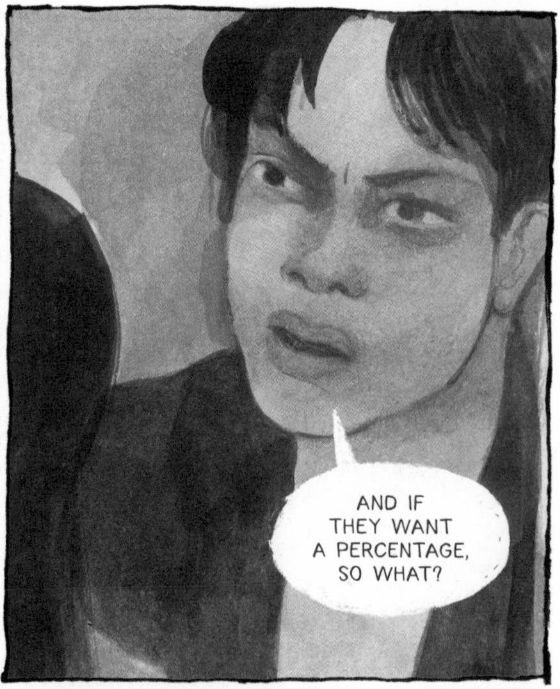
AND IF THEY WANT A PERCENTAGE, SO WHAT?

A FEW DAYS LATER MARCELLO APPEARED AGAIN.

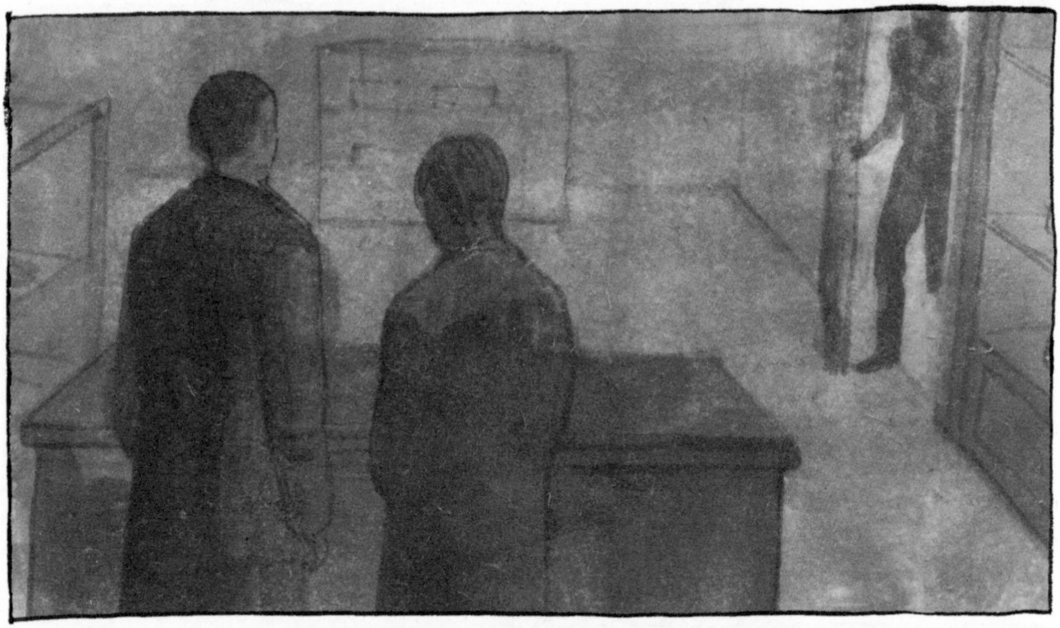

BUT HE NO LONGER SEEMED TOO INTERESTED IN THE SHOES...

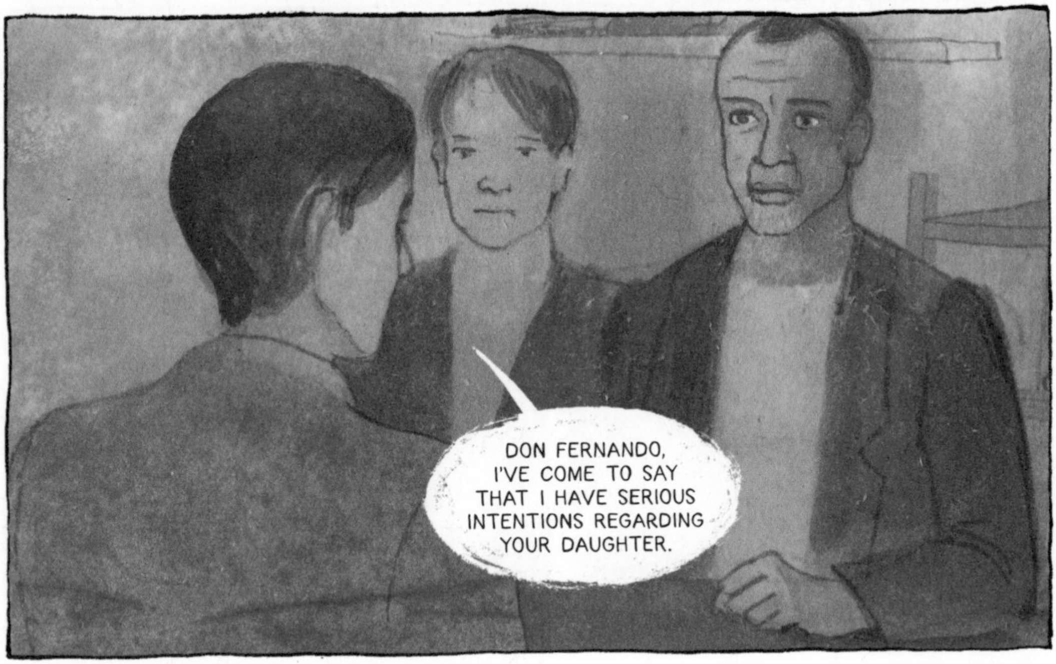
DON FERNANDO, I'VE COME TO SAY THAT I HAVE SERIOUS INTENTIONS REGARDING YOUR DAUGHTER.

ALL THIS LILA TOLD ME LATER.

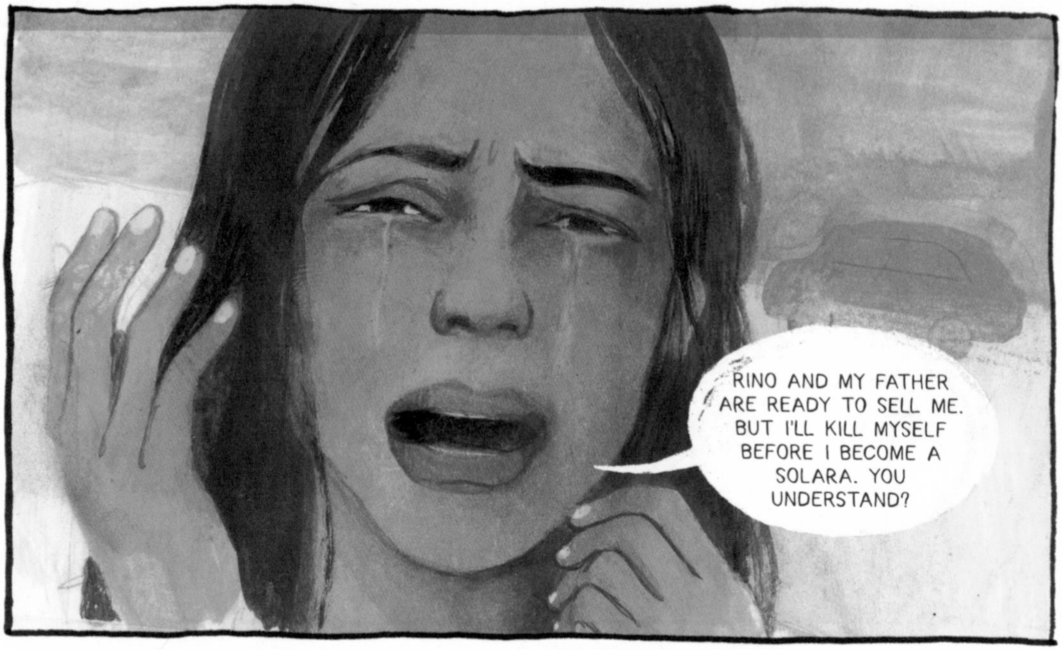
RINO AND MY FATHER ARE READY TO SELL ME. BUT I'LL KILL MYSELF BEFORE I BECOME A SOLARA. YOU UNDERSTAND?

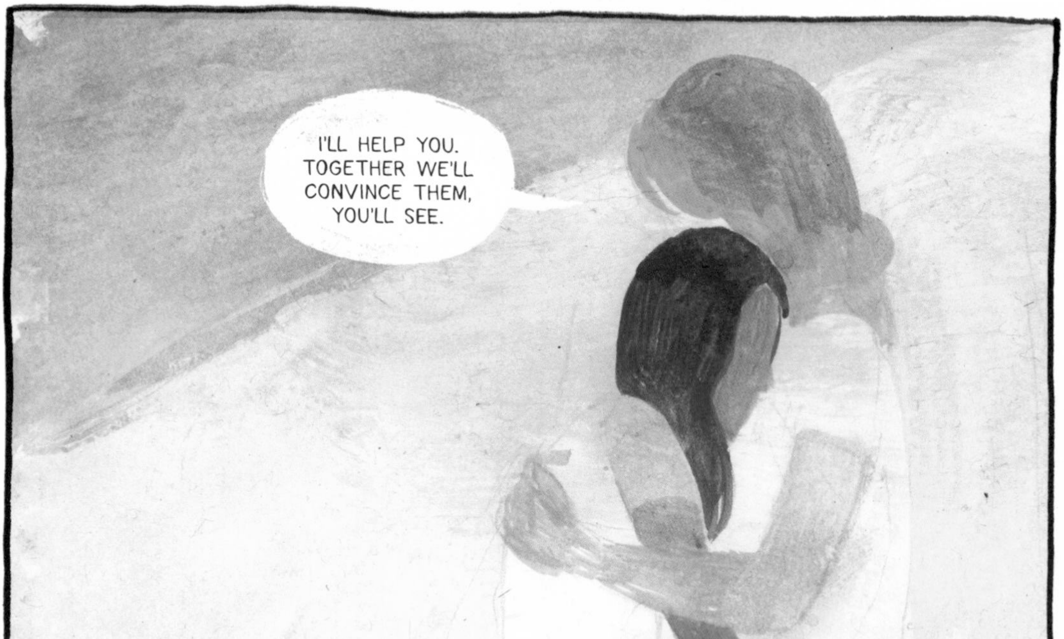
I'LL HELP YOU. TOGETHER WE'LL CONVINCE THEM, YOU'LL SEE.

BUT FATE HAD OTHER PLANS FOR ME.

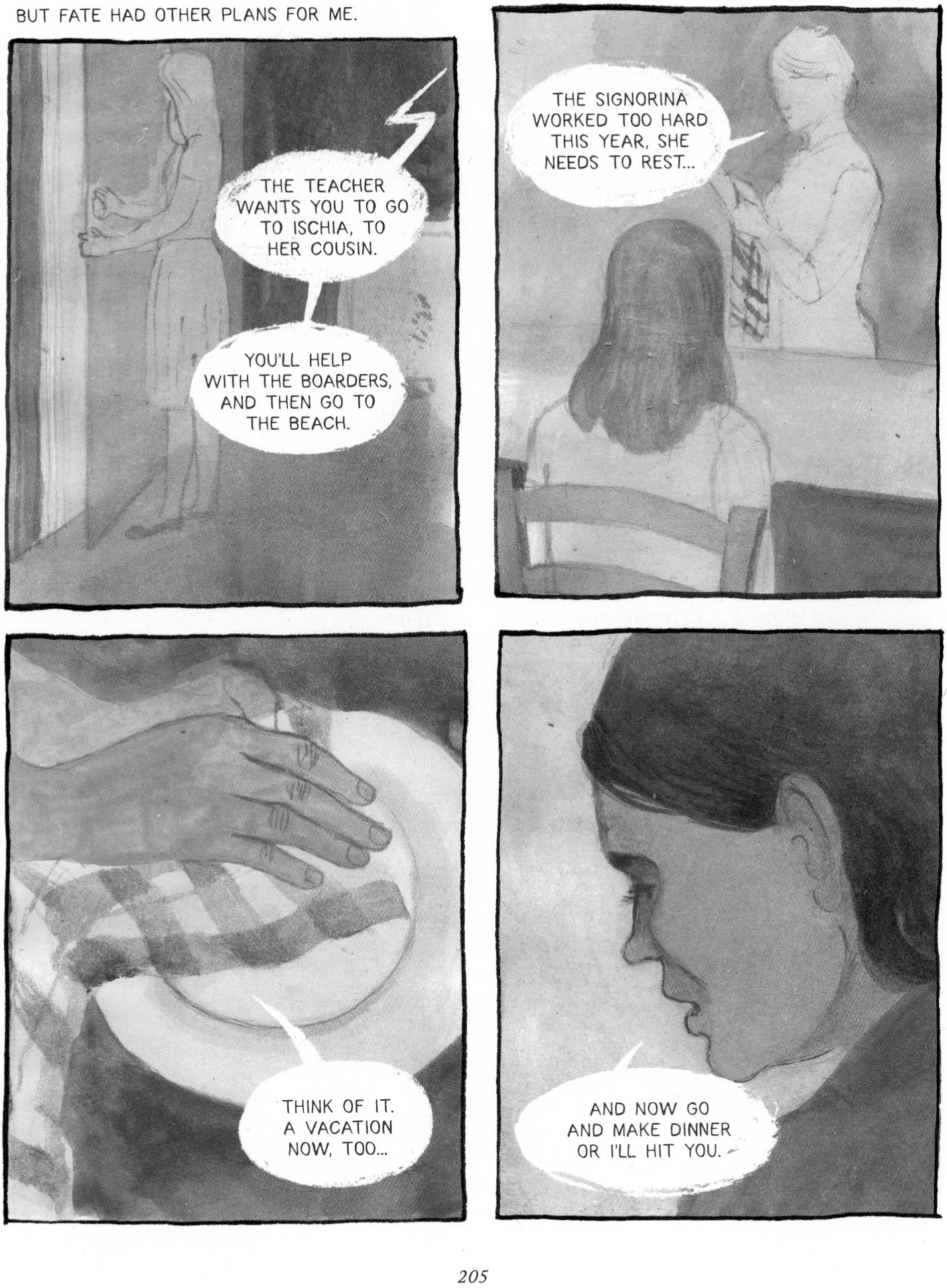
THE TEACHER WANTS YOU TO GO TO ISCHIA, TO HER COUSIN.
YOU'LL HELP WITH THE BOARDERS, AND THEN GO TO THE BEACH.
THE SIGNORINA WORKED TOO HARD THIS YEAR, SHE NEEDS TO REST...
THINK OF IT. A VACATION NOW, TOO...
AND NOW GO AND MAKE DINNER OR I'LL HIT YOU.

TWO DAYS LATER, HOWEVER, SHE HERSELF TOOK ME TO THE FERRY. I FELT BOTH TERRIFIED AND HAPPY. IT WAS MY FIRST JOURNEY ALONE.

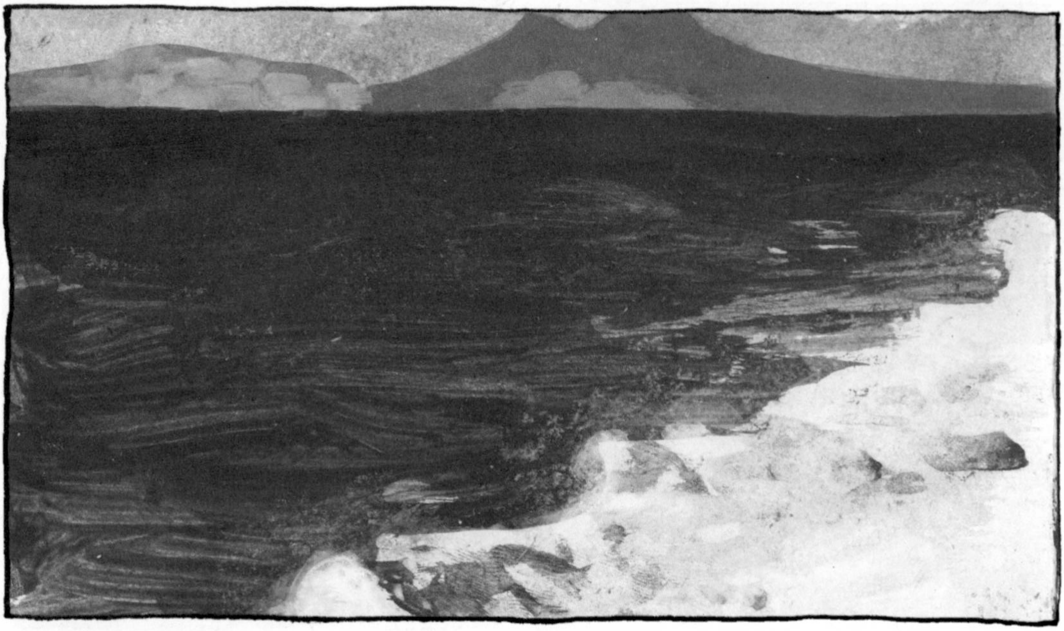

MY MOTHER'S LARGE BODY, THE NEIGHBORHOOD, LILA'S TROUBLES... IT ALL GREW INCREASINGLY DISTANT.

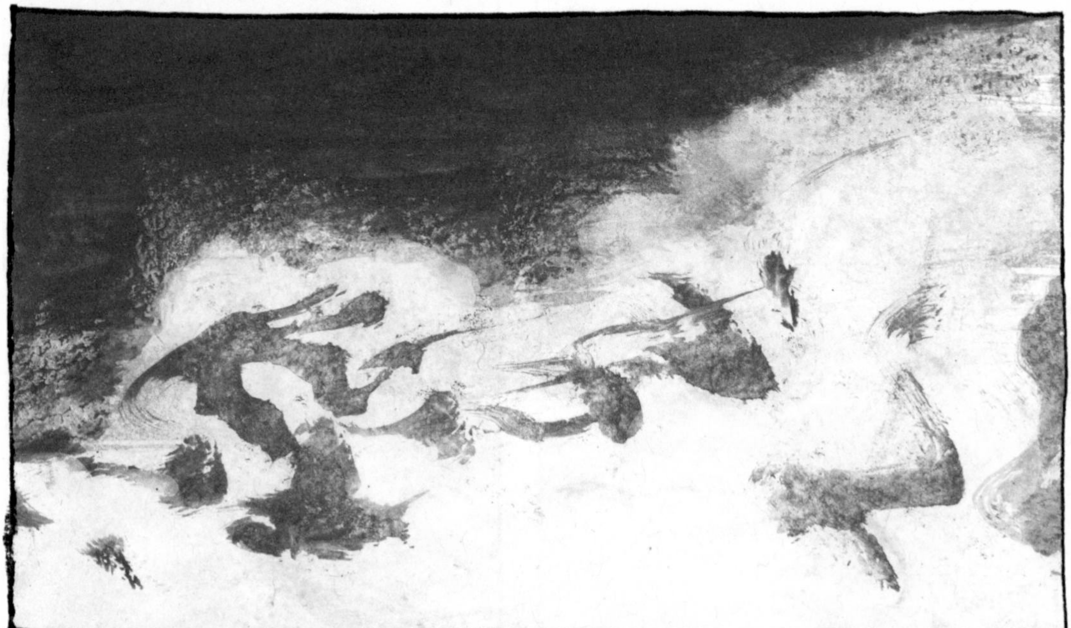

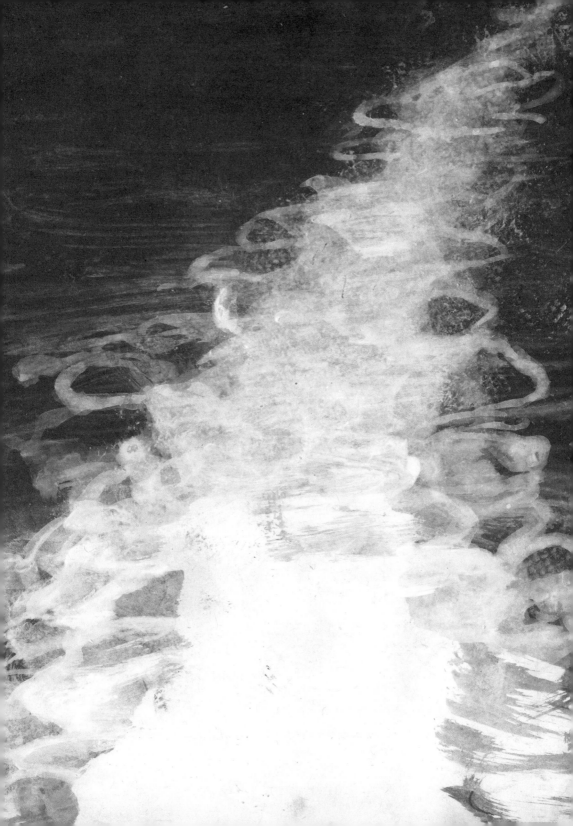

ON ISCHIA I FLOURISHED.

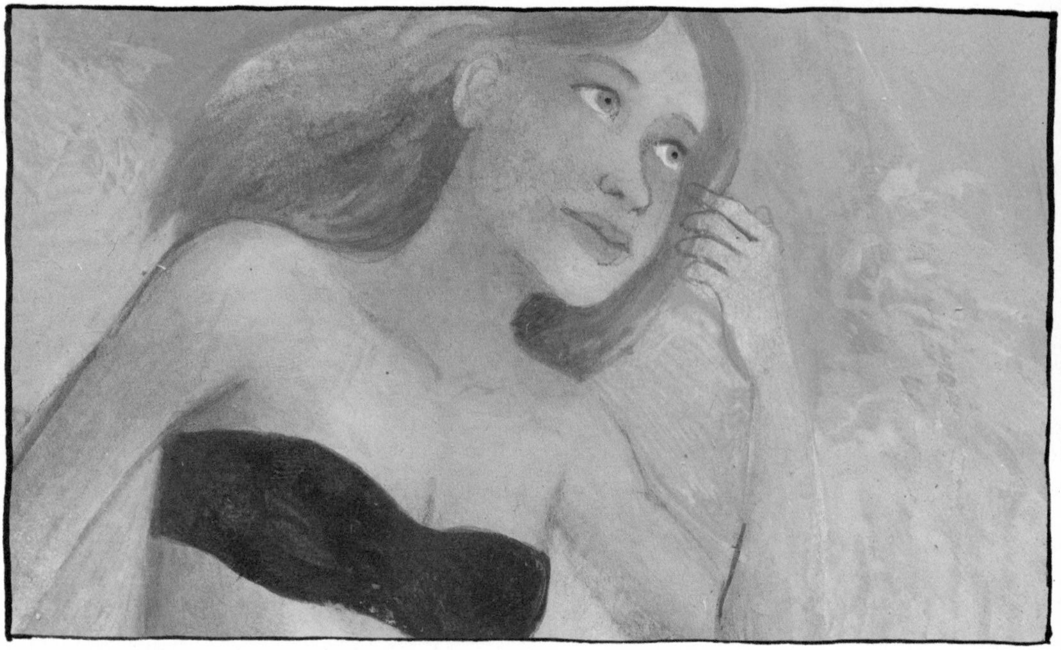

IN THE MORNING I HELPED NELLA, THE TEACHER'S COUSIN, WITH THE GUESTS.
IN THE AFTERNOON I WENT TO THE MARONTI BEACH.

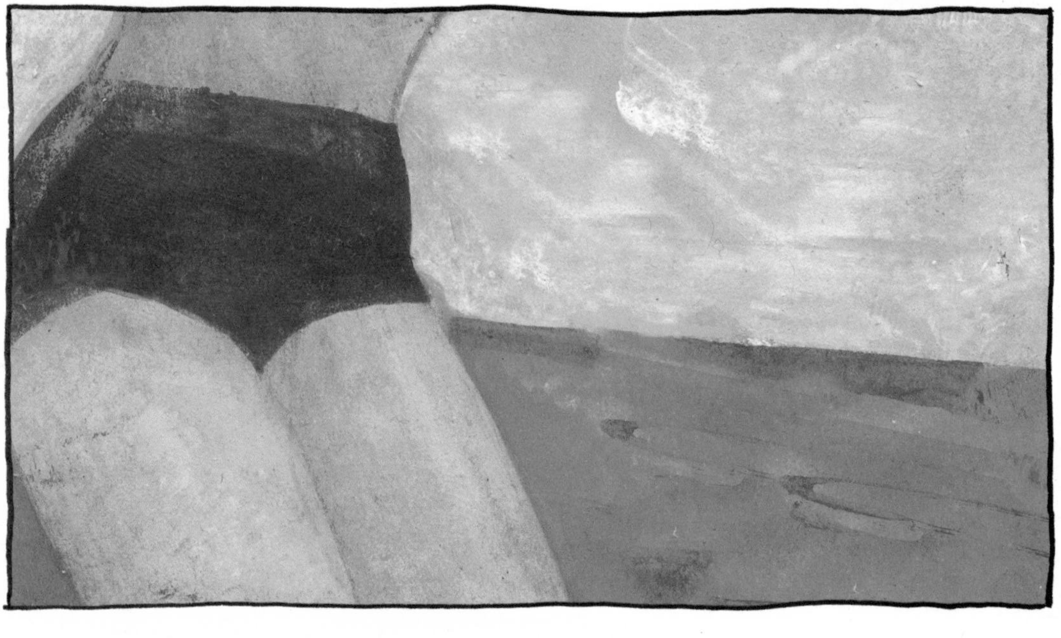

NELLA HAD TOLD ME THAT A FAMILY FROM NAPLES WAS ARRIVING. THEY HAD A WONDERFUL SON, A BOY MY AGE.

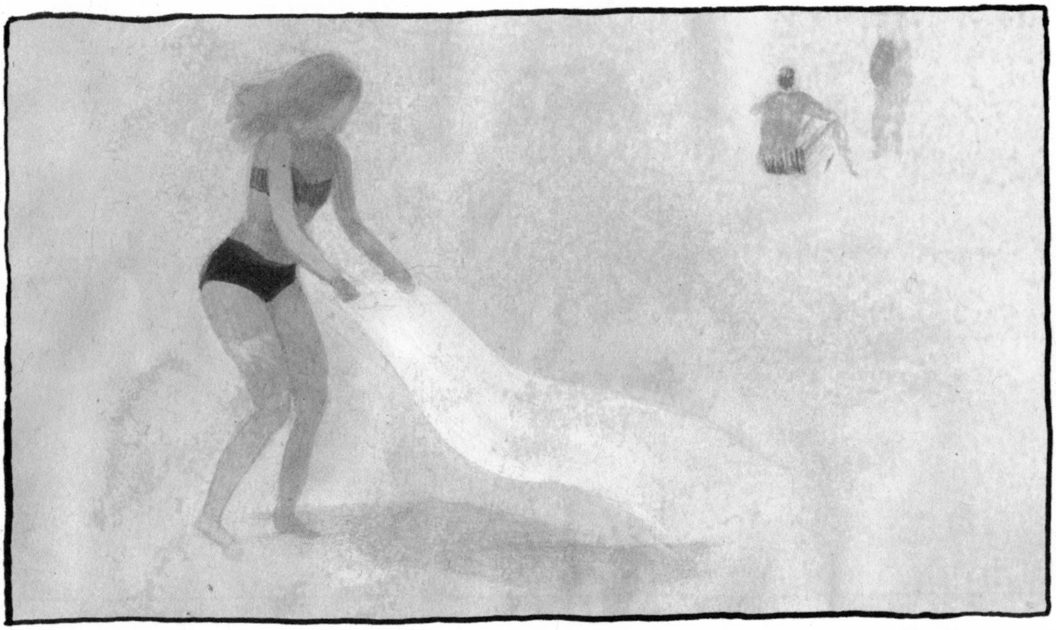

I WAS IMMEDIATELY ANXIOUS ABOUT THIS YOUNG MAN: FEARFUL THAT HE WOULDN'T LIKE ME, THAT WE'D BE UNABLE TO SAY A WORD TO EACH OTHER.

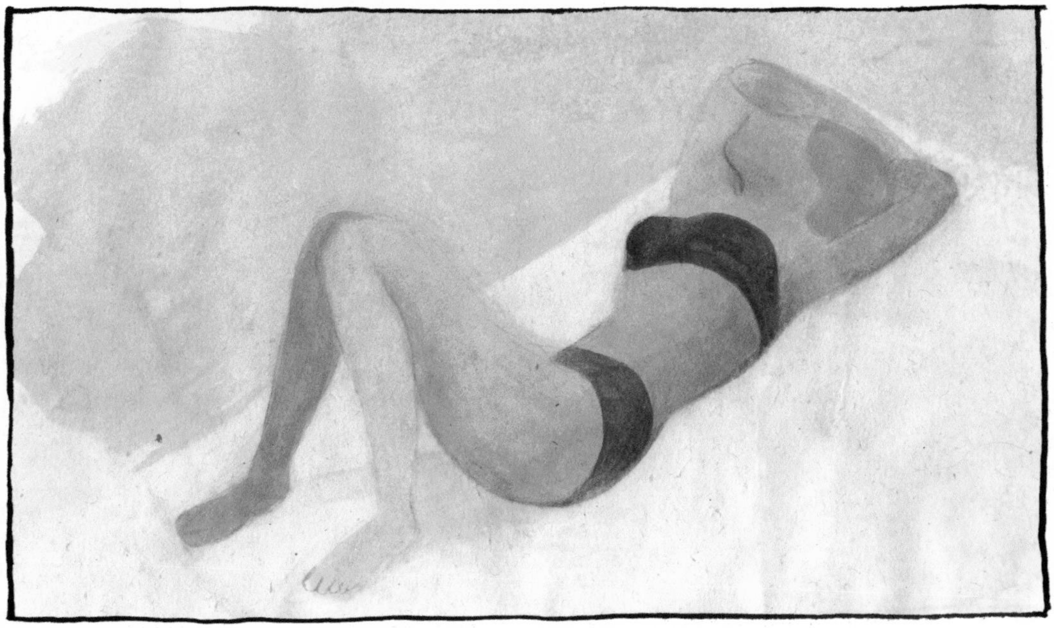

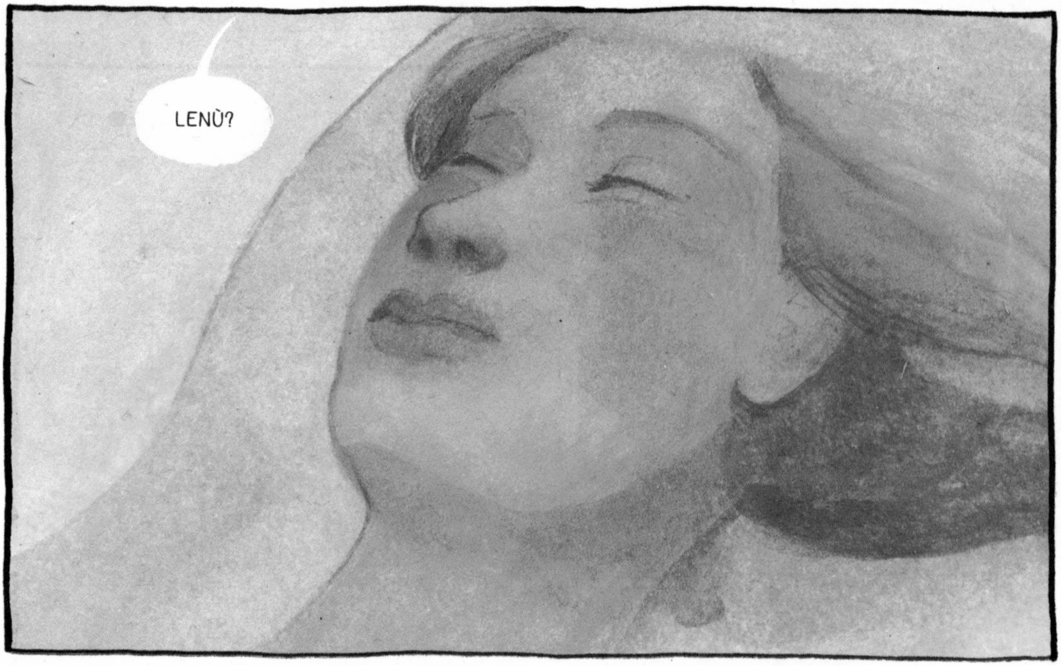
LENÙ?

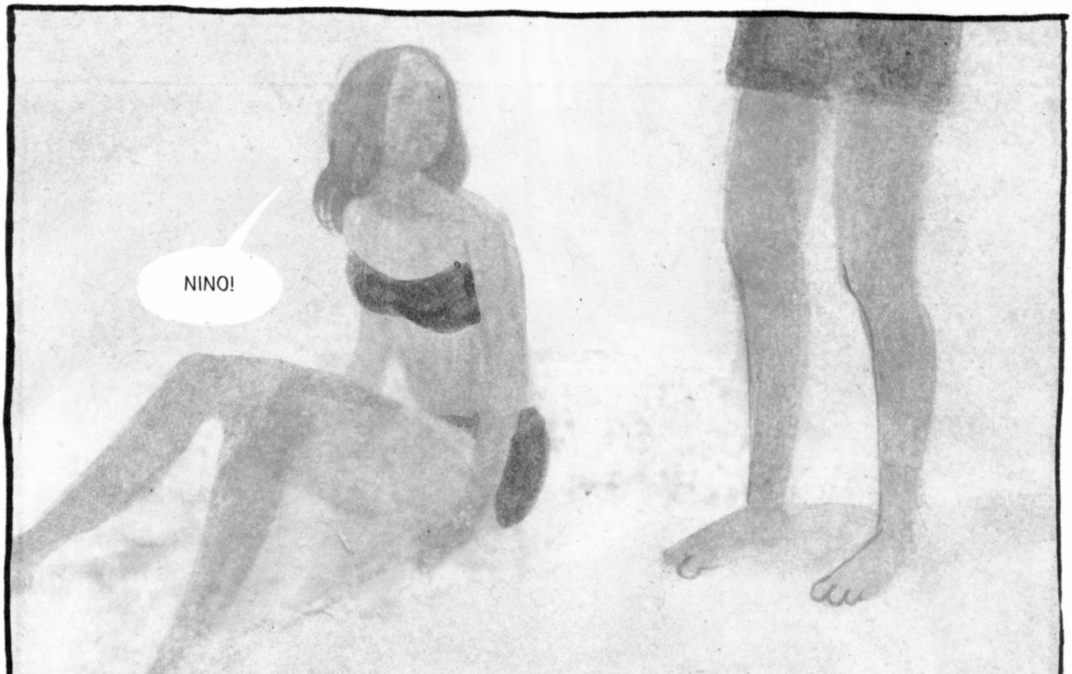
NINO!

WAS IT POSSIBLE? THE FAMILY WE WERE EXPECTING...

...WAS NINO SARRATORE'S?

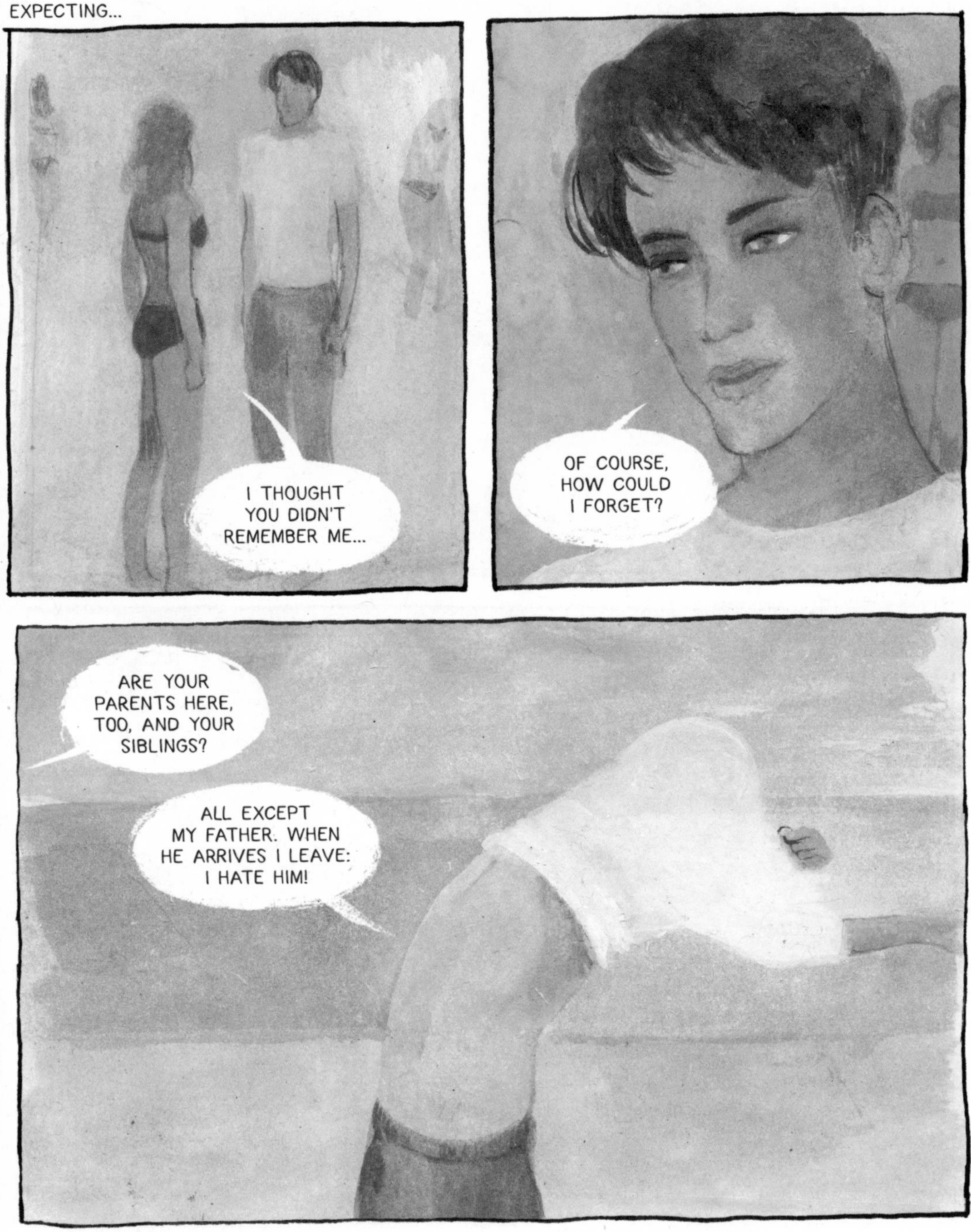
I THOUGHT YOU DIDN'T REMEMBER ME...
OF COURSE, HOW COULD I FORGET?
ARE YOUR PARENTS HERE, TOO, AND YOUR SIBLINGS?
ALL EXCEPT MY FATHER. WHEN HE ARRIVES I LEAVE: I HATE HIM!

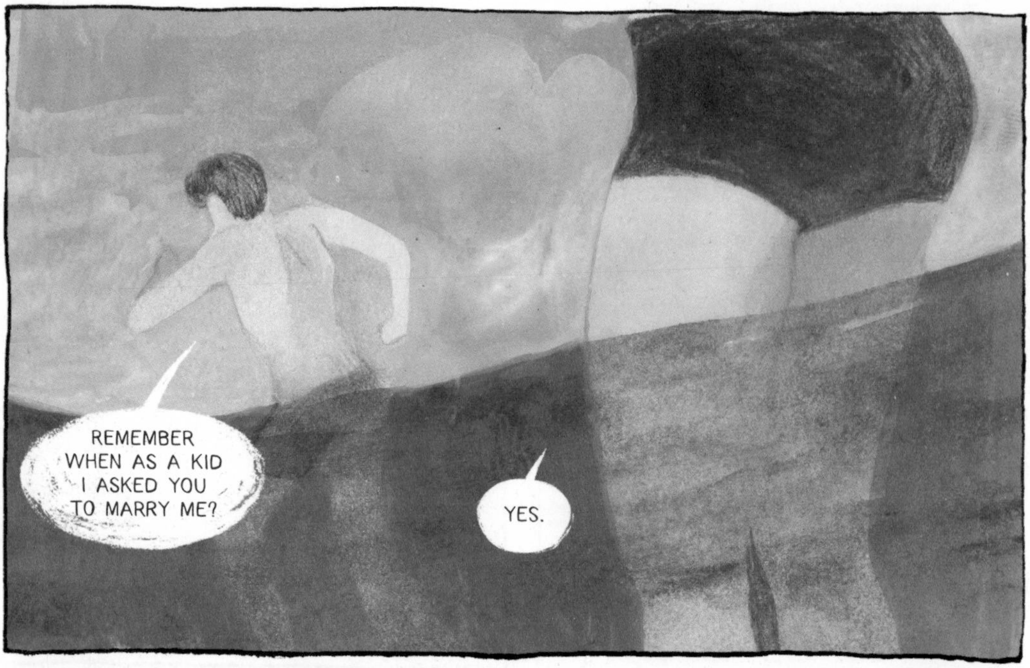
REMEMBER WHEN AS A KID I ASKED YOU TO MARRY ME?
YES.

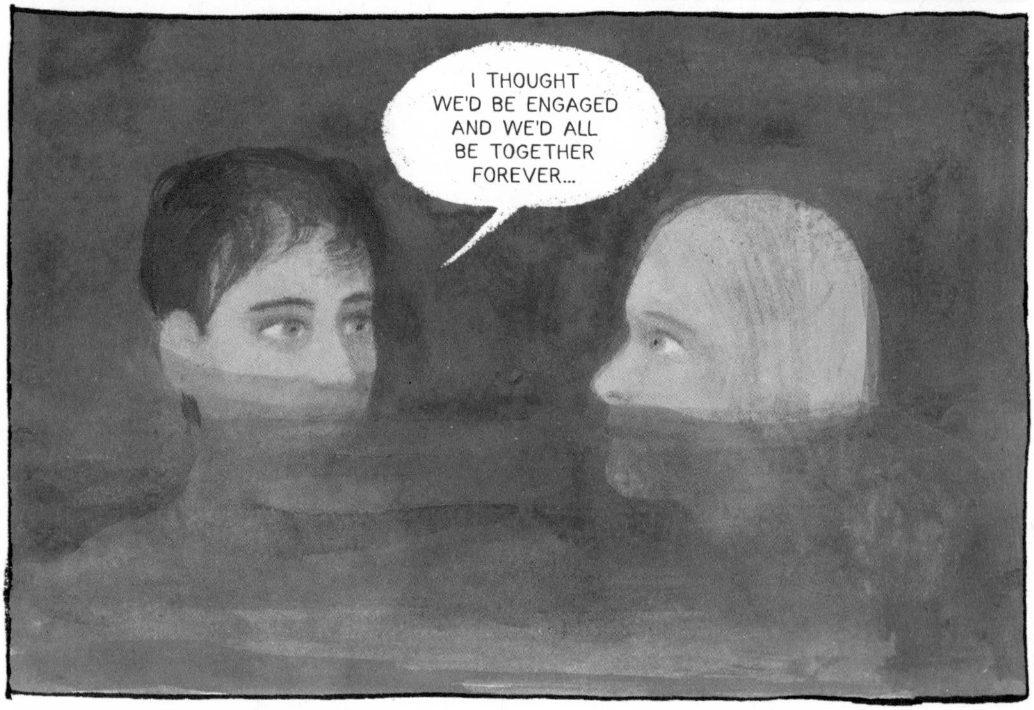
I THOUGHT WE'D BE ENGAGED AND WE'D ALL BE TOGETHER FOREVER...

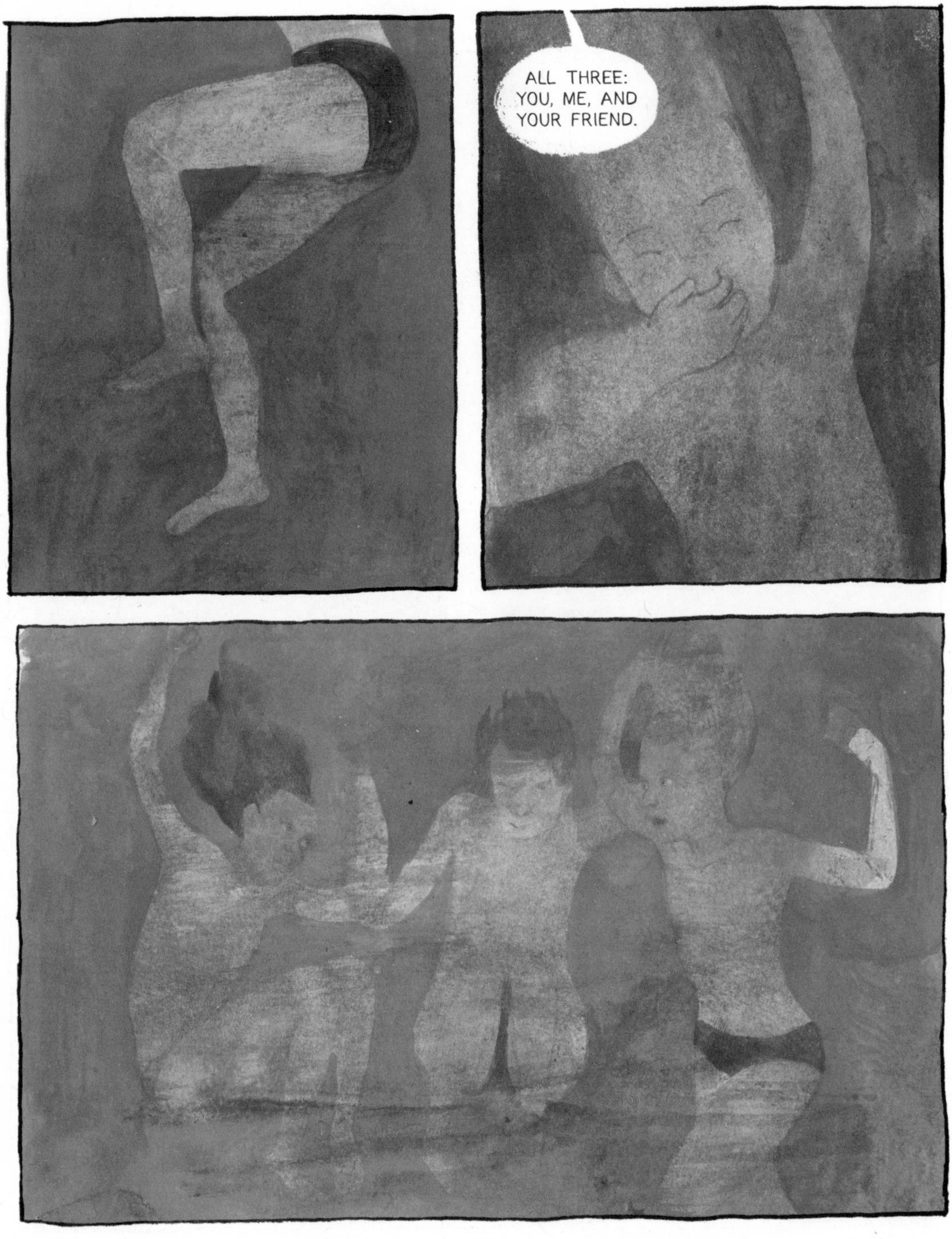
ALL THREE: YOU, ME, AND YOUR FRIEND.

I FELT A SHARP PAIN IN MY CHEST: LILA WAS EVEN HERE, BETWEEN US.

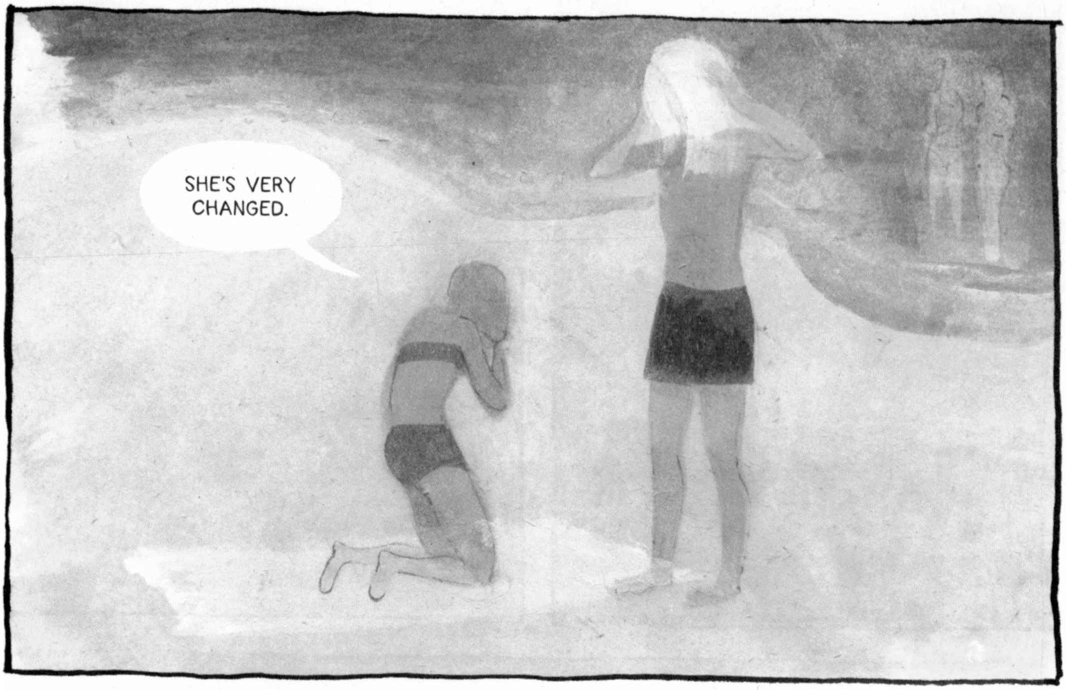
SHE'S VERY CHANGED.

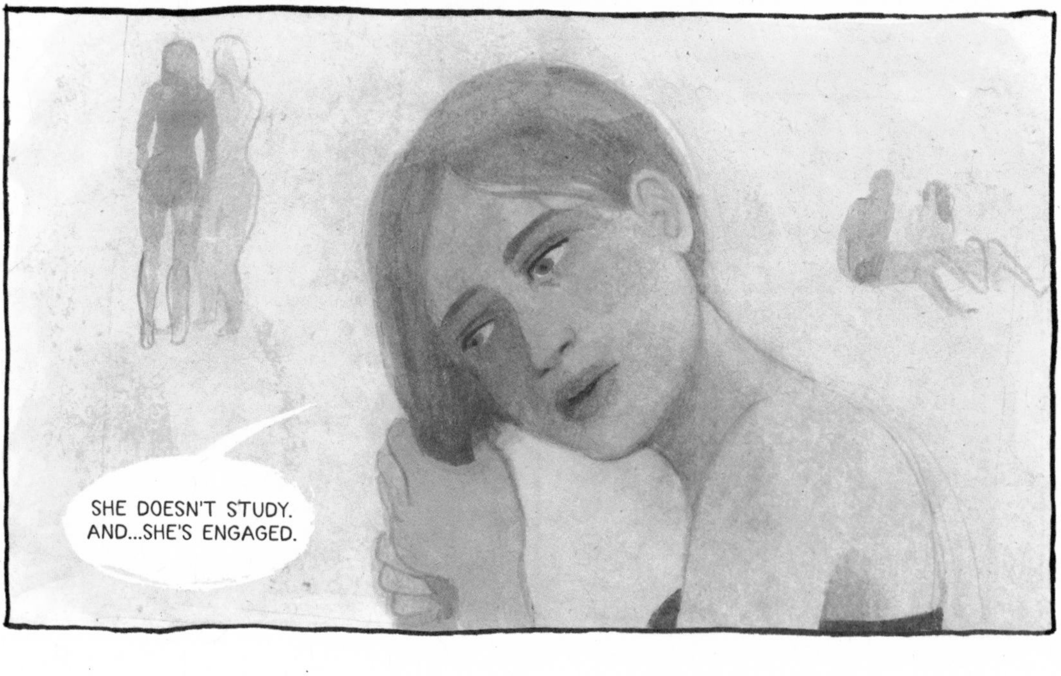
SHE DOESN'T STUDY. AND...SHE'S ENGAGED.

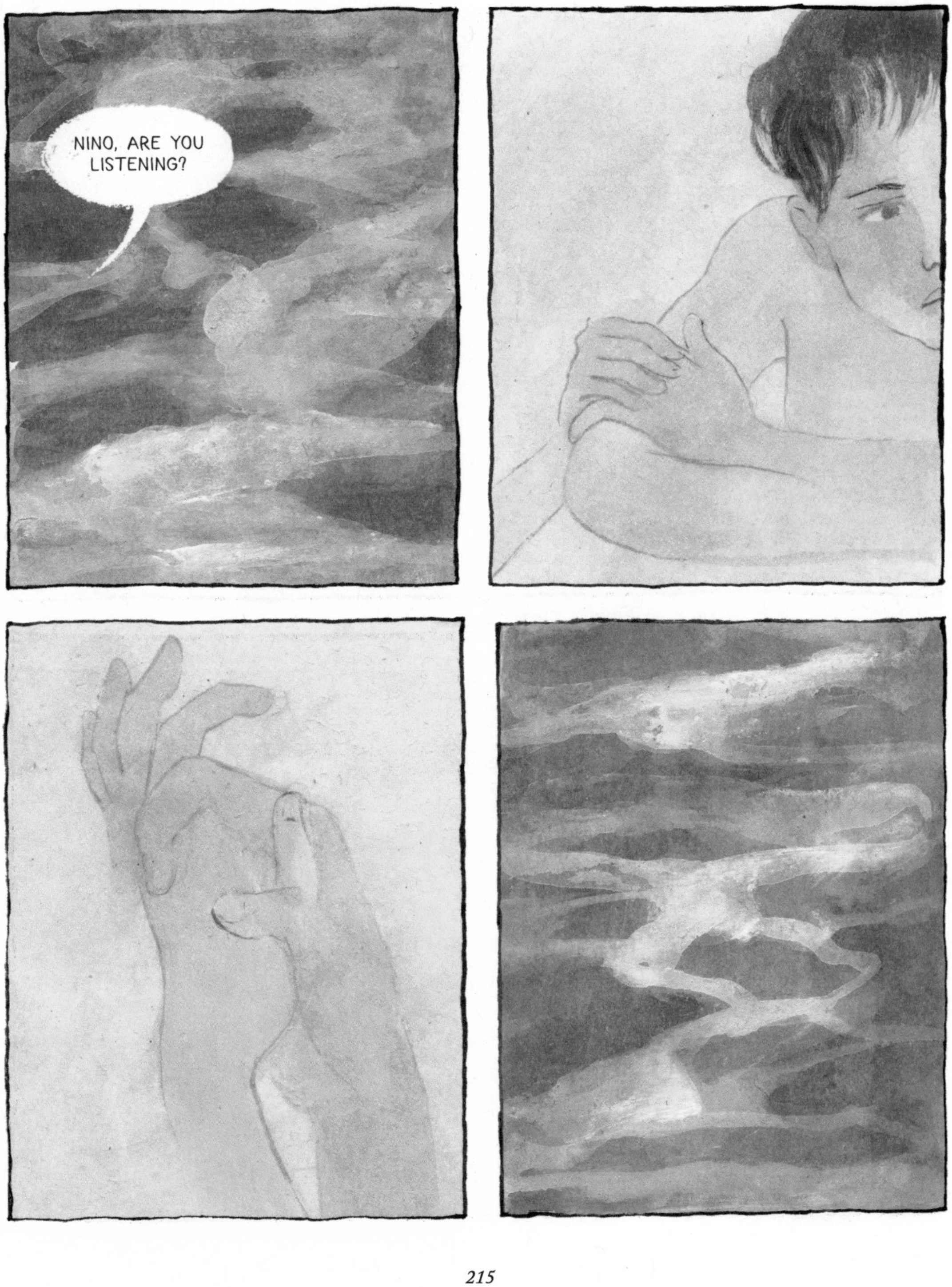
NINO, ARE YOU LISTENING?

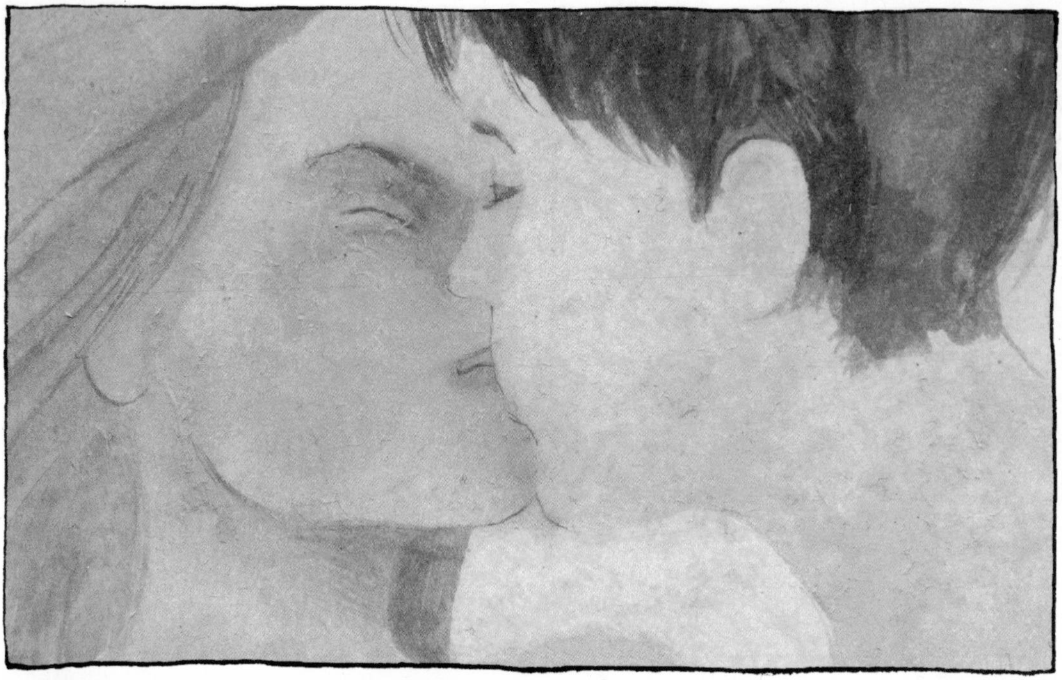

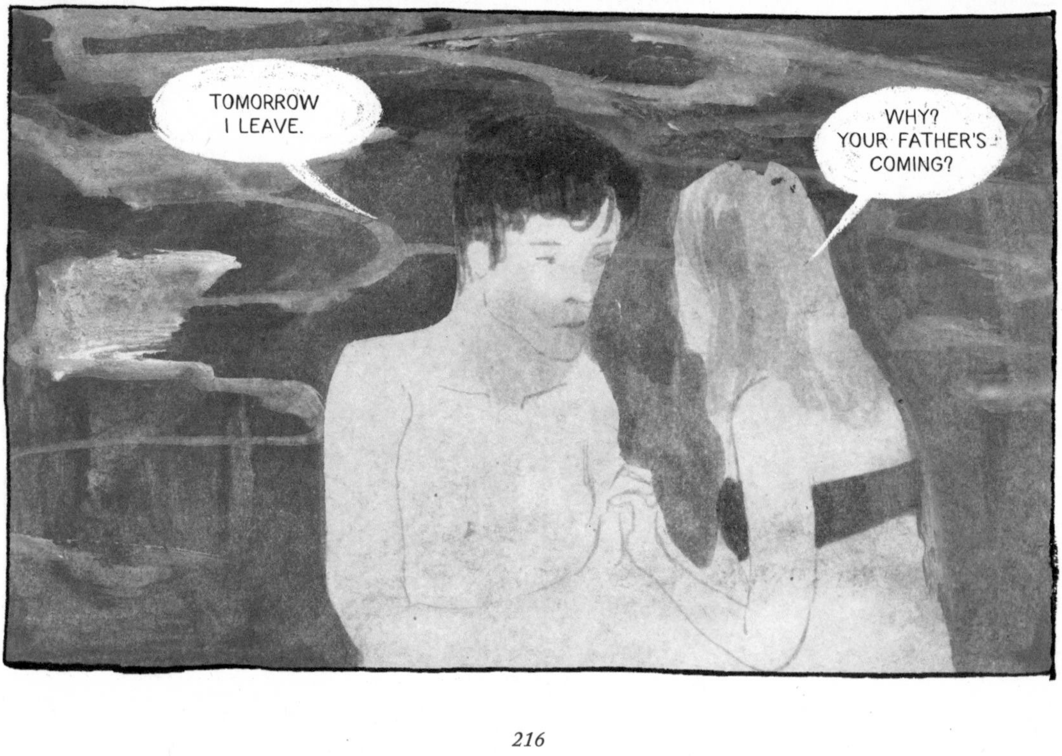
TOMORROW I LEAVE.
WHY? YOUR FATHER'S COMING?

I CRIED ALL NIGHT AND WHEN I WOKE UP NINO WAS GONE.

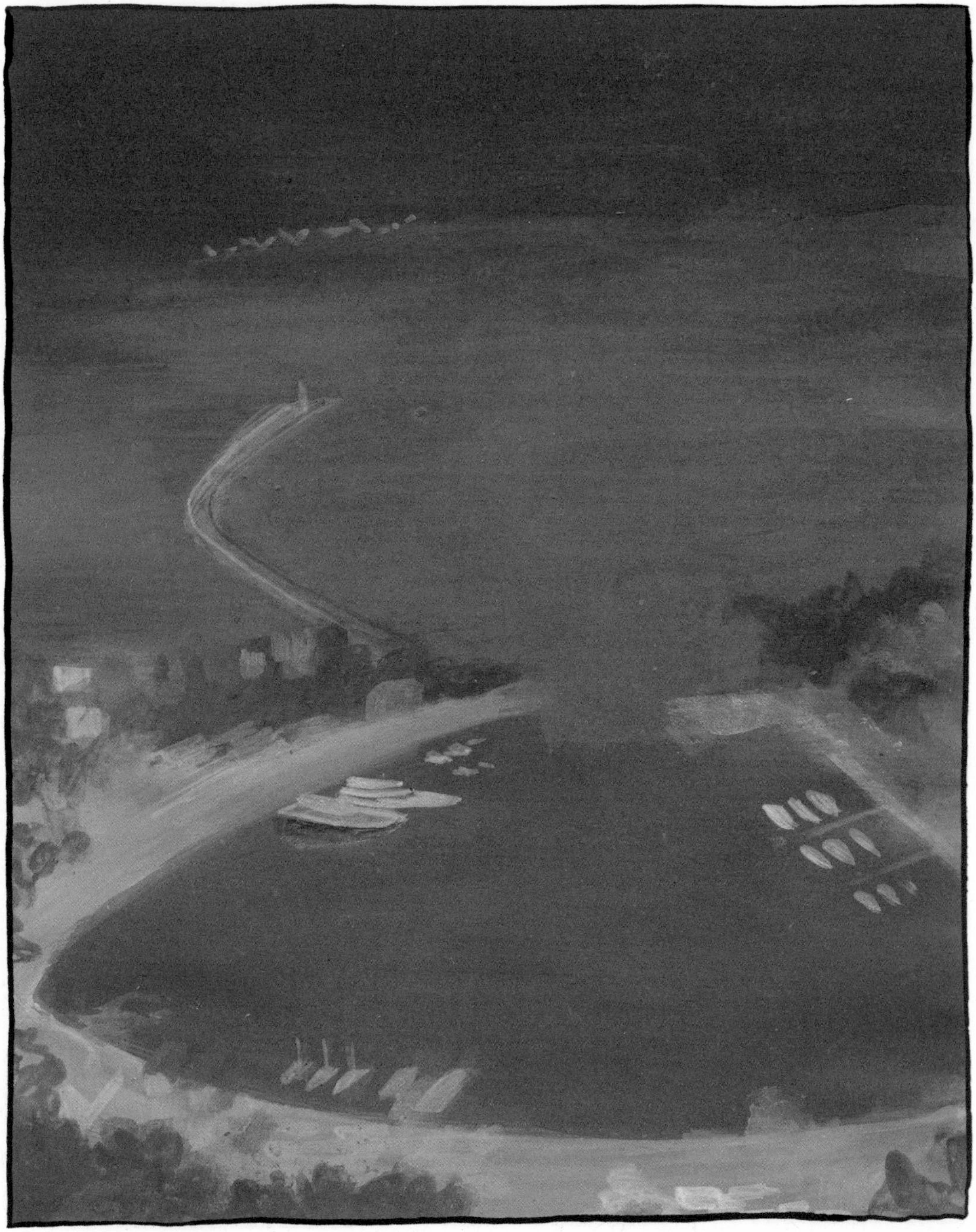

THAT SAME DAY I GOT A LETTER.

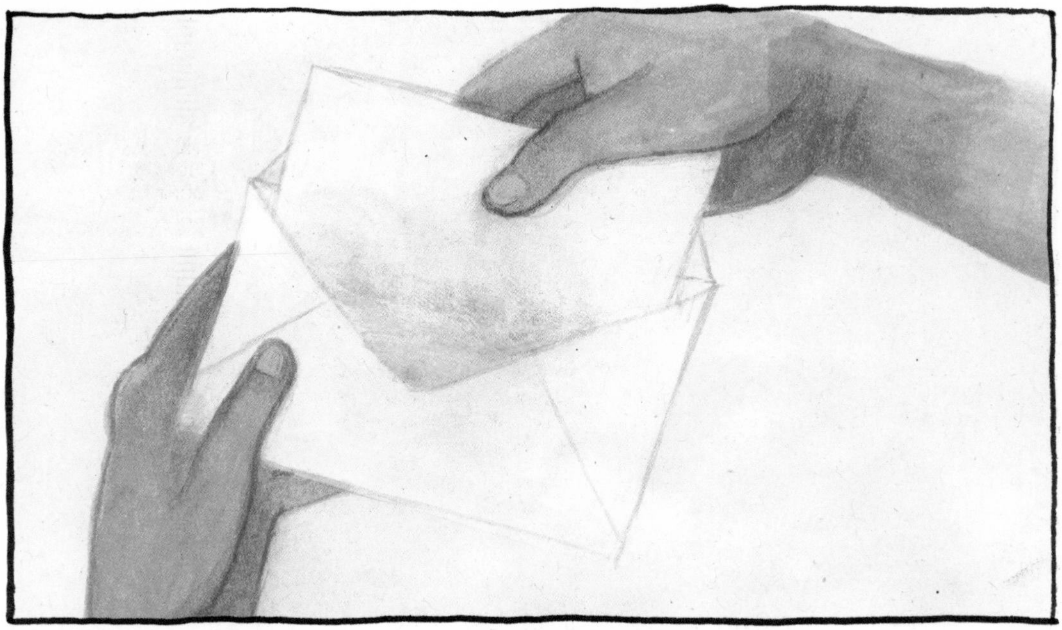

IT WAS FROM LILA. I READ IT AND I SAW HER, HEARD HER. HER WRITING WAS BEAUTIFUL.

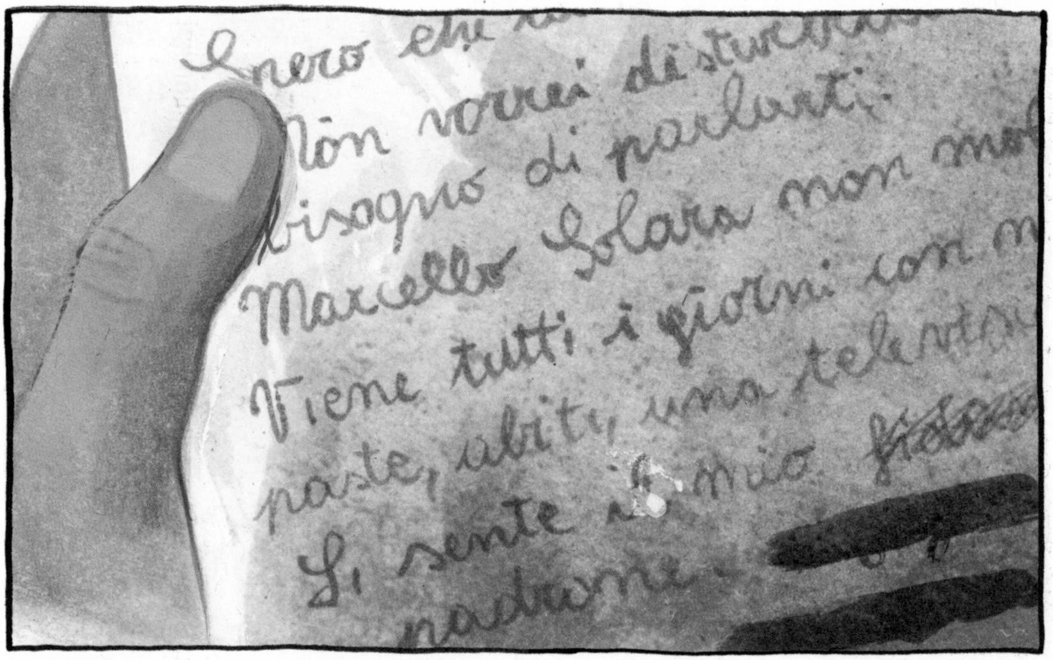
Spero che
Non vorrei
bisogno di parlarti.
Marcello Solara non
Viene tutti i giorni con
paste, abiti, una
Si sente il mio

HER WORLD RAPIDLY SUPERIMPOSED ITSELF ON MINE.

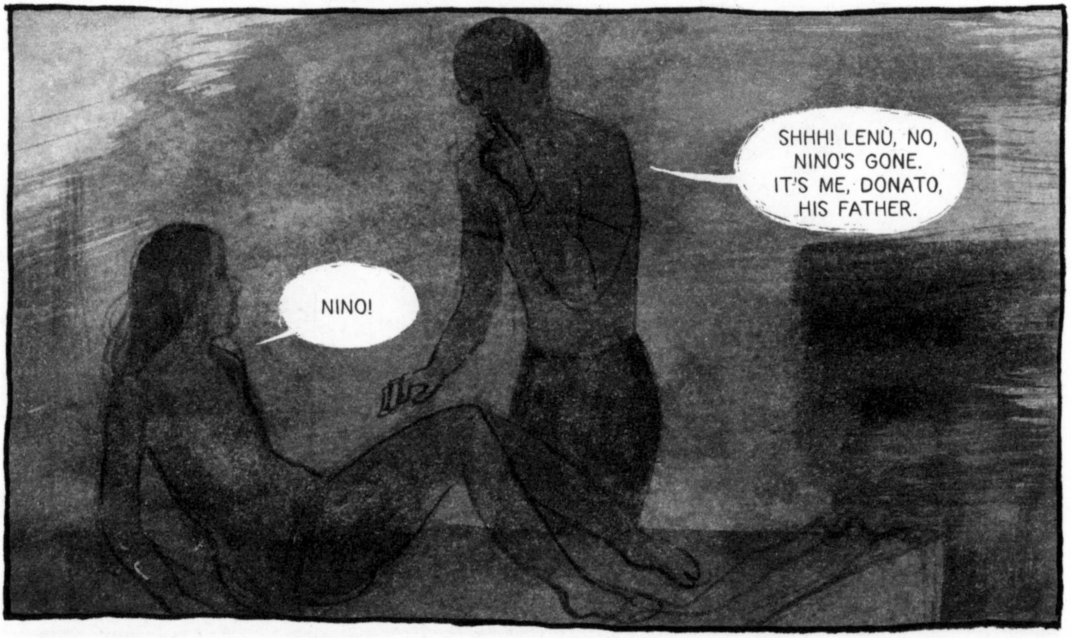
NINO!
SHHH! LENÙ, NO, NINO'S GONE. IT'S ME, DONATO, HIS FATHER.

MARCELLO CONSIDERED HIMSELF HER FIANCÉ, RATHER, HER MASTER: HE FOLLOWED HER, SPIED ON HER...

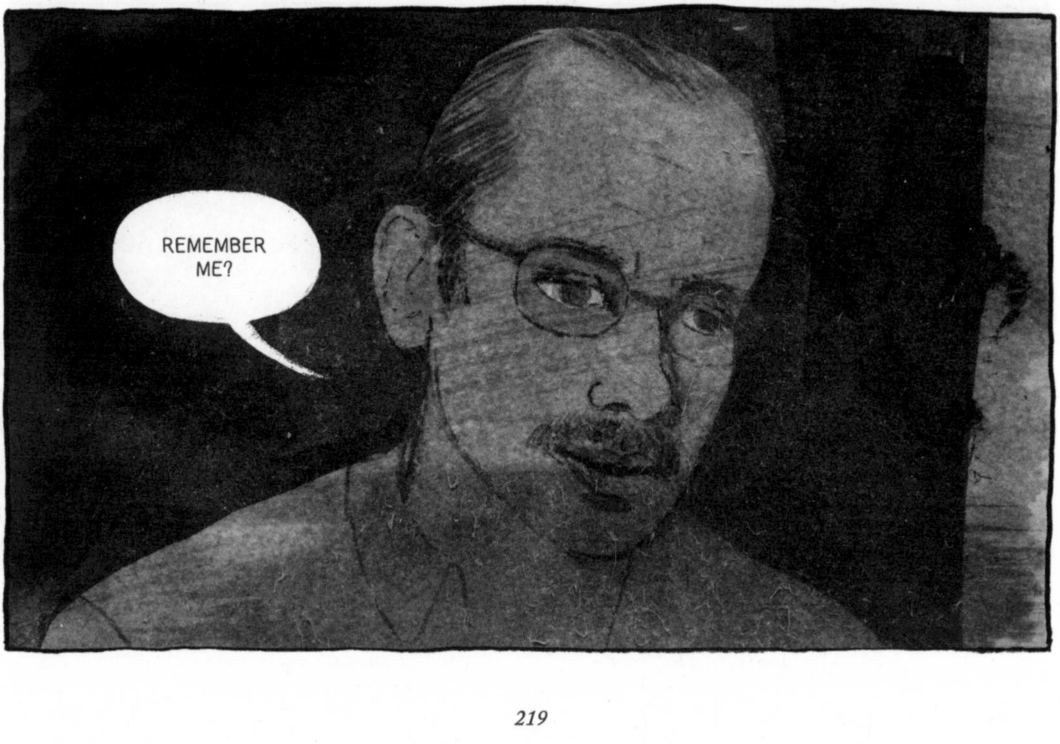
REMEMBER ME?

...HE WANTED TO KNOW ALL ABOUT HER AND, WORSE, WAS ALWAYS TRYING TO KISS HER.

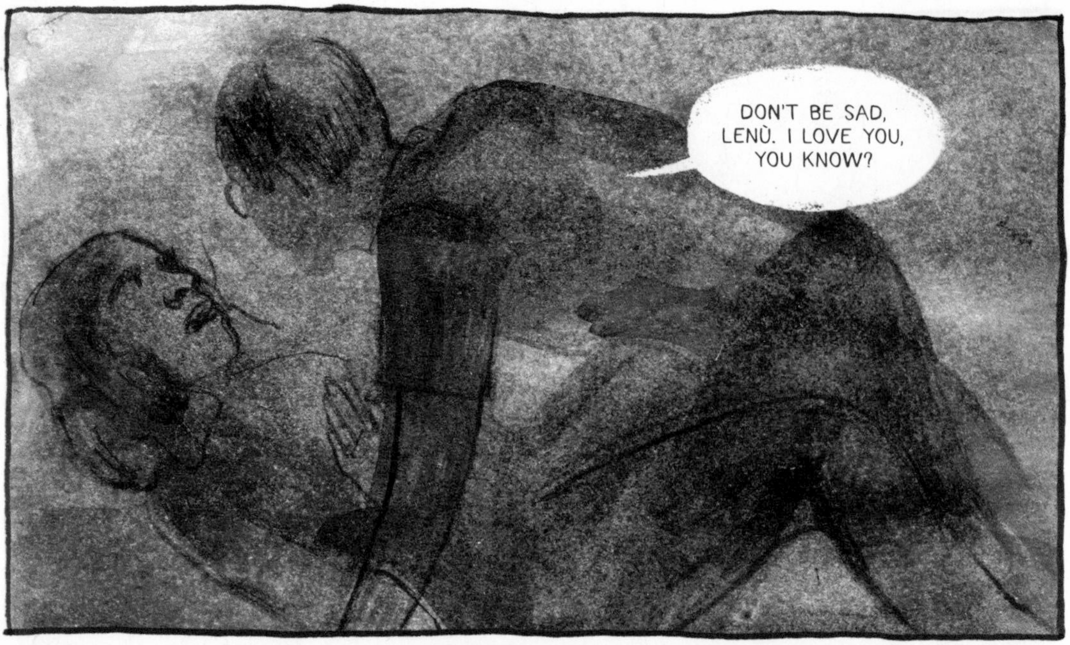
DON'T BE SAD, LENÙ. I LOVE YOU, YOU KNOW?

SHE FELT THE WEIGHT OF THE WORLD: GOOD AND EVIL MIXED TOGETHER REINFORCED EACH OTHER.

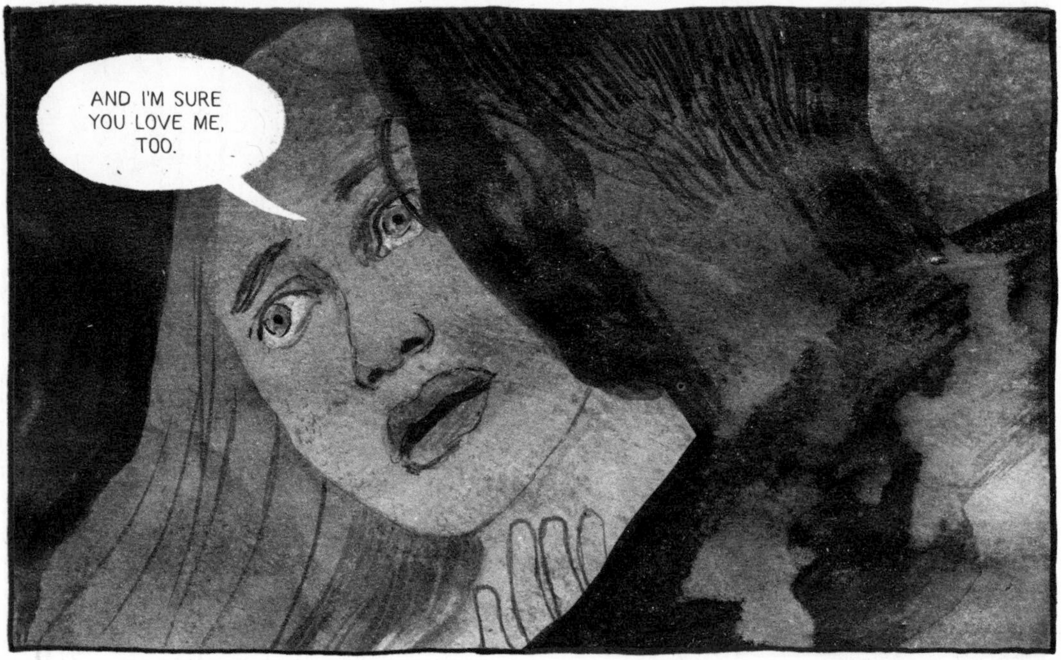
AND I'M SURE YOU LOVE ME, TOO.

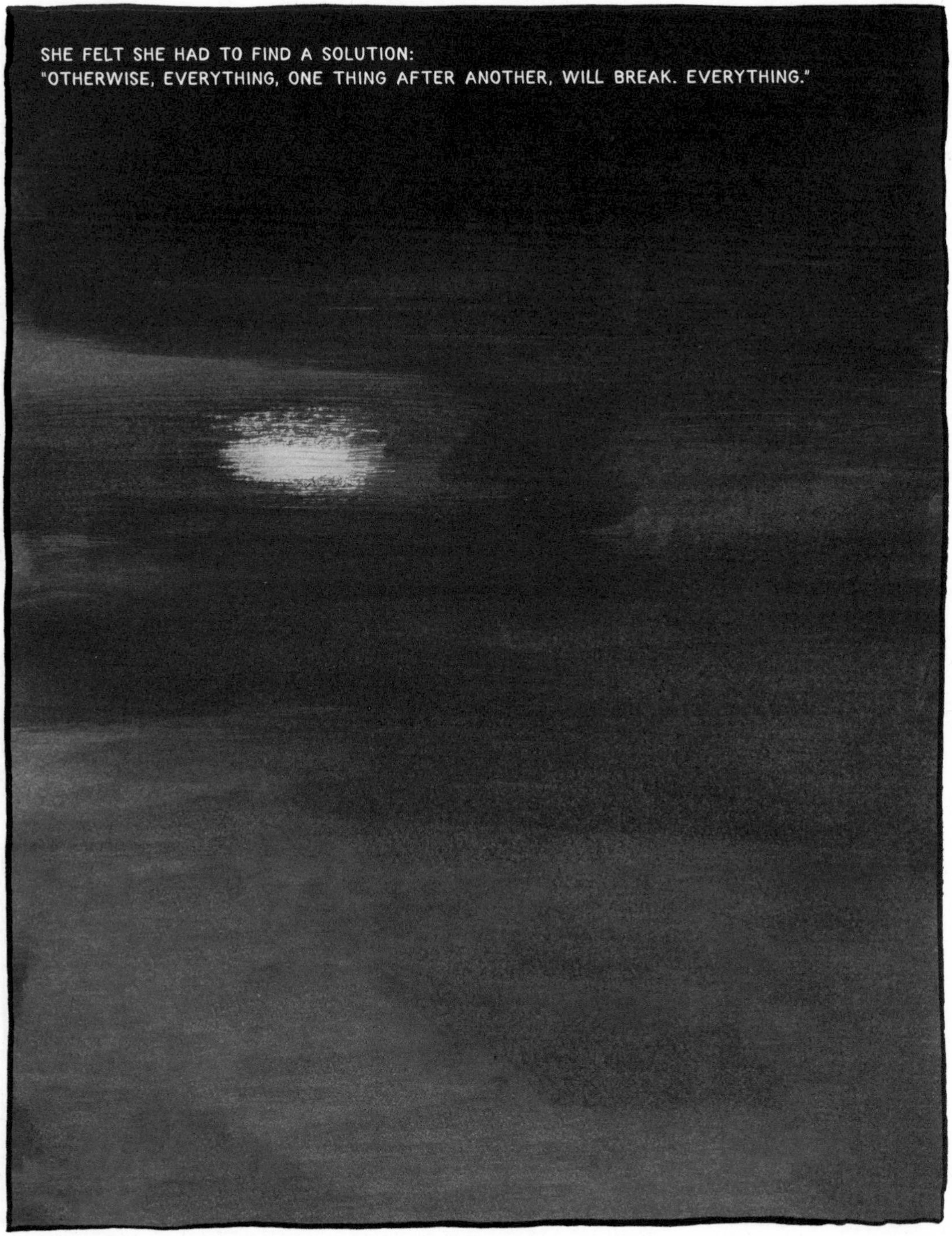
SHE FELT SHE HAD TO FIND A SOLUTION:
"OTHERWISE, EVERYTHING, ONE THING AFTER ANOTHER, WILL BREAK. EVERYTHING."

"I NEED TO SEE YOU, LENÙ. BUT YOU WHO CAN SHOULD NOT RETURN TO THIS TERRIBLE PLACE."

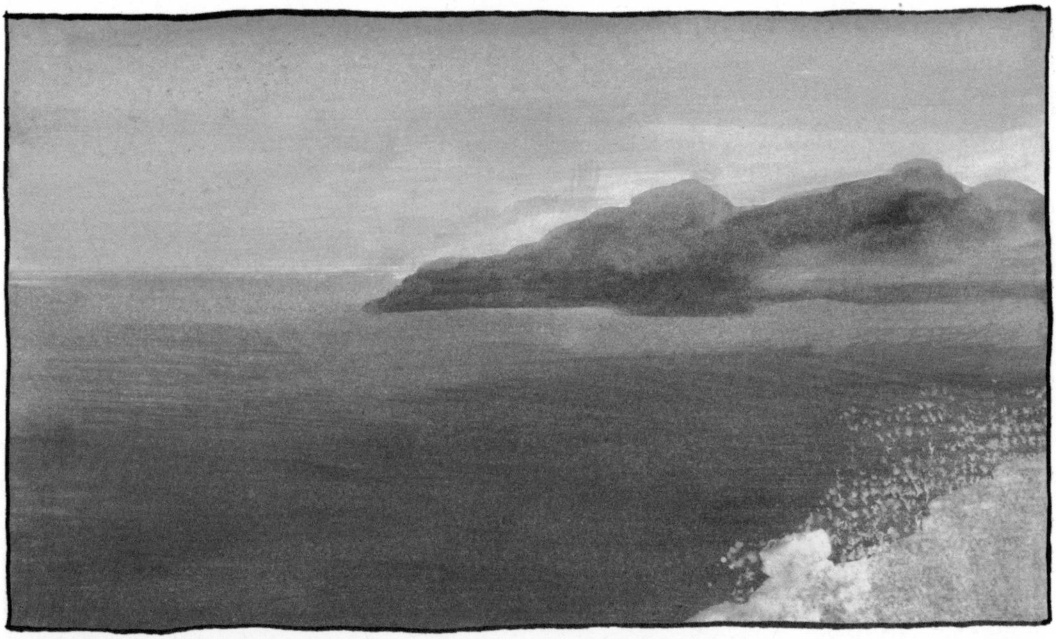

"YOU UNDERSTAND? DON'T EVER COME BACK."

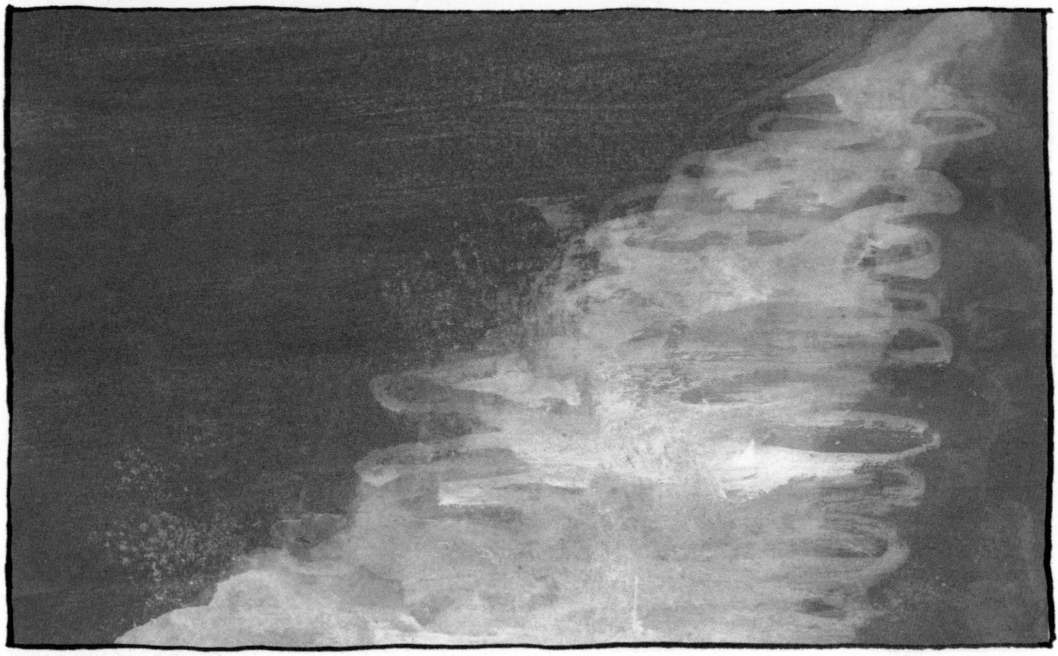

I FOUND NAPLES SUBMERGED IN A STINKING, DEVASTATING HEAT.

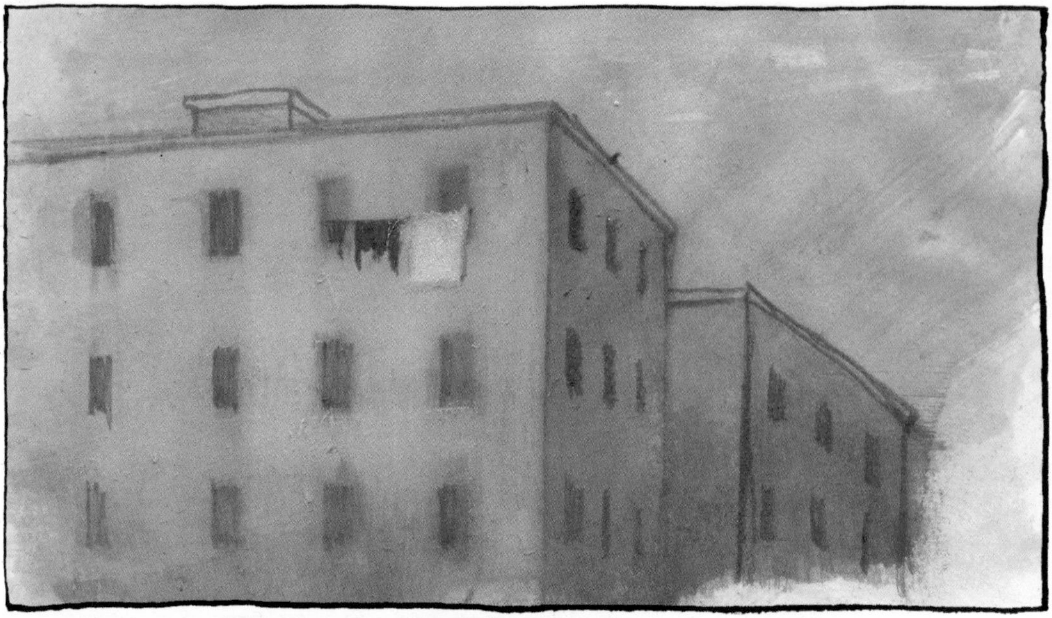

I STILL FELT ON ME THE ODOR OF DONATO SARRATORE.
HIS HANDS HAD FONDLED ME EVERYWHERE.

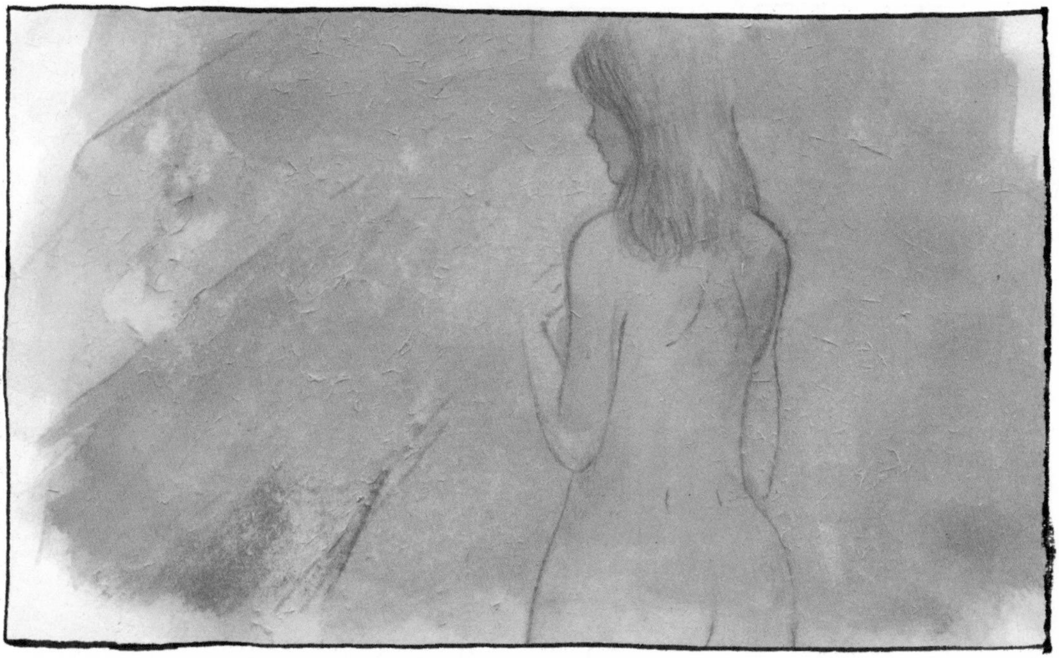

I HURRIED TO FIND LILA RIGHT AWAY.

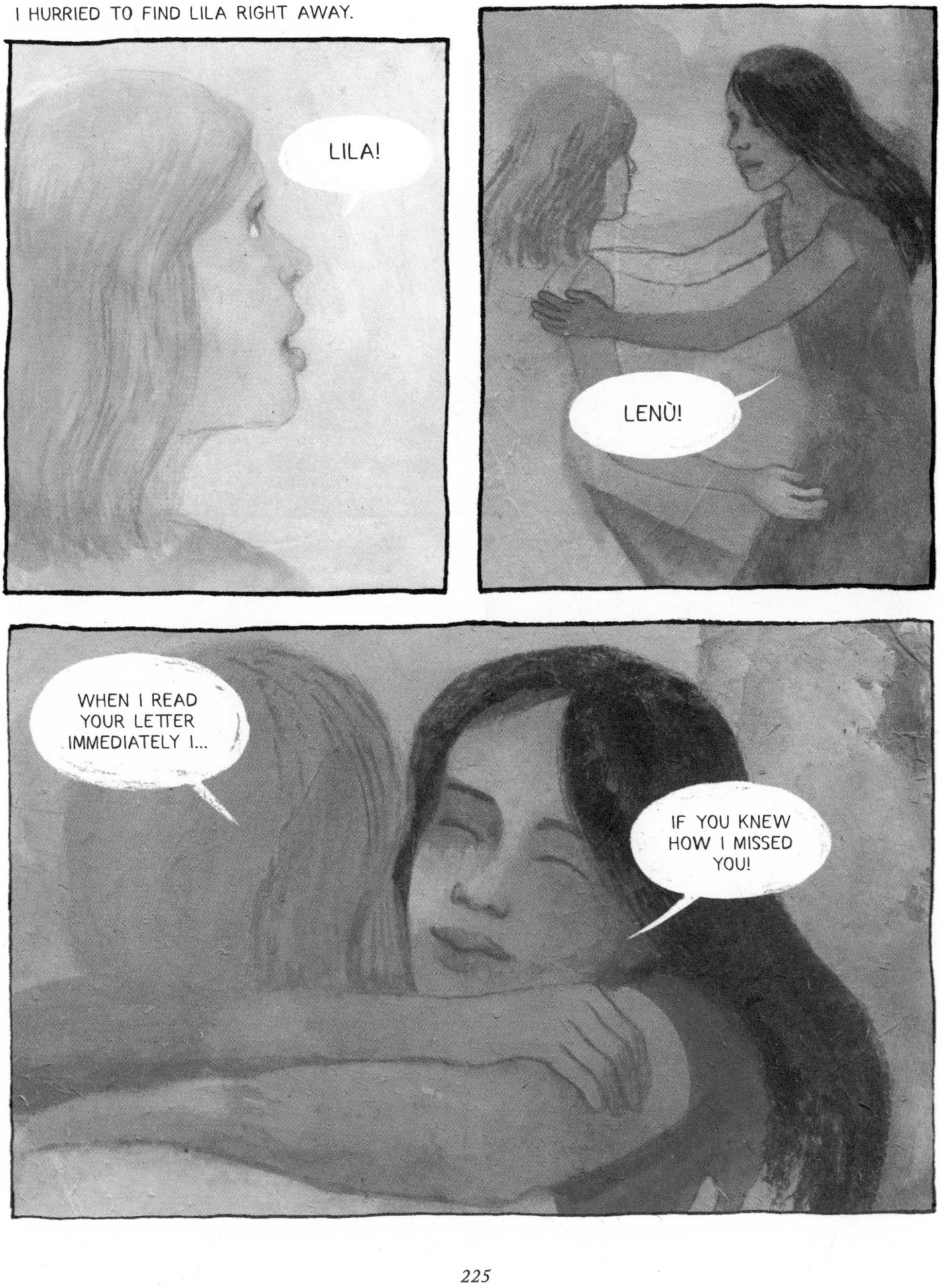
LILA!
LENÙ!
WHEN I READ YOUR LETTER IMMEDIATELY I...
IF YOU KNEW HOW I MISSED YOU!

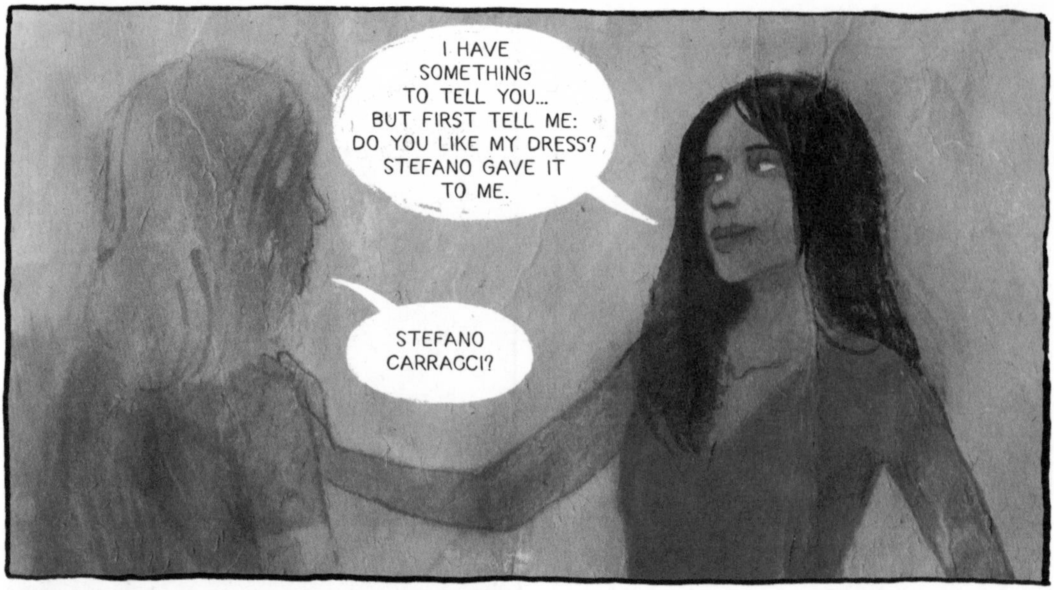
I HAVE SOMETHING TO TELL YOU... BUT FIRST TELL ME: DO YOU LIKE MY DRESS? STEFANO GAVE IT TO ME.
STEFANO CARRACCI?

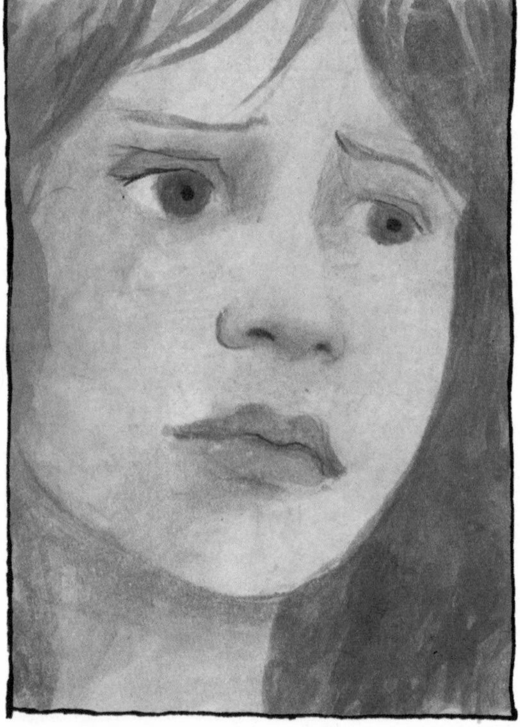

I THOUGHT I'D FIND HER DESPERATE, SAD...

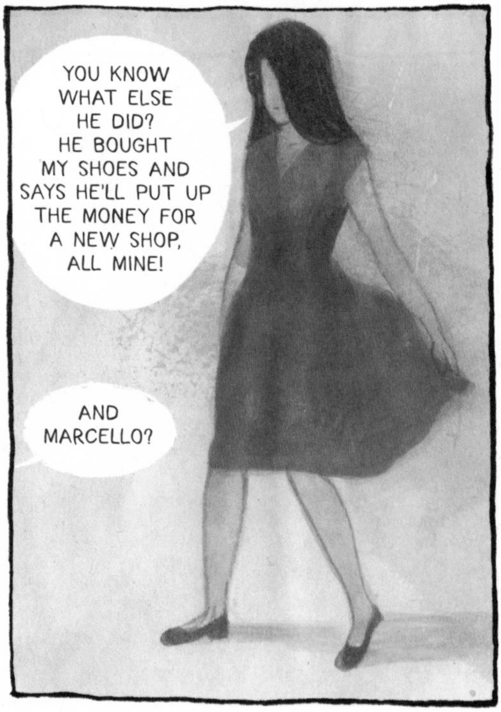
YOU KNOW WHAT ELSE HE DID? HE BOUGHT MY SHOES AND SAYS HE'LL PUT UP THE MONEY FOR A NEW SHOP, ALL MINE!
AND MARCELLO?

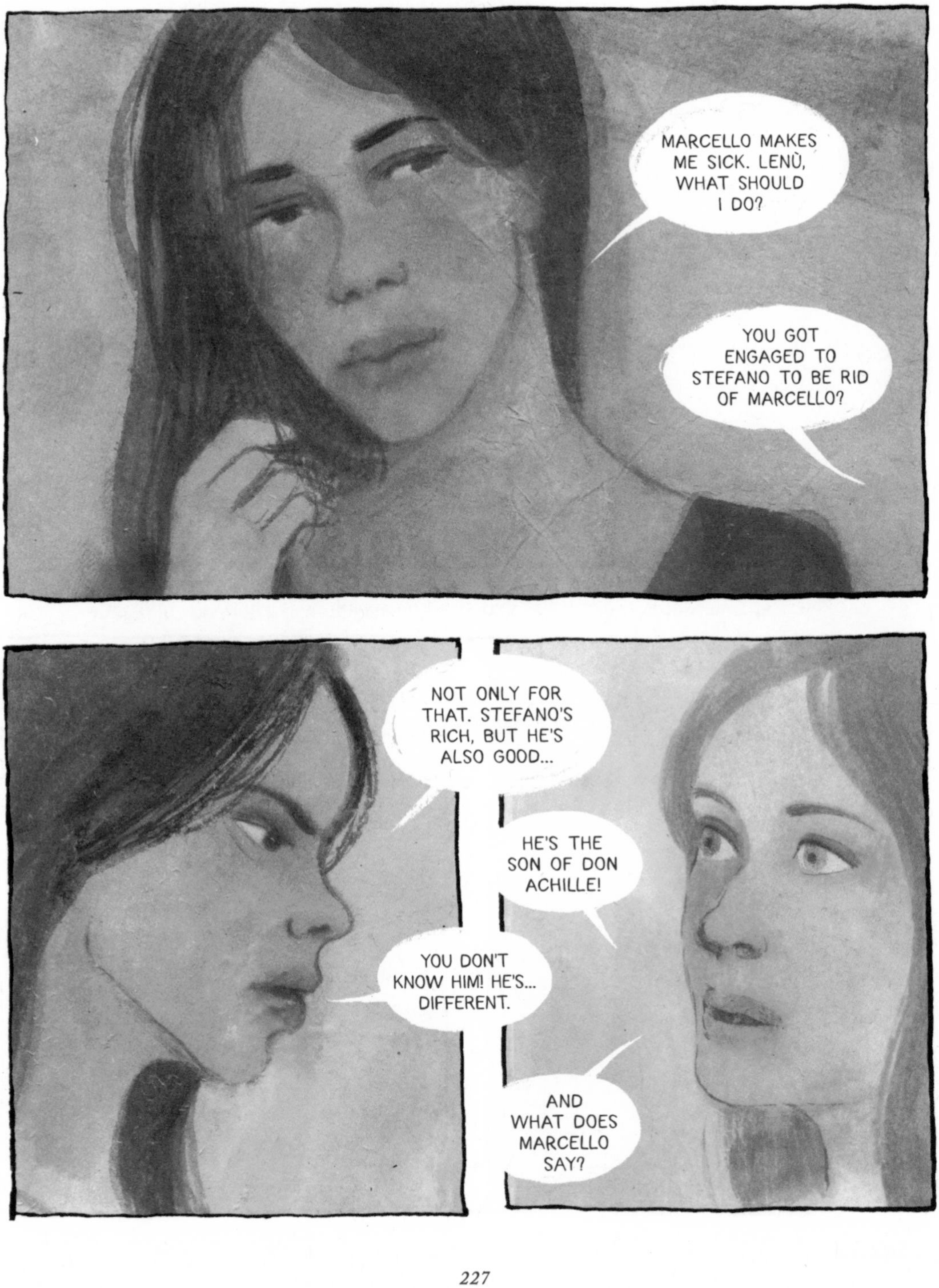
MARCELLO MAKES ME SICK. LENÙ, WHAT SHOULD I DO?
YOU GOT ENGAGED TO STEFANO TO BE RID OF MARCELLO?
NOT ONLY FOR THAT. STEFANO'S RICH, BUT HE'S ALSO GOOD...
HE'S THE SON OF DON ACHILLE!
YOU DON'T KNOW HIM! HE'S... DIFFERENT.
AND WHAT DOES MARCELLO SAY?

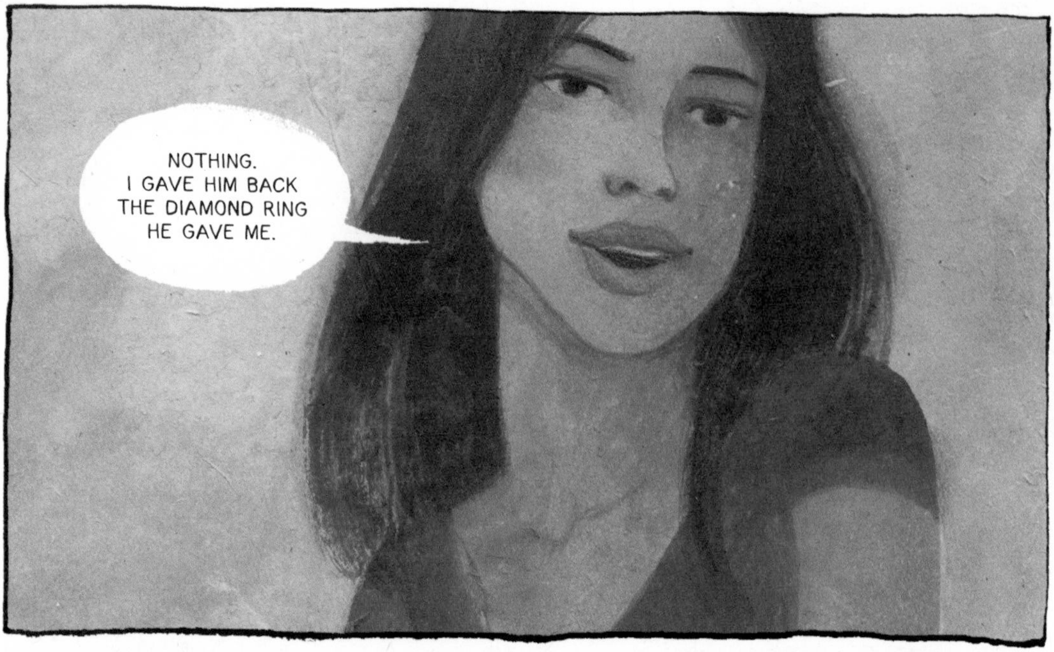
NOTHING. I GAVE HIM BACK THE DIAMOND RING HE GAVE ME.

WHY HAD SHE MADE ME COME BACK? WHAT DID SHE WANT FROM ME? FROM ALL OF US?

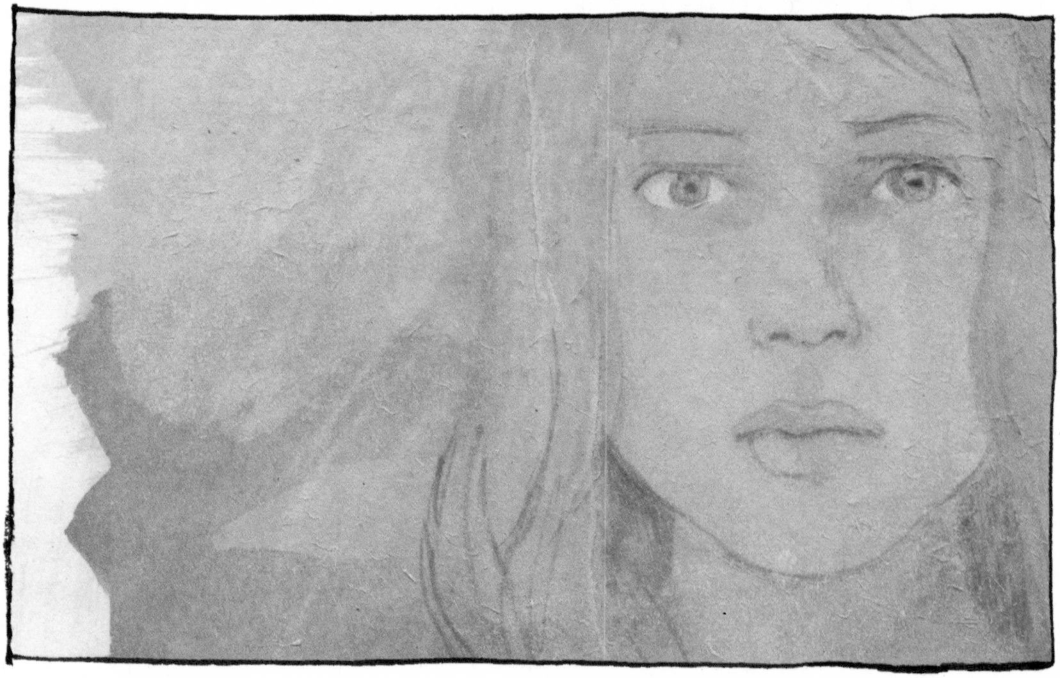

DID SHE WANT TO LEAVE THE NEIGHBORHOOD BY STAYING THERE?

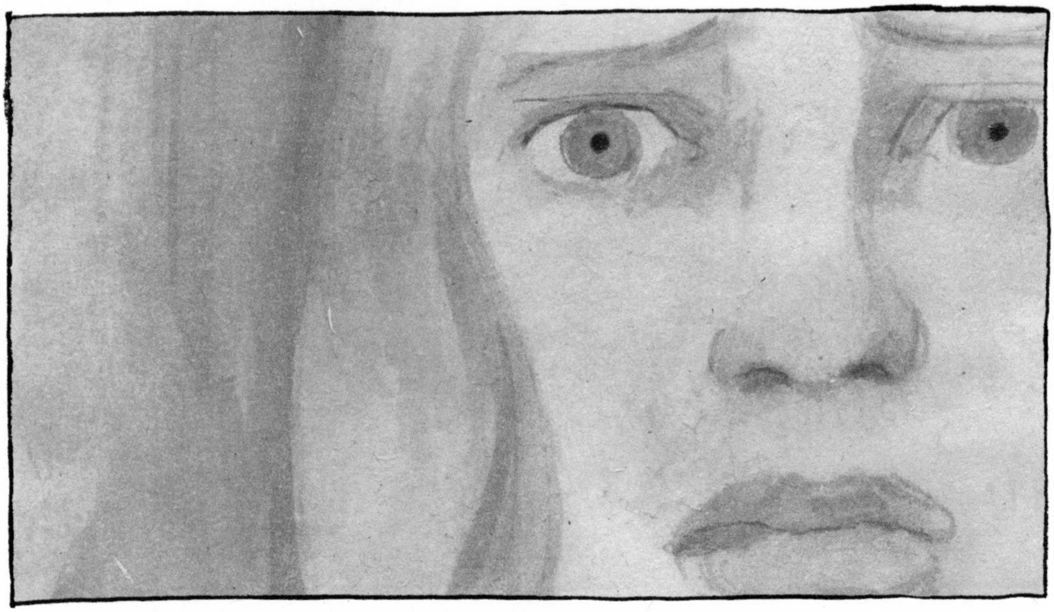

DID SHE WANT TO DRAW US OUT OF OURSELVES, TEAR OFF THE OLD SKIN AND PUT ON A NEW ONE, SUITABLE FOR WHAT SHE WAS INVENTING?

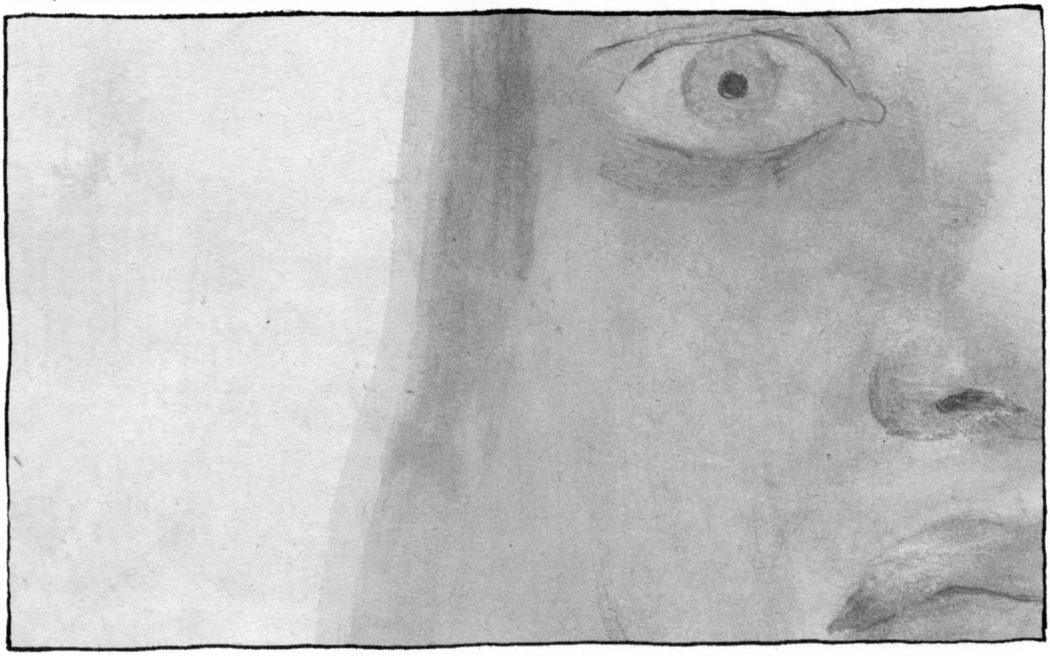

WHILE I WAS TAKING MY EXAMS IN THE SECOND YEAR OF HIGH SCHOOL, THE NEWS ARRIVED...

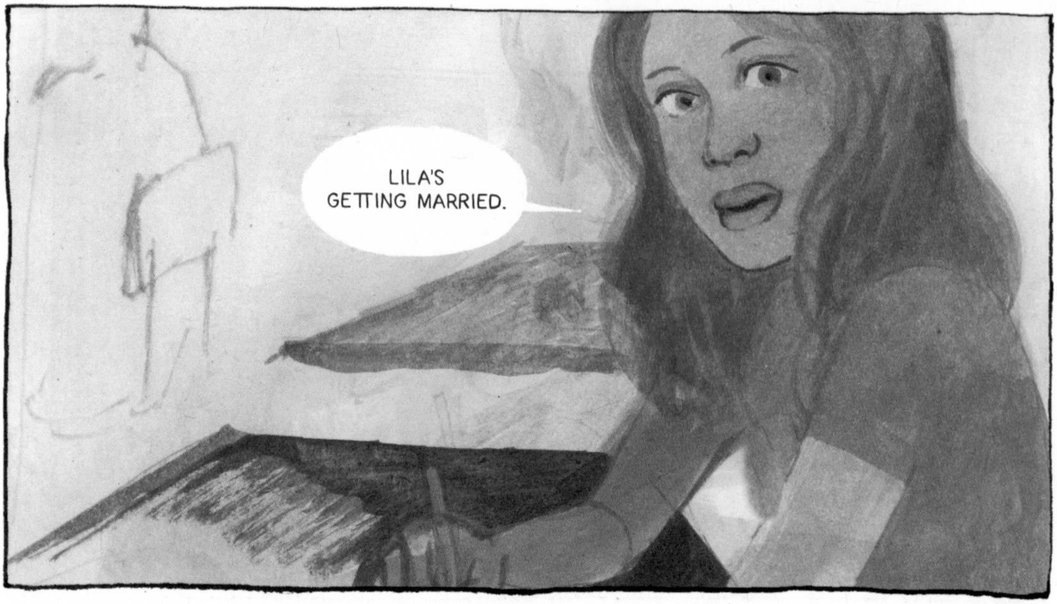
LILA'S GETTING MARRIED.

SHE WAS ALWAYS ONE STEP AHEAD.

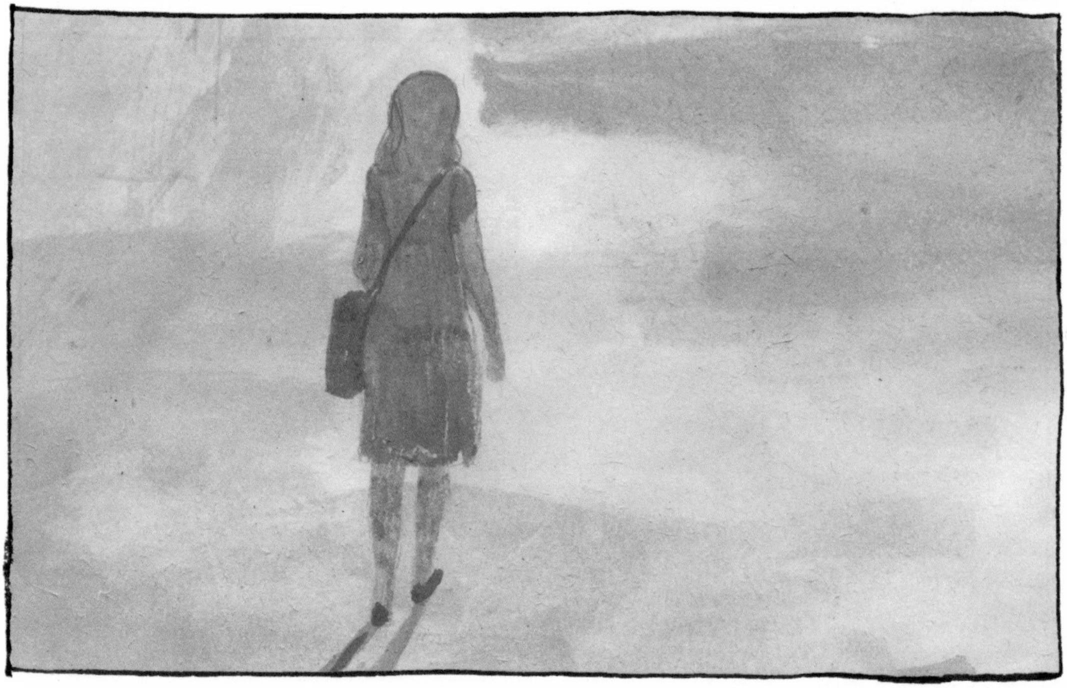

I FELT THE MEANINGLESSNESS OF MY LIFE, OF SCHOOL. I HAD ALWAYS MADE CHOICES ONLY TO MAKE HER ENVIOUS...

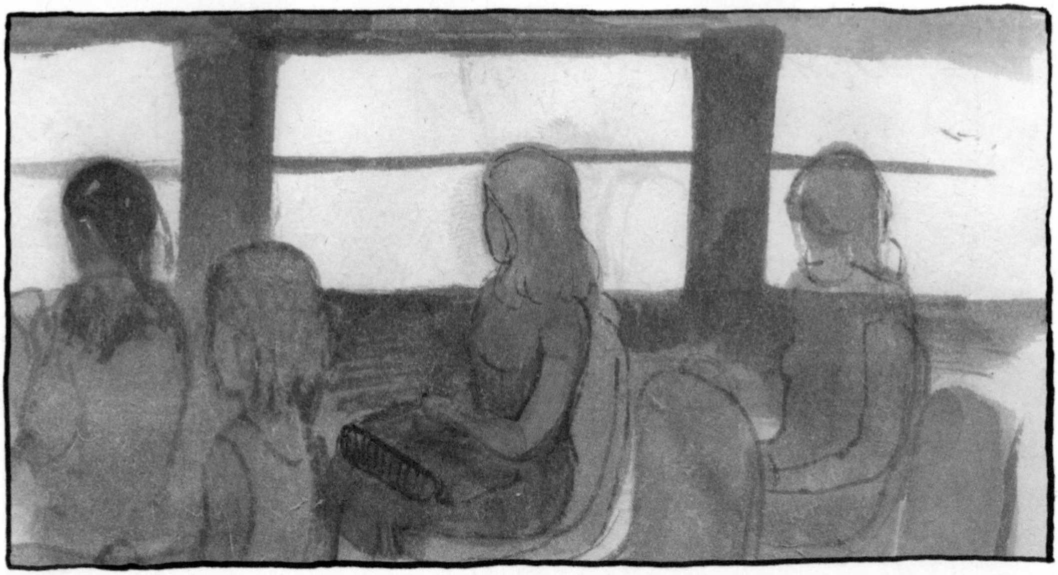

AND WHEN ANTONIO, THE MECHANIC, ASKED ME TO BE HIS GIRLFRIEND, EVEN THOUGH I LOVED NINO I'D SAID YES. BUT ONLY IN ORDER NOT TO FALL BEHIND HER.

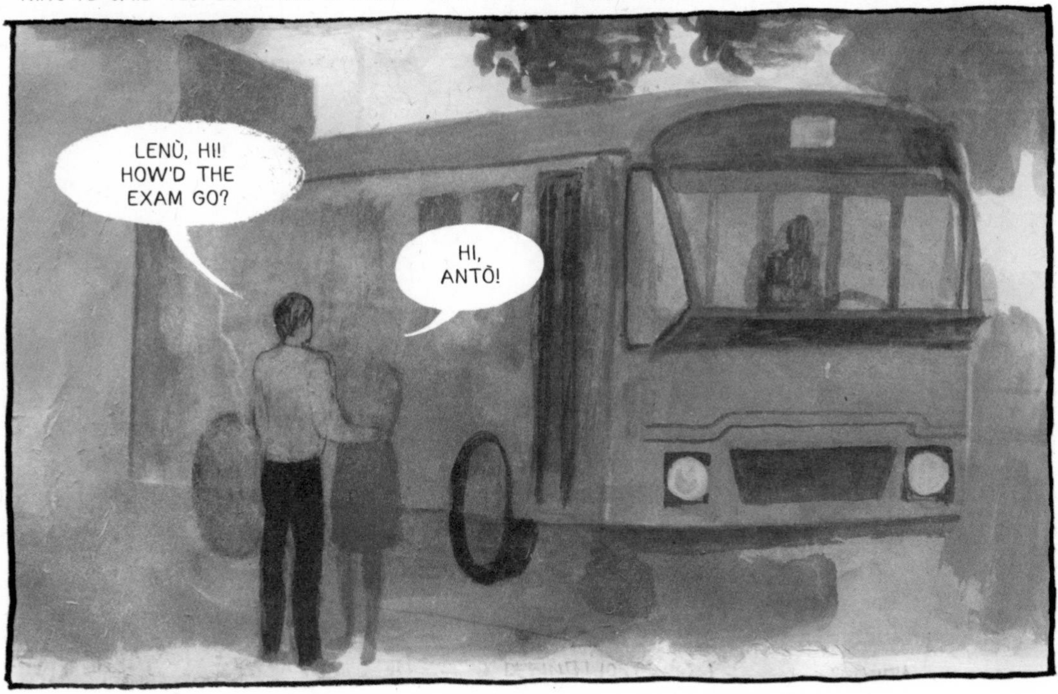
LENÙ, HI! HOW'D THE EXAM GO?
HI, ANTÒ!

LILA HAD MADE A DEFINITIVE LEAP, WITH NO RETURN.

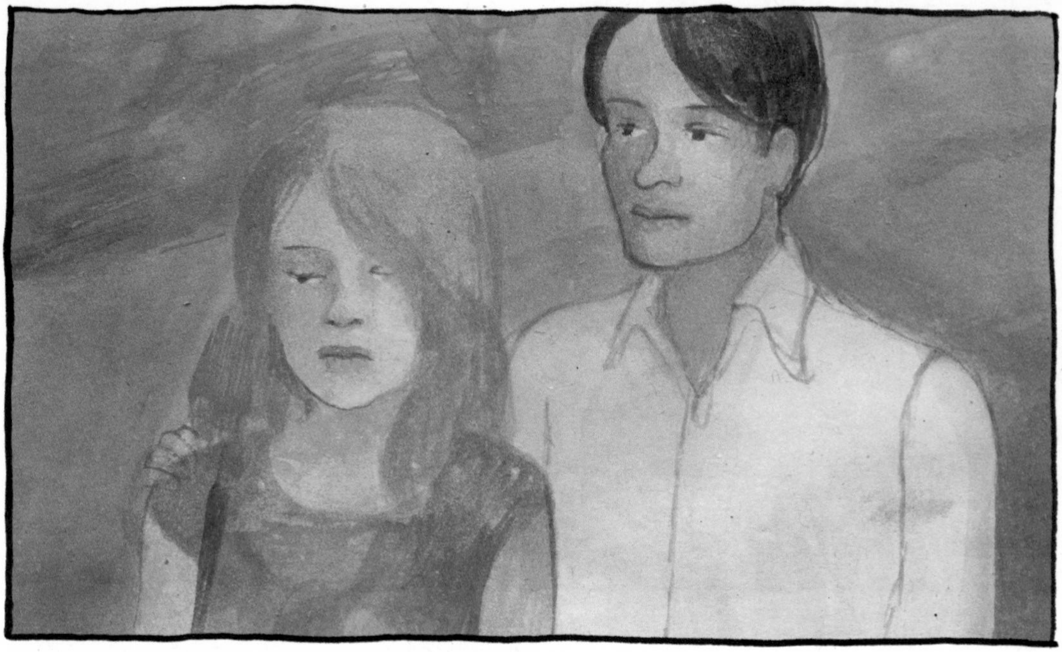

I WOULD NO LONGER BE ABLE TO REACH HER.

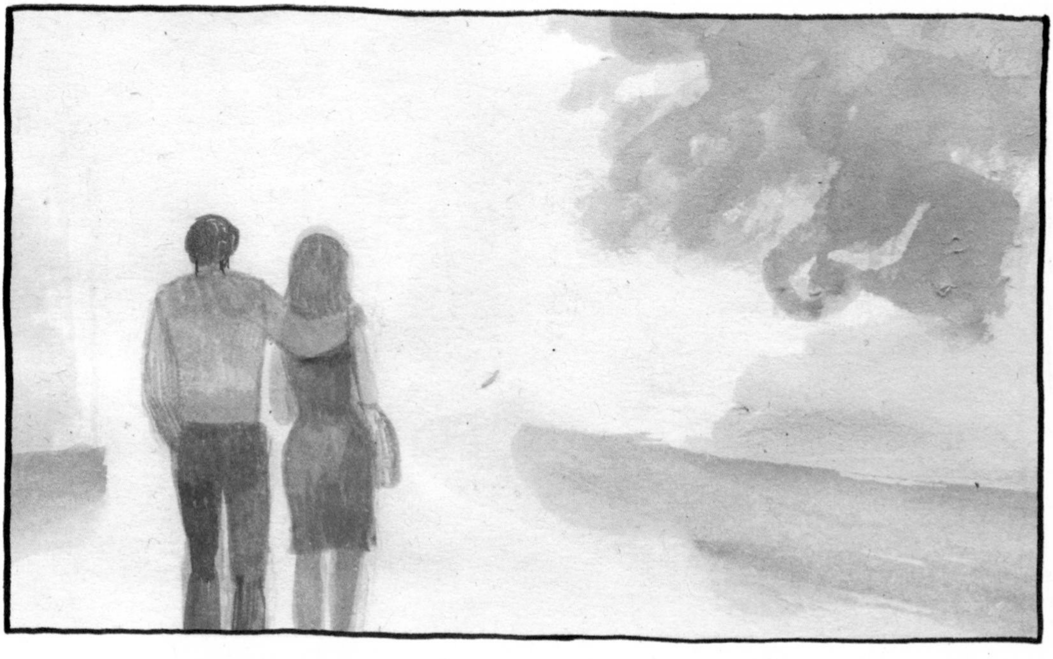

THE WEDDING DAY ARRIVED.

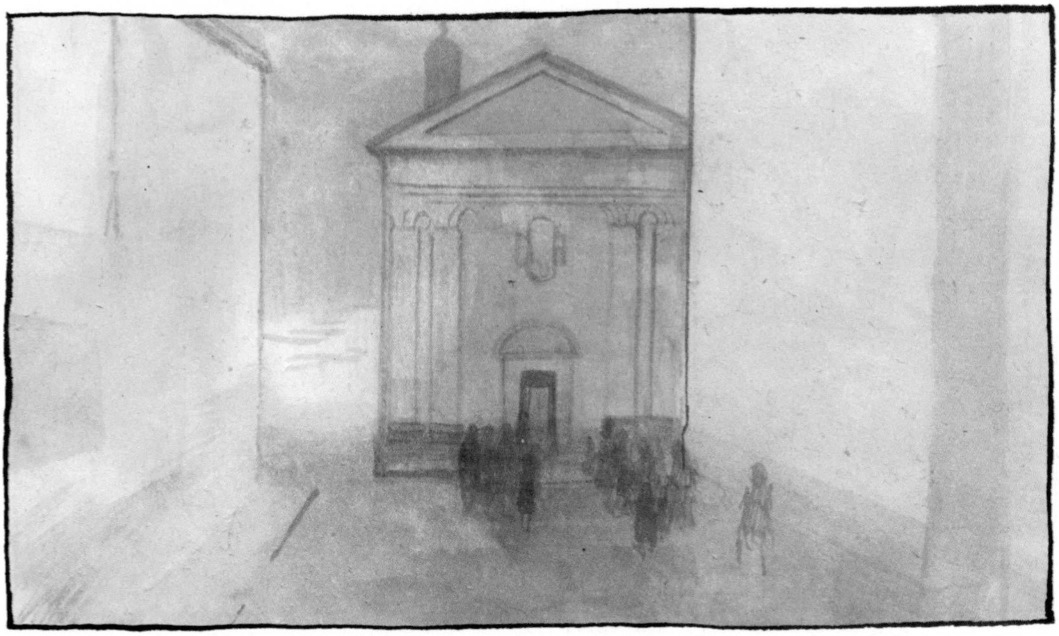

THE WHOLE NEIGHBORHOOD WAS THERE.

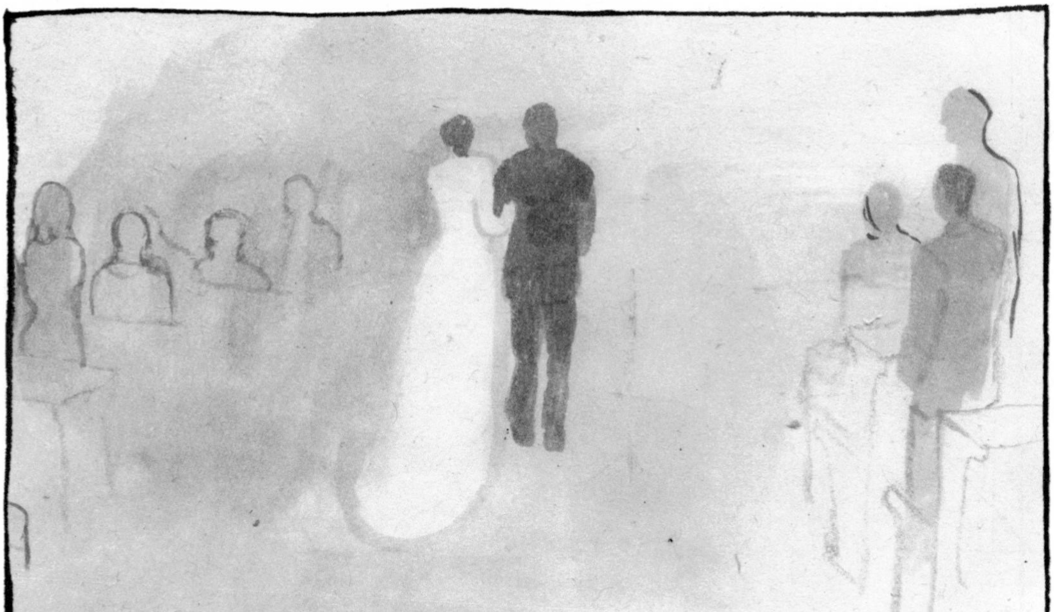

EVEN NINO, WITH HIS SISTER MARISA.

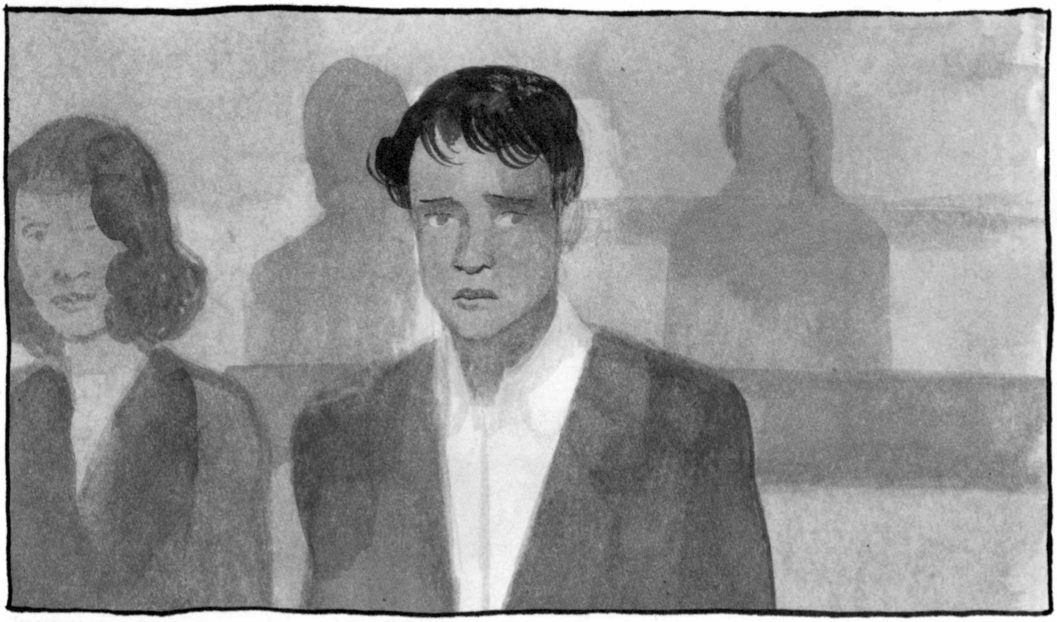

I HADN'T SEEN HIM SINCE THE DAY OF THE KISS.

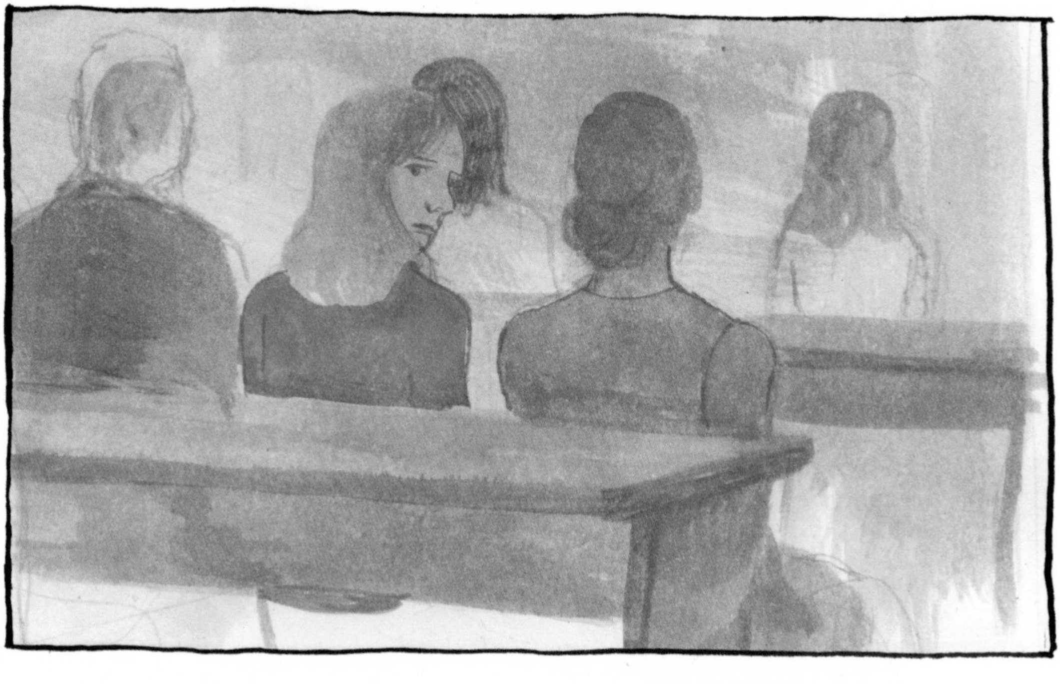

ONLY THE SOLARA BROTHERS WERE ABSENT: LILA HAD BEEN FIRM ABOUT THAT.

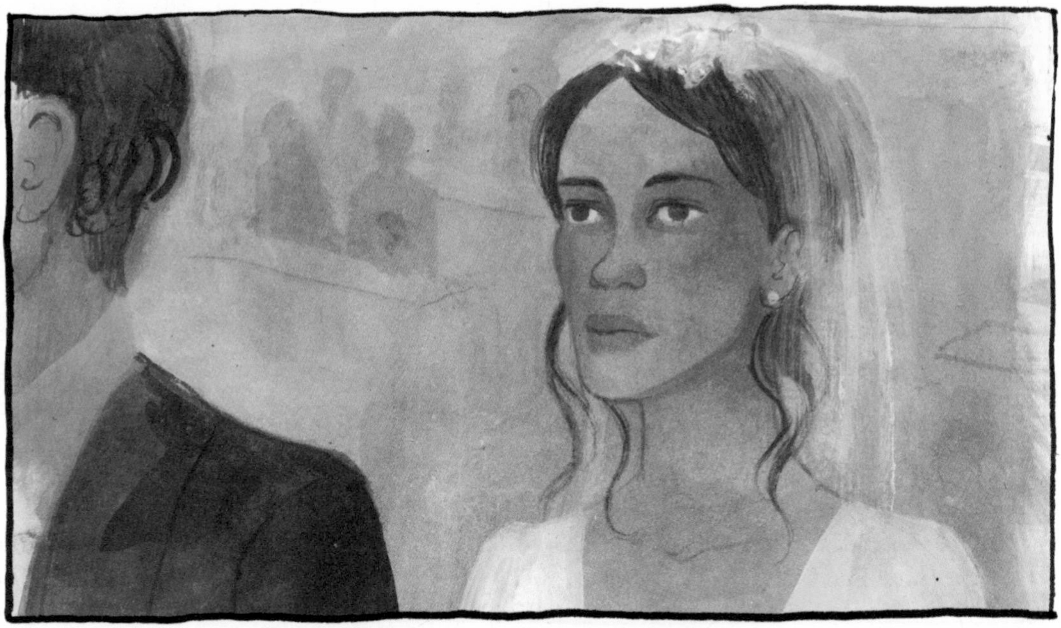

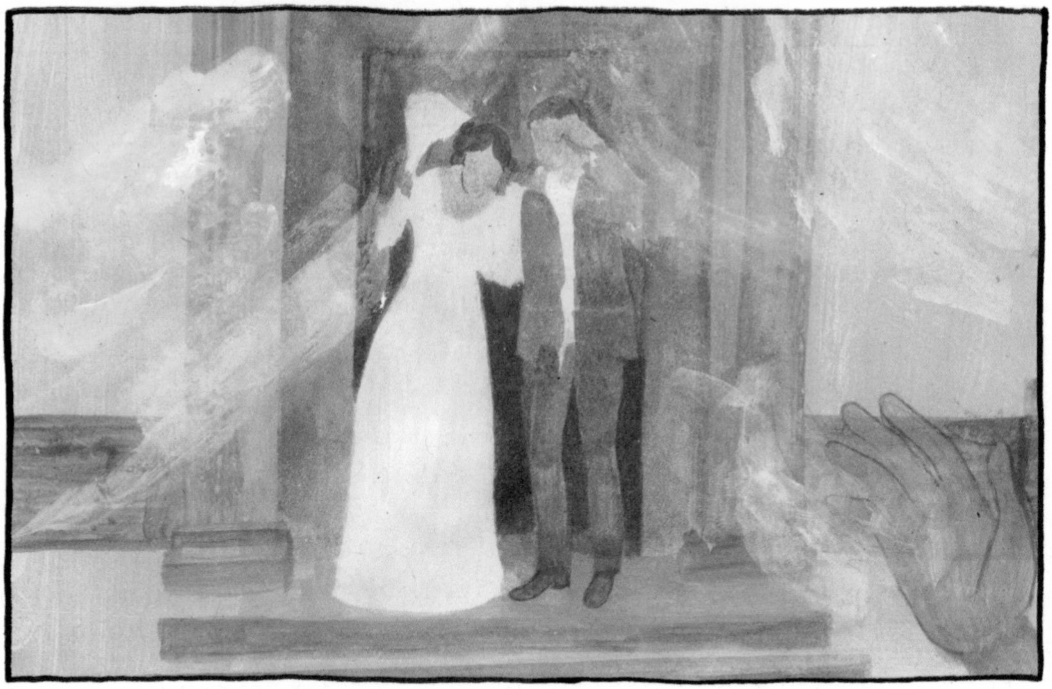

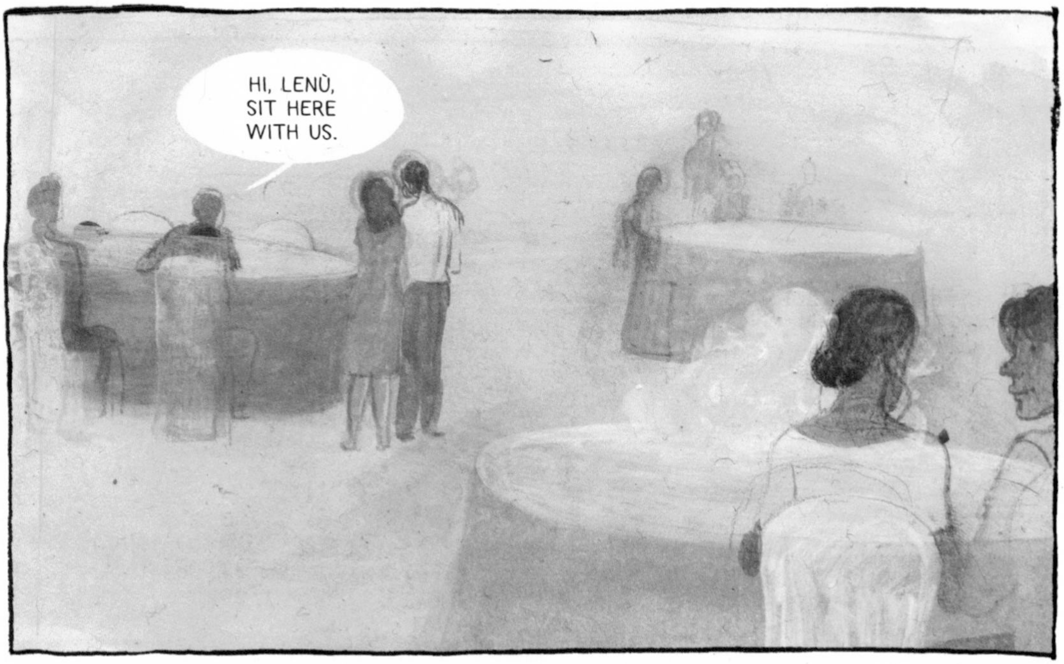
HI, LENÙ, SIT HERE WITH US.

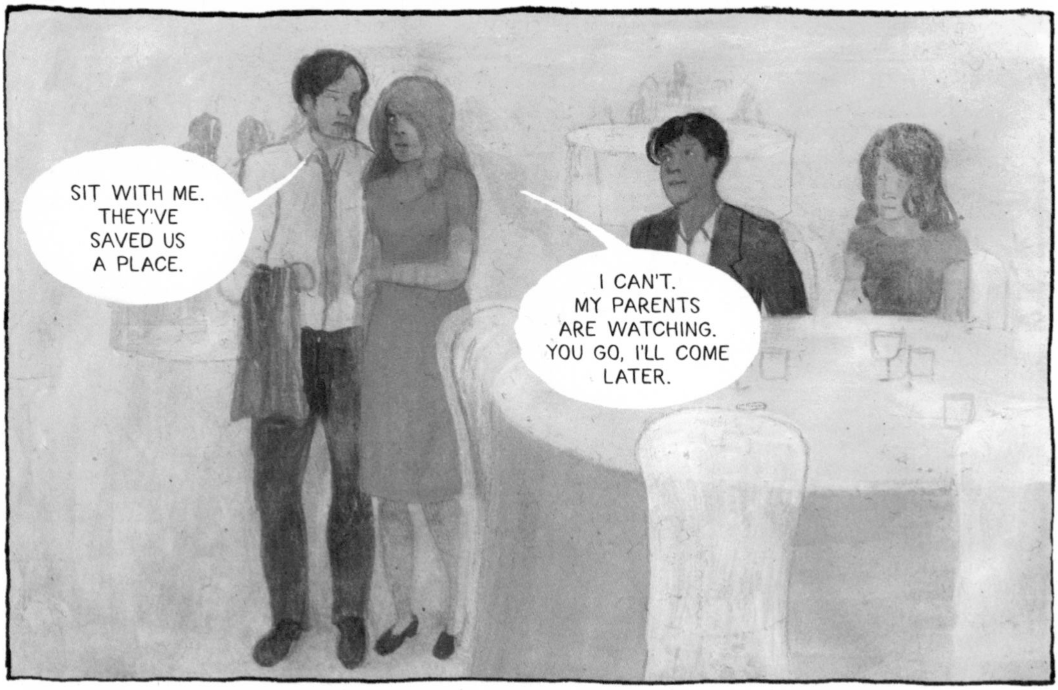
SIT WITH ME. THEY'VE SAVED US A PLACE.
I CAN'T. MY PARENTS ARE WATCHING. YOU GO, I'LL COME LATER.

I SAT AT THE TABLE WITH NINO AND MARISA.

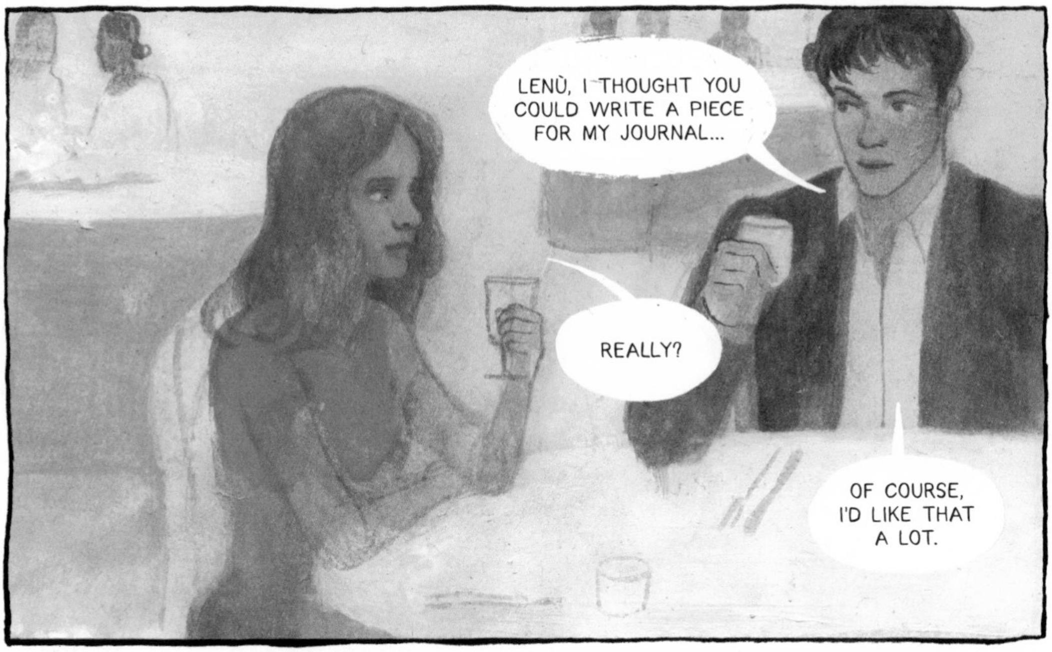
LENÙ, I THOUGHT YOU COULD WRITE A PIECE FOR MY JOURNAL...
REALLY?
OF COURSE, I'D LIKE THAT A LOT.

LILA WAS ON THE OPPOSITE SIDE OF THE ROOM.

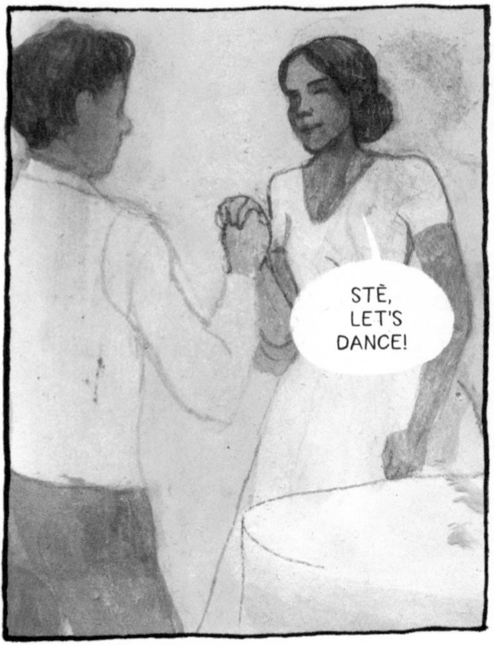
STÊ, LET'S DANCE!

SHE WAS THE QUEEN OF THE CELEBRATION.

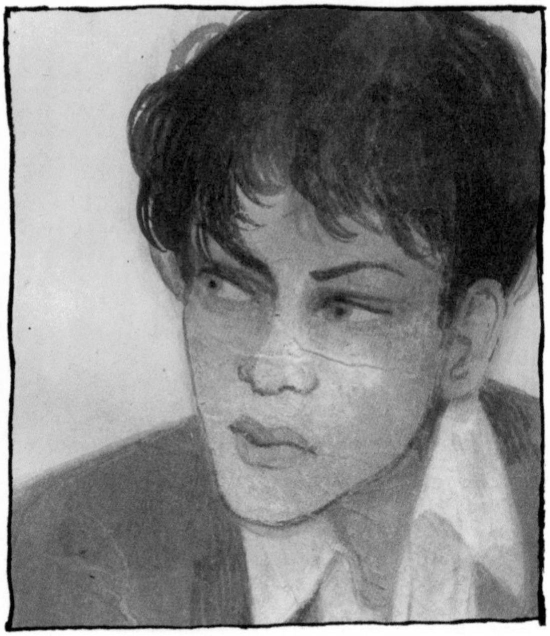

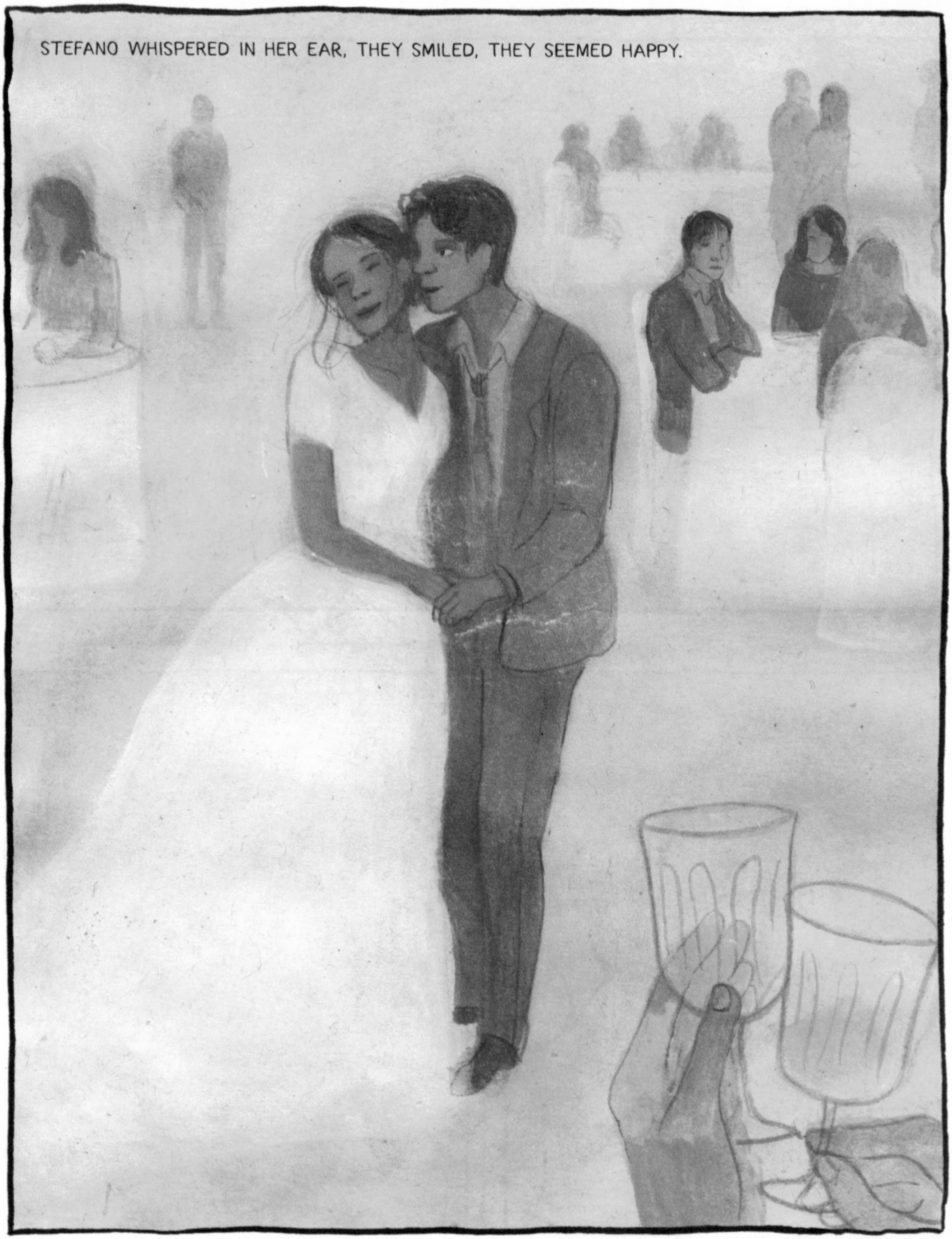
STEFANO WHISPERED IN HER EAR, THEY SMILED, THEY SEEMED HAPPY.

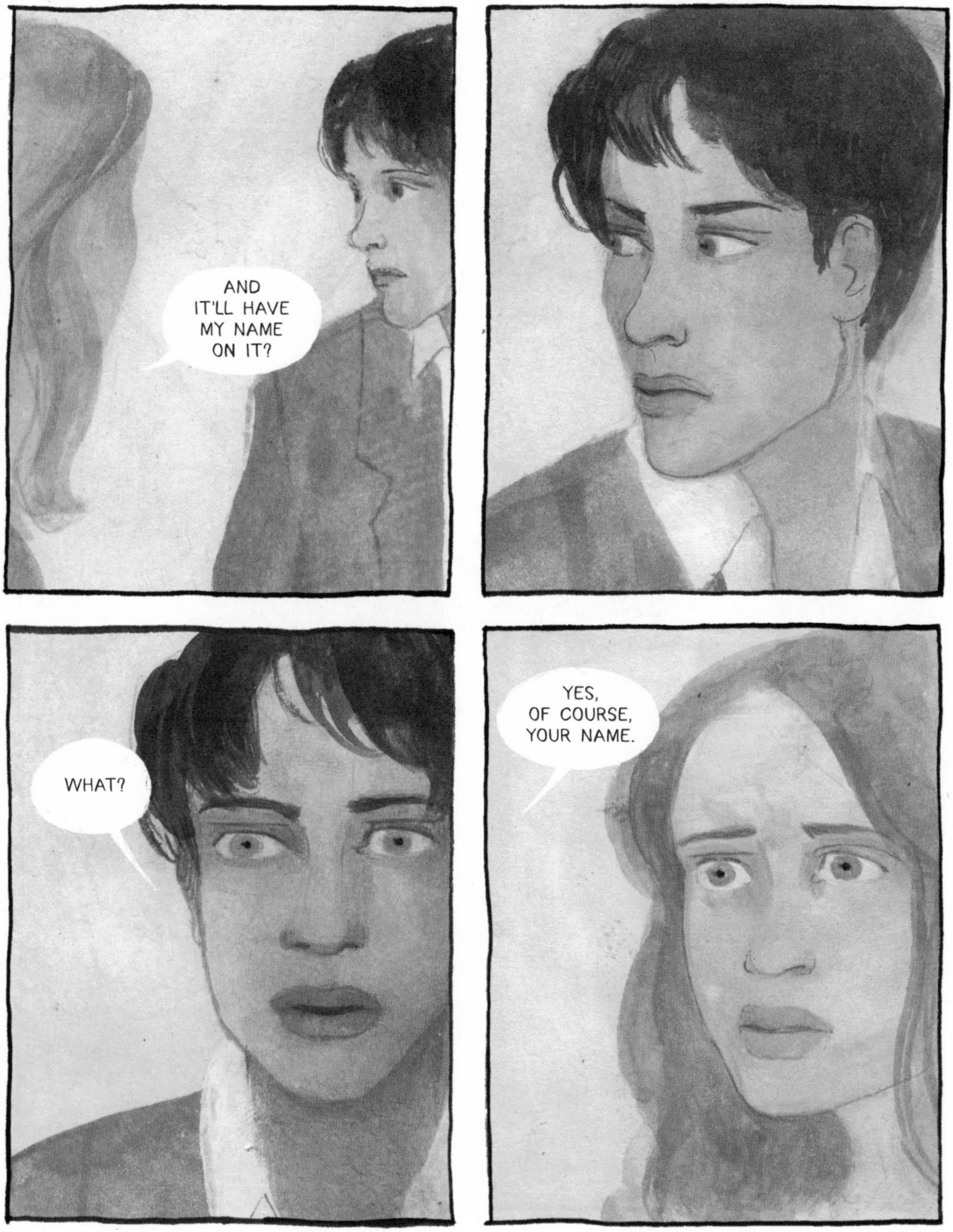
AND IT'LL HAVE MY NAME ON IT?
WHAT?
YES, OF COURSE, YOUR NAME.

AS A CHILD I HAD COUNTED ON LILA TO ESCAPE THE NEIGHBORHOOD.
BUT SHE WAS STILL THERE, CHAINED TO THAT WORLD FROM WHICH SHE THOUGHT SHE'D TAKEN THE BEST.

ALL AROUND WAS A LOUD DIN, A DRUNKEN GAIETY.
BEHIND THE FESTIVE APPEARANCE I FELT A QUARRELSOME DISCONTENT: LOVES AND INTERESTS, NEW BUILDINGS AND OLD, HATRED AND SPITE...

I KNEW THEM ALL, WOMEN AND MEN.

WAS I LIKE THEM?

WAS I STILL?

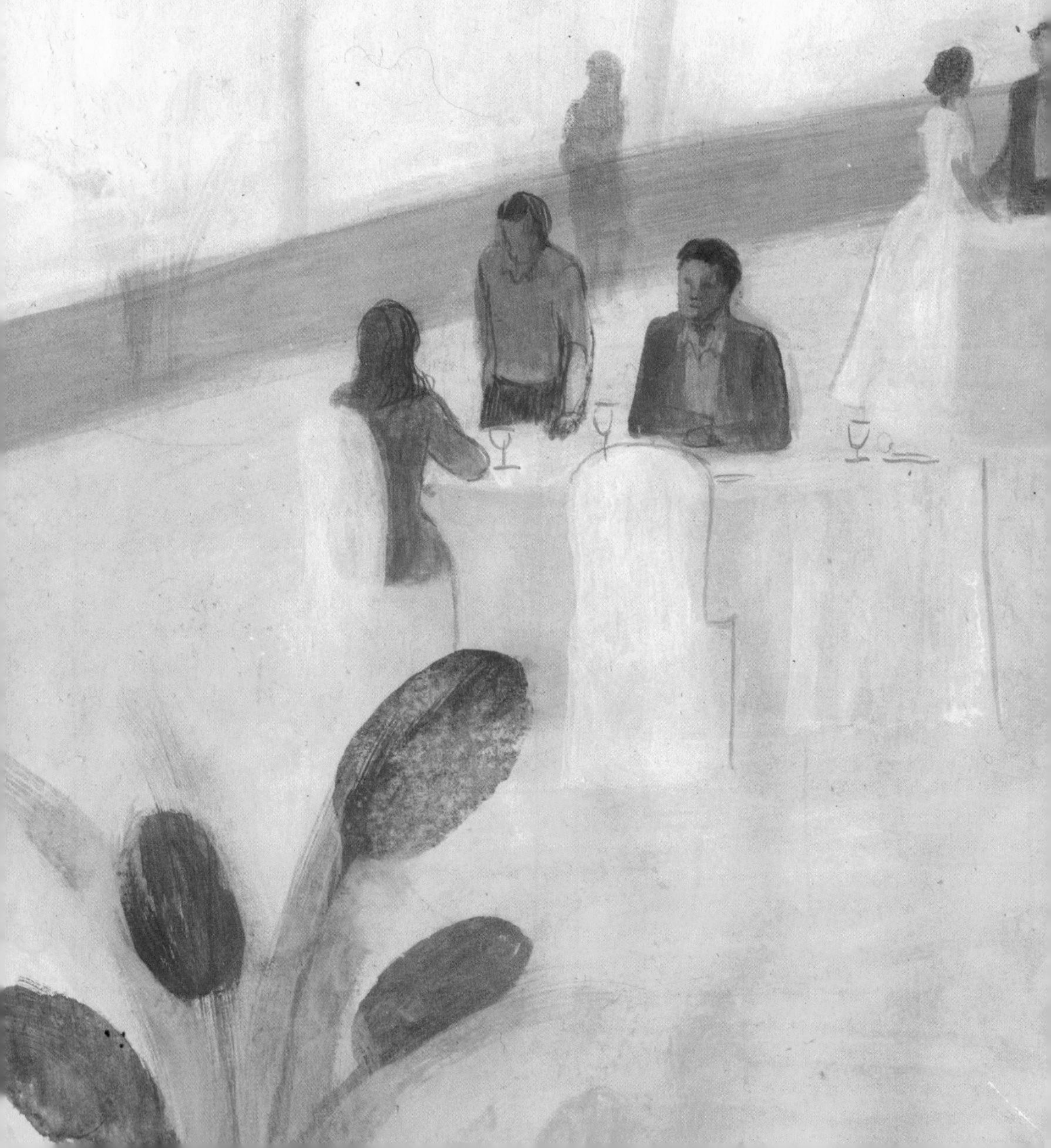

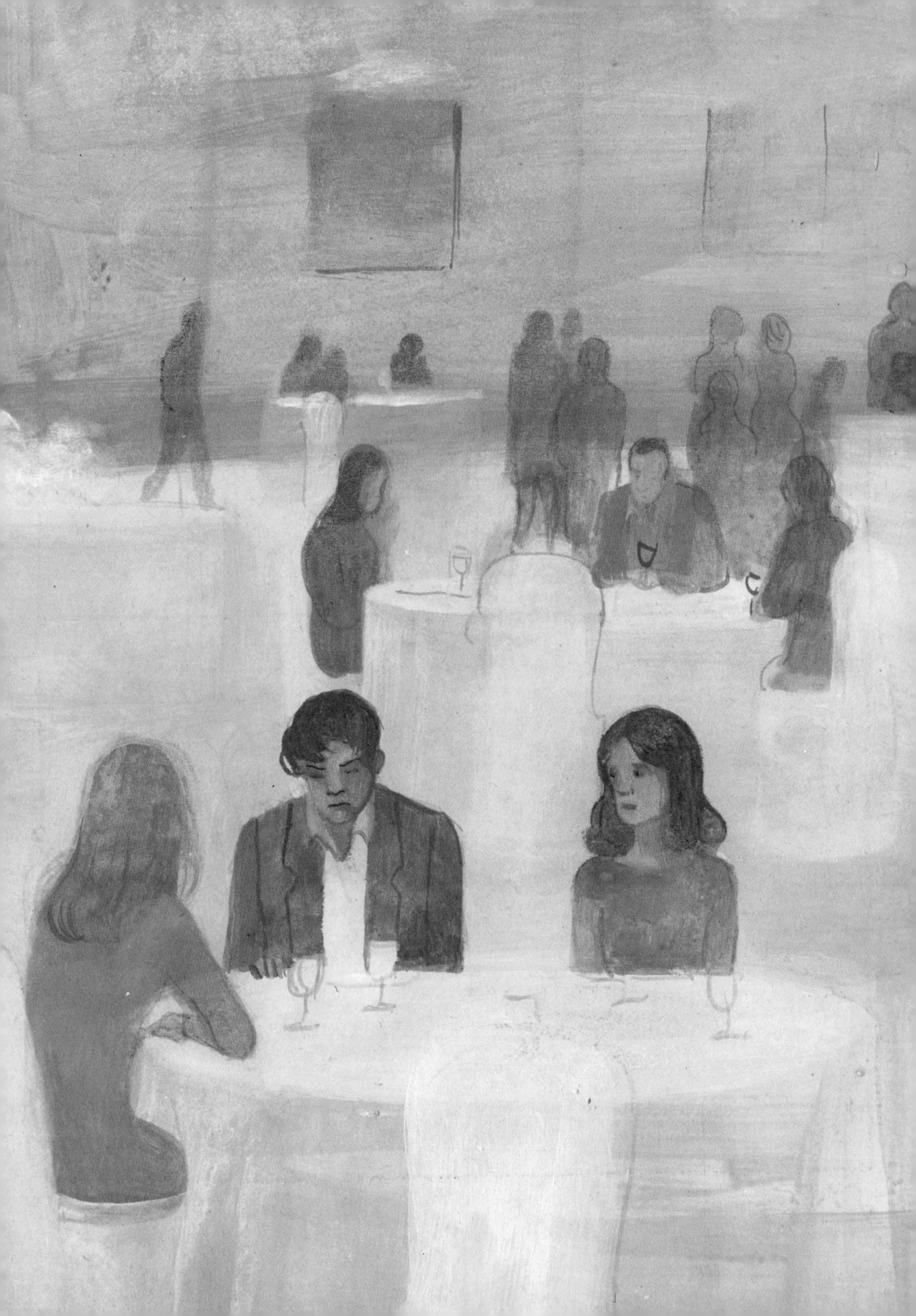

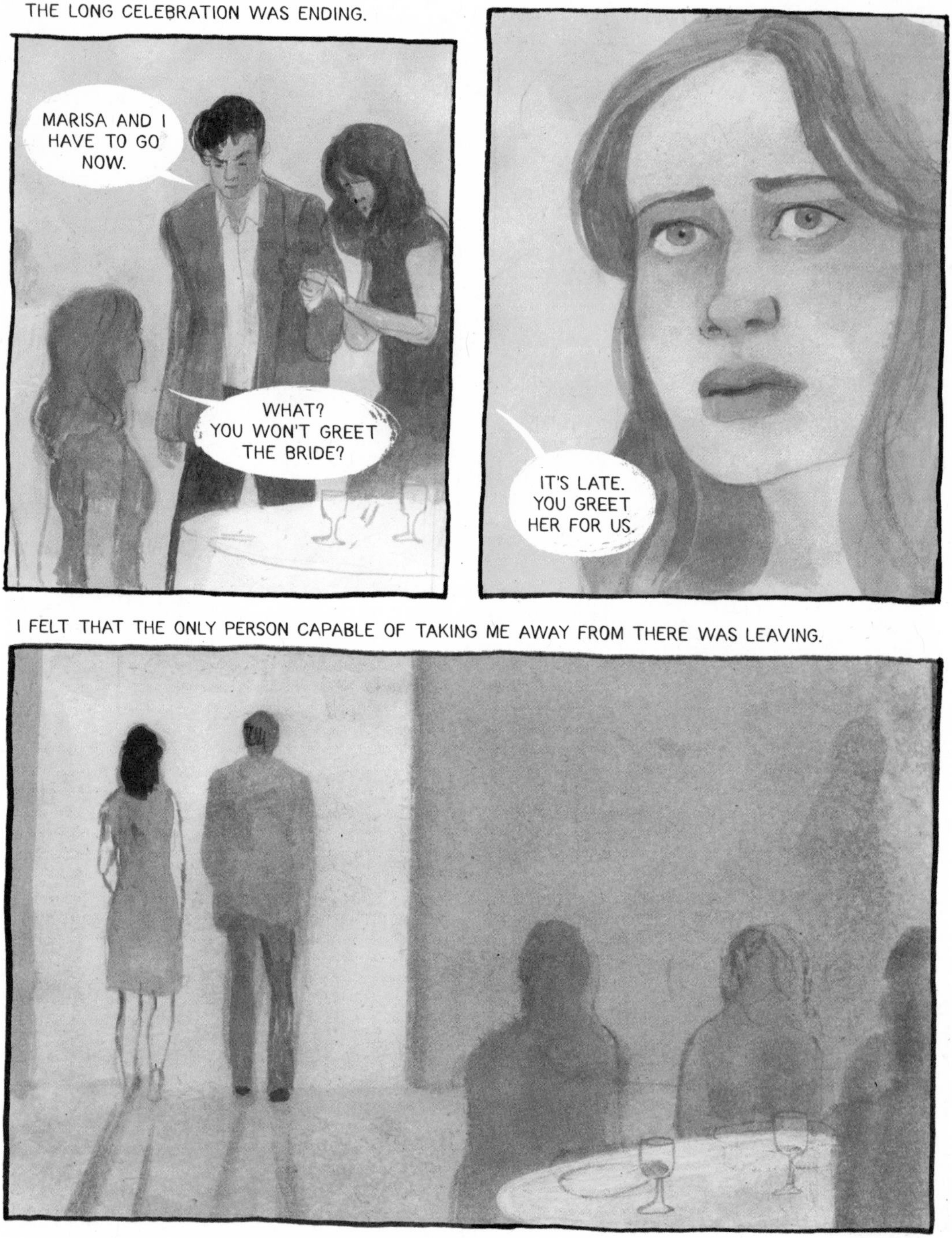
THE LONG CELEBRATION WAS ENDING.
MARISA AND I HAVE TO GO NOW.
WHAT? YOU WON'T GREET THE BRIDE?
IT'S LATE. YOU GREET HER FOR US.
I FELT THAT THE ONLY PERSON CAPABLE OF TAKING ME AWAY FROM THERE WAS LEAVING.

WHEN THE DOOR CLOSED BEHIND HIM...

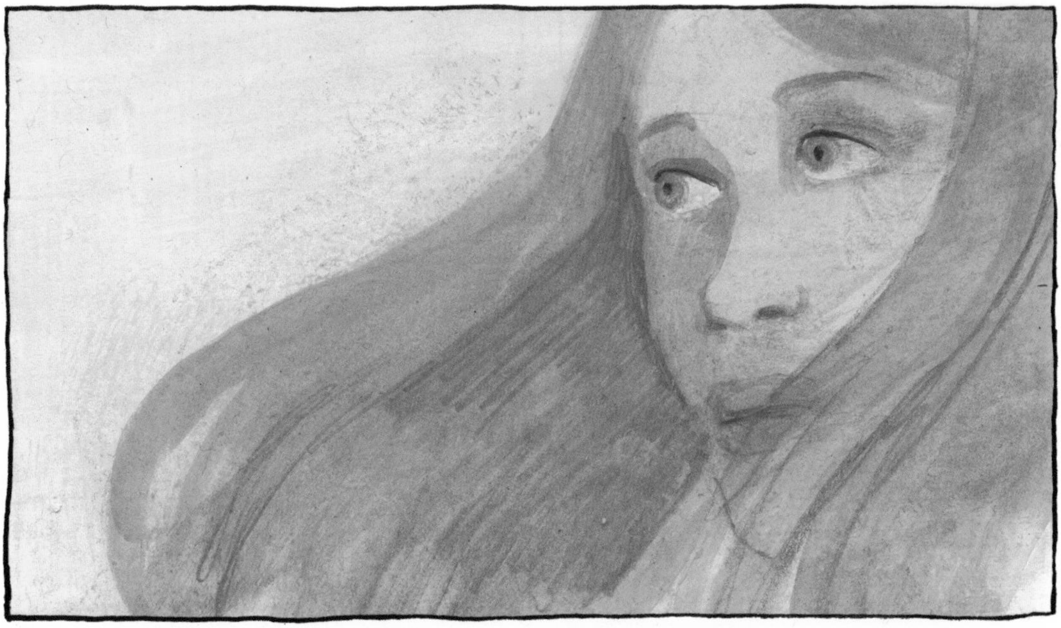

...I SEEMED TO FEEL A GUST OF WIND.

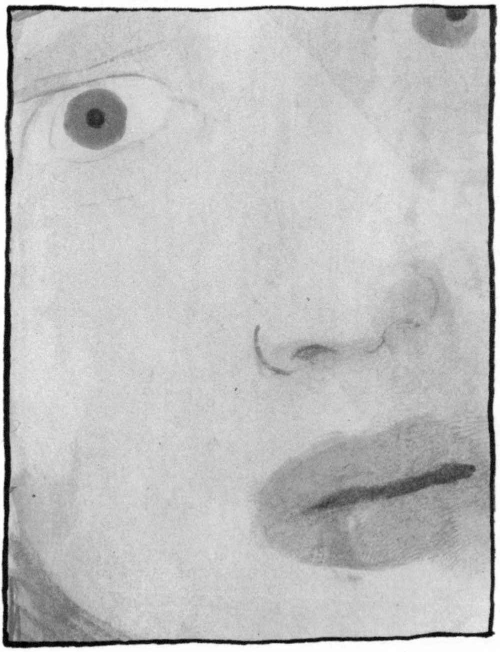

BUT THERE WAS NO WIND.

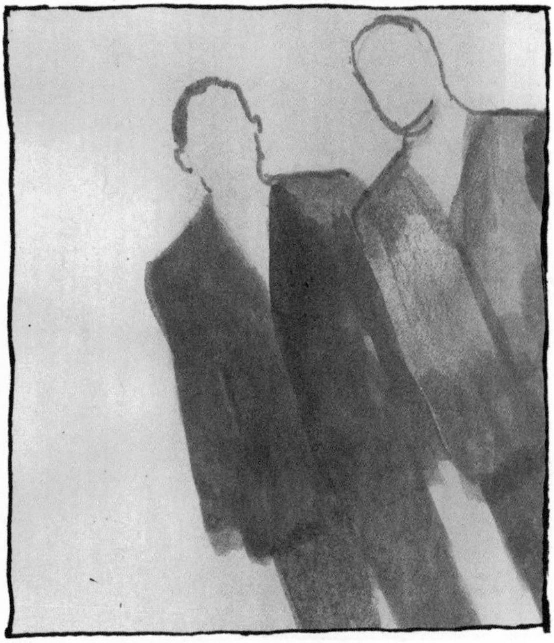

IT WAS THE SOLARA BROTHERS.

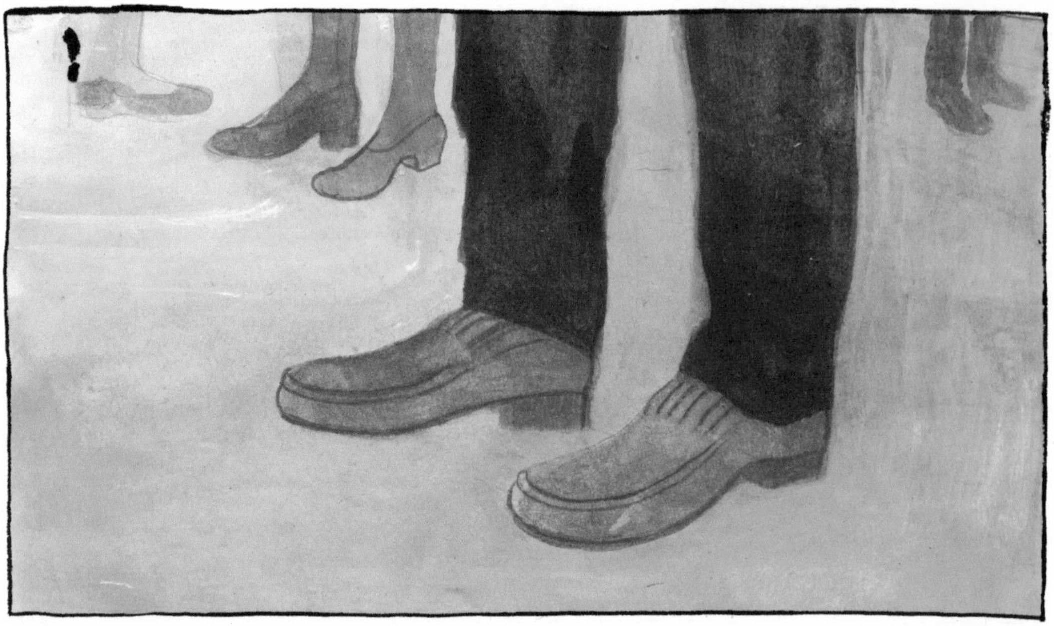

MARCELLO HAD ON HIS FEET...

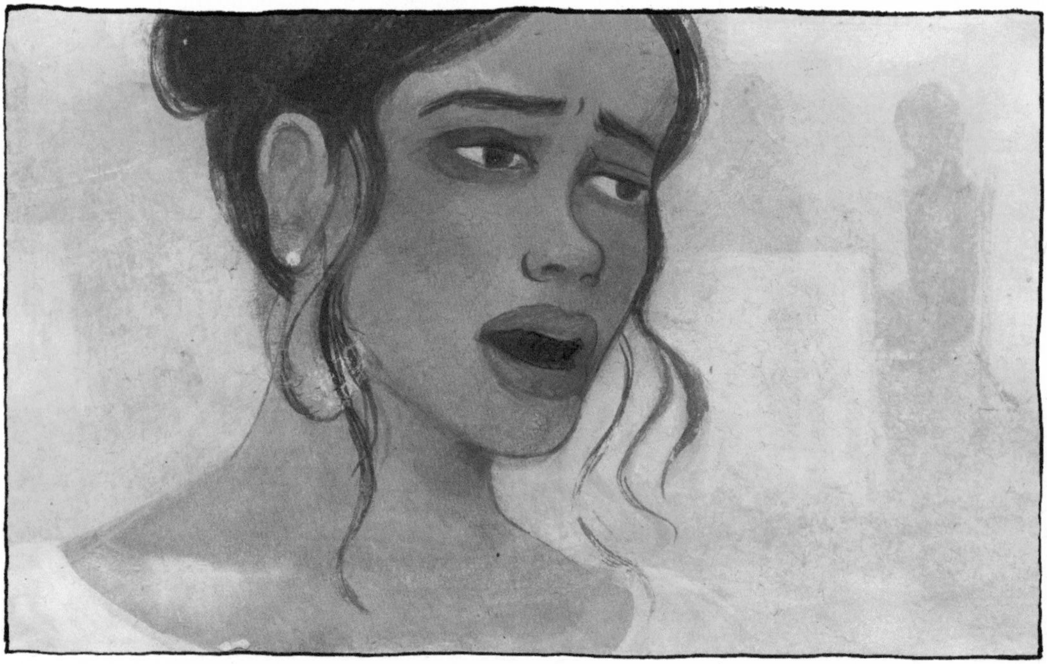

...A PAIR OF CERULLO SHOES!

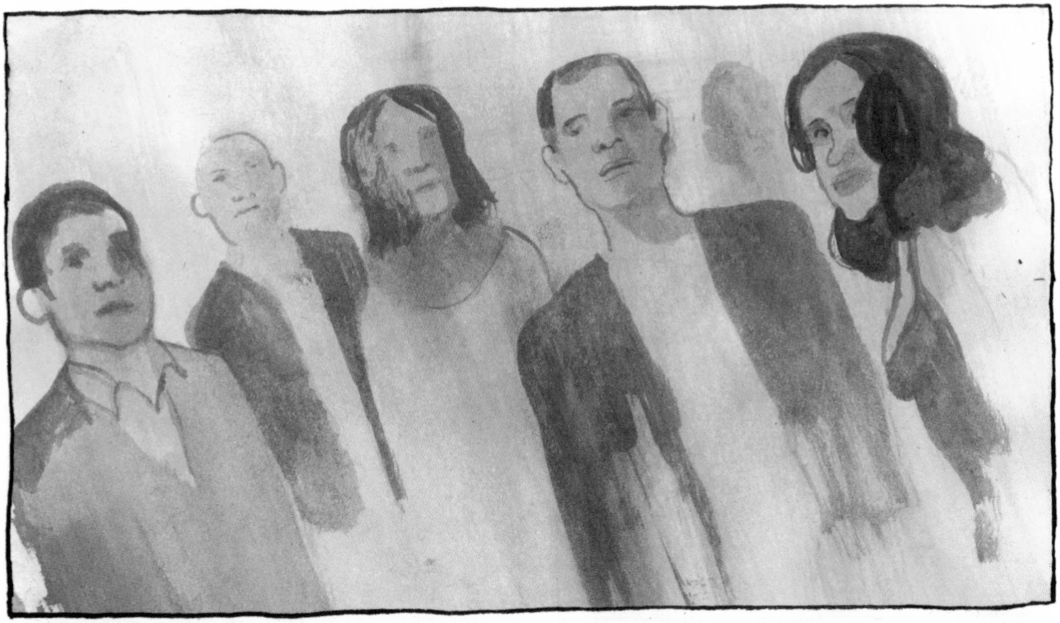

THE SHOES THAT LILA HAD DESIGNED AS A CHILD,

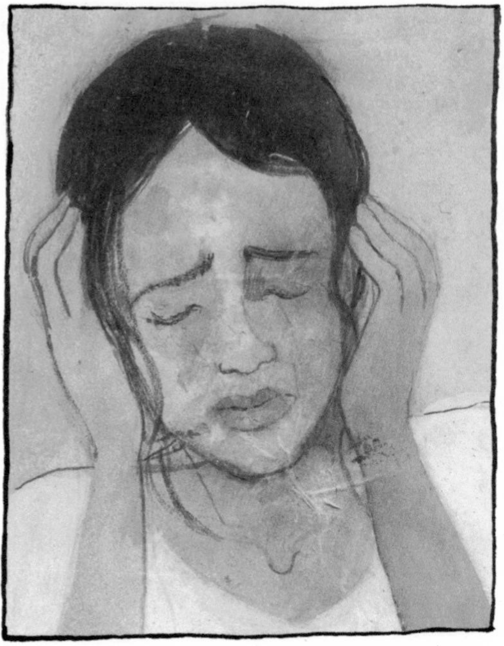

AND THAT STEFANO HAD BOUGHT, SAYING HOW MUCH HE LIKED THEM.

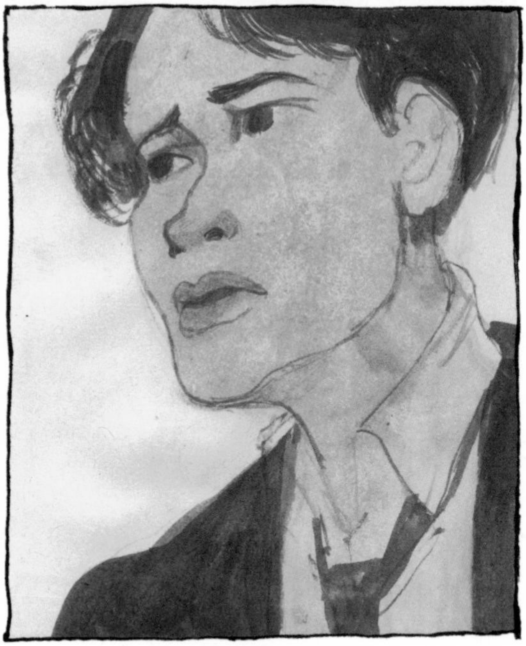

WHAT WERE THEY DOING ON THE FEET...

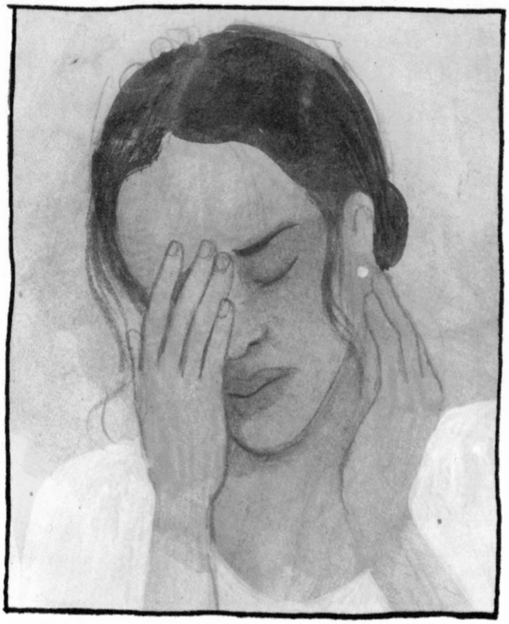

...OF THAT PIG MARCELLO?

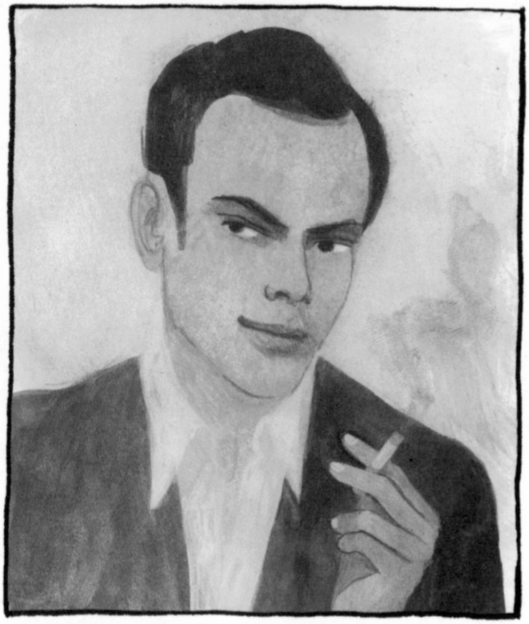

THOSE VERY SHOES!

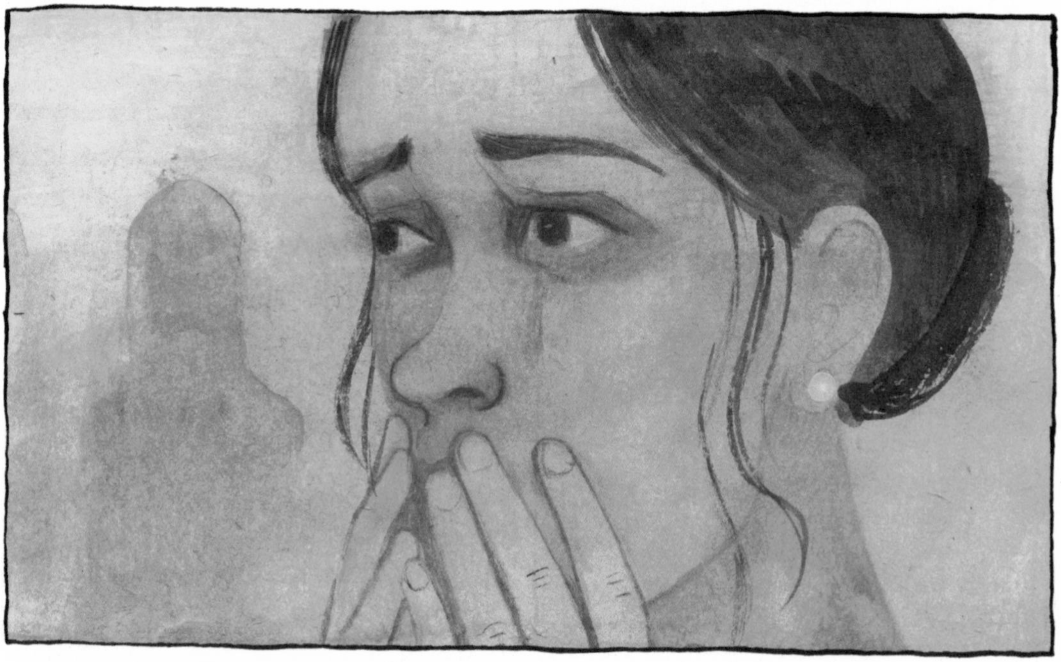

THE ONES LILA HAD MADE WITH HER BROTHER RINO...

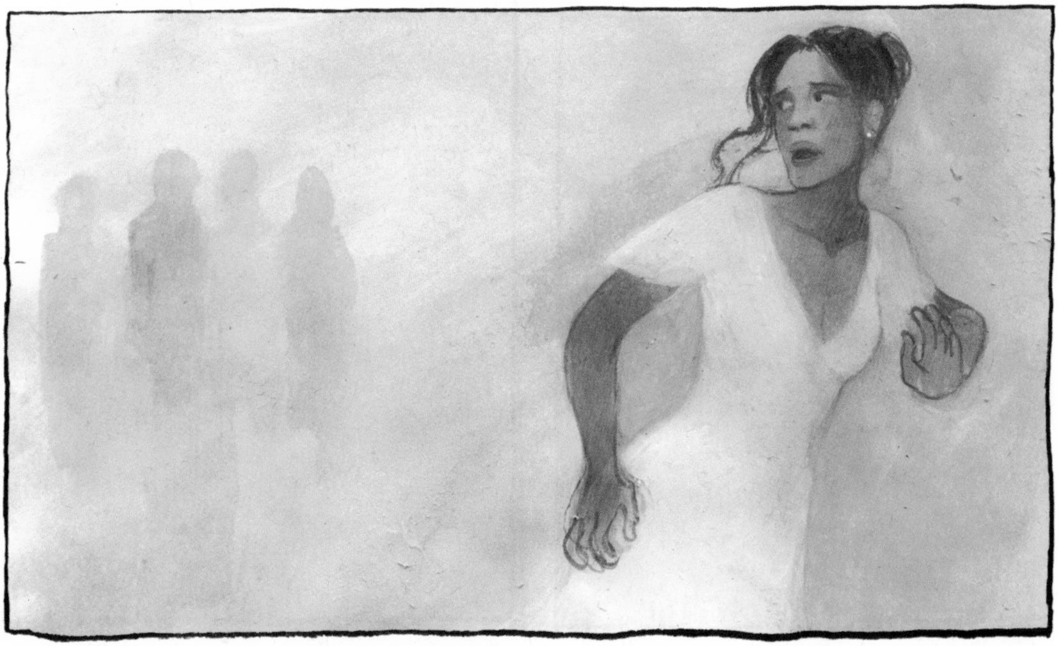

...WORKING LOVINGLY FOR MONTHS AND MONTHS.

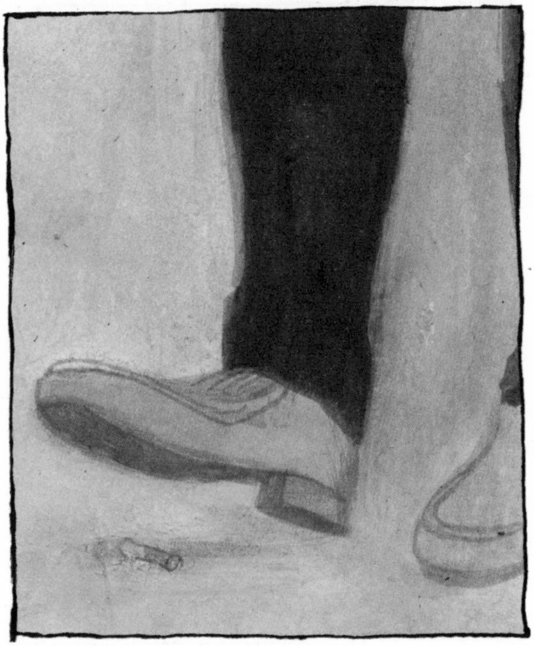

MAKING.

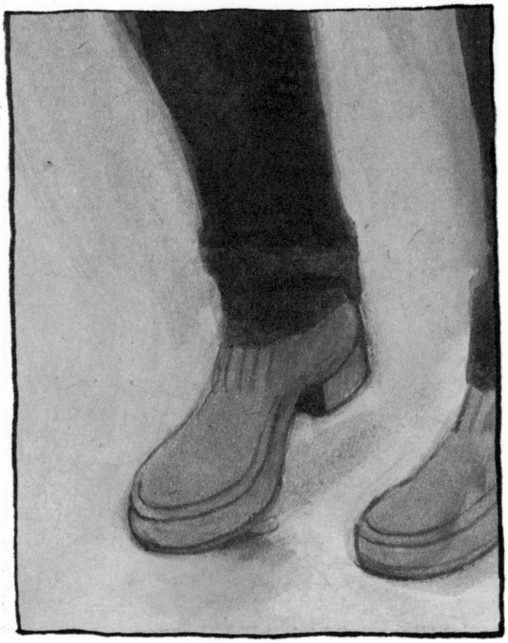

UNMAKING.

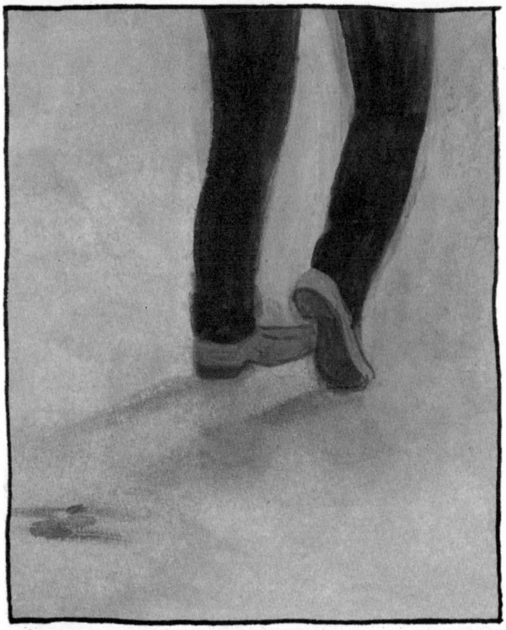

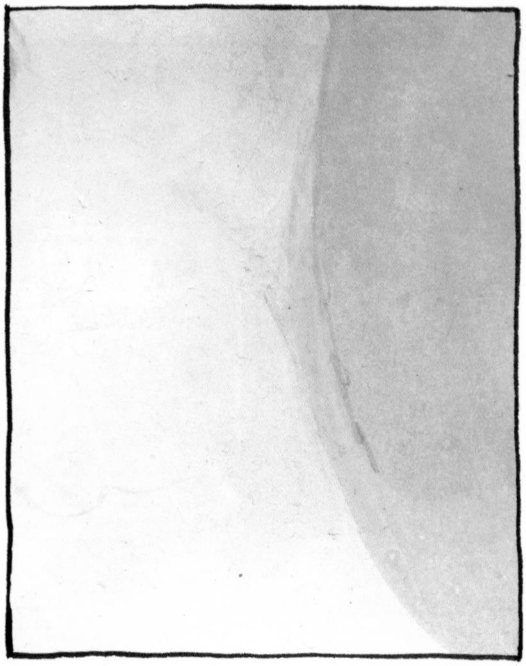

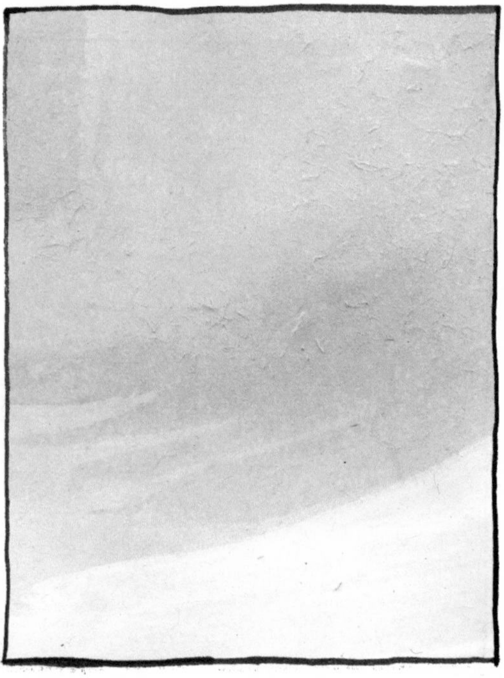

AND RUINING HER HANDS.

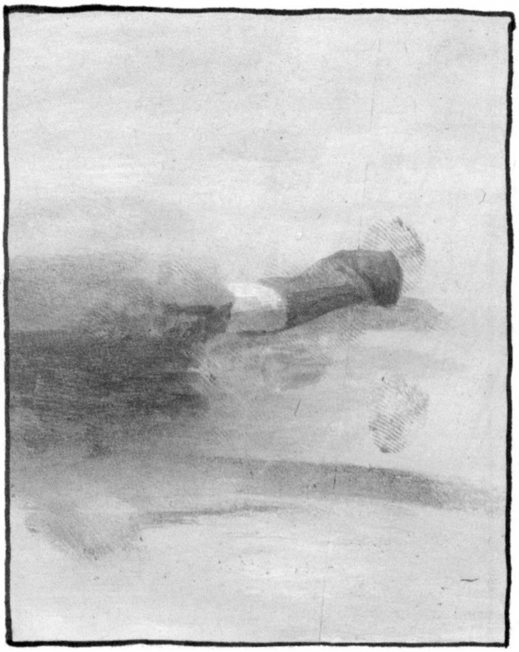

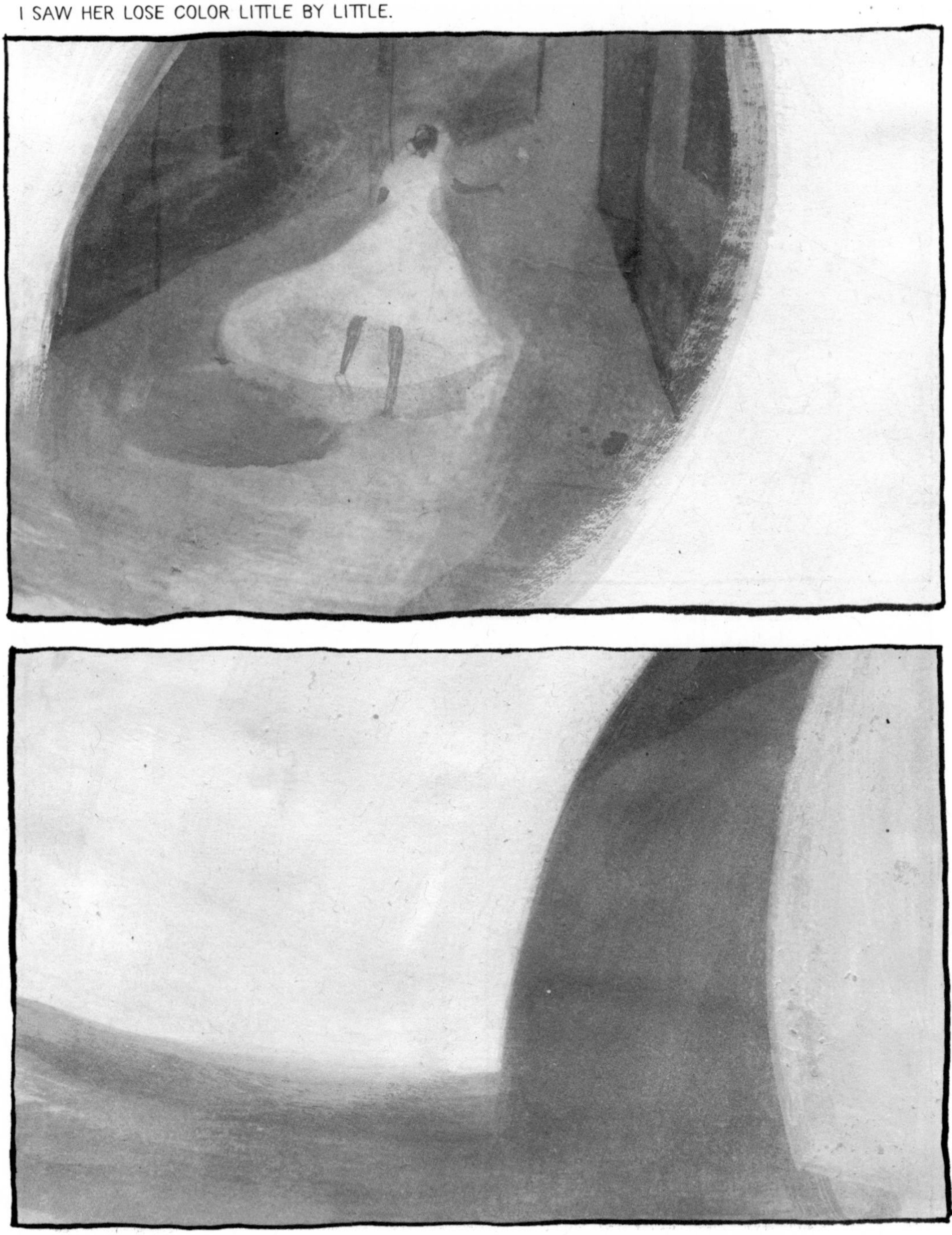
I SAW HER LOSE COLOR LITTLE BY LITTLE.

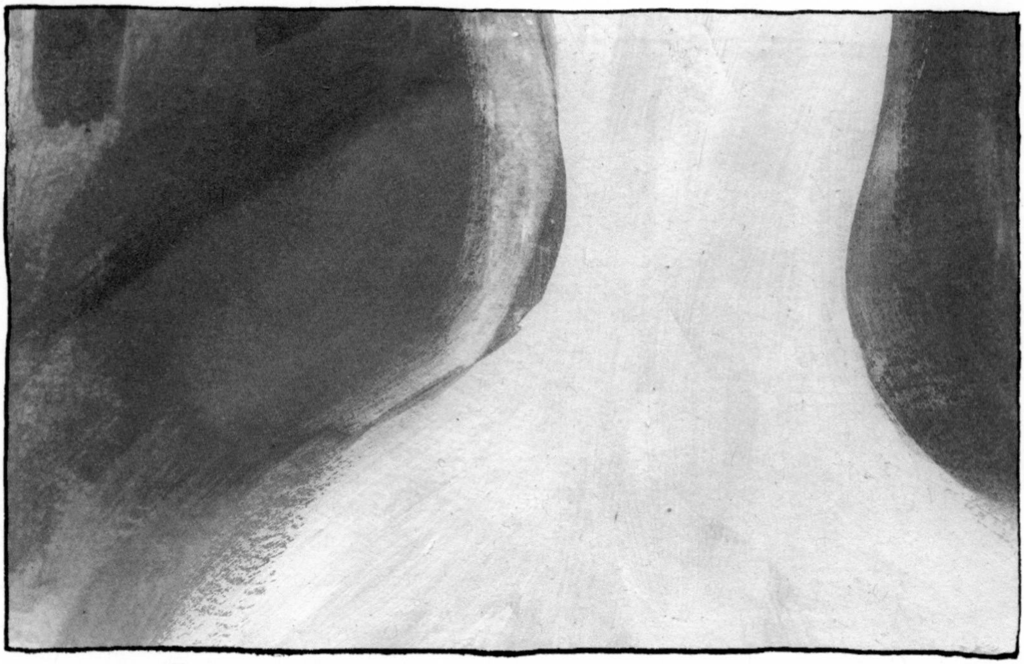
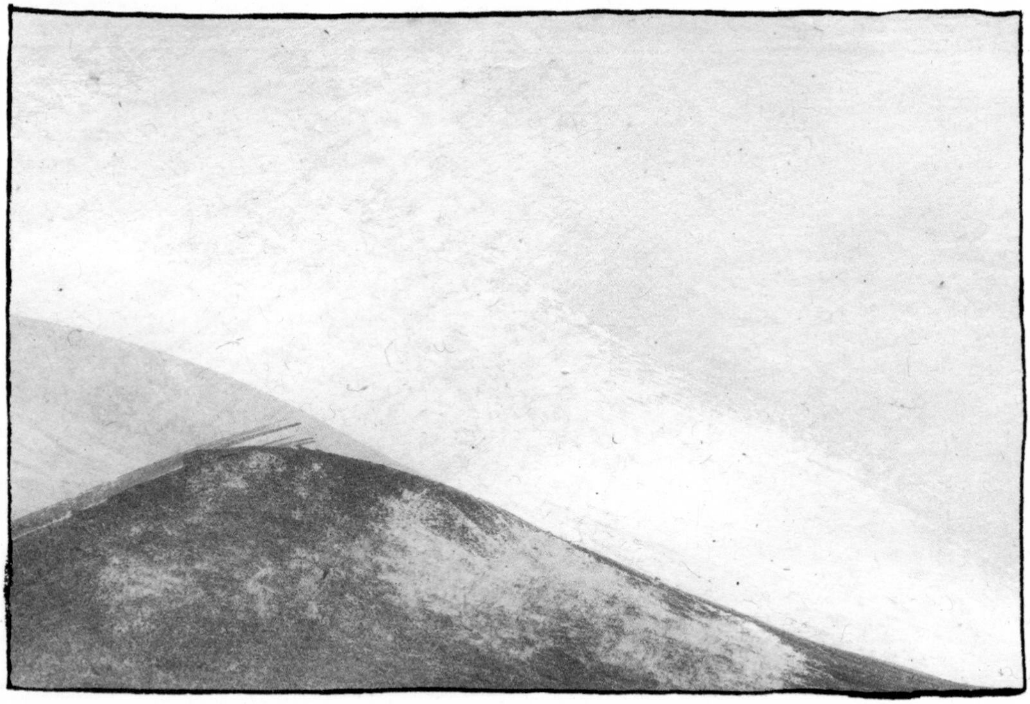

GROW EXTREMELY PALE.

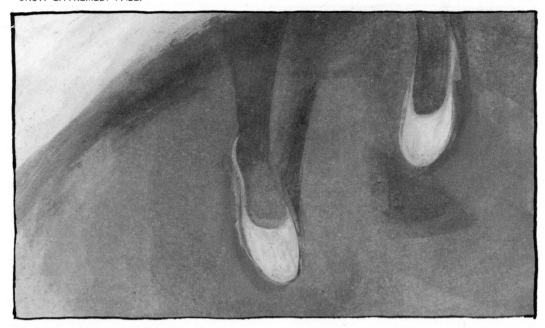

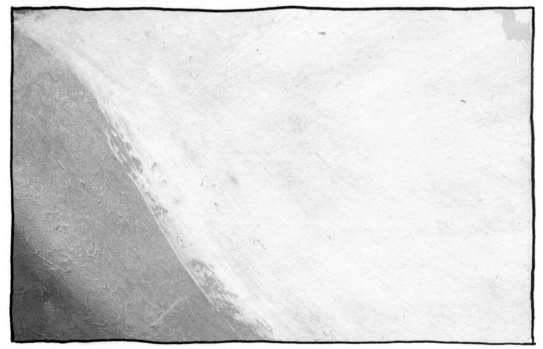

WHITER THAN HER WEDDING DRESS.

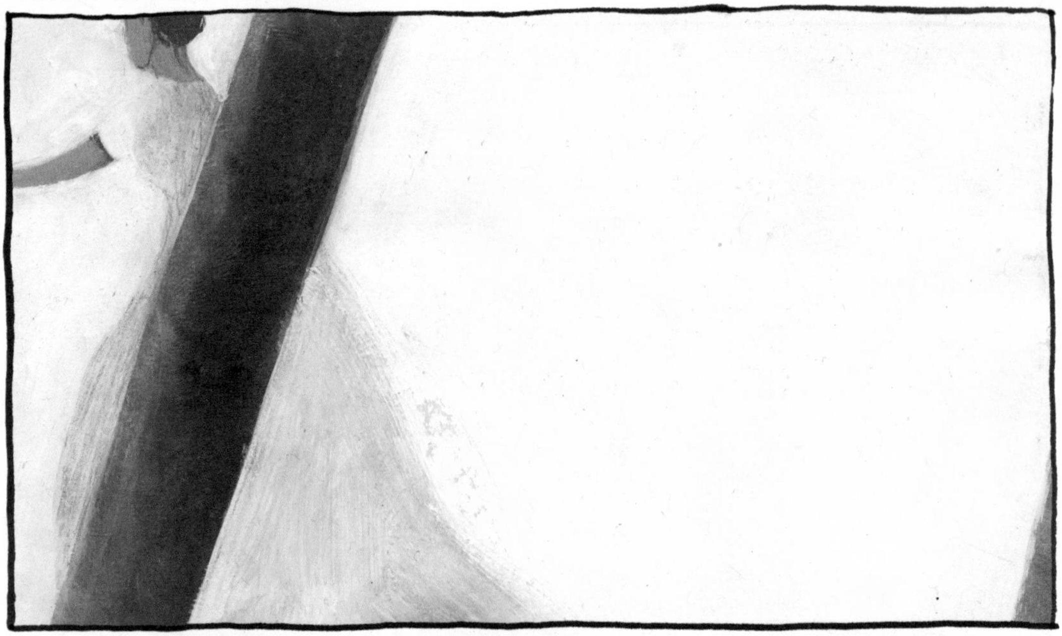

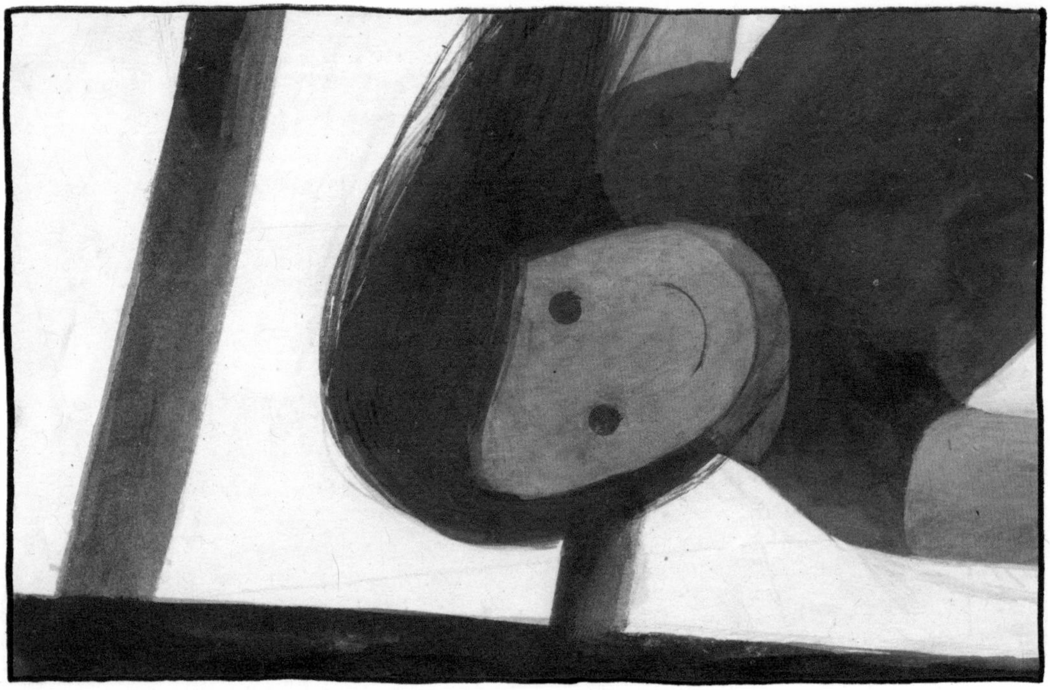

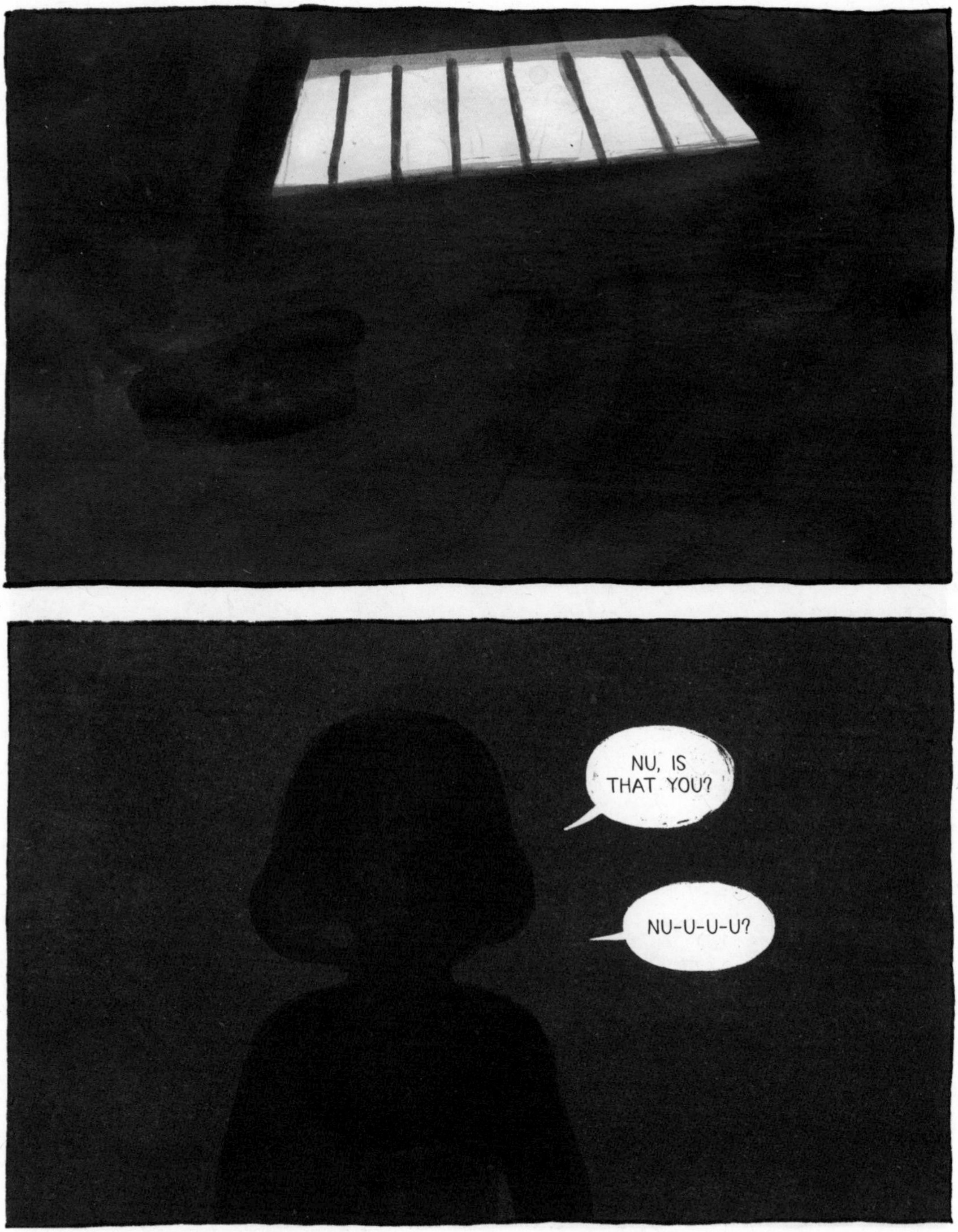
NU, IS THAT YOU?
NU-U-U-U?

JUST AS WHEN SHE WAS A CHILD.

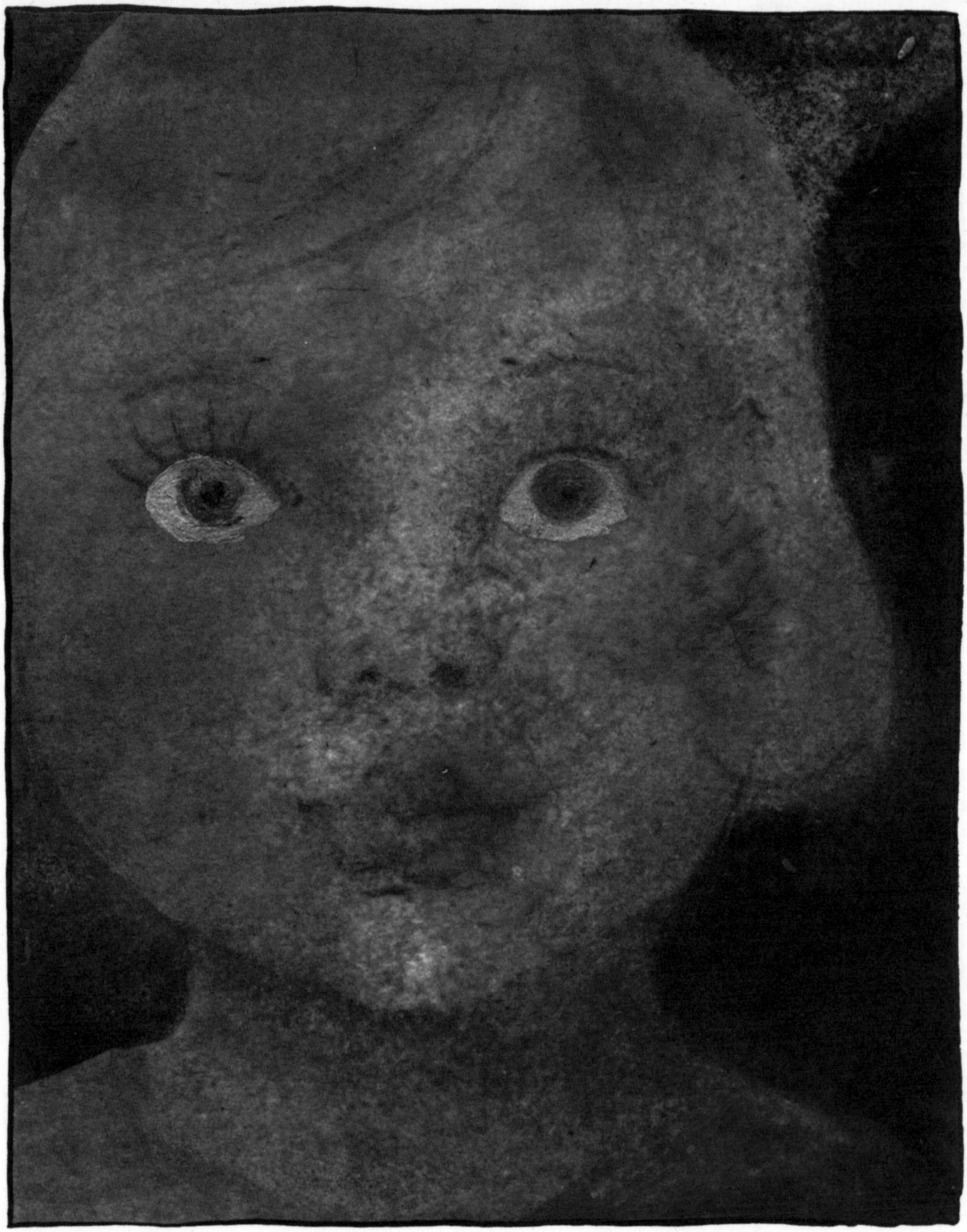

The authors would like to thank the following for their help and support:

Luigi De Angelis, Stefano and Paolo Gabici,
Lorenzo and Geppy Gleijeses, Laura Magnini,
Chiara Mammarella, Rodolfo Sacchettini,
Elena Zagaglia.

Special thanks to Davide Reviati
and to the whole fantastic Coconino team.

Thanks to Elena Ferrante.